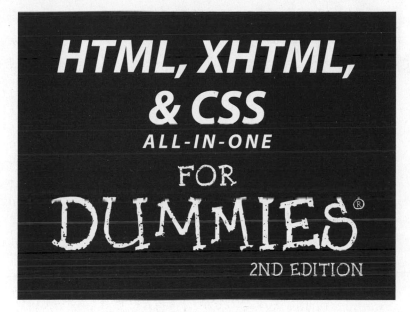

HTML, XHTML, & CSS
ALL-IN-ONE

FOR
DUMMIES®

2ND EDITION

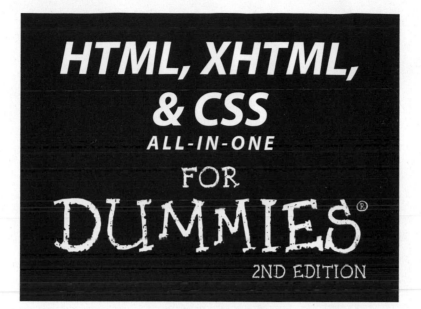

HTML, XHTML, & CSS
ALL-IN-ONE
FOR DUMMIES®
2ND EDITION

by Andy Harris

WILEY

Wiley Publishing, Inc.

HTML, XHTML, & CSS All-in-One For Dummies®, 2nd Edition

Published by
Wiley Publishing, Inc.
111 River Street
Hoboken, NJ 07030-5774

www.wiley.com

WILEY

About the Author

Andy Harris began his teaching life as a special education teacher. As he was teaching young adults with severe disabilities, he taught himself enough computer programming to support his teaching habit with freelance programming. Those were the exciting days when computers started to have hard drives, and some computers began communicating with each other over an arcane mechanism some were calling the Internet.

All this time Andy was teaching computer science part time. He joined the faculty of the Indiana University-Purdue University Indianapolis Computer Science department in 1995. He serves as a Senior Lecturer, teaching the introductory courses to freshmen as well as numerous courses on Web development, general programming, and game programming. As manager of the Streaming Media Laboratory, he developed a number of online video-based courses, and worked on a number of international distance education projects including helping to start a computer science program in Tetevo, Macedonia FYR.

Andy is the author of several other computing books including *JavaScript For Dummies*, *Flash Game Programming For Dummies*, and *Game Programming: the L Line*. He invites your comments and questions at andy@aharris books.net. You can visit his main site and find a blog, forum, and links to other books at http://www.aharrisbooks.net.

Dedication

I dedicate this book to Jesus Christ, my personal savior, and to Heather, the joy in my life. I also dedicate this project to Elizabeth, Matthew, Jacob, and Benjamin. I love each of you.

Author's Acknowledgments

Thank you first to Heather. Even though I type all the words, this book is a real partnership, like the rest of our life. Thanks for being my best friend and companion. Thanks also for doing all the work it takes for us to sustain a family when I'm in writing mode.

Thank you to Mark Enochs. It's great to have an editor who gets me, and who's willing to get excited about a project. I really enjoy working with you.

Thanks very much to Katie Feltman. It's fun to see how far a few wacky ideas have gone. Thanks for continuing to believe in me, and for helping me to always find an interesting new project.

Thank you to the copy editors: first and foremost, I thank Brian Walls for all his hard work in making this edition presentable. Thanks also go to Teresa Artman, John Edwards, and Melba Hopper for their help. I appreciate your efforts to make my geeky mush turn into something readable. Thanks for improving my writing.

A special thanks to Jeff Noble for his technical editing. I appreciate your vigilance. You have helped to make this book as technically accurate as possible.

Thank you to the many people at Wiley who contribute to a project like this. The author only gets to meet a few people, but so many more are involved in the process. Thank you very much for all you've done to help make this project a reality.

Thanks to Chris McCulloh for all you did on the first edition, and I thank you for your continued friendship.

A big thank you to the open source community which has created so many incredible tools and made them available to all. I'd especially like to thank the creators of Firefox, Firebug, Aptana, HTML Validator, the Web Developer toolbar, Ubuntu and the Linux community, Notepad++, PHP, Apache, jQuery, and the various jQuery plugins. This is an amazing and generous community effort.

I'd finally like to thank the IUPUI computer science family for years of support on various projects. Thank you especially to all my students, current and past. I've learned far more from you than the small amount I've taught. Thank you for letting me be a part of your education.

Publisher's Acknowledgments

We're proud of this book; please send us your comments through our online registration form located at `http://dummies.custhelp.com`. For other comments, please contact our Customer Care Department within the U.S. at 877-762-2974, outside the U.S. at 317-572-3993, or fax 317-572-4002.

Some of the people who helped bring this book to market include the following:

Acquisitions, Editorial, and Media Development

Senior Project Editor: Mark Enochs

Senior Acquisitions Editor: Katie Feltman

Copy Editors: Brian Walls, Teresa Artman, John Edwards, Melba Hopper

Technical Editor: Jeff Noble

Editorial Manager: Leah Cameron

Media Development Project Manager: Laura Moss-Hollister

Media Development Assistant Project Manager: Jenny Swisher

Media Development Assistant Producer: Shawn Patrick

Editorial Assistant: Amanda Graham

Sr. Editorial Assistant: Cherie Case

Cartoons: Rich Tennant (www.the5thwave.com)

Composition Services

Project Coordinators: Katherine Crocker, Lynsey Stanford

Layout and Graphics: Carl Byers, Timothy C. Detrick

Proofreaders: Lauren Mandelbaum, Christine Sabooni

Indexer: BIM Indexing & Proofreading Services

Special Help: Tonya Cupp, Colleen Totz Diamond

Publishing and Editorial for Technology Dummies

Richard Swadley, Vice President and Executive Group Publisher

Andy Cummings, Vice President and Publisher

Mary Bednarek, Executive Acquisitions Director

Mary C. Corder, Editorial Director

Publishing for Consumer Dummies

Diane Graves Steele, Vice President and Publisher

Composition Services

Debbie Stailey, Director of Composition Services

Contents at a Glance

Table of Contents

        Setting up the arrays 410
        Getting a city 411
        Creating a main( ) function 411
    Creating Your Own Objects... 413
        Building a basic object... 413
        Adding methods to an object 414
        Building a reusable object 415
        Using your shiny new objects 417
    Introducing JSON 417
        Storing data in JSON format 418
        Building a more complex JSON structure........................... 419

Chapter 5: Talking to the Page **423**

    Understanding the Document Object Model 423
        Navigating the DOM.. 423
        Changing DOM properties with Firebug 425
        Examining the document object 425
    Harnessing the DOM through JavaScript 427
        Getting the blues, JavaScript-style 427
        Writing JavaScript code to change colors 428
    Managing Button Events 428
        Embedding quotes within quotes 431
        Writing the changeColor function 431
    Managing Text Input and Output... 432
        Introducing event-driven programming............................. 432
        Creating the XHTML form 433
        Using GetElementById to get access to the page 434
        Manipulating the text fields 435
    Writing to the Document 436
        Preparing the HTML framework 436
        Writing the JavaScript.. 437
        Finding your innerHTML 438
    Working with Other Text Elements.. 438
        Building the form 440
        Writing the function... 441
        Understanding generated source 442

Chapter 6: Getting Valid Input **445**

    Getting Input from a Drop-Down List..................................... 445
        Building the form 446
        Reading the list box... 447
    Managing Multiple Selections 448
        Coding a multiple selection select object.......................... 449
        Writing the JavaScript code 450

Introduction

1 love the Internet, and if you picked up this book, you probably do, too. The Internet is dynamic, chaotic, exciting, interesting, and useful, all at the same time. The Web is pretty fun from a user's point of view, but that's only part of the story. Perhaps the best part of the Internet is how participatory it is. You can build your own content — free! It's really amazing. There's never been a form of communication like this before. Anyone with access to a minimal PC and a little bit of knowledge can create his or her own homestead in one of the most exciting platforms in the history of communication.

The real question is how to get there. A lot of Web development books are really about how to use some sort of software you have to buy. That's okay, but it isn't necessary. Many software packages have evolved that purport to make Web development easier — and some work pretty well — but regardless what software package you use, there's still a need to know what's really going on under the surface. That's where this book comes in.

You'll find out exactly how the Web works in this book. You'll figure out how to use various tools, but, more importantly, you'll create your piece of the Web. You'll discover:

+ **How Web pages are created:** You'll figure out the basic structure of Web pages. You'll understand the structure well because you build pages yourself. No mysteries here.

+ **How to separate content and style:** You'll understand the foundation of modern thinking about the Internet — that style should be separate from content.

+ **How to use Web standards:** The Web is pretty messy, but, finally, some standards have arisen from the confusion. You'll discover how these standards work and how you can use them.

+ **How to create great-looking Web pages:** Of course, you want a terrific-looking Web site. With this book, you'll find out how to use layout, style, color, and images.

+ **How to build modern layouts:** Many Web pages feature columns, menus, and other fancy features. You'll figure out how to build all these things.

+ **How to add interactivity:** Adding forms to your pages, validating form data, and creating animations are all possible with the JavaScript language.

✦ **How to write programs on the server:** Today's Web is powered by programs on Web servers. You'll discover the powerful PHP language and figure out how to use it to create powerful and effective sites.

✦ **How to harness the power of data:** Every Web developer eventually needs to interact with data. You'll read about how to create databases that work. You'll also discover how to connect databases to your Web pages and how to create effective and useful interfaces.

✦ **How AJAX is changing everything:** The hottest Web technology on the horizon is AJAX (Asynchronous JavaScript and XML). You'll figure out how to harness this way of working and use it to create even more powerful and interesting applications.

No Experience Necessary

I'm not assuming anything in this book. If you've never built a Web page before, you're in the right hands. You don't need any experience, and you don't have to know anything about HTML, programming, or databases. I discuss everything you need.

If you're reasonably comfortable with a computer (you can navigate the Web and use a word processor), you have all the skills you need.

Great for Advanced Folks, Too!

If you've been around Web development for a while, you'll still find this book handy.

If you've used HTML but not XHTML, see how things have changed and discover the powerful combination of XHTML and CSS.

If you're still using table-based layouts, you'll definitely want to read about newer ways of thinking. After you get over the difference, you'll be amazed at the power, the flexibility, and the simplicity of CSS-based layout and design.

If you're already comfortable with XHTML and CSS, you're ready to add JavaScript functionality for form validation and animation. If you've never used a programming language before, JavaScript is a really great place to start.

If you're starting to get serious about Web development, you've probably already realized that you'll need to work with a server at some point. PHP is a really powerful, free, and easy language that's extremely prominent on the Web landscape. You'll use this to have programs send e-mails, store and load information from files, and work with databases.

If you're messing with commercial development, you'll definitely need to know more about databases. I get e-mails every week from companies looking for people who can create a solid relational database and connect it to a Web site with PHP.

If you're curious about AJAX, you can read about what it is, how it works, and how to use it to add functionality to your site. You'll also read about a very powerful and easy AJAX library that can add tremendous functionality to your bag of tricks.

I wrote this book as the reference I wish I had. If you have only one Web development book on your shelf, this should be the one. Wherever you are in your Web development journey, you can find something interesting and new in this book.

Use Any Computer

One of the great things about Web development is how accessible it can be. You don't need a high-end machine to build Web sites. Whatever you're using now will probably do fine. I built most of the examples in this book with Windows XP and Ubuntu Linux, but a Mac is perfectly fine, too. Most of the software I use in the book is available free for all major platforms. Similar alternatives for all platforms are available in the few cases when this isn't true.

Don't Buy Any Software

Everything you need for Web development is on the CD-ROM. I've used only open-source software for this book. The CD contains a ton of tools and helpful programs. See Appendix A in the back of this book for a complete listing. Following are the highlights:

✦ **Aptana:** A full-featured programmer's editor that greatly simplifies creating Web pages, CSS documents, and code in multiple languages.

✦ **Firefox extensions:** I've included several extensions to the Firefox Web browser that turn it into a thoroughbred Web development platform. The Web Developer toolbar adds all kinds of features for creating and testing pages; the HTML Validator checks your pages for standards compliance; and the Firebug extension adds incredible features for JavaScript and AJAX debugging.

✦ **XAMPP:** When you're ready to move to the server, XAMPP is a complete server package that's easy to install and incredibly powerful. This includes the incredible Apache Web server, the PHP programming language, the MySQL database manager, and tons of useful utilities.

✦ **Useful tools:** Every time I use a tool (such as a data mapper, a diagram tool, or an image editor) in this book, I make it available on the CD-ROM.

There's no need to buy any expensive Web development tools. Everything you need is here and no harder than the more expensive Web editors.

How This Book Is Organized

Web development is about solving a series of connected but different problems. This book is organized into eight minibooks based on specific technologies. You can read them in any order you wish, but you'll find that the later books tend to rely on topics described in the earlier books. (For example, JavaScript doesn't make much sense without XHTML because it's usually embedded in a Web page.) The following describes these eight minibooks:

✦ **Book I: Creating the HTML/XHTML Foundation** — Web development incorporates a lot of languages and technologies, but HTML is the foundation. Here I show you *XHTML,* the latest incarnation of HTML, and describe how it's used to form the basic skeleton of your pages. I also preview the upcoming HTML 5 standard.

✦ **Book II: Styling with CSS** — In the old days, HTML had a few tags to spruce up your pages, but they weren't nearly powerful enough. Today, developers use Cascading Style Sheets (CSS) to add color and formatting to your pages.

✦ **Book III: Using Positional CSS** — Discover the best ways to set up layouts with floating elements, fixed positioning, and absolute positioning. Figure out how to build various multicolumn page layouts and how to create dynamic buttons and menus.

✦ **Book IV: Client-Side Programming with JavaScript** — Figure out essential programming skills with the easy and powerful JavaScript language — even if you've never programmed before. Manipulate data in Web forms and use powerful regular expression technology to validate form entries. Also discover how to create animations with JavaScript.

✦ **Book V: Server-Side Programming with PHP** — Move your code to the server and take advantage of this powerful language. Figure out how to respond to Web requests; work with conditions, functions, objects, and text files; and connect to databases.

✦ **Book VI: Managing Data with MySQL** — Most serious Web projects are eventually about data. Figure out how databases are created, how to set up a secure data server, the basics of data normalization, and how to create a reliable and trustworthy data back end for your site.

✦ **Book VII: Into the Future with AJAX** — Look forward to the technology that has the Web abuzz. AJAX isn't really a language but rather a new way of thinking about Web development. Get the skinny on what's going on here, build an AJAX connection or two by hand, and use the really cool jQuery library for adding advanced features and functionality to your pages.

✦ **Book VIII: Moving from Pages to Sites** — This minibook ties together many of the threads throughout the rest of the book. Discover how to create your own complete Web server solution or pick a Web host. Walk through the process of designing a complex multipage Web site. Build graphics for your Web site. Discover how to use content management systems to simplify complex Web sites and, finally, to build your own content management system with skills taught throughout the book.

New for the Second Edition

This second edition keeps the organization and content of the first edition. I have made a few changes to keep up with advances in technology:

✦ **Preview of HTML 5:** HTML 5 and CSS 3 offer promising new features. While it may be too early to incorporate these features into every page, it's time to learn what's coming. Book I, Chapter 8 highlights these welcome new advances.

✦ **Improved PHP coverage:** I greatly enhanced and streamlined the PHP content, making it easier to follow. You'll see these improvements throughout Book V.

✦ **Enhanced jQuery coverage:** The jQuery AJAX library has improved dramatically since the first edition. I provide much more detailed coverage including full support for jQuery UI and numerous cool widgets and tools. Book VII is much longer and more detailed than it was in the first edition.

✦ **A new graphics chapter:** A number of readers asked for more coverage of graphics tools, especially Gimp. I added a new chapter to Book VIII describing how to use Gimp to enhance your Web pages.

✦ **Support for the Website Baker CMS:** I use this CMS quite a bit in my Web business, and I find it especially easy to modify. I changed Book VIII, Chapter 3 to explain how to use and modify this excellent CMS.

✦ **Various tweaks and improvements:** No book is perfect (though I really try). There were a few passages in the previous edition that readers found difficult. I tried hard to clean up each of these areas. Many thanks to those who provided feedback!

Icons Used in This Book

This is a *For Dummies* book, so you have to expect some snazzy icons, right? I don't disappoint. Here's what you'll see:

This is where I pass along any small insights I may have gleaned in my travels.

I can't really help being geeky once in a while. Every so often, I want to explain something a little deeper. Read this to impress people at your next computer science cocktail party or skip it if you really don't need the details.

A lot of details are here. I point out something important that's easy to forget with this icon.

Watch out! Anything I mark with this icon is a place where things have blown up for me or my students. I point out any potential problems with this icon.

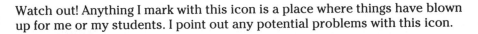

A lot of really great examples and software are on the CD. Whenever I mention software or examples that are available on the CD, I highlight it with this icon.

What's Next?

Well, that's really up to you. I sincerely believe you can use this book to turn into a top-notch Web developer. That's my goal for you.

Although this is a massive book, there's still more to figure out. If you have questions or just want to chat, feel free to e-mail me at andy@ aharrisbooks.net. You can also visit my Web site at www.aharris books.net for code examples, updates, and other good stuff. (You can also visit www.dummies.com/go/htmlxhtmlandcssaiofd2e for code examples from the book.)

I try hard to answer all reader e-mails but sometimes I get behind. Please be patient with me, and I'll do my best to help.

I can't wait to hear from you and see the incredible Web sites you develop. Have a great time, discover a lot, and stay in touch!

Book I

Creating the HTML/ XHTML Foundation

The 5th Wave   By Rich Tennant

FREELANCER NED WILLIS CONSULTS WITH A MEMBER OF HIS TECHNICAL STAFF

©RICHTENNANT

"...and that's pretty much all there is to converting a document to an HTML file."

Contents at a Glance

Chapter 1: Sound HTML Foundations

In This Chapter

✓ Creating a basic Web page

✓ Understanding the most critical HTML tags

✓ Setting up your system to work with HTML

✓ Viewing your pages

This chapter is your introduction to building Web pages. Before this slim chapter is finished, you'll have your first page up and running. Creating a basic page isn't difficult, but building pages that can grow and expand while you discover more sophisticated techniques takes a little foresight. Most of this book uses the XHTML standard. In this first chapter, I show part of an older standard called HTML. HTML is a little bit easier to start with, and everything I show in this chapter translates perfectly to the XHTML you use throughout the book.

In this minibook, you discover the modern form of Web design using XHTML. Your Web pages will be designed from the ground up, which makes them easy to modify and customize. While you figure out more advanced techniques throughout this book, you'll take the humble pages you discover in this chapter and make them do all kinds of exciting things.

Creating a Basic Page

Here's the great news: The most important Web technology you need is also the easiest. You don't need any expensive or complicated software, and you don't need a powerful computer. You probably have everything you need to get started already.

No more talking! Fire up a computer and let's build a Web page!

1. **Open a text editor.**

You can use any text editor you want, as long as it lets you save files as plain text. If you're using Windows, Notepad is fine for now. (Later, I show you some other free alternatives, but start with something you already know.)

Don't use a word processor like Microsoft Word. It doesn't save things in the right format, and not all the nifty features, like fonts and centering, work right. I promise that you'll figure out how to do all that stuff but without using a word processor. Even the Save as HTML feature doesn't work right. You really need a very simple text editor, and that's it. In Chapter 3 of this minibook, I show you a few more editors that make your life easier. You'll never use Word.

2. **Type the following code.**

Really. Type it in your text editor so you get some experience writing the actual code. I explain very soon what all this means, but type it now to get a feel for it:

```
<html>
<head>
<!-- myFirst.html -->

<title>My very first web page!</title>
</head>

<body>

<h1>This is my first web page!</h1>

<p>
This is the first web page I've ever made,
and I'm extremely proud of it.
It is so cool!
</p>

</body>
</html>
```

3. **Save the file as `myFirst.html`.**

It's important that your filename has no spaces and ends with the .html extension. Spaces cause problems on the Internet (which is, of course, where all good pages go to live), and the .html extension is how most computers know that this file is an HTML file (which is another name for a Web page). It doesn't matter where you save the file, as long as you can find it in the next step.

4. **Open your Web browser.**

The *Web browser* is the program used to look at pages. After you post your page on a Web server somewhere, your Great Aunt Gertrude can use her Web browser to view your page. You also need one (a browser, not a Great Aunt Gertrude) to test your page. For now, use whatever browser you ordinarily use. Most Windows users already have Internet Explorer installed. If you're a Mac user, you probably have Safari. Linux folks generally have Firefox. Any of these are fine. In Chapter 3 of this minibook, I explain why you probably need more than one browser and how to configure them for maximum usefulness.

5. **Load your page into the browser.**

You can do this a number of ways. You can use the browser's File menu to open a local file, or you can simply drag the file from your Desktop (or wherever) to the open browser window.

6. **Bask in your newfound genius.**

Your simple text file is transformed! If all went well, it looks like Figure 1-1.

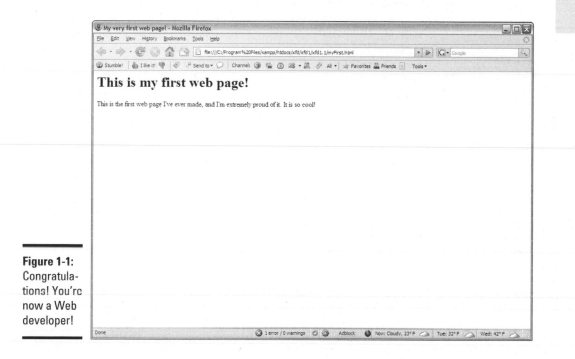

Figure 1-1:
Congratula-
tions! You're
now a Web
developer!

Understanding the HTML in the Basic Page

The page you create in the previous section uses an extremely simple notation — HTML (HyperText Markup Language), which has been around since the beginning of the Web. HTML is a terrific technology for several reasons:

✦ **It uses plain text.** Most document systems (like word processors) use special *binary encoding schemes* that incorporate formatting directly into the computer's internal language, which locks a document into a particular computer or software. That is, a document stored in Word format can't be read without a program that understands Word formatting. HTML gets past this problem by storing everything in plain text.

✦ **It works on all computers.** The main point of HTML is to have a universal format. Any computer should be able to read and write it. The plain-text formatting aids in this.

✦ **It describes what documents *mean*.** HTML isn't really designed to indicate how a page or its elements look. HTML is about describing the meaning of various elements (more on that very soon). This has some distinct advantages when you figure out how to use HTML properly.

✦ **It *doesn't* describe how documents *look*.** This one seems strange. Of course, when you look at Figure 1-1, you can see that the appearance of the text on the Web page has changed from the way the text looked in your text editor. Formatting a document in HTML does cause the document's appearance to change. That's not the point of HTML, though. You discover in Book II and Book III how to use another powerful technology — *CSS* — to change the appearance of a page after you define its meaning. This separation of meaning from layout is one of the best features of HTML.

✦ **It's easy to write.** Sure, HTML gets a little more complicated than this first example, but you can easily figure out how to write HTML without any specialized editors. You only have to know a handful of elements, and they're pretty straightforward.

✦ **It's free.** HTML doesn't cost anything to use, primarily because it isn't owned by anyone. No corporation has control of it (although a couple have tried), and nobody has a patent on it. The fact that this technology is freely available to anyone is a huge advantage.

Meeting Your New Friends, the Tags

The key to writing HTML code is the special text inside angle braces (<>). These special elements are tags. They aren't meant to be displayed on the Web page but offer instructions to the Web browser about the meaning of the text. The tags are meant to be embedded into each other to indicate the organization of the page. This basic page introduces you to all the major tags you'll encounter. (There are more, but they can wait for a chapter or two.) Each tag has a beginning and an end tag. The end tag is just like the beginning tag, except the end tag has a slash (/):

✦ **<html></html>:** The <html> tag is the foundation of the entire Web page. The tag begins the page. Likewise, </html> ends the page. For example, the page begins with <html> and ends with </html>. The <html></html> combination indicates that everything in the page is defined as HTML code.

Some books teach you to write your HTML tags in uppercase letters. This was once a standard, but it is no longer recommended. When you move to XHTML code (which is a slightly stricter form of HTML) in Chapter 2 of this minibook, you'll see that XHTML requires all tags to be lowercase.

✦ **`<head></head>`:** These tags define a special part of the Web page called the head (or sometimes header). This part of the Web page reminds me of the engine compartment of a car. This is where you put some great stuff later, but it's not where the main document lives. For now, the only thing you'll put in the header is the document's title. Later, you'll add styling information and programming code to make your pages sing and dance.

✦ **`<!-- -->`:** This tag indicates a *comment,* which is ignored by the browser. However, a comment is used to describe what's going on in a particular part of the code.

✦ **`<title></title>`:** This tag is used to determine the page's title. The title usually contains ordinary text. Whatever you define as the title will appear in some special ways. Many browsers put the title text in the browser's title bar. Search engines often use the title to describe the page.

Throughout this book, I use the filename of the HTML code as the title. That way, you can match any figure or code listing to the corresponding file on the Web site that accompanies this book. Typically, you'll use something more descriptive, but this is a useful technique for a book like this.

It's not quite accurate to say that the title text always shows up in the title bar because a Web page is designed to work on lots of different browsers. Sure, the title does show up on most major browsers that way, but what about cellphones and personal digital assistants? HTML never legislates what will happen; it only suggests. This may be hard to get used to, but it's a reality. You trade absolute control for widespread capability, which is a good deal.

✦ **`<body></body>`:** The page's main content is contained within these tags. Most of the HTML code and the stuff the user sees are in the body area. If the header area is the engine compartment, the body is where the passengers go.

✦ **`<h1></h1>`:** H1 stands for *heading level one.* Any text contained within this markup is treated as a prominent headline. By default, most browsers add special formatting to anything defined as H1, but there's no guarantee. An H1 heading doesn't really specify any particular font or formatting, just the *meaning* of the text as a level one heading. When you find out how to use CSS in Book II, you'll discover that you can make your headline look however you want. In this first minibook, keep all the default layouts for now and make sure you understand that HTML is about semantic meaning, not about layout or design. There are other levels of headings, of course, through <h6> where <h2> indicates a heading slightly less important than <h1>, <h3> is less important than <h2>, and so on.

A few notes about the basic page

Be proud of this first page. It may be simple, but it's the foundation of greater things to come. Before moving on, take a moment to ponder some important HTML/XHTML principles shown in this humble page you've created:

✔ **All tags are lowercase.** Although HTML does allow uppercase tags, the XHTML variation you'll be using throughout most of this book requires only lowercase tags.

✔ **Tag pairs are containers, with a beginning and an end.** Tags contain other tags or text.

✔ **Some elements can be repeated.** There's only one `<html>`, `<title>`, and `<body>` tag per page, but a lot of the other elements (`<h1>` and `<p>`) can be repeated as many times as you like.

✔ **Carriage returns are ignored.** In the Notepad document, there are a number of carriage returns. The formatting of the original document has no effect on the HTML output. The markup tags indicate how the output looks.

Beginners are sometimes tempted to make their first headline an `<h1>` tag and then use an `<h2>` for the second headline and an `<h3>` for the third. That's not how it works. Web pages, like newspapers and books, use different headlines to point out the relative importance of various elements on the page, often varying the point size of the text. You can read more about that in Book II.

✦ **`<p></p>`:** In HTML, p stands for the paragraph tag. In your Web pages, you should enclose each standard paragraph in a `<p></p>` pair. You might notice that HTML doesn't preserve the carriage returns or white space in your HTML document. That is, if you press Enter in your code to move text to a new line, that new line isn't necessarily preserved in the final Web page.

The `<p></p>` structure is one easy way to manage spacing before and after each paragraph in your document.

Some older books recommend using `<p>` without a `</p>` to add space to your documents, similar to pressing the Enter key. This way of thinking could cause you problems later because it doesn't truthfully reflect the way Web browsers work. Don't think of `<p>` as the carriage return. Instead, think of `<p>` and `</p>` as defining a paragraph. The paragraph model is more powerful because soon enough, you'll figure out how to take any properly defined paragraph and give it yellow letters on a green background with daisies (or whatever else you want). If things are marked properly, they'll be much easier to manipulate later.

Setting Up Your System

You don't need much to make Web pages. Your plain text editor and a Web browser are about all you need. Still, some things can make your life easier as a Web developer.

Displaying file extensions

The method discussed in this section is mainly for Windows users, but it's a big one. Windows uses the *extension* (the part of the filename after the period) to determine what type of file you're dealing with. This is very important in Web development. The files you create are simple text files, but if you store them with the ordinary .txt extension, your browser can't read them properly. What's worse, the default Windows setting hides these extensions from you, so you have only the icons to tell you what type of file you're dealing with, which causes all kinds of problems. I recommend you have Windows explicitly describe your file extensions. Here's how to set that up:

1. **Open the file manager (My Computer in XP or Computer in Vista and Windows 7).**

   Use the My Computer window to open a directory on your hard drive. It doesn't matter which directory you're looking at. You just need the tool open.

2. **Choose Tools⇨Folder Options.**

   The Folder Options dialog box appears.

3. **Select the View tab.**

   You see the Folder Options dialog box.

4. **Don't hide extensions.**

   By default, Windows likes to hide the extensions for known file types. However, you're a programmer now, so you deserve to see these things. Uncheck the Hide Extensions for Known File Types box, as shown in Figure 1-2.

5. **Show the path and hidden folders.**

   I like to see my hidden files and folders (after all, they're mine, right?) and I like to list the full path. Click the appropriate check boxes to enable these features. You'll often find them to be helpful.

6. **Apply these change to all the folders on your computer by clicking the Apply to All Folders button.**

   This causes the file extensions to appear everywhere, including the Desktop.

Figure 1-2: Don't hide file extensions (deselect that last check box).

Although my demonstration uses Windows XP, the technique is the same in Windows Vista and Windows 7.

Setting up your software

You'll write a lot of Web pages, so it makes sense to set up your system to make that process as easy as possible. I talk a lot more about some software you should use in Chapter 3 of this minibook, but for now, here are a couple of easy suggestions:

✦ **Put a Notepad icon on your Desktop.** You'll edit a lot of text files, so it's helpful to have an icon for Notepad (or whatever other text editor you use) available directly on the Desktop. That way, you can quickly edit any Web page by dragging it to the Desktop. When you use more sophisticated editors than Notepad, you'll want links to them, too.

✦ **Get another Web browser.** You may just *love* your Web browser, and that's fine, but you can't assume that everybody likes the same browser you do. You need to know how other browsers will interpret your code. Firefox is an incredibly powerful browser, and it's completely free. If you don't have them already, I suggest having links to at least two browsers directly on your Desktop.

Understanding the magic

Most of the problems people have with the Web are from misunderstandings about how this medium really works. Most people are comfortable with word processors, and we know how to make a document look how we want. Modern applications use WYSIWYG technology, promising that *what you see is what you get.* That's a reasonable promise when it comes to print documents, but it doesn't work that way on the Web.

How a Web page looks depends on a lot of things that you don't control. The user may read your pages on a smaller or larger screen than you. She may use a different operating system than you. She may have a dialup connection or may turn off the graphics for speed. She may be blind and use screen-reader technology to navigate Web pages. She may be reading your page on a PDA or a cellphone. You can't make a document that looks the same in all these situations.

A good compromise is to make a document that clearly indicates how the information fits together and makes suggestions about the visual design. The user and her browser can determine how much of those suggestions to use.

You get control of the visual design but never complete control, which is okay because you're trading total control for accessibility. People with devices you've never heard of can visit your page.

Practice a few times until you can easily build a page without looking anything up. Soon enough, you're ready for the next step — building pages like the pros.

Chapter 2: It's All about Validation

In This Chapter

- ✓ Introducing the concept of valid pages
- ✓ Using a doctype
- ✓ Introducing XHTML 1.0 Strict
- ✓ Setting the character set
- ✓ Meeting the W3C validator
- ✓ Fixing things when they go wrong
- ✓ Using HTML Tidy to clean your pages

Web development is undergoing a revolution. As the Web matures and becomes a greater part of everyday life XX, it's important to ensure that Web pages perform properly—thus, a call for Web developers to follow voluntary standards of Web development.

Somebody Stop the HTML Madness!

In the bad old days, the Web was an informal affair. People wrote HTML pages any way they wanted. Although this was easy, it led to a lot of problems:

- ✦ **Browser manufacturers added features that didn't work on all browsers.** People wanted prettier Web pages with colors, fonts, and doodads, but there wasn't a standard way to do these things. Every browser had a different set of tags that supported enhanced features. As a developer, you had no real idea if your Web page would work on all the browsers out there. If you wanted to use some neat feature, you had to ensure your users had the right browser.

- ✦ **The distinction between meaning and layout was blurred.** People expected to have some kind of design control of their Web pages, so all kinds of new tags popped up that blurred the distinction between describing and decorating a page.

- ✦ **Table-based layout was used as a hack.** HTML didn't have a good way to handle layout, so clever Web developers started using tables as a layout mechanism. This worked, after a fashion, but it wasn't easy or elegant.

✦ **People started using tools to write pages.** Web pages soon became so ugly that people began to believe that they couldn't do HTML by hand anymore and that some kind of editor was necessary to handle all that complexity for them. Although these editing programs introduced new features that made things easier upfront, these tools also made code almost impossible to change without the original editor. Web developers began thinking they couldn't design Web pages without a tool from a major corporation.

✦ **The nature of the Web was changing.** At the same time, these factors were making ordinary Web development more challenging. Innovators were recognizing that the Web wasn't really about documents but was about applications that could dynamically create documents. Many of the most interesting Web pages you visit aren't Web pages at all but programs that produce Web pages dynamically every time you visit. This meant that developers had to make Web pages readable by programs, as well as humans.

In short, the world of HTML was a real mess.

XHTML to the rescue

In 2000, the World Wide Web Consortium (usually abbreviated as W3C) got together and proposed some fixes for HTML. The basic plan was to create a new form of HTML that complied with a stricter form of markup, or *eXtensible Markup Language (XML)*. The details are long and boring, but essentially, they came up with some agreements about how Web pages are standardized. Here are some of those standards:

✦ **All tags have endings.** Every tag comes with a beginning and an end tag. (Well, a few exceptions come with their own ending built in. I'll explain when you encounter the first such tag in Chapter 6 of this minibook.) This was a new development because end tags were considered optional in old-school HTML, and many tags didn't even have end tags.

✦ **Tags can't be overlapped.** In HTML, sometimes people had the tendency to be sloppy and overlap tags, like this: `<a><b>my stuff</a></b>`. That's not allowed in XHTML, which is a good thing because it confuses the browser. If a tag is opened inside some container tag, the tag must be closed before that container is closed.

✦ **Everything's lowercase.** Some people wrote HTML in uppercase, some in lowercase, and some just did what they felt like. It was inconsistent and made it harder to write browsers that could read all the variations.

✦ **Attributes must be in quotes.** If you've already done some HTML, you know that quotes used to be optional — not anymore. (Turn to Chapter 4 for more about attributes.)

✦ **Layout must be separate from markup.** Old-school HTML had a bunch of tags (like `<font>` and `<center>`) that were more about formatting than markup. These were useful, but they didn't go far enough. XHTML (at least the Strict version covered here) eliminates all these tags. Don't worry, though; CSS gives you all the features of these tags and a lot more.

This sounds more like strict librarian rules. Really, they aren't restricting at all because most of the good HTML coders were already following these guidelines or something similar.

There's XHTML and there's good XHTML

In old-style HTML, you never really knew how your pages would look on various browsers. In fact, you never really knew if your page was even written properly. Some mistakes would look fine on one browser but cause another browser to blow up.

The idea of *validation* is to take away some of the uncertainty of HTML. It's like a spell checker for your code. My regular spell checker makes me feel a little stupid sometimes because I make mistakes. I like it, though, because I'm the only one who sees the errors. I can fix the spelling errors before I pass the document on to you, so I look smart. (Well, maybe.)

It'd be cool if you could have a special kind of checker that does the same things for your Web pages. Instead of checking your spelling, it'd test your page for errors and let you know if you made any mistakes. It'd be even cooler if you could have some sort of certification that your page follows a standard of excellence.

That's how page validation works. You can designate that your page will follow a particular standard and use a software tool to ensure that your page meets that standard's specifications. The software tool is a *validator*. I show you two different validators in the upcoming "Validating Your Page" section.

The browsers also promise to follow a particular standard. If your page validates to a given standard, any browser that validates to that same standard can reproduce your document correctly, which is a big deal.

XHTML isn't perfect

While XHTML is the standard emphasized in this book, it has a few problems of its own. Not all browsers read it the same way, and it's a bit wordier than it needs to be. It looks like the next generation will go back to a form of HTML (HTML 5). However, proper HTML 5 coding will resemble XHTML more than HTML 4. In this edition, I focus on XHTML Strict. See Chapter 8 of this minibook for a complete overview of this important standard.

Building an XHTML Document

You create an XHTML document the same way you build ordinary HTML. You can still use an ordinary text editor, but the code is slightly more involved. Look at the following code (`template.html` on this book's CD-ROM) to see a bare-bones XHTML document:

```
<!DOCTYPE html PUBLIC "-//W3C//DTD XHTML 1.0 Strict//EN"
    "http://www.w3.org/TR/xhtml1/DTD/xhtml1-strict.dtd">
<html xmlns="http://www.w3.org/1999/xhtml">
<head>
<meta http-equiv="Content-Type" content="text/html; charset=utf-8" />
<title></title>
</head>
<body>
<h1></h1>
<p>
</p>

</body>
</html>
```

At first, this new document looks a lot more complicated than the HTML you see in Chapter 1 of this minibook, but it isn't as bad as it seems.

Don't memorize all this!

Before you freak out, don't feel you have to memorize this nonsense. Even people who write books about Web development (um, like me) don't have this stuff memorized because it's too awkward and too likely to change.

Keep a copy of `template.html` on your local drive (I keep a copy on my Desktop) and begin all your new pages with this template. When you start to use a more complex editor (see Chapter 3 of this minibook), you can often customize the editor so that it automatically starts with the framework you want.

You don't have to have all this stuff down cold, but you should understand the basics of what's going on, so the following is a quick tour.

The DOCTYPE tag

The scariest looking XHTML feature is the `<!DOCTYPE>` tag. This monster is ugly, no doubt, but it does serve a purpose. Officially, it's a *document type definition*. Your doctype declares to the world what particular flavor of HTML or XHTML you're using. When you begin your page with the doctype that I suggest here, you're telling the browser: "Hey, browser, my page follows the XHTML Strict guidelines, and if you aren't sure what that is, go to this Web site to get it."

```
<!DOCTYPE html PUBLIC "-//W3C//DTD XHTML 1.0 Strict//EN"
    "http://www.w3.org/TR/xhtml1/DTD/xhtml1-strict.dtd">
```

Many doctypes are available, but it's really a lot simpler than it seems. In this book, I show you XHTML 1.0 Strict, which is the primary doctype you need today. The other variations you might find on the Web (HTML 4.0, Frameset, and Transitional doctypes) are really designed for backwards compatibility. If you're going to go the standards-compliant route, you might as well go whole hog. (And, until Microsoft supports HTML 5, it's not a meaningful option for real development.)

Even though standards will change, the techniques you learn with XHTML Strict will serve you well as you move to other standards.

The doctype for the upcoming HTML 5 standard is a lot easier than this XHTML nonsense. HTML 5 replaces this complicated doctype with one that's a lot easier to remember: `<!DOCTYPE html>`. That's it. I can't wait . . . .

The xmlns attribute

The `html` tag looks a little different from the one in Chapter 1 of this mini-book. It has the term `xmlns` after it, which stands for *XML NameSpace*. This acronym helps clarify the definitions of the tags in your document:

```
<html xmlns="http://www.w3.org/1999/xhtml">
```

Truthfully, not all validators require this part, but it doesn't hurt to add it.

The meta tag

The last tag is the funky `meta` tag, which has been part of HTML for a long time. They allow you to describe various characteristics of a Web page:

```
<meta http-equiv="Content-Type" content="text/html; charset=utf-8" />
```

The particular form of the `meta` tag you see here defines the character set to use. The `utf` character set handles a number of Western languages well.

The truth is, if you start with this framework, you'll have everything you need to make official XHTML pages that validate properly.

You validate me

All this doctype and `xmlns` nonsense is worth it because of a nifty program — a *validator*. The most important validator is the W3C validator at `http://validator.w3.org`, as shown in Figure 2-1.

Figure 2-1:
The W3C
validator
page isn't
exciting,
but it sure is
useful.

A validator is actually the front end of a piece of software that checks pages for validity. It looks at your Web page's doctype and sees if the page conforms to the rules of that doctype. If not, it tells you what might have gone wrong.

You can submit code to a validator in three ways:

✦ **Validate by URL.** This option is used when a page is hosted on a Web server. Files stored on local computers can't be checked with this technique. Book VIII describes all you need to know about working with Web servers, including how to create your own.

✦ **Validate by File Upload.** This technique works fine with files you haven't posted to a Web server. It works great for pages you write on your computer but you haven't made visible to the world. This is the most common type of validation for beginners.

✦ **Validate by Direct Input.** The validator page has a text box you can simply paste your code into. It works, but I usually prefer to use the other methods because they're easier.

Validation might sound like a big hassle, but it's really a wonderful tool because sloppy HTML code can cause lots of problems. Worse, you might think everything's okay until somebody else looks at your page, and suddenly, the page doesn't display correctly.

As of this writing, there is not yet a validator for HTML 5 code. That will change as soon as HTML 5 becomes mainstream. In the meantime, validate for XHTML Strict and you'll be more than prepared for the HTML 5 switch.

Validating Your Page

To explain all this, I created a Web page the way Aesop might have done in ancient Greece. Okay, maybe Aesop didn't write his famous fables as Web pages, but if he had, they might have looked like the following code listing:

```
<!DOCTYPE html PUBLIC "-//W3C//DTD XHTML 1.0 Strict//EN"
    "http://www.w3.org/TR/xhtml1/DTD/xhtml1-strict.dtd">
<html xmlns="http://www.w3.org/1999/xhtml">
<head>
<meta http-equiv="Content-Type" content="text/html; charset=iso-8859-1" />

<!-- oxWheels1.html -->

<!-- note this page has deliberate errors!  Please see the text
    and oxWheelsCorrect.html for a corrected version.
-->

</head>
<body>
<title>The Oxen and the Wheels</title>
<h1>The Oxen and the Wheels
<h2></h1>From Aesop's Fables</h2>

<p>
    A pair of Oxen were drawing a heavily loaded wagon along a
    miry country road. They had to use all their strength to pull
    the wagon, but they did not complain.
<p>

<p>
    The Wheels of the wagon were of a different sort. Though the
    task they had to do was very light compared with that of the
    Oxen, they creaked and groaned at every turn. The poor Oxen,
    pulling with all their might to draw the wagon through the
    deep mud, had their ears filled with the loud complaining of
    the Wheels. And this, you may well know, made their work so
    much the harder to endure
</p>

<p>
    "Silence!" the Oxen cried at last, out of patience. "What have
    you Wheels to complain about so loudly? We are drawing all the
    weight, not you, and we are keeping still about it besides."
</p>

<h2>
They complain most who suffer least.
</h2>

</body>
</html>
```

The code looks okay, but actually has a number of problems. Aesop may have been a great storyteller, but from this example, it appears he was a sloppy coder. The mistakes can be hard to see, but trust me, they're there. The question is how do you find the problems before your users do?

You might think that the problems would be evident if you viewed the page in a Web browser. The Firefox and Internet Explorer Web browsers seem to handle the page decently, even if they don't display it in an identical way. Figure 2-2 shows `oxWheels1.html` in Firefox, and Figure 2-3 shows it in Internet Explorer.

Firefox appears to handle the page pretty well, but `From Aesop's Fables` is supposed to be a headline level two, or *H2,* and it appears as plain text. Other than that, there's very little indication that something is wrong.

Microsoft Internet Explorer also tries to display the page, and it does a decent job. Notice that `From Aesop's Fables` appears to be a level one header, or H1. That's odd. Still, the page looks pretty good in both browsers, so you might assume everything's just fine. That gets you into trouble.

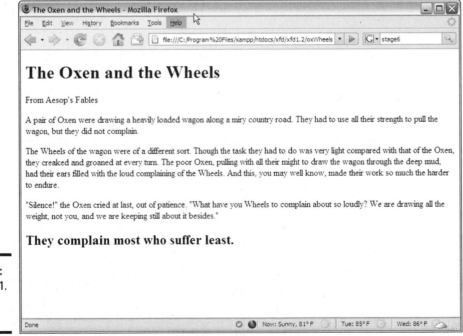

Figure 2-2:
oxWheels1.
html in
Firefox.

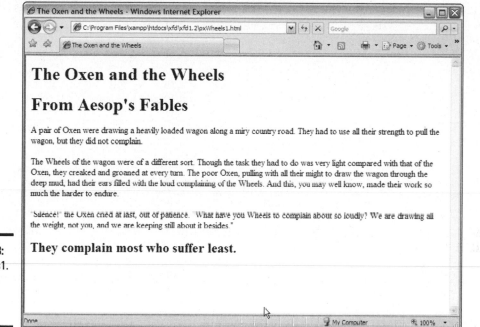

Figure 2-3:
oxWheels1.
html in
Internet
Explorer.

If it looks fine, who cares if it's exactly right? You might wonder why we care if there are mistakes in the underlying code, as long as everything works okay. After all, who's going to look at the code if the page displays properly?

The problem is, you don't know if it'll display properly, and mistakes in your code will eventually come back to haunt you. If possible, you want to know immediately what parts of your code are problematic so you can fix them and not worry.

Aesop visits W3C

To find out what's going on with this page, pay a visit to the W3C validator at http://validator.w3.org. Figure 2-4 shows me visiting this site and uploading a copy of oxWheels1.html to it.

Hold your breath and hit the Check button. You might be surprised at the results shown in Figure 2-5.

The validator is a picky beast, and it doesn't seem to like this page at all. The validator does return some useful information and gives enough hints that you can decode things soon enough.

Figure 2-4: I'm checking the oxWheels page to look for any problems.

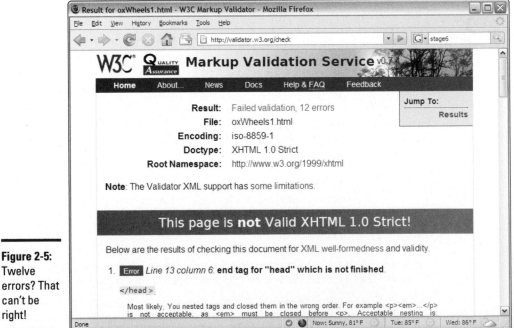

Figure 2-5: Twelve errors? That can't be right!

Examining the overview

Before you look at the specific complaints, take a quick look at the Web page the validator sends you. The Web page is chock-full of handy information. The top of the page tells you a lot of useful things:

✦ **Result:** This is really the important thing. You'll know the number of errors remaining by looking at this line. Don't panic, though. The errors in the document are probably fewer than the number you see here.

✦ **File:** The name of the file you're working on.

✦ **Encoding:** The text encoding you've set. If you didn't explicitly set text encoding, you may see a warning here.

✦ **Doctype:** This is the doctype extracted from your document. It indicates the rules that the validator is using to check your page. This should usually say XHTML 1.0 Strict.

✦ **Root Namespace:** If you use the template I give you, you always see the same namespace, and you don't have any surprises.

✦ **The dreaded red banner:** Experienced Web developers don't even have to read the results page to know if there is a problem. If everything goes well, there's a green congratulatory banner. If there are problems, the banner is red. It doesn't look good, Aesop.

Don't panic because you have errors. The mistakes often overlap, so one problem in your code often causes more than one error to pop up. Most of the time, you have far fewer errors than the page says, and a lot of the errors are repeated, so after you find the error once, you'll know how to fix it throughout the page.

Validating the page

The validator doesn't always tell you everything you need to know, but it does give you some pretty good clues. Page validation is tedious but not as difficult as it might seem at first. Here are some strategies for working through page validation:

✦ **Focus only on the first error.** Sure, 100 errors might be on the page, but solve them one at a time. The only error that matters is the first one on the list. Don't worry at all about other errors until you've solved the first one.

✦ **Note where the first error is.** The most helpful information you get is the line and column information about where the validator recognized the error. This isn't always where the error is, but it does give you some clues.

✦ **Look at the error message.** It's usually good for a laugh. The error messages are sometimes helpful and sometimes downright mysterious.

✦ **Look at the verbose text.** Unlike most programming debuggers, the W3C validator tries to explain what went wrong in something like English. It still doesn't always make sense, but sometimes the text gives you a hint.

✦ **Scan the next couple of errors.** Sometimes, one mistake shows up as more than one error. Look over the next couple of errors, as well, to see if they provide any more insight; sometimes, they do.

✦ **Revalidate.** Check the page again after you save it. If the first error is now at a later line number than the previous one, you've succeeded.

✦ **Don't worry if the number of errors goes up.** The number of perceived errors will sometimes go up rather than down after you successfully fix a problem. This is okay. Sometimes, fixing one error uncovers errors that were previously hidden. More often, fixing one error clears up many more. Just concentrate on clearing errors from the beginning to the end of the document.

✦ **Lather, rinse, and repeat.** Look at the new top error and get it straightened out. Keep going until you get the coveted Green Banner of Validation. (If I ever write an XHTML adventure game, the Green Banner of Validation will be one of the most powerful talismans.)

Examining the first error

Look again at the results for the `oxWheels1.html` page. The first error message looks like Figure 2-6.

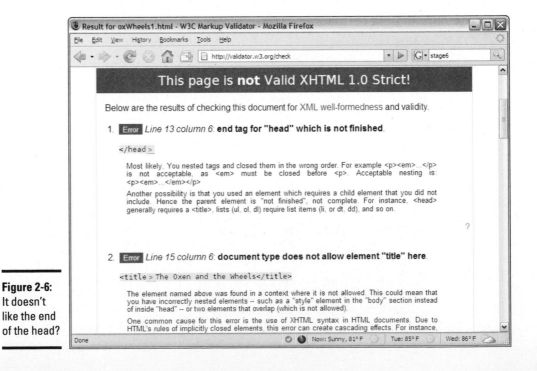

Figure 2-6: It doesn't like the end of the head?

Figure 2-6 shows the first two error messages. The first complains about where the `</head>` tag is. The second message complains about the `<title>` tag. Look at the source code, and you see that the relevant code looks like this:

```
<head>
<meta http-equiv="Content-Type" content="text/html; charset=iso-8859-1" />

<!-- oxWheels1.html -->

<!-- note this page has deliberate errors!  Please see the text
    and oxWheelsCorrect.html for a corrected version.
-->

</head>
<body>
<title>The Oxen and the Wheels</title>
<h1>The Oxen and the Wheels
```

Look carefully at the head and title tag pairs, and review the notes in the error messages, and you'll probably see the problem. The `<title>` element is supposed to be in the heading, but I accidentally put it in the body! (Okay, it wasn't accidental; I made this mistake deliberately here to show you what happens. However, I have made this mistake for real in the past.)

Fixing the title

If the title tag is the problem, a quick change in the HTML should fix this problem. `oxWheels2.html` shows another form of the page with my proposed fix:

```
<head>
<meta http-equiv="Content-Type" content="text/html; charset=iso-8859-1" />

<!-- oxWheels2.html -->

<!-- Moved the title tag inside the header -->

<title>The Oxen and the Wheels</title>
</head>

<body>
```

Note: I'm only showing the parts of the page that I changed. The entire page is available on this book's CD-ROM.

The fix for this problem is pretty easy:

1. **Move the title inside the head.**

I think the problem here is having the `<title>` element inside the body, rather than in the head where it belongs. If I move the title to the body, the error should be eliminated.

2. **Change the comments to reflect the page's status.**

   It's important that the comments reflect what changes I make.

3. **Save the changes.**

   Normally, you simply make a change to the same document, but I've elected to change the filename so you can see an archive of my changes as the page improves. This can actually be a good idea because you then have a complete history of your document's changes, and you can always revert to an older version if you accidentally make something worse.

4. **Note the current first error position.**

   Before you submit the modified page to the validator, make a mental note of the position of the current first error. Right now, the validator's first complaint is on line 13, column 6. I want the first mistake to be somewhere later in the document.

5. **Revalidate by running the validator again on the modified page.**

6. **Review the results and do a happy dance.**

   It's likely you still have errors, but that's not a failure! Figure 2-7 shows the result of my revalidation. The new first error is on line 16, and it appears to be very different from the last error. I solved it!

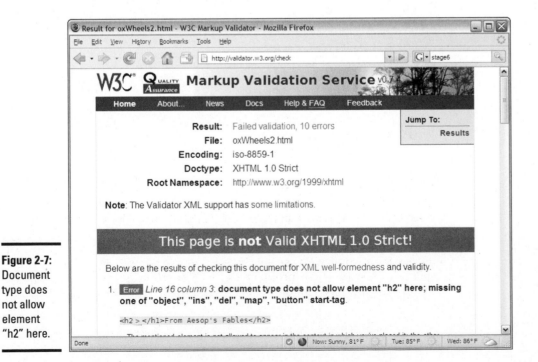

Figure 2-7: Document type does not allow element "h2" here.

Solving the next error

One down, but more to go. The next error (refer to Figure 2-7) looks strange, but it's one you see a lot.

The `document type does not allow` error is very common. What it usually means is you forgot to close something or you put something in the wrong place. The error message indicates a problem in line 16. The next error is line 16, too. See if you can find the problem here in the relevant code:

```
<body>
<h1>The Oxen and the Wheels
<h2></h1>From Aesop's Fables</h2>
```

After you know where to look, the problem becomes a bit easier to spot. I got sloppy and started the `<h2>` tag before I finished the `<h1>`. In many cases, one tag can be completely embedded inside another, but you can't have tag definitions overlap as I've done here. The `<h1>` has to close before I can start the `<h2>` tag.

This explains why the two main browsers displayed `From Aesop's Fables` differently. It isn't clear whether this code should be displayed in H1 or H2 format, or perhaps with no special formatting at all. It's much better to know the problem and fix it than to remain ignorant until something goes wrong.

The third version — `oxWheels3.html` — fixes this part of the program:

```
<!-- oxWheels3.html -->

<!-- sort out the h1 and h2 tags at the top -->

<title>The Oxen and the Wheels</title>
</head>

<body>
<h1>The Oxen and the Wheels</h1>
<h2>From Aesop's Fables</h2>
```

Checking the headline repair

The heading tags look a lot better, and a quick check of the validator confirms this fact, as shown in Figure 2-8, which now shows only six errors.

Here's another form of that `document type does not allow` error. This one seems strange because surely `<p>` tags are allowed in the body! The secret to this particular problem is to look carefully at the error message. This document has a lot of `<p>` tags in it. Which one is it complaining about?

```
    A pair of Oxen were drawing a heavily loaded wagon along a
    miry country road. They had to use all their strength to pull
    the wagon, but they did not complain.
<p>

<p>
    The Wheels of the wagon were of a different sort. Though the
    task they had to do was very light compared with that of the
    Oxen, they creaked and groaned at every turn. The poor Oxen,
    pulling with all their might to draw the wagon through the
    deep mud, had their ears filled with the loud complaining of
    the Wheels. And this, you may well know, made their work so
    much the harder to endure.
</p>
```

Aha! Line 22 is supposed to be the *end* of the paragraph, but I somehow forgot the slash character, so the validator thinks I'm beginning a new paragraph inside the previous one, which isn't allowed. This causes a bunch of other errors, too. Because the validator can't see the end of this paragraph, it thinks that all the rest of the code is inside this first paragraph. Try changing the <p> of line 22 into a </p> and see if it works better:

```
<p>
    A pair of Oxen were drawing a heavily loaded wagon along a
    miry country road. They had to use all their strength to pull
    the wagon, but they did not complain.
</p>
```

Figure 2-8: Document type doesn't allow "p" here. That's odd.

The complaint is about the <p> tag on line 22. Unfortunately, Notepad doesn't have an easy way to know which line you're on, so you just have to count until I show you some better options in Chapter 3 of this minibook. To make things easier, I've reproduced the key part of the code here and high-lighted line 22. Try to find the problem before I explain it to you:

```
<h1>The Oxen and the Wheels</h1>
<h2>From Aesop's Fables</h2>

<p>
```

Figure 2-9 shows the validation results for oxWheels4.html.

Showing off your mad skillz

Sometimes, that green bar makes little tears of joy run down my cheeks. Congratulations! It's only the second chapter in this minibook, and you're already writing better Web pages than many professionals.

Seriously, a Web page that validates to XHTML Strict is a big deal, and you deserve to be proud of your efforts. The W3C is so proud of you that they offer you a little badge of honor you can put on your page.

Figure 2-10 shows more of the page you get when your page finally validates correctly. You can see a little button and some crazy-looking HTML code.

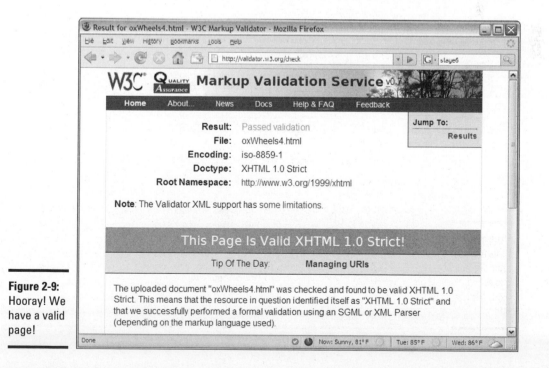

Figure 2-9:
Hooray! We
have a valid
page!

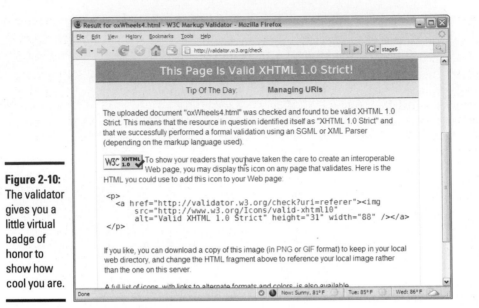

Figure 2-10:
The validator
gives you a
little virtual
badge of
honor to
show how
cool you are.

If you want, you can copy and paste that code into your page. `oxWheels5.html` has that special code added at the end of the body, shown in Figure 2-11.

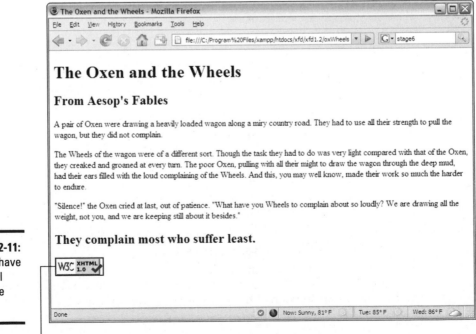

Figure 2-11:
Look, I have
a medal
from the
W3C!

Special code

Is validation really that big a deal?

I can hear the angry e-mails coming in. "Andy, I've been writing Web pages since 1998, and I never used a validator." Okay, it's true. A lot of people, even some professional Web developers, work without validating their code. Some of my older Web pages don't validate at all. (You can run the W3C validator on any page you want, not just one you wrote. This can be a source of great joy if you like feeling superior to sloppy coders.) When I became more proficient and more prolific in my Web development, I found that those little errors often caused a whole lot of grief down the road. I really believe you should validate every single page you write. Get into the habit now, and it'll pay huge dividends. When you're figuring out this stuff for the first time, do it right.

If you already know some HTML, you're gonna hate the validator for a while because it rejects coding habits that you might think are perfectly fine. Unlearning a habit is a lot harder than learning a new practice, so I feel your pain. It's still worth it.

After you discipline yourself to validate your pages, you'll find you've picked up good habits, and validation becomes a lot less painful. Experienced programmers actually like the validation process because it becomes much easier and prevents problems that could cause lots of grief later.

This little code snippet does a bunch of neat things, such as

+ **Establishing your coding prowess:** Any page that has this image on it has been tested and found compliant to XHTML Strict standards. When you see pages with this marker, you can be confident of the skill and professionalism of the author.

+ **Placing a cool image on the page:** You'll read how to add your own images in Chapter 6 of this minibook, but it's nice to see one already. This particular image is hosted at the W3C site.

+ **Letting users check the page for themselves:** When the user clicks the image, they're taken directly to the W3C validator to prove that the page is in fact valid XHTML Strict. Unfortunately, this link works only on pages that are posted to a Web server, so it doesn't work correctly on a page just sitting on your computer. Scope out Book VIII for suggestions on finding and using a server.

Using Tidy to repair pages

The W3C validator isn't the only game in town. Another great resource — HTML Tidy — can be used to fix your pages. You can download Tidy or just use the online version at `http://infohound.net/tidy`. Figure 2-12 illustrates the online version with `oxWheels1.html` being loaded.

Figure 2-12:
HTML
Tidy is an
alternative
to the W3C
validator.

Unlike W3C's validator, Tidy actually attempts to fix your page. Figure 2-13 displays how Tidy suggests the oxWheels.html page be fixed.

Figure 2-13:
Tidy fixes
the page,
but the fix
is a little
awkward.

Tidy examines the page for a number of common errors and does its best to fix the errors. However, the result is not quite perfect:

✦ **Tidy adds a new meta tag, indicating the page was created by Tidy.** I always get nervous when a program I didn't write starts messing with my pages.

✦ **Tidy tends to choose a sloppier doctype.** If you don't specify otherwise, Tidy checks against XHTML 1.0 Transitional, rather than Strict. This definition isn't as stringent. You can (and should) specify the Strict doctype manually in the submission form.

✦ **Tidy got confused by the title.** Tidy correctly diagnosed the title in the wrong place, but it added a blank title, as well as the intended one.

✦ **Sometimes, the indentation is off.** I set Tidy to indent every element, so it is easy to see how tag pairs are matched up. If I don't set up the indentation explicitly, I find Tidy code very difficult to read.

✦ **The changes aren't permanent.** Anything Tidy does is just a suggestion. If you want to keep the changes, you need to save the results in your editor.

I sometimes use Tidy when I'm stumped because I find the error messages are easier to understand than the W3C validator. However, I never trust it completely. There's really no substitute for good old detective skills and the official W3C validator.

If you find the W3C validator and Tidy to be a little tedious to use, look over the HTML validator extension described in Chapter 3 of this minibook. This handy tool adds both the W3C validator and Tidy to Firefox and automatically checks every page you visit. It also has Tidy support, so it can even fix most of your errors. That's how I do it.

Chapter 3: Choosing Your Tools

In This Chapter

✓ Choosing a text editor

✓ Using a dedicated HTML editor

✓ Comparing common browsers

✓ Introducing Integrated Development Environments (IDEs)

✓ Adding important Firefox extensions

Web development is a big job. You don't go to a construction site without a belt full of tools (and a cool hat), and the same thing is true with Web development (except you don't normally need a hard hat for Web development). An entire industry has evolved trying to sell tools that help make Web development easier. The funny thing is that the tools you need might not be the ones that people are trying to sell you. Some of the very best Web development tools are free, and some of the most expensive tools aren't that helpful.

This chapter tells you what you need and how to set up your workshop with great programs that simplify Web development.

What's Wrong with the Big Boys?

Many Web development books are really books about how to use a particular type of software. Microsoft's FrontPage/Expression Web and Macromedia/Adobe Dreamweaver are the two primary applications in this category. These tools are powerful and offer some *seemingly* great features:

✦ **WYSIWYG editing:** *What you see is what you get* is an idea borrowed from word processors. You can create a Web page much like a word-processing document and use menus, as well as tools, to handle all the formatting. The theory is that you don't have to know any icky codes.

✦ **Templates:** You can create a template that stays the same and build several pages from that template. If you need to change the template, everything else changes automatically.

✦ **Site management:** The interaction between the various pages on your site can be maintained automatically.

These sound like pretty good features, and they are. The tools (and the newer replacements, like Microsoft's Expression suite) are very powerful and can be an important part of your Web development toolkit. However, the same powerful programs introduce problems, such as the following:

+ **Code maintenance:** The commercial editors that concentrate on visual design tend to create pretty unmanageable code. If you find there's something you need to change by hand, it's pretty hard to fix the code.

+ **Vendor lock-in:** These tools are written by corporations that want you to buy other tools from them. If you're using Dreamweaver, you'll find it easy to integrate with other Adobe applications (like ColdFusion), but it's not as simple to connect to non-Adobe technology. Likewise, Microsoft's offerings are designed to work best with other Microsoft technologies.

+ **Cost:** The cost of these software packages keeps going up. Expression Web (Microsoft's replacement for FrontPage) costs about $300, and Dreamweaver weighs in at $400. Both companies encourage you to buy the software as part of a package, which can easily cost more than $500.

+ **Complexity:** They're complicated. You can take a full class or buy a huge book on how to use only one of these technologies. If it's that hard to figure out, is it really saving you any effort?

+ **Code:** You still need to understand it. No matter how great your platform is, at some point, you have to dig into your code. After you plunk down all that money and spend all that time figuring out an application, you still have to understand how the underlying code works because things still go wrong. For example, if your page fails to work with Safari, you'll have to find out why and fix the problem yourself.

+ **Spotty standards compliance:** The tools are getting better here, but if you want your pages to comply with the latest standards, you have to edit them heavily after the tool is finished.

+ **Display variations:** WYSIWYG is a lie. This is really the big problem. WYSIWYG works for word processors because it's possible to make the screen look like the printed page. After a page is printed, it stays the same. You don't know what a Web page will look like because that depends on the browser. What if the user loads your page on a cellphone or handheld device? The editors tend to perpetuate the myth that you can treat a Web page like a printed document when, in truth, it's a very different kind of beast.

+ **Incompatibility with other tools:** Web development is now moving toward content management systems (CMS) — programs which create Web sites dynamically. Generally, CMS systems provide the same ease-of-use as a visual editor but with other benefits. However, transitioning code created in a commercial editor to a CMS is very difficult. I describe CMS systems in detail in Book VIII, Chapter 3.

Alternative Web Development Tools

For Web development, all you really need is a text editor and a Web browser. You probably already have a basic set of tools on your computer. If you read Chapters 1 and 2 of this minibook, you've already written a couple of Web pages. However, the very basic tools that come with every computer might not be enough for serious work. Web development requires a specialized kind of text editor, and a number of tools have evolved that make the job easier.

The features you need on your computer

Here are a few features your text editor and browser might not have that you need.

✦ **Line numbers:** Notepad doesn't have an easy way to figure out what line you're on. And counting lines every time you want to find a problem noted by the validator is pretty tedious.

✦ **Help features:** Having an editor help with your code is ideal. Some tools can recognize HTML code, help with indentation, and warn you when something is wrong.

✦ **Macros:** You type the same code many times. A program that can record and play keyboard macros can save a huge amount of time.

✦ **Testing and validation:** Testing your code in one or more browsers should be simple, and there should be an easy way to check your code for standards.

✦ **Multiple browsers:** An Internet user having only one browser is fine, but a Web developer needs to know how things look in a couple different environments.

✦ **Browser features:** You can customize some browsers (especially Firefox) to help you a lot. With the right attachments, the browser can point out errors and help you see the structure of your page.

✦ **Free and open tools:** The Web is exciting because it's free and open technology. If you can find tools that follow the same philosophy, all the better.

Building a basic toolbox

I've found uses for five types of programs in Web development:

✦ **Enhanced text editors:** These tools are text editors, but they're souped-up with all kinds of fancy features, like syntax checkers, code-coloring tools, macro tools, and multiple document interfaces.

- ✦ **Browsers and plugins:** The browser you use can make a huge difference. You can also install free add-ons that can turn your browser into a powerful Web development tool.

- ✦ **Integrated Development Environments (IDE):** Programmers generally use IDEs, which combine text editing, visual layout, code testing, and debugging tools.

- ✦ **Programming technologies:** This book covers all pertinent info about incorporating other technologies, like Apache, PHP, and MySQL. I show you how to install everything you need for these technologies in Book VIII, Chapter 1. You don't need to worry about these things yet, but you should develop habits that are compatible with these enhanced technologies from the beginning.

- ✦ **Multimedia tools:** If you want various multimedia elements on your page, you'll need tools to manage them, as well. These could involve graphics and audio editors, as well as full-blown multimedia technologies, like Flash.

Picking a Text Editor

As a programmer, you come to see your text editor as a faithful companion. You spend a lot of time with this tool, so use one that works with you.

A text editor should save plain text without any formatting at all. You don't want anything that saves colors, font choices, or other text formatting because these things don't automatically translate to HTML.

Fortunately, you have several choices, as the following sections reveal.

Tools to avoid unless you have nothing else

A text editor may be a simple program, but that doesn't mean they're all the same. Some programs have a history of causing problems for beginners (and experienced developers, too). There's usually no need to use some of these weaker choices.

Microsoft Word

Just don't use it for Web development. Word is a word processor. Even though, theoretically, it can create Web pages, the HTML code it writes is absolutely horrific. As an example, I created a blank document, wrote "Hello World" in it, changed the font, and saved it as HTML. The resulting page was non-compliant code, was not quite HTML or XHTML, and was 114 lines long. Word is getting better, but it's just not a good Web development tool. In fact, don't use any word processor. They're just not designed for this kind of work.

Windows Notepad

Notepad is everywhere, and it's free. That's the good news. However, Notepad doesn't have a lot of the features you might need, such as line numbers, multiple documents, or macros. Use it if you're on an unfamiliar machine, but try something else if you can. Many people begin with Notepad, but it won't be long until you outgrow its limitations.

Mac TextEdit

Mac has a simple text editor built in — TextEdit — that's similar to Notepad, but closer to a word processor than a programmer's text editor. TextEdit saves files in a number of formats. If you want to use it to write Web pages, you must save your files in plain-text format, and you must not use any of TextEdit's formatting features. It's probably best not to use TextEdit unless you really have to.

A noteworthy editor: Notepad++

A number of developers have come up with good text editors. Some of the best are free, such as Notepad++ by Don Ho. Notepad++ is designed for text editing, especially in programming languages. Figure 3-1 shows Notepad++ with an HTML file loaded.

Figure 3-1:
Notepad++ has many of the features you need in a text editor.

Notepad++ has a lot of interesting features. Here are a few highlights:

✦ **Syntax highlighting:** Notepad++ can recognize key HTML terms and put different types of terms in different colors. For example, all HTML tags are rendered blue, and text is black, making it easy to tell if you've made certain kinds of mistakes, such as forgetting to end a tag. Note that the colors aren't saved in the document. The coloring features are there to help you understand the code.

✦ **Multiple files:** You'll often want to edit more than one document at a time. You can have several different documents in memory at the same time.

✦ **Multi-language support:** Currently, your pages consist of nothing but XHTML. Soon enough, you'll use some other languages, like SQL, CSS, and PHP. Notepad++ is smart enough to recognize these languages, too.

✦ **Macros:** Whenever you find yourself doing something over and over, consider writing a keyboard macro. Notepad++ has a terrific macro feature. Macros are easy to record and play back a series of keystrokes, which can save you a lot of work.

✦ **Page preview:** When you write a page, test it. Notepad++ has shortcut keys built in to let you quickly view your page in Internet Explorer (Ctrl+Alt+Shift+I) and Firefox (Ctrl+Alt+Shift+X).

✦ **TextFX:** The open-source design of Notepad++ makes it easy to add features. The TextFX extension (built into Notepad++) allows you to do all sorts of interesting things. One especially handy set of tools runs HTML Tidy on your page and fixes any problems.

Sadly, Notepad++ is a Windows-only editor. If you're using Mac or Linux, you need to find something else. Gedit is the closest alternative in the Linux world, but a few quality free editors exist for the Mac.

The old standards: VI and Emacs

No discussion of text editors is complete without a mention of the venerable UNIX editors that were the core of the early Internet experience. Most of the pioneering work on the Web was done in the UNIX and Linux operating systems, and these environments had two extremely popular text-editor families. Both might seem obscure and difficult to modern sensibilities, but they still have passionate adherents, even in the Windows community. (Besides, Linux is more popular than ever!)

VI and VIM

VI stands for VIsual Editor. That name seems strange now because most developers can't imagine an editor that's *not* visual. Back in the day, it was a very big deal that VI could use the entire screen for editing text. Before that time, line-oriented editors were the main way to edit text files. Trust me, you have it good now. Figure 3-2 shows a variant of VI (called VIM) in action.

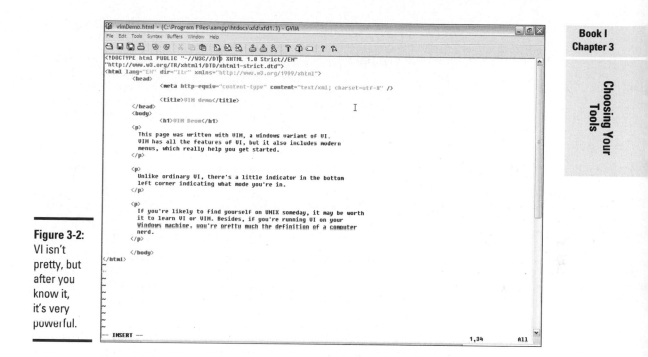

Figure 3-2:
VI isn't
pretty, but
after you
know it,
it's very
powerful.

VI is a *modal* editor, which means that the same key sometimes has more than one job, depending on the editor's current mode. For example, the I key is used to indicate where you want to insert text. The D key is used to delete text, and so on. Of course, when you're inserting text, the keys have their normal meanings. This multimode behavior is baffling to modern users, but it can be amazingly efficient after you get used to it. Skilled VI users swear by it and often use nothing else.

VI is a little too obscure for some users, so a number of variants are floating around, such as VIM, or VI Improved. (Yeah, it should be VII but maybe they were afraid people would call it the Roman numeral seven.) VIM is a little friendlier than VI. It tells you which mode it's in and includes such modern features as mouse support, menus, and icons. Even with these features, VIM is not intuitive for most people.

Versions of VI are available for nearly any operating system being used. If you already know VI, you might enjoy using it for Web page development because it has all the features you might need. If you don't already know VI, it's probably more efficient for you to start with a more standard text editor, such as Notepad++.

Emacs

The other popular editor from the UNIX world is Emacs. Like VI, you probably don't need this tool if you never use Linux or UNIX. Also like VI, if you know it already, you probably don't need anything else. Emacs has been a programmer's editor for a very long time (it has been in continuous development since 1976) and has nearly every feature you can think of.

Emacs also has a lot of features you haven't thought of, including a built-in text adventure game and even a psychotherapist simulator. I really couldn't make this stuff up if I tried.

Emacs has very powerful customization and macro features and allows you to view and edit more than one file at a time. Emacs also has the ability to view and manipulate the local file system, manage remote files, access the local operating system (OS) shell, and even browse the Web or check e-mail without leaving the program. If you're willing to invest in a program that takes some effort to understand, you'll have an incredibly powerful tool in your kit. Versions of Emacs are available for most major operating systems. Emacs is one of the first programs I install on any new computer because it's so powerful. A version of Emacs is shown in Figure 3-3.

Figure 3-3:
Emacs is powerful but somewhat eccentric.

An enhanced version — XEmacs — uses standard menus and icons like modern programs, so it's reasonably easy to get started with.

Emacs has an astonishing number of options and a nonstandard interface, so it can be challenging for beginners.

Other text editors

Many other text editors are used in Web development. The most important thing is to find one that matches the way you work. If you don't like any of the editors I've suggested so far, here are a few more you might want to try:

✦ **SynEdit:** Much like Notepad++ and very popular with Web developers

✦ **Scintilla:** Primarily a programming editor, but has nice support for XHTML coding

✦ **jEdit:** A popular text editor written in Java with nice features, but some developers consider it slower than the other choices

The Web Developer's Browser

Web pages are meant to display in a browser; so, of course, you need browsers for testing. Not all browsers are the same, though, so you need more than one. As of this writing, there are two major browsers and a number of other significant players in the browser world. It's important to know a little about the major browsers, which I discuss later in this section.

A little ancient history

You've probably already noticed that browsers are inconsistent in the way they display and handle Web pages. It's useful to understand how we got into this mess.

Mosaic/Netscape — the killer application

In the beginning, browsers were written by small teams. The most important early browser was Mosaic, written by a team based at the National Center for Supercomputing Applications (NCSA) in Champaign–Urbana, Illinois.

Several members of that NCSA team decided to create a completely commercial Web browser. Netscape was born, and it quickly became the most prominent and important browser, with 97 percent market share at the peak of its popularity.

Microsoft enters (and wins) the battle

Microsoft came onto the scene with Internet Explorer (IE). A bitter fight (sometimes called the Browser Wars) ensued between Microsoft and Netscape. Each browser added new features regularly. Eventually, entire sets of tags evolved, so a Web page written for IE would not always work in Netscape and vice versa. Developers had three bad choices: pick only one browser to support, write two versions of the page, or stick with the more limited set of features common to both browsers.

Netscape 6.0 was a technical disappointment, and Microsoft capitalized, earning a nearly complete lock on the browser market. Microsoft's version of standards became the *only* standards because there was virtually no competition. After Microsoft won the fight, there was a period of stability but very little innovation.

Firefox shakes up the world

A new browser rose from the ashes of Netscape (in fact, its original name was Firebird, after the mythical birds that rise from their own ashes). The name was later changed to Firefox, and it breathed new life into the Web. Firefox has several new features that are very appealing to Web developers:

+ **Solid compliance to standards:** Firefox followed the W3C standards almost perfectly.

+ **Tabbed browsing:** One browser window can have several panels, each with its own page.

+ **Easy customization:** Firefox developers encouraged people to add improvements and extensions to Firefox. This led to hundreds of interesting add-ons.

+ **Improved security:** By this time, a number of security loopholes in IE were publicized. Although Firefox has many of the same problems, it has a much better reputation for openness and quick solutions.

Overview of the prominent browsers

The browser is the primary tool of the Web. All your users view your page with one browser or another, so you need to know a little about each of them.

Microsoft Internet Explorer 7 and 8

Microsoft Internet Explorer (MSIE or simply IE) is the most popular browser on the planet. Before Firefox came along, a vast majority of Web users used IE. Explorer is still extremely prevalent because it comes installed with Microsoft Windows. Of course, it also works exclusively with Microsoft Windows. Mac and Linux aren't supported (users don't seem too upset about it, though).

IE7 featured some welcome additions, including tabbed browsing and improved compliance with the W3C standards. Cynics have suggested these improvements were a response to Firefox. IE7 was quickly replaced with the most recent version, Internet Explorer 8. IE8 has much improved speed and standards-compliance, but it still lags behind the other major browsers in these regards.

If you write your code to XHTML 1.0 Strict standards, it almost always displays as expected in IE7/8.

IE versions 7 and 8 do not fully support HTML 5. If you want to experience these features, you need to use one of the other modern browsers described in this chapter.

Older versions of Internet Explorer

The earlier versions of IE are still extremely important because so many computers out there don't have IE7 or IE8 installed yet.

Microsoft made a version of IE available for programmers to embed in their own software; therefore, many custom browsers are actually IE with a different skin. Most of the custom browsers that are installed with the various broadband services are simply dressed up forms of IE. Therefore, IE is even more common than you might guess because people might be using a version of it while thinking it's something else.

IE6 and earlier versions used Microsoft's own variation of standards. They display old-style HTML well, but these browsers don't comply perfectly with all the W3C standards. Having a version of one of these older browsers around is important so you can see how your pages display in them. If you write standards-compliant code, you'll find that it doesn't work perfectly in these variations. You need to do some tweaking to make some features come out right. Don't panic, because they're relatively small details, and I point out the strategies you need as we go.

Checking your pages on IE6 or earlier is necessary. Unfortunately, if you have IE8 (or whatever comes next), you probably don't have IE6 any longer. You can't have two versions of IE running on the same machine at once (at least, not easily), so you might need to keep an older machine just for testing purposes. You can use a testing site, such as Spoon.net (www.spoon.net/browsers), to check how various browsers render your pages if you don't want to install all the other browsers.

Mozilla Firefox

Developers writing standards-compliant code frequently test their pages in Firefox because it has a great reputation for standards compliance. Firefox has other advantages, as well, such as

✦ **Better code view:** If you view the HTML code of a page, you see the code in a special window. The code has syntax coloring, which makes it easy to read. IE often displays code in Notepad, which is confusing because you think you can edit the code, but you're simply editing a copy.

✦ **Better error-handling:** You'll make mistakes. Generally, Firefox does a better job of pointing out errors than IE, especially when you begin using JavaScript and other advanced technologies.

✦ **Great extensions:** As you see later in this chapter, Firefox has some wonderful extensions that make Web development a lot easier. These extensions allow you to modify your code on the fly, automatically validate your code, and explore the structure of your page dynamically.

Google Chrome

Google has jumped into the fray with an interesting browser called Chrome. Google sees the future of computing in browser-based applications using AJAX technologies. The Chrome browser is extremely fast, especially in the JavaScript technology that serves as the foundation to this strategy. Chrome complies quite well with common standards, so if your pages look good in Firefox, they'll also do well in Chrome.

Other notable browsers

Firefox and IE are the big players in the browser world, but they certainly aren't the only browsers you will encounter.

Opera

The Opera Web browser, one of the earliest standards-compliant browsers, is a technically solid browser that has never been widely used. If you design your pages with strict compliance in mind, users with Opera have no problems accessing them.

Webkit/Safari

Apple includes a Web browser in all recent versions of Mac OS. The current incarnation — Safari — is an excellent standards-compliant browser. Safari was originally designed only for the Mac, but a Windows version has been released recently. The Webkit framework, the foundation for Safari, is used in a number of other online applications, mainly on the Mac. It's also the foundation of the browsers on the iPhone and iPad.

Mozilla

There's still a Mozilla browser, but it has been replaced largely with Firefox. Because Mozilla uses the same underlying engine, it renders code the same way Firefox does.

Portable browsers

The Web isn't just about desktops anymore. Lots of people browse the Web with cellphones, iPhones, and PDAs. These devices often have specialized Web browsers designed to handle the particular needs of the portable gadget. However, these devices usually have tiny screens, small memory capacity, and slower download speeds than their desktop cousins. A portable browser rarely displays a page the way it's intended to appear on a desktop machine. Portable browsers usually do a good job of making standards-compliant code work, but they really struggle with other types of HTML (especially tables used for formatting and fixed layouts).

Text-only browsers

Some browsers that don't display any graphics at all (such as Lynx) are intended for the old command-line interfaces. This may seem completely irrelevant today, but these browsers are incredibly fast because they don't display graphics. Auditory browsers read the contents of Web pages. They were originally intended for people with visual disabilities, but people without any disabilities often use them as well. Fire Vox is a variant of Firefox that reads Web pages aloud.

Worrying about text-only readers may seem unnecessary because people with visual disabilities are a relatively small part of the population, and you may not think they're part of your target audience. You probably should think about these users anyway, because it isn't difficult to help them. There's another reason, too. The search engines (Google is the main game in town) read your page just like a text-only browser. Therefore, if an element is invisible to a text-based browser, it won't appear on the search engine.

The bottom line in browsers

Really, you need to have access to a couple browsers, but you can't possibly have them all. I tend to do my initial development testing with Firefox. I then check pages on IE7 and IE6. I also check the built-in browser on my cellphone and PDA to see how the pages look there. Generally, if you get a page that gives you suitable results on IE6, IE7, and Firefox, you can be satisfied that it works on most browsers. However, there's still no guarantee. If you follow the standards, your page displays on any browser, but you might not get the exact layout you expect.

Tricking Out Firefox

One of the best features of Firefox is its support for extensions. Hundreds of clever and generous programmers have written tools to improve and alter Firefox's performance. Three of these tools — HTML Validator, Web Developer toolbar, and Firebug — are especially important to Web developers.

Validating your pages with HTML Validator

In Chapter 2 of this minibook, I explain how important Web standards are and how to use online services such as `http://validator.w3.org` and HTML Tidy (`http://infohound.net/tidy`). These are terrific services, but it would be even better to have these validators built directly into your browser. The HTML Validator extension by Marc Gueury is a tool that does exactly that: It adds both the W3C validator and HTML Tidy to your Firefox installation.

When you have the HTML Validator extension (available on this book's CD-ROM) running, you have an error count in the footer of every page you visit. (You'll be amazed how many errors are on the Web.) You'll be able to tell immediately if a page has validation errors.

With the HTML Validator, your View Source tool is enhanced, as shown in Figure 3-4.

View Source window   Page repair

Figure 3-4:
The HTML
Validator
explains all
errors in
your page.

Validation errors

Error suggestions

The View Source tool becomes much more powerful when you run HTML Validator, as follows:

+ **Each error is listed in an errors panel.** You see this same error list from W3C.

+ **Clicking an error highlights it in the source code listing.** This makes it easy to see exactly what line of code triggers each error.

+ **Complete help is shown for every error.** The HTML Validator toolbar presents much more helpful error messages than the W3C results.

+ **Automated clean-up.** You can click the Clean Up link, and the HTML Validator extension automatically applies HTML Tidy to your page. This can be a very effective way to fix older pages with many errors.

The HTML Validator tool will revolutionize your Web development experience, helping you create standards-compliant sites easily and discover the compliance level of any page you visit. (It's fun to feel superior.)

Using the Web Developer toolbar

The Web Developer toolbar by Chris Pederick provides all kinds of useful tools for Web developers. The program installs as a new toolbar in Firefox, as shown in Figure 3-5.

CSS editor   Block outlines   Web Developer toolbar

Figure 3-5:
The Web Developer toolbar adds several features to Firefox.

Figure 3-5 shows the Wiley home page with some of the Web Developer tool-bar features active. The Edit CSS frame on the left allows you to modify the look of the page in real time, and the thick outlines help visualize the page organization. (I describe these ideas in detail in Books III and IV.)

When you activate the Web Developer toolbar (use the View⇨Toolbars menu command to hide or show it), you can use it to do the following:

✦ **Edit your page on the fly.** The Edit HTML Entry option on the Miscellaneous drop-down menu opens a small text editor on the left side of the screen. You can make changes to your HTML here and immediately see the results in the main screen. The changes aren't permanent, but you can save them.

✦ **Validate your pages.** Choosing CSS⇨Edit CSS is the command to validate your page, but the Web Developer toolbar also adds some hotkeys to Firefox so you can instantly send your page to the W3C validator. Pressing Ctrl+Shift+A contacts the W3C validator and then sends your page to it. It's much easier than memorizing the validator address. This feature alone is worth the short download time. You can also do other kinds of validation, check your CSS, or see how well your page conforms to various guidelines for people with disabilities.

✦ **Manipulate CSS code.** After you define your page with XHTML, use CSS to dress it up. The CSS menu has a number of great tools for seeing how CSS is set up and experimenting with it on the fly. I explain how to use the CSS tools in Books II and III, where I describe CSS.

✦ **View your page in different sizes.** Not everybody has a huge flat-panel display. It's important to see how your page looks in a number of standard screen resolutions.

✦ **Get a speed report.** Your Web page may load great on your broadband connection, but how does it work on Aunt Judy's dialup? Web Developer has a tool that analyzes all the components of the page, reports how long each component takes to download over various connections, and suggests ways to improve the speed of your page downloads.

✦ **Check accessibility.** You can run a number of automated tests to determine how accessible your page is. Use the accessibility tests to see how your page will work for people with various disabilities and whether you pass certain required standards (for example, requirements of government sites).

The Web Developer toolbar can do a lot more, but these are some of the highlights. The toolbar is a small and fast download, and it makes Web development a lot easier. There's really no good reason not to use it.

Using Firebug

The Firebug extension is another vital tool for Web developers. Firebug concentrates more on JavaScript development rather than pure XHTML development, but it's also useful for XHTML beginners. Figure 3-6 shows the Firebug extension opened as a panel in Firefox.

Firebug's Inspect mode allows you to compare the HTML code to the output. When you move your mouse over a part of the rendered page, Firebug highlights the relevant part of the code in the other panel. Likewise, you can move the mouse over a code fragment and see the affected code segment, which can be extremely handy when things aren't working out the way you expect.

You can view the HTML code as an outline, which helps you see the overall structure of the code. You can also edit the code in the panel and see the results immediately, as you can with the Web Developer toolbar, which I discuss in the previous section. Changes you make in Firebug aren't permanent, but you can copy them to your text editor.

Firebug really shows off when you get to more sophisticated techniques, such as CSS, DOM Manipulation, JavaScript, and AJAX. Books IV and VII show you how Firebug can be used to aid in these processes.

Figure 3-6:
Firebug gives a detailed view of your page.

Source code window   CSS information

Using a Full-Blown IDE

You might think I hate dedicated Web page editors, but I don't. I use them all the time for other kinds of programming. The problem is that up until recently, there weren't any real IDEs (Integrated Development Environments) for Web development. Most of the tools try to be visual development tools that automate the design of visual pages, rather than programming environments. They have flaws because Web development is really a programming problem with visual design aspects, rather than a visual design problem with programming underneath.

A couple of IDEs have popped up recently in the open-source community. One tries to be like the commercial tools (and ends up replicating some of their flaws). Some other editors have emerged that seem to be a good compromise between helping you write solid code and growing with you while you become more sophisticated.

Introducing Aptana

My preferred editor for beginners who intend to advance is Aptana (available on this book's CD-ROM or at www.aptana.com). Aptana Studio is a full-blown IDE, based on the popular Eclipse editor. Aptana has many features that make it a good choice for Web developers:

✦ **Syntax completion:** Aptana has built-in knowledge of HTML (and several other languages). When you start to type HTML code, it recognizes the code and pops up a list of suggestions. Figure 3-7 shows Aptana helping on some HTML code.

✦ **Automatic ending tags:** As soon as you write a beginning tag, Aptana automatically generates the corresponding end tag. This makes it much less likely that you'll forget an ending tag — one of the most common coding errors.

✦ **Automatically generated XHTML template:** When you tell Aptana to create an HTML page, it can generate the page template with all the messy doctype stuff built in. (I explain how to customize this feature in the next section.)

✦ **Error detection:** Aptana can look at the code and detect certain errors. Although it isn't a replacement for a validator, it can be a very handy tool, especially when you begin to write JavaScript code.

✦ **File management tools:** Aptana makes it easy to work with both the local file system and pages that reside on Internet servers.

✦ **Page preview:** You can preview your page directly within Aptana, or you can view it in your primary browser.

✦ **Outline view:** This panel displays the page structure as an outline to help you see the overall structure of the page. You can also use this panel as a table of contents to get to any particular part of your page in the editor quickly. Figure 3-8 shows the Outline view in action.

Syntax highlighting

Automatic code completion

Multiple files

Code outline

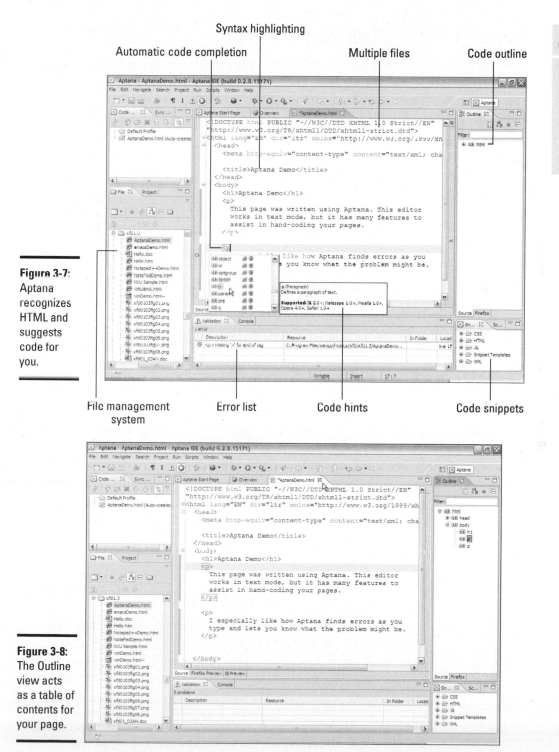

Figure 3-7:
Aptana recognizes HTML and suggests code for you.

File management system

Error list

Code hints

Code snippets

Figure 3-8:
The Outline view acts as a table of contents for your page.

✦ **Advanced features:** When you're ready to try JavaScript and AJAX, Aptana has nice support for these more advanced technologies. The syntax-highlighting features work in CSS, JavaScript, and PHP the same way they do in HTML. This means you can use the same editor for all your Web languages, which is a great thing.

Aptana Studio previously had two different versions, but now the features are combined, and the community edition is the only version offered. Studio is completely free to use and redistribute, although it has multiple licensing models. It provides all the features you might need and a few advanced features (such as integrated support for cloud-based computing) you may never use.

Customizing Aptana

Aptana is a great editor, but I recommend you change a few settings after you install it on your system.

Getting to the HTML editor preferences

Aptana can be customized in many ways. For now, the only preferences you need to change are in the HTML editor. Choose Windows➪Preferences, and in the Preferences dialog box, expand the Aptana link and select HTML Editor. The dialog box is shown in Figure 3-9.

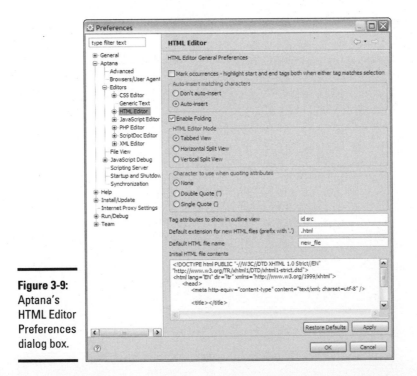

Figure 3-9: Aptana's HTML Editor Preferences dialog box.

Changing the extension

By default, Aptana saves files with the .htm extension. Because this is the extension normally used only by Microsoft servers, I prefer to save pages with the .html extension. All Web pages in this book are stored with the .html extension.

Enter **.html** in the Default Extension for New HTML Files (Prefix with '.') field to make this change, if you wish.

Changing the initial contents

When you create a new Web page in Aptana, a basic template appears. This is convenient, but it creates an HTML 4.0 doctype. Open template.html in a normal text editor, copy it, and paste it to the provided text area, and your pages will begin with the standard template.

Changing the view

Aptana allows you to split the screen with your code in one panel and a browser view in another. Every time you save your code, the browser view immediately updates. This is a really good tool, especially for a beginner, because you can get very quick feedback on how your page looks. In the HTML Editor Mode section in the Preferences dialog box (refer to Figure 3-9), you can indicate whether you want the browser preview to be in a separate tab, in a horizontal split screen, or in a vertical split screen. I use tabs because I like to see as much code as possible on-screen.

The latest version of Aptana tries to force you into a project mode, where you combine all your files into a large project. Although this is fine for large projects, it's probably not what you want when you first get started. To build a file without a project, use the File tab (on the left) to move to the directory where you want to create the file. Right-click the directory and choose New.

Aptana issues

I use Aptana quite a bit, and it's one of my favorite tools. However, it isn't perfect; it's a large program that can take some time to load. I have also run into some display bugs here and there, and the debugging model doesn't always seem to cooperate the way it should. Aptana is quite a good tool, but if these things bother you, you might want to look at the following alternative.

Introducing Komodo Edit

Komodo Edit is another very powerful Web editor (similar to Aptana) that may suit some developers more. Komodo doesn't try to do everything that Aptana does, but it's faster and a bit more reliable. Mainly a text editor, Komodo does have some great features. My favorite part about Komodo is how easy it is to modify.

✦ **Abbreviations:** Although many editors have features like this, the abbreviations tool in Komodo is especially useful. Komodo comes with a huge number of abbreviations built in, and a very easy mechanism to use them. For example, if you type **xhtml** and then press Ctrl-T, Komodo will replace the text with a complete XHTML framework. Creating new abbreviations is very easy, so you can quickly customize.

✦ **Macros:** I think one of Aptana's biggest weaknesses is the clumsy macro features. Aptana doesn't have an easy way to record keystroke commands and play them back. (To be fair, Aptana has an incredibly powerful scripting system, but it isn't super easy to use.) Komodo has a really super macro-recording feature.

✦ **Snippets:** Komodo has a terrific built-in library of code snippets containing the code you frequently use. Adding new snippets is easy, so soon enough you'll have most of the code you use a lot available at your fingertips.

✦ **Commands:** Komodo allows you to define commands you can run from within the editor. For example, you can create a DOS command to list all the files in the current directory and run the command without leaving Komodo. This can be useful if you're writing code that creates files (as you do in Book V, Chapter 7). It's also used to run external programs, such as compilers (if you were writing code in a language like C or Java that requires such things).

Figure 3-10 shows Komodo Edit being used to modify a Web page.

Keyboard macros   Code snippets

Figure 3-10:
Komodo Edit
has many
of the same
features as
Aptana, but
it's a little
smaller and
snappier.

Chapter 4: Managing Information with Lists and Tables

In This Chapter

✔ Understanding basic lists

✔ Creating unordered, ordered, and nested lists

✔ Building definition lists

✔ Building basic tables

✔ Using rowspan and colspan attributes

You'll often need to present large amounts of organized information, and XHTML has some wonderful tools to manage this task. XHTML has three kinds of lists and a powerful table structure for organizing the content of your page. Figure out how these tools work, and you can manage complex information with ease.

Making a List and Checking It Twice

XHTML supports three types of lists. *Unordered* lists generally contain bullet points. They're used when the order of elements in the list isn't important. *Ordered* lists usually have some kind of numeric counter preceding each list item. *Definition* lists contain terms and their definitions.

Creating an unordered list

All the list types in XHTML are closely related. The simplest and most common kind of list is an unordered list.

Looking at an unordered list

Look at the simple page shown in Figure 4-1. In addition to a couple of headers, it has a list of information.

Figure 4-1:
An un-
ordered
list of Web
browsers.

This list of browsers has some interesting visual characteristics:

✦ **The items are indented.** There's some extra space between the left margin and the beginning of each list item.

✦ **The list elements have bullets.** That little dot in front of each item is a *bullet.* Bullets are commonly used in unordered lists like this one.

✦ **Each item begins a new line.** When a list item is displayed, it's shown on a new line.

These characteristics help you see that you have a list, but they're just default behaviors. Defining something as a list doesn't force it to look a particular way; the defaults just help you see that these items are indeed part of a list.

Remember the core idea of XHTML here. You aren't really describing how things *look,* but what they *mean.* You can change the appearance later when you figure out CSS, so don't get too tied up in the particular appearance of things. For now, just recognize that HTML (and by extension, XHTML) can build lists, and make sure you know how to use the various types.

Building an unordered list

Lists are made with two kinds of tags. One tag surrounds the entire list and indicates the general type of list. This first example demonstrates an unordered list, which is surrounded by the <ul></ul> pair.

Note: Indenting all the code inside the <ul> set is common. The unordered list can go in the main body.

Inside the <ul></ul> set is a number of list items. Each element of the list is stored between a <li> (list item) and a </li> tag. Normally, each <li></li> pair goes on its own line of the source code, although you can make a list item as long as you want.

Look to Book II, Chapter 4 for information on how to change the bullet to all kinds of other images, including circles, squares, and even custom images.

The code for the unordered list is pretty straightforward:

```
<!DOCTYPE html PUBLIC "-//W3C//DTD XHTML 1.0 Strict//EN"
"http://www.w3.org/TR/xhtml1/DTD/xhtml1-strict.dtd">
<html lang="EN" dir="ltr" xmlns="http://www.w3.org/1999/xhtml">
  <head>
    <meta http-equiv="content type" content="text/xml; charset=utf-8" />

    <title>basicUL.html</title>
  </head>
  <body>
    <h1>Basic Lists</h1>
    <h2>Common Web Browsers</h2>
    <ul>
      <li>Firefox</li>
      <li>Internet Explorer</li>
      <li>Opera</li>
      <li>Safari</li>
    </ul>

  </body>
</html>
```

Creating ordered lists

Ordered lists are almost exactly like unordered lists. Ordered lists traditionally have numbers rather than bullets (although you can change this through CSS if you want; see Book III, Chapter 3).

Viewing an ordered list

Figure 4-2 demonstrates a page with a basic ordered list — basicOL.html.

Figure 4-2:
A simple
ordered list.

Figure 4-2 shows a list where the items are numbered. When your data is a list of steps or information with some type of numerical values, an ordered list is a good choice.

Building the ordered list

The code for basicOL.html is remarkably similar to the previous unordered list:

```
<!DOCTYPE html PUBLIC "-//W3C//DTD XHTML 1.0 Strict//EN"
"http://www.w3.org/TR/xhtml1/DTD/xhtml1-strict.dtd">
<html lang="EN" dir="ltr" xmlns="http://www.w3.org/1999/xhtml">
  <head>
    <meta http-equiv="content-type" content="text/xml; charset=utf-8" />
    <title>basicOL.html</title>
  </head>

  <body>
    <h1>Basic Ordered List</h1>
    <h2>Top ten dog names in the USA</h2>
    <ol>
      <li>Max</li>
      <li>Jake</li>
      <li>Buddy</li>
      <li>Maggie</li>
      <li>Bear</li>
      <li>Molly</li>
      <li>Bailey</li>
      <li>Shadow</li>
      <li>Sam</li>
      <li>Lady</li>
    </ol>

    <p>
      data from http://www.bowwow.com.au
    </p>
  </body>
</html>
```

The only change is the list tag itself. Rather than the `<ul>` tag, the ordered list uses the `<ol>` indicator. The list items are the same `<li></li>` pairs used in the unordered list.

You don't indicate the item number anywhere; it generates automatically based on the position of each item within the list. Therefore, you can change the order of the items, and the numbers are still correct.

This is where it's great that XHTML is about meaning, not layout. If you specified the actual numbers, it'd be a mess to move things around. All that really matters is that the element is inside an ordered list.

Making nested lists

Sometimes, you'll want to create outlines or other kinds of complex data in your pages. You can easily nest lists inside each other, if you want. Figure 4-3 shows a more complex list describing popular cat names in the U.S. and Australia.

Nested Lists

Popular Cat Names

• USA

   1. Tigger
   2. Tiger
   3. Max
   4. Smokey
   5. Sam

• Australia

   1. Oscar
   2. Max
   3. Tiger
   4. Sam
   5. Misty

Figure 4-3:
An ordered list inside an unordered list!

Figure 4-3 uses a combination of lists to do its work. This figure contains a list of two countries: the U.S. and Australia. Each country has an H3 heading and another (ordered) list inside it. You can nest various elements inside a list, but you have to do it carefully if you want the page to validate.

In this example, there's an unordered list with only two elements. Each of these elements contains an `<h3>` heading and an ordered list. The page handles all this data in a relatively clean way and validates correctly.

Examining the nested list example

The entire code for `nestedList.html` is reproduced here:

```
<!DOCTYPE html PUBLIC "-//W3C//DTD XHTML 1.0 Strict//EN"
"http://www.w3.org/TR/xhtml1/DTD/xhtml1-strict.dtd">
<html lang="EN" dir="ltr" xmlns="http://www.w3.org/1999/xhtml">
  <head>
    <meta http-equiv="content-type" content="text/xml; charset=utf-8" />
    <title>nestedList.html</title>
  </head>

  <body>
    <h1>Nested Lists</h1>

    <h2>Popular Cat Names</h2>
    <ul>
      <li>
        <h3>USA</h3>
        <ol>
          <li>Tigger</li>
          <li>Tiger</li>
          <li>Max</li>
          <li>Smokey</li>
          <li>Sam</li>
        </ol>
      </li>

      <li>
        <h3>Australia</h3>
        <ol>
          <li>Oscar</li>
          <li>Max</li>
          <li>Tiger</li>
          <li>Sam</li>
          <li>Misty</li>
        </ol>
      </li>
    </ul>
  </body>
</html>
```

Here are a few things you might notice in this code listing:

✦ There's a large <ul> set surrounding the entire main list.

✦ The main list has only two list items.

✦ Each of these items represents a country.

✦ Each country has an <h3> element, describing the country name inside the <li>.

✦ Each country also has an <ol> set with a list of names.

✦ The indentation really helps you see how things are connected.

Indenting your code

You might have noticed that I indent all the XHTML code in this book. The browsers ignore all indentation, but it's still an important coding habit.

There are many opinions about how code should be formatted, but the standard format I use in this book will serve you well until you develop your own style.

Generally, I use the following rules to indent HTML/XHTML code:

✦ **Indent each nested element.** Because the `<head>` tag is inside the `<html>` element, I indent to indicate this. Likewise, the `<li>` elements are always indented inside `<ul>` or `<ol>` pairs.

✦ **Line up your elements.** If an element takes up more than one line, line up the ending tag with the beginning tag. This way, you know what ends what.

✦ **Use spaces, not tabs.** The tab character often causes problems in source code. Different editors format tabs differently, and a mixture of tabs and spaces can make your carefully formatted page look awful when you view it in another editor.

If you are using Aptana (and you really should consider it if you're not — see Chapter 3 in this minibook for more information about it), note that Aptana's autoformatting defaults to tabs. From the Window menu, select Preferences. Then find the Aptana⇨Editors panel and select Insert Spaces Instead of Tabs.

✦ **Use two spaces.** Most coders use two or four spaces per indentation level. HTML elements can be nested pretty deeply. Going seven or eight layers deep is common. If you use tabs or too many spaces, you'll have so much white space that you can't see the code.

Aptana defaults to four spaces, but you can change it to two. From the General menu, choose Editors⇨Text Editors, and set the Displayed Tab Width option to 2.

✦ **End at the left margin.** If you finish the page and you're not back at the left margin, you've forgotten to end something. Proper indentation makes seeing your page organization easy. Each element should line up with its closing tag.

Building a nested list

When you look over the code for the nested list, it can look intimidating, but it isn't really that hard. The secret is to build the list *outside in:*

1. **Create the outer list first.**

   Build the primary list (whether it's ordered or unordered). In my example, I began with just the unordered list with the two countries in it.

2. **Add list items to the outer list.**

   If you want text or headlines in the larger list (as I did), you can put them here. If you're putting nothing but a list inside your primary list, you may want to put some placeholder `<li>` tags in there just so you can be sure everything's working.

3. **Validate before adding the next list level.**

   Nested lists can confuse the validator (and you). Validate your code with the outer list to make sure there are no problems before you add inner lists.

4. **Add the first inner list.**

   After you know the basic structure is okay, add the first interior list. For my example, this was the ordered list of cat names in the U.S.

5. **Repeat until finished.**

   Keep adding lists until your page looks right.

6. **Validate frequently.**

   It's much better to validate while you go than to wait until everything's finished. Catch your mistakes early so you don't replicate them.

Building the definition list

One more type of list — the definition list — is very useful, even if it's used infrequently. The definition list was originally designed to format dictionary-style definitions, but it's really useful any time you have name and value pairs. Figure 4-4 shows a sample definition list in action.

Basic Definition List

Common Web Browsers

Mosaic
  The mother of all modern browsers. The first widely used visual browser.
Netscape
  The commercial successor to Mosaic. Widely popular, but eventually eclipsed by Internet Explorer
IE
  Microsoft's entry into the browser market, and a dominant player.
Firefox
  An open-source browser that has shaken up the world.

Figure 4-4: A basic definition list.

Definition lists don't use bullets or numbers. Instead, they have two elements. *Definition terms* are usually words or short phrases. In Figure 4-4, the browser names are defined as definition terms. *Definition descriptions* are the extended text blocks that contain the actual definition.

The standard layout of definition lists indents each definition description. Of course, you can change the layout to what you want after you understand the CSS in Books II and III.

You can use definition lists any time you want a list marked by key terms, rather than bullets or numbers. The definition list can also be useful in other situations, such as forms, figures with captions, and so on.

Here's the code for `basicDL.html`:

```
<!DOCTYPE html PUBLIC "-//W3C//DTD XHTML 1.0 Strict//EN"
"http://www.w3.org/TR/xhtml1/DTD/xhtml1-strict.dtd">
<html lang="EN" dir="ltr" xmlns="http://www.w3.org/1999/xhtml">
  <head>
    <meta http-equiv="content-type" content="text/xml; charset=utf-8" />
    <title>BasicDL.html</title>
  </head>

  <body>
    <h1>Basic Definition List</h1>
    <h2>Common Web Browsers</h2>
    <dl>
      <dt>Mosaic</dt>
      <dd>
        The mother of all modern browsers. The first widely used
        visual browser.
      </dd>

      <dt>Netscape</dt>
      <dd>
        The commercial successor to Mosaic. Widely popular, but
        eventually eclipsed by Internet Explorer
      </dd>

      <dt>IE</dt>
      <dd>
        Microsoft's entry into the browser market, and a dominant
        player.
      </dd>

      <dt>Firefox</dt>
      <dd>
        An open-source browser that has shaken up the world.
      </dd>
    </dl>
  </body>
</html>
```

As you can see, the definition list uses three tag pairs:

✦ **<dl></dl>** defines the entire list.

✦ **<dt></dt>** defines each definition term.

✦ **<dd></dd>** defines the definition data.

Definition lists aren't used often, but they can be extremely useful. Any time you have a list that will be a combination of terms and values, a definition list is a good choice.

Building Tables

Sometimes, you'll encounter data that fits best in a tabular format. XHTML supports several table tags for this kind of work. Figure 4-5 illustrates a very basic table.

A Basic Table

XHTML Super Heroes

Hero	Power	Nemesis
The XMLator	Standards compliance	Sloppy Code Boy
Captain CSS	Super-layout	Lord Deprecated
Browser Woman	Mega-Compatibility	Ugly Code Monster

Sometimes, the best way to show data in a meaningful way is to organize it in a table. XHTML defines a table with the (cleverly named) `<table>` tag. The table contains a number of table rows (defined with the `<tr>` tag). Each table row can consist of a number of table data (`<td>`) or table header (`<th>`) tags.

Compare the output in Figure 4-5 with the code for `basicTable.html` that creates it:

```
<!DOCTYPE html PUBLIC "-//W3C//DTD XHTML 1.0 Strict//EN"
"http://www.w3.org/TR/xhtml1/DTD/xhtml1-strict.dtd">
<html lang="EN" dir="ltr" xmlns="http://www.w3.org/1999/xhtml">
  <head>
    <meta http-equiv="content-type" content="text/xml; charset=utf-8" />
    <title>basicTable.html</title>
  </head>

  <body>
    <h1>A Basic Table</h1>
    <h2>XHTML Super Heroes</h2>
    <table border = "1">
      <tr>
        <th>Hero</th>
        <th>Power</th>
        <th>Nemesis</th>
      </tr>

      <tr>
        <td>The XMLator</td>
        <td>Standards compliance</td>
        <td>Sloppy Code Boy</td>
      </tr>

      <tr>
        <td>Captain CSS</td>
```

```
      <td>Super-layout</td>
      <td>Lord Deprecated</td>
   </tr>

   <tr>
      <td>Browser Woman</td>
      <td>Mega-Compatibility</td>
      <td>Ugly Code Monster</td>
   </tr>

   </table>
  </body>
</html>
```

Defining the table

The XHTML table is defined with the `<table></table>` pair. It makes a lot of sense to indent and space your code carefully so you can see the structure of the table in the code. Just by glancing at the code, you can guess that the table consists of three rows and each row consists of three elements.

In a word processor, you typically create a blank table by defining the number of rows and columns, and then fill it in. In XHTML, you define the table row by row, and the elements in each row determine the number of columns. It's up to you to make sure each row has the same number of elements.

By default (in most browsers, anyway), tables don't show their borders. If you want to see basic table borders, you can turn on the table's `border` attribute. (An *attribute* is a special modifier you can attach to some tags.)

```
<table border = "1">
```

This tag creates a table and specifies that it will have a border of size `1`. If you leave out the `border = "1"` business, some browsers display a border and some don't. You can set the border value to `0` or to a larger number. The larger number makes a bigger border, as shown in Figure 4-6.

Although this method of making table borders is perfectly fine, I show a much more flexible and powerful technique in Book II, Chapter 4.

Figure 4-6:
I set the border attribute to 10.

A Basic Table

XHTML Super Heroes

Hero	Power	Nemesis
The XMLator	Standards compliance	Sloppy Code Boy
Captain CSS	Super-layout	Lord Deprecated
Browser Woman	Mega-Compatibility	Ugly Code Monster

Setting a table border is a good idea because you can't count on browsers to have the same default. Additionally, the border value is always in quotes. When you read about CSS in Book II (are you getting tired of hearing that?), you discover how to add more complex and interesting borders than this simple attribute allows.

Adding your first row

After you define a table, you need to add some rows. Each row is indicated by a `<tr></tr>` pair.

Inside the `<tr></tr>` set, you need some table data. The first row often consists of *table headers.* These special cells are formatted differently to indicate that they're labels, rather than data.

Table headers have some default formatting to help you remember they're headers, but you can change the way they look. You can change the table header's appearance in all kinds of great ways in Books II and III. Define the table header so when you discover formatting and decide to make all your table headers chartreuse, you'll know where in the HTML code all the table headers are.

Indent your headers inside the `<tr>` set. If your table contains three columns, your first row might begin like this:

```
<tr>
  <th></th>
  <th></th>
  <th></th>
</tr>
```

Place the text you want shown in the table headers between the `<th>` and `</th>` elements. The contents appear in the order they're defined.

Headings don't have to be on the top row. If you want headings on the left, just put a `<th></th>` pair as the first element of each row. You can have headings at both the top and the left, if you want. In fact, you can have headings anywhere, but it usually makes sense to put headings only at the top or left.

Making your data rows

The next step is to create another row. The data rows are just like the heading row, except they use `<td></td>` pairs, rather than `<th></th>` pairs, to contain the data elements. Typically, a three-column table has blank rows that look like this:

```
<tr>
  <td></td>
  <td></td>
  <td></td>
</tr>
```

Place the data elements inside the `<td></td>` segments and you're ready to go.

Building tables in the text editor

Some people think that tables are a good reason to use WYSIWYG (what you see is what you get) editors because they think it's hard to create tables in text mode. You have to plan a little, but it's really quite quick and easy to build an HTML table without graphical tools if you follow this plan:

1. **Plan ahead.**

   Know how many rows and columns will be in the table. Sketch it on paper first might be helpful. Changing the number of rows later is easy, but changing the number of columns can be a real pain after some of the code has been written.

2. **Create the headings.**

   If you're going to start with a standard headings-on-top table, begin by creating the heading row. Save, check, and validate. You don't want mistakes to multiply when you add more complexity. This heading row tells how many columns you'll need.

3. **Build a sample empty row.**

   Make a sample row with the correct number of `td` elements with one `<td></td>` pair per line. Build one `td` set and use copy and paste to copy this data cell as many times as you need. Make sure the number of `<td>` pairs equals the number of `<th>` sets in the heading row.

4. **Copy and paste the empty row to make as many rows as you need.**

5. **Save, view, and validate.**

   Be sure everything looks right and validates properly before you put a lot of effort into adding data.

6. **Populate the table with the data you need.**

   Go row by row, adding the data between the `<td></td>` pairs.

7. **Test and validate again to make sure you didn't accidentally break something.**

Spanning rows and columns

Sometimes, you need a little more flexibility in your table design. Figure 4-7 shows a page from an evil overlord's daily planner.

Figure 4-7:
Some
activities
take up
more than
one cell.

Using colspan and rowspan

My Schedule

	Monday	Tuesday	Wednesday	Thursday	Friday
Breakfast	In lair	with cronies	In lair	in lair	in lair
Morning	Design traps		Improve Hideout		
Afternoon	train minions	train minions	train minions	train minions	world domination
Evening	manaical laughter	manaical laughter	manaical laughter	manaical laughter	

Being an evil overlord is clearly a complex business. From a code stand-point, the items that take up more than one cell are the most interesting. Designing traps takes two mornings, and improving the lair takes three. All Friday afternoon and evening are spent on world domination. Take a look at the code, and you'll see how it works:

```
<!DOCTYPE html PUBLIC "-//W3C//DTD XHTML 1.0 Strict//EN"
"http://www.w3.org/TR/xhtml1/DTD/xhtml1-strict.dtd">
<html lang="EN" dir="ltr" xmlns="http://www.w3.org/1999/xhtml">
  <head>
    <meta http-equiv="content-type" content="text/xml; charset=utf-8" />
    <title>tableSpan.html</title>
  </head>

  <body>
    <h1>Using colspan and rowspan</h1>
    <table border = "1">
      <caption>My Schedule</caption>
      <tr>
        <th></th>
        <th>Monday</th>
        <th>Tuesday</th>
        <th>Wednesday</th>
        <th>Thursday</th>
        <th>Friday</th>
      </tr>

      <tr>
        <th>Breakfast</th>
        <td>In lair</td>
        <td>with cronies</td>
        <td>In lair</td>
        <td>in lair</td>
        <td>in lair</td>
      </tr>

      <tr>
        <th>Morning</th>
        <td colspan = "2">Design traps</td>
        <td colspan = "3">Improve Hideout</td>
      </tr>

      <tr>
        <th>Afternoon</th>
        <td>train minions</td>
        <td>train minions</td>
        <td>train minions</td>
```

```
      <td>train minions</td>
      <td rowspan = "2">world domination</td>
    </tr>

    <tr>
      <th>Evening</th>
      <td>maniacal laughter</td>
      <td>maniacal laughter</td>
      <td>maniacal laughter</td>
      <td>maniacal laughter</td>
    </tr>

  </table>

  </body>
</html>
```

The secret to making cells larger than the default is two special attributes: `rowspan` and `colspan`.

Spanning multiple columns

The morning activities tend to happen over several days. Designing traps will take both Monday and Tuesday morning, and improving the hideout will occupy the remaining three mornings. Take another look at the Morning row; here's how this is done:

```
<tr>
  <th>Morning</th>
  <td colspan = "2">Design traps</td>
  <td colspan = "3">Improve Hideout</td>
</tr>
```

The Design Traps cell spans over two normal columns. The `colspan` attribute tells how many columns this cell will take. The Improve Hideout cell has a `colspan` of 3.

The Morning row still takes up six columns. The `<th>` is one column wide, like normal, but the Design Traps cell spans two columns and the Improve Hideout cell takes three, which totals six columns wide. If you increase the width of a cell, you need to eliminate some other cells in the row to compensate.

Spanning multiple rows

A related property — `rowspan` — allows a cell to take up more than one row of a table. Look back at the Friday column in Figure 4-7, and you'll see the World Domination cell takes up two time slots. (If world domination was easy, everybody would do it.) Here's the relevant code:

```
<tr>
  <th>Afternoon</th>
  <td>train minions</td>
  <td>train minions</td>
  <td>train minions</td>
```

```
   <td>train minions</td>
   <td rowspan = "2">world domination</td>
</tr>

<tr>
  <th>Evening</th>
  <td>maniacal laughter</td>
  <td>maniacal laughter</td>
  <td>maniacal laughter</td>
  <td>maniacal laughter</td>
</tr>
```

The Evening row has only five entries because the World Domination cell extends into the space that would normally be occupied by a <td> pair.

If you want to use rowspan and colspan, don't just hammer away at the page in your editor. Sketch out what you want to accomplish first. I'm pretty good at this stuff, and I still needed a sketch before I was able to create the tableSpan.html code.

Avoiding the table-based layout trap

Tables are pretty great. They're a terrific way to present certain kinds of data. When you add the colspan and rowspan concepts, you can use tables to create some pretty interesting layouts. In fact, because old-school HTML didn't really have any sort of layout technology, a lot of developers came up with some pretty amazing layouts based on tables. You still see a lot of Web pages today designed with tables as the primary layout mechanism.

Using tables for layout causes some problems though, such as

✦ **Tables aren't meant for layout.** Tables are designed for data presentation, not layout. To make tables work for layout, you have to do a lot of sneaky hacks, such as tables nested inside other tables or invisible images for spacing.

✦ **The code becomes complicated fast.** Tables involve a lot of HTML markup. If the code involves tables nested inside each other, it's very difficult to remember which <td> element is related to which row of which table. Table-based layouts are very difficult to modify by hand.

✦ **Formatting is done cell by cell.** A Web page could be composed of hundreds of table cells. Making a change in the font or color often involves making changes in hundreds of cells throughout the page. This makes your page less flexible and harder to update.

✦ **Presentation is tied tightly to data.** A table-based layout tightly intertwines the data and its presentation. This runs counter to a primary goal of Web design — separation of data from its presentation.

✦ **Table-based layouts are hard to change.** After you create a layout based on tables, it's very difficult to make modifications because all the table cells have a potential effect on other cells.

✦ **Table-based layouts cause problems for screen-readers.** People with visual disabilities use special software to read Web pages. These screen-readers are well adapted to read tables as they were intended (to manage tabular data), but the screen-readers have no way of knowing when the table is being used as a layout technique rather than a data presentation tool. This makes table-based layouts less compliant to accessibility standards.

Resist the temptation to use tables for layout. Use tables to do what they're designed for: data presentation. Book III is entirely about how to use CSS to generate any kind of visual layout you might want. The CSS-based approaches are easier, more dependable, and much more flexible.

Chapter 5: Making Connections with Links

In This Chapter

✔ **Understanding hyperlinks**

✔ **Building the anchor tag**

✔ **Recognizing absolute and relative links**

✔ **Building internal links**

✔ **Creating lists of links**

The basic concept of the hyperlink is common today, but it was a major breakthrough back in the day. The idea is still pretty phenomenal, if you think about it: When you click a certain piece of text (or a designated image, for that matter), your browser is instantly transported somewhere else. The new destination might be on the same computer as the initial page, or it could be literally anywhere in the world.

Any page is theoretically a threshold to any other page, and all information has the ability to be linked. This is still a profound idea. In this chapter, you discover how to add links to your pages.

Making Your Text Hyper

The hyperlink is truly a wonderful thing. Believe it or not, there was a time when you had to manually type in the address of the Web page you wanted to go to. Not so anymore. Figure 5-1 illustrates a page that describes some of my favorite Web sites.

In Figure 5-1, the underlined words are hyperlinks. Clicking a hyperlink takes you to the indicated Web site. Although this is undoubtedly familiar to you as a Web user, a few details are necessary to make this mechanism work:

✦ **Something must be linkable.** Some text or other element must provide a trigger for the linking behavior.

✦ **Things that are links should look like links.** This is actually easy to do when you write plain XHTML because all links have a standard (if ugly) appearance. Links are usually underlined blue text. When you can create color schemes, you may no longer want links to look like the default appearance, but they should still be recognizable as links.

✦ **The browser needs to know where to go.** When the user clicks the link, the browser is sent to some address somewhere on the Internet. Sometimes that address is visible on the page, but it doesn't need to be.

✦ **It should be possible to integrate links into text.** In this example, each link is part of a sentence. It should be possible to make some things act like links without necessarily standing on their own (like heading tags do).

✦ **The link's appearance sometimes changes.** Links sometimes begin as blue underlined text, but after a link has been visited, the link is shown in purple, instead. After you know CSS, you can change this behavior.

Of course, if your Web page mentions some other Web site, you should provide a link to that other Web site.

Figure 5-1:
You can
click the
links to visit
the other
sites.

Introducing the anchor tag

The key to hypertext is an oddly named tag called the *anchor* tag. This tag is encased in an `<a></a>` set of tags and contains all the information needed to manage links between pages.

The code for the `basicLinks.html` page is shown here:

```
<!DOCTYPE html PUBLIC "-//W3C//DTD XHTML 1.0 Strict//EN"
"http://www.w3.org/TR/xhtml1/DTD/xhtml1-strict.dtd">
<html lang="EN" dir="ltr" xmlns="http://www.w3.org/1999/xhtml">
  <head>
    <meta http-equiv="content-type" content="text/xml; charset=utf-8" />
    <title>basicLinks.html</title>
  </head>

  <body>
    <h1>Some of my favorite sites</h1>
      <h2>Wikipedia</h2>
      <p>
        One of my favorite Web sites is called
        <a href = "http://www.wikipedia.org">wikipedia.</a>
        This terrific site allows ordinary users to enter
        encyclopedia definitions. Over time, the entries
        can be as reliable as a commercial encyclopedia,
        and a lot more complete.
      </p>

      <h2>Dummies</h2>
      <p>
        You can find out a lot about upcoming and current
        Dummies books at <a href = "http://www.dummies.com">
        www.dummies.com</a>. You might even find this
        book mentioned there.
      </p>

      <h2>PopURLS</h2>
      <p>
        Web 2.0 is all about social networking. If you want
        to know what's happening on the Internet today,
        check out <a href = "http://popurls.com">
        popurls.com</a>. This site aggregates a bunch of
        social networking sites.
      </p>
  </body>
</html>
```

As you can see, the anchor tag is embedded into paragraphs. The text generally flows around an anchor, and you can see the anchor code is embedded inside the paragraphs.

Comparing block-level and inline elements

All the tags described so far in this book have been *block-level* tags. Block-level tags typically begin and end with carriage returns. For example, three `<h1>` tags occupy three lines. Each `<p></p>` set has implied space above and below it. Most XHTML tags are block-level.

Some tags are meant to be embedded inside block-level tags and don't interrupt the flow of the text. The anchor tag is one such tag. Anchors never stand on their own in the HTML body. This type of tag is an *inline* tag. They're meant to be embedded inside block-level tags, such as list items, paragraphs, and headings.

Analyzing an anchor

The first link shows all the main parts of an anchor in a pretty straightforward way:

```
<a href = "http://www.wikipedia.org">wikipedia.</a>
```

✦ **The anchor tag itself:** The anchor tag is simply the `<a></a>` pair. You don't type the entire word *anchor,* just the *a.*

✦ **The hypertext reference (href) attribute:** Almost all anchors contain this attribute. It's very rare to write `<a` without `href`. The `href` attribute indicates a Web address will follow.

✦ **A Web address in quotes:** The address that the browser will follow is encased in quotes. See the next section in this chapter for more information on Web addresses. In this example, `http://www.wikipedia.org` is the address.

✦ **The text that appears as a link:** The user will typically expect to click specially formatted text. Any text that appears between the `<a href>` part and the `</a>` part is visible on the page and formatted as a link. In this example, the word *wikipedia* is the linked text.

✦ **The `</a>` marker:** This marker indicates that the text link is finished.

Introducing URLs

The special link addresses are a very important part of the Web. You probably already type Web addresses into the address bar of your browser (`http://www.google.com`), but you may not be completely aware of how they work. Web addresses are technically URLs (Uniform Resource Locators), and they have a very specific format.

Sometimes, you'll see the term *URI* (Uniform Resource Identifier) instead of URL. URI is technically a more correct name for Web addresses, but the term URL has caught on. The two terms are close enough to be interchangeable.

A URL usually contains the following parts:

✦ **Protocol:** A Web *protocol* is a standardized agreement on how communication occurs. The Web primarily uses HTTP (hypertext transfer protocol), but occasionally, you encounter others. Most addresses begin with `http://` because this is the standard on the Web. Protocols usually end with a colon and two slashes (`://`).

✦ **Host name:** It's traditional to name your primary Web server www. There's no requirement for this, but it's common enough that users expect to type **www** right after the `http://` stuff. Regardless, the text right after `http://` (and up to the first period) is the name of the actual computer you're linking to.

✦ **Domain name:** The last two or three characters indicate a particular type of Web server. These letters can indicate useful information about the type of organization that houses the page. Three-letter domains usually indicate the type of organization, and two-letter domains indicate a country. Sometimes, you'll even see a combination of the two. See Table 5-1 for a list of common domain names.

✦ **Subdomain:** Everything between the host name (usually www) and the domain name (often .com) is the subdomain. This is used so that large organizations can have multiple servers on the same domain. For example, my department Web page is http://www.cs.iupui.edu. www is the name of the primary server, and this is the computer science department at IUPUI (Indiana University–Purdue University Indianapolis), which is an educational organization.

✦ **Page name:** Sometimes, an address specifies a particular document on the Web. This page name follows the address and usually ends with .html. Sometimes, the page name includes subdirectories and user-name information, as well. For example, my Web design course is in the N241 directory of my (aharris) space at IUPUI, so the page's full address is http://www.cs.iupui.edu/~aharris/n241/index.html.

✦ **Username:** Some Web servers are set up with multiple users. Sometimes, an address will indicate a specific user's account with a tilde (~) character. My address has ~aharris in it to indicate the page is found in my (aharris) account on the machine.

The page name is sometimes optional. Many servers have a special name set up as the default page, which appears if no other name is specified. This name is usually index.html but sometimes home.htm. On my server, index.html is the default name, so I usually just point to www.cs.iupui.edu/~aharris/n241, and the index page appears.

Table 5-1	Common Domain Names
Domain	*Explanation*
.org	Non-profit institution
.com	Commercial enterprise
.edu	Educational institution
.gov	Governing body
.ca	Canada
.uk	United Kingdom
.tv	Tuvali

Making Lists of Links

Many Web pages turn out to be lists of links. Because lists and links go so well together, it's good to look at an example. Figure 5-2 illustrates a list of links to books written by a certain (cough) devilishly handsome author.

Some nice programming books

- HTML / XHTML / CSS AIO for Dummies A complete resource to web development
- JavaScript / AJAX for Dummies Using JavaScript, AJAX, and jQuery
- Game Programming - the L Line Game development in Python
- Flash Game Programming for Dummies Game development using Flash

This example has no new code to figure out, but the page shows some interesting components:

✦ **The list:** An ordinary unordered list.

✦ **Links:** Each list item contains a link. The link has a reference (which you can't see immediately) and linkable text (which is marked like an ordinary link).

✦ **Descriptive text:** After each link is some ordinary text that describes the link. Writing some text to accompany the actual link is very common.

This code shows the way the page is organized:

```
<html lang="EN" dir="ltr" xmlns="http://www.w3.org/1999/xhtml">
  <head>
    <meta http-equiv="content-type" content="text/xml; charset=utf-8" />
    <title>listLinks.html</title>
  </head>

  <body>
    <h1>Some nice programming books</h1>
    <ul>
      <li><a href = "http://www.aharrisbooks.net/xfd_2ed">
          HTML / XHTML / CSS AIO for Dummies</a>
          A complete resource to web development</li>
      <li><a href = "http://www.aharrisbooks.net/jad">
          JavaScript / AJAX for Dummies</a>
          Using JavaScript, AJAX, and jQuery</li>
      <li><a href="http://www.aharrisbooks.net/pythonGame">
          Game Programming - the L Line</a>
          Game development in Python</li>
      <li><a href="http://www.aharrisbooks.net/flash">
          Flash Game Programming for Dummies</a>
          Game development using Flash</li>
```

```
    </ul>
  </body>
</html>
```

The indentation is interesting here. Each list item contains an anchor and some descriptive text. To keep the code organized, Web developers tend to place the anchor inside the list item. The address sometimes goes on a new line if it's long, with the anchor text on a new line and the description on succeeding lines. I normally put the `<li>` tag at the end of the last line, so the beginning `<li>` tags look like the bullets of an unordered list. This makes it easier to find your place when editing a list later.

Working with Absolute and Relative References

There's more than one kind of address. So far, you've seen only absolute references, used for links to outside pages. Another kind of reference — a relative reference — links multiple pages inside your own Web site.

Understanding absolute references

The type of link used in `basicLinks.html` is an *absolute reference*. Absolute references always begin with the protocol name (usually `http://`). An absolute reference is the complete address to a Web page, just as you'd use in the browser's address bar. Absolute references are used to refer to a site somewhere else on the Internet. Even if your Web site moves (say, from your desktop machine to a Web server somewhere on the Internet), all the absolute references will work fine because they don't rely on the current page's position for any information.

Introducing relative references

Relative references are used when your Web site includes more than one page. You might choose to have several pages and a link mechanism for moving among them. Figure 5-3 shows a page with several links on it.

Destinations of Porcine Mammals

- This little pig went to <u>market</u>
- This little pig stayed <u>home</u>.
- This little pig had <u>roast beef</u>
- This little pig had <u>none</u>.
- This little pig went '<u>wee wee wee</u>' all the way home.

Figure 5-3:
These little piggies sure get around.

The page isn't so interesting on its own, but it isn't meant to stand alone. When you click one of the links, you go to a brand-new page. Figure 5-4 shows what happens when you click the market link.

Figure 5-4: The market page lets you move back.

I'm in the market

back

The market page is pretty simple, but it also contains a link back to the initial page. Most Web sites aren't single pages at all, but an interconnected web of pages. The relative reference is very useful when you have a set of pages with interlacing links.

The code for `pigs.html` shows how relative references work:

```
<!DOCTYPE html PUBLIC "-//W3C//DTD XHTML 1.0 Strict//EN"
"http://www.w3.org/TR/xhtml1/DTD/xhtml1-strict.dtd">
<html lang="EN" dir="ltr" xmlns="http://www.w3.org/1999/xhtml">
  <head>
    <meta http-equiv="content-type" content="text/xml; charset=utf-8" />
    <title>pigs.html</title>
  </head>

  <body>
    <h1>Destinations of Porcine Mammals</h1>
    <ul>
      <li>This little pig went to
          <a href = "market.html">market</a></li>
      <li>This little pig stayed
          <a href = "home.html">home</a>.</li>
      <li>This little pig had
          <a href = "roastBeef.html">roast beef</a></li>
      <li>This little pig had
          <a href = "none.html">none</a>.</li>
      <li>This little pig went
          <a href = "wee.html">'wee wee wee'</a>
          all the way home.</li>
    </ul>
  </body>
</html>
```

Most of the code is completely familiar. The only thing surprising is what's *not* there. Take a closer look at one of the links:

```
<a href = "market.html">home</a>.</li>
```

There's no protocol (the `http://` part) and no address at all, just a file-name. This is a *relative reference*. Relative references work by assuming the address of the current page. When the user clicks `market.html`, the browser sees no protocol, so it assumes that `market.html` is in the same directory on the same server as `pigs.html`.

Relative references work like directions. For example, if you're in my lab and ask where the water fountain is, I'd say, "Go out into the hallway, turn left, and turn left again at the end of the next hallway." Those directions get you to the water fountain if you start in the right place. If you're somewhere else and you follow the same directions, you don't really know where you'll end up.

Relative references work well when you have a bunch of interconnected Web pages. If you create a lot of pages about the same topic and put them in the same directory, you can use relative references between the pages. If you decide to move your pages to another server, all the links still work correctly.

In Book VIII, you discover how to set up a permanent Web server. It's often most convenient to create and modify your pages on the local machine and then ship them to the Web server for the world to see. If you use relative references, it's easy to move a group of pages together and know the links will still work.

If you're referring to a page on somebody else's site, you have to use an absolute reference. If you're linking to another page on your site, you typically use a relative reference.

Chapter 6: Adding Images

*Y*ou have the basics of text, but pages without images are . . . well, a little boring. Pictures do a lot for a Web page, and they're not that hard to work with. Still, you should know some things about using pictures in your pages. In this chapter, you get all the fundamentals of adding images to your pages.

Adding Images to Your Pages

Every time you explore the Web, you're bound to run into tons of pictures on just about every page you visit. Typically, images are used in four ways on Web pages:

✦ **External link:** The page has text with a link embedded in it. When the user clicks the link, the image replaces the page in the Web browser. To make an externally linked image, just make an ordinary link (as I describe in Chapter 5 of this minibook) but point toward an image file, rather than an HTML (HyperText Markup Language) file.

✦ **Embedded images:** The image is embedded into the page. The text of the page usually flows around the image. This is the most common type of image used on the Web.

✦ **Background images:** An image can be used as a background for the entire page or for a specific part of the page. Images usually require some special manipulation to make them suitable for background use.

✦ **Custom bullets:** With CSS, you can assign a small image to be a bullet for an ordered or unordered list. This allows you to make any kind of customized list markers you can draw.

The techniques you read about in this chapter apply to all type of images, but a couple of specific applications (such as backgrounds and bullets) use CSS. For details on using images in CSS, see Book II, Chapter 4.

Adding links to images

The easiest way to incorporate images is to link to them. Figure 6-1 shows the externalImage.html page.

The page's code isn't much more than a simple link:

```
<!DOCTYPE html PUBLIC "-//W3C//DTD XHTML 1.0 Strict//EN"
"http://www.w3.org/TR/xhtml1/DTD/xhtml1-strict.dtd">
<html lang="EN" dir="ltr" xmlns="http://www.w3.org/1999/xhtml">
  <head>
    <meta http-equiv="content-type" content="text/xml; charset=utf-8" />
    <title>externalImage.html</title>
  </head>

  <body>
    <h1>Linking to an External Image</h1>
    <p>
      <a href = "shipStandard.jpg">
        Susan B. Constant
      </a>
    </p>
  </body>
</html>
```

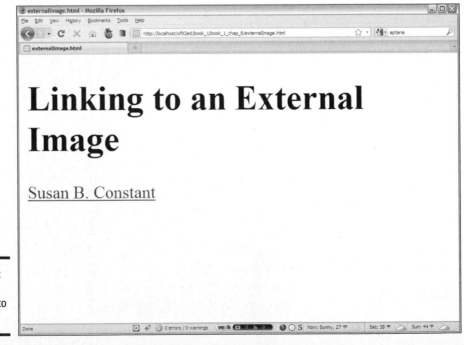

Figure 6-1:
This page
has a link to
an image.

The `href` points to an image file, not an HTML page. You can point to any type of file you want in an anchor tag. If the browser knows the file type (for example, HTML and standard image formats), the browser displays the file. If the browser doesn't know the file format, the user's computer tries to display the file using whatever program it normally uses to open that type of file.

See Chapter 5 of this minibook for a discussion of anchor tags if you need a refresher.

This works fine for most images because the image is displayed directly in the browser.

You can use this anchor trick with any kind of file, but the results can be very unpredictable. If you use the link trick to point to some odd file format, there's no guarantee the user has the appropriate software to view it. Generally, save this trick for very common formats, like GIF and JPG. (If these formats are unfamiliar to you, they are described later in this chapter.)

Most browsers automatically resize the image to fit the browser size. This means a large image may appear to be smaller than it really is, but the user still has to wait for the entire image to download.

Because this is a relative reference, the indicated image must be in the same directory as the HTML file. When the user clicks the link, the page is replaced by the image, as shown in Figure 6-2.

Figure 6-2:
The image appears in place of the page.

External links are easy to create, but they have some problems:

✦ **They don't preview the image.** The user has only the text description to figure out what the picture might be.

✦ **They interrupt the flow.** If the page contains a series of images, the user has to keep leaving the page to view images.

✦ **The user must back up to return to the main page.** The image looks like a Web page, but it isn't. No link or other explanatory text in the image indicates how to get back to the Web page. Most users know to click the browser's Back button, but don't assume all users know what to do.

Adding inline images using the <img> tag

The alternative to providing links to images is to embed your images into the page. Figure 6-3 displays an example of this technique.

The code shows how this image was included into the page:

```
<!DOCTYPE html PUBLIC "-//W3C//DTD XHTML 1.0 Strict//EN"
"http://www.w3.org/TR/xhtml1/DTD/xhtml1-strict.dtd">
<html lang="EN" dir="ltr" xmlns="http://www.w3.org/1999/xhtml">
  <head>
    <meta http-equiv="content-type" content="text/xml; charset=utf-8" />
    <title>embeddedImage.html</title>
  </head>

  <body>
    <h1>The Susan B. Constant</h1>
    <p>
      <img src = "shipStandard.jpg"
           height = "480"
           width = "640"
           alt = "Susan B. Constant" />
    </p>

    <p>
      The <em>Susan B. Constant</em> was flagship of the
      fleet of three small ships that brought settlers to Jamestown, the first
      successful English Colony in the new world.  This is a replica housed
      near Jamestown, Virginia.
    </p>
  </body>
</html>
```

The image (img) tag is the star of this page. This tag allows you to grab an image file and incorporate it into the page directly. The image tag is a one-shot tag. It doesn't end with </img>. Instead, use the /> characters at the end of the img definition to indicate that this tag doesn't have content.

You might have noticed that I italicized *Susan B. Constant* in the page, and I used the <em> tag to get this effect. <em> stands for *emphasis,* and <strong> means *strong emphasis.* By default, any text within an <em></em> pair is italicized, and <strong></strong> text is boldfaced. Of course, you can change this behavior with CSS.

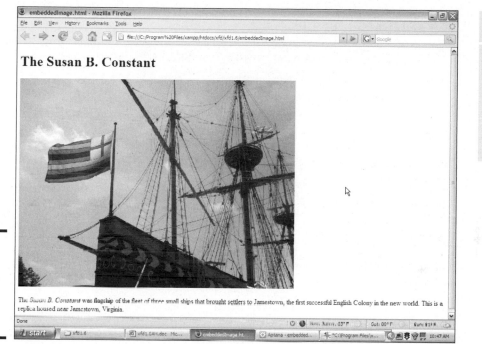

Figure 6-3:
The ship image is embedded into the page.

The image tag has a number of important attributes, which I discuss in the following sections.

src (source)

The `src` attribute allows you to indicate the URL (Uniform Resource Locator) of the image. This can be an absolute or relative reference. Linking to an image in your own directory structure is generally best because you can't be sure an external image will still be there when the user gets to the page. (For more on reference types, turn to Chapter 5 of this minibook.)

height and width

The `height` and `width` attributes are used to indicate the size of the image. The browser uses this information to indicate how much space to reserve on the page.

Using `height` and `width` attributes to change the size of an image on a Web page is tempting, but it's a bad idea. Change the image size with your image editor (I show you how later in this chapter). If you use the `height` and `width` attributes, the user has to wait for the full image, even if she'll see a smaller version. Don't make the user wait for information she won't see. If you use these attributes to make the image larger than its default size, the resulting image has poor resolution. Find the image's actual size by looking at it in your image tool and use these values. If you leave out `height` and `width`, the browser determines the size automatically, but you aren't guaranteed to see the text until all the images have downloaded. Adding these attributes lets the browser format the page without waiting for the images.

alt (alternate text)

The `alt` attribute gives you an opportunity to specify alternate text describing the image. Alternate text information is used when the user has images turned off and by screen-readers. Internet Explorer (IE) automatically creates a *ToolTip* (floating text) based on the alternate text.

You can actually add a floating ToolTip to any element using the `title` attribute. This works in all standards-compliant browsers, with nearly any HTML element.

The `alt` attribute is required on all images if you want to validate XHTML Strict.

Additionally, the `<img>` tag is an inline tag, so it needs to be embedded inside a block-level tag, like a `<p>` or `<li>`.

Choosing an Image Manipulation Tool

You can't just grab any old picture off your digital camera and expect it to work on a Web page. The picture might work, but it could cause problems for your viewers. It's important to understand that *digital images* (any kind of images you see on a computer or similar device) are different from the kind of images you see on paper.

An image is worth 3.4 million words!

Digital cameras and scanners are amazing these days. Even moderately priced cameras can now approach the resolution of old-school analog cameras. Scanners are also capable of taking traditional images and converting them into digital formats that computers use. In both cases, though, the default image can be in a format that causes problems. Digital images are stored as a series of dots, or *pixels*. In print, the dots are very close together, but computer screens have larger dots. Figure 6-4 shows how the ship image looks straight from the digital camera.

My camera handles pictures at 6 megapixels (MP). That's a pretty good resolution, and it sounds very good in the electronics store. If I print that picture on paper, all those dots are very tiny, and I get a nice picture. If I try to show the same picture on the computer screen, I see only one corner. This actual picture came out at 2,816 pixels wide by 2,112 pixels tall. You only see a small corner of the image because the screen shots for this book are taken at 1024 x 768 pixels. Less than a quarter of the image is visible.

Figure 6-4:
Wow. That
doesn't look
like much.

When you look at a large image in most browsers, it's automatically resized
to fit the page. The cursor usually turns into some kind of magnifying glass,
and if you click the image, you can see it in its full size or the smaller size.

Some image viewers take very large images and automatically resize them so
they fit the screen. (This is the default behavior of Windows' default image
viewer and most browsers.) The image may appear to be a reasonable size
because of this feature, but it'll be huge and difficult to download in an actual
Web page. Make sure you know the actual size of an image before you use it.

Although shrinking an image so that it's completely visible is obvious,
there's an even more compelling reason to do so. Each pixel on the screen
requires 3 bytes of computer memory. (A *byte* is the basic unit of memory
in a computer.) For comparison purposes, one character of text requires
roughly 1 byte. The uncompressed image of the ship weighs a whopping 17
megabytes (MB). If you think of a word as five characters long, one picture
straight from the digital camera takes up the same amount of storage space
and transmission time as roughly 3,400,000 words. This image requires
nearly three minutes to download on a 56K modem!

In a Web page, small images are often shown at about 320 x 240 pixels, and
larger images are often 640 x 480 pixels. If I use software to resample the
image to the size I actually need and use an appropriate compression algorithm, I can get the image to look like Figure 6-5.

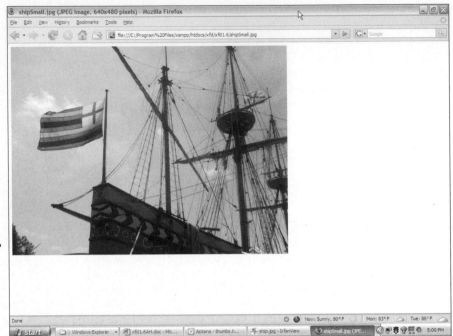

Figure 6-5:
The resized
image is
a lot more
manageable.

The new version of the image is the size and file format I need, it looks just as good, and it weighs a much more reasonable 88 kilobytes. That's 2 percent of the original image size.

Although this picture is a lot smaller than the original image, it still takes up a lot more memory than text. Even this smaller image takes up as much transmission time and storage space as 1,600 words! It still takes 10 seconds to download on a 56K modem. Use images wisely.

Images are great, but keep some things in mind when you use them:

✦ **Make sure the images are worth displaying.** Don't use a picture without some good reason because each picture makes your page dramatically slower to access.

✦ **Use software to resize your image.** Later in this chapter, I show you how to use free software to change the image to exactly the size you need.

✦ **Use a compressed format.** Images are almost never used in their native format on the Web because they're just too large. Several formats have emerged that are useful for working with various types of images. I describe these formats in the section "Choosing an Image Format," later in this chapter.

If you're curious how I determined the download speed of these images, it's pretty easy. The Web Developer toolbar (which I mention in Chapter 3 of this minibook) has a View Speed Report option on the Tools menu that does the job for you.

Introducing IrfanView

IrfanView, by Irfan Skiljan, is a freeware program that can handle your basic image manipulation needs and quite a bit more. I used it for all the screenshots in this book, and I use it as my primary image viewer. A copy is included on the CD-ROM that accompanies this book, or you can get a copy at www.irfanview.net. Of course, you can use any software you want, but if something's really good and free, it's a great place to start. In the rest of this chapter, I show you how to do the main image-processing jobs with IrfanView, but you can use any image editor you want.

A Web developer needs to have an image manipulation program to help with all these chores. Like other Web development tools, you can pay quite a bit for an image manipulation tool, but you don't have to. Your image tool should have at least the following capabilities:

✦ **Resizing:** Web pages require smaller images than printing on paper. You need a tool that allows you to resize your image to a specific size for Web display.

✦ **Saving to different formats:** There's a dizzying number of image formats available, but only three formats work reliably on the Web (which I discuss in the next section). You need a tool that can take images in a wide variety of formats and reliably switch it to a Web-friendly format.

✦ **Cropping:** You may want only a small part of the original picture. A cropping tool allows you to extract a rectangular region from an image.

✦ **Filters:** You may find it necessary to modify your image in some way. You may want to reduce red-eye, lighten or darken your image, or adjust the colors. Sometimes, images can be improved with sharpen or blur filters, or more artistic filters, such as canvas or oil-painting tools.

✦ **Batch processing:** You may have a number of images you want to work with at one time. A batch processing utility can perform an operation on a large number of images at once, as you see later in this chapter.

You may want some other capabilities, too, such as the ability to make composite images, images with transparency, and more powerful effects. You can use commercial tools or the excellent open-source program Gimp, which is included on this book's CD-ROM. This chapter focuses on IrfanView because it's simpler, but investigate Gimp (or its cousin GimpShop, for people used to Photoshop) for a more complete and even more powerful tool. I use IrfanView for basic processing, and I use Gimp when I need a little more power. See Book VIII, Chapter 4 for a more complete discussion of Gimp.

Here are a few free alternatives if you want some other great software to try:

✦ **XnView:** Similar to IrfanView, allows you to preview and modify pictures in hundreds of formats, create thumbnails, and more. It's available for Mac and Linux. (IrfanView is Windows-only.)

✦ **Pixia:** A full-blown graphic editor from Japan. Very powerful.

✦ **GimpShop:** A version of Gimp modified to have menus like Photoshop.

✦ **Paint.net:** A powerful Windows-only paint program.

Use Google or another search engine to locate any of these programs.

Choosing an Image Format

Almost nobody uses raw images on the Web because they're just too big and unwieldy. Usually, Web images are compressed to take up less space. All the types of image files you see in the computer world (BMP, JPG, GIF, and so on) are essentially different ways to make an image file smaller. Not all the formats work on the Web, and they have different characteristics, so it's good to know a little more about them.

BMP

The BMP format is Microsoft's standard image format. Although it's compressed sometimes, usually it isn't. The BMP format creates very detailed images with little to no compression, and the file is often too large to use on the Web. Many Web browsers can handle BMP images, but you shouldn't use them. Convert to one of the other formats, instead.

JPG/JPEG

The JPG format (also called JPEG) is a relatively old format designed by the Joint Photographic Experts Group. (Get it? JPEG!) It works by throwing away data that's less important to human perception. Every time you save an image in the JPG format, you lose a little information. This sounds terrible, but it really isn't. The same image that came up as 13MB in its raw format is squeezed down to 1.5MB when stored as a JPG. Most people can't tell the difference between the compressed and non-compressed version of the image by looking at them.

The JPG algorithm focuses on the parts of the image that are important to perception (brightness and contrast, for example) and throws away data that isn't as important. (Actually, much of the color data is thrown away, but the colors are re-created in an elaborate optical illusion.)

JPG works best on photographic-style images with a lot of color and detail. Many digital cameras save images directly as JPGs.

One part of the JPG process allows you to determine the amount of compression. When you save an image as a JPG, you can often determine the quality on a scale between accuracy and compression.

The JPG compression scheme causes some particular problems with text. JPG is not good at preserving sharp areas of high contrast (such as letters on a background). JPG is not the best format for banner images or other images with text on them. Use GIF or PNG instead.

Even if you choose 100 percent accuracy, the file is still greatly compressed. The adjustable compression operates only on a small part of the process. Compressing the file too much can cause visible square shadows, or *artifacts*. Experiment with your images to see how much compression they can take and still look like the original.

> **WARNING!** Keep a high-quality original around when you're making JPG versions of an image because each copy loses some detail. If you make a JPG from a JPG that came from another JPG, the loss of detail starts to add up, and the picture loses some visual quality.

GIF

The GIF format was developed originally for CompuServe, way before the Web was invented. This format was a breakthrough in its time and still has some great characteristics.

GIF is a *lossless* algorithm so, potentially, no data is lost when converting an image to GIF (compare that to the *lossy* JPG format). GIF does its magic with a *color palette* trick and a *run-length encoding* trick.

The color palette works like a paint-by-number set where an image has a series of numbers printed on it, and each of the paint colors has a corresponding number. What happens in a GIF image is similar. GIF images have a list of 256 colors, automatically chosen from the image. Each of the colors is given a number. A *raw* (uncompressed) image requires 3 bytes of information for each pixel (1 each to determine the amount of red, green, and blue) In a GIF image, all that information is stored one time in the color palette. The image itself contains a bunch of references to the color palette.

For example, if blue is stored as color 1 in the palette, a strip of blue might look like this:

1, 1, 1, 1, 1, 1, 1, 1, 1, 1

GIF uses its other trick — run-length encoding — when it sees a list of identical colors. Rather than store the above value as 1, 1, 1, 1, 1, 1, 1, 1, 1, 1, the GIF format can specify a list of 10 ones. That's the general idea of run-length encoding. The ship image in this example weighs 2.92MB as a full-size GIF image.

The GIF format works best for images with a relatively small number of colors and large areas of the same color. Most drawings you make in a drawing program convert very well to the GIF format. Photos aren't ideal because they usually have more than 256 colors in them, and the subtle changes in color mean there are very few solid blotches of color to take advantage of run-length encoding.

GIF does have a couple of great advantages that keep it popular. First, a GIF image can have a transparent color defined. Typically, you'll choose some awful color not found in nature (kind of like choosing bridesmaid dresses) to be the transparent color. Then, when the GIF encounters a pixel that color, it displays whatever is underneath instead. This is a crude but effective form of transparency. Figure 6-6 shows an image with transparency.

Whenever you see an image on a Web page that doesn't appear to be rectangular, there's a good chance the image is a GIF. The image is still a rectangle, but it has transparency to make it look more organic. Typically, whatever color you set as the background color when you save a GIF becomes the transparent color.

Creating a complex transparent background, like the statue, requires a more complex tool than IrfanView. I used Gimp, but any high-end graphics tool can do the job. IrfanView is more suited to operations that work on the entire image.

Figure 6-6:
This statue
is a GIF with
transparency.

Coming soon — vector formats

Here's another form of image format that I hope will gain more prominence. All the formats described so far are *raster-based* image formats. This type of image stores an image as a series of dots. *Vector-based* image formats use formulas to store the instructions to draw an image. Certain kinds of images (especially charts and basic line art) can be far more efficient when stored as vector formats. Unfortunately, IE and Firefox support different and incompatible vector formats, so it doesn't look like vector-based images will be a factor

soon. Flash also uses vector-based techniques, but this technique requires expensive proprietary software to create vector images and a third-party plugin to use them.

The most promising new technology is the <canvas> tag in HTML 5. This tag allows programmers to draw directly on a portion of the screen using JavaScript code. If it becomes a standard, the <canvas> tag will unleash many new possibilities for Web-based graphics.

Another interesting feature of GIF is the ability to create animations. Animated GIFs are a series of images stored in the same file. You can embed information, determining the interval between images. You can create animated GIFs with Gimp, which is included on this book's CD-ROM.

Animated GIFs were overused in the early days of the Web, and many now consider them the mark of an amateur. Nobody really thinks that animated mailbox is cute anymore.

For a while, there were some legal encumbrances regarding a part of the GIF scheme. The owners of this algorithm tried to impose a license fee. This was passed on to people using commercial software but became a big problem for free software creators.

Fortunately, it appears that the legal complications have been resolved for now. Still, you'll see a lot of open-software advocates avoiding the GIF algorithm altogether because of this problem.

PNG

Open-source software advocates created a new image format that combines some of the best features of both JPG and GIF, with no legal problems. The resulting format is *Portable Network Graphics,* or *PNG*. This format has a number of interesting features, such as

✦ **Lossless compression:** Like GIF, PNG stores data without losing any information.

✦ **Dynamic color palette:** PNG supports as many colors as you want. You aren't limited to 256 colors as you are with GIF.

✦ **No software patents:** The underlying technology of PNG is completely open source, with no worries about whether somebody will try to enforce a copyright down the road.

✦ **True alpha transparency:** The PNG format has a more sophisticated form of transparency than GIF. Each pixel can be stored with an alpha value. *Alpha* refers to the amount of transparency. The alpha can be adjusted from completely transparent to completely opaque.

With all its advantages, you might expect PNG to be the most popular image format on the Web. Surprisingly, it's been slow to catch on. The main reason for this is spotty support for PNG in Internet Explorer (IE). Most versions of IE don't support PNG's alpha transparency correctly.

Summary of Web image formats

All these formats may seem overwhelming, but choosing an image format is easy because each format has its own advantages and disadvantages:

✦ **GIF** is best when you need transparency or animation. Avoid using GIF on photos, as you won't get optimal compression, and you'll lose color data.

✦ **JPG** is most useful for photographic images, which are best suited for the JPG compression technique. However, keep in mind that JPG isn't suitable for images that require transparency. Text in JPG images tends to become difficult to read because of the lossy compression technique.

✦ **PNG** is useful in most situations, but be aware that IE (especially version 6) doesn't handle PNG transparency correctly. (You sometimes see strange color blotches where you expect transparency.)

✦ **BMP and other formats** should be avoided entirely. Although you can make other formats work in certain circumstances, there's no good reason to use any other image formats most of the time.

Manipulating Your Images

All this talk of compression algorithms and resizing images may be dandy, but how do you do it?

Fortunately, IrfanView can do nearly anything you need for free. IrfanView has nice features for all the main types of image manipulation you need.

Changing formats in IrfanView

Changing image formats with IrfanView is really easy. For example, find an image file on your computer and follow these steps:

1. **Load the image into IrfanView by dragging the image into IrfanView or using the File⇨Open menu command.**

2. **Make any changes you may want to the image before saving.**

3. **Use the File⇨Save As command to save the file.**

4. **Pick the image format from the Save Picture As dialog box, as shown in Figure 6-7.**

5. **Save the file with a new filename.**

Keep the original file and save any changes in a new file. That way, you don't overwrite the original file. This is especially important if you're converting to JPG because each successive save of a JPG causes some image loss.

Save Picture As ...

Save in: xfd1.0

thumbs
xfd0106fig01.png
xfd0106fig02.png
xfd0106fig03.png
xfd0106fig04.png
xfd0106fig05.png
xfd0106fig06.png

File name: shipStandard   Save

Save as type: PNG - Portable Network Graphics   Cancel

BMP - Windows Bitmap
ECW - Enhanced Compressed Wavelet
EMF - Enhanced Windows Metafile
FSH - EA Sports Format
GIF - Compuserve GIF
ICO - Windows Icon
JP2 - JPEG2000 Format
JPG - JPEG Files
JPM - JPM Format
LDF - LuraDocument Format
LWF - LuraWave Format
PCX - Zsoft Paintbrush
PBM - Portable Bitmap
PDF - Portable Document Format
PGM - Portable Graymap
PNG - Portable Network Graphics
PPM - Portable Pixelmap
RAW - RAW Image Data
TGA - Truevision Targa
TIF - Tagged Image File Format

Figure 6-7: IrfanView can save in all these formats.

Don't use spaces in your filenames. Your files may move to other computers on the Internet, and some computers have trouble with spaces. It's best to avoid spaces and punctuation (except the underscore character) on any files that will be used on the Internet. Also, be very careful about capitalization. It's likely that your image will end up on a Linux server someday, and the capitalization makes a big difference there.

Resizing your images

All the other image-manipulation tricks may be optional, but you should *really* resize your images. Although high-speed modems may have no trouble with a huge image, nothing makes a Web page inaccessible to dialup users faster than bloated image sizes.

To resize an image with IrfanView, perform the following steps:

1. **Load the image into IrfanView.**

   You can do this by dragging the image onto the IrfanView icon, dragging into an open instance of IrfanView, or using the menus within IrfanView.

2. **From the Image menu, choose Resize/Resample.**

   You can also use Ctrl+R for this step. Figure 6-8 shows the resulting dialog box.

Figure 6-8: IrfanView's Resize/ Resample Image dialog box.

3. **Determine the new image size.**

   A number of standard image sizes are available. 800 x 600 pixels will create a large image in most browsers. If you want the image smaller, you need to enter a size in the text boxes. Images embedded in Web pages are often 320 pixels wide by 240 pixels tall. That's a very good starting point. Anything smaller will be hard to see, and anything larger might take up too much screen space.

4. **Preserve the aspect ratio using the provided check box.**

   This makes sure the ratio between height and width is maintained. Otherwise, the image may be distorted.

5. **Save the resulting image as a new file.**

When you make an image smaller, you lose data. That's perfectly fine for the version you put on the Web, but you should hang on to the original large image in case you want to resize again.

6. Resample, rather than resize.

Resampling is a slower but more accurate technique for changing the image size. This is IrfanView's default behavior, so leave it alone. It's still quite fast on a modern computer. The default (Lanczos) filter is fine, although you can experiment with other filters to get a faster conversion, if you want.

Enhancing image colors

Sometimes, you can make improvements to an image by modifying the colors. The Enhance Colors dialog box on the Images menu gives you a wide range of options, as shown in Figure 6-9.

Figure 6-9: You can change several options in the Enhance Colors dialog box.

You can do a surprising number of helpful operations on an image with this tool:

✦ **Brightness:** When adjusted to a higher value, the image becomes closer to white. When adjusted to a negative value, the image becomes closer to black. This is useful when you want to make an image lighter or darker for use as a background image.

If your image is too dark or too bright, you may be tempted to use the Brightness feature to fix it. The Gamma Correction feature described later in this section is more useful for this task.

✦ **Contrast:** You usually use the Contrast feature in conjunction with the Brightness feature to adjust an image. Sometimes, an image can be improved with small amounts of contrast adjustments.

✦ **Color Balance:** Sometimes, an image has poor color balance (for example, indoor lighting sometimes creates a bluish cast). You can adjust the amount of red, green, and blue with a series of sliders. The easiest way to manage color balance is to look at a part of the image that's supposed to be white and play with the slider until it looks truly white.

✦ **Gamma Correction:** This is used to correct an image that is too dark or too light. Unlike the Brightness adjustment, Gamma Correction automatically adjusts the contrast. Small adjustments to this slider can sometimes fix images that are a little too dark or too light.

✦ **Saturation:** When saturation is at its smallest value, the image becomes black and white. At its largest value, the colors are enhanced. Use this control to create a grayscale image or to enhance colors for artistic effect.

Using built-in effects

IrfanView has a few other effects available that can sometimes be extremely useful. These effects can be found individually on the Image menu or with the Image Effects browser on the Image menu. The Image Effects browser (as shown in Figure 6-10) is often a better choice because it gives you a little more control of most effects and provides interactive feedback on what the effect will do. Sometimes, effects are called *filters* because they pass the original image through a math function, which acts like a filter or processor to create the modified output.

Figure 6-10: The Image Effects browser lets you choose special effects.

Here's a rundown of some of the effects, including when you would use them:

✦ **None:** Just for comparison purposes, Figure 6-11 shows the ship image without any filters turned on.

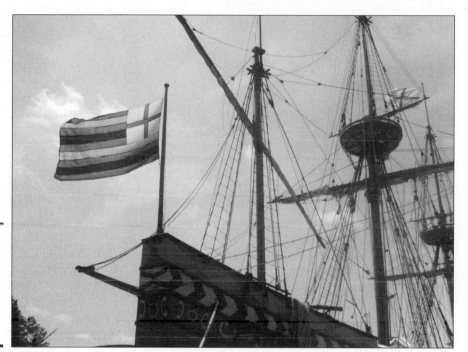

Figure 6-11:
Here's the standard ship image, at full-screen resolution.

I've exaggerated the effects for illustration purposes, but it may still be difficult to see the full effect of these filters on the printed page. The grayscale images in this book are a poor representation of the actual color images. Use the images in this chapter as a starting point, but to understand these filters, you really need to experiment with your own images in IrfanView or a similar tool. I've also added all these images to my Web site so you can see them there (www.aharrisbooks.net/xfd2ed).

✦ **Blur:** This filter reduces contrast between adjacent pixels. (Really, we could go over the math, but let's leave that for another day, huh?) You might wonder why you'd make an image blurry on purpose. Sometimes, the Blur filter can fix graininess in an image. You can also use Blur in conjunction with Sharpen (which I cover in just a moment) to fix small flaws in an image. I applied the Blur filter to the standard ship image in Figure 6-12.

✦ **Sharpen:** The opposite of Blur, the Sharpen filter enhances the contrast between adjacent pixels. When used carefully, it can sometimes improve an image. The Sharpen filter is most effective in conjunction with the Blur filter to remove small artifacts. Figure 6-13 shows the ship image with the Sharpen filter applied.

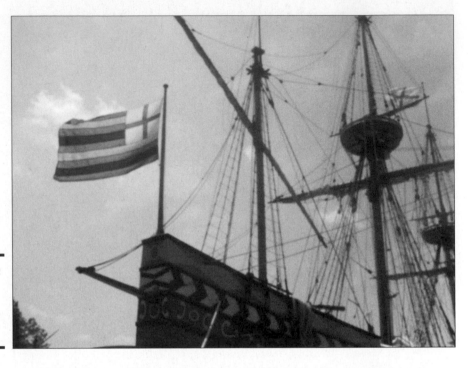

Figure 6-12:
The Blur filter reduces contrast.

Figure 6-13:
The Sharpen filter increases contrast.

If you believe crime shows on TV, you can take a blurry image and keep applying a sharpen filter to read a license plate on a blurry image from a security camera. However, it just doesn't usually work that way. You can't make detail emerge from junk, but sometimes, you can make small improvements.

✦ **Emboss:** This filter creates a grayscale image that looks like embossed metal, as shown in Figure 6-14. Sometimes, embossing can convert an image into a useful background image because embossed images have low contrast. You can use the Enhance Colors dialog box to change the gray embossed image to a more appealing color.

✦ **Oil Paint:** This filter applies a texture reminiscent of an oil painting to an image, as shown in Figure 6-15. It can sometimes clean up a picture and give it a more artistic appearance. The higher settings make the painting more abstract.

✦ **3D Button:** This feature can be used to create an image, similar to Figure 6-16, that appears to be a button on the page. This will be useful later when you figure out how to use CSS or JavaScript to swap images for virtual buttons. You can set the apparent height of the image in the filter. Normally, you apply this filter to smaller images that you intend to make into buttons the user can click.

Figure 6-14: Embossing creates a low-contrast 3D effect.

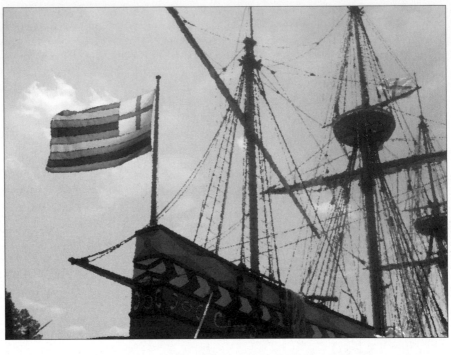

Figure 6-15: Oil Paint makes an image slightly more abstract.

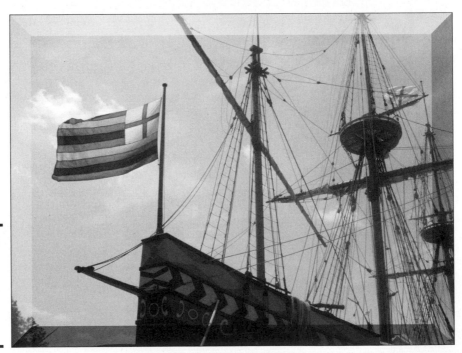

Figure 6-16: The image appears to stick up from the page like a button.

✦ **Red Eye Reduction:** You use this filter to fix a common problem with flash photography. Sometimes, a person's eyes appear to have a reddish tinge to them. Unlike the other filters, this one is easier to access from the Image menu. Use the mouse to select the red portion of the image and then apply the filter to turn the red areas black. It's best not to perform this filter on the entire image because you may inadvertently turn other red things black.

Other effects you can use

Many more effects and filters are available. IrfanView has a few more built in that you can experiment with. You can also download a huge number of effects in the Adobe Photoshop 8BF format. These effects filters can often be used in IrfanView and other image-manipulation programs.

Some effects allow you to explode the image, add sparkles, map images onto 3D shapes, create old-time sepia effects, and much more.

If you want to do even more image manipulation, consider a full-blown image editor. Adobe Photoshop is the industry standard, but Gimp is an open-source alternative (included on this book's CD-ROM) that does almost as much. See Book VIII, Chapter 4 for more about using Gimp for image processing.

Batch processing

Often, you'll have a lot of images to modify at one time. IrfanView has a wonderful *batch-processing* tool that allows you to work on several images at once. I frequently use this tool to take all the images I want to use on a page and convert them to a particular size and format. The process seems a little complicated, but after you get used to it, you can modify a large number of images quickly and easily.

If you want to convert a large number of images at the same time, follow these steps:

1. **Identify the original images and place them in one directory.**

   I find it easiest to gather all the images into one directory, whether they come from a digital camera, scanner, or other device.

2. **Open the Batch Conversion dialog box by choosing File⇨Batch Conversion — Rename.**

   This Batch Conversion dialog box appears, as shown in Figure 6-17.

3. **Find your original images by navigating the directory window in the Batch Conversion dialog box.**

Files to convert   File selector

Figure 6-17:
IrfanView
has a
powerful
batch
conversion
tool.

Conversion options

4. **Copy your images to the Input Files workspace by clicking the Add button.**

Select the images you want to modify and press the Add button. The selected image names are copied to the Input Files workspace.

5. **Specify the output directory.**

If you want to put the new images in the same directory as the input files, click the Use This Directory as Output button. If not, choose the directory where you want the new images to go.

6. **In the Work As box, choose Batch Conversion — Rename Result Files.**

You can use this setting to rename your files, to do other conversions, or both. Generally, I recommend both.

7. **Set the output format to the format you want.**

For photos, you probably want JPG format.

8. **Change renaming settings in the Batch Rename Settings area if you want to specify some other naming convention for your images.**

By default, each image is called *image*### where ### is a three-digit number. They are numbered according to the listing in the Input Files workspace. You can use the Move Up and Move Down buttons to change the order images appear in this listing.

9. **Click the Set Advanced Options button to change the image size.**

This displays the Settings for All Images dialog box, as shown in Figure 6-18.

Figure 6-18:
Use the
Settings for
All Images
dialog box
to resize
images in
batch mode.

10. **Specify the new size of the image in the Resize area.**

Several common sizes are preset. If you want another size, use the given options. I set my size to 320 x 240.

11. **Close the Settings for All Images dialog box and then, in the Batch Conversion dialog box, press the Start button.**

In a few seconds, the new images are created.

Using Images as Links

Sometimes, you'll want to use images as links. For example, look at `thumbs.html`, as shown in Figure 6-19.

This page uses thumbnail images. A *thumbnail* is a small version of the full-size image. The thumbnail is embedded, and the user clicks it to see the full-size version in the browser.

Thumbnails are good because they allow the user to preview a small version of each image without having to wait for the full-size versions to be rendered on-screen. If the user wants to see a complete image, he can click the thumbnail to view it on its own page.

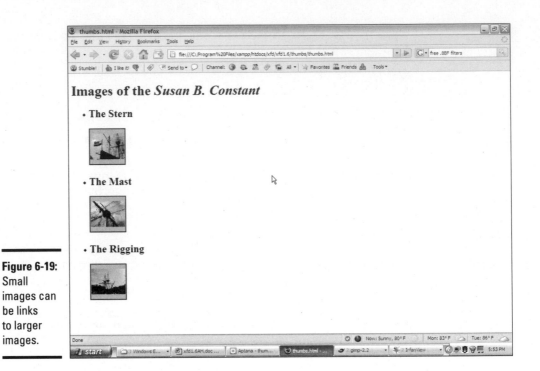

Figure 6-19:
Small
images can
be links
to larger
images.

Creating thumbnail images

Thumbnails are simply scaled-down versions of ordinary images. Because this process is fairly common, IrfanView comes with a wonderful tool to automate thumbnail creation. To make a batch of thumbnails in IrfanView

1. **Organize your images.**

Any page that has a large number of images can get confusing. I prefer to organize everything that will be used by a particular page into its own directory. I created a *thumbs* directory that contains `thumbs.html`, all the full-size images, and all the thumbnails. I usually don't find it helpful to have separate directories for images. It's more helpful to organize by project or page than by media type.

2. **Rename images, if necessary.**

Images that come from a digital camera or scanner often have cryptic names. Your life is a lot easier if your image names are easier to understand. I named my images `ship_1.jpg`, `ship_2.jpg`, and `ship_3.jpg`.

3. **Make any changes you want to the originals before you make the thumbnails.**

Use the tips described in this chapter to clean up or improve your images before you make thumbnails, or the thumbnails won't represent the actual images accurately.

4. Open the IrfanView Thumbnails tool by choosing File➪Thumbnails or by pressing the T key.

The Thumbnails tool appears, as shown in Figure 6-20.

5. Select the thumbnails you want to create.

Use the mouse to select any images you want to make thumbnails from.

6. Choose Save Selected Thumbs as Individual Images from the File menu.

You have other options, but this gives the behavior you probably want. The other options create automatic contact sheets, open the batch editor, or create slide shows. These are great things, but for now, you want thumbnails.

7. Specify the output directory.

You can put the thumbnails in the same directory as the originals. The thumbnails have the same name as the originals, but the filenames end with _t.

8. Review the new thumbnail images.

You should see a new set of smaller images (default size is 80 x 80 pixels) in the directory.

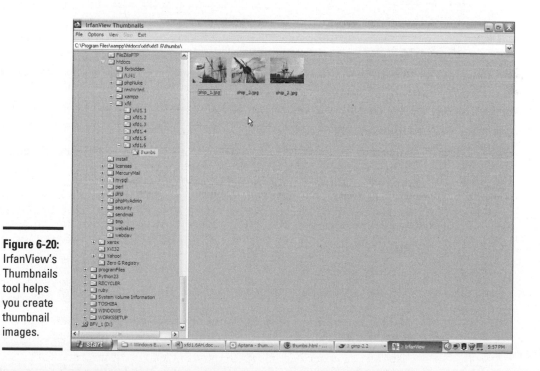

Figure 6-20:
IrfanView's
Thumbnails
tool helps
you create
thumbnail
images.

Creating a thumbnail-based image directory

Now, you have everything you need to build a page similar to thumbs.html. Here's an overview of the code:

```html
<!DOCTYPE html PUBLIC "-//W3C//DTD XHTML 1.0 Strict//EN"
"http://www.w3.org/TR/xhtml1/DTD/xhtml1-strict.dtd">
<html lang="EN" dir="ltr" xmlns="http://www.w3.org/1999/xhtml">
  <head>
    <meta http-equiv="content-type" content="text/xml; charset=utf-8" />
    <title>thumbs.html</title>
  </head>

  <body>
    <h1>Images of the <em>Susan B. Constant</em></h1>
    <ul>
      <li>
        <h2>The Stern</h2>
        <a href = "ship_1.jpg">
          <img src = "ship_1_t.jpg"
               height = "80"
               width = "80"
               alt = "ship 1" />
        </a>
      </li>

      <li>
        <h2>The Mast</h2>
        <a href = "ship_2.jpg">
          <img src = "ship_2_t.jpg"
               height = "80"
               width = "80"
               alt = "ship 2" />
        </a>
      </li>

      <li>
        <h2>The Rigging</h2>
        <a href = "ship_3.jpg">
          <img src = "ship_3_t.jpg"
               height = "80"
               width = "80"
               alt = "ship 3" />
        </a>
      </li>
    </ul>
  </body>
</html>
```

This code looks complicated, but it's really just a combination of techniques described in this chapter. Look over the code and use the indentation to determine the structure.

The page is an unordered list. Each list item contains an H2 headline and an anchor. The anchor contains an image, rather than text. When you include an image inside an anchor tag, it's outlined in blue.

The key is to use the thumbnails as inline images inside the page, and the full-size image as the href of the anchor. The user sees the small image, but this small image is also a link to the full-size version of the image. This way, the user can see the small image easily but can view the full-size image if she wishes.

Chapter 7: Creating Forms

In This Chapter

✔ Adding form to your pages

✔ Creating input and password text boxes

✔ Building multi-line text inputs

✔ Making list boxes and check boxes

✔ Building groups of radio buttons

✔ Creating buttons

XHTML gives you the ability to describe Web pages, but today's Web isn't a one-way affair. Users want to communicate through Web pages, by typing in information, making selections from drop-down lists, and interacting, rather than simply reading. In this chapter, you learn how to build these interactive elements in your pages.

You Have Great Form

There's one more aspect to XHTML that you need to understand — the ability to make forms. *Forms* are the parts of the page that allow user interaction. Figure 7-1 shows a page with all the primary form elements in place.

The form demo (or `formDemo.html` on this book's CD-ROM, if you're playing along at home) exemplifies the main form elements in XHTML. In this chapter, you discover how to build all these elements.

You can create forms with ordinary XHTML, but to make them *do* something, you need a programming language. Book IV explains how to use JavaScript to interact with your forms, and Book V describes the PHP language. Use this chapter to figure out how to build the forms and then jump to another minibook to figure out how to make them do stuff. If you aren't ready for full-blown programming yet, feel free to skip this chapter for now and move on to CSS in Books II and III. Come back here when you're ready to make forms to use with JavaScript or PHP.

Figure 7-1:
Form
elements
allow user
interaction.

The `formDemo.html` page shows the following elements:

+ **A form:** A container for form elements. Although the form element itself isn't usually a visible part of the page (like the body tag), it could be with appropriate CSS.

+ **Text boxes:** These standard form elements allow the user to type text into a one-line element.

+ **Password boxes:** These boxes are like text boxes, except they automatically obscure the text to discourage snooping.

+ **Text areas:** These multi-line text boxes accommodate more text than the other types of text boxes. You can specify the size of the text area the user can type into.

+ **Select lists:** These list boxes give the user a number of options. The user can select one element from the list. You can specify the number of rows to show or make the list drop down when activated.

+ **Check boxes:** These non-text boxes can be checked or not. Check boxes act *independently* — more than one can be selected at a time (unlike radio buttons).

+ **Radio buttons:** Usually found in a group of options, only one radio button in a group can be selected at a time. Selecting one radio button deselects the others in its group.

✦ **Buttons:** These elements let the user begin some kind of process. The Input button is used in JavaScript coding (which I describe in Book IV), whereas the Standard and Submit buttons are used for server-side programming (see Book V). The Reset button is special because it automatically resets all the form elements to their default configurations.

✦ **Labels:** Many form elements have a small text label associated with them. Although labels are not required, they can make a form easier to style with CSS and easier for the user.

✦ **Fieldsets and legends:** These set off parts of the form. They're optional, but they can add a lot of visual appeal to a form.

Now that you have an overview of form elements, it's time to start building some forms!

Forms must have some form

All the form elements must be embedded inside a <form></form> pair. The code for basicForm.html illustrates the simplest possible form:

```
<!DOCTYPE html PUBLIC "-//W3C//DTD XHTML 1.0 Strict//EN"
"http://www.w3.org/TR/xhtml1/DTD/xhtml1-strict.dtd">
<html lang="EN" dir="ltr" xmlns="http://www.w3.org/1999/xhtml">
  <head>
    <meta http-equiv="content-type" content="text/xml; charset=utf-8" />
    <title>basicForm.html</title>
  </head>

  <body>
    <h1>A basic form</h1>
    <form action = "">
      <h2>Form elements go here</h2>
      <h3>Other HTML is fine, too.</h3>
    </form>

  </body>
</html>
```

The <form></form> pair indicates a piece of the page that may contain form elements. All the other form doohickeys and doodads (buttons, select objects, and so on) must be inside a <form> pair.

The action attribute indicates what should happen when the form is submitted. This requires a programming language, so a full description of the action attribute is in Book IV. Still, you must indicate an action to validate, so for now just leave the action attribute null with a pair of quotes (" ").

Organizing a form with fieldsets and labels

Forms can contain many components, but the most important are the *input elements* (text boxes, buttons, drop-down lists, and the like) and the *text labels* that describe the elements. Traditionally, Web developers used tables to set up forms, but this isn't really the best way to go because forms aren't tabular information. XHTML includes some great features to help you describe the various parts of a form. Figure 7-2 shows a page with fieldsets, layouts, and basic input.

A *fieldset* is a special element used to supply a visual grouping to a set of form elements.

The form still doesn't look very good, I admit, but that's not the point. Like all XHTML tags, the form elements aren't about describing how the form looks; they're about what all the main elements mean. (Here I go again. . . .) You use CSS to make the form look the way you want. The XHTML tags describe the parts of the form, so you have something to hook your CSS to. It all makes sense very soon, I promise.

Here's the code for the fieldset demo (`fieldsetDemo.html` on this book's CD-ROM):

```
<!DOCTYPE html PUBLIC "-//W3C//DTD XHTML 1.0 Strict//EN"
"http://www.w3.org/TR/xhtml1/DTD/xhtml1-strict.dtd">
<html lang="EN" dir="ltr" xmlns="http://www.w3.org/1999/xhtml">
  <head>
    <meta http-equiv="content-type" content="text/xml; charset=utf-8" />
    <title>fieldsetDemo.html</title>
  </head>

  <body>
    <h1>Sample Form with a Fieldset</h1>
    <form action = "">
      <fieldset>
        <legend>Personal Data</legend>
        <p>
          <label>Name</label>
          <input type = "text" />
        </p>

        <p>
          <label>Address</label>
          <input type = "text" />
        </p>

        <p>
          <label>Phone</label>
          <input type = "text" />
        </p>

      </fieldset>
    </form>
  </body>
</html>
```

Legend

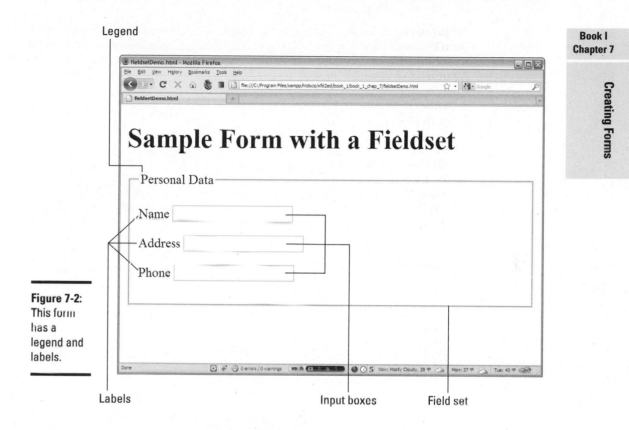

Figure 7-2:
This form
has a
legend and
labels.

Labels   Input boxes   Field set

The form has these elements:

✦ **The `<form>` and `</form>` tags:** These define the form as a part of the page. Don't forget the null `action` attribute.

✦ **The `<fieldset>` pair:** This pair describes the included elements as a set of fields. This element isn't necessary, but it does give you some nice organization and layout options later when you use CSS. You can think of the fieldset as a blank canvas for adding visual design to your forms. By default, the fieldset places a border around all the contained elements.

✦ **The `<legend>` tag:** A part of the fieldset, this tag allows you to specify a legend for the entire fieldset. The legend is visible to the user.

✦ **The paragraphs:** I sometimes place each label and its corresponding input element in a paragraph. This provides some nice formatting capabilities and keeps each pair together.

✦ **The `<label>` tag:** This tag allows you to specify a particular chunk of text as a label. No formatting is done by default, but you can add formatting later with CSS.

✦ **The `<input>` elements:** The user types data into these elements. For now, I'm just using very basic text inputs so the form has some kind of input. In the next section, I explain how to build more complete text inputs.

Building Text-Style Inputs

Most of the form elements are variations of the same tag. The `<input>` tag can create single-line text boxes, password boxes, buttons, and even invisible content (such as hidden fields). Most of these objects share the same basic attributes, although the outward appearance can be different.

Making a standard text field

Figure 7-3 shows the most common form of the input element — a *plain text field.*

Figure 7-3: The input element is often used to make a text field.

To make a basic text input, you need a form and an input element. Adding a label so that the user knows what he's supposed to enter into the text box is also common. Here's the code:

```
<!DOCTYPE html PUBLIC "-//W3C//DTD XHTML 1.0 Strict//EN"
"http://www.w3.org/TR/xhtml1/DTD/xhtml1-strict.dtd">
<html lang="EN" dir="ltr" xmlns="http://www.w3.org/1999/xhtml">
  <head>
    <meta http-equiv="content-type" content="text/xml; charset=utf-8" />
    <title>textbox.html</title>
  </head>

  <body>
    <form action = "">
      <p>
        <label>Name</label>
        <input type = "text"
               id = "txtName"
               value = "Joe"/>
      </p>
    </form>

  </body>
</html>
```

An input element has three common attributes:

+ **type:** The type attribute indicates the type of input element this is. This first example sets type to text, creating a standard text box. Other types throughout this chapter create passwords, hidden fields, check boxes, and buttons.

+ **id:** The id attribute creates an identifier for the field. When you use a programming language to extract data from this element, use id to specify which field you're referring to. An id field often begins with a hint phrase to indicate the type of object it is (for instance, txt indicates a text box).

+ **value:** This attribute determines the default value of the text box. If you leave this attribute out, the text field begins empty.

Text fields can also have other attributes, which aren't used as often, such as

+ **size:** This attribute determines the number of characters that are displayed.

+ **maxlength:** Use this attribute to set the largest number of characters that are allowed.

There is no `</input>` tag. Input tags are a holdover from the days when many tags did not have ending tags. You just end the original tag with a slash character (/), as shown in the preceding sample code.

You might wonder why I added the `<label>` tag if it doesn't have any effect on the appearance or behavior of the form. In this particular example, the `<label>` tag doesn't have an effect, but like everything else in HTML, you can do amazing style things with it in CSS. Even though labels don't typically have a default style, they are still useful.

Building a password field

Passwords are just like text boxes, except the text isn't displayed. Instead, a series of asterisks appears. Figure 7-4 shows a basic password field.

Figure 7-4:
Enter the secret password.

The following code reveals that passwords are almost identical to ordinary text fields:

```
<!DOCTYPE html PUBLIC "-//W3C//DTD XHTML 1.0 Strict//EN"
"http://www.w3.org/TR/xhtml1/DTD/xhtml1-strict.dtd">
<html lang="EN" dir="ltr" xmlns="http://www.w3.org/1999/xhtml">
  <head>
    <meta http-equiv="content-type" content="text/xml; charset=utf-8" />
    <title>password.html</title>
  </head>

  <body>
    <form action = "">
      <fieldset>
        <legend>Enter a password</legend>
        <p>
          <label>Type password here</label>
          <input type = "password"
                 id = "pwd"
                 value = "secret" />
        </p>
      </fieldset>
    </form>
  </body>
</html>
```

In this example, I've created a password field with the ID pwd. The default value of this field is secret. The term *secret* won't actually appear in the field; it will be replaced with six asterisk characters.

The password field offers virtually no meaningful security. It protects the user from the KGB glancing over his shoulder to read a password, but that's about it. The open standards of XHTML and the programming languages mean passwords are often passed in the open. There are solutions — such as the SSL (Secure Socket Layer) technology — but for now, just be aware that the password field just isn't suitable for protecting the recipe of your secret sauce.

This example doesn't really do anything with the password, but you'll use other technologies for that.

Making multi-line text input

The single-line text field is a powerful feature, but sometimes, you want something with a bit more space. The essay.html program, as shown in Figure 7-5, demonstrates how you might create a page for an essay question.

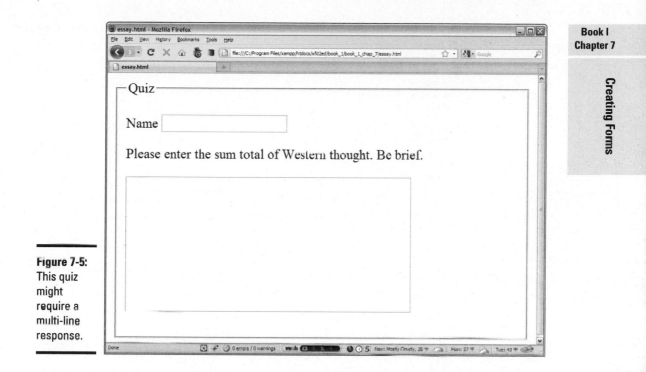

Figure 7-5:
This quiz
might
require a
multi-line
response.

The star of this program is a new tag — <textarea>:

```
<!DOCTYPE html PUBLIC "-//W3C//DTD XHTML 1.0 Strict//EN"
"http://www.w3.org/TR/xhtml1/DTD/xhtml1-strict.dtd">
<html lang="EN" dir="ltr" xmlns="http://www.w3.org/1999/xhtml">
  <head>
    <meta http-equiv="content-type" content="text/xml; charset=utf-8" />
    <title>essay.html</title>
  </head>

  <body>
    <form action = "">
      <fieldset>
        <legend>Quiz</legend>

        <p>
          <label>Name</label>
          <input type = "text"
                  id = "txtName" />
        </p>

        <p>
          <label>
            Please enter the sum total of
            Western thought. Be brief.
          </label>
        </p>

        <p>
          <textarea id = "txtAnswer"
```

```
                    rows = "10"
                    cols = "40"></textarea>
        </p>
      </fieldset>
    </form>
  </body>
</html>
```

Here are a few things to keep in mind when using the `<textarea>` tag:

✦ **It needs an `id` attribute, just like an input element.**

✦ **You can specify the size with `rows` and `cols` attributes.**

✦ **The content goes between the tags.** The text area can contain a lot more information than the ordinary `<input>` tags, so rather than placing the data in the `value` attribute, the content of the text goes between the `<textarea>` and `</textarea>` tags.

 Anything placed between `<textarea>` and `</textarea>` in the code ends up in the output, too. This includes spaces and carriage returns. If you don't want any blank spaces in the text area, place the ending tag right next to the beginning tag, as I did in the essay example.

Creating Multiple Selection Elements

Sometimes, you want to present the user with a list of choices and then have the user pick one of these elements. XHTML has a number of interesting ways to do this.

Making selections

The drop-down list is a favorite selection tool of Web developers for the following reasons:

✦ **It saves screen space.** Only the current selection is showing. When the user clicks the list, a series of choices drop down and then disappear again after the selection is made.

✦ **It limits input.** The only things the user can choose are things you've put in the list. This makes it much easier to handle the potential inputs because you don't have to worry about typing errors.

✦ **The value can be different from what the user sees.** This seems like an odd advantage, but it does turn out to be very useful sometimes. I show an example when I describe color values later in this chapter.

Figure 7-6 shows a simple drop-down list in action.

Figure 7-6:
The user
can choose
from a list of
colors.

The code for this simple drop-down list follows:

```
<!DOCTYPE html PUBLIC "-//W3C//DTD XHTML 1.0 Strict//EN"
"http://www.w3.org/TR/xhtml1/DTD/xhtml1-strict.dtd">
<html lang="EN" dir="ltr" xmlns="http://www.w3.org/1999/xhtml">
  <head>
    <meta http-equiv="content-type" content="text/xml; charset=utf-8" />
    <title>basicSelect.html</title>
  </head>

  <body>
    <form action = "">
      <p>
        <label>What is your favorite color?</label>
        <select id = "selColor">
          <option value = "#ff0000">Red</option>
          <option value = "#00ff00">Green</option>
          <option value = "#0000ff">Blue</option>
          <option value = "#00ffff">Cyan</option>
          <option value = "#ff00ff">Magenta</option>
          <option value = "#ffff00">Yellow</option>
          <option value = "#000000">Black</option>
          <option value = "#ffffff">White</option>
        </select>
      </p>
    </form>
  </body>
</html>
```

What are those funky #ff00ff things?

If you look carefully at the code for `basic-Select.html`, you see that the values are all strange text with pound signs and weird characters. These are *hex codes,* and they're a good way to describe colors for computers. I explain all about how these work in Book II, Chapter 1. This coding mechanism is not nearly as hard to understand as it seems. For now though, this code with both color names and hex values is a good example of wanting to show the user one thing (the name of a color in English) and send some other value (the hex code) to a program. You see this code again in Book IV, Chapter 5, where I use a list box just like this to change the background color of the form with JavaScript.

The `select` object is a bit different from some of the other input elements you're used to, such as

+ **It's surrounded by a `<select></select>` pair.** These tags indicate the entire list.

+ **The `select` object has an `id` attribute.** Although the `select` object has many other tags inside, typically only the `select` object itself has an `id` attribute.

+ **It contains a series of `<option></option>` pairs.** Each individual selection is housed in an `<option></option>` set.

+ **Each `<option>` tag has a value associated with it.** The value is used by code. The value isn't necessarily what the user sees. (See the sidebar "What are those funky #ff00ff things?" for an example.)

+ **The content between `<option></option>` is visible to the user.** The content is what the user actually sees.

Select boxes don't require the drop-down behavior. If you want, you can specify the number of rows to display with the `size` attribute. In this case, the number of rows you specify will always be visible on the screen.

Building check boxes

Check boxes are used when you want the user to turn a particular choice on or off. For example, look at Figure 7-7.

Each check box represents a true or false value that can be selected or not selected, and the status of each check box is completely independent from the others. The user can check none of the options, all of them, or any combination.

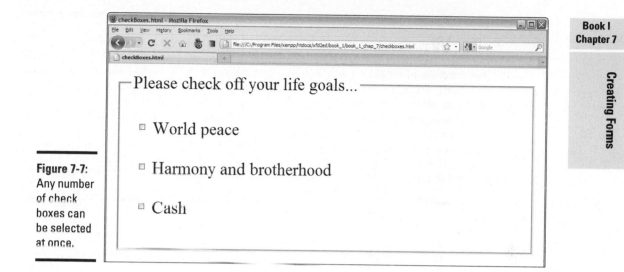

Figure 7-7:
Any number
of check
boxes can
be selected
at once.

This code shows that check boxes use your old friend the `<input>` tag:

```
<!DOCTYPE html PUBLIC "-//W3C//DTD XHTML 1.0 Strict//EN"
"http://www.w3.org/TR/xhtml1/DTD/xhtml1-strict.dtd">
<html lang="EN" dir="ltr" xmlns="http://www.w3.org/1999/xhtml">
  <head>
    <meta http-equiv="content-type" content="text/xml; charset=utf-8" />
    <title>checkBoxes.html</title>
  </head>

  <body>
    <form action = "">
      <fieldset>
        <legend>Please check off your life goals...</legend>
        <p>
          <input type = "checkbox"
                 id = "chkPeace"
                 value = "peace" />World peace
        </p>

        <p>
          <input type = "checkbox"
                 id = "chkHarmony"
                 value = "harmony" />Harmony and brotherhood
        </p>

        <p>
          <input type = "checkbox"
                 id = "chkCash"
                 value = "cash" />Cash
        </p>

      </fieldset>
    </form>
  </body>
</html>
```

This all seems inconsistent

Sometimes, the value of a form element is visible to users, and sometimes it's hidden. Sometimes, the text the user sees is inside the tag, and sometimes it isn't. It's a little confusing. The standards evolved over time, and they honestly could have been a little more consistent.

Still, this is the set of elements you have, and they're not really that hard to understand. Write forms a few times, and you'll remember. You can always start by looking over my code and borrowing it as a starting place.

You're using the same attributes of the `<input>` tag, but they work a bit differently than the way they do in a plain old text box:

✦ **The `type` is `checkbox`.** That's how the browser knows to make a check box, rather than a text field.

✦ **The checkbox still requires an ID.** If you'll be writing programming code to work with this thing (and you will, eventually), you'll need an ID for reference.

✦ **The value is hidden from the user.** The user doesn't see the actual value. That's for the programmer (like the `select` object). Any text following the check box only *appears* to be the text associated with it.

Creating radio buttons

Radio buttons are used when you want to let the user pick only one option from a group. Figure 7-8 shows an example of a radio button group in action.

Figure 7-8: You can choose only one of these radio buttons.

Radio buttons might seem similar to check boxes, but they have some important differences:

✦ **Only one can be checked at a time.** The term *radio button* came from the old-style car radios. When you pushed the button for one station, all the other buttons popped out. I still have one of those radios. (I guess I have a Web-design car.)

✦ **They have to be in a group.** Radio buttons make sense only in a group context. The point of a radio button is to interact with its group.

✦ **They all have the same name!** Each radio button has its own ID (like other input elements), but they also have a name attribute. The name attribute indicates the *group* a radio button is in.

✦ **You can have more than one group on a page.** Just use a different name attribute for each group.

✦ **One of them has to be selected.** The group should always have one value and only one. Some browsers check the first element in a group by default, but just in case, you should select the element you want selected. Add the checked = "checked" attribute (developed by the Department of Redundancy Department) to the element you want selected when the page appears. In this example, I preselected the most expensive option, all in the name of good capitalistic suggestive selling.

Here's some code that explains it all:

```
<!DOCTYPE html PUBLIC "-//W3C//DTD XHTML 1.0 Strict//EN"
"http://www.w3.org/TR/xhtml1/DTD/xhtml1-strict.dtd">
<html lang="EN" dir="ltr" xmlns="http://www.w3.org/1999/xhtml">
  <head>
    <meta http-equiv="content-type" content="text/xml; charset=utf-8" />
    <title>radioButtons.html</title>
  </head>

<body>
  <form action = "">
    <fieldset>
      <legend>How much do you want to spend?</legend>
      <p>
        <input type = "radio"
               name = "radPrice"
               id = "rad100"
               value = "100" />Too much
      </p>

      <p>
        <input type = "radio"
               name = "radPrice"
               id = "rad200"
               value = "200" />Way too much
      </p>

      <p>
        <input type = "radio"
```

```
                    name = "radPrice"
                    id = "rad5000"
                    value = "5000"
                    checked = "checked" />You've got to be kidding.
            </p>
        </fieldset>
      </form>
    </body>
</html>
```

Pressing Your Buttons

XHTML also comes with several types of buttons. You use these guys to make something actually happen. Generally, the user sets up some kind of input by typing in text boxes and then selecting from lists, options, or check boxes. Then, the user clicks a button to trigger a response. Figure 7-9 demonstrates four types of buttons.

The code for this button example is shown here:

```
<!DOCTYPE html PUBLIC "-//W3C//DTD XHTML 1.0 Strict//EN"
"http://www.w3.org/TR/xhtml1/DTD/xhtml1-strict.dtd">
<html lang="EN" dir="ltr" xmlns="http://www.w3.org/1999/xhtml">
  <head>
    <meta http-equiv="content-type" content="text/xml; charset=utf-8" />
    <title>buttons.html</title>
  </head>

  <body>
    <h1>Button Demo</h1>
    <form action = "">
      <fieldset>
        <legend>
          input-style buttons
        </legend>

        <input type = "button"
               value = "input type = button" />

        <input type = "submit" />
        <input type = "reset" />
      </fieldset>

      <fieldset>
        <legend>button tag buttons</legend>

        <button type = "button">
          button tag
        </button>
        <button>
          <img src = "clickMe.gif"
               alt = "click me" />
        </button>
      </fieldset>
    </form>
  </body>
</html>
```

Figure 7-9:
XHTML
supports
several
types of
buttons.

Each button type is described in this section.

Making input-style buttons

The most common form of button is just another form of your old friend, the
<input> tag. If you set the input's type attribute to "button", you gener-
ate a basic button:

```
<input type = "button"
       value = "input type = button" />
```

The ordinary Input button has a few key features:

+ **The input type is set to "button".** This makes an ordinary button.

+ **The value attribute sets the button's caption.** Change the value
  attribute to make a new caption. This button's caption shows how the
  button was made: input type = "button".

+ **This type of button doesn't imply a link.** Although the button appears
  to depress when it's clicked, it doesn't do anything. You have to write
  some JavaScript code to make it work.

✦ **Later, you'll add event-handling to the button.** After you discover JavaScript in Book IV, you use a special attribute to connect the button to code.

✦ **This type of button is for client-side programming.** This type of code resides on the user's computer. I discuss client-side programming with JavaScript in Book IV.

Building a Submit button

Submit buttons are usually used in server-side programming. In this form of programming, the code is on the Web server. In Book V, you use PHP to create server-side code. The `<input>` tag is used to make a Submit button, too!

```
<input type = "submit" />
```

Although they look the same, the Submit button is different than the ordinary button in a couple subtle ways:

✦ **The `value` attribute is optional.** If you leave it out, the button displays Submit Query. Of course, you can change the `value` to anything you want, and this becomes the caption of the Submit button.

✦ **Clicking it causes a link.** This type of button is meant for server-side programming. When you click the button, all the information in the form is gathered and sent to some other page on the Web.

✦ **Right now, it goes nowhere.** When you set the form's `action` attribute to null (" "), you told the Submit button to just reload the current page. When you figure out real server-side programming, you change the form's `action` attribute to a program that works with the data.

✦ **Submit buttons aren't for client-side.** Although you can attach an event to the Submit button (just like the regular Input button), the linking behavior often causes problems. Use regular Input buttons for client-side and Submit buttons for server-side.

It's a do-over: The Reset button

Yet another form of the versatile `<input>` tag creates the Reset button:

```
<input type = "reset" />
```

This button has a very specific purpose. When clicked, it resets all the elements of its form to their default values. Like the Submit button, it has a default value (`"reset"`), and it doesn't require any code.

Introducing the <button> tag

The button has been a useful part of the Web for a long time, but it's a bit boring. HTML 4.0 introduced the `<button>` tag, which works like this:

```
<button type = "button">
  button tag
</button>
```

The `<button>` tag acts more like a standard XHTML tag, but it can also act like a Submit button. Here are the highlights:

✦ **The `type` attribute determines the style.** You can set the button to `ordinary` (by setting its type to `button`), `submit`, or `reset`. If you don't specify the type, buttons use the Submit style. The button's `type` indicates its behavior, just like the Input-style buttons.

✦ **The caption goes between the `<button></button>` pair.** There's no `value` attribute. Instead, just put the intended caption inside the `<button>` pair.

✦ **You can incorporate other elements.** Unlike the Input button, you can place images or styled text inside a button. This gives you some other capabilities. The second button in the `buttons.html` example uses a small GIF image to create a more colorful button.

Chapter 8: The Future of HTML: HTML 5

The Web world is always changing. A new version of HTML — HTML 5 — is on the horizon, and it has some very interesting features. In this chapter, I preview the new features in HTML 5 and show you a few examples. When HTML becomes the standard, you'll be ahead of the game.

Can't We Just Stick with XHTML?

XHTML is great. When you add CSS to it, you can do a lot with XHTML. However, it isn't perfect. The Web is evolving, and we're now commonly doing things with Web pages that were once unheard of:

✦ **Sophisticated structure:** Web-based documents frequently have navigation elements, footer elements, page sections, and individual articles. Developers often use many variations of the <div> tag to manage these elements. HTML 5 has them built in.

✦ **Multimedia:** It's now common for Web pages to incorporate audio and video, yet these elements aren't built into HTML like image support. Instead, developers have to rely on external software, such as Flash.

✦ **Vector/real-time graphics:** The graphics capabilities of current browsers are fine, but they don't allow real-time modification. Programmers often use third-party software, such as Flash or Silverlight, to bring in this capability.

✦ **Enhanced programming:** Developers are no longer satisfied with Web pages as documents. Today's Web pages are the foundation of entire applications. Developers (and their customers) want advanced capabilities, such as dragging and dropping, local data storage, and geolocation (a fancy term for a browser that can tell where the device using the page is in the world).

Using the HTML 5 doctype

The XHTML doctype is remarkably ugly. I'll be honest. I can't code it from memory, and I write books about this stuff. My favorite part about HTML 5 might be the sensible doctype:

```
<!DOCTYPE html>
```

That's it. No messy XMLNS business, no crazy URLs, no http-equiv nonsense. Just <!DOCTYPE html>. This replaces both the <doctype> and the <HTML> tags. It's beautiful, in a geeky sort of way.

You might still want to add this line inside your heading:

```
<meta http-equiv="Content-Type" content="text/html;charset=utf-8" >
```

It specifies the character set as a standard text encoding. Typically, the server sends this, so it isn't really necessary, but including the line eliminates a possible validator warning that no typeface was defined.

Browser support for HTML 5

Before you get too excited about HTML 5, you have to realize it's still experimental. All the examples in this chapter were tested in Firefox 3.5, which supports many HTML 5 features. The latest versions of Chrome, Safari, and Opera all have support for key features of HTML 5, but Microsoft Internet Explorer (at least up to version 8) does not incorporate most features of HTML 5.

Validating HTML 5

Because the final specification for HTML 5 is still under review, validating HTML 5 code is not an exact science. The W3C validator has provisional support for HTML 5, but HTML 5 validation isn't built into Tidy or other validation tools, yet.

Still, it makes sense to validate your HTML 5 code as much as you can because validation will prevent problems down the road.

Semantic Elements

One of the key features of HTML is the support for new semantic features. HTML is supposed to be about describing the meaning of elements, yet Web pages frequently have elements without HTML tags. Look at the following example of HTML 5 code:

```
<!DOCTYPE html>
  <head>
    <title>semanticTags.html</title>
  </head>
  <body>
    <h1>Semantic Tags Demo</h1>
    <nav>
      <h2>Navigation</h2>
      <ul>
        <li>one</li>
        <li>two</li>
        <li>three</li>
        <li>four</li>
        <li>five</li>
      </ul>
    </nav>

    <section>
      <h2>Section</h2>

      <article>
        <h3>Article 1</h3>
        <p>
          This is an article. It's just a logical part of a page.
        </p>
      </article>

      <article>
        <h3>Article 1</h3>
        <p>
          This is an article. It's just a logical part of a page.
        </p>
      </article>
    </section>
  </body>
</html>
```

This code validates perfectly as HTML 5, but it has several tags that were not allowed in XHTML or previous versions of HTML:

✦ **<nav>:** It's very common for Web pages to have navigation sections. These often are menus or some other list of links. You can have several navigation elements on the page. The <nav> </nav> tags indicate that the block contains some sort of navigation elements.

✦ **<section>:** This is a generic tag for a section of the page. You can have several sections if you wish. Sections are indicated by the <section> </section> pair.

✦ **<article>:** The <article> tag is used to denote an article, say a blog posting. In my example, I put two articles inside the section.

None of these tags has any particular formatting. The tags just indicate the general layout of the page. You'll use CSS to make these sections look exactly how you want. (I didn't show a screen shot for this reason; you won't see anything special.)

The semantic tags aren't absolutely necessary. They were added because many Web developers already do something similar with the generic <div> tag. Use of these semantic tags will clarify your code and reduce some of the excessive use of divs that tends to clutter even modern XHTML designs.

Using New Form Elements

Even the earliest forms of HTML had support for user forms — tools for retrieving information from a user. The basic form elements have changed very little since the original versions of HTML. HTML 5 finally adds a few form elements to make certain kinds of data input much easier to manage. Although browsers have been slow to accept these features, they promise a much-improved user experience while the Web becomes a primary form of application development. Figure 8-1 shows a number of the new HTML 5 elements.

As with any HTML tag, the tag itself indicates a certain kind of data, not any particular appearance or behavior. Likely, these specialized input elements will make data entry easier for users.

Figure 8-1: HTML 5 supports several new variants of the input elements.

The screen captures of the code that follows are shown in Opera 10.10. As of this writing, Opera is the only major browser that supports these form elements. As you look over the code, you'll see that the extensions to the input element make a lot of sense.

```html
<!DOCTYPE html>
<head>
  <title>formDemo.html</title>
  <link rel = "stylesheet"
        type = "text/css"
        href = "formDemo.css" />

</head>

<body>
  <h1>HTML 5 Form Demo</h1>
  <form action = "">
    <label for = "email">email</label>
    <input type = "email"
           id = "email"/>

    <label for = "url">url</label>
    <input type = "url"
           id = "url" />

    <label for = "number">number</label>
    <input type = "number"
           id = "number"
           min = "0"
           max = "10"
           step = "2"
           value = "5" />

    <label for = "range">range</label>
    <input type = "range"
           id = "range"
           min = "0"
           max = "10"
           step = "2"
           value = "5" />

    <label for = "date">date</label>
    <input type = "date">

    <label for = "time">time</label>
    <input type = "time">

  </form>

</body>
</html>
```

Nothing surprising in these elements, but the new capabilities are interesting:

✦ **E-mail:** An `email` input element is optimized for accepting e-mail addresses. Some browsers may incorporate format-checking for this type. Mobile browsers may pop up specialized keyboards (making the @ sign more prominent, for example) when a user is entering data into an e-mail field.

✦ **Url:** Like an `email` input element, a `url` input element creates a field for entering links. Usually, the `url` input element doesn't have any particular formatting, but it may have a specialized pop-up keyboard in mobile devices.

✦ **Number:** A `number` input element specifies a numeric field. If you designate a field a `number` input element, you can indicate maximum (`max`) and minimum (`min`) values as well as a `step` value that indicates how much the data will change. Some browsers will check to see that the data is within the given range, and some will add a visual component that allows a user to select a number with small arrow buttons.

✦ **Range:** A `range` input element is similar to a `number` input element, but browsers that support it often use a small scrollbar to simplify user input.

✦ **Date:** Dates are especially difficult to get accurately from a user. By using a `date` input element, a date field can show an interactive calendar when a user begins to enter a date. Figure 8-2 illustrates this field in action.

✦ **Time:** By using the `time` input element, a time field can show a small dialog simplifying the process of retrieving time information from a user.

Figure 8-2:
When a user enters a date, a small calendar appears.

These effects aren't guaranteed. Different browsers will respond differently. Right now, Opera is the only browser that supports these features. However, since the effects are all variants of the input element, you can use these tags without penalty in earlier versions of HTML and XHTML. Any browser that does not understand these fancier form elements will simply replace them with ordinary text input fields.

Using Embedded Fonts

Technically, it's not part of HTML 5, but the new browsers have another great feature: embeddable fonts. Until now, there was no reliable way to use an arbitrary font in a Web page. You could suggest any font you wished, but that font would only work if the user already had it installed on her computer.

The current crop of browsers finally supports an embedded font technique that allows you to post a font file on your server and use that font in your page (much like the background image mechanism). This means you can finally have much better control of your typography on the Web. Figure 8-3 illustrates a page with an embedded font.

```
File  Edit  View  History  Bookmarks  Tools  Help

           C              file:///opt/lampp/htdocs/xfd2ed/book_1/book_1_chap_8/embedd      Google

   EmbeddedFont


        Embedded Font Demo



      HERE'S ANOTHER CUSTOM FONT




Done
```

Figure 8-3:
The fonts are embedded directly into the page.

The code for including a font is not difficult. Take a look at the code for embeddedFont.html to see how it's done:

```
<!DOCTYPE html>
  <head>
    <title>EmbeddedFont</title>
    <style type = "text/css">
      @font-face {
        font-family: "Miama";
        src: url("Miama.otf");
      }

      @font-face {
        font-family: "spray";
        src: url("ideoma_SPRAY.otf");
      }

      h1 {
        font-family: Miama;
        font-size: 300%;
      }

      h2 {
        font-family: spray;
      }
    </style>
  </head>

  <body>
    <h1>Embedded Font Demo</h1>
    <h2>Here's another custom font</h2>
  </body>

</html>
```

Here's how you do it.

1. **Identify your font:** Find a font file you want to use. Most commercial fonts are licensed for single-computer use, so stick with open font formats, such as the ones you'll find at http://openfontlibrary.org.

2. **Pick a font format:** Unfortunately, this part of the standard is still non-standard. Most browsers that support embedded fonts use TTF (the most common font format) or OTF (a somewhat more open variant of TTF). A new standard, WOFF, is on the horizon and may be more acceptable to font developers, but it isn't widely used yet. Internet Explorer uses only the proprietary EOT format. Look up the WEFT utility for converting fonts for use in Internet Explorer.

3. **Place the font file near your code:** Your Web page will need a copy of the font file somewhere on the server; put it in the same directory as your page. Remember, when you move the page to the server, you also need to make a copy of the font file on the server.

4. **Build a font-face:** Near the top of your CSS, designate a new font face using your custom font. This is slightly different CSS syntax than you may have used before. The @ sign indicates you are preparing a new CSS element.

5. **Specify the font-family:** This is the name used to designate the font in the rest of your CSS. Typically, this is similar to the font name, but easier to type.

6. **Indicate where the font file can be found:** The `src` attribute indicates where the file can be found. Typically, this is the filename of the font file in the same directory as the page. You can include several `src` attributes if you want to have more than one version of the file. (You might include EOT and OTF formats, for example, so the font is likely to work on any browser.)

7. **Use your new font in your CSS:** You now can use the font-family name in your CSS the same way you do with any other font. If the user doesn't have that font installed, the font is used for this Web page but not installed on the client's machine. Some fonts (like Miama in my example) may require some size adjustments to look right.

Just because you can use any font file doesn't mean you should. Many fonts are commercial products and cannot be distributed without permission. However, many excellent free and open-source fonts are available. See the open font library at `http://openfontlibrary.org` to find several great fonts.

Audio and Video Tags

Multimedia has been a promise of Web technology since the beginning but isn't integrated fully into HTML. Developers have had to rely on third-party technologies, such as plugins and the embed tag, to incorporate audio and video into Web pages. HTML 5 finally supports audio (with an `<audio>` tag) and video (with a `<video>` tag). For the first time, audio and video components can play natively in Web browsers without requiring any external technology.

This is a major breakthrough, or it will be if the browser developers cooperate. As an example, look at this code:

```
<!DOCTYPE html>
<head>
  <title>audioDemo.html</title>
</head>

<body>
  <h1>HTML 5 Audio Demo</h1>
  <audio src = "Do You Know Him.ogg" controls>
    This example uses the HTML 5 audio tag.
    Try using Firefox 3.5 or greater.
  </audio>

  <p>
    This song was written by a friend of mine, Daniel Rassum. He sings about
    hard life and redemption.
```

```
      If you like this song, I encourage you to check out his album at
      <a href = "http://www.noisetrade.com">www.noisetrade.com</a>.
      It's a "free trade" music site where you pay
      what you think is fair for an artist's work.
  </p>
</body>
</html>
```

The only new feature is the `<audio>` tag. This tag pair allows you to place an audio file directly into the Web page. You can set the audio to play automatically, or you can indicate player controls. Player controls are the preferred approach because it's considered polite to let the user choose whether audio plays when the page is loaded. If the browser does not support the `<audio>` tag, any text between the `<audio>` and `</audio>` tags is displayed.

Figure 8-4 illustrates `audioDemo.html` playing a song.

The HTML 5 specification (at the moment) does not specify any particular file format for the audio tag. The key browsers support the open-source Ogg Vorbis format and uncompressed `.wav` files. Browser manufacturers are having difficulty agreeing on what the standard should be. Some organizations with a stake in proprietary formats aren't excited about supporting an unencumbered format that currently is known only to geeks.

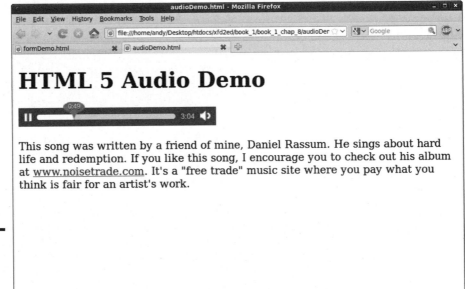

Figure 8-4:
The HTML 5 audio tag puts a simple audio player on the page.

If you remember old-school HTML, you might wonder if the `<audio>` tag is an improvement over the old `<embed>` tag. The `<embed>` tag was power-ful but very difficult to use. If you use the `<embed>` tag to embed an audio file into a Web page, the client machine looks for the default player for the particular file format and attempts to embed that player into the page (which might or might not work). The developer has no control of exactly what plugin will be used, which makes it very difficult to manage or control the element's behavior. The `<audio>` tag is built into the browser, and the browser manages the audio rather than some external program. This gives the developer much more control over what happens.

The `<video>` tag works much the same way as the audio tag but gives the Web browser native support for video. The following code shows a sample video playing in Firefox 3.5:

```
<!DOCTYPE html>
<head>
  <title>videoDemo</title>
</head>

<body>
  <h1>Video Demo</h1>
  <video src = "bigBuck.ogv" controls>
    Your browser does not support embedded video
    through HTML 5. Try Firefox 3.5 or greater.
  </video>

  <p>
    This video is a trailer for the incredible short move
    "Big Buck Bunny." This experiment proves that talented
    volunteers can produce a high-quality professional video
    using only open-source tools.
    Go to <a href = "http://www.bigbuckbunny.org">
    http://www.bigbuckbunny.org</a> to see the entire video.
  </p>
</body>
</html>
```

As with audio, the W3 standard does not specify any particular video format, so the various browser manufacturers are free to interpret this require-ment differently. Most of the current browsers support the open-source Ogg Theora format. (Yep, it's related to Ogg Vorbis.)

Video is more complex because the file format doesn't necessarily imply a particular coding mechanism. I encoded this video with the Ogg Vorbis wrapper using the AVI codec for the video portion and MP3 for the audio portion. This approach seems to be working in the two HTML 5 browsers I access.

Figure 8-5 is an example of a page showing a fun video created with free tools.

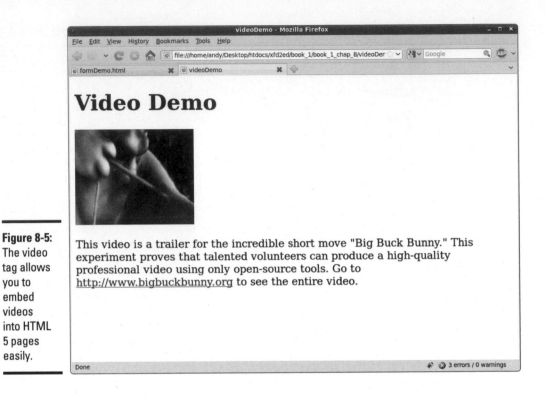

Figure 8-5:
The video
tag allows
you to
embed
videos
into HTML
5 pages
easily.

The actual movie I show in the example is a trailer to the excellent short movie *Big Buck Bunny*. This incredible cartoon shows what can be done with completely open-source tools and rivals works from commercial studios. Thanks to the Blender foundation for releasing this hilarious and impressive film under a creative commons license.

The Canvas Tag

HTML 5 offers at least one more significant new feature. The <canvas> tag allows developers to draw directly on a portion of the form using programming commands. Although this technique requires some JavaScript skills, it opens substantial new capabilities. Figure 8-6 shows a simple page illustrating the <canvas> tag.

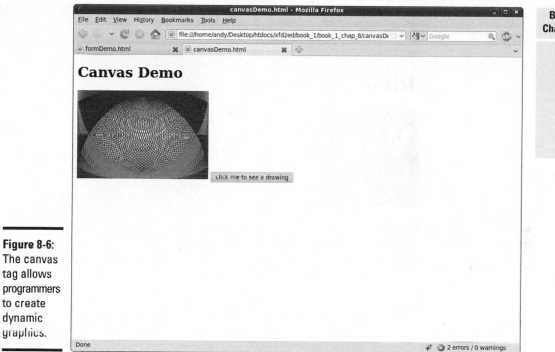

Figure 8-6:
The canvas
tag allows
programmers
to create
dynamic
graphics.

The code for `canvasDemo.html` relies on JavaScript, so check Book IV for details on how to write this code and much more. As an overview, though, here's the code:

```
<!DOCTYPE html>
<head>
  <title>canvasDemo.html</title>
  <script type = "text/javascript">
    //<![CDATA[

    function draw(){
      var myCanvas = document.getElementById("myCanvas"),
      var context = myCanvas.getContext("2d");
      context.fillStyle = "blue";
      context.strokeStyle = "red";
      circle(context, 1, 1, 1);

      for (i = 1; i <= 200; i+= 2){
        circle(context, i, i, i, "blue");
        circle(context, 300-i, 200-i, i, "red");
        circle(context, 300-i, i, i, "blue");
        circle(context, i, 200-i, i, "red");
      } // end for

    } // end draw

    function circle(context, x, y, radius, color){
      context.strokeStyle = color;
```

```
      context.beginPath();
      context.arc(x, y, radius, 0, Math.PI * 2, true);
      context.stroke();
    } // end circle
    //]]>
  </script>
</head>

<body>
  <h1>Canvas Demo</h1>

  <canvas id = "myCanvas"
          width = "300"
          height = "200">
    This example requires HTML 5 canvas support
  </canvas>

  <button type = "button"
          onclick = "draw()">
    click me to see a drawing
  </button>

</body>
</html>
```

There's quite a bit going on in this program. The image doesn't come from the server as most Web images do; it's drawn on demand by a small JavaScript program.

+ **Create an HTML page with a <canvas> tag:** Of course, you need the <canvas> tag in your document; the element designates a part of the page that displays a graphic. The image of a canvas element is not pulled from an external file but created with JavaScript code.

+ **Extract a drawing context from the canvas:** It's only possible to do 2D graphics with a <canvas> tag, but 3D canvases are expected in the future.

+ **Use special drawing commands to modify the context:** The canvas mechanism supports a number of special JavaScript commands that allow you to draw and manipulate shapes directly on the surface. This example draws a number of circles in different colors to create an interesting pattern.

Although the <canvas> tag may not be that interesting, it's one of the most important features of HTML 5 because it changes the way programmers think about Web development. Because the client program draws the image, the image can be modified in real time and interact with the user. Here are some examples:

+ **Dynamic graphs:** A Web page describing data can have graphs that automatically change when the underlying data changes.

+ **Custom components:** A programmer can create entire new widgets to replace the ordinary buttons and list boxes. This will likely lead to Web-based user interfaces as rich as those now on the desktop.

✦ **Gaming and animation:** Until now, online gaming has required third-party applications (such as Flash or Java). The <canvas> tag promises full graphics capability directly in the browser. Enterprising programmers have already written some very interesting games using the <canvas> tag.

✦ **An entire operating system:** It's possible that high-powered Web browsers with very fast JavaScript engines will be able to recreate much of an entire operating system using the <canvas> tag as a graphical interface. A number of interesting devices are already using Web-based tools as the foundation of the GUI. It's probably not a coincidence that the new browser and the new operating system by Google have the exact same name (Chrome).

The <canvas> tag will likely have a profound effect on Web development, but it isn't heavily used yet. One major browser (guess which one) has decided not to implement the <canvas> tag. (Okay, I'll tell you. It's Internet Explorer.) Canvas is so important to the Web that Google has built a canvas plugin so canvas-based apps will work in IE.

Other Promising Features

HTML 5 offers some other very interesting capabilities. Most of the advanced tools won't be used by beginning Web developers, but they'll add very interesting new capabilities to the Web if they are adopted universally.

✦ **Geolocation:** If a device has GPS or Wi-Fi triangulation hardware built in (as many high-end cellphones, PDAs, and smartphones do), the geolocation tool will allow the programmer to determine the current position of the browser. This will have interesting consequences, as a search for gas stations can be automatically limited to gas stations within a certain radius of the current position (as one example).

✦ **Local storage:** Developers are working to build complete applications (replacements for word processors, spreadsheets, and other common tools) that are based on the Web browser. Of course, this won't work when the computer is not online. HTML 5 will have mechanisms for automatically storing data locally when the machine is not online, and synchronizing it when possible.

✦ **Drag-and-drop:** Currently, you can implement a form of drag and drop inside the Web browser (see Book VII, Chapter 4 for an example). The next step is to allow users to drag a file from the desktop to an application running in the browser and have the browser app use that data. HTML 5 supports this mechanism.

Limitations of HTML 5

HTML 5 looks very exciting, and it points to fascinating new capabilities. However, it isn't here yet. Most of the browser manufacturers support at least some form of HTML 5, but none support every feature. One notable developer has stayed far away from the HTML 5 specification. As of IE8, Microsoft does not support the `<audio>` or `<video>` tags, the `<canvas>` tag, or the semantic elements described in this chapter. To be fair, Microsoft has allowed embedded fonts for quite some time, but only using the proprietary EOT font format. Microsoft has not committed to including any HTML 5 features in IE9. If Microsoft continues to go its own way and Internet Explorer remains a dominant browser, HTML 5 technologies may never gain traction. It's also possible that Microsoft's refusal to abide by standards will finally erode its market share enough that they will decide to go along with developer requests and support these new standards in an open way.

HTML 5 is not yet an acknowledged standard, and one of the most prominent browsers in use doesn't support it. For that reason, I still use XHTML 1.0 strict as my core language, and most examples in this book use that standard. However, I do highlight potential uses of HTML 5 when they occur in this book.

Book II

Styling with CSS

Change your fonts, colors, and backgrounds with CSS.

Contents at a Glance

Chapter 1: Coloring Your World

XHTML does a good job of setting up the basic design of a page, but face it: The pages it makes are pretty ugly. In the old days, developers added a lot of other tags to HTML to make it prettier, but it was a haphazard affair. Now, XHTML disallows all the tags that made pages more attractive. That sounds bad, but it isn't really a loss. Today, XHTML is almost always written in concert with CSS (Cascading Style Sheets). It's amazing how much you can do with CSS to beautify your XHTML pages.

CSS allows you to change the color of any image on the page, add backgrounds and borders, change the visual appearance of elements (like lists and links), as well as customize the entire layout of your page. Additionally, CSS allows you to keep your XHTML simple because all the formatting is stored in the CSS. CSS is efficient, too, because it allows you to reuse a style across multiple pages. If XHTML gives your pages structure, CSS gives them beauty.

This chapter gets you started by describing how to add color to your pages.

Now You Have an Element of Style

The secret to CSS is the *style sheet*, a set of rules for describing how various objects will display. For example, look at `basicColors.html` in Figure 1-1.

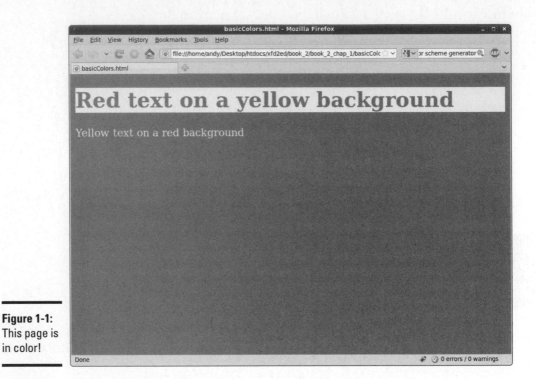

Figure 1-1:
This page is
in color!

As always, don't take my word for it. This chapter is about color, and you need to look at these pages from the CD or Web site to see what I'm talking about.

Nothing in the XHTML code provides color information. What makes this page different from plain XHTML pages is a new section that I've stashed in the header. Take a gander at the code to see what's going on:

```
<!DOCTYPE html PUBLIC "-//W3C//DTD XHTML 1.0 Strict//EN"
"http://www.w3.org/TR/xhtml1/DTD/xhtml1-strict.dtd">
<html lang="EN" dir="ltr" xmlns="http://www.w3.org/1999/xhtml">
  <head>
    <meta http-equiv="content-type" content="text/xml; charset=utf-8" />
    <title>basicColors.html</title>
    <style type = "text/css">
      body {
        color: yellow;
        background-color: red;
      }

      h1 {
        color: red;
        background-color: yellow;
      }
    </style>
  </head>
```

```
<body>
  <h1>Red text on a yellow background</h1>
  <p>
    Yellow text on a red background
  </p>
</body>
</html>
```

As you can see, nothing is dramatically different in the XHTML code. The body simply contains an h1 and a p. Although the text mentions the colors, nothing in the XHTML code makes the colors really happen.

The secret is the new `<style></style>` pair I put in the header area:

```
<style type = "text/css">
  body {
    color: yellow;
    background-color: red;
  }

  h1 {
    color: red;
    background-color: yellow;
  }
</style>
```

The `<style>` tag is an HTML tag, but what it does is special: It switches languages! Inside the style elements, you're not writing XHTML anymore. You're in a whole new language — CSS. CSS has a different job than XHTML, but they're made to work well together.

It may seem that the CSS code is still part of HTML because it's inside the XHTML page, but it's best to think of XHTML and CSS as two distinct (if related) languages. XHTML describes the content, and CSS describes the layout. CSS (as you soon see) has a different syntax and style than XHTML and isn't always embedded in the Web page.

Setting up a style sheet

Style sheets describe presentation rules for XHTML elements. If you look at the preceding style sheet (the code inside the `<style>` tags), you can see that I've described presentation rules for two elements: the `<body>` and `<h1>` tags. Whenever the browser encounters one of these tags, it attempts to use these style rules to change that tag's visual appearance.

Styles are simply a list of *selectors* (places in the page that you want to modify). For now, I use tag names (body and h1) as selectors. However, in Chapter 3 of this minibook, I show many more selectors that you can use.

Each selector can have a number of style *rules*. Each rule describes some attribute of the selector. To set up a style, keep the following in mind:

✦ **Begin with the style tags.** The type of style you'll be working with is embedded into the page. You should describe your style in the header area.

✦ **Include the style type in the header area.** The style type is always `"text/css"`. The beginning `<style>` tag always looks like this:

```
<style type = "text/css">
```

✦ **Define an element.** Use the element name (the tag name alone) to begin the definition of a particular element's style. You can define styles for all the XHTML elements (and other things, too, but not today). The style rule for the body is designated like this:

```
body {
```

✦ **Use braces ({ }) to enclose the style rules.** Each style's rules are enclosed in a set of braces. Similar to many programming languages, braces mark off special sections of code. It's traditional to indent inside the braces.

✦ **Give a rule name.** In this chapter, I'm working with two very simple rules: `color` and `background-color`. Throughout this minibook, you can read about many more CSS rules (sometimes called attributes) that you can modify. A colon (`:`) character always follows the rule name.

✦ **Enter the rule's value.** Different rules take different values. The attribute value is followed by a semicolon. Traditionally, each name-value pair is on one line, like this:

```
body {
  color: yellow;
  background-color: red;
}
```

Changing the colors

In this very simple example, I just changed some colors around. Here are the two primary color attributes in CSS:

✦ `color:` This refers to the foreground color of any text in the element.

✦ `background-color:` The background color of the element. (The hyphen is a formal part of the name. If you leave it out, the browser won't know what you're talking about.)

With these two elements, you can specify the color of any element. For example, if you want all your paragraphs to have white text on a blue background, add the following text to your style:

```
p {
  color: white;
  background-color: blue;
}
```

Like XHTML Strict, CSS is case-sensitive. CSS styles should be written entirely in lowercase.

You'll figure out many more style elements in your travels, but they all follow the same principles illustrated by the color attributes.

Specifying Colors in CSS

Here are the two main ways to define colors in CSS. You can use color names, such as pink and fuchsia, or you can use *hex values.* (Later in this chapter, in the section "Creating Your Own Color Scheme," you find out how to use special numeric designators to choose colors.) Each approach has its advantages.

Using color names

Color names seem like the easiest solution, and, for basic colors like red and yellow, they work fine. However, here are some problems with color names that make them troublesome for Web developers:

✦ **Only 16 color names will validate.** Although most browsers accept hundreds of color names, only 16 are guaranteed to validate in CSS and XHTML validators. See Table 1-1 for a list of those 16 colors.

✦ **Color names are somewhat subjective.** You'll find different opinions on what exactly constitutes any particular color, especially when you get to the more obscure colors. (I personally wasn't aware that PeachPuff and PapayaWhip are colors. They sound more like dessert recipes to me.)

✦ **It can be difficult to modify a color.** For example, what color is a tad bluer than Gainsboro? (Yeah, that's a color name, too. I had no idea how extensive my color disability really was.)

✦ **They're hard to match.** Let's say you're building an online shrine to your cat and you want the text to match your cat's eye color. It'll be hard to figure out exactly what color name corresponds to your cat's eyes. I guess you could ask.

Table 1-1	Legal Color Names and Hex Equivalents
Color	*Hex Value*
Black	#000000
Silver	#C0C0C0
Gray	#808080

(continued)

Table 1-1 *(continued)*

Color	Hex Value
White	#FFFFFF
Maroon	#800000
Red	#FF0000
Purple	#800080
Fuchsia	#FF00FF
Green	#008800
Lime	#00FF00
Olive	#808000
Yellow	#FFFF00
Navy	#000080
Blue	#0000FF
Teal	#008080
Aqua	#00FFFF

The mysterious hex codes are included in this table for completeness. It's okay if you don't understand what they're about. All is revealed in the next section.

Obviously, I can't show you actual colors in this black-and-white book, so I added a simple page to the CD-ROM and Web site that displays all the named colors. Check `namedColors.html` to see the actual colors.

Putting a hex on your colors

Colors in HTML are a strange thing. The "easy" way (with color names) turns out to have many problems. The method most Web developers *really* use sounds a lot harder, but it isn't as bad as it may seem at first. The *hex color* scheme uses a seemingly bizarre combination of numbers and letters to determine color values. #00FFFF is aqua. #FFFF00 is yellow. It's a scheme only a computer scientist could love. Yet, after you get used to it, you'll find the system has its own geeky charm. (And isn't geeky charm the best kind?)

Hex colors work by describing exactly what the computer is doing, so you have to know a little more about how computers work with color. Each dot (or *pixel*) on the screen is actually composed of three tiny beams of light (or LCD diodes or something similar). Each pixel has tiny red, green, and blue beams.

The light beams work kind of like stage lights. Imagine a black stage with three spotlights (red, green, and blue) trained on the same spot. If all the lights are off, the stage is completely dark. If you turn on only the red light, you see red. You can turn on combinations to get new colors. For example, turning on red and green creates a spot of yellow light. Turning on all three lights makes white.

Coloring by number

You could devise a simple system to describe colors by using 1 to represent on and 0 to represent off. In this system, three digits represent each color, with one digit each for red, green, and blue. So, red would be 100 (turn on red, but turn off green and blue), and 111 would be white (turn on all three lights).

This system produces only eight colors. In a computer system, each of the little lights can be adjusted to various levels of brightness. These values measure from 0 (all the way off) to 255 (all the way on). Therefore, you could describe red as rgb(255, 0, 0) and yellow as rgb(255, 255, 0).

The 0 to 255 range of values seems strange because you're probably used to base 10 mathematics. The computer actually stores values in binary notation. The way a computer sees it, yellow is actually 111111111111111100000000. Ack! There has to be an easier way to handle all those binary values. That's why we use *hexadecimal notation*. Read on. . . .

Hex education

All those 1s and 0s get tedious. Programmers like to convert to another format that's easier to work with. It's easier to convert numbers to base 16 than base 10, so that's what programmers do. You can survive just fine without understanding base 16 (also called *hexadecimal* or *hex*) conversion, but you should understand a few key features, such as:

✦ **Each hex digit is shorthand for four digits of binary.** The whole reason programmers use hex is to simplify working with binary.

✦ **Each digit represents a value between 0 and 15.** Four digits of binary represent a value between 0 and 15.

✦ **We have to invent some digits.** The whole reason hex looks so weird is the inclusion of characters. This is for a simple reason: There aren't enough numeric digits to go around! Table 1-2 illustrates the basic problem.

Table 1-2	Hex Representation of Base Ten Numbers
Decimal (Base 10)	*Hex (Base 16)*
0	0
1	1
2	2
3	3
4	4
5	5
6	6
7	7
8	8
9	9
10	A
11	B
12	C
13	D
14	E
15	F

The ordinary digits 0–9 are the same in hex as they are in base 10, but the values from 10–15 (base ten) are represented by alphabetic characters in hexadecimal.

You're very used to seeing the value 10 as equal to the number of fingers on both hands, but that's not always the case when you start messing around with numbering systems like we're doing here. The number 10 simply means one of the current base. Until now, you may have never used any base but base ten, but all that changes here. 10 is ten in base ten, but in base two, 10 means two. In base eight, 10 means eight, and in base sixteen, 10 means sixteen. This is important because when you want to talk about the number of digits on your hands in hex, you can't use the familiar notation 10 because in hex 10 means sixteen. We need a single-digit value to represent ten, so computer scientists legislated themselves out of this mess by borrowing letters. 10 is A, 11 is B, and 15 is F.

If all this math theory is making you dizzy, don't worry. I show in the next section some shortcuts for creating great colors using this scheme. For now, though, here's what you need to understand to use hex colors:

✦ **A color requires six digits of hex.** A pixel requires three colors, and each color uses eight digits of binary. Two digits of hex cover each color. Two digits represent red, two for green, and finally two for blue.

✦ **Hex color values usually begin with a pound sign.** To warn the browser that a value will be in hexadecimal, the value is usually preceded with a pound sign (#). So, yellow is #FFFF00.

Working with colors in hex may seem really crazy and difficult, but it has some important advantages:

Book II
Chapter 1

✦ **Precision:** Using this system gives you a huge number of colors to work with (over 16 million, if you really want to know). There's no way you could come up with that many color names on your own. Well, you could, but you'd be very, very old by the time you were done.

Coloring Your World

✦ **Objectivity:** Hex values aren't a matter of opinion. There could be some argument about the value of burnt sienna, but hex value #666600 is unambiguous.

✦ **Portability:** Most graphic editors use the hex system, so you can pick any color of an image and get its hex value immediately. This would make it easy to find your cat's eye color for that online shrine.

✦ **Predictability:** After you understand how it works, you can take any hex color and convert it to a value that's a little darker, a little brighter, or that has a little more blue in it. This is difficult to do with named colors.

✦ **Ease of use:** This one may seem like a stretch, but after you understand the Web-safe palette, which I describe in the next section, it's very easy to get a rough idea of a color and then tweak it to make exactly the form you're looking for.

Using the Web-safe color palette

A long time ago, browsers couldn't even agree on what colors they'd display reliably. Web developers responded by working within a predefined palette of colors that worked pretty much the same on every browser. Today's browsers have no problems showing lots of colors, but the so-called *Web-safe color palette* is still sometimes used because it's an easy starting point.

The basic idea of the Web-safe palette (shown in Table 1-3) is this: Each color can have only one of the following values: 00, 33, 66, 99, CC, or FF. 00 is the darkest value for each color, and FF is the brightest. The primary colors are all made of 0s and Fs: #FF0000 is red (all red, no green, no blue). A Web-safe color uses any combination of these values, so #33CC00 is Web-safe, but #112233 is not.

Table 1-3	Web-Safe Color Values		
Description	*Red*	*Green*	*Blue*
Very bright	FF	FF	FF
	CC	CC	CC
	99	99	99
	66	66	66
	33	33	33
Very dark	00	00	00

To pick a Web-safe value from this chart, determine how much of each color you want. A bright red will have red turned on all the way (FF) with no green (00) and no blue (00), making #FF0000. If you want a darker red, you might turn the red down a little. The next darker Web-safe red is #CC0000. If that isn't dark enough, you might try #990000. Let's say you like that, but you want it a little purple. Simply add a notch or two of blue: #990033 or #990066.

If you're having trouble following this, look at `colorTester.html` on the CD-ROM. It allows you to pick a Web-safe color by clicking buttons organized like Table 1-3.

The original problem Web-safe colors were designed to alleviate is long resolved, but they're still popular as a starting point. Web-safe colors give you a dispersed and easily understood subset of colors you can start with. You don't have to stay there, but it's a great place to start.

Choosing Your Colors

Figure 1-2 shows the `colorTester.html` program I added to the Web page and CD-ROM. This page lets you experiment with colors. I refer to it during this discussion.

The `colorTester.html` page uses techniques that I describe primarily in Book IV, Chapter 5. Feel free to look over the source code to get a preview of JavaScript and Dynamic HTML (DHTML) concepts. By the end of Book IV, you can write this program.

The best way to understand colors is to do some hands-on experimentation. You can use the `colorTester.html` page to do some quick tests, or you can write and modify your own pages that use color.

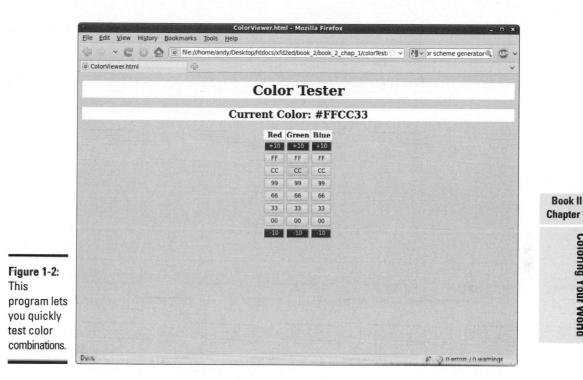

Figure 1-2:
This program lets you quickly test color combinations.

Starting with Web-safe colors

The `colorTester.html` program works by letting you quickly enter a Web-safe value. To make red, press the FF button in the red column. The blue and green values have the default value of 00, so the background is red.

The Web-safe colors give you a lot of room to play, and they're very easy to work with. In fact, they're so common that you can use a shortcut. Because the Web-safe colors are all repeated, you can write a repeated digit (FF) as a single digit (F). You can specify magenta as either #FF00FF or as #F0F and the browser understands, giving you a headache-inducing magenta.

To make a darker red, change the FF to the next smallest value, making #CC0000. If you want it darker yet, try #990000. Experiment with all the red values and see how easy it is to get several different types of red. If you want a variation of pink, raise the green and blue values together. #FF6666 is a dusty pink color; #FF9999 is a bit brighter; and #FFCCCC is a very white pink.

Modifying your colors

The Web-safe palette is convenient, but it gives you a relatively small number of colors (216, if you're counting). Two hundred and sixteen crayons in the box are pretty nice, but you might need more. Generally, I start with Web-safe colors and then adjust as I go. If you want a lighter pink than #FFCCCC, you can jump off the Web-safe bandwagon and use #FFEEEE or any other color you wish!

In the `colorTester.html` program, you can use the top and bottom button in each row to fine-tune the adjustments to your color.

Doing it on your own pages

Of course, it doesn't really matter how the colors look on *my* page. The point is to make things look good on *your* pages. To add color to your pages, do the following:

1. **Define the XHTML as normal.**

The XHTML shouldn't have any relationship to the colors. Add the color strictly in CSS.

2. **Add a <style> tag to the page in the header area.**

Don't forget to set the `type = "text/css"` attribute.

3. **Add a selector for each tag you want to modify.**

You can modify any HTML tag, so if you want to change all the paragraphs, add a `p { }` selector. Use the tag name without the angle braces, so `<h1>` becomes `h1{ }`.

4. **Add `color` and `background-color` attributes.**

You'll discover many more CSS elements you can modify throughout Books II and III but for now, stick to `color` and `background-color`.

5. **Specify the color values with color names or hex color values.**

Changing CSS on the fly

If you've installed the Web Developer toolbar to Firefox (which I describe in Book I, Chapter 3) you have some nifty CSS tools at your disposal. I really love the CSS editor. To make it work, take any page (with or without CSS) and open it in Firefox. For this example, I use a list example from Book I, Chapter 4.

Be sure the Web Developer toolbar is installed and then choose Edit CSS from the CSS menu. A new panel that looks similar to Figure 1-3 appears.

You can simply type CSS code into the little text editor, and the page updates instantly! Figure 1-4 shows the same page after I made a few changes.

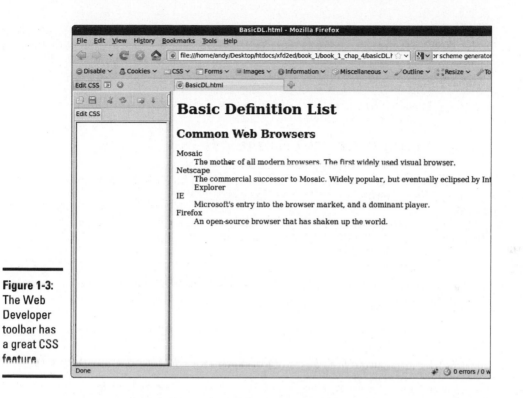

**Book II
Chapter 1**

Coloring Your World

Figure 1-3:
The Web
Developer
toolbar has
a great CSS
feature.

Figure 1-4:
The CSS
changes
show
immediately.

I used color to make the definition list easier to view. I changed both the foreground and background colors in the heading level 1. I set the definition terms (dt) to red and added a yellow background to the definitions (dd). Check Book I, Chapter 4 if you need a refresher on definition lists in XHTML.

The Web Developer CSS editor is great because you can see the results in real time. It's a super way to play around with your colors (and other CSS elements). You can also use it to view and modify an existing CSS document. Pull up any page you want and open the CSS editor. You can change colors all you want without making a commitment.

The changes made using the Web Developer CSS editor aren't permanent. You're making changes only in the copy in your own browser. If you really like the CSS code that you've written in the editor, copy it to the clipboard and paste it into your page to make it permanent, or save it to a file for later use.

Creating Your Own Color Scheme

The technical side of setting colors isn't too difficult, but deciding *what* colors to use can be a challenge. Entire books have been written about how to determine a color scheme. A little bit of subjectivity is in the process, but a few tools and rules can get you started.

Understanding hue, saturation, and value

The RGB color model is useful because it relates directly to how computers generate color, but it's not perfect. It's a bit difficult to visualize variations of a color in RGB. For that reason, other color schemes are often used. The most common variation is *Hue, Saturation, and Value,* or *HSV.* The HSV system organizes colors in a way more closely related to the color wheel.

To describe a color using HSV, you specify three characteristics of a color using numeric values:

✦ **Hue:** The basic color. The color wheel is broken into a series of hues. These are generally middle of the road colors that can be made *brighter* (closer to white) and *darker* (closer to black).

✦ **Saturation:** How pervasive the color is. A high saturation is very bright. A low saturation has very little color. If you reduce all the saturation in an image, the image is *grayscale,* with no color at all.

✦ **Value:** The brightness of the color. The easiest way to view value is to think about how the image would look when reduced to grayscale (by pulling down the saturation). All the brighter colors will be closer to white, and the darker colors will be nearly black.

The HSV model is useful because it allows you to pick colors that go well together. Use the hue property to pick the basic colors. Because there's a mathematical relationship between the various color values, it becomes easy to predict which colors work well together. After you have all the hues worked out, you can change the saturation and value to modify the overall tone of the page. Generally, all the colors in a particular scheme have similar saturation and values.

Unfortunately, you can't specify CSS colors in HSV mode. Instead, you have to use another tool to get the colors you want and convert them to RGB format.

Using the Color Scheme Designer

Some people have great color sense. Others (like me) struggle a little bit because it all seems a little subjective. If you're already confident with colors, you may not need this section — although, you still might find it interesting validation of what you already know. On the other hand, if you get perplexed in a paint store, you might find it helpful to know that some really useful tools are available.

One great way to get started is with a free tool: the Color Scheme Designer, shown in Figure 1-5. This tool created by Petr Stanicek uses a variation of the HSV model to help you pick color schemes. You can find this program at `http://colorschemedesigner.com`.

Figure 1-5:
The Color Scheme Designer helps you pick colors.

The Color Scheme Designer has several areas, such as:

+ **The color wheel:** This tool may bring back fond memories of your elementary school art class. The wheel arranges the colors in a way familiar to artists. You can click the color wheel to pick a primary color for your page.

+ **The color scheme selector:** You can pick from a number of color schemes. I describe these schemes a little later in this section.

+ **A preview area:** This area displays the selected colors in action so you can see how the various colors work together.

+ **Hex values:** The hex values for the selected colors display on the page so you can copy them to your own application.

+ **Variations:** You can look at variations of the selected scheme. These variations are often useful because they show differences in the saturation and value without you doing the math.

+ **Color-blindness simulation:** This very handy tool lets you see your color scheme as it appears to people with various types of color-blindness.

This won't make sense without experimentation. Be sure to play with this tool and see how easy it is to create colors that work well together.

Selecting a base hue

The Color Scheme Designer works by letting you pick one main hue and then uses one of a number of schemes for picking other hues that work well with the base one. To choose the base hue you want for your page, click a color on the color wheel.

The color wheel is arranged according to the traditional artist's color scheme based on HSV rather than the RGB scheme used for computer graphics. When you select a color, the closest RGB representation is returned. This is nice because it allows you to apply traditional (HSV-style) color theory to the slightly different RGB model.

When you pick a color on the color wheel, you're actually picking a hue. If you want any type of red, you can pick the red that appears on the wheel. You can then adjust the variations to modify the saturation and value of all the colors in the scheme together.

To pick a color using this scheme, follow these steps:

1. **Pick a hue.**

The colors on the color wheel represent hues in the HSV model. Find a primary color you want to use as the foundation of your page.

2. **Determine a scheme.**

   The scheme indicates which other colors you will use and how they relate to the primary hue. More information on the various schemes is available in the next section.

3. **Adjust your scheme.**

   The main schemes are picked using default settings for saturation and value. The Adjust Scheme tab allows you to modify the saturation and value settings to get much more control of your color scheme. You can also adjust the level of contrast to get very interesting effects.

4. **Preview the scheme.**

   The Designer has several options for previewing your color scheme, including the ability to create quick Web pages using the scheme. You might also look at the color blindness simulators to see how your page appears to people with different kinds of color blindness.

5. **Export the color settings.**

   If you want, you can export the color settings to a number of formats, including a very nice HTML/CSS format. You can also save the colors to a special file for importing into GIMP or Photoshop, so the exact colors used in your page will be available to your image editor, too.

Picking a color scheme

The various color schemes use mathematical relationships around the color wheel to predict colors that work well with the primary color. Here are the basic schemes, including what they do:

✦ **Mono (monochromatic):** Takes the base hue and offers a number of variations in saturation and value. This scheme is nice when you really want to emphasize one particular color (for example, if you're doing a Web site about rain forests and want a lot of greens). Be sure to use high contrast between the foreground and background colors so your text is readable.

✦ **Complement:** Uses the base hue and the *complementary* (opposite) color. Generally, this scheme uses several variations of the base hue and a splash of the complementary hue for contrast.

✦ **Triad:** Selects the base hue and two opposite hues. When you select the Triad scheme, you can also choose the angular distance between the opposite colors. If this distance is zero, you have the complementary color scheme. When the angle increases, you have a *split complementary* system, which uses the base hue and two hues equidistant from the contrast. Such schemes can be jarring at full contrast, but when adjusted for saturation and value, you can create some very nice color schemes.

+ **Tetrad:** Generates four hues. As with the Triad scheme, when you add more hues, keeping your page unified becomes more difficult unless you adjust the variations for lower contrast.

+ **Analogic:** Schemes use the base hue and its two neighbors.

+ **Accented Analogic:** Just like the Analogic scheme, but with the addition of the complementary color.

Chapter 2: Styling Text

In This Chapter

✔ Introducing fonts and typefaces

✔ Specifying the font family

✔ Determining font size

✔ Understanding CSS measurement units

✔ Managing other font characteristics

✔ Using the font rule to simplify font styles

*W*eb pages are still primarily a text-based media, so you'll want to add some formatting capabilities. XHTML doesn't do any meaningful text formatting on its own, but CSS adds a wide range of tools for choosing the typeface, font size, decorations, alignment, and much more. In this chapter, you discover how to manage text the CSS way.

A bit of semantics is in order. The thing most people dub a *font* is more properly a *typeface*. Technically, a font is a particular typeface at a particular size with a specific set of decorations (underlining, italic, and so on). The distinction is honestly not that important in a digital setting. You don't explicitly set the font in CSS. You determine the *font family* (which is essentially a typeface), and then you modify its characteristics (creating a font as purists would think of it). Still, when I'm referring to the thing that most people call a font (a file in the operating system that describes the appearance of an alphabet set), I use the familiar term *font*.

Setting the Font Family

To assign a font family to part of your page, use some new CSS. Figure 2-1 illustrates a page with the heading set to Comic Sans MS.

If this page is viewed on a Windows machine, it generally displays the font correctly because Comic Sans MS is installed with most versions of Windows. If you're on another type of machine, you may get something else. More on that in a moment, but for now, look at the simple case.

Here's the code:

```
<!DOCTYPE html PUBLIC "-//W3C//DTD XHTML 1.0 Strict//EN"
"http://www.w3.org/TR/xhtml1/DTD/xhtml1-strict.dtd">
<html lang="EN" dir="ltr" xmlns="http://www.w3.org/1999/xhtml">
  <head>
    <meta http-equiv="content-type" content="text/xml; charset=utf-8" />
    <title>comicHead.html</title>
    <style type = "text/css">
      h1 {
        font-family: "Comic Sans MS";
      }
    </style>
  </head>

  <body>
    <h1>This is a heading</H1>
    <p>
      This is ordinary text.
    </p>
  </body>
</html>
```

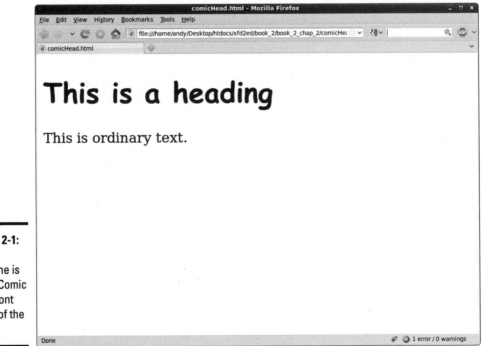

Figure 2-1:
The headline is in the Comic Sans font (most of the time).

Applying the font-family style attribute

The secret to this page is the CSS font-family attribute. Like most CSS elements, this can be applied to any HTML tag on your page. In this particular case, I applied it to my level one heading.

```
h1 {
    font-family: "Comic Sans MS";
}
```

You can then attach any font name you wish, and the browser attempts to use that font to display the element.

Even though a font may work perfectly fine on your computer, it may not work if that font isn't installed on the user's machine.

If you run exactly the same page on a Linux machine, you might see the result shown in Figure 2-2.

The specific font Comic Sans MS is installed on Windows machines, but the *MS* stands for Microsoft. This font isn't always installed on Linux or Mac. (Sometimes it's there, and sometimes it isn't.) You can't count on users having any particular fonts installed.

The Comic Sans font is fine for an example, but it has been heavily over-used in Web development. Serious Web developers avoid using it in real applications because it tends to make your page look amateurish.

Figure 2-2:
Under Linux, the heading might not be the same font!

> Applications Places System 🕑🕑🕑🕑🕑   6:00 PM 🔊
>
> comicHead.html - Mozilla Firefox
>
> File Edit View Go Bookmarks Tools Help
>
> ◄ · ► · 🔄 ✖ 🏠 📄 http://xfd.freehostia.com/xfd2.2/comicHead.html ▼ ⊙ Go G
>
> 📄 Release Notes 📄 Fedora Project 📄 Fedora Weekly News 📄 Community Support 📄 Fedora Core 6 🔴 Red Hat Magazine
>
> ## This is a heading
>
> This is ordinary text.

Using generic fonts

It's a little depressing. Even though it's easy to use fonts, you can't use them freely because you don't know if the user has them. Fortunately, you can do a few things that at least increase the odds in your favor. The first trick is to use *generic font names*. These are *virtual* font names that every compliant browser agrees to support. Figure 2-3 shows a page with all the generic fonts.

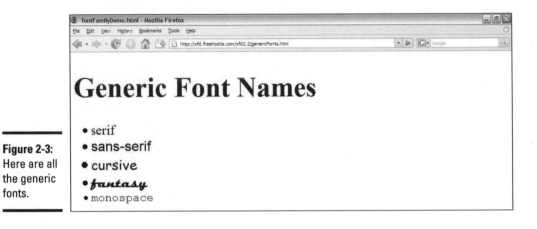

Figure 2-3:
Here are all
the generic
fonts.

I used browser controls to make the fonts larger than normal so you can see the details in this figure. Both the programmer and the user should be able to change the font size. Later, I describe how to change the font size through code.

The generic fonts really are families of fonts:

✦ **Serif:** These fonts have those little serifs (the tiny cross strokes that enhance readability). Print text (like the paragraph you're reading now) tends to use serif fonts, and they're the default font for most browsers. The most common serif typeface is Times New Roman or Times.

✦ **Sans Serif:** Sans serif fonts don't have the little feet. Generally, they're used for headlines or other emphasis. Sometimes, they're seen as more modern and cleaner than serif fonts, so sometimes they're used for body text. Arial is the most common sans serif font. In this book, the figure captions use a sans serif font.

✦ **Cursive:** These fonts look a little like handwriting. In Windows, the script font is usually Comic Sans MS. Script fonts are used when you want a less formal look. *For Dummies* books use script fonts all over the place for section and chapter headings.

✦ **Fantasy:** Fantasy fonts are decorative. Just about any theme you can think of is represented by a fantasy font, from Klingon to Tolkien. You can also find fonts that evoke a certain culture, making English text appear to be Persian or Chinese. Fantasy fonts are best used sparingly, for emphasis, as they often trade readability for visual appeal.

✦ **Monospace:** Monospace fonts produce a fixed-width font like typewritten text. Monospace fonts are frequently used to display code. Courier is a common monospace font. All code listings in this book use a monospaced font.

Because the generic fonts are available on all standards-compliant browsers, you'd think you could use them confidently. Well, you can be sure they'll appear, but you still might be surprised at the result. Figure 2-4 shows the same page as Figure 2-3 (in Windows) but in Linux.

Macs display yet another variation because the fonts listed here aren't *actual* fonts. Instead, they're *virtual* fonts. A standards-compliant browser promises *to select an* appropriate *stand in.* For example, if you choose sans serif, one browser may choose to use Arial. Another may choose Chicago. You can always use these generic font names and know the browser can find something close, but there's no guarantee exactly what font the browser will choose. Still, it's better than nothing. When you use these fonts, you're assured something in the right neighborhood, if not exactly what you intended.

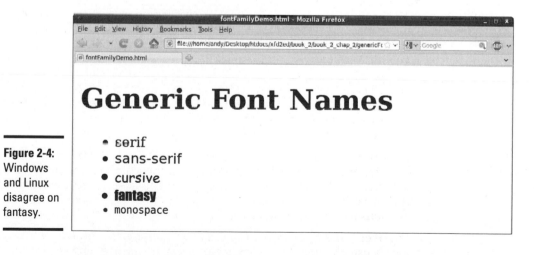

Figure 2-4:
Windows
and Linux
disagree on
fantasy.

Making a list of fonts

This uncertainty is frustrating, but you can take some control. You can specify an entire list of font names if you want. The browser tries each font in turn. If it can't find the specified font, it goes to the next font and on down the line.

You might choose a font that you know is installed on all Windows machines, a font found on Macs, and finally one found on all Linux machines. The last font on your list should be one of the generic fonts, so you'll have some control over the worst-case scenario.

Table 2-1 shows a list of fonts commonly installed on Windows, Mac, and Linux machines.

Table 2-1	Font Equivalents	
Windows	*Mac*	*Linux*
Arial	Arial	Nimbus Sans L
Arial Black	Arial Black	
Comic Sans MS	Comic Sans MS	TSCu_Comic
Courier New	Courier New	Nimbus Mono L
Georgia	Georgia	Nimbus Roman No9 L
Lucida Console	Monaco	
Palatino	Palatino	FreeSerif
Tahoma	Geneva	Kalimati
Times New Roman	Times	FreeSerif
Trebuchet MS	Helvetica	FreeSans
Verdana	Verdana	Kalimati

You can use this chart to derive a list of fonts to try. For example, look at the following style:

```
p {
    font-family: "Trebuchet MS", Helvetica, FreeSans, sans-serif;
}
```

This style has a whole smorgasbord of options. First, the browser tries to load Trebuchet MS. If it's a Windows machine, this font is available, so that one displays. If that doesn't work, the browser tries Helvetica (a default Mac font). If that doesn't work, it tries FreeSans, a font frequently installed on Linux machines. If this doesn't work, it defaults to the old faithful sans serif, which simply picks a sans serif font.

Note that font names of more than one word must be encased in quotes, and commas separate the list of font names.

The death of the font tag

There used to be a tag in old-school HTML called the `<font>` tag. You could use this tag to change the size, color, and font family. There were also specific tags for italic (`<i>`), boldface (`<b>`), and centering (`<center>`). These tags were very easy to use, but they caused some major problems. To use them well, you ended up littering your page with all kinds of tags trying to describe the markup, rather than the meaning. There was no easy way to reuse font information, so you often had to repeat things many times throughout the page, making it difficult to change. XHTML Strict no longer allows the `<font>`, `<i>`, `<b>`, or `<center>` tags. The CSS elements I show in this chapter more than compensate for this loss. You now have a more flexible, more powerful alternative.

 Don't get too stressed about Linux fonts. It's true that the equivalencies are harder to find, but Linux users tend to fall into two camps: They either don't care if the fonts are exact, or they do care and they've installed equivalent fonts that recognize the common names. In either case, you can focus on Mac and Windows people for the most part, and, as long as you've used a generic font name, things work okay on a Linux box. Truth is, I mainly use Linux, and I've installed all the fonts I need.

The Curse of Web-Based Fonts

Fonts seem pretty easy at first, but some big problems arise with actually using them.

Understanding the problem

The problem with fonts is this: Font resources are installed in each operating system. They aren't downloaded with the rest of the page. Your Web page can call for a specific font, but that font isn't displayed unless it's already installed on the user's computer.

Say I have a cool font called Happygeek. (I just made that up. If you're a font designer, feel free to make a font called that. Just send me a copy. I can't wait.) It's installed on my computer, and when I choose a font in my word processor, it shows up in the list. I can create a word-processing document with it, and everything will work great.

If I send a printout of a document using Happygeek to my grandma, everything's great because the paper doesn't need the actual font. It's just ink. If I send her the digital file and tell her to open it on her computer, we'll have a problem. See, she's not that hip and doesn't have Happygeek installed. Her computer will pick some other font.

This isn't a big problem in word processing because people don't generally send around digital copies of documents with elaborate fonts in them. However, Web pages are passed around *only* in digital form. To know which fonts you can use, you have to know what fonts are installed on the user's machine, and that's impossible.

Part of the concern is technical (figuring out how to transfer the font information to the browser), but the real issue is digital rights management. If you've purchased a font for your own use, does that give you the right to transfer it to others, so now they can use it without paying?

Examining possible solutions

This has been a problem since the beginning of the Web. Many people have tried to come up with solutions. None of the solutions are good, but here are a few compromises:

+ **Embedded fonts:** Netscape and Internet Explorer (IE) both came up with techniques to embed fonts into a Web page. Both techniques involved using a piece of software to convert the font into a proprietary format that allows it to be used for the specific page and nothing else. The two systems were incompatible, and both were a little awkward. Almost nobody used them. Firefox now completely ignores this technology, and IE can do it but with a separate tool. Until browsers come up with a compatible solution, I don't recommend this technique.

+ **CSS 3 embedded fonts:** CSS 3 (the next version of CSS on the horizon) promises a way to import a font file purely through CSS. You'll be able to specify a particular filename and pass a URL (Uniform Resource Locator) to the file on your server, and it'll be used for that particular page but not installed on the user's system. Custom fonts have been handled this way in games for years. Take a look at Book I, Chapter 8 for a preview of this technology. It looks extremely promising.

+ **Flash:** Flash is a vector format that's very popular on the Web. Flash has very nice features for converting fonts to a binary format within the flash output, and most users have some kind of flash player installed. The Flash editor is expensive, somewhat challenging to figure out, and defeats many of the benefits of XHTML. These disadvantages outweigh the potential benefit of custom fonts.

I'm certainly not opposed to using Flash. I just don't think it's a good idea to build entire Web pages in Flash, or to use Flash simply to get access to fonts. If you're interested in using Flash, you might want to check out another book I wrote, *Flash Game Programming For Dummies*. In the book, you learn how to make Flash *literally* sing and dance.

+ **Images:** Some designers choose to forego HTML altogether and create their pages as huge images. This requires a huge amount of bandwidth, makes the pages impossible to search, and makes them difficult to modify. This is a really bad idea. Although you have precise control of the visual layout, you lose most of the advantages of XHTML. Content in images cannot be read by search engines and is entirely inaccessible to people with screen-readers. An image large enough to fill the screen will take many times longer to download than equivalent XHTML markup. The user cannot resize an image-based page, and this type of page does not scale well to phones or other portable browsers.

Using images for headlines

Generally, you should use standard fonts for the page's main content, so having a limited array of fonts isn't such a big problem. Sometimes, though, you want to use fonts in your headlines. You can use a graphical editor, like GIMP, to create text-based images and then incorporate them into your pages. Figure 2-5 shows an example of this technique.

Figure 2-5:
The font shows up because it's an image.

In this case, I want to use my special cow font. (I *love* my cow font.)

Here's the process:

1. Plan your page.

   When you use graphics, you lose a little flexibility. You need to know exactly what the headlines should be. You also need to know what headline will display at what level. Rather than relying on the browser to display your headlines, you're creating graphics in your graphic tool (I'm using GIMP) and placing them directly in the page.

2. Create your images.

   I used the wonderful Logos feature in GIMP (choose Xtns⇨Script-fu⇨logos) to create my cow text. I built an image for each headline with the *Bovination* tool. I'm just happy to have a Bovination tool. It's something I've always wanted. If only it could be converted to a weapon.

3. **Specify font sizes directly.**

   In the image, it makes sense to specify font sizes in pixels because here you're really talking about a specific number of pixels. You're creating "virtual text" in your graphic editor, so make the text whatever size you want it to be in the finished page.

4. **Use any font you want.**

   You don't have to worry about whether the user has the font because you're not sending the font, just an image composed with the font.

5. **Create a separate image for each headline.**

   This particular exercise has two images — a level 1 heading and a level 2. Because I'm creating images directly, it's up to me to keep track of how the image will communicate its headline level.

6. **Consider the headline level.**

   Be sure to make headline level 2 values look a little smaller or less emphasized than level 1. That is, if you have images that will be used in a heading 1 setting, they should use a larger font than images that will be used in a less emphasized heading level. Usually, this is done by adjusting the font size in your images.

7. **Build the page the way you normally would.**

   After you create these specialty images, build a regular Web page. Put <h1> and <h2> tags in exactly the same places you usually do.

8. **Put <img> tags inside the headings.**

   Rather than ordinary text, place image tags inside the <h1> and <h2> tags. See the upcoming code imageTitles.html if you're a little confused.

9. **Put headline text in the alt attribute.**

   The alt attribute is especially important here because if the user has graphics turned off, the text still appears as an appropriately styled heading. People with slow connections see the text before the images load, and people using text readers can still read the image's alt text.

Here's the code used to generate the image-based headers:

```
<!DOCTYPE html PUBLIC "-//W3C//DTD XHTML 1.0 Strict//EN"
"http://www.w3.org/TR/xhtml1/DTD/xhtml1-strict.dtd">
<html lang="EN" dir="ltr" xmlns="http://www.w3.org/1999/xhtml">
  <head>
    <meta http-equiv="content-type" content="text/xml; charset=utf-8" />
    <title>imageTitles.html</title>
  </head>

  <body>
    <h1>
      <img src = "cowsHistory.png"
           alt = "Cows in History" />
    </h1>
```

```
<p>
  This page describes famous cows in history
</p>

<h2>
  <img src = "cowpens.png"
       alt = "Battle of Cowpens" />
</h2>

<p>
  Most people are unaware that cattle actually took
  part in the battle. They didn't of course. I just
  made that up.
</p>

  </body>
</html>
```

This technique is a nice compromise between custom graphics and ordinary XHTML as follows:

✦ **You have great control of your images.** If you're skilled with your graphics tool, you can make any type of image you want act as a headline. There's literally no limit except your skill and creativity.

✦ **The page retains its structure.** You still have heading tags in place, so it's easy to see that you mean for a particular image to act as a headline. You can still see the page organization in the XHTML code.

✦ **You have fallback text.** The alt attributes will activate if the images can't be displayed.

✦ **The semantic meaning of image headlines is preserved.** The alt tags provide another great feature. If they replicate the image text, this text is still available to screen readers and search engines, so the text isn't buried in the image.

This technique is great for headlines or other areas, but notice that I was careful to repeat the headline text in the <alt> tag. This is important because I don't want to lose the text. Search engine tools and screen readers need the text.

Don't be tempted to use this technique for larger amounts of body text. Doing so causes some problems:

✦ **The text is no longer searchable.** Search engines can't find text if it's buried in images.

✦ **The text is harder to change.** You can't update your page with a text editor. Instead, you have to download the image, modify it, and upload it again.

✦ **Images require a lot more bandwidth than text.** Don't use images if they don't substantially add to your page. You can make the case for a few heading images, but it's harder to justify having your entire page stored as an image just to use a particular font.

Specifying the Font Size

Like font names, font sizes are easy to change in CSS, but there are some hidden traps.

Size is only a suggestion!

In print media, after you determine the size of the text, it pretty much stays there. The user can't change the font size in print easily. By comparison, Web browsers frequently change the size of text. A cellphone-based browser displays text differently than one on a high-resolution LCD panel. Further, most browsers allow the user to change the size of all the text on the screen. Use Ctrl++ (plus sign) and Ctrl+– (minus sign) to make the text larger or smaller. In older versions of IE (prior to IE7), choose the Text Size option from the Page menu to change the text size.

The user should really have the ability to adjust the font size in the browser. When I display a Web page on a projector, I often adjust the font size so students in the back can read. Some pages have the font size set way too small for me to read. (It's probably my high-tech monitor. It couldn't possibly have anything to do with my age.)

Determining font sizes precisely is counter to the spirit of the Web. If you declare that your text will be exactly 12 points, for example, one of two things could happen:

✦ **The browser might enforce the 12-point rule literally.** This takes control from the user, so users who need larger fonts are out of luck. Older versions of IE do this.

✦ **The user might still change the size.** If this is how the browser behaves (and it usually is), 12 points doesn't always mean 12 points. If the user can change font sizes, the literal size selection is meaningless.

The Web developer should set up font sizes, but only in *relative* terms. Don't bother using absolute measurements (in most cases) because they don't really mean what you think. Let the user determine the base font size and specify relative changes to that size.

Using the font-size style attribute

The basic idea of font size is pretty easy to grasp in CSS. Take a look at `fontSize.html` in Figure 2-6.

This page obviously shows a number of different font sizes. The line "Font Sizes" is an ordinary `h1` element. All the other lines are paragraph tags. They appear in different sizes because they have different styles applied to them.

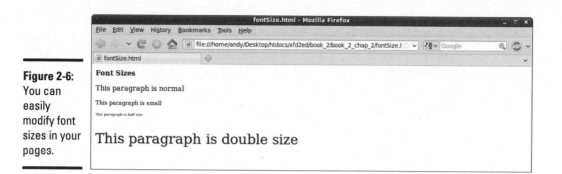

**Book II
Chapter 2**

Styling Text

Figure 2-6:
You can easily modify font sizes in your pages.

Font sizes are changed with the (cleverly named) `font-size` attribute:

```
p {
  font-size: small;
}
```

Simply indicate the `font-size` rule, and, well, the size of the font. In this example, I used the special value `small`, but there are many other ways to specify sizes in CSS.

Absolute measurement units

Many times, you need to specify the size of something in CSS. Of course, font size is one of these cases. The different types of measurement have different implications. It's important to know there are two distinct kinds of units in CSS. *Absolute measurements* attempt to describe a particular size, as in the real world. *Relative measurements* are about changes to some default value. Generally, Web developers are moving toward relative measurement for font sizes.

Points (pt)

In word processing, you're probably familiar with *points* as a measurement of font size. You can use the abbreviation `pt` to indicate you're measuring in points, for example:

```
p {
  font-size: 12pt;
}
```

There is no space between `12` and `pt`.

Unfortunately, points aren't an effective unit of measure for Web pages. Points are an absolute scale, useful for print, but they aren't reliable on the Web because you don't know what resolution the user's screen has. A 12-point font might look larger or smaller on different monitors.

In some versions of IE, after you specify a font size in points, the user can no longer change the size of the characters. This is unacceptable from a usability standpoint. Relative size schemes (which I describe later in this chapter) prevent this problem.

Pixels (px)

Pixels refer to the small dots on the screen. You can specify a font size in pixels, although that's not the way it's usually done. For one thing, different monitors make pixels in different sizes. You can't really be sure how big a pixel will be in relationship to the overall screen size. Different letters are different sizes, so the pixel size is a rough measurement of the width and height of the average character. Use the px abbreviation to measure fonts in pixels:

```
p {
  font-size: 20px;
}
```

Traditional measurements (in, cm)

You can also use inches (in) and centimeters (cm) to measure fonts, but this is completely impractical. Imagine you have a Web page displayed on both your screen and a projection system. One inch on your own monitor may look like ten inches on the projector. Real-life measurement units aren't meaningful for the Web. The only time you might use them is if you'll be printing something and you have complete knowledge of how the printer is configured. If that's the case, you're better off using a print-oriented layout tool (like a word processor) rather than HTML.

Relative measurement units

Relative measurement is a wiser choice in Web development. Use these schemes to change sizes in relationship to the standard size.

Named sizes

CSS has a number of font size names built in:

xx-small	large
x-small	x-large
small	xx-large
medium	

It may bother you that there's nothing more specific about these sizes: How big is large? Well, it's bigger than medium. That sounds like a flip answer, but it's the truth. The user sets the default font size in the browser (or leaves it alone), and all other font sizes should be in relation to this preset size. The medium size is the default size of paragraph text on your page. For comparison purposes, <h1> tags are usually xx-large.

Percentage (%)

The percentage unit is a relative measurement used to specify the font in relationship to its normal size. Use 50% to make a font half the size it would normally appear and 200% to make it twice the normal size. Use the % symbol to indicate percentage, as shown here:

```
p {
  font-size: 150%;
}
```

Percentages are based on the default size of ordinary text, so an <h1> tag at 100% is the same size as text in an ordinary paragraph.

Em (em)

In traditional typesetting, the em is a unit of measurement equivalent to the width of the "m" character in that font. In actual Web use, it's really another way of specifying the relative size of a font. For instance, 0.5 ems is half the normal size, and 3 ems is three times the normal size. The term em is used to specify this measurement.

```
p {
  font-size: 1.5em;
}
```

Here are the best strategies for font size:

✦ **Don't change sizes without a good reason.** Most of the time, the browser default sizes are perfectly fine, but there may be some times when you want to adjust fonts a little more.

✦ **Define an overall size for the page.** If you want to define a font size for the entire page, do so in the <body> tag. Use a named size, percentage, or ems to avoid the side effects of absolute sizing. The size defined in the body is applied to every element in the body automatically.

✦ **Modify any other elements.** You might want your links a little larger than ordinary text, for example. You can do this by applying a font size attribute to an element. Use relative measurement if possible.

Determining Other Font Characteristics

In addition to size and color (see Chapter 1 of this minibook), you can change fonts in a number of other ways.

Figure 2-7 shows a number of common text modifications you can make.

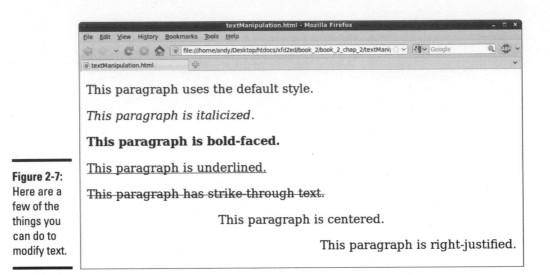

Figure 2-7:
Here are a few of the things you can do to modify text.

The various paragraphs in this page are modified in different ways. You can change the alignment of the text as well as add italic, bold, underline, or strikethrough to the text.

CSS uses a potentially confusing set of rules for the various font manipulation tools. One rule determines the font style, and another determines boldness.

I describe these techniques in the following sections for clarity.

I used a trick I haven't shown yet to produce this comparison page. I have multiple paragraphs, each with their own style. Look to Chapter 3 of this minibook to see how to have more than one paragraph style in a particular page.

Using font-style for italics

The `font-style` attribute allows you to make italic text, as shown in Figure 2-8.

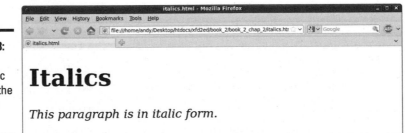

Figure 2-8:
You can make italic text with the font-style attribute.

Here's some code illustrating how to add italic formatting:

```
<!DOCTYPE html PUBLIC "-//W3C//DTD XHTML 1.0 Strict//EN"
"http://www.w3.org/TR/xhtml1/DTD/xhtml1-strict.dtd">
<html lang="EN" dir="ltr" xmlns="http://www.w3.org/1999/xhtml">
  <head>
    <meta http-equiv="content-type" content="text/xml; charset=utf-8" />
    <title>italics.html</title>
    <style type = "text/css">
      p {
        font-style: italic;
      }
    </style>
  </head>

  <body>
    <h1>Italics</h1>
    <p>This paragraph is in italic form.</p>
  </body>
</html>
```

Book II
Chapter 2

Styling Text

The `font-style` values can be `italic`, `normal`, or `oblique` (tilted toward the left).

If you want to set a particular segment to be set to italic, normal, or oblique style, use the `font-style` attribute.

Using font-weight for bold

You can make your font bold by using the `font-weight` CSS attribute, as shown in Figure 2-9.

Figure 2-9:
The font-weight attribute affects the boldness of your text.

If you want to make some of your text bold, use the `font-weight` CSS attribute, like this:

```
<!DOCTYPE html PUBLIC "-//W3C//DTD XHTML 1.0 Strict//EN"
"http://www.w3.org/TR/xhtml1/DTD/xhtml1-strict.dtd">
<html lang="EN" dir="ltr" xmlns="http://www.w3.org/1999/xhtml">
  <head>
    <meta http-equiv="content-type" content="text/xml; charset=utf-8" />
```

```
      <title>bold.html</title>
      <style type = "text/css">
        p {
          font-weight: bold;
        }
      </style>
  </head>

  <body>
    <h1>Boldface</h1>
    <p>
      This paragraph is bold.
    </p>
  </body>
</html>
```

Font weight can be defined a couple ways. Normally, you simply indicate bold in the font-weight rule, as I did in this code. You can also use a numeric value from 100 (exceptionally light) to 900 (dark bold).

Using text-decoration

Text-decoration can be used to add a couple other interesting formats to your text, including underline, strikethrough, overline, and blink.

For example, the following code produces an underlined paragraph:

```
<!DOCTYPE html PUBLIC "-//W3C//DTD XHTML 1.0 Strict//EN"
"http://www.w3.org/TR/xhtml1/DTD/xhtml1-strict.dtd">
<html lang="EN" dir="ltr" xmlns="http://www.w3.org/1999/xhtml">
  <head>
    <meta http-equiv="content-type" content="text/xml; charset=utf-8" />
    <title>underline.html</title>
    <style type = "text/css">
      p {
        text-decoration: underline;
      }
    </style>
  </head>

  <body>
    <h1>Underline</h1>
    <p>
      This paragraph is underlined.
    </p>
  </body>
</html>
```

Be careful using underline in Web pages. Users have been trained that under-lined text is a link, so they may click your underlined text expecting it to take them somewhere.

The underline.html code produces a page similar to Figure 2-10.

Figure 2-10:
You can underline text with text-decoration.

You can also use `text-decoration` for other effects, such as strikethrough (called "line-through" in CSS,) as shown in the following code:

```
C "-//W3C//DTD XHTML 1.0 Strict//EN"
"http://www.w3.org/TR/xhtml1/DTD/xhtml1-strict.dtd">
<html lang="EN" dir="ltr" xmlns="http://www.w3.org/1999/xhtml">
  <head>
    <meta http-equiv="content-type" content="text/xml; charset=utf-8" />
    <title>strikethrough.html</title>
    <style type = "text/css">
      p {
        text-decoration: line-through;
      }
    </style>
  </head>

  <body>
    <h1>Strikethrough</h1>
    <p>
      This paragraph has strikethrough text.
    </p>
  </body>
</html>
```

The `strikethrough.html` code produces a page similar to Figure 2-11.

Figure 2-11:
Text-decoration can be used for a strikethrough effect.

`Text-decoration` has a few other rarely used options, such as

+ **Overline:** The `overline` attribute places a line over the text. Except for a few math and chemistry applications (which would be better done in an equation editor and imported as images), I can't see when this might be used.

+ **Blink:** The `blink` attribute is a distant cousin of the legendary `<blink>` tag in Netscape and causes the text to blink on the page. The `<blink>` tag (along with gratuitous animated GIFs) has long been derided as the mark of the amateur. Avoid blinking text at all costs.

There's an old joke among Internet developers: The only legitimate place to use the `<blink>` tag is in this sentence: Schrodinger's cat is `<blink>`not`</blink>` dead. Nothing is funnier than quantum mechanics illustrated in HTML.

Using text-align for basic alignment

You can use the `text-align` attribute to center, left-align, or right-align text, as shown in the following code:

```
<!DOCTYPE html PUBLIC "-//W3C//DTD XHTML 1.0 Strict//EN"
"http://www.w3.org/TR/xhtml1/DTD/xhtml1-strict.dtd">
<html lang="EN" dir="ltr" xmlns="http://www.w3.org/1999/xhtml">
  <head>
    <meta http-equiv="content-type" content="text/xml; charset=utf-8" />
    <title>center.html</title>
    <style type = "text/css">
      p {
        text-align: center;
      }
    </style>
  </head>

  <body>
    <h1>Centered</h1>
    <p>This paragraph is centered.</p>

  </body>
</html>
```

You can also use the `text-align` attribute to right- or left-justify your text. The page shown in Figure 2-12 illustrates the `text-align` attribute.

You can apply the `text-align` attribute only to text. The old `<center>` tag could be used to center nearly anything (a table, some text, or images), which was pretty easy but caused problems. Book III explains how to position elements in all kinds of powerful ways, including centering anything. Use `text-align` to center text inside its own element (whether that's a heading, a paragraph, a table cell, or whatever).

Figure 2-12:
This text is
centered
with text-
align.

Other text attributes

CSS offers a few other text manipulation tools, but they're rarely used:

✦ **Font-variant:** Can be set to `small-caps` to make your text use only capital letters. Lowercase letters are shown in a smaller font size.

✦ **Letter-spacing:** Adjusts the spacing between letters. It's usually measured in ems. (See the section "Relative measurement units" earlier in the chapter for more on ems.) Fonts are so unpredictable on the Web that if you're trying to micromanage this much, you're bound to be disappointed by the results.

✦ **Word-spacing:** Allows you to adjust the spacing between words.

✦ **Text-indent:** Lets you adjust the indentation of the first line of an element. This value uses the normal units of measurement. Indentation can be set to a negative value, causing an outdent if you prefer.

✦ **Vertical-align:** Used when you have an element with a lot of vertical space (often a table cell). You can specify how the text behaves in this situation.

✦ **Text-transform:** Helps you convert text into uppercase, lowercase, or capitalized (first letter uppercase) forms.

✦ **Line-height:** Indicates the vertical spacing between lines in the element Like letter and word spacing, you'll probably be disappointed if you're this concerned about exactly how things are displayed.

Using the font shortcut

It can be tedious to recall all the various font attributes and their possible values. Aptana and other dedicated CSS editors make it a lot easier, but there's another technique often used by the pros. The `font` rule provides an easy shortcut to a number of useful font attributes. The following code shows you how to use the `font` rule:

```
<!DOCTYPE html PUBLIC "-//W3C//DTD XHTML 1.0 Strict//EN"
"http://www.w3.org/TR/xhtml1/DTD/xhtml1-strict.dtd">
<html lang="EN" dir="ltr" xmlns="http://www.w3.org/1999/xhtml">
```

```
<head>
  <meta http-equiv="content-type" content="text/xml; charset=utf-8" />
  <title>fontTag.html</title>
  <style type = "text/css">
    p {
        font: bold italic 150% "Dadhand", cursive;
    }
  </style>
</head>

<body>
  <h1>Using Font shortcut</h1>
  <p>
     This paragraph has many settings.
  </p>
</body>
</html>
```

Figure 2-13 illustrates the powerful `font` rule in action.

Figure 2-13:
The font rule
can change
many things
at once.

The great thing about the `font` rule is how it combines many of the other font-related rules for a simpler way to handle most text-formatting needs.

The `font` attribute is extremely handy. Essentially, it allows you to roll all the other font attributes into one. Here's how it works:

✦ **Specify the `font` rule in the CSS.**

✦ **List any `font-style` attributes.** You can mention any attributes normally used in the `font-style` rule (`italic` or `oblique`). If you don't want either, just move on.

✦ **List any `font-variant` attributes.** If you want small caps, you can indicate it here. If you don't, just leave this part blank.

✦ **List any `font-weight` values.** This can be "bold" or a font-weight number (100–900).

✦ **Specify the font-size value in whatever measurement system you want (but ems or percentages are preferred).** Don't forget the measurement unit symbol (`em` or `%`) because that's how the `font` rule recognizes that this is a size value.

✦ **Indicate a font-family list last.** The last element is a list of font families you want the browser to try. This list must be last, or the browser may not interpret the font attribute correctly. (Dadhand is a custom font I own; cursive will be used if Dadhand is not available.)

The font rule is great, but it doesn't do everything. You still may need separate CSS rules to define your text colors and alignment. These attributes aren't included in the font shortcut.

Don't use commas to separate values in the font attribute list. Use commas only to separate values in the list of font-family declarations.

You can skip any values you want as long as the order is correct. For example

```
font: italic "Comic Sans MS", cursive;
```

is completely acceptable, as is

```
font: 70% sans-serif;
```

Working with subscripts and superscripts

Occasionally, you'll need *superscripts* (characters that appear a little bit higher than normal text, like exponents and footnotes) or *subscripts* (characters that appear lower, often used in mathematical notation). Figure 2-14 demonstrates a page with these techniques.

Figure 2-14: This page has super-scripts and subscripts (and, ooooh, math!).

$$A^2 + B^2 = C^2$$

$$i_0 = 0$$

Surprisingly, you don't need CSS to produce superscripts and subscripts. These properties are managed through HTML tags. You can still style them the way you can any other HTML tag.

```
<!DOCTYPE html PUBLIC "-//W3C//DTD XHTML 1.0 Strict//EN"
"http://www.w3.org/TR/xhtml1/DTD/xhtml1-strict.dtd">
<html lang="EN" dir="ltr" xmlns="http://www.w3.org/1999/xhtml">
  <head>
    <meta http-equiv="content-type" content="text/xml; charset=utf-8" />
    <title>SuperSub.html</title>
```

```
    </head>

    <body>
      <p>
        A<sup>2</sup> + B<sup>2</sup> = C<sup>2</sup>
      </p>

      <p>
        i<sub>0</sub> = 0
      </p>
    </body>
  </html>
```

Chapter 3: Selectors, Class, and Style

In This Chapter

✔ Modifying specific named elements

✔ Adding and modifying emphasis and strong emphasis

✔ Creating classes

✔ Introducing span and div

✔ Using pseudo-classes and the link tag

✔ Selecting specific contexts

✔ Defining multiple styles

*Y*ou know how to use CSS to change all the instances of a particular tag, but what if you want to be more selective? For example, you might want to change the background color of only one paragraph, or you might want to define some special new type of paragraph. Maybe you want to specify a different paragraph color for part of your page, or you want visited links to appear differently from unselected links. The part of the CSS style that indicates what element you want to style is a *selector*. In this chapter, you discover powerful new ways to select elements on the page.

Selecting Particular Segments

Figure 3-1 illustrates how you should refer to someone who doesn't appreciate your Web development prowess.

Defining more than one kind of paragraph

Apart from its cultural merit, this page is interesting because it has three different paragraph styles. The introductory paragraph is normal. The quote is set in italicized font, and the attribution is monospaced and right-aligned.

The quote in the following code was generated by one of my favorite sites on the Internet: the Shakespearean insult generator. Nothing is more satisfying than telling somebody off in iambic pentameter.

```
<!DOCTYPE html PUBLIC "-//W3C//DTD XHTML 1.0 Strict//EN"
"http://www.w3.org/TR/xhtml1/DTD/xhtml1-strict.dtd">
<html lang="EN" dir="ltr" xmlns="http://www.w3.org/1999/xhtml">
  <head>
    <meta http-equiv="content-type" content="text/xml; charset=utf-8" />
    <title>quote.html</title>
    <style type = "text/css">
      #quote {
        font: bold italic 130% Garamond, Comic Sans MS, fantasy;
        text-align: center;
      }

      #attribution {
        font: 80% monospace;
        text-align: right;
      }
    </style>
  </head>

  <body>
    <h1>Literature Quote of the day</h1>
    <p>
      How to tell somebody off the classy way:
    </p>

    <p id = "quote">
      [Thou] leathern-jerkin, crystal-button, knot-pated,
      agatering, puke-stocking, caddis-garter, smooth-tongue, Spanish pouch!
    </p>

    <p id = "attribution">
      -William Shakespeare (Henry IV Part I)
    </p>

  </body>
</html>
```

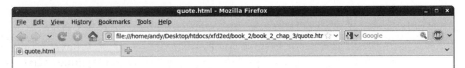

Figure 3-1:
This page
has three
kinds of
paragraphs.

Styling identified paragraphs

Until now, you've used CSS to apply a particular style to an element all across the page. For example, you can add a style to the <p> tag, and that style applies to all the paragraphs on the page.

Sometimes (as in the Shakespeare insult page), you want to give one element more than one style. You can do this by naming each element and using the name in the CSS style sheet. Here's how it works:

1. **Add an `id` attribute to each HTML element you want to modify.**

   For example, the paragraph with the attribution now has an `id` attribute with the value `attribution`.

   ```
   <p id = "attribution">
   ```

**Book II
Chapter 3**

2. **Make a style in CSS.**

   Use a pound sign followed by the element's ID in CSS to specify you're not talking about a tag type any more, but a specific element: For example, the CSS code contains the selector `#attribution`, meaning, "Apply this style to an element with the attribution id."

   ```
   #attribution {
   ```

Selectors, Class, and Style

3. **Add the style.**

   Create a style for displaying your named element. In this case, I want the paragraph with the `attribution` ID right-aligned, monospace, and a little smaller than normal. This style will be attached only to the specific element.

   ```
   #attribution {
     font: 80% monospace;
     text-align: right;
   }
   ```

The ID trick works great on any named element. IDs have to be *unique* (you can't repeat the same ID on one page), so this technique is best when you have a style you want to apply to only one element on the page. It doesn't matter what HTML element it is (it could be an h1, a paragraph, a table cell, or whatever). If it has the ID `quote`, the `#quote` style is applied to it. You can have both ID selectors and ordinary (element) selectors in the same style sheet.

Using Emphasis and Strong Emphasis

You may be shocked to know that XHTML doesn't allow italics or bold. Old-style HTML had the <i> tag for italics and the <b> tag for bold. These seem easy to use and understand. Unfortunately, they can trap you. In your XHTML, you shouldn't specify *how* something should be styled. You should specify instead the *purpose* of the styling. The <i> and <b> tags are removed from XHTML Strict and replaced with <em> and <strong>.

Adding emphasis to the page

The `<em>` tag means *emphasized*. By default, em italicizes your text. The `<strong>` tag stands for *strong emphasis*. It defaults to bold.

Figure 3-2 illustrates a page with the default styles for em and strong.

The code for the `emphasis.html` page is pretty straightforward. It has no CSS at all:

```
<!DOCTYPE html PUBLIC "-//W3C//DTD XHTML 1.0 Strict//EN"
"http://www.w3.org/TR/xhtml1/DTD/xhtml1-strict.dtd">
<html lang="EN" dir="ltr" xmlns="http://www.w3.org/1999/xhtml">
  <head>
    <meta http-equiv="content-type" content="text/xml; charset=utf-8" />
    <title>emphasis.html</title>
  </head>

  <body>
    <h1>Emphasis and Strong Emphasis</h1>
    <p>
      This paragraph illustrates two main kinds of emphasis.
      <em>This sentence uses the em tag.</em>
      By default, emphasis is italic.
      <strong>This sentence uses strong emphasis.</strong>
      The default formatting of strong emphasis is bold.
    </p>

    <p>
      Of course you can change the formatting with CSS.
      This is a great example of <em>semantic</em> formatting.
      Rather than indicating the <strong>formatting</strong>
      of some text, you indicate <strong>how much it is emphasized.</strong>
    </p>

    <p>
      This way, you can go back and change things, like adding color
      to emphasized text without the formatting commands
      muddying your actual text.
    </p>
  </body>
</html>
```

It'd be improper to think that em is just another way to say *italic* and strong is another way to say *bold*. In the old scheme, after you define something as italic, you're pretty much stuck with that. The XHTML way describes the meaning, and you can define it how you want.

Modifying the display of em and strong

Figure 3-3 shows how you might modify the levels of emphasis. I used yellow highlighting (without italics) for em and a larger red font for strong.

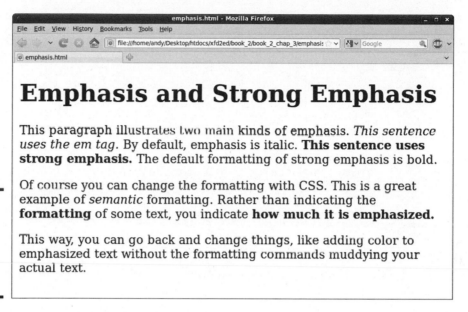

Book II
Chapter 3

Selectors, Class,
and Style

Figure 3-2:
You can
use em
and strong
to add
emphasis.

Figure 3-3:
You can
change the
way that em
and strong
modify text.

The code for emphasisStyle.html (as shown in Figure 3-3) is *identical* to the code for emphasis.html (as shown in Figure 3-2). The only difference is the addition of a style sheet. The style sheet is embedded in the Web page between style tags. Check out Chapter 1 of this minibook for a refresher on how to incorporate CSS styles in your Web pages.

```
<style type = "text/css">
  em {
    font-style: normal;
```

```
    background-color: yellow;
  }

  strong {
    color: red;
    font-size: 110%;
  }
</style>
```

The style is used to modify the XHTML. The meaning in the XHTML stays the same — only the style changes.

The semantic markups are more useful than the older (more literal) tags because they still tell the truth even if the style has been changed. (In the XHTML code, the important thing is whether the text is emphasized, not what it means to emphasize the text. That job belongs to CSS.)

What's funny about the following sentence?

<strong> is always bold.

Get it? *That's a bold-faced lie!* Sometimes I crack myself up.

Defining Classes

You can easily apply a style to all the elements of a particular type in a page, but sometimes you might want to have tighter control of your styles. For example, you might want to have more than one paragraph style. As an example, look at the classes.html page featured in Figure 3-4.

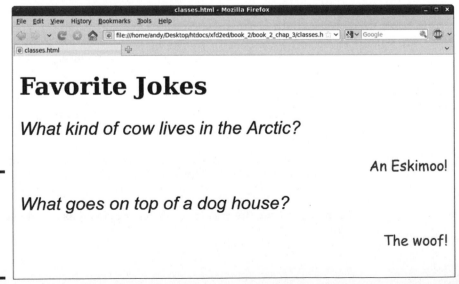

Figure 3-4: Each joke has a question and an answer.

Once again, multiple formats are on this page:

✦ **Questions have a large italic sans serif font.** There's more than one question.

✦ **Answers are smaller, blue, and in a cursive font.** There's more than one answer, too.

Questions and answers are all paragraphs, so you can't simply style the paragraph because you need two distinct styles. There's more than one question and more than one answer, so the ID trick would be problematic. Two different elements can't have the same ID — you don't want to create more than one identical definition. This is where the notion of classes comes into play.

Adding classes to the page

CSS allows you to define classes in your XHTML and make style definitions that are applied across a class. It works like this:

1. **Add the `class` attribute to your XHTML questions.**

Unlike ID, several elements can share the same class. All my questions are defined with this variation of the <p> tag. Setting the class to `question` indicates these paragraphs will be styled as questions:

```
<p class = "question">
  What kind of cow lives in the Arctic?
</p>
```

2. **Add similar class attributes to the answers by setting the class of the answers to answer:**

```
<p class = "answer">
  An Eskimoo!
</p>
```

Now you have two different subclasses of paragraph: `question` and `answer`.

3. **Create a class style for the questions.**

The class style is defined in CSS. Specify a class with the period (`.`) before the class name. Classes are defined in CSS like this:

```
<style type = "text/css">
  .question {
    font: italic 150% arial, sans-serif;
    text-align: left;
  }
```

In this situation, the `question` class is defined as a large sans serif font aligned to the left.

4. Define the look of the answers.

The `answer` class uses a right-justified cursive font.

```
.answer {
    font: 120% "Comic Sans MS", cursive;
    text-align: right;
    color: #00F;
}
</style>
```

Combining classes

Here's the code for the `classes.html` page, showing how to use CSS classes:

```
<!DOCTYPE html PUBLIC "-//W3C//DTD XHTML 1.0 Strict//EN"
"http://www.w3.org/TR/xhtml1/DTD/xhtml1-strict.dtd">
<html lang="EN" dir="ltr" xmlns="http://www.w3.org/1999/xhtml">
  <head>
    <meta http-equiv="content-type" content="text/xml; charset=utf-8" />
    <title>classes.html</title>
    <style type = "text/css">
      .question {
        font: italic 150% arial, sans-serif;
        text-align: left;
      }

      .answer {
        font: 120% "Comic Sans MS", cursive;
        text-align: right;
        color: #00F;
      }
    </style>
  </head>

  <body>
    <h1>Favorite jokes</h1>

    <p class = "question">
      What kind of cow lives in the Arctic?
    </p>

    <p class = "answer">
      An Eskimoo!
    </p>

    <p class = "question">
      What goes on top of a dog house?
    </p>

    <p class = "answer">
      The woof!
    </p>
  </body>
</html>
```

Sometimes you see selectors, like

`p.fancy`

that include both an element and a class name. This style is applied only to paragraphs with the `fancy` class attached. Generally, I like classes because they can be applied to all kinds of things, so I usually leave the element name out to make the style as reusable as possible.

One element can use more than one class. Figure 3-5 shows an example of this phenomenon.

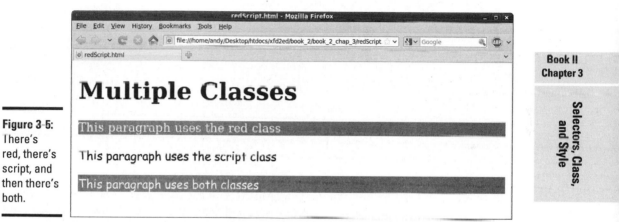

**Book II
Chapter 3**

Selectors, Class,
and Style

Figure 3-5: There's red, there's script, and then there's both.

The paragraphs in Figure 3-5 appear to be in three different styles, but only red and script are defined. The third paragraph uses both classes. Here's the code:

```
<!DOCTYPE html PUBLIC "-//W3C//DTD XHTML 1.0 Strict//EN"
"http://www.w3.org/TR/xhtml1/DTD/xhtml11-strict.dtd">
<html lang="EN" dir="ltr" xmlns="http://www.w3.org/1999/xhtml">
  <head>
    <meta http-equiv="content-type" content="text/xml; charset=utf-8" />
    <title>redScript.html</title>
    <style type = "text/css">
      .red {
        color: white;
        background-color: red;
      }

      .script {
        font-family: cursive;
      }
    </style>
  </head>

  <body>
    <h1>Multiple Classes</h1>
    <p class = "red">
      This paragraph uses the red class
    </p>
```

```
<p class = "script">
  This paragraph uses the script class
</p>

<p class = "red script">
  This paragraph uses both classes
</p>
</body>
</html>
```

The style sheet introduces two classes. The red class makes the paragraph red (well, white text with a red background), and the script class applies a cursive font to the element.

The first two paragraphs each have a class, and the classes act as you'd expect. The interesting part is the third paragraph because it has two classes.

```
<p class = "red script">
```

This assigns both the red and script classes to the paragraph. Both styles will be applied to the element in the order they are written. Note that both class names occur inside quotes and no commas are needed (or allowed). You can apply more than two classes to an element if you wish. If the classes have conflicting rules (say one makes the element green and the next makes it blue), the latest class in the list will overwrite earlier values.

An element can also have an ID. The ID style, the element style, and all the class styles are taken into account when the browser tries to display the object.

Normally, I don't like to use colors or other specific formatting instructions as class names. Usually, it's best to name classes based on their meaning (like mainColorScheme). You might decide that green is better than red, so you either have to change the class name or you have to have a red class that colored things green. That'd be weird.

Introducing div and span

So far, I've applied CSS styles primarily to paragraphs (with the <p> tag), but you can really use any element you want. In fact, you may want to invent your own elements. Perhaps you want a particular style, but it's not quite a paragraph. Maybe you want a particular style inside a paragraph. XHTML has two very useful elements that are designed as *generic* elements. They don't have any predefined meaning, so they're ideal candidates for modification with the id and class attributes.

✦ **div:** A block-level element (like the p element). It acts just like a paragraph. A div usually has carriage returns before and after it. Generally, you use div to group a series of paragraphs.

✦ **span:** An inline element. It doesn't usually cause carriage returns because it's meant to be embedded into some other block-level element (usually a paragraph or a div). Usually, a span is used to add some type of special formatting.

Organizing the page by meaning

To see why div and span are useful, take a look at Figure 3-6.

Figure 3-6:
This page has names and phone numbers.

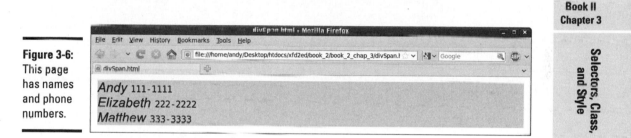

The formatting of the page isn't complete (read about positioning CSS in Book III), but some formatting is in place. Each name and phone number pair is clearly a group of things. Names and phone numbers are formatted differently. The interesting thing about this page is the code:

```html
<!DOCTYPE html PUBLIC "-//W3C//DTD XHTML 1.0 Strict//EN"
"http://www.w3.org/TR/xhtml1/DTD/xhtml1-strict.dtd">
<html lang="EN" dir="ltr" xmlns="http://www.w3.org/1999/xhtml">
  <head>
    <meta http-equiv="content-type" content="text/xml; charset=utf-8" />
    <title>divSpan.html</title>
    <style type = "text/css">
      .contact {
        background-color: #CCCCFF;
      }
      .name {
        font: italic 110% arial, sans-serif;
      }

      .phone {
        font: 100% monospace;
      }

    </style>
  </head>

<body>
  <div class = "contact">
    <span class = "name">Andy</span>
    <span class = "phone">111-1111</span>
  </div>
```

```
<div class = "contact">
  <span class = "name">Elizabeth</span>
  <span class = "phone">222-2222</span>
</div>

<div class = "contact">
  <span class = "name">Matthew</span>
  <span class = "phone">333-3333</span>
</div>

  </body>
</html>
```

What's exciting about this code is its clarity. When you look at the XHTML, it's very clear what type of data you're talking about because the structure describes the data. Each div represents a contact. A contact has a name and a phone number.

The XHTML doesn't specify how the data displays, just what it means.

Why not make a table?

This is where experienced HTML 4 people shake their heads in disbelief. This page seems like a table, so why not make it one? What matters here isn't that the information is in a table, but that names and phone numbers are part of contacts. There's no need to bring in artificial table elements if you can describe the data perfectly well without them.

If you still want to make the data *look* like a table, that's completely possible, as shown in Figure 3-7. See Book III to see exactly how some of the styling code works. Of course, you're welcome to look at the source code for this styled version (dubbed divSpanStyled.html on the CD-ROM) if you want a preview.

Figure 3-7:
After you define the data, you can style it as a table if you want.

divSpan.html - Mozilla Firefox	
Andy	111-1111
Elizabeth	222-2222
Matthew	333-3333

The point is this: After you define the data, you can control it as much as you want. Using span and div to define your data gives you far more control than tables and leaves your XHTML code much cleaner.

div and span aren't simply a replacement for tables. They're tools for organizing your page into segments based on *meaning*. After you have them in place, you can use CSS to apply all kinds of interesting styles to the segments.

Using Pseudo-Classes to Style Links

Now that you have some style going in your Web pages, you may be a bit concerned about how ugly links are. The default link styles are useful, but they may not fit with your color scheme.

Styling a standard link

Adding a style to a link is easy. After all, <a> (the tag that defines links) is just an XHTML tag, and you can add a style to any tag. Here's an example, where I make my links black with a yellow background:

```
a {
  color: black;
  background-color: yellow;
}
```

That works fine, but links are a little more complex than some other elements. Links actually have three *states:*

+ **Normal:** This is the standard state. With no CSS added, most browsers display unvisited links as blue underlined text.

+ **Visited:** This state is enabled when the user visits a link and returns to the current page. Most browsers use a purple underlined style to indicate that a link has been visited.

+ **Hover:** The hover state is enabled when the user's mouse is lingering over the element. Most browsers don't use the hover state in their default settings.

If you apply a style to the <a> tags in a page, the style is applied to all the states of all the anchors.

Styling the link states

You can apply a different style to each state, as illustrated by Figure 3-8. In this example, I make ordinary links black on a white background. A visited link is black on yellow; and, if the mouse is hovering over a link, the link is white with a black background.

Take a look at the code and see how it's done:

```
<!DOCTYPE html PUBLIC "-//W3C//DTD XHTML 1.0 Strict//EN"
"http://www.w3.org/TR/xhtml1/DTD/xhtml1-strict.dtd">
<html lang="EN" dir="ltr" xmlns="http://www.w3.org/1999/xhtml">
  <head>
    <meta http-equiv="content-type" content="text/xml; charset=utf-8" />
    <title>linkStates.html</title>
    <style type = "text/css">
      a{
        color: black;
        background-color: white;
      }

      a:visited {
        color: black;
        background-color: #FFFF33;
      }

      a:hover {
        color: white;
        background-color: black;
      }
    </style>
  </head>

  <body>
    <h1>Pseudo-classes and links</h1>

    <p>
      <a href = "http://www.google.com">This link is normal</a>
    </p>

    <p>
      <a href = "http://www.reddit.com">This link has been visited</a>
    </p>

    <p>
      <a href = "http://www.digg.com">The mouse is hovering over this link</a>
    </p>
  </body>
</html>
```

Nothing is special about the links in the HTML part of the code. The links
change their state dynamically while the user interacts with the page. The
style sheet determines what happens in the various states. Here's how you
approach putting the code together:

1. Determine the ordinary link style first by making a style for the <a> tag.

If you don't define any other pseudo-classes, all links will follow the ordinary link style.

2. Make a style for visited links.

A link will use this style after that site is visited during the current browser session. The a:visited selector indicates links that have been visited.

3. Make a style for hovered links.

The a:hover style is applied to the link only when the mouse is hovering over the link. As soon as the mouse leaves the link, the style reverts to the standard or visited style, as appropriate.

Best link practices

Link styles have some special characteristics. You need to be a little bit careful how you apply styles to links. Consider the following issues when applying styles to links:

✦ **The order is important.** Be sure to define the ordinary anchor first. The pseudo-classes are based on the standard anchor style.

✦ **Make sure they still look like links.** It's important that users know something is intended to be a link. If you take away the underlining and the color that normally indicates a link, your users might be confused. Generally, you can change colors without trouble, but links should be either underlined text or something that clearly looks like a button.

✦ **Test visited links.** Testing visited links is a little tricky because, after you visit a link, it stays visited. If you have the Web Developer toolbar installed on Firefox, you can choose the Miscellaneous⇨Visited Links command to mark all links as visited or unvisited. In IE, choose Tools⇨Delete Browsing History and then select the Delete History button. You then need to refresh the page for the change to take effect.

✦ **Don't change font size in a hover state.** Unlike most styles, hover changes the page in real time. A hover style with a different font size than the ordinary link can cause problems. The page is automatically reformatted to accept the larger (or smaller) font, which can move a large amount of text on the screen rapidly. This can be frustrating and disconcerting for users. It's safest to change colors or borders on hover but not the font family or font size.

The hover pseudo-class is supposed to be supported on other elements, but browser support is spotty. You can define a hover pseudo-class for div and <p> elements with some confidence if users are using the latest browsers. Earlier browsers are less likely to support this feature, so don't rely on it too much.

Selecting in Context

CSS allows some other nifty selection tricks. Take a look at Figure 3-9 and you see a page with two kinds of paragraphs in it.

The code for the `context-style.html` page is deceptively simple:

```
<!DOCTYPE html PUBLIC "-//W3C//DTD XHTML 1.0 Strict//EN"
"http://www.w3.org/TR/xhtml1/DTD/xhtml1-strict.dtd">
<html lang="EN" dir="ltr" xmlns="http://www.w3.org/1999/xhtml">
  <head>
    <meta http-equiv="content-type" content="text/xml; charset=utf-8" />
    <title>context-style</title>
    <style type = "text/css">
      #special p {
        text-align: right;
      }
    </style>
  </head>

  <body>
    <h1>Selecting By Context</h1>

    <div>
      <p>This paragraph is left-justified.</p>
      <p>This paragraph is left-justified.</p>
      <p>This paragraph is left-justified.</p>
    </div>

    <div id = "special">
      <p>The paragraphs in this div are different.</p>
      <p>The paragraphs in this div are different.</p>
      <p>The paragraphs in this div are different.</p>
    </div>
  </body>
</html>
```

Figure 3-9: Obviously two kinds of paragraphs are here — or are there?

If you look at the code for `context-style.html`, you see some interesting things:

+ **The page has two `div`s.** One `div` is anonymous, and the other is `special`.

+ **None of the paragraphs has an ID or class.** The paragraphs in this page don't have names or classes defined, yet they clearly have two different types of behavior. The first three paragraphs are aligned to the left, and the last three are aligned to the right.

+ **The style rule affects paragraphs inside the `special div`.** Take another look at the style:

  ```
  #special p {
  ```

  This style rule means, "Apply this style to any paragraph appearing inside something called `special`." You can also define a rule that could apply to an image inside a list item or emphasized items inside a particular class. When you include a list of style selectors without commas, you're indicating a nested style.

+ **Paragraphs defined outside `special` aren't affected.** This nested selection technique can help you create very complex style combinations. It becomes especially handy when you start building positioned elements, like menus and columns.

Defining Multiple Styles at Once

Sometimes, you want a number of elements to share similar styles. As an example, look at Figure 3-10.

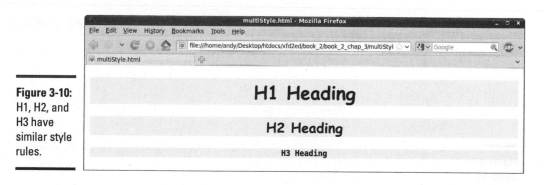

Figure 3-10:
H1, H2, and
H3 have
similar style
rules.

As shown in Figure 3-10, the top three headings all have very similar styles. Creating three different styles would be tedious, so CSS includes a shortcut:

```
<!DOCTYPE html PUBLIC "-//W3C//DTD XHTML 1.0 Strict//EN"
"http://www.w3.org/TR/xhtml1/DTD/xhtml1-strict.dtd">
<html lang="EN" dir="ltr" xmlns="http://www.w3.org/1999/xhtml">
  <head>
    <meta http-equiv="content-type" content="text/xml; charset=utf-8" />
    <title>multiStyle.html</title>
    <style type = "text/css">
      h1, h2, h3 {
        text-align: center;
        font-family: "Bradley Hand ITC", cursive;
        background-color: yellow;
      }

      h3 {
        font-family: monospace;
      }
    </style>
  </head>

  <body>
    <h1>H1 Heading</h1>
    <h2>H2 Heading</h2>
    <h3>H3 Heading</h3>
  </body>
</html>
```

One style element (the one that begins h1, h2, h3) provides all the information for all three heading types. If you include more than one element in a style selector separated by commas, the style applies to all the elements in the list. In this example, the centered cursive font with a yellow background is applied to heading levels 1, 2, and 3 all in the same style.

If you want to make modifications, you can do so. I created a second h3 rule, changing the font-family attribute to monospace. Style rules are applied in order, so you can always start with the general rule and then modify specific elements later in the style if you wish.

If you have multiple elements in a selector rule, it makes a huge difference whether you use commas. If you separate elements with spaces (but no commas), CSS looks for an element nested within another element. If you include commas, CSS applies the rule to all the listed elements.

Chapter 4: Borders and Backgrounds

In This Chapter

✔ Creating borders

✔ Managing border size, style, and color

✔ Using the border shortcut style

✔ Understanding the box model

✔ Setting padding and margin

✔ Creating background and low-contrast images

✔ Changing background image settings

✔ Adding images to list items

C SS offers some great features for making your elements more colorful, including a flexible and powerful system for adding borders to your elements. You can also add background images to all or part of your page. This chapter describes how to use borders and backgrounds for maximum effect.

Joining the Border Patrol

You can use CSS to draw borders around any HTML element. You have some freedom in the border size, style, and color. Here are two ways to define border properties: using individual border attributes, and using a shortcut. Borders don't actually change the layout, but they do add visual separation that can be appealing, especially when your layouts are more complex.

Using the border attributes

Figure 4-1 illustrates a page with a simple border drawn around the heading.

Figure 4-1: This page features a double red border.

Shades of danger

Several border styles rely on shading to produce special effects. Here are a couple things to keep in mind when using these shaded styles:

✔ **You need a wide border.** The shading effects are typically difficult to see if the border is very thin.

✔ **Browsers shade differently.** All the shading tricks modify the *base* color (the color you indicate with the `border-color` attribute) to simulate depth. Unfortunately, the browsers don't all do this in the same way. The Firefox/Mozilla browsers create a new color *lighter* than the base color to simulate areas in the light (the top and left

sides of an outset border, for example). Internet Explorer (IE) uses the base color for the lighter regions and creates a *darker* shade to simulate areas in darkness. I show a technique to define different color schemes for each browser in Chapter 5 of this minibook. For now, avoid shaded styles if this bothers you.

✔ **Black shading doesn't work in IE.** IE makes colors darker to get shading effects. If your base color is black, IE can't make anything darker, so you don't see the shading effects at all. Likewise, white shading doesn't work well on Firefox.

The code for the `borderProps.html` page demonstrates the basic principles of borders in CSS:

```
<!DOCTYPE html PUBLIC "-//W3C//DTD XHTML 1.0 Strict//EN"
"http://www.w3.org/TR/xhtml1/DTD/xhtml1-strict.dtd">
<html lang="EN" dir="ltr" xmlns="http://www.w3.org/1999/xhtml">
  <head>
    <meta http-equiv="content-type" content="text/xml; charset=utf-8" />
    <title>borderProps.html</title>
    <style type = "text/css">
      h1 {
        border-color: red;
        border-width: .25em;
        border-style: double;
      }
    </style>
  </head>

  <body>
    <h1>This has a border</h1>
  </body>
</html>
```

Each element can have a border defined. Borders require three attributes:

✦ **width:** The width of the border. This can be measured in any CSS unit, but border width is normally described in pixels (px) or ems. (***Remember:*** An *em* is roughly the width of the capital letter "M" in the current font.)

✦ **color:** The color used to display the border. The color can be defined like any other color in CSS, with color names or hex values.

✦ `style:` CSS supports a number of border styles. For the example in the following section, I chose a double border. This draws a border with two thinner lines around the element.

You must define all three attributes if you want borders to appear properly. You can't rely on the default values to work in all browsers.

Defining border styles

After you define the three attributes, it's time to pick your border style. CSS has a predetermined list of border styles you can choose from. Figure 4-2 shows a page with all the primary border styles displayed.

Figure 4-2: This page shows the main border styles.

You can choose any of these styles for any border:

✦ **Solid:** A single solid line around the element.

✦ **Double:** Two lines around the element with a gap between them. The border width is the combined width of both lines and the gap.

✦ **Groove:** Uses shading to simulate a groove etched in the page.

✦ **Ridge:** Uses shading to simulate a ridge drawn on the page.

✦ **Inset:** Uses shading to simulate a pressed-in button.

✦ **Outset:** Uses shading to simulate a button *sticking out* from the page.

✦ **Dashed:** A dashed line around the element.

✦ **Dotted:** A dotted line around the element.

I didn't reprint the source of `borderStyles.html` here, but it's included on the CD-ROM and Web site if you want to look it over. I added a small margin to each list item to make the borders easier to distinguish. Margins are discussed later in this chapter in the "Borders, margin, and padding" section.

Using the border shortcut

Defining three different CSS attributes for each border is a bit tedious. Fortunately, CSS includes a handy border shortcut that makes borders a lot easier to define, as Figure 4-3 demonstrates.

Figure 4-3:
This border is defined with only one CSS rule.

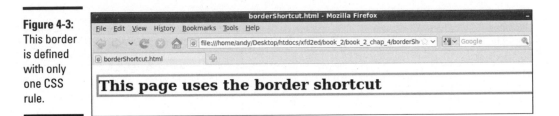

You can't tell the difference from the output, but the code for `border-Shortcut.html` is extremely simple:

```
<!DOCTYPE html PUBLIC "-//W3C//DTD XHTML 1.0 Strict//EN"
"http://www.w3.org/TR/xhtml1/DTD/xhtml1-strict.dtd">
<html lang="EN" dir="ltr" xmlns="http://www.w3.org/1999/xhtml">
  <head>
    <meta http-equiv="content-type" content="text/xml; charset=utf-8" />
    <title>borderShortcut.html</title>
    <style type = "text/css">
      h1 {
        border: red 5px solid;
      }
    </style>
  </head>

  <body>
    <h1>This page uses the border shortcut</h1>
  </body>
</html>
```

The order in which you describe border attributes doesn't matter. Just specify a color, a size, and a border style.

Creating partial borders

If you want, you can have more precise control of each side of a border. There are a number of specialized border shortcuts for each of the sub-borders. Figure 4-4 shows how you can add borders to the top, bottom, or sides of your element.

Figure 4-4 applies a border style to the bottom of the heading and to the left side of the paragraph. Partial borders are pretty easy to build, as you can see from the code listing:

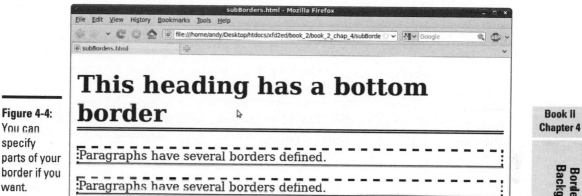

Figure 4-4:
You can specify parts of your border if you want.

```
<!DOCTYPE html PUBLIC "-//W3C//DTD XHTML 1.0 Strict//EN"
"http://www.w3.org/TR/xhtml1/DTD/xhtml1-strict.dtd">
<html lang="EN" dir="ltr" xmlns="http://www.w3.org/1999/xhtml">
  <head>
    <meta http-equiv="content-type" content="text/xml; charset=utf-8" />
    <title>subBorders.html</title>
    <style type = "text/css">
      h1 {
        border-bottom: 5px black double;
      }

      p {
        border-left:3px black dotted;
        border-right: 3px black dotted;
        border-top: 3px black dashed;
        border-bottom: 3px black groove;
      }
    </style>
  </head>

  <body>
    <h1>This heading has a bottom border</h1>

    <p>
      Paragraphs have several borders defined.
    </p>

    <p>
      Paragraphs have several borders defined.
    </p>

  </body>
</html>
```

Notice the border styles. CSS has style rules for each side of the border: `border-top`, `border-bottom`, `border-left`, and `border-right`. Each of these styles acts like the border shortcut, but it only acts on one side of the border.

 There's also specific border attributes for each side (bottom-border-width adjusts the width of the bottom border, for example), but they're almost never used because the shortcut version is so much easier.

Introducing the Box Model

XHTML and CSS use a specific type of formatting called the *box model*. Understanding how this layout technique works is important. If you don't understand some of the nuances, you'll be surprised by the way your pages flow.

The box model relies on two types of elements: inline and block-level. Block-level elements include `<div>` tags, paragraphs, and all headings (h1–h6); whereas, `strong`, `a`, and `image` are examples of inline elements.

The main difference between inline and block-level elements is this: Block-level elements always describe their own space on the screen; whereas, inline elements are allowed only within the context of a block-level element.

Your overall page is defined in block-level elements, which contain inline elements for detail.

Each block-level element (at least in the default setting) takes up the entire width of the screen. The next block-level element goes directly underneath the last element defined.

Inline elements flow differently. They tend to go immediately to the right of the previous element. If there's no room left on the current line, an inline element drops down to the next line and goes to the far left.

Borders, margin, and padding

Each block-level element has several layers of space around it, such as:

+ **Padding:** The space between the content and the border.

+ **Border:** Goes around the padding.

+ **Margin:** Space outside the border between the border and the parent element.

Figure 4-5 shows the relationship among margin, padding, and border.

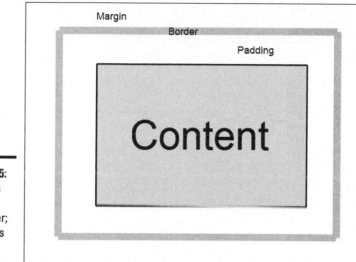

Figure 4-5:
Margin is outside the border; padding is inside.

You can change settings for the margin, border, and padding to adjust the space around your elements. The `margin` and `padding` CSS rules are used to set the sizes of these elements, as shown in Figure 4-6.

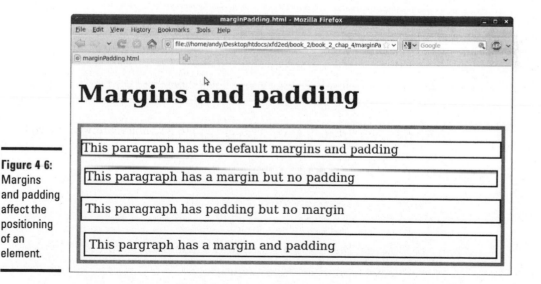

Figure 4-6:
Margins and padding affect the positioning of an element.

In Figure 4-6, I applied different combinations of margin and padding to a series of paragraphs. To make things easier to visualize, I drew a border around the `<div>` containing all the paragraphs and each individual paragraph element. You can see how the spacing is affected.

```
<!DOCTYPE html PUBLIC "-//W3C//DTD XHTML 1.0 Strict//EN"
"http://www.w3.org/TR/xhtml1/DTD/xhtml1-strict.dtd">
<html lang="EN" dir="ltr" xmlns="http://www.w3.org/1999/xhtml">
  <head>
    <meta http-equiv="content-type" content="text/xml; charset=utf-8" />
    <title>marginPadding.html</title>
    <style type = "text/css">
      div {
        border: red 5px solid;
      }
      p {
        border: black 2px solid;
      }
      #margin {
        margin: 5px;
      }
      #padding {
        padding: 5px;
      }
      #both {
        margin: 5px;
        padding: 5px;
      }
    </style>
  </head>

  <body>
    <h1>Margins and padding</h1>
    <div id = "main">
      <p>This paragraph has the default margins and padding</p>
      <p id = "margin">This paragraph has a margin but no padding</p>
      <p id = "padding">This paragraph has padding but no margin</p>
      <p id = "both">This paragraph has a margin and padding</p>
    </div>
  </body>
</html>
```

You can determine margin and padding using any of the standard CSS measurement units, but the most common are pixels and ems.

Positioning elements with margins and padding

As with borders, you can use variations of the margin and padding rules to affect spacing on a particular side of the element. One particularly important form of this trick is *centering*.

In old-style HTML, you could center any element or text with the <center> tag. This was pretty easy, but it violated the principle of separating content from style. The text-align: center rule is a nice alternative, but it only works on the contents of an element. If you want to center an entire block-level element, you need another trick, as you can see in Figure 4-7.

This page illustrates a few interesting ideas:

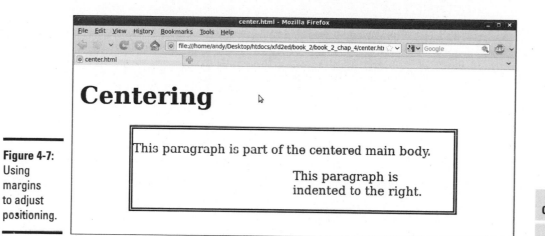

✦ **You can adjust the width of a block.** The main `div` that contains all the paragraphs has its width set to 75 percent of the page body width.

✦ **Center an element by setting `margin-left` and `margin-right` to auto.** Set both the left and right margins to `auto` to make an element center inside its parent element. This trick is most frequently used to center `div`s and tables.

✦ **Use `margin-left` to indent an entire paragraph.** You can use `margin-left` or `margin-right` to give extra space between the border and the contents.

✦ **Percentages refer to percent of the parent element.** When you use percentages as the unit measurement for margins and padding, you're referring to the percentage of the parent element; so a `margin-left` of 50 percent leaves the left half of the element blank.

✦ **Borders help you see what's happening.** I added a border to the main-Body `div` to help you see that the `div` is centered.

✦ **Setting the margins to auto doesn't center the *text*.** It centers the `div` (or other block-level element). Use `text-align: center` to center text inside the `div`.

The code that demonstrates these ideas is shown here:

```
<!DOCTYPE html PUBLIC "-//W3C//DTD XHTML 1.0 Strict//EN"
"http://www.w3.org/TR/xhtml1/DTD/xhtml1-strict.dtd">
<html lang="EN" dir="ltr" xmlns="http://www.w3.org/1999/xhtml">
  <head>
    <meta http-equiv="content-type" content="text/xml; charset=utf-8" />
    <title>center.html</title>
    <style type = "text/css">
      #mainBody {
        border: 5px double black;
        width: 75%;
```

```
      margin-left: auto;
      margin-right: auto;
    }
    .indented {
      margin-left: 50%;
    }
  </style>
</head>

<body>
  <h1>Centering</h1>
  <div id = "mainBody">
    <p>
      This paragraph is part of the centered main body.
    </p>
    <p class = "indented">
      This paragraph is indented to the right.
    </p>
  </div>
</body>
</html>
```

Changing the Background Image

You can use another CSS rule — `background-image` — to apply a background image to a page or elements on a page. Figure 4-8 shows a page with this feature.

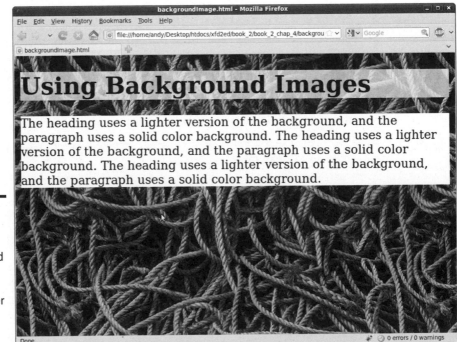

Figure 4-8: This page has a background image for the body and another for the heading.

Background images are easy to apply. The code for `backgroundImage.html` shows how:

```
<!DOCTYPE html PUBLIC "-//W3C//DTD XHTML 1.0 Strict//EN"
"http://www.w3.org/TR/xhtml1/DTD/xhtml1-strict.dtd">
<html lang="EN" dir="ltr" xmlns="http://www.w3.org/1999/xhtml">
  <head>
    <meta http-equiv="content-type" content="text/xml; charset=utf-8" />
    <title>backgroundImage.html</title>
    <style type = "text/css">
      body {
        background-image: url("ropeBG.jpg");
      }
      h1 {
        background-image: url("ropeBGLight.jpg");
      }
      p {
        background-color: white;
      }
    </style>
  </head>

  <body>
    <h1>Using Background Images</h1>

    <p>
      The heading uses a lighter version of the background,
      and the paragraph uses a solid color background.
      The heading uses a lighter version of the background,
      and the paragraph uses a solid color background.
      The heading uses a lighter version of the background,
      and the paragraph uses a solid color background.
    </p>
  </body>
</html>
```

**Book II
Chapter 4**

**Borders and
Backgrounds**

Attaching the background image to an element through CSS isn't difficult. Here are the general steps:

1. **Find or create an appropriate image and place it in the same directory as the page so it's easy to find.**

2. **Attach the `background-image` style rule to the page you want to apply the image to.**

If you want to apply the image to the entire page, use the `body` element.

3. **Tell CSS where `background-image` is by adding a `url` identifier.**

Use the keyword `url()` to indicate that the next thing is an address.

4. **Enter the address of the image.**

It's easiest if the image is in the same directory as the page. If that's the case, you can simply type the image name. Make sure you surround the URL with quotes.

5. **Test your background image by viewing the Web page in your browser.**

   A lot can go wrong with background images. The image may not be in the right directory, you might have misspelled its name, or you may have forgotten the url() bit. (I do all those things sometimes.)

Getting a background check

It's pretty easy to add backgrounds, but background images aren't perfect. Figure 4-9 demonstrates a page with a nice background. Unfortunately, the text is difficult to read.

Background images can add a lot of *zing* to your pages, but they can introduce some problems, such as:

+ **Background images can add to the file size.** Images are very large, so a big background image can make your page much larger and harder to download.

+ **Some images can make your page harder to read.** An image in the background can interfere with the text, so the page can be much harder to read.

+ **Good images don't make good backgrounds.** A good picture draws the eye and calls attention to it. The job of a background image is to fade into the background. If you want people to look at a picture, embed it. Background images shouldn't jump into the foreground.

+ **Backgrounds need to be low contrast.** If your background image is dark, you can make light text viewable. If the background image is light, dark text shows up. If your image has areas of light and dark (like nearly all good images), it'll be impossible to find a text color that looks good against it.

Solutions to the background conundrum

Web developers have come up with a number of solutions to background image issues over the years. I used several of these solutions in the backgroundImage.html page (the readable one shown in Figure 4-8).

Using a tiled image

If you try to create an image the size of an entire Web page, the image will be so large that dialup users will almost never see it. Even with compression techniques, a page-sized image is too large for quick or convenient loading.

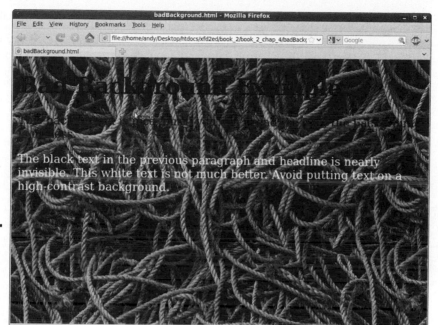

Figure 4-9:
The text is
very hard to
read. Don't
do this to
your users!

Fortunately, you can use a much smaller image and fool the user into thinking it takes up the entire screen. Figure 4-10 shows the ropeDG.jpg that I used to cover the entire page.

Figure 4-10:
The image
is only 500 x
500 pixels.

Image courtesy of Julian Burgess (Creative Commons License)

I used a specially created image for the background. Even though it's only 500 pixels wide by 500 pixels tall, it's been carefully designed to repeat so you can't see the seams. If you look carefully, you can tell that the image repeats, but you can't tell exactly where one copy ends and the next one begins.

This type of image is a *tiled background* or sometimes a *seamless texture*.

Getting a tiled image

If you want an image that repeats seamlessly, you have two main options:

✦ **Find an image online.** A number of sites online have free seamless backgrounds for you to use on your site. Try a search and see what you come up with.

✦ **Make your own image.** If you can't find a pre-made image that does what you want, you can always make your own. All the main image editing tools have seamless background tools. In GIMP, choose Filters➪Map➪Make Seamless. Check Book VIII, Chapter 4 for a technique to build your own tiled backgrounds in GIMP.

By default, a background image repeats as many times as necessary in both the horizontal and vertical dimensions to fill up the entire page. This fills the entire page with your background, but you only have to download a small image.

Setting background colors

Background colors can be a great tool for improving readability. If you set the background color of a specific element, that background color will appear on top of the underlying element's background image. For the `background Image.html` example, I set the background color of all p objects to white, so the text will appear on white regardless of the complex background. This is a useful technique for body text (like <p> tags) because text tends to be smaller and readability is especially important. If you want, you can set a background color that's similar to the background image. Just be sure the foreground color contrasts with the background color so the text is easy to read.

When you use a dark background image with light text, be sure to also set the `background-color` to a dark color. This way the text is readable. Images take longer to load than colors and may be broken. Make sure the user can read the text immediately.

Reducing the contrast

In `backgroundImage.html`, the heading text is pretty dark, which won't show up well against the dark background image. I used a different trick for the h1 heading. The heading uses a different version of the ropes image; this one is adjusted to be much brighter. The image is shown in Figure 4-11.

Figure 4-11:
This is the ropes image with the brightness turned way up.

With this element, I kept the ropes image, but I made a much brighter background so the dark text would show up well underneath. This technique allows you to use the background image even underneath text, but here are a few things to keep in mind if you use it:

✦ **Make the image very dark or very light.** Use the Adjust Colors command in IrfanView or your favorite image editor to make your image dark or light. Don't be shy. If you're creating a lighter version, make it *very* light. (See Book I, Chapter 6 for details on color manipulation in IrfanView and Book VIII, Chapter 4 for how to change colors in GIMP.)

✦ **Set the foreground to a color that contrasts with the background.** If you have a very light version of the background image, you can use dark text on it. A dark background will require light text. Adjust the text color with your CSS code.

✦ **Set a background color.** Make the background color representative of the image. Background images can take some time to appear, but the background color appears immediately because it is defined in CSS. This is especially important for light text because white text on the default white background is invisible. After the background image appears, it overrides the background color. Be sure the text color contrasts with the background, whether that background is an image or a solid color.

✦ **Use this trick for large text.** Headlines are usually larger than body text, and they can be easier to read, even if they have a background behind them. Try to avoid putting background images behind smaller body text. This can make the text much harder to read.

Manipulating Background Images

After you place your background image, you might not be completely pleased with the way it appears. Don't worry. You still have some control. You can specify how the image repeats and how it's positioned.

Turning off the repeat

Background images repeat both horizontally and vertically by default. You may not want a background image to repeat, though. Figure 4-12 is a page with the ropes image set to not repeat at all.

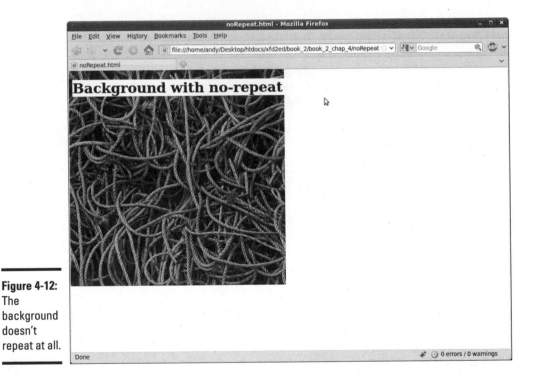

Figure 4-12: The background doesn't repeat at all.

The code uses the `background-repeat` attribute to turn off the automatic repetition.

```
<!DOCTYPE html PUBLIC "-//W3C//DTD XHTML 1.0 Strict//EN"
"http://www.w3.org/TR/xhtml1/DTD/xhtml1-strict.dtd">
<html lang="EN" dir="ltr" xmlns="http://www.w3.org/1999/xhtml">
  <head>
    <meta http-equiv="content-type" content="text/xml; charset=utf-8" />
    <title>noRepeat.html</title>
```

```
<style type = "text/css">
  body {
    background-image: url("ropeBG.jpg");
    background-repeat: no-repeat;
  }
  h1 {
    background-color: white;
  }
</style>
</head>

<body>
  <h1>Background with no-repeat</h1>
</body>
</html>
```

The `background-repeat` attribute can be set to one of four values:

✦ `repeat`: The default value; the image is repeated indefinitely in both *x*- and *y*-axes.

✦ `no-repeat`: Displays the image one time; no repeat in *x*- or *y*-axis.

✦ `repeat-x`: Repeats the image horizontally but not vertically.

✦ `repeat-y`: Repeats the image vertically but not horizontally.

Making effective gradients with repeat-x and repeat-y

Gradients are images that smoothly flow from one color to another. They can have multiple colors, but simplicity is a virtue here. The `repeat-x` and `repeat-y` techniques discussed in the previous section can be combined with a special image to create a nice gradient background image that's very quick to download. Figure 4-13 shows an example of this technique.

Book II
Chapter 4

Borders and Backgrounds

Figure 4-13: The page appears to have a large background image.

Even though the entire page is covered in a background image, I made the actual background quite small. The outlined area in Figure 4-13 is the actual image used in the background (displayed with an `img` tag and a border). You can see that the image used is very short (5 pixels tall). I used `background-repeat: y` to make this image repeat as many times as necessary to fill the height of the page.

The code is pretty straightforward:

```
<!DOCTYPE html PUBLIC "-//W3C//DTD XHTML 1.0 Strict//EN"
"http://www.w3.org/TR/xhtml1/DTD/xhtml1-strict.dtd">
<html lang="EN" dir="ltr" xmlns="http://www.w3.org/1999/xhtml">
  <head>
    <meta http-equiv="content-type" content="text/xml; charset=utf-8" />
    <title>gradient.html</title>
    <style type = "text/css">
      body {
        background-image: url("blueGrad.jpg");
        background-repeat: repeat-y;
      }
      img {
        border: 1px solid black;
      }
    </style>
  </head>

  <body>
    <h1>Using a thin gradient background</h1>
    <p>
    Here's the actual gradient height: <br />
    <img src = "blueGrad.jpg" />
        alt = "blue gradient" />
    </p>

  </body>
</html>
```

Here's how you make a gradient background:

1. **Obtain or create a gradient image.**

   Most image editing tools can make gradient fills easily. In GIMP, you simply select the gradient tool, choose an appropriate foreground and background color, and apply the gradient to the image.

2. **Set the image size.**

   If you want your image to tile vertically (as I did), you'll want to make it very short (5 px) and very wide (I chose 1,600 px, so it would fill nearly any browser).

3. **Apply the image as the background image of the body or of any other element, using the `background-image` attribute.**

4. **Set the `background-repeat` attribute to `repeat-x` to make the image repeat as many times as necessary vertically.**

Use a vertical gradient image if you prefer. If you want to have a color that appears to change down the page, create a tall, skinny gradient and set background-repeat to repeat-x.

The great thing about this technique is how it uses a relatively small image to fill a large Web site. It looks good, but it'll still download reasonably fast.

Using Images in Lists

It's not quite a background, but you can also use images for list items. Sometimes, you might want some type of special bullet for your lists, as shown in Figure 4-14.

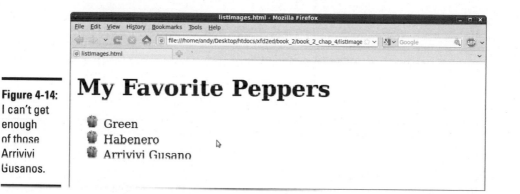

Figure 4-14:
I can't get enough of those Arrivivi Gusanos.

On this page, I've listed some of my (many) favorite varieties of peppers. For this kind of list, a custom pepper bullet is just the thing. Of course, CSS is the answer:

```
<!DOCTYPE html PUBLIC "-//W3C//DTD XHTML 1.0 Strict//EN"
"http://www.w3.org/TR/xhtml1/DTD/xhtml1-strict.dtd">
<html lang="EN" dir="ltr" xmlns="http://www.w3.org/1999/xhtml">
  <head>
    <meta http-equiv="content-type" content="text/xml; charset=utf-8" />
    <title>listImages.html</title>
    <style type = "text/css">
      li {
        list-style-image: url("pepper.gif");
      }
    </style>
  </head>

  <body>
    <h1>My Favorite Peppers</h1>
    <ul>
      <li>Green</li>
      <li>Habenero</li>
      <li>Arrivivi Gusano</li>
```

```
      </ul>
    </body>
  </html>
```

The list-style-image attribute allows you to attach an image to a list item. To create custom bullets:

1. **Begin with a custom image.**

   Bullet images should be small, so you may have to make something little. I took a little pepper image and resized it to be 25 x 25 pixels. The image will be trimmed to an appropriate width, but it will have all the height of the original image, so make it small.

2. **Specify the list-style-image with a url attribute.**

   You can set the image as the list-style-image, and all the bullets will be replaced with that image.

3. **Test the list in your browser.**

   Be sure everything is working correctly. Check to see that the browser can find the image, that the size is right, and that everything looks like you expect.

Chapter 5: Levels of CSS

In This Chapter

✔ Building element-level styles

✔ Creating external style sheets

✔ Creating a multipage style

✔ Managing cascading styles

✔ Using conditional comments

C SS is a great tool for setting up the visual display of your pages. When you first write CSS code, you're encouraged to place all your CSS rules in a `style` element at the top of the page. CSS also allows you to define style rules inside the body of the HTML and in a separate document. In this chapter, you read about these alternative methods of applying style rules, when to use them, and how various style rules interact with each other.

Managing Levels of Style

Styles can be applied to your pages at three levels:

✦ **Local styles:** Defined by specifying a style within an XHTML element's attributes.

✦ **Page-level styles:** Defined in the page's header area. This is the type of style used in Chapters 1 through 4 of this minibook.

✦ **External styles:** Defined on a separate document and linked to the page.

Using local styles

A style can be defined directly in the HTML body. Figure 5-1 is an example of this type of code. A local style is also sometimes called an *element-level* style, because it modifies a particular instance of an element on the page.

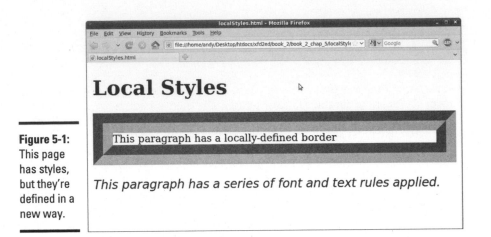

Figure 5-1:
This page
has styles,
but they're
defined in a
new way.

You can't see the difference from Figure 5-1, but if you look over the code, you'll see it's not like the style code you see in the other chapters in this minibook:

```
<!DOCTYPE html PUBLIC "-//W3C//DTD XHTML 1.0 Strict//EN"
"http://www.w3.org/TR/xhtml1/DTD/xhtml1-strict.dtd">
<html lang="EN" dir="ltr" xmlns="http://www.w3.org/1999/xhtml">
  <head>
    <meta http-equiv="content-type" content="text/xml; charset=utf-8" />
    <title>localStyles.html</title>
  </head>

  <body>
    <h1>Local Styles</h1>
    <p style = "border: 2em #FF00FF groove">
      This paragraph has a locally-defined border
    </p>

    <p style = "font-family: sans-serif;
                font-size: 1.2em;
                font-style: italic">
      This paragraph has a series of font and text rules applied.
    </p>
  </body>
</html>
```

While you look over this code, a couple things should become evident:

✦ **No `<style>` element is in the header.** Normally, you use a `<style>` section in the page header to define all your styles. This page doesn't have such a segment.

✦ **Paragraphs have their own style attributes.** I added a `style` attribute to each paragraph in the HTML body. All XHTML elements support the `style` attribute.

✦ **The entire style code goes in a single pair of quotes.** For each styled element, the entire style goes into a pair of quotes because it's one HTML attribute. You can use indentation and white space (as I did) to make things easier to understand.

When to use local styles

Local styles should not be your first choice, but they can be useful in some circumstances.

If you're writing a program to translate from a word processor or other tool, local styles are often the easiest way to make the translation work. If you use a word processor to create a page and you tell it to save the page as HTML, it will often use local styles because word processors often use this technique in their own proprietary format. Usually when you see an HTML page with a lot of local styles, it's because an automatic translation tool made the page.

Sometimes, you see local styles used in code examples. For example, the following code could be used to demonstrate different border styles:

```
<!DOCTYPE html PUBLIC "-//W3C//DTD XHTML 1.0 Strict//EN"
"http://www.w3.org/TR/xhtml1/DTD/xhtml1-strict.dtd">
<html lang="EN" dir="ltr" xmlns="http://www.w3.org/1999/xhtml">
  <head>
    <meta http-equiv="content-type" content="text/xml; charset=utf-8" />
    <title>localBorders.html</title>
  </head>

  <body>
    <h1>Inline Borders</h1>
    <p style = "border: 5px solid black">
      This paragraph has a solid black border
    </p>

    <p style = "border: 5px double black">
      This paragraph has a double black border
    </p>

  </body>
</html>
```

For example purposes, it's helpful to see the style right next to the element. This code would be fine for demonstration or testing purposes (if you just want to get a quick look at some border styles), but it wouldn't be a good idea for production code.

Local styles have very high priority, so anything you apply in a local style overrides the other style rules. This can be a useful workaround if things aren't working like you expect, but it's better to get your styles working correctly than to rely on a workaround.

The other place you'll occasionally see local styles is in Dynamic HTML (DHTML) applications, such as animation and motion. This technique often involves writing JavaScript code to change various style elements on the fly. The technique is more reliable when the style elements in question are defined locally. See Book IV, Chapter 7 for a complete discussion of this topic.

The drawbacks of local styles

It's pretty easy to apply a local style, but for the most part, the technique isn't usually recommended because it has some problems, such as:

✦ **Inefficiency:** If you define styles at the element level with the `style` attribute, you're defining only the particular instance. If you want to set paragraph colors for your whole page this way, you'll end up writing a lot of style rules.

✦ **Readability:** If style information is interspersed throughout the page, it's much more difficult to find and modify than if it's centrally located in the header (or in an external document, as you'll see shortly).

✦ **Lack of separation:** Placing the styles at the element level defeats the goal of separating content from style. It becomes much more difficult to make changes, and the mixing of style and content makes your code harder to read and modify.

✦ **Awkwardness:** An entire batch of CSS rules has to be stuffed into a single HTML attribute with a pair of quotes. This can be tricky to read because you have CSS integrated directly into the flow of HTML.

✦ **Quote problems:** The XHTML attribute requires quotes, and some CSS elements also require quotes (font families with spaces in them, for example). Having multiple levels of quotes in a single element is a recipe for trouble.

Using an external style sheet

CSS supports another way to use styles, called *external style sheets*. This technique allows you to define a style sheet as a separate document and import it into your Web pages. To see why this might be attractive, take a look at the following figure.

Figure 5-2 shows a page with a distinctive style.

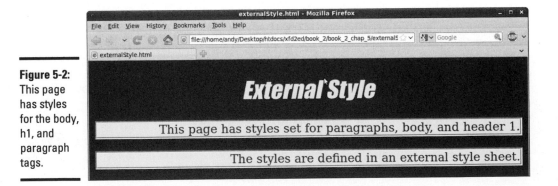

Figure 5-2: This page has styles for the body, h1, and paragraph tags.

When you look at the code for externalStyle.html, you might be surprised to see no obvious style information at all!

```
<!DOCTYPE html PUBLIC "-//W3C//DTD XHTML 1.0 Strict//EN"
"http://www.w3.org/TR/xhtml1/DTD/xhtml1-strict.dtd">
<html lang="EN" dir="ltr" xmlns="http://www.w3.org/1999/xhtml">
  <head>
    <meta http-equiv="content-type" content="text/xml; charset=utf-8" />
    <title>externalStyle.html</title>
    <link rel = "stylesheet"
          type = "text/css"
          href = "myStyle.css" />
  </head>

  <body>
    <h1>External Style</h1>
    <p>
      This page has styles set for paragraphs, body, and header 1.
    </p>

    <p>
      The styles are defined in an external style sheet.
    </p>
  </body>
</html>
```

Book II
Chapter 5

Levels of CSS

Where you normally see style tags (in the header), there is no style. Instead, you see a <link> tag. This special tag is used to connect the current document with another document.

Defining the external style

When you use a page-level style, the style elements aren't embedded in the page header but in an entirely separate document.

In this case, the page is connected to a special file called myStyle.css. This file contains all the CSS rules:

```
/* myStyle.css */

body {
  background-color: #333300;
  color: #FFFFFF;
}

h1 {
  color: #FFFF33;
  text-align: center;
  font: italic 200% fantasy;
}

p {
  background-color: #FFFF33;
  color: #333300;
  text-align: right;
  border: 3px groove #FFFF33;
}
```

The style sheet looks just like a page-level style, except for a few key differences:

✦ **The style sheet rules are contained in a separate file.** The style is no longer part of the HTML page but is an entirely separate file stored on the server. CSS files usually end with the `.css` extension.

✦ **There are no `<style></style>` tags.** These aren't needed because the style is no longer embedded in HTML.

✦ **The code begins with a comment.** The `/* */` pair indicates a comment in CSS. Truthfully, you can put comments in CSS in the page level just like I did in this external file. External CSS files frequently have comments in them.

✦ **The style document has no HTML.** CSS documents contain nothing but CSS. This comes closer to the goal of separating style (in the CSS document) and content (in the HTML document).

✦ **The document isn't tied to any particular page.** The great advantage of external CSS is reuse. The CSS document isn't part of any particular page, but any page can use it.

Reusing an external CSS style

External style sheets are really fun when you have more than one page that needs the same style. Most Web sites today use multiple pages, and they should share a common style sheet to keep consistency. Figure 5-3 shows a second page using the same `myStyle.css` style sheet.

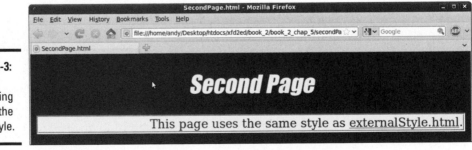

Figure 5-3: Another page using exactly the same style.

The code shows how easily this is done:

```
<!DOCTYPE html PUBLIC "-//W3C//DTD XHTML 1.0 Strict//EN"
"http://www.w3.org/TR/xhtml1/DTD/xhtml1-strict.dtd">
<html lang="EN" dir="ltr" xmlns="http://www.w3.org/1999/xhtml">
  <head>
    <meta http-equiv="content-type" content="text/xml; charset=utf-8" />
    <title>SecondPage.html</title>
    <link rel = "stylesheet"
          type = "text/css"
```

```
            href = "myStyle.css" />
   </head>

   <body>
     <h1>Second Page</h1>
     <p>
       This page uses the same style as
       <a href = "externalStyle.html">externalStyle.html</a>.
     </p>
   </body>
</html>
```

External style sheets have some tremendous advantages:

Book II
Chapter 5

Levels of CSS

✦ **One style sheet can control many pages:** Generally, you have a large number of different pages in a Web site that all share the same general style. You can define the style sheet in one document and have all the HTML files refer to the CSS file.

✦ **Global changes are easier:** Say you have a site with a dozen pages, and you decide you want some kind of chartreuse background (I don't know why — go with me here). If each page has its own page-level style definition, you have to make the change 12 times. If you're using external styles, you make the change in one place and it's automatically propagated to all the pages in the system.

✦ **Separation of content and design:** With external CSS, all the design is housed in the CSS, and the data is in XHTML.

✦ **Easy upgrades:** Because the design parameters of the entire site are defined in one file, you can easily change the site without having to mess around with individual HTML files.

Understanding the link tag

The `<link>` tag is the key to adding a CSS reference to an HTML document. The `<link>` tag has the following characteristics:

✦ **The `<link>` tag is part of the HTML page.** Use a `<link>` tag in your HTML document to specify which CSS document will be used by the HTML page.

✦ **The `<link>` tag only occurs in the header.** Unlike the `<a>` tag, the `<link>` tag can occur only in the header.

✦ **The tag has no visual presence.** The user can't see the `<link>` tag, only its effects.

✦ **The `link` tag is used to relate the document with another document.** You use the `<link>` tag to describe the relationship between documents.

✦ **The `<link>` tag has a `rel` attribute, which defines the type of relationship.** For now, the only relationship you'll use is the `stylesheet` attribute.

✦ **The `<link>` tag also has an `href` attribute, which describes the location of the other document.**

Link tags are often used to connect a page to an externally defined style document (more on them in the next section).

Most people refer to the hyperlinks created by the anchor (<a>) tag as hyperlinks or links. This can lead to some confusion because, in this sense, the link tag doesn't create that type of link. If it were up to me, the <a> tag would have been called the <link> tag, and the tag now called link would have been called rel or something. Maybe Tim Berners-Lee meant to call me the day he named these elements, and he just forgot. That's what I'm thinking.

Specifying an external link

To use the <link> tag to specify an external style sheet, follow these steps:

1. **Define the style sheet.**

External style sheets are very similar to the ones you already know. Just put all the styles in a separate text document without the <style> and </style> tags. In my example, I created a new text file called myStyle.css.

2. **Create a link element in the HTML page's head area to define the link between the HTML and CSS pages.**

My link element looks like this:

```
<link rel = "stylesheet"
      type = "text/css"
      href = "myStyle.css" />
```

3. **Set the link's relationship by setting the rel = "stylesheet" attribute.**

Honestly, stylesheet is almost the only relationship you'll ever use, so this should become automatic.

4. **Specify the type of style by setting type = "text/css" (just like you do with page-level styles).**

5. **Determine the location of the style sheet with the href attribute.**

Understanding the Cascading Part of Cascading Style Sheets

The *C* in CSS stands for *cascading,* which is an elegant term for an equally elegant and important idea. Styles cascade or flow among levels. An element's visual display may be affected by rules in another element or even another document.

Inheriting styles

When you apply a style to an element, you change the appearance of that element. If the element contains other elements, the style is often passed on to those containers. Take a look at Figure 5-4 for an illustration.

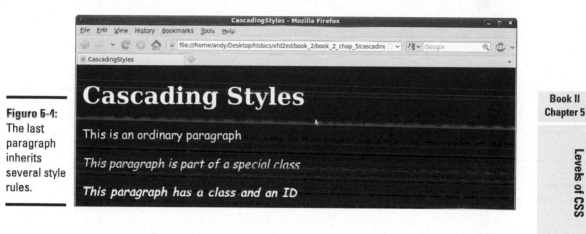

Figure 5-4: The last paragraph inherits several style rules.

Figure 5-4 shows several paragraphs, all with different font styles. Each paragraph is white with a black background. All the paragraphs use a fantasy font. Two of the paragraphs are italicized, and one is also bold. Look at the code to see how the CSS is defined.

```
<!DOCTYPE html PUBLIC "-//W3C//DTD XHTML 1.0 Strict//EN"
"http://www.w3.org/TR/xhtml1/DTD/xhtml1-strict.dtd">
<html lang="EN" dir="ltr" xmlns="http://www.w3.org/1999/xhtml">
  <head>
    <meta http-equiv="content-type" content="text/xml; charset=utf-8" />
    <title>CascadingStyles</title>
    <style type = "text/css">
      body {
        color: white;
        background-color: black;
      }

      p {
        font-family: comic sans ms, fantasy;
      }

      .italicized {
        font-style: italic;
      }

      #bold {
        font-weight: bold;
      }
    </style>
  </head>

<body>
  <h1>Cascading Styles</h1>
```

```
<p>This is an ordinary paragraph</p>

<p class = "italicized">
  This paragraph is part of a special class
</p>

<p class = "italicized"
   id = "bold">
  This paragraph has a class and an ID</p>
</body>

</html>
```

Take a look at the page, and you'll notice some interesting things:

✦ **Everything is white on a black background.** These styles were defined in the body. Paragraphs without specific colors will inherit the colors of the parent element (in this case, the body). There's no need to specify the paragraph colors because the body takes care of them.

✦ **Paragraphs all use the fantasy font.** I set the paragraph's font-family attribute to fantasy. All paragraphs without an explicit font-family attribute will use this rule.

✦ **A class is used to define italics.** The second paragraph is a member of the italicized class, which gives it italics. Because it's also a paragraph, it gets the paragraph font, and it inherits the color rules from the body.

✦ **The bold ID only identifies font weight.** The third paragraph has all kinds of styles associated with it. This paragraph displays all the styles of the second, plus the added attributes of its own ID.

In the cascadingStyles.html example, the final paragraph inherits the font from the generic p definition, italics from its class, and boldfacing from its ID. Any element can attain style characteristics from any of these definitions.

Hierarchy of styles

An element will display any style rules you define for it, but certain rules are also passed on from other places. Generally, this is how style rules cascade through the page:

✦ **The body defines overall styles for the page.** Any style rules that you want the entire page to share should be defined in the body. Any element in the body begins with the style of the page. This makes it easy to define an overall page style.

✦ **A block-level element passes its style to its children.** If you define a div with a particular style, any elements inside that div will inherit the div's style attributes. Likewise, defining a list will also define the list items.

✦ **You can always override inherited styles.** Of course, if you don't want paragraphs to have a particular style inherited from the body, you can just change them.

Not all style rules are passed on to child elements. The text formatting and color styles are inherited, but border and positioning rules are not. This actually makes sense. Just because you define a border around a `div` doesn't mean you want the same border around the paragraphs inside that `div`.

Overriding styles

The other side of inherited style is the ability to override an inherited style rule. For example, take a look at this code:

```
<!DOCTYPE html PUBLIC "-//W3C//DTD XHTML 1.0 Strict//EN"
"http://www.w3.org/TR/xhtml1/DTD/xhtml1-strict.dtd">
<html lang="EN" dir="ltr" xmlns="http://www.w3.org/1999/xhtml">
  <head>
    <meta http-equiv="content-type" content="text/xml; charset=utf-8" />
    <title>overRide.html</title>
    <style type = "text/css">
      body { color: red; }
      p {color: green; }
      .myClass { color: blue; }
      #whatColor { color: purple; }
    </style>
  </head>

  <body>
    <p class = "myClass"
       id = "whatColor">
      This paragraph is a member of a class and has an ID,
      both with style rules. It has four conflicting
      color rules!
    </p>
  </body>
</html>
```

The code listing has a different indentation scheme than I've used in the rest of the chapter. Because all the styles had one rule, I chose not to indent to save space.

The question is this: What color will the `whatColor` element display? It's a member of the body, so it should be red. It's also a paragraph, and paragraphs are green. It's also a member of the `myClass` class, so it should be blue. Finally, it's named `whatColor`, and elements with this ID should be purple.

Four seemingly conflicting color rules are all dropped on this poor element. What color will it be?

CSS has a clear ranking system for handling this type of situation. In general, more specific rules trump more general rules. Here's the precedence (from highest to lowest precedence):

1. **User preference:** The user always has the final choice about what styles are used. Users aren't required to use any styles at all and can always change the style sheet for their own local copy of the page. If a user needs to apply a special style (for example, high contrast for people with visual disabilities), he should always have that option.

2. **Local style:** A local style (defined with the `style` attribute in the HTML) has the highest precedence of developer-defined styles. It overrules any other styles.

3. **id:** A style attached to an element `id` has a great deal of weight because it overrides any other styles defined in the style sheet.

4. **Class:** Styles attached to a class override the style of the object's element. So, if you have a paragraph with a color green that belongs to a class colored blue, the element will be blue because class styles outrank element styles.

5. **Element:** The element style takes precedence over any of its containers. For example, if a paragraph is inside a `div`, the paragraph style has the potential to override both the `div` and the body.

6. **Container element:** `div`s, tables, lists, and other elements used as containers pass their styles on. If an element is inside one or more of these containers, it can inherit style attributes from them.

7. **Body:** Anything defined in the body style is an overall page default, but it will be overridden by any other styles.

In the `overRide.html` example, the `id` rule will take precedence, so the paragraph will display in green.

If you want to see a more complete example, look at `cascadingStyles.html` on the CD-ROM. It extends the `whatColor` example with other paragraphs that demonstrate the various levels of the hierarchy.

Precedence of style definitions

When you have styles defined in various places (locally, page level, or externally) the placement of the style rule also has a ranking. Generally, an external style has the weakest rank. You can write a page-level style rule to override an external style.

You might do this if you decide all your paragraphs will be blue, but you have one page where you want the paragraphs green. Define paragraphs as green in the page-level style sheet, and your page will have the green paragraphs without interfering with the other page's styles.

Page-level styles (defined in the header) have medium weight. They can override external styles but are overridden by local styles.

Locally defined styles (using the HTML style attribute) have the highest precedence, but they should be avoided as much as possible. Use classes or IDs if you need to override the page-level default styles.

Using Conditional Comments

While we're messing around with style sheets, there's one more thing you should know. Every once in a while, you'll encounter a page that needs one set of style rules for most browsers and has some exceptions for Internet Explorer.

Most of what you know works equally well in any browser. I've focused on the established standards, which work very well on most browsers. Unfortunately, Internet Explorer (especially before version 7) is notorious for not following the standards exactly. Internet Explorer (IE) doesn't do everything exactly right. When IE had unquestioned dominance, everybody just made things work for IE. Now you have a bigger problem. You need to make your code work for standards-compliant browsers, and sometimes you need to make a few changes to make sure that IE displays things correctly.

**Book II
Chapter 5**

Levels of CSS

Coping with incompatibility

This has been a problem since the beginning of Web development, and a number of solutions have been proposed over the years, such as:

+ **"Best viewed with" disclaimers:** One common technique is to code for one browser or another and then ask users to agree with your choice by putting up this disclaimer. This isn't a good technique because the user shouldn't have to adapt to you. Besides, sometimes the choice is out of the user's hands. More and more small devices (such as PDAs and cellphones) have browsers built in, which are difficult to change. IE isn't available on Linux machines, and not everyone can install a new browser.

+ **Parallel pages:** You might be tempted to create two versions of your page, one for IE and one for the standards-compliant browsers (Firefox, Netscape Navigator, Opera, Safari, and so on). This is also a bad solution because it's twice (or more) as much work. You'll have a lot of trouble keeping track of changes in two different pages. They'll inevitably fall out of synch.

+ **JavaScript-based browser detection:** In Book IV, you see that JavaScript has features for checking on the browser. This is good, but it still doesn't quite handle the differences in style sheet implementation between the browsers.

✦ **CSS hacks:** The CSS community has frequently relied on a series of hacks (unofficial workarounds) to handle CSS compatibility problems. This approach works by exploiting certain flaws in IE to overcome others. The biggest problem with this is that when Microsoft fixes some flaws (as they've done with IE 7), many of the flaws you relied on to fix a problem may be gone, but the original problem is still there.

✦ **Conditional comments:** Although IE has bugs, it also has some innovative features. One of these features, *conditional comments,* lets you write code that displays only in IE. Because the other browsers don't support this feature, the IE-specific code is ignored in any browser not based on IE. This is the technique currently preferred by coders who adhere to Web standards.

Making Internet Explorer–specific code

It's a little easier for you to see how conditional comments work if I show you a simple example and then show you how to use the conditional comment trick to fix CSS incompatibility problems.

Figure 5-5 shows a simple page with Firefox. Figure 5-6 shows the exact same page displayed in IE 7.

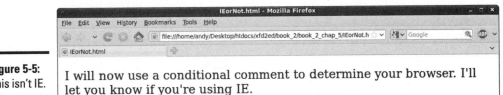

Figure 5-5: This isn't IE.

Figure 5-6: And this is IE. Somehow the code knows the difference.

Take a look at the code for `whatBrowser.html` and see how it works.

```
<!DOCTYPE html PUBLIC "-//W3C//DTD XHTML 1.0 Strict//EN"
"http://www.w3.org/TR/xhtml1/DTD/xhtml1-strict.dtd">
<html lang="EN" dir="ltr" xmlns="http://www.w3.org/1999/xhtml">
  <head>
    <meta http-equiv="content-type" content="text/xml; charset=utf-8" />
```

```
   <title>IEorNot.html</title>

</head>

<body>
  <p>
    I will now use a conditional comment to determine your
    browser. I'll let you know if you're using IE.
  </p>

  <!--[if IE]>
    <h1>You're using IE</h1>
  <![endif]-->

</body>
</html>
```

The only part that's new is the strange comments:

```
  <!--[if IE]>
    <h1>You're using IE</h1>
  <![endif]-->
```

Conditional comments are a special feature available only in Internet Explorer. They allow you to apply a test to your browser. You can place any XHTML code you wish between `<!-- [if IE]>` and `<![endif]-->`, but that code will only be rendered by versions of Internet Explorer. Any other browser will read the entire block as a comment and ignore it completely.

So, when you look at `whatBrowser` in IE, it sees the conditional comment, says to itself, "Why yes, I'm Internet Explorer," and displays the "Using IE" headline. If you look at the same page with Firefox, the browser doesn't understand the conditional comment but sees an HTML comment (which begins with `<!--` and ends with `-->`). HTML comments are ignored, so the browser does nothing.

Using a conditional comment with CSS

Conditional comments on their own aren't that interesting, but they can be a very useful tool for creating compatible CSS. You can use conditional comments to create two different style sheets, one that works for IE and one that works with everything else. Figures 5-7 and 5-8 illustrate a simple example of this technique:

Figure 5-7:
This page has a yellow background in most browsers.

Most browsers will read a standard style sheet that creates a yellow background.

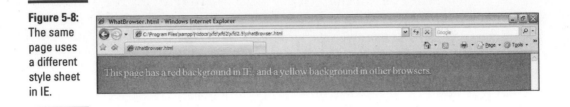

If the page is rendered in IE, it uses a second style sheet.

Look at the code, and you'll see it's very similar to the `IEorNot.html` page.

```
<!DOCTYPE html PUBLIC "-//W3C//DTD XHTML 1.0 Strict//EN"
"http://www.w3.org/TR/xhtml1/DTD/xhtml1-strict.dtd">
<html lang="EN" dir="ltr" xmlns="http://www.w3.org/1999/xhtml">
  <head>
    <meta http-equiv="content-type" content="text/xml; charset=utf-8" />
    <title>WhatBrowser.html</title>

    <!-- default style -->
    <style type = "text/css">
      body {
        background-color: yellow;
        color: blue;
      }
    </style>

    <!-- IE only style overrides default -->
    <!--[if IE]>
      <style type = "text/css">
        body {
          background-color: red;
          color: yellow;
        }
      </style>
    <![endif]-->

  </head>

  <body>

    <p>
      This page has a red background in IE, and a yellow
      background in other browsers.
    </p>
  </body>
</html>
```

If you want a page to use different styles in IE and other browsers, do the following:

1. **Define the default style first.**

   Begin by creating the style that will work in most browsers. Most of the time, this style will also work in IE. You can create the style at the page level (with the `<style></style>` pair) or externally (with the `<link>` tag).

2. **Create a conditional comment in the header.**

   Create a conditional comment *after* the primary style, as shown in this code snippet.

   ```
   <!-- default style -->
   <style type = "text/css">
     body {
        background-color: yellow;
        color: blue;
     }
   </style>

   <!-- IE only style overrides default -->
   <!--[if IE]>

   <![endif] >
   ```

3. **Build a new IE-specific style inside the comment.**

   The style inside the comment will be applied only to IE browsers, such as in the following lines:

   ```
   <!--[if IE]>
     <style type = "text/css">
       body {
          background-color: red;
          color: yellow;
       }
     </style>
   <![endif]-->
   ```

4. **The commented style can be page level or external.**

   Like the default style, you can use the `<style></style>` pair to make a page-level style or you can use the `<link>` tag to pull in an externally defined style sheet.

5. **Only place code that solves IE issues in the conditional style.**

   IE will read the code in both styles, so there's no need to repeat everything. Use the conditional style for only those areas where IE doesn't do what you expect.

6. **Don't forget to end the conditional comment.**

   If you leave off the end of your conditional comment (or any comment, for that matter), most of your page won't appear. That could be bad.

Checking the Internet Explorer version

So far, you haven't encountered many situations that require conditional comments, but they're handy when you need them. One more trick can be useful. You can specify which version of IE you're using. This is important when you read about positionable CSS in Book III because IE 7 works pretty well with standards-compliant code, but the earlier versions do not. You can use this variation to specify code only for IE 6 and earlier.

```
<!--[if lte IE 6]>
...
<[endif]-->
```

The lte signifies *less than or equal to,* so code inside this condition will run only on early versions of IE.

Book III

Using Positional CSS

Contents at a Glance

Chapter 1: Fun with the Fabulous Float

In This Chapter

✔ Understanding the pitfalls of traditional layout tools

✔ Using float with images and block-level tags

✔ Setting the width and margins of floated elements

✔ Creating attractive forms with float

✔ Using the clear attribute with float

*O*ne of the big criticisms against HTML is that it lacks real layout tools. You can do a lot with your page, but it's still basically a list of elements arranged vertically on the screen. As the Web matures and screen resolutions improve, people want Web pages to look more like print matter, with columns, good-looking forms, and more layout options. CSS provides several great tools for building nice layouts. After you get used to them, you can build just about any layout you can imagine. This chapter describes the amazing float attribute and how it can be used as the foundation of great page layouts.

Avoiding Old-School Layout Pitfalls

Back in the prehistoric (well, pre-CSS) days, no good option was built into HTML for creating a layout that worked well. Clever Web developers and designers found some ways to make things work, but these proposed solutions all had problems.

Problems with frames

Frames were a feature of the early versions of HTML. They allowed you to break a page into several segments. Each segment was filled with a different page from the server. You could change pages independently of each other, to make a very flexible system. You could also specify the width and height of each frame.

At first glance, frames sound like an ideal solution to layout problems. In practice, they had a lot of disadvantages, such as

✦ **Complexity:** If you had a master page with four segments, you had to keep track of five Web pages. A *master* page kept track of the relative positions of each section but had no content of its own. Each of the other pages had content but no built-in awareness of the other pages.

✦ **Linking issues:** The default link action caused content to pop up in the same frame as the original link, which isn't usually what you want. Often, you'd put a menu in one frame and have the results of that menu pop up in another frame. This meant most anchors had to be modified to make them act properly.

✦ **Backup nightmares:** If the user navigated to a page with frames and then caused one of the frames to change, what should the backup button do? Should it return to the previous state (with only the one segment returned to its previous state) or was the user's intent to move entirely off the master page to what came before? There are good arguments for either and no good way to determine the user's intention. Nobody ever came up with a reasonable compromise for this problem.

✦ **Ugliness:** Although it's possible to make frames harder to see, they did become obvious when the user changed the screen size and scroll bars would automatically pop up.

✦ **Search engine problems:** Search engines had a lot of problems with frame-based pages. The search engine might only index part of a frame-based site, and the visitor might get incomplete Web sites missing navigation or sidebars.

For all these reasons, frames aren't allowed in XHTML Strict documents. The layout techniques you read about in this chapter more than compensate for the loss of frames as layout tools. Read how to integrate content from other pages on the server with AJAX in Book VIII, Chapter 5.

Problems with tables

When it became clear that frames weren't the answer, Web designers turned to tables. HTML has a flexible and powerful table tool, and it's possible to do all kinds of creative things with that tool to create layouts. Many HTML developers still do this, but you'll see that flow-based layout is cleaner and easier. Tables are meant for tabular data, not as a layout tool. When you use tables to set up the visual layout of your site, you'll encounter these problems:

✦ **Complexity:** Although table syntax isn't that difficult, a lot of nested tags are in a typical table definition. To get exactly the look you want, you probably won't use an ordinary table but tricks, like `rowspan` and `colspan`, special spacer images, and tables inside tables. It doesn't take long for the code to become bulky and confusing.

✦ **Content and display merging:** Using a table for layout violates the principle of separating content from display. If your content is buried inside a complicated mess of table tags, it'll be difficult to move and update.

✦ **Inflexibility:** If you create a table-based layout and then decide you don't like it, you basically have to redesign the entire page from scratch. It's no simple matter to move a menu from the left to the top in a table-based design, for example.

Tables are great for displaying tabular data. Avoid using them for layout because you have better tools available.

Problems with huge images

Some designers skip HTML altogether and create Web pages as huge images. Tools, like Photoshop, include features for creating links in a large image. Again, this seems ideal because a skilled artist can have control over exactly what is displayed. Like the other techniques, this has some major drawbacks, such as

✦ **Size and shape limitations:** When your page is based on a large image, you're committed to the size and shape of that image for your page. If a person wants to view your page on a cellphone or PDA, it's unlikely to work well, if at all.

✦ **Content issues:** If you create all the text in your graphic editor, it isn't really stored to the Web page as text. In fact, the Web page will have no text at all. This means that search engines can't index your page, and screen-readers for people with disabilities won't work.

✦ **Difficult updating:** If you find an error on your page, you have to modify the image, not just a piece of text. This makes updating your page more challenging than it would be with a plain XHTML document.

✦ **File size issues:** An image large enough to fill a modern browser window will be extremely large and slow to download. Using this technique will all but eliminate users with dialup access from using your site.

**Book III
Chapter 1**

**Fun with the
Fabulous Float**

Problems with Flash

Another tool that's gained great popularity is the Flash animation tool from Adobe (formerly Macromedia). This tool allows great flexibility in how you position things on a page and supports techniques that are difficult or impossible in ordinary HTML, such as sound and video integration, automatic motion tweening, and path-based animation. Flash certainly has a place in Web development (especially for embedded games — check out my earlier book, *Beginning Flash Game Programming For Dummies*). Even though Flash has great possibilities, you should avoid its use for ordinary Web development for the following reasons:

✦ **Cost:** The Flash editor isn't cheap, and it doesn't look like it'll get cheaper. The tool is great, but if free or low-cost alternatives work just as well, it's hard to justify the cost.

✦ **Binary encoding:** All text in a Flash Web page is stored in the Flash file itself. It's not visible to the browser. Flash pages (like image-based pages) don't work in Web searches and aren't useful for people with screen-readers.

✦ **Updating issues:** If you need to change your Flash-based page, you need the Flash editor installed. This can make it more difficult to keep your page up to date.

✦ **No separation of content:** As far as the browser is concerned, there's no content but the Flash element, so there's absolutely no separation of content and layout. If you want to make a change, you have to change the Flash application.

✦ **Search engine problems:** Code written in Flash can't always be read by search engines (though Google is working on the problem).

✦ **Technical issues:** Flash is not integrated directly into the browser, which leads to a number of small complications. The Forward and Back buttons don't work as expected, printing can be problematic, and support is not universal.

Adobe has recently released a very interesting tool called Flex. It's based on the Flash engine, and it's specifically designed to overcome some of the shortcomings I list here. It'll be interesting to see if this becomes an important technology. Advances in HTML 5 and CSS3 also show some promise, so perhaps Flash will become less necessary.

Introducing the Floating Layout Mechanism

CSS supplies a couple techniques for layout. The preferred technique for most applications is a *floating layout.* The basic idea of this technique is to leave the XHTML layout as simple as possible but to provide style hints that tell the various elements how to interact with each other on the screen.

In a floating layout, you don't legislate exactly where everything will go. Instead, you provide hints and let the browser manage things for you. This ensures flexibility because the browser will try to follow your intentions, no matter what size or shape the browser window becomes. If the user resizes the browser, the page will flex to fit to the new size and shape, if possible.

Floating layouts typically involve less code than other kinds of layouts because only a few elements need specialized CSS. In most of the other layout techniques, you need to provide CSS for every single element to make things work as you expect.

Using float with images

The most common place to use the `float` attribute is with images. Figure 1-1 has a paragraph with an image embedded inside.

It's more likely that you want the image to take up the entire left part of the paragraph. The text should flow around the paragraph, similar to Figure 1-2.

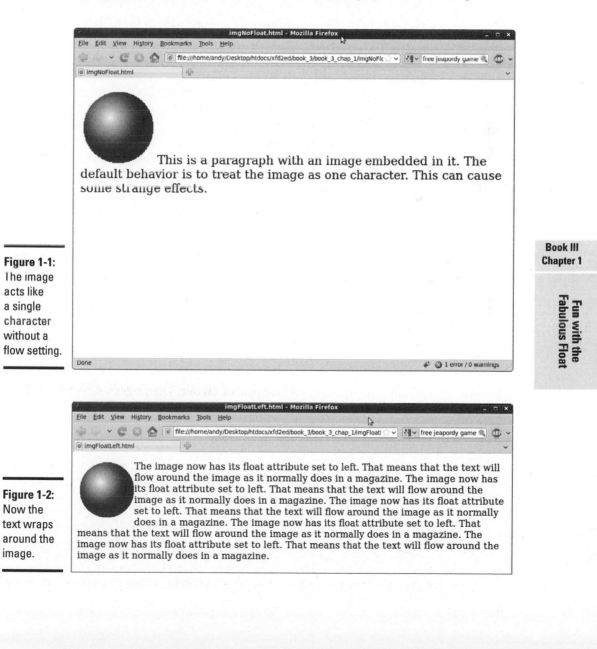

Figure 1-1:
The image acts like a single character without a flow setting.

Figure 1-2:
Now the text wraps around the image.

Book III
Chapter 1

Fun with the Fabulous Float

When you add a `float:left` attribute to the `img` element, the image tends to move to the left, pushing other content to the right. Now, the text flows around the image. The image is actually removed from the normal flow of the page layout, so the paragraph takes up all the space. Inside the paragraph, the text avoids overwriting the image.

Adding the float property

The code for adding the `float` property is pretty simple:

```
<!DOCTYPE html PUBLIC "-//W3C//DTD XHTML 1.0 Strict//EN"
"http://www.w3.org/TR/xhtml1/DTD/xhtml1-strict.dtd">
<html lang="EN" dir="ltr" xmlns="http://www.w3.org/1999/xhtml">
  <head>
    <meta http-equiv="content-type" content="text/xml; charset=utf-8" />
    <title>imgFloat.html</title>
    <style type = "text/css">
      img {
        float: left;
      }
    </style>
  </head>

  <body>
    <p>
      <img src = "ball.gif"
           alt = "ball" />
      The image now has its float attribute set to left. That means
      that the text will flow around the image as it normally does
      in a magazine.
      The image now has its float attribute set to left. That means
      that the text will flow around the image as it normally does
      in a magazine.
      The image now has its float attribute set to left. That means
      that the text will flow around the image as it normally does
      in a magazine.
      The image now has its float attribute set to left. That means
      that the text will flow around the image as it normally does
      in a magazine.
      The image now has its float attribute set to left. That means
      that the text will flow around the image as it normally does
      in a magazine.
    </p>
  </body>
</html>
```

The only new element in the code is the CSS `float` attribute. The `img` object has a `float:left` attribute. It isn't necessary to change any other attributes of the paragraph because the paragraph text knows to float around the image.

Of course, you don't have to simply float to the left. Figure 1-3 shows the same page with the image's `float` attribute set to the right.

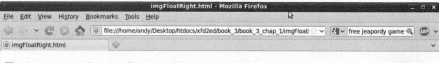

Figure 1-3:
Now the
image is
floated to
the right.

Using Float with Block-Level Elements

The `float` attribute isn't only for images. You can also use it with any element (typically `p` or `div`) to create new layouts. Using the `float` attribute to set the page layout is easy after you understand how things really work.

Floating a paragraph

Paragraphs and other block-level elements have a well-defined default behavior. They take the entire width of the page, and the next element appears below. When you apply the `float` element to a paragraph, the behavior of that paragraph doesn't change much, but the behavior of *succeeding* paragraphs is altered.

To illustrate, I take you all the way through the process of building two side-by-side paragraphs.

Begin by looking at a page with three paragraphs. Paragraph 2 has its `float` property set to `left`. Figure 1-4 illustrates such a page.

**Book III
Chapter 1**

**Fun with the
Fabulous Float**

floatDemo - Mozilla Firefox

File   Edit   View   History   Bookmarks   Tools   Help

file:///home/andy/Desktop/htdocs/xfd2ed/book_3/book_3_chap_1/floatDem | free jeapordy game

floatDemo

Float Demo

Paragraph 1. This paragraph has the normal behavior of a block-level element. It takes up the entire width of the page, and the next element is placed underneath.

Paragraph 2. This paragraph is floated left. It is placed to the left, and the next element will be placed to the right of it.

Paragraph 3. This paragraph has no floating, width or margin. It takes whatever space it can to the right of the floated element, and then flows to the next line.

Figure 1-4:
Paragraphs
2 and 3
are acting
strangely.

As you can see, some strange formatting is going on here. I improve on things later to make the beginnings of a two-column layout, but for now, just take a look at what's going on:

✦ **I've added borders to the paragraphs.** As you'll see, the width of an element isn't always obvious by looking at its contents. When I'm messing around with `float`, I often put temporary borders on key elements so I can see what's going on. You can always remove the borders when you have it working right.

✦ **The first paragraph acts normally.** The first paragraph has the same behavior you see in all block-style elements. It takes the entire width of the page, and the next element will be placed below it.

✦ **The second paragraph is pretty normal.** The second paragraph has its `float` attribute set to `left`. This means that the paragraph will be placed in its normal position, but that other text will be placed to the left of this element.

✦ **The third paragraph seems skinny.** The third paragraph seems to surround the second, but the text is pushed to the right. The `float` parameter in the previous paragraph causes this one to be placed in any remaining space (which currently isn't much). The remaining space is on the right and eventually underneath the second paragraph.

The code to produce this is simple HTML with equally simple CSS markup:

```
<!DOCTYPE html PUBLIC "-//W3C//DTD XHTML 1.0 Strict//EN"
"http://www.w3.org/TR/xhtml1/DTD/xhtml1-strict.dtd">
<html lang="EN" dir="ltr" xmlns="http://www.w3.org/1999/xhtml">
  <head>
    <meta http-equiv="content-type" content="text/xml; charset=utf-8" />
    <title>floatDemo</title>
    <style type = "text/css">
      p {
        border: 2px black solid;
      }
      .floated {
        float: left;
      }
    </style>

  </head>

  <body>
    <h1>Float Demo</h1>
    <p>
      Paragraph 1.
      This paragraph has the normal behavior of a block-level element.
      It takes up the entire width of the page, and the next element
      is placed underneath.
    </p>

    <p class = "floated">
      Paragraph 2.
      This paragraph is floated left. It is placed to the left, and the
```

```
      next element will be placed to the right of it.
    </p>

    <p>
      Paragraph 3.
      This paragraph has no floating, width or margin. It takes whatever
      space it can to the right of the floated element, and then flows
      to the next line.
    </p>
  </body>
</html>
```

As you can see from the code, I have a simple class called `floated` with the `float` property set to `left`. The paragraphs are defined in the ordinary way. Even though paragraph 2 seems to be embedded inside paragraph 3 in the screen shot, the code clearly shows that this isn't the case. The two paragraphs are completely separate.

I added a black border to each paragraph so you can see that the size of the element isn't always what you'd expect.

Adjusting the width

When you float an element, the behavior of succeeding elements is highly dependent on the width of the first element. This leads to a primary principle of float-based layout:

> If you float an element, you must also define its width.

The exception to this rule is elements with a predefined width, such as images and many form elements. These elements already have an implicit width, so you don't need to define width in the CSS. If in doubt, try setting the width at various values until you get the layout you're looking for.

Figure 1-5 shows the page after I adjusted the width of the floated paragraph to 50 percent of the page width.

Book III
Chapter 1

Fun with the
Fabulous Float

Figure 1-5:
The floated paragraph has a width of 50 percent of the page.

Specifying the width

Paragraph 1. This paragraph has the normal behavior of a block-level element. It takes up the entire width of the page, and the next element is placed underneath.

Paragraph 2. I've adjusted this paragraph to have a width of 50%. This paragraph is floated left. It is placed to the left, and the next element will be placed to the right of it.

Paragraph 3. This paragraph has no floating, width or margin. It takes whatever space it can to the right of the floated element, and then flows to the next line.

Things look better in Figure 1-5, but paragraph 2 still seems to be embedded inside paragraph 3. The only significant change is in the CSS style:

```
<style type = "text/css">
  p {
    border: 2px black solid;
  }
  .floated {
    float: left;
    width: 50%;
  }
</style>
```

I've added a `width` property to the floated element.

Elements that have the `float` attribute enabled will generally also have a width defined, except for images or other elements with an inherent width.

When you use a percentage value in the context of width, you're expressing a percentage of the *parent* element (in this case, the `body` because the paragraph is embedded in the document body). Setting the `width` to 50% means I want this paragraph to span half the width of the document body.

Setting the next margin

Things still don't look quite right. I added the borders around each paragraph so you can see an important characteristic of floating elements. Even though the text of paragraph 3 wraps to the right of paragraph 2, the actual paragraph element still extends all the way to the left side of the page. The *element* doesn't necessarily flow around the floated element, but its *contents* do. The background color and border of paragraph 3 still take as much space as they normally would if paragraph 2 didn't exist.

This is because a floated element is removed from the normal flow of the page. Paragraph 3 has access to the space once occupied by paragraph 2, but the text in paragraph 3 will try to find its own space without stepping on text from paragraph 2.

Somehow, you need to tell paragraph 3 to move away from the paragraph 2 space. This isn't a difficult problem to solve once you recognize it. Figure 1-6 shows a solution.

The `margin-left` property of paragraph 3 is set to 53 percent. Because the width of paragraph 2 is 50 percent, this provides a little gap between the columns. Take a look at the code to see what's going on here:

```
<!DOCTYPE html PUBLIC "-//W3C//DTD XHTML 1.0 Strict//EN"
"http://www.w3.org/TR/xhtml1/DTD/xhtml1-strict.dtd">
<html lang="EN" dir="ltr" xmlns="http://www.w3.org/1999/xhtml">
  <head>
```

```
<meta http-equiv="content-type" content="text/xml; charset=utf-8" />
<title>floatWidthMargin.html</title>
<style type = "text/css">
  p {
    border: 2px black solid;
  }
  .floated {
    float: left;
    width: 50%;
  }
  .right {
    margin-left: 52%;
  }
</style>

</head>

<body>
  <h1>Specifying the width</h1>
  <p>
    Paragraph 1.
    This paragraph has the normal behavior of a block-level element.
    It takes up the entire width of the page, and the next element
    is placed underneath.
  </p>

  <p class = "floated">
   Paragraph 2.
    This paragraph is floated left. The
    next element will be placed to the right of it. Now this has a width
    of 50%.
   </p>

  <p class = "right">
    Paragraph 3.
    This paragraph now has a margin-left so it is separated from the
    previous paragraph. Its width is still automatically
    determined.
  </p>

  </body>
</html>
```

Book III
Chapter 1

Fun with the
Fabulous Float

Figure 1-6:
The left margin of paragraph 3 is set to give a two-column effect.

Using Float to Style Forms

Many page layout problems appear to require tables. Some clever use of the CSS `float` can help elements with multiple columns without the overhead of tables.

Forms cause a particular headache because a form often involves labels in a left column followed by `input` elements in the right column. You'd probably be tempted to put such a form in a table. Adding table tags will make the HTML much more complex and isn't required. It's much better to use CSS to manage the layout.

You can float elements to create attractive forms without requiring tables. Figure 1-7 shows a form with `float` used to line up the various elements.

Figure 1-7: This is a nice-looking form defined without a table.

As page design gets more involved, it makes more sense to think of the HTML and the CSS separately. The HTML will give you a sense of the overall intent of the page, and the CSS can be modified separately. Using external CSS is a natural extension of this philosophy. Begin by looking at `floatForm.html` and concentrate on the XHTML structure before worrying about style:

```
<!DOCTYPE html PUBLIC "-//W3C//DTD XHTML 1.0 Strict//EN"
"http://www.w3.org/TR/xhtml1/DTD/xhtml1-strict.dtd">
<html lang="EN" dir="ltr" xmlns="http://www.w3.org/1999/xhtml">
  <head>
    <meta http-equiv="content-type" content="text/xml; charset=utf-8" />
    <title>floatForm.html</title>
    <link rel = "stylesheet"
          type = "text/css"
          href = "floatForm.css" />

  </head>

  <body>
    <form action = "">
      <fieldset>
        <label>Name</label>
        <input type = "text"
               id = "txtName" />
        <label>Address</label>
```

```
            <input type = "text"
                    id = "txtAddress" />
            <label>Phone</label>
            <input type = "text"
                    id = "txtPhone" />
            <button type = "button">
               submit request
            </button>
          </fieldset>
        </form>
    </body>
</html>
```

While you look over this code, note several interesting things about how the page is designed:

+ **The CSS is external.** CSS is defined in an external document. This makes it easy to change the style and helps you to focus on the XHTML document in isolation.

+ **The XHTML code is minimal.** The code is very clean. It includes a form with a `fieldset`. The `fieldset` contains labels, `input` elements, and a `button`.

+ **There isn't a table.** There's no need to add a table as an artificial organization scheme. A table wouldn't add to the clarity of the page. The form elements themselves provide enough structure to allow all the formatting you need.

+ **Labels are part of the design.** I used the `label` element throughout the form, giving me an element that can be styled however I wish.

+ **Everything is selectable.** I'll want to apply one CSS style to labels, another to `input` elements, and a third style to the `button`. I've set up the XHTML so I can use CSS selectors without requiring any `id` or `class` attributes.

+ **There's a button.** I used a `button` element instead of `<input type = "button">` on purpose. This way, I can apply one style to all the `input` elements and a different style to the `button` element.

Designing a page like this one so its internal structure provides all the selectors you need is wonderful. This keeps the page very clean and easy to read. Still, don't be afraid to add classes or IDs if you need them.

Figure 1-8 demonstrates how the page looks with no CSS.

It's often a good idea to look at your page with straight XHTML before you start messing around with CSS.

If you have a page with styles and you want to see how it will look without the style rules, use the Web Developer toolbar. You can temporarily disable some or all CSS style rules to see the default content underneath. This can sometimes be extremely handy.

Figure 1-8:
The plain
XHTML is
a start, but
some CSS
would help
a lot.

Using float to beautify the form

It'd be very nice to give the form a tabular feel, with each row containing a label and its associated input element. My first attempt at a CSS file for this page looked like this:

```
/* floatNoClear.css
   CSS file to go with float form
   Demonstrates use of float, width, margin
   Code looks fine but the output is horrible.
*/

fieldset {
  background-color: #AAAAFF;
}
label {
  float: left;
  width: 5em;
  text-align: right;
  margin-right: .5em;
}
input {
  background-color: #CCCCFF;
  float: left;
}
button {
  float: left;
  width: 10em;
  margin-left: 7em;
  margin-top: 1em;
  background-color: #0000CC;
  color: #FFFFFF;
}
```

This CSS looks reasonable, but you'll find it doesn't quite work right. (I show the problem and how to fix it later in this chapter.) Here are the steps to build the CSS:

1. **Add colors to each element.**

Colors are a great first step. For one thing, they ensure that your selectors are working correctly so that everything's where you think it is. This color scheme has a nice modern feel to it, with a lot of blues.

2. **Float the labels to the left.**

   Labels are all floated to the left, meaning they should move as far left as possible, and other things should be placed to the right of them.

3. **Set the label width to 5em.**

   This gives you plenty of space for the text the labels will contain.

4. **Set the labels to be right-aligned.**

   Right-aligning the labels will make the text snug up to the input elements but give them a little margin-right so the text isn't too close.

5. **Set the input's float to left.**

   This tells each input element to go as far to the left (toward its label) as it can. The input element goes next to the label if possible and on the next line, if necessary. Like images, input elements have a default width, so it isn't absolutely necessary to define the width in CSS.

6. **Float the button, too, but give the button a little top margin so it has a respectable space at the top. Set the width to 10em.**

This seems to be a pretty good CSS file. It follows all the rules, but if you apply it to floatForm.html, you'll be surprised by the results shown in Figure 1-9.

Figure 1-9:
This form
is…well…
ugly.

After all that talk about how nice float-based layout is, you're probably expecting something a bit neater. If you play around with the page in your browser, you'll find that everything works well when the browser is narrow, but when you expand the width of the browser, it gets ugly. Figure 1-10 shows the form when the page is really skinny. (I used the CSS editor on the Web Developer toolbar to adjust the width of the page display.)

Things get worse when the page is a little wider, as you can see in Figure 1-11.

Figure 1-10: The form looks great when the page is skinny.

Figure 1-11: With a slightly wider browser, things get strange.

If you make the page as wide as possible, you'll get a sense of what the browser was trying to accomplish in Figure 1-12.

When CSS doesn't do what you want, it's usually acting on some false assumptions, which is the case here. Floating left causes an element to go as far to the left as possible and on the next line, if necessary. However, that's not really what you want on this page. The inputs should float next to the labels, but each label should begin its own line. The labels should float all the way to the left margin with the inputs floating left next to the labels.

Adjusting the fieldset width

One approach is to consider how well the page behaves when it's skinny because the new label and input combination will simply wrap down to the next line. You can always make a container narrow enough to force the behavior you're expecting. Because all the field elements are inside the fieldset, you can simply make it narrower to get a nice layout, as shown in Figure 1-13.

When you want to test changes in CSS, nothing beats the CSS editor in the Web Developer Extension. I made Figure 1-13 by editing the CSS on the fly with this tool. You can see that the new line of CSS is still highlighted.

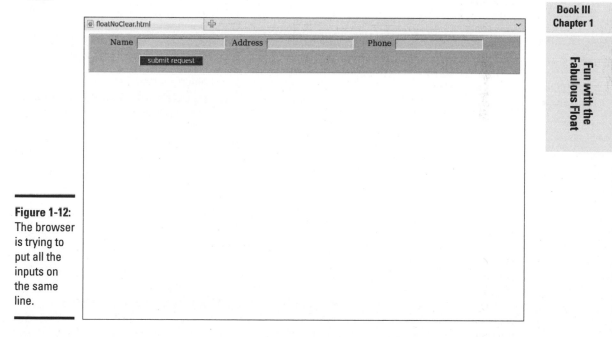

Figure 1-12:
The browser is trying to put all the inputs on the same line.

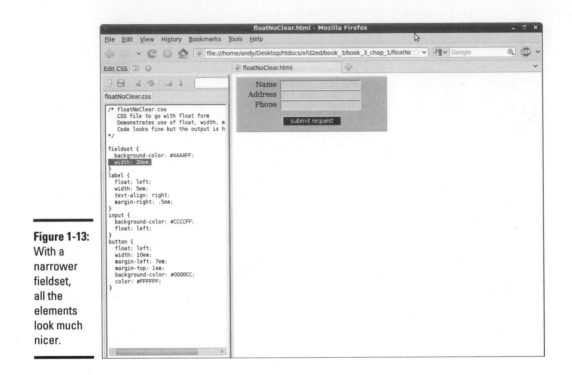

Figure 1-13:
With a narrower fieldset, all the elements look much nicer.

Setting the width of the `fieldset` to `15em` does the job. Because the widths of the other elements are already determined, forcing them into a `15em`-wide box makes everything line up nicely with the normal wrapping behavior of the `float` attribute. If you don't want the width change to be so obvious, you can apply it to the `form` element, which doesn't have any visible attributes (unless you add them, such as `color` or `border`).

Unfortunately, this doesn't always work because the user may adjust the font size and mess up all your careful design.

Using the clear attribute to control page layout

Adjusting the width of the container is a suitable solution, but it does feel like a bit of a hack. There should be some way to make the form work right, regardless of the container's width. There is exactly such a mechanism.

The `clear` attribute is used on elements with a `float` attribute. The `clear` attribute can be set to `left`, `right`, or `both`. Setting the `clear` attribute to `left` means you want nothing to the left of this element. In other words, the element should be on the left margin of its container. That's exactly what you want here. Each label should begin its own line, so set its `clear` attribute to `left`.

To force the button onto its own line, set its `clear` attribute to `both`. This means that the button should have no elements to the left or the right. It should occupy a line all its own.

If you want an element to start a new line, set both its `float` and `clear` attributes to `left`. If you want an element to be on a line alone, set `float` to `left` and `clear` to `both`.

Using the `clear` attribute allows you to have a flexible-width container and still maintain reasonable control of the form design. Figure 1-14 shows that the form can be the same width as the page and still work correctly. This version works, no matter the width of the page.

Figure 1-14: When you apply clear to floating elements, you can control the layout.

```
floatForm.html                    ⊕                              ⌄

    Name  [                                              ]
 Address  [                                              ]
   Phone  [                                              ]
          [ submit request ]
```

Here's the final CSS code, including `clear` attributes in the labels and button:

```
/* floatForm.css
   CSS file to go with float form
   Demonstrates use of float, width, margin, and clear
*/

fieldset {
  background-color: #AAAAFF;
}

label {
  clear: left;
  float: left;
  width: 5em;
  text-align: right;
  margin-right: .5em;
}

input {
  float: left;
  background-color: #CCCCFF;
}

button {
  float: left;
  clear: both;
```

```
    margin-left: 7em;
    margin-top: 1em;
    background-color: #0000CC;
    color: #FFFFFF;
}
```

You now have the basic tools in place to use flow layout. Look to Chapter 2 of this minibook to see how these tools are put together to build a complete page layout.

Chapter 2: Building Floating Page Layouts

In This Chapter

↙ **Creating a classic two-column page**

↙ **Creating a page-design diagram**

↙ **Using temporary borders**

↙ **Creating fluid layouts and three-column layouts**

↙ **Working with and centering fixed-width layouts**

The floating layout technique provides a good alternative to tables, frames, and other layout tricks formerly used. You can build many elegant multi-column page layouts with ordinary XHTML and CSS styles.

Creating a Basic Two-Column Design

Many pages today use a two-column design with a header and footer. Such a page is quite easy to build with the techniques you read about in this chapter.

Designing the page

It's best to do your basic design work on paper, not on the computer. Here's my original sketch in Figure 2-1.

Draw the sketch first so you have some idea what you're aiming for. Your sketch should include the following information:

✦ **Overall page flow:** How many columns do you want? Will it have a header and footer?

✦ **Section names:** Each section needs a name, which will be used in both the XHTML and the CSS.

✦ **Width indicators:** How wide will each column be? (Of course, these widths should add up to 100 percent or less.)

✦ **Fixed or percentage widths:** Are the widths measured in percentages (of the browser size) or in a fixed measurement (pixels)? This has important implications. For this example, I'm using a dynamic width with percentage measurements.

A note to perfectionists

If you're really into detail and control, you'll find this chapter frustrating. People accustomed to having complete control of a design (as you often do in the print world) tend to get really stressed when they realize how little actual control they have over the appearance of a Web page.

Really, it's okay. This is a good thing. When you design for the Web, you give up absolute control, but you gain unbelievable flexibility. Use the ideas outlined in this chapter to get your page looking right on a standards-compliant browser. Take a deep breath and look at it on something else (like Internet Explorer 6 if you want to suffer a heart attack!). Everything you positioned so carefully is all messed up! Take another deep breath and use conditional comments to fix the offending code without changing how it works in those browsers that do things correctly.

✦ **Font considerations:** Do any of the sections require any specific font styles, faces, or colors?

✦ **Color scheme:** What are the main colors of your site? What will be the color and background color of each section?

This particular sketch (in Figure 2-1) is very simple because the page will use default colors and fonts. For a more complex job, you need a much more detailed sketch. The point of the sketch is to separate design decisions from coding problems. Solve as much of the design stuff as possible first so you can concentrate on building the design with XHTML and CSS.

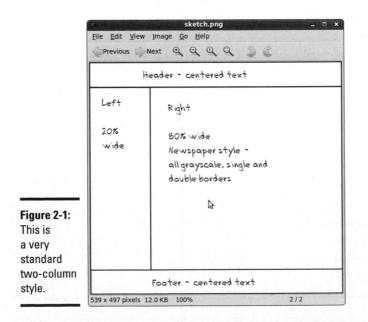

Figure 2-1:
This is
a very
standard
two-column
style.

Building the XHTML

After you have a basic design in place, you're ready to start building the XHTML code that will be the framework. Start with basic CSS but create a `div` for each section that will be in your final work. You can put a place-holder for the CSS, but don't add any CSS yet. Here's my basic code (I removed some of the redundant text to save space):

```
<!DOCTYPE html PUBLIC "-//W3C//DTD XHTML 1.0 Strict//EN"
"http://www.w3.org/TR/xhtml1/DTD/xhtml1-strict.dtd">
<html lang="EN" dir="ltr" xmlns="http://www.w3.org/1999/xhtml">
  <head>
    <meta http-equiv="content-type" content="text/xml; charset=utf-8" />
    <title>twoColumn.html</title>
    <link rel = "stylesheet"
          type = "text/css"
          href = "twoCol.css" />
  </head>

  <body>
    <div id = "head">
      <h1>Two Columns with Float</h1>
    </div>

    <div id = "left">
      <h2>Left Column</h2>
    </div>

    <div id = "right">
      <h2>Right Column</h2>
    </div>

    <div id = "footer">
      <h3>Footer</h3>
    </div>
  </body>
</html>
```

What's up with the Latin?

The flexible layouts built throughout this chapter require some kind of text so the browser knows how big to make things. The actual text isn't important, but something needs to be there.

Typesetters have a long tradition of using phony Latin phrases as filler text. Traditionally, this text has begun with the words "Lorem Ipsum," so it's called *Lorem Ipsum* text.

This particular version is semi-randomly generated from a database of Latin words.

If you want, you can also use Lorem Ipsum in your page layout exercises. Conduct a search for Lorem Ipsum generators on the Web to get as much fake text as you want for your mockup pages.

Although Lorem Ipsum text is useful in the screen shots, it adds nothing to the code listings. Throughout this chapter, I remove the Lorem Ipsum text from the code listings to save space. See the original files on the CD-ROM or Web site for the full pages in all their Cesarean goodness.

Nothing at all is remarkable about this XHTML code, but it has a few important features, such as

✦ **It's standards-compliant.** It's good to check and make sure the basic XHTML code is well formed before you do a lot of CSS work with it. Sloppy XHTML can cause you major headaches later.

✦ **It contains four divs.** The parts of the page that will be moved later are all encased in div elements.

✦ **Each div has an ID.** All the divs have an ID determined from the sketch.

✦ **No formatting is in the XHTML.** The XHTML code contains no formatting at all. That's left to the CSS.

✦ **It has no style yet.** Although a <link> tag is pointing to a style sheet, the style is currently empty.

Figure 2-2 shows what the page looks like before you add any CSS to it.

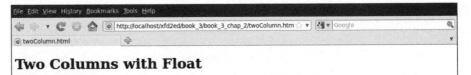

Figure 2-2:
The plain
XHTML
is plain
indeed;
some CSS
will come in
handy.

Adding preliminary CSS

You can write CSS in your editor, but the Web Developer toolbar's CSS editor is an especially handy tool because it allows you to see the effects of your CSS immediately. Here's how to use this tool:

1. **Use Firefox for your primary testing.**

Firefox has much better standards support than IE. Get your code working in Firefox first. Besides, the extremely handy Web Developer isn't available for Internet Explorer.

2. **Be sure the Web Developer toolbar is installed.**

See Chapter 3 of Book I for more information on this wonderful free tool. You use this tool to modify your CSS and see the results immediately in the Web browser.

3. **Activate the CSS editor by choosing Tools➪Edit CSS or pressing Ctrl+Shift+E.**

4. **Create CSS rules.**

Type the CSS rules in the provided window. Throughout this chapter, I show what rules you use and the order in which they go. The key thing about this editor is you can type a rule in the text window, and the page in the browser is immediately updated.

5. **Check the results.**

Watch the main page for interactive results. As soon as you finish a CSS rule, the Web page automatically refreshes, showing the results of your work.

6. **Save your work.**

The changes made during an edit session are temporary. If you specified a CSS file in your document, but it doesn't exist, the Save button automatically creates and saves that file.

Using temporary borders

And now for one of my favorite CSS tricks. . . . Before doing anything else, create a selector for each of the named divs and add a temporary border to each div. Make each border a different color. The CSS might look like this:

```css
#head {
  border: 1px black solid;
}

#left {
  border: 1px red solid;
}

#right {
  border: 1px blue solid;
}

#footer {
  border: 1px green solid;
}
```

You won't keep these borders, but they provide some very useful cues while you're working with the layout:

+ **Testing the selectors:** While you create a border around each selector, you can see whether you've remembered the selector's name correctly. It's amazing how many times I've written code that I thought was broken just because I didn't write the selector properly.

+ **Identifying the divs:** If you make each border a different color, it'll be easier to see which div is which when they begin to overlap.

+ **Specifying the size of each div:** The text inside a div isn't always a good indicator of the actual size. The border tells you what's really going on.

Of course, you won't leave these borders in place. They're just helpful tools for seeing what's going on during the design process. Look at `borders.html` and `borders.css` on the CD-ROM or Web site to see the full code.

Figure 2-3 displays how the page looks with the color borders turned on.

It's fine that you can't see the actual colors in the black-and-white image in Figure 2-3. Just appreciate that when you see the page in its full-color splendor, the various colors will help you see what's going on.

File Edit View History Bookmarks Tools Help

http://localhost/xfd2ed/book_3/book_3_chap_2/borders.html ☆ ▼ Google

borders.html

Two Columns with Float

Left Column

This is the left column. This is the left column.

Right Column

This is the right column. This is the right column. This is the right column. This is the right column. This is the right column. This is the right column. This is the right column. This is the right column. This is the right column. This is the right column. This is the right column. This is the right column. This is the right column. This is the right column. This is the right column. This is the right column. This is the right column. This is the right column. This is the right column. This is the right column.

Right Column

This is the right column. This is the right column. This is the right column. This is the right column. This is the right column. This is the right column. This is the right column. This is the right column. This is the right column. This is the right column. This is the right column. This is the right column. This is the right column. This is the right column. This is the right column. This is the right column. This is the right column. This is the right column. This is the right column. This is the right column.

Right Column

This is the right column. This is the right column. This is the right column. This is the right column. This is the right column. This is the right column. This is the right column. This is the right column.

Done   0 errors / 0 warnings

Figure 2-3: Colored borders make it easier to manipulate the divs.

Setting up the floating columns

This particular layout doesn't require major transformation. A few CSS rules will do the trick:

```
#head {
  border: 3px black solid;
}

#left {
  border: 3px red solid;
  float: left;
  width: 20%;
}

#right {
  border: 3px blue solid;
  float: left;
  width: 75%
}

#footer {
  border: 3px green solid;
  clear: both;
}
```

I made the following changes to the CSS:

+ **Float the #left div.** Set the #left div's float property to left so other divs (specifically the #right div) are moved to the right of it.

+ **Set the #left width.** When you float a div, you must also set its width. I've set the margin to 20 percent of the page width as a starting point.

+ **Float the #right div, too.** The right div can also be floated left, and it'll end up snug to the left div. Don't forget to add a width. I set the width of #right to 75 percent, leaving another 5 percent available for padding, margins, and borders.

+ **Clear the footer.** The footer should take up the entire width of the page, so set its clear property to both.

Figure 2-4 shows how the page looks with this style sheet in place (see floated.html and floated.css on the CD-ROM or Web site for complete code).

Tuning up the borders

The colored borders in Figure 2-4 point out some important features of this layout scheme. For instance, the two columns are not the same size. This can have important implications.

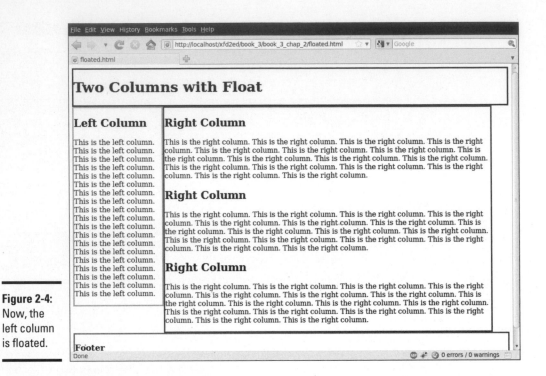

Figure 2-4:
Now, the
left column
is floated.

You can change the borders to make the page look more like a column layout. I'm going for a newspaper-style look, so I use simple double borders. I put a black border under the header, a gray border to the left of the right column, and a gray border on top of the bottom segment. Tweaking the padding and centering the footer complete the look. Here's the complete CSS:

```
#head {
  border-bottom: 3px double black;
}
#left {
  float: left;
  width: 20%;
}
#right {
  float: left;
  width: 75%;
  border-left: 3px double gray;
}
#footer {
  clear: both;
  text-align: center;
  border-top: 3px double gray;
}
```

The final effect is shown in Figure 2-5.

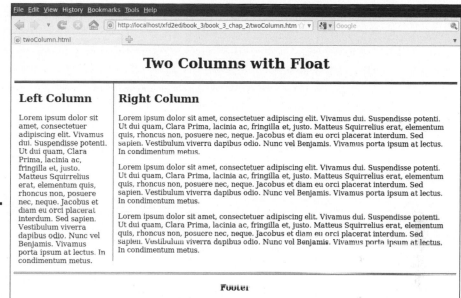

**Book III
Chapter 2**

Building Floating
Page Layouts

Figure 2-5:
This is a decent design, which adjusts with the page width.

Advantages of a fluid layout

This type of layout scheme (with floats) is often called a *fluid* layout because it has columns but the sizes of the columns are dependent on the browser width. This is an important issue because, unlike layout in the print world, you really have no idea what size the browser window that displays your page will be. Even if the user has a widescreen monitor, the browser may be in a much smaller window. Fluid layouts can adapt to this situation quite well.

Fluid layouts (and indeed all other float-based layouts) have another great advantage. If the user turns off CSS or can't use it, the page still displays. The elements will simply be printed in order vertically, rather than in the intended layout. This can be especially handy for screen readers or devices with exceptionally small screens, like phones and PDAs.

Building a Three-Column Design

Sometimes, you'll prefer a three-column design. It's a simple variation of the two-column approach. Figure 2-6 shows a simple three-column layout.

This design uses very basic CSS with five named divs. Here's the code (with the dummy paragraph text removed for space):

```
<!DOCTYPE html PUBLIC "-//W3C//DTD XHTML 1.0 Strict//EN"
"http://www.w3.org/TR/xhtml1/DTD/xhtml1-strict.dtd">
<html lang="EN" dir="ltr" xmlns="http://www.w3.org/1999/xhtml">
  <head>
    <meta http-equiv="content-type" content="text/xml; charset=utf-8" />
    <title>threeColumn.html</title>
    <link rel = "stylesheet"
          type = "text/css"
          href = "threeColumn.css" />
  </head>

  <body>
    <div id = "head">
      <h1>Three-Column Layout</h1>
    </div>

    <div id = "left">
      <h2>Left Column</h2>
    </div>

    <div id = "center">
      <h2>Center Column</h2>
    </div>

    <div id = "right">
      <h2>Right Column</h2>
    </div>

    <div id = "footer">
      <h3>Footer</h3>
    </div>
  </body>
</html>
```

Figure 2-6:
This is
a three-
column
floating
layout.

Styling the three-column page

As you can see from the HTML, there isn't really much to this page. It has five named divs, and that's about it. All the really exciting stuff happens in the CSS:

```
#head {
  text-align: center;
}

#left {
  float: left;
  width: 20%;
  padding-left: 1%;
}

#center {
  float: left;
  width: 60%;
  padding-left: 1%;
}

#right {
  float: left;
  width: 17%;
  padding-left: 1%;
}

#footer {
  border: 1px black solid;
  float: left;
  width: 100%;
  clear: both;
  text-align: center;
}
```

Each element (except the head) is floated with an appropriate width. The process for generating this page is similar to the two-column layout:

1. **Diagram the layout.**

   Begin with a general sense of how the page will look and the relative width of the columns. Include the names of all segments in this diagram.

2. **Create the XHTML framework.**

   Create all the necessary divs, including id attributes. Add representative text so you can see the overall texture of the page.

3. **Add temporary borders.**

   Add a temporary border to each element so you can see what's going on when you start messing with float attributes. This also ensures you have all the selectors spelled properly.

4. **Float the leftmost element.**

   Add the float attribute to the leftmost column. Don't forget to specify a width (in percentage).

5. **Check your work.**

   Work in the Web Developer CSS editor (where you can see changes on the fly) or frequently save your work and view it in a browser.

6. **Float the center element.**

   Add `float` and `width` attributes to the center element.

7. **Float the right-most element.**

   Incorporate `float` and `width` in the right element.

8. **Ensure the widths total around 95 percent.**

   You want the sum of the widths to be nearly 100 percent but not quite. Generally, you need a little space for margins and padding. Final adjustments come later, but you certainly don't want to take up more than 100 percent of the available real estate.

9. **Float and clear the footer.**

   To get the footer acting right, you need to float it and clear it on both margins. Set its width to 100 percent, if you want.

10. **Tune up.**

    Remove the temporary borders, adjust the margins and padding, and set alignment as desired. Use percentages for margins and padding, and then adjust so all percentages equal 100 percent.

Early versions of Internet Explorer (6 and earlier) have a well-documented problem with margins and padding. According to the standards, the width of an element is supposed to be the width of the *content,* with borders, margins, and padding outside. A properly behaved browser won't shrink your content when you add borders and margins. The early versions of Internet Explorer (IE) counted the width as *including* all borders, padding, and margin, effectively shrinking the content when you added these elements. If your page layout is looking a little off with IE, this may be the problem. Use the conditional comment technique described in Chapter 5 of Book II to make a variant style for IE if this bothers you.

Problems with the floating layout

The floating layout solution is very elegant, but it does have one drawback. Figure 2-7 shows the three-column page with the borders drawn around each element.

Figure 2-7 shows an important aspect of this type of layout. The columns are actually blocks, and each is a different height. Typically, I think of a column as stretching the entire height of a page, but this isn't how CSS does it. If you want to give each column a different background color, for example, you'll want each column to be the same height. This can be done with a CSS trick (at least, for the compliant browsers).

Figure 2-7:
The columns aren't really columns; each is a different height.

Specifying a min-height

The standards-compliant browsers (all versions of Firefox and Opera, and IE 7) support a `min-height` property. This specifies a minimum height for an element. You can use this property to force all columns to the same height. Figure 2-8 illustrates this effect.

The CSS code simply adds the `min-height` attribute to all the column elements:

```
#head {
  text-align: center;
  border-bottom: 3px double gray;
}

#left {
  float: left;
  width: 20%;
  min-height: 30em;
  background-color: #EEEEEE;
}

#center {
  float: left;
  width: 60%;
  padding-left: 1%;
  padding-right: 1%;
  min-height: 30em;
}

#right {
```

```
  float: left;
  width: 17%;
  padding-left: 1%;
  min-height: 30em;
  background-color: #EEEEEE;
}

#footer {
  border: 1px black solid;
  float: left;
  width: 100%;
  clear: both;
  text-align: center;
}
```

Some guesswork is involved still. You have to experiment a bit to determine what the min-height should be. If you guess too short, one column will be longer than the min-height, and the columns won't appear correctly. If you guess too tall, you'll have a lot of empty space at the bottom of the screen.

Unfortunately, the min-height trick works only with the latest browsers. IE versions 6 and earlier don't support this attribute. For these browsers, you may need a fixed-width layout.

Figure 2-8:
The min-height attribute forces all columns to be the same height.

Building a Fixed-Width Layout

Fluid layouts are terrific. They're very flexible, and they're not hard to build. Sometimes, though, it's nice to use a fixed-width layout, particularly if you want your layout to conform to a particular background image.

The primary attribute of a fixed-width layout is the use of a fixed measurement (almost always pixels), rather than the percentage measurements used in a fluid layout.

Figure 2-9 shows a two-column page with a nicely colored background.

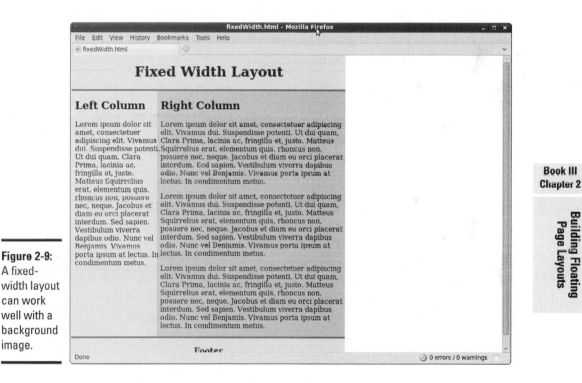

Figure 2-9: A fixed-width layout can work well with a background image.

Setting up the XHTML

As usual, the XHTML code is minimal. It contains a few named divs. (Like usual, I've removed filler text for space reasons.)

```
<!DOCTYPE html PUBLIC "-//W3C//DTD XHTML 1.0 Strict//EN"
"http://www.w3.org/TR/xhtml1/DTD/xhtml1-strict.dtd">
<html lang="EN" dir="ltr" xmlns="http://www.w3.org/1999/xhtml">
  <head>
    <meta http-equiv="content-type" content="text/xml; charset=utf-8" />
    <title>fixedWidth.html</title>
```

```
    <link rel = "stylesheet"
          type = "text/css"
          href = "fixedWidth.css" />
  </head>

  <body>
    <div id = "header">
      <h1>Fixed Width Layout</h1>
    </div>

    <div id = "left">
      <h2>Left Column</h2>
    </div>

    <div id = "right">
      <h2>Right Column</h2>
    </div>

    <div id = "footer">
      <h3>Footer</h3>
    </div>
  </body>
</html>
```

Using an image to simulate true columns

If you need to overcome the limitations of older browsers, you can use a
background image to simulate colored columns. Figure 2-10 shows the basic
background image I'm using for this page.

Figure 2-10:
This image
is repeated
vertically
to simulate
two
columns.

The image has been designed with two segments. The image is exactly 640
pixels wide, with one color spanning 200 pixels and the other 440 pixels.
When you know the exact width you're aiming for, you can position the columns to exactly that size. Here's the CSS code:

```
body {  background-image: url("fixedBG.gif");
  background-repeat: repeat-y;
}

#header {
  background-color: #e2e393;
  border-bottom: 3px double black;
  text-align: center;
  float: left;
  width: 640px;
```

```
    clear: both;
    margin-left: -8px;
    margin-top: -10px;
}

#left {
    float: left;
    width: 200px;
    clear: left;
}

#right {
    float: left;
    width: 440px;
}

#footer {
    float: left;
    width: 640px;
    clear: both;
    text-align: center;
    background-color: #e2e393;
    margin-left:-8px;
    border-top: 3px double black;
}
```

This code works a lot like the other floating layouts, except for the following changes:

+ **The body has a background image attached.** I attached the two-color background image to the entire body. This makes the page look like it has two columns. Remember to set the `background-repeat` attribute to `repeat-y` so the background repeats indefinitely in the vertical *y*-axis.

+ **The header and footer areas need background colors or images defined so the *fake* columns don't appear to stretch underneath these segments.**

+ **Header and footer will need some margin adjustments.** The browsers tend to put a little bit of margin on the header and footer divs, so compensate by setting negative values for `margin-left` on these elements.

+ **All measurements are now in pixels.** This will ensure that the layout corresponds to the image, also measured in pixels.

If you use a fixed-width layout and the user changes the font size, the results will be unpredictable. A fluid layout will change with the font size, but a fixed layout may have problems rendering a larger font in the indicated space.

Building a Centered Fixed-Width Layout

Fixed-width layouts are common, but they look a little strange if the browser isn't the width specified in the CSS. If the browser is too narrow, the layout won't work, and the second column will (usually) drop down to the next line.

If the browser is too wide, the page will appear to be scrunched onto the left margin with a great deal of white space on the right.

The natural solution would be to make a relatively narrow fixed-width design that's centered inside the entire page. Figure 2-11 illustrates a page with this technique.

Some have called this type of design (fixed-width floating centered in the browser) a *jello* layout because it's not quite fluid and not quite fixed.

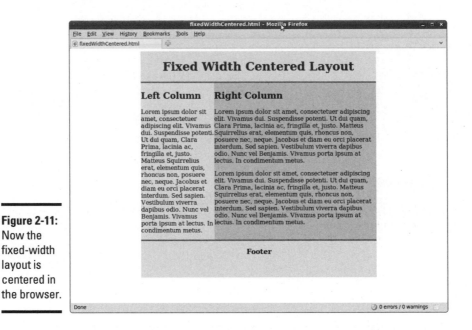

Figure 2-11: Now the fixed-width layout is centered in the browser.

Making a surrogate body with an all div

In any case, the HTML requires only one new element, an `all` div that encases everything else inside the body (as usual, I removed the placeholder text):

```
<!DOCTYPE html PUBLIC "-//W3C//DTD XHTML 1.0 Strict//EN"
"http://www.w3.org/TR/xhtml1/DTD/xhtml1-strict.dtd">
<html lang="EN" dir="ltr" xmlns="http://www.w3.org/1999/xhtml">
  <head>
    <meta http-equiv="content-type" content="text/xml; charset=utf-8" />
    <title>fixedWidthCentered.html</title>
    <link rel = "stylesheet"
          type = "text/css"
          href = "fixedWidthCentered.css" />
  </head>

  <body>
    <div id = "all">
```

```
      <div id = "header">
        <h1>Fixed Width Centered Layout</h1>
      </div>

      <div id = "left">
        <h2>Left Column</h2>
      </div>

      <div id = "right">
        <h2>Right Column</h2>
      </div>

      <div id = "footer">
        <h3>Footer</h3>
      </div>
    </div>
  </body>
</html>
```

The entire page contents are now encapsulated in a special `all` div. This div will be resized to a standard width (typically 640 or 800 pixels). The `all` element will be centered in the body, and the other elements will be placed inside `all` as if it were the body:

```css
#all {
  background-image: url("fixedBG.gif");
  background-repeat: repeat-y;
  width: 640px;
  height: 600px;
  margin-left: auto;
  margin-right: auto;
}

#header {
  background-color: #e2e393;
  border-bottom: 3px double black;
  text-align: center;
  float: left;
  width: 640px;
  clear: both;
}

#left {
  float: left;
  width: 200px;
  clear: left;
}

#right {
  float: left;
  width: 440px;
}

#footer {
  float: left;
  width: 640px;
  clear: both;
  text-align: center;
  background-color: #e2e393;
  border-top: 3px double black;
}
```

How the jello layout works

This code is very similar to the `fixedWidth.css` style, but it has some important new features:

- **The background image is now applied to `all`.** The `all` div is now acting as a surrogate body element, so the background image is applied to it instead of the background.

- **The `all` element has a fixed width.** This element's width will determine the width of the fixed part of the page.

- **`all` also needs a fixed height.** If you don't specify a height, `all` will be 0 pixels tall because all the elements inside it are floated. Set the height large enough to make the background image extend as far down as necessary.

- **Center `all`.** Remember, to center divs (or any other block-level elements) you set `margin-left` and `margin-right` both to `auto`.

- **Do *not* float `all`.** The `margin: auto` trick doesn't work on floated elements. `all` shouldn't have a `float` attribute set.

- **Ensure the interior widths add up to `all`'s width.** If `all` has a width of 640 pixels, be sure that the widths, borders, and margins of all the elements inside `all` add up to exactly 640 pixels. If you go even one pixel over, something will spill over and mess up the effect.

Limitations of the jello layout

Jello layouts represent a compromise between fixed and fluid layouts, but they aren't perfect:

- **Implicit minimum width:** Very narrow browsers (like cellphones) can't render the layout at all. Fortunately, these browsers usually allow you to turn off CSS, so the page will still be visible.

- **Wasted screen space:** If you make the rendered part of the page narrow, a lot of space isn't being used in higher-resolution browsers. This can be frustrating.

- **Complexity:** Although this layout technique is far simpler than table-based layouts, it's still a bit involved. You do have to plan your divs to make this type of layout work.

- **Browser support:** Layout is an area where little differences in browser implementations can lead to big headaches. Be prepared to use conditional comments to handle inconsistencies, like IE's strange margin and padding support.

Chapter 3: Styling Lists and Menus

In This Chapter

✓ Using CSS styles with lists

✓ Building buttons from lists of links

✓ Dynamically displaying sublists

✓ Managing vertical and horizontal lists

✓ Building CSS-based menus

*M*ost pages consist of content and navigation tools. Almost all pages have a list of links somewhere on the page. Navigation menus are lists of links, but lists of links in plain HTML are ugly. There has to be a way to make 'em prettier.

It's remarkably easy to build solid navigation tools with CSS alone (at least, in the modern browsers that support CSS properly). In this chapter, you rescue your lists from the boring 1990s sensibility, turning them into dynamic buttons, horizontal lists, and even dynamically cascading menus.

Revisiting List Styles

XHTML does provide some default list styling, but it's pretty dull. You often want to improve the appearance of a list of data. Most site navigation is essentially a list of links. One easy trick is to make your links appear as a set of buttons, as shown in Figure 3-1.

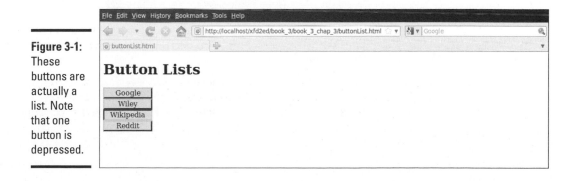

Figure 3-1: These buttons are actually a list. Note that one button is depressed.

The buttons in Figure 3-1 are pretty nice. They look like buttons, with the familiar three-dimensional look of buttons. They also act like buttons, with each button *depressing* when the mouse hovers over it. When you click one of these buttons, it acts like a link, taking you to another page.

Defining navigation as a list of links

If you look at the HTML, you'll be astonished at its simplicity:

```
<!DOCTYPE html PUBLIC "-//W3C//DTD XHTML 1.0 Strict//EN"
"http://www.w3.org/TR/xhtml1/DTD/xhtml1-strict.dtd">
<html lang="EN" dir="ltr" xmlns="http://www.w3.org/1999/xhtml">
  <head>
    <meta http-equiv="content-type" content="text/xml; charset=utf-8" />
    <title>buttonList.html</title>
    <link rel = "stylesheet"
          type = "text/css"
          href = "buttonList.css" />
  </head>

  <body>
    <h1>Button Lists</h1>
    <div id = "menu">
      <ul>
        <li><a href = "http://www.google.com">Google</a></li>
        <li><a href = "http://www.wiley.com">Wiley</a></li>
        <li><a href = "http://www.wikipedia.org">Wikipedia</a></li>
        <li><a href = "http://www.reddit.com">Reddit</a></li>
      </ul>
    </div>
  </body>
</html>
```

Turning links into buttons

As far as the XHTML code is concerned, it's simply a list of links. There's nothing special here that makes this act like a group of buttons, except the creation of a div called menu. All the real work is done in CSS:

```
#menu li {
  list-style-type: none;
  width: 7em;
  text-align: center;
  margin-left: -2.5em;
}

#menu a {
  text-decoration: none;
  color: black;
  display: block;
  border: 3px blue outset;
  background-color: #CCCCFF;
}

#menu a:hover {
  border: 3px blue inset;
}
```

The process for turning an ordinary list of links into a button group like this is simply an application of CSS tricks:

1. **Begin with an ordinary list that will validate properly.**

It doesn't matter if you use an unordered or ordered list. Typically, the list will contain anchors to other pages. In this example, I'm using this list of links to some popular Web sites:

```
<div id = "menu">
  <ul>
    <li><a href = "http://www.google.com">Google</a></li>
    <li><a href = "http://www.wiley.com">Wiley</a></li>
    <li><a href = "http://www.wikipedia.org">Wikipedia</a></li>
    <li><a href = "http://www.reddit.com">Reddit</a></li>
  </ul>
</div>
```

2. **Enclose the list in a named div.**

Typically, you still have ordinary links on a page. To indicate that these menu links should be handled differently, put them in a div named `menu`. All the CSS-style tricks described here refer to lists and anchors only when they're inside a `menu` div.

3. **Remove the bullets by setting the `list-style-type` to `none`.**

This removes the bullets or numbers that usually appear in a list because these features distract from the effect you're aiming for (a group of buttons). Use CSS to specify how list items should be formatted when they appear in the context of the menu ID:

```
#menu li {
  list-style-type: none;
  width: 5em;
  text-align: center;
  margin-left: -2.5em;
}
```

4. **Specify the width of each button:**

```
width: 5em;
```

A group of buttons looks best if they're all the same size. Use the CSS `width` attribute to set each `li` to 5em.

5. **Remove the margin by using a negative `margin-left` value, as shown here:**

```
margin-left: -2.5em;
```

Lists have a default indentation of about 2.5em to make room for the bullets or numbers. Because this list won't have bullets, it doesn't need the indentations. Overwrite the default indenting behavior by setting `margin-left` to a negative value.

6. **Clean up the anchor by setting `text-decoration` to `none` and setting the anchor's color to something static, such as black text on light blue in this example:**

**Book III
Chapter 3**

**Styling Lists and
Menus**

```
#menu a {
  text-decoration: none;
  color: black;
  display: block;
  border: 3px blue outset;
  background-color: #CCCCFF;
}
```

The button's appearance will make it clear that users can click it, so this is one place you can remove the underlining that normally goes with links.

7. Give each button an outset border, as shown in the following:

```
border: 3px blue outset;
```

The outset makes it look like a 3D button sticking out from the page. This is best attached to the anchor, so you can swap the border when the mouse is hovering over the button.

8. Set the anchor's `display` to `block`.

This is a sneaky trick. Block display normally makes an element act like a block-level element inside its container. In the case of an anchor, the entire button becomes clickable, not just the text. This makes your page easier to use:

```
display: block;
```

9. Swap for an inset border when the mouse hovers on an anchor by using the `#menu a:hover` selector to change the border to an inset:

```
#menu a:hover {
  border: 3px blue inset;
}
```

When the mouse hovers on the button, it appears to be pressed down, enhancing the 3D effect.

This list makes an ideal navigation menu, especially when placed inside one column of a multicolumn floating layout.

The inset/outset border trick is easy, but the results are a tad ugly. If you prefer, you can build two empty button images (one up and one down) in your image editor and simply swap the background images rather than the borders.

Building horizontal lists

Sometimes, you want horizontal button bars. Because XHTML lists tend to be vertical, you might be tempted to think that a horizontal list is impossible. In fact, CSS provides all you need to convert exactly the same XHTML to a horizontal list. Figure 3-2 shows such a page.

Figure 3-2:
This list uses
the same
XHTML but
different
CSS.

Button Lists

| Google | Wiley | Wikipedia | Reddit |

There's no need to show the XHTML again because it hasn't changed at all (ain't CSS grand?). Even the CSS hasn't changed much:

```
#menu ul {
  margin-left: -2.5em;
}

#menu li {
  list-style-type: none;
  float: left;
  width: 5em;
  text-align: center;
}

#menu a {
  text-decoration: none;
  color: black;
  display: block;
  border: 3px blue outset;
  background-color: #CCCCFF;
}

#menu a:hover {
  border: 3px blue inset;
}
```

The modifications are incredibly simple:

1. **Float each list item by giving each `li` a `float:left` value:**

```
#menu li {
  list-style-type: none;
  float: left;
  width: 5em;
  text-align: center;
}
```

2. **Move the `margin-left` of the entire `ul` by taking the `margin-left` formatting from the `li` elements and transferring it to the `ul`:**

```
#menu ul {
  margin-left: -2.5em;
}
```

3. **Add a horizontal element.**

Now that the button bar is horizontal, it makes more sense to put in some type of horizontal page element. For example, you may want to use this type of element inside a `heading` div.

Creating Dynamic Lists

A simple list of buttons can look better than ordinary XHTML links, but sometimes, your page needs to have a more complex navigation scheme. For example, you may want to create a menu system to help the user see the structure of your site.

When you think of a complex hierarchical organization (which is how most multipage Web sites end up), the easiest way to describe the structure is in a set of *nested* lists. XHTML lists can contain other lists, and this can be a great way to organize data.

Nested lists are a great way to organize a lot of information, but they can be complicated. You can use some special tricks to make parts of your list appear and disappear when needed. In the sections "Hiding the inner lists" and "Getting the inner lists to appear on cue," later in this chapter, you expand this technique to build a menu system for your pages.

Building a nested list

Begin by creating a system of nested lists without any CSS at all. Figure 3-3 shows a page with a basic nested list.

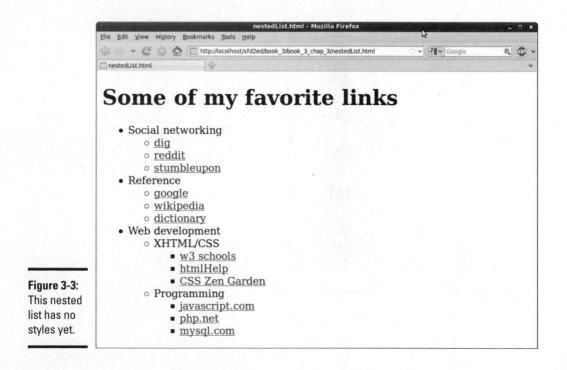

Figure 3-3: This nested list has no styles yet.

No CSS styling is in place yet, but the list has its own complexities:

✦ **The primary list has three entries.** This is actually a multilayer list. The top level indicates categories, not necessarily links.

✦ **Each element in the top list has its own sublist.** A second layer of links has various links in most elements.

✦ **The Web Development element has another layer of sublists.** The general layout of this list entry corresponds to a complex hierarchy of information — like most complex Web sites.

✦ **The list validates to the XHTML Strict standard.** It's especially important to validate your code before adding CSS when it involves somewhat complex XHTML code, like the multilevel list. A small problem in the XHTML structure that may go unnoticed in a plain XHTML document can cause all kinds of strange problems in your CSS.

Here is the code for the nested list in plain XHTML:

```
<!DOCTYPE html PUBLIC "-//W3C//DTD XHTML 1.0 Strict//EN"
"http://www.w3.org/TR/xhtml1/DTD/xhtml1-strict.dtd">
<html lang="EN" dir="ltr" xmlns="http://www.w3.org/1999/xhtml">
  <head>
    <meta http-equiv="content-type" content="text/xml; charset=utf-8" />
    <title>nestedList.html</title>
  </head>

  <body>
    <h1>Some of my favorite links</h1>
    <ul>
      <li>Social networking
        <ul>
          <li><a href = "http://www.digg.com">digg</a></li>
          <li><a href = "http://www.reddit.com">reddit</a></li>
          <li><a href = "http://www.stumbleupon.com">stumbleupon</a></li>
        </ul>
      </li>
      <li>Reference
        <ul>
          <li><a href = "http://www.google.com">google</a></li>
          <li><a href = "http://wikipedia.org">wikipedia</a></li>
          <li><a href = "http://dictionary.com">dictionary</a></li>
        </ul>
      </li>
      <li>Web development
        <ul>
          <li>XHTML/CSS
            <ul>
              <li><a href = "http://www.w3schools.com">w3 schools</a></li>
              <li><a href = "http://htmlhelp.com">htmlHelp</a></li>
              <li><a href = "http://www.csszengarden.com">CSS Zen Garden</a></li>
            </ul>
          </li>
          <li>Programming
            <ul>
              <li><a href = "http://javascript.com">javascript.com</a></li>
              <li><a href = "http://php.net">php.net</a></li>
              <li><a href = "http://www.mysql.com">mysql.com</a></li>
            </ul>
```

**Book III
Chapter 3**

Styling Lists and Menus

```
            </li>
          </ul>
        </li>
      </ul>
    </body>
</html>
```

Take special care with your indentation when making a complex nested list like this one. Without proper indentation, it becomes very difficult to establish the structure of the page. Also, a list item can contain text and another list. Any other arrangement (putting text between list items, for example) will cause a validation error and big headaches when you try to apply CSS.

Hiding the inner lists

The first step of creating a dynamic menu system is to hide any lists that are embedded in a list item. Add the following CSS style to your page:

```
li ul {
  display: none;
}
```

In reality, you usually apply this technique only to a specially marked div, like a menu system. Don't worry about that for now. Later in this chapter, I show you how to combine this technique with a variation of the button technique for complex menu systems.

Your page will undergo a startling transformation, as shown in Figure 3-4.

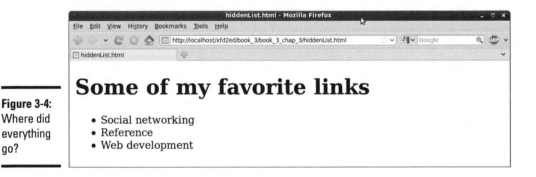

Figure 3-4:
Where did everything go?

That tiny little snippet of CSS code is a real powerhouse. It does some fascinating things, such as

+ **Operating on unordered lists that appear inside list items:** What this really means is the topmost list won't be affected, but any unordered list that appears inside a list item will have the style applied.

+ **Using `display: none` to make text disappear:** Setting the `display` attribute to `none` tells the XHTML page to hide the given data altogether.

This code works well on almost all browsers. It's pretty easy to make text disappear. Unfortunately, it's a little trickier to make all the browsers bring it back.

Getting the inner lists to appear on cue

The fun part is getting the interior lists to pop up when the mouse is over the parent element. A second CSS style can make this happen:

```
li ul {
  display: none;
}

li:hover ul {
  display: block;
}
```

The new code is pretty interesting. When the page initially loads, It appears the same as what's shown in Figure 3-4, but see the effect of holding the mouse over the Social Networking element in Figure 3-5.

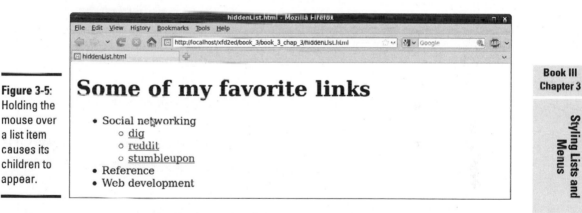

Figure 3-5:
Holding the mouse over a list item causes its children to appear.

This code doesn't work on all browsers! Internet Explorer 6 (IE6) and earlier versions don't support the :hover pseudo-class on any element except a. Provide a conditional comment with an alternative style for early versions of IE. All modern browsers (including IE 7 and 8) work fine.

Here's how the list-reappearing code works:

✦ **All lists inside lists are hidden.** The first style rule hides any list that's inside a list element.

✦ **li:hover refers to a list item that's being hovered on.** That is, if the mouse is situated on top of a list item, this rule pertains to it.

✦ **li:hover ul refers to an unordered list inside a hovered list item.** In other words, if some content is an unordered list that rests inside a list that currently has the mouse hovering over it, apply this rule. *(Whew!)*

✦ **Display the list as a block.** `display:block` overrides the previous `display:none` instruction and displays the particular element as a block. The text reappears magically.

This hide-and-seek trick isn't all that great on its own. It's actually quite annoying to have the contents pop up and go away like that. There's another more annoying problem. Look at Figure 3-6 to see what can go wrong.

To see why this happens, take another look at the CSS code that causes the segment to reappear:

```
li:hover ul {
  display: block;
}
```

This code means set display to block for any `ul` that's a child of a hovered `li`. The problem is that the Web Development `li` contains a `ul` that contains *two more* `ul`s. All the lists under Web Development appear, not just the immediate child.

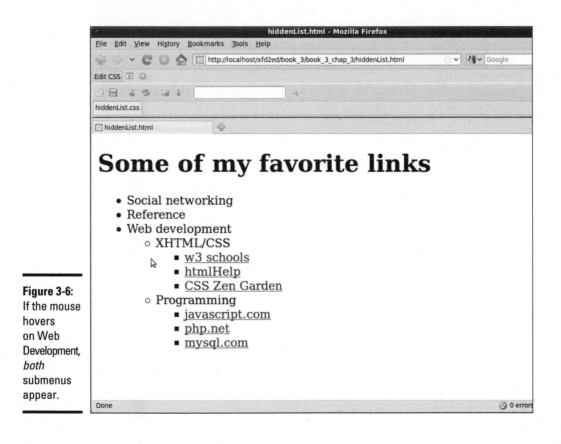

Figure 3-6:
If the mouse hovers on Web Development, *both* submenus appear.

One more modification of the CSS fixes this problem:

```
li ul {
  display: none;
}

li:hover > ul {
  display: block;
}
```

The greater than symbol (>) is a special selector tool. It indicates a direct relationship. In other words, the ul must be a direct child of the hovered li, not a grandchild or great-grandchild. With this indicator in place, the page acts correctly, as shown in Figure 3-7.

Book III
Chapter 3

Styling Lists and Menus

Figure 3-7:
Now, only the next menu level shows up on a mouse hover.

This trick allows you to create nested lists as deeply as you wish and to open any segment by hovering on its parent.

My current code has a list with three levels of nesting, but you can add as many nested lists as you want and use this code to make it act as a dynamic menu.

Figure 3-8 illustrates how to open the next section of the list.

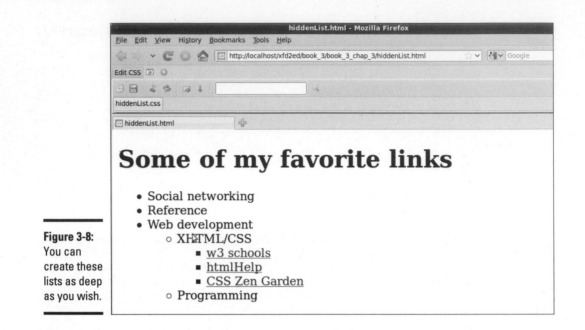

Figure 3-8:
You can
create these
lists as deep
as you wish.

I'm not suggesting that this type of menu is a good idea. Having stuff pop around like this is actually pretty distracting. With a little more formatting, you can use these ideas to make a functional menu system. I'm just starting here so you can see the hide-and-seek behavior in a simpler system before adding more details.

Building a Basic Menu System

You can combine the techniques of buttons and collapsing lists to build a menu system entirely with CSS. Figure 3-9 shows a page with a vertically arranged menu.

When the user hovers over a part of the menu, the related subelements appear, as shown in Figure 3-10.

This type of menu has a couple interesting advantages, such as:

✦ **It's written entirely with CSS.** You don't need any other code or programming language.

✦ **The menus are simply nested lists.** The XHTML is simply a set of nested lists. If the CSS turns off, the page is displayed as a set of nested lists, and the links still function normally.

✦ **The relationships between elements are illustrated.** When you select an element, you can see its parent and sibling relationships easily.

Figure 3-9:
Only the
top-level
elements
are visible
by default.

Figure 3-10:
The user
can select
any part of
the original
nested list.

WARNING!

Nice as this type of menu system is, it isn't perfect. Because it relies on the
`li:hover` trick, it doesn't work in versions of Internet Explorer (IE) prior to
7.0. You need alternate CSS for these users.

Building a vertical menu with CSS

The vertical menu system works with exactly the same HTML as the `hidden List` example — only the CSS changed. Here's the new CSS file:

```css
/* horizMenu.css */
/* unindent entire list */
#menu ul {
  margin-left: -2.5em;
}

/* set li as buttons */
#menu li {
  list-style-type: none;
  border: 1px black solid;;
  width: 10em;
  background-color: #cccccc;
  text-align: center;
}

/* display anchors as buttons */
#menu a {
  color: black;
  text-decoration: none;
  display: block;
}

/* flash white on anchor hover */
#menu a:hover {
  background-color: white;
}

/* collapse menus */
#menu li ul {
  display: none;
}

/* show submenus on hover */
#menu li:hover > ul {
  display: block;
  margin-left: -2em;
}
```

Of course, the CSS uses a few tricks, but there's really nothing new. It's just a combination of techniques you already know:

1. **Un-indent the entire list by setting the `ul`'s `margin-left` to a negative value to compensate for the typical indentation. `2.5em` is about the right amount.**

Because you're removing the `list-style` types, the normal indentation of list items will become a problem.

2. **Format the li tags.**

   Each li tag inside the menu structure should look something like a button. Use CSS to accomplish this task:

   ```
   /* set li as buttons */
   #menu li {
     list-style-type: none;
     border: 1px black solid;;
     width: 10em;
     background-color: #cccccc;
     text-align: center;
   }
   ```

   a. *Set* list-style-type *to none.*

   b. *Set a border with the* border *attribute.*

   c. *Center the text by setting* text-align *to* center.

   d. *Add a background color or image, or you'll get some strange border bleed-through later when the buttons overlap.*

3. **Format the anchors as follows:**

   ```
   /* display anchors as buttons */
   #menu a {
     color: black;
     text-decoration: none;
     display: block;
   }
   ```

   a. *Take out the underline with* text-decoration: none.

   b. *Give the anchor a consistent color.*

   c. *Set* display *to* block *(so the entire area will be clickable, not just the text).*

4. **Give some indication it's an anchor by changing the background when the user hovers on the element:**

   ```
   /* flash white on anchor hover */
   #menu a:hover {
     background-color: white;
   }
   ```

   Because the anchors no longer look like anchors, you have to do something else to indicate there's something special about these elements. When the user moves the mouse over any anchor tag in the menu div, that anchor's background color will switch to white.

5. **Collapse the menus using the hidden menus trick (discussed in the section "Hiding the inner lists," earlier in this chapter) to hide all the sublists:**

   ```
   /* collapse menus *#menu li ul {
     display: none;
   }
   ```

6. **Display the hidden menus when the mouse hovers on the parent element by adding the code described in the "Getting the inner lists to appear on cue" section:**

```
/* show submenus on hover */
#menu li:hover > ul {
  display: block;
  margin-left: -2em;
}
```

This trick won't work on IE6 or earlier versions. You have to provide an alternate style sheet (with conditional commenting) or a JavaScript technique for these earlier browsers.

Building a horizontal menu

You can make a variation of the menu structure that will work along the top of a page. Figure 3-11 shows how this might look.

The submenus come straight down from their parent elements. I find a little bit of indentation helpful for deeply nested lists, as shown in Figure 3-12.

Again, the HTML is identical. The CSS for a horizontal menu is surprisingly close to the vertical menu. The primary difference is floating the list items:

```
/* vertMenu.css */
/* unindent each unordered list */

#menu ul {
  margin-left: -2.5em;
}

/* turn each list item into a solid gray block */
#menu li {
  list-style-type: none;
  border: black solid 1px;
  float: left;
  width: 10em;
  background-color: #CCCCCC;
  text-align: center;
}

/* set anchors to act like buttons */
#menu a {
  display: block;
  color: black;
  text-decoration: none;
}

/* flash anchor white when hovered */
#menu a:hover {
  background-color: white;
}

/* collapse nested lists */
```

```
#menu li ul {
  display: none;
}

/* display sublists on hover */
#menu li:hover > ul {
  display: block;
}

/* indent third-generation lists */
#menu li li li{
  margin-left: 1em;
}
```

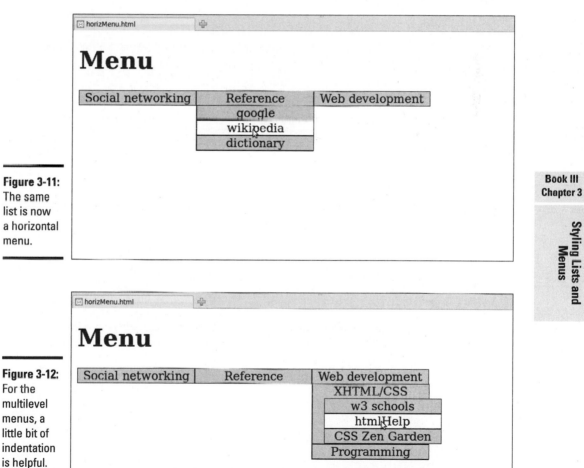

Figure 3-11:
The same
list is now
a horizontal
menu.

Figure 3-12:
For the
multilevel
menus, a
little bit of
indentation
is helpful.

The CSS code has just a few variations from the vertical menu CSS:

✦ Float each list item by adding `float` and `width` attributes.

```
/* turn each list item into a solid gray block */
#menu li {
  list-style-type: none;
  border: black solid 1px;
  float: left;
  width: 10em;
  background-color: #CCCCCC;
  text-align: center;
}
```

This causes the list items to appear next to each other in the same line.

✦ Give each list item a width. In this case, `10em` seems about right.

✦ Indent a deeply nested list by having the first-order sublists appear directly below the parent.

A list nested deeper than its parent is hard to read. A little indentation helps a lot with clarity.

✦ Use `#menu li li li` to indent nested list items, as shown here:

```
/* indent third-generation lists */
#menu li li li{
  margin-left: 1em;
}
```

This selector is active on an element which has `#menu` and three list items in its *family tree*. It will work only on list items three levels deep. This special formatting isn't needed at the other levels but is helpful to offset the third-level list items.

These tricks are just the beginning of what you can do with some creativity and the amazing power of CSS and HTML. You can adopt the simple examples presented here to create your own marvels of navigation.

These menu systems work pretty well, but if they're used in a standard layout system, the rest of the page can shift around to fit the changing shape of the menus. To avoid this, place the menu using the fixed mechanisms described in Chapter 4 of this minibook.

Chapter 4: Using Alternative Positioning

In This Chapter

✓ Setting position to absolute

✓ Managing z-index

✓ Creating fixed and flexible layouts

✓ Working with fixed and relative positioning

*F*loating layouts (described in Chapter 3 of this minibook) are the preferred way to set up page layouts today but, sometimes, other alternatives are useful. You can use *absolute, relative, or fixed positioning* techniques to put all your page elements exactly where you want them. Well, *almost* exactly. It's still Web development, where nothing's exact.

Still, the techniques described in this chapter will give you even more capabilities when it comes to setting up great-looking Web sites.

Working with Absolute Positioning

Begin by considering the default layout mechanism. Figure 4-1 shows a page with two paragraphs on it.

I used CSS to give each paragraph a different color (to aid in discussion later) and to set a specific height and width. The positioning is left to the default layout manager, which positions the second (black) paragraph directly below the first (blue) one.

Figure 4-1:
These two paragraphs have a set height and width, but default positioning.

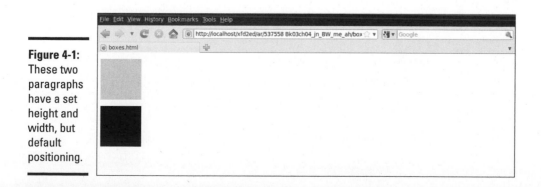

Setting up the HTML

The code is unsurprising:

```
<!DOCTYPE html PUBLIC "-//W3C//DTD XHTML 1.0 Strict//EN"
"http://www.w3.org/TR/xhtml1/DTD/xhtml1-strict.dtd">
<html lang="EN" dir="ltr" xmlns="http://www.w3.org/1999/xhtml">
  <head>
    <meta http-equiv="content-type" content="text/xml; charset=utf-8" />
    <title>boxes.html</title>
    <style type = "text/css">
      #blueBox {
        background-color: blue;
        width: 100px;
        height: 100px;
      }
      #blackBox {
        background-color: black;
        width: 100px;
        height: 100px;
      }
    </style>
  </head>

  <body>
    <p id = "blueBox"></p>
    <p id = "blackBox"></p>
  </body>
</html>
```

If you provide no further guidance, paragraphs (like other block-level elements) tend to provide carriage returns before and after themselves, stacking on top of each other. The default layout techniques ensure that nothing ever overlaps.

Adding position guidelines

Figure 4-2 shows something new: The paragraphs are overlapping!

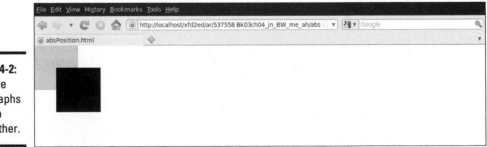

Figure 4-2:
Now the paragraphs overlap each other.

This feat is accomplished through some new CSS attributes:

```
<!DOCTYPE html PUBLIC "-//W3C//DTD XHTML 1.0 Strict//EN"
"http://www.w3.org/TR/xhtml1/DTD/xhtml1-strict.dtd">
```

```
<html lang="EN" dir="ltr" xmlns="http://www.w3.org/1999/xhtml">
  <head>
    <meta http-equiv="content-type" content="text/xml; charset=utf-8" />
    <title>absPosition.html</title>
    <style type = "text/css">

      #blueBox {
        background-color: blue;
        width: 100px;
        height: 100px;
        position: absolute;
        left: 0px;
        top: 0px;
        margin: 0px;
      }
      #blackBox {
        background-color: black;
        width: 100px;
        height: 100px;
        position: absolute;
        left: 50px;
        top: 50px;
        margin: 0px;
      }
    </style>
  </head>

  <body>
    <p id = "blueBox"></p>
    <p id = "blackBox"></p>
  </body>
</html>
```

Book III
Chapter 4

Using Alternative
Positioning

So, why do I care if the boxes overlap? Well, you might not care, but the interesting part is this: You can have much more precise control over where elements live and what size they are. You can even override the browser's normal tendency to keep elements from overlapping, which gives you some interesting options.

Making absolute positioning work

A few new parts of CSS allow this more direct control of the size and position of these elements. Here's the CSS for one of the boxes:

```
#blueBox {
  background-color: blue;
  width: 100px;
  height: 100px;
  position: absolute;
  left: 0px;
  top: 0px;
  margin: 0px;
}
```

1. Set the position attribute to absolute.

Absolute positioning can be used to determine exactly (more or less) where the element will be placed on the screen:

```
position: absolute;
```

2. **Specify a `left` position in the CSS.**

   After you determine that an element will have `absolute` position, it's removed from the normal flow, so you're obligated to fix its position. The `left` attribute determines where the left edge of the element will go. This can be specified with any of the measurement units, but it's typically measured in pixels:

   ```
   left: 0px;
   ```

3. **Specify a `top` position with CSS.**

   The `top` attribute indicates where the top of the element will go. Again, this is usually specified in pixels:

   ```
   top: 0px;
   ```

4. **Use the `height` and `width` attributes to determine the size.**

   Normally, when you specify a position, you also want to determine the size:

   ```
   width: 100px;
   height: 100px;
   ```

5. **Set the margins to 0.**

   When you're using absolute positioning, you're exercising quite a bit of control. Because browsers don't treat margins identically, you're better off setting margins to 0 and controlling the spacing between elements manually:

   ```
   margin: 0px;
   ```

Generally, you use absolute positioning only on named elements, rather than classes or general element types. For example, you won't want all the paragraphs on a page to have the same size and position, or you couldn't see them all. Absolute positioning works on only one element at a time.

Managing z-index

When you use absolute positioning, you can determine exactly where things are placed, so it's possible for them to overlap. By default, elements described later in HTML are positioned on top of elements described earlier. This is why the black box appears over the top of the blue box in Figure 4-2.

Handling depth

You can use a special CSS attribute called `z-index` to change this default behavior. The *z*-axis refers to how close an element appears to be to the viewer. Figure 4-3 demonstrates how this works.

Figure 4-3:
The z-index allows you to change which elements appear closer to the user.

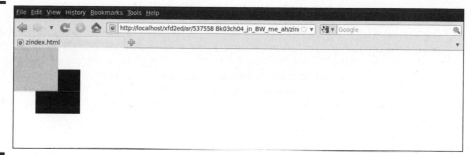

The z-index attribute requires a numeric value. Higher numbers mean the element is closer to the user (or on *top*). Any value for z-index places the element higher than elements with the default z-index. This can be very useful when you have elements that you want to appear over the top of other elements (for example, menus that temporarily appear on top of other text).

Here's the code illustrating the z-index effect:

```
<!DOCTYPE html PUBLIC "-//W3C//DTD XHTML 1.0 Strict//EN"
"http://www.w3.org/TR/xhtml1/DTD/xhtml1-strict.dtd">
<html lang="EN" dir="ltr" xmlns="http://www.w3.org/1999/xhtml">
  <head>
    <meta http-equiv="content-type" content="text/xml; charset=utf-8" />
    <title>zindex.html</title>
    <style type = "text/css">

      #blueBox {
        background-color: blue;
        width: 100px;
        height: 100px;
        position: absolute;
        left: 0px;
        top: 0px;
        margin: 0px;
        z-index: 1;
      }
      #blackBox {
        background-color: black;
        width: 100px;
        height: 100px;
        position: absolute;
        left: 50px;
        top: 50px;
        margin: 0px;
      }
    </style>
  </head>

  <body>
    <p id = "blueBox"></p>
    <p id = "blackBox"></p>
  </body>
</html>
```

Working with z-index

The only change in this code is the addition of the z-index property. Here are a couple things to keep in mind when using z-index:

✦ **One element can totally conceal another.** When you start positioning things absolutely, one element can seem to disappear because it's completely covered by another. The z-index attribute is a good way to check for this situation.

✦ **Negative z-index is undefined.** The value for z-index must be positive. A negative value is undefined and may cause your element to disappear.

✦ **It may be best to give all values a z-index.** If you define the z-index for some elements and leave the z-index undefined for others, you have no guarantee exactly what will happen. If in doubt, just give every value its own z-index, and you'll know exactly what should overlap what.

✦ **Don't give two elements the same z-index.** The point of the z-index is to clearly define which element should appear closer. Don't defeat this purpose by assigning the same z-index value to two different elements on the same page.

Building a Page Layout with Absolute Positioning

You can use absolute positioning to create a page layout. This process involves some trade-offs. You tend to get better control of your page with absolute positioning (compared to floating techniques), but absolute layout requires more planning and more attention to detail. Figure 4-4 shows a page layout created with absolute positioning techniques.

The technique for creating an absolutely positioned layout is similar to the floating technique (in the general sense).

Overview of absolute layout

Before you begin putting your page together with absolute positioning, it's good to plan the entire process. Here's an example of how the process should go:

1. **Plan the site.**

Having a drawing that specifies how your site layout will look is really important. In absolute positioning, your planning is even more important than the floating designs because you'll need to specify the size and position of every element.

**Book III
Chapter 4**

**Using Alternative
Positioning**

Figure 4-4:
This layout
was created
with
absolute
positioning.

2. Specify an overall size.

This particular type of layout has a fixed size. Create an `all` div housing all the other elements and specify the size of this div (in a fixed unit for now, usually `px` or `em`).

3. Create the XHTML.

The XHTML page should have a named div for each part of the page (so if you have headers, columns, and footers, you need a div for each).

4. Build a CSS style sheet.

The CSS styles can be internal or linked, but because absolute positioning tends to require a little more markup than floating, external styles are preferred.

5. Identify each element.

It's easier to see what's going on if you assign a different colored border to each element.

6. Make each element absolutely positioned.

Set `position: absolute` in the CSS for each element in the layout.

7. Specify the size of each element.

Set the `height` and `width` of each element according to your diagram. (You *did* make a diagram, right?)

8. **Determine the position of each element.**

   Use the `left` and `top` attributes to determine where each element goes in the layout.

9. **Tune-up your layout.**

   You'll probably want to adjust margins and borders. You may need to do some adjustments to make it all work. For example, the menu is 150px wide, but I added `padding-left` and `padding-right` of 5px each. This means the width of the menu needs to be adjusted to 140px to make everything still fit.

Writing the XHTML

The HTML code is pretty straightforward:

```
<!DOCTYPE html PUBLIC "-//W3C//DTD XHTML 1.0 Strict//EN"
"http://www.w3.org/TR/xhtml1/DTD/xhtml1-strict.dtd">
<html lang="EN" dir="ltr" xmlns="http://www.w3.org/1999/xhtml">
  <head>
    <meta http-equiv="content-type" content="text/xml; charset=utf-8" />
    <title>absLayout.html</title>
    <link rel = "stylesheet"
          type = "text/css"
          href = "absLayout.css" />
  </head>

  <body>
    <div id = "all">
      <div id = "head">
        <h1>Layout with Absolute Positioning</h1>
      </div>

      <div id = "menu">
      </div>

      <div id = "content">
      </div>
    </div>
  </body>
</html>
```

The HTML file calls an external style sheet called absLayout.css.

Adding the CSS

The CSS code is a bit lengthy but not too difficult:

```
/* absLayout.css */
#all {
  border: 1px solid black;
  width: 800px;
  height: 600px;
  position: absolute;
  left: 0px;
  top: 0px;
}
```

```
#head {
  border: 1px solid green;
  position: absolute;
  width: 800px;
  height: 100px;
  top: 0px;
  left: 0px;
  text-align: center;
}

#menu {
  border: 1px solid red;
  position: absolute;
  width: 140px;
  height: 500px;
  top: 100px;
  left: 0px;
  padding-left: 5px;
  padding-right: 5px;
}

#content{
  border: 1px solid blue;
  position: absolute;
  width: 645px;
  height: 500px;
  top: 100px;
  left: 150px;
  padding-left: 5px;
}
```

A static layout created with absolute positioning has a few important features to keep in mind:

✦ **You're committed to position everything.** After you start using absolute positioning, you need to use it throughout your site. All the main page elements require absolute positioning because the normal flow mechanism is no longer in place.

You can still use floating layout *inside* an element with absolute position, but all your main elements (heading, columns, and footing) need to have absolute position if one of them does.

✦ **You should specify size and position.** With a floating layout, you're still encouraging a certain amount of fluidity. Absolute positioning means you're taking the responsibility for both the shape and size of *each* element in the layout.

✦ **Absolute positioning is less adaptable.** With this technique, you're pretty much bound to a specific screen width and height. You'll have trouble adapting to PDAs and cellphones. (A more flexible alternative is shown in the next section.)

✦ **All the widths and the heights have to add up.** When you determine the size of your display, all the heights, widths, margins, padding, and borders have to add up, or you'll get some strange results. When you use absolute positioning, you're also likely to spend some quality time with your calculator, figuring out all the widths and the heights.

Creating a More Flexible Layout

You can build a layout with absolute positioning and some flexibility. Figure 4-5 illustrates such a design.

The size of this layout is attached to the size of the browser screen. It attempts to adjust to the browser while it's resized. You can see this effect in Figure 4-6.

The page simply takes up a fixed percentage of the browser screen. The proportions are all maintained, no matter what the screen size is.

Having the page resize with the browser works, but it's not a complete solution. When the browser window is small enough, the text will no longer fit without some ugly bleed-over effects.

Designing with percentages

This *absolute but flexible* trick is achieved by using percentage measurements. The position is still set to absolute, but rather than defining size and position with pixels, use percentages instead. Here's the CSS:

```
/* absPercent.css */

#all {
  border: 1px black solid;
  position: absolute;
  left: 5%;
  top: 5%;
  width: 90%;
  height: 90%;
}

#head {
  border: 1px black solid;
  position: absolute;
  left: 0%;
  top: 0%;
  width: 100%;
  height: 10%;
  text-align: center;
}

#head h1 {
  margin-top: 1%;
}

#menu {
  border: 1px green solid;
  position: absolute;
  left: 0%;
  top: 10%;
  width: 18%;
  height: 90%;
  padding-left: 1%;
  padding-right: 1%;
}
```

```
#content {
  border: 1px black solid;
  position: absolute;
  left: 20%;
  top: 10%;
  width: 78%;
  height: 90%;
  padding-left: 1%;
  padding-right: 1%;
}
```

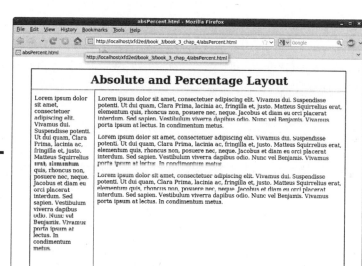

Figure 4-5:
This page uses absolute layout, but it doesn't have a fixed size.

Figure 4-6:
The layout resizes in proportion to the browser window.

The key to any absolute positioning (even this flexible kind) is math. When you just look at the code, it isn't clear where all those numbers come from. Look at the diagram for the page in Figure 4-7 to see where all these numbers come from.

Figure 4-7:
The diagram is the key to a successful layout.

Building the layout

Here's how the layout works:

1. **Create an `all` container by building a div with the `all` ID.**

   The `all` container will hold *all* the contents of the page. It isn't absolutely necessary in this type of layout, but it does allow for a centering effect.

2. **Specify the size and position of `all`.**

   I want the content of the page to be centered in the browser window, so I set its height and width to 90 percent, and its `margin-left` and `margin-top` to 5 percent. In effect, this sets the `margin-right` and `margin-bottom` to 5 percent also. These percentages refer to the `all` div's container element, which is the body, with the same size as the browser window.

3. **Other percentages are in relationship to the `all` container.**

   Because all the other elements are placed inside `all`, the percentage values are no longer referring to the entire browser window. The widths and heights for the menu and content areas are calculated as percentages of their container, which is `all`.

4. **Determine the heights.**

   Height is usually pretty straightforward because you don't usually have to change the margins. Remember, though, that the head accounts for 10 percent of the page space, so the height of both the menu and content needs to be 90 percent.

5. **Figure the general widths.**

   In principle, the width of the menu column is 20 percent, and the content column is 80 percent. This isn't entirely accurate, though.

6. **Compensate for margins.**

   You probably want some margins, or the text looks cramped. If you want 1 percent margin-left and 1 percent margin-right on the menu column, you have to set the menu's width to 18 percent to compensate for the margins. Likewise, set the content width to 78 percent to compensate for margins.

As if this weren't complex enough, remember that Internet Explorer 6 (IE6) and earlier browsers calculate margins differently! In these browsers, the margin happens *inside* the content, so you don't have to compensate for them (but you have to remember that they make the useable content area smaller). You'll probably have to make a conditional comment style sheet to handle IE6 if you use absolute positioning.

Exploring Other Types of Positioning

If you use the position attribute, you're most likely to use absolute. However, here are other positioning techniques that can be handy in certain circumstances:

✦ **Relative:** Set position: relative when you want to move an element from its default position. For example, if you set position to relative and top: -10px, the element would be placed 10 pixels higher on the screen than normal.

✦ **Fixed:** Use fixed position when you want an element to stay in the same place, even when the page is scrolled. This is sometimes used to keep a menu on the screen when the contents are longer than the screen width. If you use fixed positioning, be sure you're not overwriting something already on the screen.

The real trick is to use appropriate combinations of positioning schemes to solve interesting problems.

Creating a fixed menu system

Figure 4-8 illustrates a very common type of Web page — one with a menu on the left and a number of stories or topics in the main area.

Something is interesting about this particular design. The button list on the left refers to specific segments of the page. When you click one of these buttons (say, the Gamma button), the appropriate part of the page is called up, as shown in Figure 4-9.

Normally, when you scroll down the page, things on the top of the page (like the menu) disappear. In this case, the menu stays on the screen, even though the part of the page where it was originally placed is now off the screen.

Gamma isn't necessarily moved to the top of the page. Linking to an element ensures that it's visible but doesn't guarantee where it will appear.

You can achieve this effect using a combination of positioning techniques.

Figure 4-8: At first glance, this is yet another two-column layout.

Book III
Chapter 4

Using Alternative
Positioning

Figure 4-9:
The page
scrolls to
the Gamma
content, but
the menu
stays put.

Setting up the XHTML

The HTML for the fixed menu page is simple (as you'd expect by now):

```
<!DOCTYPE html PUBLIC "-//W3C//DTD XHTML 1.0 Strict//EN"
"http://www.w3.org/TR/xhtml1/DTD/xhtml1-strict.dtd">
<html lang="EN" dir="ltr" xmlns="http://www.w3.org/1999/xhtml">
  <head>
    <meta http-equiv="content-type" content="text/xml; charset=utf-8" />
    <title>fixedRelative.html</title>
    <link rel = "stylesheet"
          type = "text/css"
          href = "fixedRelative.css" />
  </head>

  <body>
    <h1>Fixed Position</h1>
    <div id = "menu">
      <ul>
        <li><a href = "#alpha">Alpha</a></li>
        <li><a href = "#beta">Beta</a></li>
        <li><a href = "#gamma">Gamma</a></li>
        <li><a href = "#delta">Delta</a></li>
      </ul>
    </div>

    <div class = "content"
         id = "alpha">
      <h2>Alpha</h2>
    </div>
```

```
<div class = "content"
     id = "beta">
    <h2>Beta</h2>
</div>

<div class = "content"
     id = "gamma">
    <h2>Gamma</h2>
</div>

<div class = "content"
     id = "delta">
    <h2>Delta</h2>
</div>

  </body>
</html>
```

The XHTML has only a few noteworthy characteristics:

+ **It has a menu.** The div named `menu` contains a list of links (like most menus).

+ **The menu has internal links.** A menu can contain links to external documents or (like this one) links inside the current document. The `<a href = "#alpha">Alpha</a>` code means create a link to the element in this page with the ID `alpha`.

+ **The page has a series of `content` divs.** Most of the page's content appears in one of the several divs with the `content` class. This class indicates all these divs will share some formatting.

+ **The `content` divs have separate IDs.** Although all the `content` divs are part of the same class, each has its own ID. This allows the menu to select individual items (and would also allow individual styling, if desired).

As normal for this type of code, I left out the filler paragraphs from the code listing.

Setting the CSS values

The interesting work happens in CSS. Here's an overview of the code:

```
/* fixedRelative.css */

body {
  background-color: #fff9bf;
}

h1 {
 text-align: center;
}

#menu {
  position: fixed;
  width: 18%;
}
```

```
#menu li {
  list-style-type: none;
  margin-left: -2em;
  text-align: center;
}

#menu a{
  display: block;
  border: 2px gray outset;
  text-decoration: none;
  color: black;
}

#menu a:hover{
  color: white;
  background-color: black;
  border: 2px gray inset;
}

#menu h2 {
  text-align: center;
}

.content {
  position: relative;
  left: 20%;
  width: 80%;
}

.content h2 {
  border-top: 3px black double;
}
```

Most of the CSS is familiar if you've looked over the other chapters in this minibook. I changed the menu list to make it look like a set of buttons, and I added some basic formatting to the headings and borders. The interesting thing here is how I positioned various elements.

Here's how you build a fixed menu:

1. **Set the menu position to `fixed` by setting the `position` attribute to `fixed`.**

   The menu div should stay on the same spot, even while the rest of the page scrolls. Fixed positioning causes the menu to stay put, no matter what else happens on the page.

2. **Give the menu a width with the `width` attribute.**

   It's important that the width of the menu be predictable, both for aesthetic reasons and to make sure the content isn't overwritten by the menu. In this example, I set the menu width to 18 percent of the page width (20 percent minus some margin space).

3. **Consider the menu position by explicitly setting the `top` and `left` attributes.**

When you specify a fixed position, you can determine where the element is placed on the screen with the `left` and `top` attributes. I felt that the default position was fine, so I didn't change it.

4. **Set content position to `relative`.**

   By default, all members of the `content` class will fill out the entire page width. Because the menu needs the leftmost 20 percent of the page, set the `content` class position to `relative`.

5. **Change content's `left` attribute to 20 percent.**

   Because `content` has `relative` positioning, setting the left to 20 percent will add 20 percent of the parent element to each `content`'s `left` value. This will ensure that there's room for the menu to the left of all the content panes.

6. **Give content a `width` property.**

   If you don't define the width, `content` panels may bleed off the right side of the page. Use the `width` property to ensure this doesn't happen.

Determining Your Layout Scheme

All these layout options might just make your head spin. What's the right strategy? Well, that depends.

The most important thing is to find a technique you're comfortable with that gives you all the flexibility you need.

Absolute positioning seems very attractive at first because it promises so much control. The truth is, it's pretty complicated to pull off well, it isn't quite as flexible as the floating layout techniques, and it's hard to make it work right in older browsers.

Floating layouts are generally your best bet, but it's good to know how absolute positioning works. Every once in a while, you find a situation where absolute positioning is a good idea. You see another example of absolute positioning in Chapter 7 of Book IV: animating the position of an element on the screen.

Sometimes, fixed and relative positioning schemes are handy, as in the example introduced in the preceding section.

Sometimes, you'll find it's best to combine schemes. (It's difficult to combine absolute positioning with another scheme, but you can safely combine floating, fixed, and relative positioning techniques most of the time.)

There really aren't any set answers. CSS layout is still an art in progress, and there's plenty to find out about that I can't describe in this book. Keep practicing and keep exploring, and you'll be building beautiful and functional layouts in no time.

Book IV

Client-Side Programming with JavaScript

JavaScript code adds interactivity for checking input and even making games and animations.

Contents at a Glance

Chapter 1: Getting Started with JavaScript

In This Chapter

↙ **Adding JavaScript code to your pages**

↙ **Setting up your environment for JavaScript**

↙ **Creating variables**

↙ **Inputting and outputting with modal dialogs**

↙ **Using concatenation to build text data**

↙ **Understanding data types**

↙ **Using string methods and properties**

↙ **Using conversion functions**

W eb pages are defined by the XHTML code and fleshed out by CSS. But to make them move and breathe, sing, and dance, you need to add a programming language or two. If you thought building Web pages was cool, you're going to love what you can do with a little programming. Programming is what makes pages interact with the user. Interactivity is the "new" in "new media" (if you ask me, anyway). Learn to program, and your pages come alive.

Sometimes people are nervous about programming. It seems difficult and mysterious, and only super-geeks do it. That's a bunch of nonsense. Programming is no more difficult than XHTML and CSS. It's a natural extension, and you're going to like it.

In this chapter, you discover how to add code to your Web pages. You use a language called JavaScript, which is already built into most Web browsers. You don't need to buy any special software, compilers, or special tools because you build JavaScript just like XHTML and CSS — in an ordinary text editor or a specialty editor such as Aptana.

Working in JavaScript

JavaScript is a programming language first developed by Netscape Communications. It is now standard on nearly every browser. You should know a few things about JavaScript right away:

✦ **It's a real programming language.** Don't let anybody tell you otherwise. Sure, JavaScript doesn't have all the same features as a monster, such as C++ or VB.NET, but it still has all the hallmarks of a complete programming language.

✦ **It's not Java.** Sun Microsystems developed a language called Java, which is also sometimes used in Web programming. Despite the similar names, Java and JavaScript are completely different languages. The original plan was for JavaScript to be a simpler language for controlling more complex Java applets, but that never really panned out.

Don't go telling people you're programming in Java. Java people love to act all superior and condescending when JavaScript programmers make this mistake. If you're not sure, ask a question on my Web page. I can help you with either language.

✦ **It's a scripting language.** As programming languages go, JavaScript's pretty friendly. It's not quite as strict or wordy as some other languages. It also doesn't require any special steps (such as compilation), so it's pretty easy to use. These things make JavaScript a great first language.

Choosing a JavaScript editor

Even though JavaScript is a programming language, it is still basically text. Because it's normally embedded in a Web page, you can work in the same text editor you're using for XHTML and CSS. If you aren't already, I recommend that you use the powerful Aptana editor. Aptana is great for XHTML and CSS, but it's very useful when you use it to incorporate JavaScript code in your pages.

JavaScript is an entirely different language and syntax than HTML and CSS. It isn't hard to learn, but there's a lot to learning any programming language. Aptana has a number of great features that help you tremendously when writing JavaScript code:

✦ **Syntax highlighting:** Like HTML and CSS, Aptana automatically adjusts code colors to help you see what's going on in your program. As you see in the later sidebar "Concatenation and your editor," this adjustment can be a big benefit when things get complicated.

✦ **Code completion:** When you type the name of an object, Aptana provides you with a list of possible completions. This shortcut can be really helpful because you don't have to memorize all the details of the various functions and commands.

✦ **Help files:** The Start page (available from the File menu if you've dismissed it) has links to great help pages for HTML, CSS, and JavaScript. The documentation is actually easier to read than some of what you'll find on the Web.

✦ **Integrated help:** Hover the mouse on a JavaScript command or method, and a nifty little textbox pops up to explain exactly how the feature works. Often, it even includes an example or two.

✦ **Error warnings:** When Aptana can tell something is going wrong, it gives you an error message and places a red squiggly (such as the one spell checkers use) under the suspect code.

While Aptana is a very good choice, not everyone likes it. I'm also a big fan of Komodo edit, which has all the same features as Aptana, works on any OS, and is a little bit faster than Aptana. If you find Aptana too complicated, take a look at Komodo and see if it fits your style better.

Of course, you can use any text editor if you don't want or need those features. Any of the following text editors (all mentioned in Book I, Chapter 3) are suitable for JavaScript work:

✦ Notepad++

✦ VI / VIM

✦ Emacs

✦ Scintilla

✦ jEdit

There's one strange characteristic I've noticed in Aptana. The Preview tab isn't as reliable a technique for checking JavaScript code as it was in XHTML and CSS. I find it better to run the code directly in my browser or use the Run button to have Aptana run it in the external browser for me.

Picking your test browser

In addition to your editor, you should think again about your browser when you're testing JavaScript code. All the major browsers support JavaScript; and the support for JavaScript is relatively similar across the browsers (at least for the stuff in this chapter). However, browsers aren't equal when it comes to testing your code.

Things will go wrong when you write JavaScript code, and the browser is responsible for telling you what went wrong. Firefox is way ahead of Internet Explorer when it comes to reporting errors. Firefox errors are much easier to read and understand, and Firefox supports a thing called the *javascript console* (described in Chapter 3) that makes it much easier to see what's going on. If at all possible, use Firefox to test your code and then check for discrepancies in Internet Explorer.

You can discover more about finding and fixing errors in Chapter 3 of this minibook.

Writing Your First JavaScript Program

The foundation of any JavaScript program is a standard Web page like the ones featured in the first three minibooks.

To create your first JavaScript program, you need to add JavaScript code to your pages. Figure 1-1 shows the classic first program in any language.

This page has a very simple JavaScript program in it that pops up the phrase "Hello, World!" in a special element called a dialog box. It's pretty cool.

Here's an overview of the code:

```
<!DOCTYPE html PUBLIC "-//W3C//DTD XHTML 1.0 Strict//EN"
"http://www.w3.org/TR/xhtml1/DTD/xhtml1-strict.dtd">
<html lang="EN" dir="ltr" xmlns="http://www.w3.org/1999/xhtml">
  <head>
    <meta http-equiv="content-type" content="text/xml; charset=utf-8" />
    <title>HelloWorld.html</title>
    <script type = "text/javascript">
      //<![CDATA[
        // Hello, world!
        alert("Hello, World!");
      //]]>
    </script>
  </head>

  <body>

  </body>
</html>
```

Figure 1-1: A Java Script program caused this little dialog box to pop up!

Hello World?

There's a long tradition in programming languages that your first program in any language should simply say, "Hello, World!" and do nothing else. There's actually a very good practical reason for this habit. Hello World is the simplest possible program you can write that you can prove works. Hello World programs are used to help you figure out the mechanics of the programming environment — how the program is written, what special steps you have to do to make the code run, and how it works. There's no point in making a more complicated program until you know you can get code to pop up and say hi.

As you can see, this page contains nothing in the HTML body. You can incorporate JavaScript with XHTML content. For now, though, you can simply place JavaScript code in the head area in a special tag and make it work.

Embedding your JavaScript code

JavaScript code is placed in your Web page via the `<script>` tag. JavaScript code is placed inside the `<script></script>` pair. The `<script>` tag has one required attribute, `type`, which will usually be `text/javascript`. (Other types are possible, but they're rarely used.)

The other funny thing in this page is that crazy CDATA stuff. Immediately inside the script tag, the next line is

```
//<![CDATA[
```

This bizarre line is a special marker explaining that the following code is character information and shouldn't be interpreted as XHTML. The end of the script finishes off the character data marker with this code:

```
//]]>
```

In modern browsers, it's a good idea to mark your JavaScript code as character data. If you don't, the XHTML validator can sometimes get confused and claim you have errors when you don't.

That CDATA business is bizarre. It's hard to memorize, I know, but just type it a few times, and you'll own it.

A lot of older books and Web sites don't recommend the character data trick, but it's well worth learning. You've invested too much effort into building standards-compliant pages to have undeserved error messages pop up because the browser thinks your JavaScript is badly formatted XHTML.

Creating comments

Just like XHTML and CSS, comments are important. Because programming code can be more difficult to decipher than XHTML or CSS, it's even more important to comment your code in JavaScript than it is in these environments. The comment character in JavaScript is two slashes (//).The browser ignores everything from the two slashes to the end of the line. You can also use a multi-line comment (/* */) just like the one in CSS.

Using the alert ( ) method for output

You can output data in JavaScript in a number of ways. In this chapter, I focus on the simplest to implement and understand — the *alert ()*.

This technique pops up a small dialog box containing text for the user to read. The alert box is an example of a *modal dialog*. Modal dialogs interrupt the flow of the program until the user pays attention to them. Nothing else will happen in the program until the user acknowledges the dialog by clicking the OK button. The user can't interact with the page until he clicks the button.

Modal dialogs may seem a bit rude. In fact, you probably won't use them much once you discover other input and output techniques. The fact that the dialog box demands attention makes it a very easy tool to use when you start programming. I use it (and one of its cousins) throughout this chapter because it's easy to understand and use.

Adding the semicolon

Each command in JavaScript ends with a semicolon (;) character. The semicolon in most computer languages acts like the period in English. It indicates the end of a logical thought. Usually, each line of code is also one line in the editor.

To tell the truth, JavaScript will usually work fine if you leave out the semicolons. However, you should add them anyway because they help clarify your meaning. Besides, most other languages, including PHP (see Book V), require semicolons. You may as well start a good habit now.

Introducing Variables

Computer programs get their power by working with information. Figure 1-2 shows a program that gets user data from the user to include in a customized greeting.

Figure 1-2:
First, the
program
asks the
user for her
name.

This program introduces a new kind of dialog that allows the user to enter some data. The information is stored in the program for later use. After the user enters her name, she gets a greeting, as shown in Figure 1-3.

Figure 1-3:
The
beginning of
the greeting.
Press the
button for
the rest.

The rest of the greeting happens in a second dialog box, shown in Figure 1-4. It incorporates the username supplied in the first dialog box.

Figure 1-4:
Now the
greeting is
complete.

The output may not seem that incredible, but take a look at the source code to see what's happening:

```
<!DOCTYPE html PUBLIC "-//W3C//DTD XHTML 1.0 Strict//EN"
"http://www.w3.org/TR/xhtml1/DTD/xhtml1-strict.dtd">
<html lang="EN" dir="ltr" xmlns="http://www.w3.org/1999/xhtml">
  <head>
    <meta http-equiv="content-type" content="text/xml; charset=utf-8" />
    <title>prompt.html</title>
    <script type = "text/javascript">
      //<![CDATA[

      var person = "";
      person = prompt("What is your name?");
```

```
     alert("Hi");
     alert(person);

     //]]>
   </script>
 </head>

 <body>

 </body>
</html>
```

Creating a variable for data storage

This program is interesting because it allows user interaction. The user can enter a name, which is stored in the computer and then returned in a greeting. The key to this program is a special element called a *variable*. Variables are simply places in memory for holding data. Any time you want a computer program to "remember" something, you can create a variable and store your information in it.

Variables typically have the following characteristics:

✦ **The `var` statement:** You can indicate that you're creating a variable with the `var` command.

✦ **A name:** When you create a variable, you're required to give it a name.

✦ **An initial value:** It's useful to give each variable a value immediately.

✦ **A data type:** JavaScript automatically determines the type of data in a variable (more on this in the upcoming "Understanding Variable Types" section), but you should still be clear in your mind what type of data you expect a variable to contain.

Asking the user for information

The `prompt` statement does several interesting things:

✦ **Pops up a dialog box.** This modal dialog box is much like the one the `alert()` method creates.

✦ **Asks a question.** The `prompt()` command expects you to ask the user a question.

✦ **Provides space for a response.** The dialog box contains a space for the user to type a response and buttons for the user to click when he's finished or wants to cancel the operation.

✦ **Passes the information to a variable.** The purpose of a `prompt()` command is to get data from the user, so prompts are nearly always connected to a variable. When the code is finished, the variable contains the indicated value.

Responding to the user

This program uses the `alert()` statement to begin a greeting to the user. The first alert works just like the one from the `helloWorld` program, described earlier in this chapter in the "Writing Your First JavaScript Program" section:

```
alert("Hi");
```

The content of the parentheses is the text you want the user to see. In this case, you want the user to see the literal value `"Hi"`.

The second `alert()` statement is a little bit different:

```
alert(person);
```

This `alert()` statement has a parameter with no quotes. Because the parameter has no quotes, JavaScript understands that you don't really want to say the text *person*. Instead, it looks for a variable named `person` and returns the value of that variable.

The variable can take any name, store it, and return a customized greeting.

Using Concatenation to Build Better Greetings

To have a greeting and a person's name on two different lines seems a little awkward. Figure 1-5 shows a better solution.

The program asks for a name again and stores it in a variable. This time, the greeting is combined into one alert (see Figure 1-6), which looks a lot better.

Figure 1-5:
Once again, I ask the user for a name.

[JavaScript Application]

What is your name?

Matthew

OK   Cancel

Figure 1-6:
Now the user's name is integrated into the greeting.

The page at http://localhost says:

Hi there, Matthew!

OK

Concatenation and your editor

The hard part about concatenation is figuring out which part of your text is a literal value and which part is a string. It won't take long before you go cross-eyed trying to understand where the quotes go.

Modern text editors (like Aptana and Komodo) have a wonderful feature that can help you here. They color different kinds of text. By default, Aptana colors variable names black and literal text dark green (at least when you're in JavaScript — in HTML, literal text is blue).

I find it hard to differentiate the dark green from black, so I changed the Aptana color scheme. I have string literals blue whether I'm in JavaScript or HTML. I find this color more consistent and easier for me to read. With this setting, I can easily see what part of the statement is literal text and what's being read as a variable name. That makes concatenation a lot easier.

To change the color scheme in Aptana, choose Window⇨Preferences. An expandable outline appears in the resulting dialog box. In the section Aptana — Editors — JavaScript Editor — Colors, scroll down to find color settings for any type of data. I found string (another term for text) under literals and changed the color from dark green to blue.

If you make a mistake, clicking the Restore Defaults button reverts to the default values.

Most editors that have syntax highlighting allow you to change settings to fit your needs. Don't be afraid to use these tools to help you program better.

The secret to Figure 1-6 is one of those wonderful gems of the computing world: a really simple idea with a really complicated name. The term *concatenation* is a delightfully complicated word for a basic process. Look at the following code, and you see that combining variables with text is not all that complicated:

```
<script type = "text/javascript">
  //<![CDATA[
  // from concat.html

  var person = "";
  person = prompt("What is your name?");
  alert("Hi there, " + person + "!");

  //]]>
</script>
```

 For the sake of brevity, I include only the script tag and its contents throughout this chapter. The rest of this page is a standard blank XHTML page. You can see the complete document on the Web site or CD-ROM. I do include a comment in each JavaScript snippet that indicates where you can get the entire file on the CD-ROM.

Comparing literals and variables

The program `concat.html` contains two kinds of text. `"Hi there, "` is a *literal* text value. That is, you really mean to say "Hi there, " (including the comma and the space). `person` is a variable. (For more on variables, see the section "Introducing Variables," earlier in this chapter.)

You can combine literal values and variables in one phrase if you want:

```
alert("Hi there, " + person + "!");
```

The secret to this code is to follow the quotes. `"Hi there, "` is a literal value because it is in quotes. On the other hand, `person` is a variable name because it is *not* in quotes; `"!"` is a literal value. You can combine any number of text snippets together with the plus sign.

Using the plus sign to combine text is called *concatenation*. (I told you it was a complicated word for a simple idea.)

Including spaces in your concatenated phrases

You may be curious about the extra space between the comma and the quote in the output line:

```
alert("Hi there, " + person + "!");
```

This extra space is important because you want the output to look like a normal sentence. If you don't have the space, the computer doesn't add one, and the output looks like this:

```
Hi there,Rachael!
```

You need to construct the output as it should look, including spaces and punctuation.

Understanding the String Object

The `person` variable used in the previous program is designed to hold text. Programmers (being programmers) devised their own mysterious term to refer to text. In programming, text is referred to as *string* data.

The term *string* comes from the way text is stored in computer memory. Each character is stored in its own cell in memory, and all the characters in a word or phrase reminded the early programmers of beads on a string. Surprisingly poetic for a bunch of geeks, huh?

Introducing object-based programming (and cows)

JavaScript (and many other modern programming languages) uses a powerful model called *object-oriented programming (OOP)*. This style of programming has a number of advantages. Most important for beginners, it allows you access to some very powerful objects that do interesting things out of the box.

Objects are used to describe complicated things that can have a lot of characteristics — like a cow. You can't really put an adequate description of a cow in an integer variable.

In many object-oriented environments, objects can have the following characteristics. (Imagine a cow object for the examples.)

✦ **Properties:** Characteristics about the object, such as `breed` and `age`

✦ **Methods:** Things the objects can do, such as `moo()` and `giveMilk()`

✦ **Events:** Stimuli the object responds to, such as `onTip`

I describe each of these ideas throughout this minibook, as not all objects support all these characteristics.

If you have a variable of type `cow`, it describes a pretty complicated thing. This thing might have properties, methods, and events, all which can be used together to build a good representation of a cow. (Believe it or not, I've built cow programming constructs more than once in my life — and you thought programming was dull!)

Most variable types in Java are actually objects, and most JavaScript objects have a full complement of properties and methods; many even have event handlers. Master how these things work and you've got a powerful and compelling programming environment.

Okay, before you send me any angry e-mails, I know debate abounds about whether JavaScript is a *truly* object-oriented language. I'm not going to get into the (frankly boring and not terribly important) details in this beginner book. We're going to call JavaScript object-oriented for now, because it's close enough for beginners. If that bothers you, you can refer to JavaScript as an object-based language. Nearly everyone agrees with that. You can find out more information on this topic throughout this minibook while you discover how to make your own objects in Chapter 4 and use HTML elements as objects in Chapter 5.

Investigating the length of a string

When you assign text to a variable, JavaScript automatically treats the variable as a string object. The object instantly takes on the characteristics of a string object. Strings have a couple of properties and a bunch of methods. The one interesting property (at least for beginners) is `length`. Look at the example in Figure 1-7 to see the `length` property in action.

Figure 1-7:
This
program
reports the
length of
any text.

[JavaScript Application]

⚠ The name Jacob is 5 characters long.

OK

That's kind of cool how the program can figure out the length of a phrase. The cooler part is the way it works. As soon as you assign a text value to a variable, JavaScript treats that variable as a string, and because it's a string, it now has a `length` property. This property returns the length of the string in characters. Here's how it's done in the code.

```
<script type = "text/javascript">
  //<![CDATA[
  //from nameLength.html

  var person = prompt("Please enter your name.");
  var length = person.length;

  alert("Hi, " + person + "!");
  alert("The name " + person + " is " + length + " characters long.");

  //]]>
</script>
```

A property is used like a special subvariable. For example, `person` is a variable in the previous example. `person.length` is the `length` property of the `person` variable. In JavaScript, an object and a variable are connected by a period (with no spaces).

The `string` object in JavaScript has only two other properties (con-structor and prototype). Both of these properties are needed only for advanced programming, so I skip them for now.

Using string methods to manipulate text

The `length` property is kind of cool, but the string object has a lot more up its sleeve. Objects also have *methods* (things the object can do). Strings in JavaScript have all kinds of methods. Here are a few of my favorites:

✦ `toUpperCase()` makes an entirely uppercase copy of the string.

✦ `toLowerCase()` makes an entirely lowercase copy of the string.

**Book IV
Chapter 1**

Getting Started
with JavaScript

✦ `substring()` returns a specific part of the string.

✦ `indexOf()` determines whether one string occurs within another.

The string object has many other methods, but I'm highlighting the preceding because they're useful for beginners. Many string methods, such as `big()` and `fontColor()`, simply add HTML code to text. They aren't used very often because they produce HTML code that won't validate, and they don't really save a lot of effort anyway. Some other methods, such as `search()`, `replace()`, and `slice()`, use advanced constructs like arrays and regular expressions that aren't necessary for beginners. (To find out more about working with arrays, see Chapter 4 of this minibook. You can find out more about regular expressions in Chapter 6.)

Don't take my word for it. Look up the JavaScript string object in the Aptana's online help (or one of the many other online JavaScript references) and see what properties and methods it has.

Like properties, methods are attached to an object by the period. Methods are distinguished by a pair of parentheses, which sometimes contain special information called *parameters*.

The best way to see how methods work is to look at some in action. Look at the code for `stringMethods.html`:

```
<script type = "text/javascript">
  //<![CDATA[
  //from stringMethods.html

  var text = prompt("Please enter some text.");

  alert("I'll shout it out:");
  alert(text.toUpperCase());

  alert("Now in lowercase...");
  alert(text.toLowerCase());

  alert("The first 'a' is at letter...");
  alert(text.indexOf("a"));

  alert("The first three letters are ...");
  alert(text.substring(0, 3));

  //]]>
</script>
```

Figure 1-8 displays the output produced by this program.

Please enter some text.

javascript rocks

Cancel   OK

I'll shout it out:

OK

The first 'a' is at letter...

OK

JAVASCRIPT ROCKS

OK

1

OK

Now in lowercase...

OK

The first three letters are ...

OK

Figure 1-8:
String
methods
can be fun.

javascript rocks

OK

jav

OK

Here's another cool thing about Aptana. When you type text, Aptana understands that you're talking about a string variable and automatically pops up a list of all the possible properties and methods. I wish I had that when I started doing this stuff!

You can see from the preceding code that methods are pretty easy to use. When you have a string variable, you can invoke the variable name followed by a period and the method name. Some methods require more information to do their job. Here are the specifics:

✦ toUpperCase() and toLowerCase() take the value of the variable and convert it entirely to the given case. This method is often used when you aren't concerned about the capitalization of a variable.

✦ indexOf(substring) returns the character position of the substring within the variable. If the variable doesn't contain the substring, it returns the value –1.

✦ substring(begin, end) returns the substring of the variable from the beginning character value to the end.

Why are the first three characters (0, 3)?

The character locations for JavaScript (and most programming languages) will seem somewhat strange to you until you know the secret. You may expect `text.substring(1,3)` to return the first three characters of the variable `text`, yet I used `text.substring(0,3)`. Here's why: The indices don't refer to the character numbers but to the indices *between* characters.

```
|a|b|c|d|
 0 1 2 3 4
```

So, if I want the first three characters of the string "abcd", I use `substring(0,3)`. If I want the "cd" part, it's `substring(2,4)`.

Understanding Variable Types

JavaScript isn't too fussy about whether a variable contains text or a number, but the distinction is still important because it can cause some surprising problems. To illustrate, take a look at a program that adds two numbers together, and then see what happens when you try to get numbers from the user to add.

Adding numbers

First, take a look at the following program:

```
<script type = "text/javascript">
  //<![CDATA[
  //from addNumbers.html

  var x = 5;
  var y = 3;
  var sum = x + y;

  alert(x + " plus " + y + " equals " + sum);

  //]]>
</script>
```

(As usual for this chapter, I'm only showing the script part because the rest of the page is blank.)

This program features three variables. I've assigned the value 5 to x and 3 to y. I then add x + y and assign the result to a third variable, sum. The last line prints the results, which are also shown in Figure 1-9.

Figure 1-9:
This
program
(correctly)
adds two
numbers
together.

[JavaScript Application]

⚠ 5 plus 3 equals 8

OK

Note a few important things from this example:

✦ **You can assign values to variables.** It's best to read the equal sign as "gets" so that the first assignment is read as "variable x gets the value 5."

```
var x = 5;
```

✦ **Numeric values aren't enclosed in quotes.** When you refer to a text literal value, it's always enclosed in quotes. Numeric data, such as the value 5, isn't placed in quotes.

✦ **You can add numeric values.** Because x and y both contain numeric values, you can add them together.

✦ **You can replace the results of an operation in a variable.** The result of the calculation x + y is placed in a variable called sum.

✦ **Everything works as expected.** The behavior of this program works as expected. That's important because it's not always true. (You can see an example of this behavior in the next section — I love writing code that blows up on purpose!)

Adding the user's numbers

The natural extension of the addNumbers.html program is a feature that allows the user to input two values and then returns the sum. This program can be the basis for a simple adding machine. Here's the JavaScript code:

```
<script type = "text/javascript">
  //<![CDATA[
  //from addInputWrong.html

  var x = prompt("first number:");
  var y = prompt("second number:");
  var sum = x + y;

  alert(x + " plus " + y + " equals " + sum);

  //]]>
</script>
```

This code seems reasonable enough. It asks for each value and stores them in variables. It then adds the variables and returns the results, right? Well, look at Figure 1-10 to see a surprise.

Figure 1-10:
Wait a
minute . . .
3 + 5 = 35?

Something's obviously not right here. To understand the problem, you need to see how JavaScript makes guesses about data types (see the next section).

The trouble with dynamic data

Ultimately, all the information stored in a computer, from music videos to e-mails, is stored as a bunch of ones and zeroes. The same value 01000001 can mean all kinds of things: It may mean the number 65 or the character A. (In fact, it does mean both those things in the right context.) The same binary value may mean something entirely different if it's interpreted as a real number, a color, or a part of a sound file.

The theory isn't critical here, but one point is really important: Somehow the computer has to know what kind of data is stored in a specific variable. Many languages, such as C and Java, have all kinds of rules about defining data. If you create a variable in one of these languages, you have to define exactly what kind of data will go in the variable, and you can't change it.

JavaScript is much more easygoing about variable types. When you make a variable, you can put any kind of data in it that you want. In fact, the data type can change. A variable can contain an integer at one point, and the same variable may contain text in another part of the program.

JavaScript uses the context to determine how to interpret the data in a particular variable. When you assign a value to a variable, JavaScript puts the data in one of the following categories:

✦ *Integers* are whole numbers (no decimal part). They can be positive or negative values.

✦ A *floating point number* has a decimal point — for example, 3.14. You can also express floating point values in scientific notation, such as 6.02e23 (Avogadro's number –6.02 times 10 to the 23rd). Floating point numbers can also be negative.

✦ A *Boolean* value can only be true or false.

✦ Text is usually referred to as *string* data in programming languages. String values are usually enclosed in quotes.

✦ *Arrays* and *objects* are more complex data types that you can ignore for now.

Most of the time, when you make a variable, JavaScript guesses right, and you have no problems. But sometimes, JavaScript makes some faulty assumptions, and things go wrong.

The pesky plus sign

I use the plus sign in two ways throughout this chapter. The following code uses the plus sign in one way (concatenating two string values):

```
var x = "Hi, ";
var y = "there!",

result = x + y;
alert(result);
```

In this code, x and y are text variables. The result = x + y line is interpreted as "concatenate x and y," and the result is "Hi, there!"

Here's the strange thing: The following code is almost identical.

```
var x = 3;
var y = 5;

result = x + y;
alert(result);
```

Strangely, the behavior of the plus sign is different here, even though the statement result = x + y is identical in the two code snippets.

In this second case, x and y are numbers. The plus operator has two entirely different jobs. If it's surrounded by numbers, it adds. If it's surrounded by text, it concatenates.

That's what happened to the first adding machine program. When the user enters data in prompt dialogs, JavaScript assumes that the data is text. When I try to add x and y, it "helpfully" concatenates instead.

There's a fancy computer science word for this phenomenon (an operator doing different things in different circumstances). Those Who Care about Such Things call this mechanism an *overloaded operator*. Smart people sometimes have bitter arguments about whether overloaded operators are a good idea because they can cause problems like this one, but they can also make things easier in other contexts. I'm not going to enter into that debate here. It's not really a big deal, as long as you can see the problem and fix it.

Changing Variables to the Desired Type

If JavaScript is having a hard time figuring out what type of data is in a variable, you can give it a friendly push in the right direction with some handy conversion functions, as shown in Table 1-1.

Table 1-1		Variable Conversion Functions		
Function	*From*	*To*	*Example*	*Result*
parseInt()	String	Integer	parseInt("23")	23
parse Float()	String	Floating point	parseFloat("21.5")	21.5
toString()	Any variable	String	myVar.toString()	*varies*
eval()	Expression	Result	eval("5 + 3")	8
Math. ceil()	Floating point	Integer	Math.ceil(5.2)	6
Math. floor()			Math.floor(5.2)	5
Math. round()			Math.round(5.2)	5

Using variable conversion tools

The conversion functions are incredibly powerful, but you only need them if the automatic conversion causes you problems. Here's how they work:

✦ parseInt() is used to convert text to an integer. If you put a text value inside the parentheses, the function returns an integer value. If the string has a floating-point representation ("4.3" for example) an integer value (4) is returned.

✦ parseFloat() converts text to a floating-point value.

✦ toString() takes any variable type and creates a string representation. Usually, using this function isn't necessary to use because it's invoked automatically when needed.

✦ eval() is a special method that accepts a string as input. It then attempts to evaluate the string as JavaScript code and return the output. You can use this method for variable conversion or as a simple calculator — eval("5 + 3") returns the integer 8.

✦ Math.ceil() is one of several methods of converting a floating-point number to an integer. This technique always rounds *upward,* so Math.ceil(1.2) is 2, and Math.ceil(1.8) is also 2.

✦ Math.floor() is similar to Math.ceil(), except it always rounds *downward,* so Math.floor(1.2) and Math.floor(1.8) will both evaluate to 1.

✦ Math.round() works like the standard rounding technique used in grade school. Any fractional value less than .5 rounds down, and greater than or equal to .5 rounds up, so Math.round(1.2) is 1, and Math.round(1.8) is 2.

Fixing the addInput code

With all this conversion knowledge in place, it's pretty easy to fix up the addInput program so that it works correctly. Just use parseFloat() to force both inputs into floating-point values before adding them. You don't have to explicitly convert the result to a string. That's automatically done when you invoke the alert() method.

```
//<![CDATA[
// from addInput.html

var x = prompt("first number:");
var y = prompt("second number:");
var sum = parseFloat(x) + parseFloat(y);

alert(x + " plus " + y + " equals " + sum);

//]]>
```

You can see the program works correctly in Figure 1-11.

Figure 1-11:
Now the
program
asks for
input and
correctly
returns
the sum.

Conversion methods allow you to ensure that the data is in exactly the format you want.

Chapter 2: Making Decisions with Conditions

In This Chapter

✔ Generating random numbers and integers

✔ Working with conditions

✔ Using the if-else and switch structures

✔ Handling unusual conditions

*O*ne of the most important aspects of computers is their apparent ability to make decisions. Computers can change their behavior based on circumstances. In this chapter, you discover how to maximize this decision-making ability.

Working with Random Numbers

Random numbers are a big part of computing. They add uncertainty to games, but they're also used for serious applications, such as simulations, security, and logic. Most languages have a feature for creating random numbers, and JavaScript is no exception. The Math.random() function returns a random floating-point value between zero and one.

Technically, computers can't create truly random numbers. Instead, they use a complex formula that starts with one value and creates a second semi-predictable value. In JavaScript, the first value (called the random *seed*) is taken from the system clock in milliseconds, so the results of a random number call seem truly random.

Creating an integer within a range

Creating a random floating-point number between zero and one is easy, thanks to the Math.random() function. What if you want an integer within a specific range? For example, say that you want to simulate rolling a six-sided die. How do you get from the 0-to-1 floating-point value to a 1-to-6 integer?

Here's the standard approach:

1. **Get a random float between 0 and 1 using the `Math.random()` function.**

2. **Multiply that value by 6.**

    This step gives you a floating-point value between 0 and 5.999 (but never 6).

3. **Use `math.ceil()` to round up.**

    At this point, you need to convert the number to an integer. In Book IV, Chapter 1, I mention three functions you can use to convert from a float to an integer. `Math.ceil()` always rounds up, which means you'll always get an integer between 1 and 6.

Building a program that rolls dice

The following `rollDie.html` code helps you simulate rolling a six-sided die.

```
<!DOCTYPE html PUBLIC "-//W3C//DTD XHTML 1.0 Strict//EN"
"http://www.w3.org/TR/xhtml1/DTD/xhtml1-strict.dtd">
<html lang="EN" dir="ltr" xmlns="http://www.w3.org/1999/xhtml">
  <head>
    <meta http-equiv="content-type" content="text/xml; charset=utf-8" />
    <title>rollDie.html</title>
    <script type = "text/javascript">
      //<![CDATA[
      // from rollDie.html

      var number = Math.random();
      alert(number);

      var biggerNumber = number * 6;
      alert(biggerNumber);

      var die = Math.ceil(biggerNumber);
      alert(die);

      //]]>

    </script>
  </head>

  <body>
    <div id = "output">

    </div>
  </body>
</html>
```

As you can see, I converted the strategy from the previous section directly into JavaScript code:

1. **Create a random float.**

    The `Math.random()` function creates a random floating-point number and stores it in the variable `number`.

2. **Multiply the number by 6 to move the number into the appropriate range (6 values).**

   I multiplied by 6 and stored the result in `biggerNumber`.

3. **Round up.**

   I used the `Math.ceil()` function to round the number up to the next highest integer.

Figure 2-1 shows the program running.

0.48863943067028326

Figure 2-1:
This program generates a value between 1 and 6.

2.9318365840216996

OK

3

OK

You may need to run the `rollDice.html` page a few times to confirm that it works as suspected.

If you want to rerun a program you've loaded into the browser, just hit the page refresh button on the browser toolbar.

Using if to Control Flow

If you can roll a die, you'll eventually want different things to happen based on the results of the die roll. Figure 2-2 shows two different runs of a simple game called `deuce.html`.

Okay, it's not that exciting. I promise to add dancing hippos in a later version.

In any case, the "You got a Deuce!" message happens only when you roll a 2. The code is simple but profound:

```
<script type = "text/javascript">
  //<![CDATA[
  // get a random number
  // If it's a two, you win
```

```
var die = Math.ceil(Math.random() * 6);
alert(die);
if (die == 2){
  alert ("You got a Deuce!");
} // end if

//]]>
</script>
```

As usual, I'm showing only the script tag and its contents here, because the rest of the page is blank.

> ⚠ 5
>
> ✓ OK

Figure 2-2: Something exciting happens when you roll a two.

> ⚠ 2
>
> ✓ OK

> ⚠ You got a Duece!
>
> ✓ OK

The basic if statement

The key to deuce.html is the humble if statement. This powerful command does a number of important things:

✦ **It sets up a condition.** The main idea behind a condition is that it's a true or false question. An if statement always includes some type of condition in parentheses. (For more on conditions, see the next section.)

✦ **It begins a block of code.** An if statement sets up a chunk of code that doesn't always execute. The end of the if line includes a left brace ({).

✦ **It usually has indented code under it.** The line or lines immediately after the if statement are part of the block, so they're indented to indicate that they're special.

✦ **It ends several lines later.** The end of the if statement is actually the right brace (}) several lines down in the code. In essence, an if statement contains other code.

✦ **It's indented.** The convention is to indent all the code between the if statement and its ending brace.

Although not required, many programmers add a comment to indicate that the right brace ends an `if` statement. In the C-like languages, the same symbol (`}`) is used to end a bunch of things, so it's nice to remind yourself what you think you're ending here.

All about conditions

A condition is the central part of `if` and several other important structures. Conditions deserve a little respect of their own. A *condition* is an expression that can be evaluated to true or false. Conditions come in three flavors:

+ **Comparison:** By far the most common kind of condition. Typically, you compare a variable to a value, or two variables to each other. Table 2-1 describes a number of different types of comparisons.

+ **Boolean variable:** A variable that contains only `true` or `false`. In JavaScript, any variable can be a Boolean, if you assign it `true` or `false` as a value. You don't need to compare a Boolean to anything else because it's already true or false.

+ **Boolean function:** Returns a `true` or `false` value, and you can also use this type of function as a condition.

Incidentally, Boolean variables are the only primitive variable type capitalized in most languages. They were named after a person, George Boole, a nineteenth-century mathematician who developed a form of binary arithmetic. Boole died thinking his research a failure. His work eventually became the foundation of modern computing. Drop a mention of George at your next computer science function to earn mucho geek points.

Comparison operators

JavaScript supports a number of comparison types, summarized in Table 2-1.

Table 2-1		Comparison Operators	
Name	*Operator*	*Example*	*Notes*
Equality	==	(x==3)	Works with all variable types, including strings.
Not equal	!=	(x != 3)	`True` if values are not equal
Less than	<	(x < 3)	Numeric or alphabetical comparison
Greater than	>	(x > 3)	Numeric or alphabetical comparison
Less than or equal to	<=	(x <= 3)	Numeric or alphabetical comparison
Greater than or equal to	>=	(x >= 3)	Numeric or alphabetical comparison

You should consider a few things when working with conditions:

+ **Be sure the variable types are compatible.** You'll get unpredictable results if you compare a floating-point value to a string.

+ **You can compare string values.** In JavaScript, you can use the inequality operators to determine the alphabetical order of two values. (This ability isn't possible in most other languages.)

+ **Equality uses a double equal sign.** The single equal sign (=) is used to indicate assignment. When you're comparing variables, use a double equal (==) instead.

Don't confuse assignment with comparison! If you accidentally say (x = 3) instead of (x == 3), your code won't crash, but it won't work properly. The first statement simply assigns the value 3 to the variable *x*. It returns the value `true` if the assignment was successful (which it will be). You'll think you're comparing *x* to *3*, but you're assigning *3* to *x*, and the condition will always be true. Keeping these two straight is a nightmare. I still mess it up once in a while.

Using the else Clause

The `deuce.html` game, described in the section "Using if to control flow," is pretty exciting and all, but it would be even better if you had one comment when the roll is a 2 and another comment when it's something else. Figure 2-3 shows a program with exactly this behavior.

Figure 2-3:
You get one message for deuces and another message for everything else.

This program uses the same type of condition as the earlier `deuce.html` game, but it adds an important section:

```
<script type = "text/javascript">
 //<![CDATA[
 // from deuceOrNot.html

 var die = Math.ceil(Math.random() * 6);
 if (die == 2){
```

```
        alert("You got a deuce!");
    } else {
        alert("It's only a " + die + ".");
    } // end if

    //]]>
    </script>
```

The `if` statement is unchanged, but now an `else` clause appears. Here's how the program works:

1. **The `if` statement sets up a condition.**

   The `if` statement indicates the beginning of a code branch, and it prepares the way for a condition.

2. **The condition establishes a test.**

   Conditions are true or false expressions, so the condition indicates something that can be true or false.

3. **If the condition is true, the code between the condition and the `else` clause runs.**

   After this code is finished, control moves past the end of the `if` structure.

4. **If the condition is false, the code between `else` and the end of the `if` statement runs instead.**

The `else` clause acts like a fork in the road. The code goes along one path or another (depending on the condition) but never both paths at one time.

You can put as much code as you want inside an `if` or `else` clause, including more `if` statements!

The `else` clause is used only in the context of an `if` statement. You can't use `else` by itself.

Using if-else for more complex interaction

The `if else` structure is pretty useful when you have only two branches, but what if you want to have several options? Figure 2-4 shows a die only a geek could love. All its values are output in binary notation. (For more on binary notation, see the sidebar "Binary?")

Book IV
Chapter 2

Making Decisions
with Conditions

Figure 2-4:
A die for the
true geek
gamer.

[JavaScript Application]

⚠ 010

OK

Binary?

Binary notation is the underlying structure of all data in a computer. It uses ones and zeroes to store other numbers, which you can combine to form everything you see on the computer, from graphics to text to music videos and adventure games. Here's a quick conversion chart so that you can read the dice:

Die Number	Binary Notation
1	001
2	010
3	011
4	100
5	101
6	110

You can survive just fine without knowing binary (unless you're a computer science major — then you're expected to dream in binary). Still, it's kind of cool to know how things really work.

A simple `if-else` structure isn't sufficient here because you have six options. (`if-else` gives you only two choices). Here's some code that uses another variation of `if` and `else`:

```
<script type = "text/javascript">
//<![CDATA[
// from binaryDice.html

var die = Math.ceil(Math.random() * 6);
if (die == 1){
  alert("001");
} else if (die == 2){
  alert("010");
} else if (die == 3){
  alert("011");
} else if (die == 4){
  alert("100");
} else if (die == 5){
  alert("101");
} else if (die == 6){
  alert("110");
} else {
  alert("something strange is happening...");
} // end if

//]]>
</script>
```

This program begins with an ordinary `if` statement, but it has a number of `else` clauses. You can include as many `else` clauses as you want if each includes its own condition.

To see how this program works, imagine the computer generates the value 3.

1. The first condition (die == 1) is false, so the program immediately jumps to the next else.

2. Step 1 sets up another condition (die == 2), which is also false, so control goes to the next else clause.

3. This step has yet another condition (die == 3), which is true, so the code inside this clause executes (alerting the value "011").

4. A condition has finally been triggered, so the computer skips all the other else conditions and moves to the line after the end if.

5. This step is the last line of code, so the program ends.

Solving the mystery of the unnecessary else

When you use multiple conditions, you can (and should) still indicate an ordinary else clause without a condition as your last choice. This special condition sets up code that should happen if none of the other conditions is triggered. It's useful as a fallback position, in case you didn't anticipate a condition in the else if clauses.

If you think carefully about the binary dice program, the else clause seems superfluous. (I love that word.) It isn't really necessary! You went through all that trouble to create a random number scheme that guarantees you'll have an integer between 1 and 6. If you checked for all six values, why have an else clause? It should never be needed.

There's a big difference between what should happen and what does happen. Even if you think you've covered every single case, you're going to be surprised every once in a while. If you use a multiple if structure, you should always incorporate an else clause to check for surprises. It doesn't need to do much but inform you that something has gone terribly wrong.

Using switch for More Complex Branches

When you have one expression that may have multiple values — as is the case when rolling a die, as described in the preceding sections — you may want to take advantage of a handy tool called switch for exactly this type of situation. Take a look at Figure 2-5, which is a variation of the die roller.

Once again, I start with an ordinary 1–6 integer and assign a new value based on the original roll. This time, I use another structure specialized for "one expression with lots of values" situations. Take a look at the following code:

```
<script type = "text/javascript">
//<![CDATA[
// from RomanDice.html
var die = Math.ceil(Math.random() * 6);
```

```
var output = "";
switch(die){
  case 1:
    output = "I";
    break;
  case 2:
    output = "II";
    break;
  case 3:
    output = "III";
    break;
  case 4:
    output = "IV";
    break;
  case 5:
    output = "V";
    break;
  case 6:
    output = "VI";
    break;
  default:
    output = "PROBLEM!!!";
} // end switch
```

Figure 2-5:
Now we
have
ancient
Roman dice.
Useful if
we come
across any
ancient
Romans.

Creating an expression

The switch structure in the preceding code is organized a little bit differently than the if--else if business.

The switch keyword is followed immediately by an expression in parentheses. The expression is usually a variable with several possible values. The switch structure then provides a series of test values and code to execute in each case.

To create a switch statement:

1. **Begin with the switch keyword.**

This step sets up the structure. You'll indent everything until the right brace (}) that ends the switch structure.

2. **Indicate the expression.**

   The expression is usually a variable you want to compare against several values. The variable goes inside parentheses and is followed by a left brace ({).

3. **Identify the first case.**

   Indicate the first value you want to compare the variable against. Be sure the case is the same type as the variable.

4. **End the case description with a colon (:).**

   Be careful! Case lines end with a colon (indicating the beginning of a case) rather than the more typical semicolon. It's easy to forget this difference.

5. **Write code for the case.**

   You can write as many lines of code as you want inside each case. This code executes only if the expression is equal to the given case. Typically, all the code in a case is indented.

6. **Indicate the end of the case with a break statement.**

   This statement tells the computer to jump out of the switch structure as soon as this case has been evaluated (which is almost always what you want).

7. **Repeat with other cases.**

   Build similar code for all the other cases you wish to test.

8. **Trap for surprises with default.**

   The special case default works like the else in an else if structure: It manages any cases that haven't already been trapped. Even if you think you have all the bases covered, you should put some default code in place just in case.

   You don't need to put a break statement in the default clause, because it always happens at the end of the switch structure anyway.

Switching with style

The switch structure is powerful, but it can be tricky because the format is a little strange. Here are a few tips to keep in mind:

+ **You can compare any type of expression.** If you've used another language (like C or Java), you may have learned that switches only work on numeric values. You can use JavaScript switches on any data type.

+ **It's up to you to get the type correct.** If you're working with a numeric variable and you compare it against string values, you may not get the results you're looking for.

✦ **Don't forget the colons.** At first glance, the switch statement uses semicolons like most other JavaScript commands. Cases end with colons (:). Getting confused is easy to do.

✦ **Break each case.** Use the break statement to end each case, or you'll get weird results.

Wouldn't arrays be better? If you have some programming experience, you may argue that another solution involving something called *arrays* is better for this particular problem. I tend to agree, but for that solution, go to Chapter 4 of this minibook. Switches and if-else structures have their place, too.

Nesting if Statements

You can combine conditions in all kinds of crazy ways. One decision can include other decisions, which may incorporate other decisions. You can put if statements inside each other to manage this kind of (sometimes complicated) logic.

Figure 2-6 shows a particularly bizarre example. Imagine that you're watching the coin toss at your favorite sporting event. Of course, a coin can be heads or tails. Just for the sake of argument, the referee also has a complex personality. Sometimes he's a surfer, and sometimes he's an L337 94m3r (translation: elite gamer). Figure 2-6 shows a few tosses of the coin.

I don't know why the referee is sometimes a surfer and sometimes an L337 94m3r. Perhaps he faced a particularly bizarre set of childhood circumstances.

Figure 2-6:
Heads or
tails? Surfer
or gamer?

What's this L337 stuff?

Leet (L337) is a wacky social phenomenon primarily born of the online gaming community. Originally, it began as people tried to create unique screen names for multiplayer games. If you wanted to call yourself "gamer," for example, you'd usually find the name already taken. Enterprising gamers started substituting similar-looking letters and numbers (and sometimes creative spelling) to make original names that are still somewhat readable. The practice spread, and now it's combined with text messaging and online chat shortcuts as a sort of geek code. Get it? L337 94m3r is Leet Gamer, or Elite Gamer.

This example is getting pretty strange, so you may as well look at some code:

```
<script type = "text/javascript">
  //<![CDATA[
  // from coinToss.html
  coin = Math.ceil(Math.random() * 2);
  character = Math.ceil(Math.random() * 2);
  if (character == 1){
    //It's a surfer referee
    if (coin == 1){
      alert("You got heads, Dude.");
    } else {
      alert("Dude! It's totally tails!");
    } // end coin if

  } else {
    //now it's a L337 Referee
    if (coin == 1){
      alert("h34D$ r0xx0r$");
    } else {
      alert("741L$ ruL3");
    } // end coin if
  } // end character if

  //]]>
</script>
```

Building the nested conditions

If you understand how nested `if` structures work, you can see how the code all fits together.

1. Flip a coin.

I just used a variation of the die-rolling technique, described in the earlier sections. A coin can be only heads or tails, so I rolled a value that would be 1 or 2 for the `coin` variable.

2. Flip another coin for the personality.

The referee's persona is reflected in another random value between 1 and 2.

3. **Check to see whether you have a surfer.**

   If the `character` roll is 1, we have a surfer, so set up an `if` statement to handle the surfer's output.

4. **If it's the surfer, check the coin toss.**

   Now that you know a surfer is speaking, check the coin for heads or tails. Another `if` statement handles this task.

5. **Respond to the coin toss in surfer-speak.**

   Use `alert()` statements to output the result in the surfer dialect.

6. **Handle the L337 character.**

   The outer `if` structure determines which character is speaking. The `else` clause of this case will happen if `character` is not 1, so all the LEET stuff goes in the `else` clause.

7. **Check the coin again.**

   Now that you know you're speaking in gamer code, determine what to say by consulting the coin in another `if` statement.

Making sense of nested ifs

Nested `if` structures aren't all that difficult, but they can be messy, especially when you get several layers deep (as you will, eventually). The following tips help make sure that everything makes sense:

+ **Watch your indentation.** Be vigilant on your indentation scheme. An editor like Aptana, which automatically indents your code, is a big plus. Indentation is a great way to tell what level of code you're on.

+ **Use comments.** You can easily get lost in the logic of a nested condition. Add comments liberally so that you can remind yourself where you are in the logic. I specify which `if` statement is ending.

+ **Test your code.** Just because you think it works doesn't mean it will. Surprises will happen. Test thoroughly to make sure that the code does what you think it should do.

Chapter 3: Loops and Debugging

In This Chapter

- ✔ Working with for loops
- ✔ Building while loops
- ✔ Recognizing troublesome loops
- ✔ Catching crashes and logic errors
- ✔ Using the Aptana line-by-line debugger

Computer programs can do repetitive tasks easily, thanks to a series of constructs called *loops*. In this chapter, you discover the two major techniques for managing loops.

Loops are powerful, but they can be dangerous. It's possible to create loops that act improperly, and these problems are difficult to diagnose. I demonstrate several powerful techniques for identifying issues in your code.

Building Counting Loops with for

A *loop* is a structure that allows you to repeat a chunk of code. One standard type of loop — the for loop — repeats a chunk of code a certain number of times. Figure 3-1 shows a for loop in action.

Figure 3-1: This loop repeats ten times before it stops.

now on lap: 1.

now on lap: 8.

now on lap: 2.

now on lap: 9.

now on lap: 3.

now on lap: 10.

Although it looks like ten different alert statements appear, only one exists; it's just repeated ten times.

I show the first few dialogs and the last. You should be able to get the idea. Be sure to look at the actual program on the CD-ROM to see how it really works.

Building a standard for loop

You can see the structure of the for loop in the following code:

```
<script type = "text/javascript">
  //<![CDATA[
  //from BasicFor.html
  for (lap = 1; lap <= 10; lap++){
    alert("now on lap: " + lap + ".");
  } // end for
  //]]>
</script>
```

for loops are based on an integer, which is sometimes called a *sentry variable*. In this example, lap serves as the sentry variable. You typically use the sentry variable to count the number of repetitions through a loop.

The for statement has three distinct parts:

✦ **Initialization:** This segment (lap = 1) sets up the initial value of the sentry.

✦ **Condition:** The condition (lap <= 10) is an ordinary condition (although it doesn't require parentheses in this context). As long as the condition is evaluated as true, the loop will repeat.

✦ **Modification:** The last part of the for structure (lap++) indicates how the sentry will be modified throughout the loop. In this case, I add 1 to the lap variable each time through the loop.

The for structure has a pair of braces containing the code that will be repeated. As usual, all code inside this structure is indented. You can have as much code inside a loop as you want.

The lap++ operator is a special shortcut. Adding 1 to a variable is common, so the lap++ operation means "add 1 to lap." You can also write lap = lap + 1, but lap++ sounds so much cooler.

When programmers decided to improve on the C language, they called the new language C++. Get it? It's one better than C! Those computer scientists are such a wacky bunch!

When you know how many times something should happen, for loops are pretty useful.

Counting backward

You can modify the basic `for` loop so that it counts backward. Figure 3-2 shows an example of this behavior.

Figure 3-2:
This
program
counts
backward.

Backing up: 10   √ OK

Backing up: 2   √ OK

Backing up: 9   √ OK

Backing up: 1   √ OK

The backward version of the `for` loop uses the same general structure as the forward version (shown in the preceding section), but with slightly different parameters:

```
<script type = "text/javascript">
  //<![CDATA[
  //from backwards.html

  for (lap = 10; lap >= 1; lap--){
    alert("Backing up: " + lap);
  } // end for

  //]]>
</script>
```

If you want to count backward, just modify the three parts of the `for` statement:

✦ **Initialize the sentry to a large number.** If you're counting down, you need to start with a number larger than 0 or 1.

✦ **Keep going as long as the sentry is larger than some value.** The code inside the loop will execute as long as the condition is true. The number will be getting smaller, so make sure that you're doing a greater than (>) or greater than or equal to (>=) comparison.

✦ **Decrement the sentry.** If you want the number to get smaller, you need to subtract something from it. The -- operator is a quick way to do so. It subtracts 1 from the variable.

Counting by 5

You can use the `for` loop to make other kinds of counting loops. If you want to count by five, for example, you can use the following variation:

```
<script type = "text/javascript">
  //<![CDATA[

  //from byFive.html
  for (i = 5; i <= 25; i += 5){
    alert(i);
  } // end for

  //]]>

</script>
```

This code starts i as five, repeats as long as i is less than or equal to 25, and adds 5 to i on each pass through the loop. Figure 3-3 illustrates this code in action.

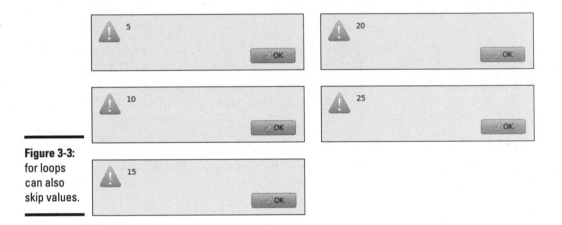

Figure 3-3: for loops can also skip values.

If you want a for loop to skip numbers, you just make a few changes to the general pattern:

+ **Build a sentry variable, using a sensible initial value.** If you want the loop to start at 5, use 5 as the initial value.

+ **Check against a condition.** It makes sense for a 5 loop to end at a multiple of 5. If you want this loop to continue until you get to 25, continue as long as i is less than or equal to 25.

+ **Modify the variable on each pass.** In the example, the statement i += 5 adds 5 to i. (It's just like saying i = i + 5.)

Fortunately, all these elements are in the for loop structure, so you probably won't overlook them. Still, if you find that your loop isn't working as expected, you may need to look into the debugging tricks described in the section "Catching Logic Errors" later in this chapter.

Looping for a while

The for loop is useful, but it has a cousin that's even more handy, the while loop. A while loop isn't tied to any particular number of repetitions. It simply repeats as long as its condition is true.

Creating a basic while loop

The basic while loop is deceptively simple to build. Here's an example:

```
<script type = "text/javascript">
  //<![CDATA[
  // from while.html

  answer = "-99";
  while (answer != "5"){
    answer = prompt("What is 3 + 2?");
    if (answer == "5"){
      alert("great!");
    } else {
      alert("try again...");
    } // end if
  } // end while

  //]]>
</script>
```

This script asks the user a simple math question and keeps asking until the user responds correctly. You can see it in action in Figure 3-4.

Figure 3-4: This loop continues until the user answers correctly.

The operation of a while loop is easy to understand. Here's how the math program works:

1. **Create a variable called answer to act as a sentry variable for the loop.**

2. **Initialize the variable.**

   The initial value of the variable is set to "-99", which can't possibly be correct. That guarantees that the loop will execute at least one time.

3. **Evaluate the answer.**

   In this particular program, the correct answer is 5. If the value of `answer` is anything but 5, the loop continues. In this example, I've preset the value of `answer` to `"-99"` so that the loop happens at least once.

4. **Ask the user a challenging math question.**

   Well, a math question, anyway. The important thing is to change the value of `answer` so that it's possible to get 5 in the answer and exit the loop.

5. **Give the user some feedback.**

   It's probably good to let the user know how she did, so provide some sort of feedback.

Avoiding loop mistakes

A `while` loop seems simpler than a `for` loop, but `while` has exactly the same basic requirements:

+ **A critical sentry variable typically controls the loop.** Some key variable usually (but not always) controls a `while` loop.

+ **The sentry must be initialized.** If the loop is going to behave properly, the sentry variable must still be initialized properly. In most cases, you'll want to guarantee that the loop happens at least one time.

+ **You must have a condition.** Like the `for` loop, `while` loops are based on conditions. As long as the condition is true, the loop continues.

+ **You must include a mechanism for changing the sentry.** Somewhere in the loop, you need to have a line that changes the value of the sentry. Be sure that it's possible to make the condition false, or you'll be in the loop forever!

If you forget one of these steps, the `while` loop may not work correctly. Making mistakes in your `while` loops is easy. Unfortunately, these mistakes don't usually result in a crash. Instead, the loop may either refuse to run altogether or continue on indefinitely. If your loop has that problem, you'll want to make sure that you read the next section.

Introducing Bad Loops

Sometimes loops don't behave. Even if you have the syntax correct, your loop still may not do what you want. The following sections describe two loop errors: Loops that never happen and loops that never quit.

Managing the reluctant loop

You may write some code and find that the loop never seems to run, as in the following program:

```
<script type = "text/javascript">
  //<![CDATA[

  //from never.html
  //Warning! this script has a deliberate error!

  i = 1;
  while (i > 10){
    i++;
  } // end while

  //]]>
</script>
```

This code looks innocent enough, but if you run it, you'll be mystified. It doesn't crash, but it also doesn't seem to do anything. If you follow the code step by step, you eventually see why. I initialize i to 1, and then repeat as long as i is greater than 10. See the problem? i is less than 10 right now, so the condition starts out false, and the loop never executes! I probably meant for the condition to be (i < 10). It's a sloppy mistake, but exactly the kind of bone-headed error I make all the time.

I'm not showing you a screenshot of this program, because nothing happens. Likewise, I don't show you a screenshot of the one in the next section because it doesn't do anything useful either.

Managing the obsessive loop

The other kind of bad-natured loop is the opposite of the reluctant loop I describe in the preceding section. This one starts just fine, but never goes away!

The following code illustrates an endless loop:

```
<script type = "text/javascript">
  //<![CDATA[

  //from endless.html
  // Warning: this program has a deliberate
  // error! You will have to stop the browser
  // to end the loop.

  i = 0;
  j = 0;

  while (i < 10){
    j++;
    alert(j);
  } // end while

  //]]>
</script>
```

If you decide to run `endless.html`, be aware that it won't work properly. What's worse, the only way to stop it will be to kill your browser through the task manager. In the upcoming section "Catching Logic Errors," I show you how to run such code in a safe environment so that you can figure out what's wrong with it.

This code is just one example of the dreaded endless loop. Such a loop usually has perfectly valid syntax, but some logic error prevents it from running properly. The logic error is usually one of the following:

+ **The variable wasn't initialized properly.** The initial value of the sentry is preventing the loop from beginning correctly.

+ **The condition is checking for something that can't happen.** Either the condition has a mistake in it, or something else is preventing it from triggering.

+ **The sentry hasn't been updated inside the loop.** If you simply forget to modify the sentry variable, you get an endless loop. If you modify the variable after the loop has completed, you get an endless loop. If you ask for input in the wrong format, you may also get a difficult-to-diagnose endless loop.

Debugging Your Code

If you've written JavaScript code, you've encountered errors. It's part of a programmer's life. Loops are especially troublesome because they can cause problems even when the syntax is perfect. Fortunately, you can use some great tricks to help track down pesky bugs.

Letting Aptana help

If you're writing your code with Aptana, you already have some great help available. Aptana gives you the same syntax-highlighting and code-completion features as you had when writing XHTML and CSS.

Also, Aptana can often spot JavaScript errors on the fly. Figure 3-5 shows a program with a deliberate error.

Aptana notifies you of errors in your code with a few mechanisms:

+ **The suspect code has a red squiggle underneath.** Similar to a word processing spell checker.

+ **A red circle indicates the troublesome line.** You can scan the margin to quickly see where the errors are.

✦ **The validation pane summarizes all errors.** You can see the errors and the line number for each. Double-click an error to enter that spot in the code. If the validation window is not visible, you can enable it by selecting Window⇨Show View⇨Validation from the menu system.

✦ **You can hover on an error to get more help.** Hover the mouse on an error to get a summary of the error.

Aptana can catch some errors, but it's most useful at preventing errors with the automatic indentation and code assist features.

Debugging JavaScript on Internet Explorer

Internet Explorer has unpredictable behavior when it comes to JavaScript errors. IE6 will take you to some type of editor, but the editors have changed over the years and can be modified (without your knowledge or permission) when you install new software. IE7 and IE8 (at least by default) simply do nothing. You won't see an error or any indication that an error occurred. (Denial — my favorite coping mechanism.)

You can force IE to give you a little bit of help, though. All you have to do is choose Tools⇨Internet Options and then click the Advanced tab. You see a dialog box that looks similar to Figure 3-6.

Figure 3-5: Aptana caught my error and provides some help.

Figure 3-6:
This dialog
box allows
you to
get error
warnings
in Internet
Explorer.

In the dialog box, select Display a Notification about Every Script Error.
Leave all the other settings alone for now. (Yep, we're going to keep script
debugging disabled, because it doesn't work very well. I show you a better
technique in the "Finding errors in Firefox" section.)

When you reload `broken.html` in Internet Explorer, you see something
similar to Figure 3-7.

Figure 3-7:
I never
thought I'd
be happy to
see an error
message.

This message is actually good news because you know what the problem is
and you have a clue about how to fix it. In this particular case, the error message is pretty useful. Sometimes that's the case, and sometimes the error
messages seem to have been written by aliens.

Be sure to have error notification turned on in IE so that you know about errors right away. Of course, you also need to check your code in Firefox.

Finding errors in Firefox

Firefox has somewhat better error-handling than IE by default, and you can use add-ons to turn it into a debugging machine. At Firefox's default setting, error notification is minimal. If you suspect JavaScript errors, open the JavaScript Errors window by choosing Tools⇨Error Console. Figure 3-8 shows the error console after running broken.html.

Error Console

| 🖂 All | ⊜ Errors | ⚠ Warnings | ⓘ Messages | 🧹 Clear |

Code: [   ] Evaluate

missing) after condition
http://localhost/xfd2ed/book_4/book_4_chap_3/broken.html   Line: 13

```
if(i == 1{
        ↑
```

Figure 3-8:
The Firefox error console is pretty useful.

Generally, I find the error messages in the Firefox console more helpful than the ones provided by IE.

The error console doesn't automatically clear itself when you load a new page. When you open the console, it may still contain a bunch of old error messages, so be sure to clear the history (with the error console's Clear button) and refresh your page to see exactly what errors are occurring on this page.

Finding errors with Firebug

One of the best things about Firefox is the add-on architecture. Some really clever people have created very useful add-ons that add wonderful functionality. Firebug is one example. This add-on (available on the CD-ROM or at https://addons.mozilla.org/en-US/firefox/addon/1843) adds to your debugging bag of tricks tremendously.

Firebug is useful for HTML and CSS editing, but it really comes into its own when you're trying to debug JavaScript code. (For more on Firebug, see Book I, Chapter 3.)

When Firebug is active, it displays a little icon at the bottom of the browser window. If it identifies any JavaScript errors, a red error icon appears. When you click this icon, the Firebug window appears and describes the problem. Figure 3-9 shows how the Firebug tool works.

If you click the offending code snippet, you can see it in context — especially useful when the error isn't on the indicated line. Generally, if I'm doing any tricky JavaScript, I turn on Firebug to catch any problems.

Figure 3-9:
Click an
error line in
the Firebug
tool to see
the error in
context.

Catching Logic Errors

The dramatic kind of error you see in broken.html is actually easy to fix. It crashes the browser at a particular part of the code, so you get a good idea what went wrong. Crashes usually result in error messages, which generally give some kind of clue about what went wrong. Most of the time, it's a problem with syntax. You spelled something wrong, forgot some punctuation, or did something else that's pretty easy to fix once you spot it. This type of error is called a *syntax error*.

Loops and branches often cause a more sinister kind of problem, called a *logic error*. Logic errors happen when your code doesn't have any syntax problems, but it's still not doing what you want. These errors can be much harder to pin down, because you don't get as much information.

Of course, if you have the right tools, you can eventually track down even the trickiest bugs. The secret is to see exactly what's going on inside your variables — stuff the user usually doesn't see.

Logging to the console with Firebug

Firebug has another nifty trick. It allows you to send quick messages to the Firebug console. Take a look at log.html:

```
<script type = "text/javascript">
  //<![CDATA[
  // from log.html
  // note this program requires firebug on firefox

  for (i = 1; i <= 5; i++){
    console.log(l);
  } // end for loop

  //another loop with a fancier output
  for (i = 1; i <= 5; i++){
    console.log("i is now %d ", i);
  }

  console.info("This is info");
  console.warn("This is a warning");
  console.error("This is an error");

  //]]>
</script>
```

This code is special because it contains several references to the console object. This object is available only to Firefox browsers with the FireBug extension installed. When you run the program with Firebug and look at the console tab, you see something similar to Figure 3-10.

The console object allows you to write special messages that only the programmer in the console sees. This ability is a great way to test your code and see what's going on, especially if things aren't working the way you want.

 If you want to test your code in IE, there's a version of Firebug (called Firebug Lite) that works on other browsers. Check the Firebug page (https://addons.mozilla.org/en-US/firefox/addon/1843) to download and install this tool if you want to use console commands on non-Firefox browsers.

Figure 3-10:
The Firebug console shows lots of new information.

Looking at console output

Here's how the console object works:

✦ **The first loop prints the value of i to the console.** Each time through the first loop, the console.log function prints the current value of i. This information is useful whenever the loop isn't working correctly. You can use the console.log() method to print the value of any variable.

✦ **The second loop demonstrates a more elaborate kind of printing.** Sometimes, you want to make clear exactly what value you're sending to the console. Firebug supports a special syntax called *formatted printing* to simplify this process.

```
console.log("i is now %d.", i);
```

The text string "i is now %d" indicates what you want written in the console. The special character %d specifies that you place a numeric variable in this position. After the comma, you can indicate the variable you want inserted into the text.

You can use other formatting characters as well. %s is for string, and %o is for object. If you're familiar with printf in C, you'll recognize this technique.

✦ **You can specify more urgent kinds of logging.** If you want, you can use alternatives to the `console.log` to impart more urgency in your messages. If you compare the code in `log.html` with the output of Figure 3-10, you can see how `info`, `warning`, and `error` are formatted.

When your program isn't working properly, try using console commands to describe exactly what's going on with each of your variables. This approach often helps you see problems and correct them.

When your program works properly, don't forget to take out the console commands! Either remove them or render them ineffective with comment characters. The console commands will cause an error in any browser that doesn't have Firebug installed. Typically, your users will not have this extension. (Nor should they need it! You've debugged everything for them!)

Using the Interactive Debug Mode

Traditional programming languages often feature a special debugging tool for fixing especially troubling problems. A typical debugger has

✦ **The ability to pause a program while it's running.** Logic errors are hard to catch because the program keeps on going. With a debugger, you can set a particular line as a *breakpoint*. When the debugger encounters the breakpoint, the program enters a pause mode. It isn't completely running, and it isn't completely stopped.

✦ **A mechanism for moving through the code a line at a time.** You can normally step through code one line at a time so that you can see what's going on.

✦ **A way to view the values of all variables and expressions.** Knowing what's happening in your variables is important. (For example, is a particular variable changing when you think it should?) A debugger should let you look at the values of all its variables.

✦ **The ability to stop runaway processes.** When you create loops, you'll accidentally create endless loops. (For more on endless loops, see the earlier section "Managing the obsessive loop.") In a typical browser, the only way out of an endless loop is to kill the browser with the task manager (or process manager in some operating systems). That step is a bit drastic. A debugger can let you stop a runaway loop without accessing the task manager.

Debuggers are extremely handy, and they're very common in most programming languages. JavaScript programmers, however, haven't had much access to debugging tools in the past because the technical considerations of an embedded language made this difficult.

Book IV
Chapter 3

Loops and
Debugging

Fortunately, Firebug has a wonderful debug mode that works very well and provides all those features. To test it, I wrote a program with a deliberate error that would be hard to find without a debugger:

```
//<![CDATA[
//from debug.html
//has a deliberate error

var i = 0;
var j = 0;
while (i <= 10){
  console.log(i);
  j++;
} // end while


//]]>
</script>
```

This code is another version of the `endless.html` program from the "Managing the obsessive loop" section earlier in this chapter. You may see the problem right away. If not, you'll see it when you run the debugger, which I describe how to do in the next sections.

Aptana also has an interactive debugger, but it's now integrated into the Firebug debugging tool. I focus on the Firebug version, because it's easier.

Interactive debugging is usually used when the program is running but not doing what you want. In this case, run the program but stop it so you can inspect the behavior of the code in a sort of "super slo-mo." Essentially, you can pause the program at a suspected trouble spot and look carefully at all the variables while the program is paused. You can then advance one line at a time and check the status of your program at each line of execution. It's a very powerful mechanism.

Setting up the Firebug debugger

The `FireBug` extension has a very powerful and easy-to-use integrated debugger. To make it work, follow these steps:

1. **Make sure Firebug is visible.**

   Use the F12 or Firebug button to make the Firebug console visible.

2. **Turn on script viewing.**

   Interactive debugging can slow the browser significantly, so it is turned off by default. Enable the drop-down list on Firebug's script tab to turn script management on.

3. **Load the page into the browser.**

   It's sometimes better to configure Firebug before you load the offending page because some types of bugs cause the browser to hang. If you set things up first and then load the page, you're less likely to run into this sort of problem. (See the upcoming section "Adding a debugger directive" if this is still a problem.)

Setting a breakpoint

A JavaScript program can get much longer than the short examples I show in this book. You usually won't want to start the line-by-line debugging from the beginning, so you need to specify a breakpoint. When you run a program in debug mode, the program runs at normal speed until it reaches a breakpoint and then it pauses so that you can control it more immediately.

To set a breakpoint:

1. **Look at the code in Firebug's script window**.

If you followed the steps in the previous list to set up the Firebug debugger, you should already see the script in this window. Find a place in the code preceding where you expect trouble. If you suspect a loop is going crazy, find the line right before that loop begins, for example.

2. **Click the left margin to set a breakpoint.**

Click the left margin of the script window to establish a breakpoint. When you reload the page, code control will pause when the browser gets to this point.

3. **Refresh the page.**

Use the browser's refresh button or the F5 key to reload your page. This time the program should stop when it gets to the breakpoint.

Adding a debugger directive

This approach works fine for most programs, but sometimes Firebug runs into a problem because the browser (and thus the debugger) doesn't get control of a program until it finishes loading. Sometimes an endless loop prevents the program from ever loading, so the debugger never gets control. If you run into this sort of situation, there's another way to set the breakpoint. You can also place a breakpoint directly in your code. Here's how:

1. **Load your script into your editor.**

2. **Find the spot where you want to pause.**

Typically, this is right before the code you expect is the problem. If you think the problem is an endless loop, move your cursor to the first line of that loop.

3. **Add the keyword `debugger;` to your code.**

This special line is a signal to Firebug that it should invoke debug mode at this point.

4. **Load the page into Firefox.**

Even if the page has an endless loop, the `debugger` directive will cause Firebug to pause so you can see what's going on in the code.

5. **Remove the `debugger;` line when you finish.**

The `debugger` directive is used only for debugging. Obviously, you don't want the page to enter debug mode on the user's machine. After you fix the problem, remove this line from your source code.

If you forget to remove the `debugger` directive, most browsers will register a JavaScript error. This directive only makes sense if Firebug is installed, and users should never need a debugger. (That's your job.)

Examining debug mode

Firebug, when in debug mode, has a few new features you may not have seen before. Figure 3-11 shows `debuggerDirective.html` in Firefox with the Firebug plugin activated.

A number of important new items occur on the page:

✦ **The main browser panel may not show anything.**

By definition, the program is not finished, so there may not be anything on the page yet. That's not a problem. We're really looking under the hood here, so we don't expect anything yet.

✦ **The current line of code is highlighted.**

In the script window, one line is highlighted: the line of code that is about to be executed. The program is paused, allowing you to look over the current state of the program before you proceed.

✦ **You can mouse over any variable to see its current value.**

If you hover the mouse on a variable in the script, you can see its value. In Figure 3-11 none of the variables have been created yet, so they do not have meaningful values.

✦ **The Watch tab window shows you the value of all variables.**

You use this window to see what is happening to your variables. Note that JavaScript has access to tons of variables in the Web page we haven't discussed yet. For now, just focus on the variables under "scopechain."

✦ **You can add another variable or expression to watch for.**

If you want to keep an eye on a variable, you can type it into the New Watch Expression textbox at the top of the Watch tab window. It's sometimes helpful to enter the condition for your `while` loop into this textbox. That way you can tell if the condition is currently true or false.

The Stack tab window shows the complete logic path that your program has taken so far. This is helpful information when your code becomes more complex, but it isn't useful yet. The Breakpoints tab window allows you to add or remove additional breakpoints.

✦ **The "remote control" toolbar lets you control the program execution.**

This panel has three ways to step to the next instruction. For now, the Step Over button (or the F10 key) is the one you'll use most often. (See the sidebar "Controlling the flow" for information on these functions' differences.)

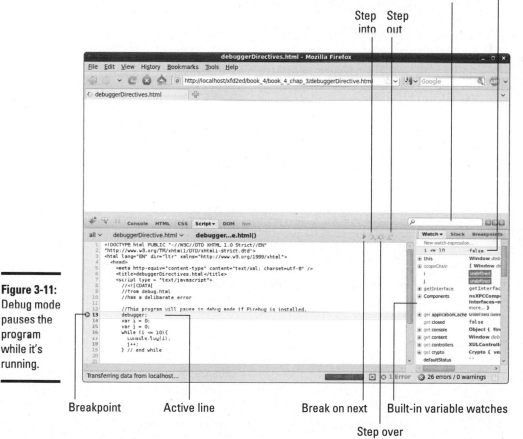

Figure 3-11: Debug mode pauses the program while it's running.

Condition added in 'New watch expression' text area

Search for a variable or term in the code with this box.

Step into   Step out

Breakpoint   Active line   Break on next   Built-in variable watches

Step over

Book IV Chapter 3

Loops and Debugging

Debugging your code

When the debugger is up and running, the process is pretty simple.

1. **Load the code.**

Load the offending code into your browser. If the browser freezes every time you try to load the code, add the debugger directive to your code to load it directly into debug mode.

2. **Add breakpoints as necessary.**

Even if you turn on the debugger directive, you may want to set break-points to ensure the program stops where you want it to stop. Click the margin of the Script tab's main browser window to set or remove breakpoints.

3. **Refresh the page.**

After you set the breakpoints, refresh the page to run the page in the browser and stop at your first breakpoint.

4. **Look over your variables.**

Normally, if your program has a logic error, it's because some variable doesn't have the value you think it does. Look carefully at the value of each variable (especially those used to control loops) and see whether it has the value you expect at this point. It may help to copy your condition from the code into the New Watch Expression box so you can tell whether a condition is currently true or false.

5. **Step to the next instruction.**

When you're sure the code is performing the way you expect, use the Step Over button to move to the next instruction.

6. **Repeat until you find the problem.**

Look at the new state of the variables. Have things changed? Are there any surprises?

Normally, the process of going through your code slowly with the ability to check the state of your variables at every turn will help you find your mistakes. Learning how to use your debugger will save you hours of time.

Sometimes, you're still stuck in an endless loop. The debugger helps you find problems, but it doesn't fix them. When you recognize you're still in an endless loop, you must regain control so you can go back to the editor and fix the problem. If you're in debug mode, you might simply redirect your browser to another page (use the home button, for example). However, endless loops are notorious; therefore, you may need a more drastic measure. Use your operating system's task management tool to kill the offending browser window and then reload the browser.

Controlling the flow

Several mechanisms step through a program in debug mode. Most of the time they work the same, but some subtle differences exist in their behavior. Here's how stepping through a program works:

The Play button (green triangle) runs the program at full speed until the program encounters the next breakpoint. This is useful when you want to stop at one point to check your variables, quickly jump through a lot of code, and stop again after all that code has executed.

The Step Into button goes to the next line of code. If that code is a function, the debugger jumps into that function and examines the code inside that function. Generally, this is useful when you want to examine how data flows into functions. (See Chapter 4 of this minibook for more information about functions.)

The Step Over button goes to the next line of code. If that code is a function, the program executes the entire function as one line and doesn't go into the details of the function. Normally, this is the behavior you want. If you're concerned about the code inside the function, you should add another breakpoint there to stop the code execution at that point.

The Step Out button completes the current function at normal speed and stops at the next line of code outside the current function. This is normally used when you accidentally step into a function you don't need to examine; so you can go back to the main code without having to step through hundreds of lines of irrelevant code.

Chapter 4: Functions, Arrays, and Objects

In This Chapter

✔ **Passing parameters into functions**

✔ **Returning values from functions**

✔ **Functions and variable scope**

✔ **Producing basic arrays**

✔ **Retrieving data from arrays**

✔ **Building a multidimensional array**

✔ **Creating objects**

✔ **Building object constructors**

✔ **Introducing JSON notation**

It doesn't take long for your code to become complex. Soon enough, you find yourself wanting to write more sophisticated programs. When things get larger, you need new kinds of organizational structures to handle the added complexity.

You can bundle several lines of code into one container and give this new chunk of code a name: that is a *function*. You can also take a whole bunch of variables, put them into a container, and give it a name. That's called an *array*. If you combine functions and data, you get another interesting structure called an *object*.

This chapter is about how to work with more code and more data without going crazy.

Breaking Code into Functions

Functions come in handy when you're making complex code easier to handle — a useful tool for controlling complexity. You can take a large, complicated program and break it into several smaller pieces. Each piece stands alone and solves a specific part of the overall problem.

You can think of each function as a miniature program. You can define variables in functions, put loops and branches in there, and do anything else you can do with a program. A program using functions is basically a program full of subprograms.

After you define your functions, they're just like new JavaScript commands. In a sense, when you add functions, you're adding to JavaScript.

To explain functions better, think back to an old campfire song, "The Ants Go Marching." Figure 4-1 re-creates this classic song for you in JavaScript format. (You may want to roast a marshmallow while you view this program.)

Figure 4-1:
Nothing reminds me of functions like a classic campfire song.

> ⚠ The ants go marching 1 by 1 hurrah, hurrah
> The ants go marching 1 by 1 hurrah, hurrah
> The ants go marching 1 by 1
> The little one stops to suck his thumb
> ✓ OK

> ⚠ The ants go marching 2 by 2 hurrah, hurrah
> The ants go marching 2 by 2 hurrah, hurrah
> The ants go marching 2 by 2
> The little one stops to tie his shoe
> ✓ OK

> ⚠ ...and they all go marching down
> to the ground
> to get out
> of the rain.
>
> boom boom boom boom boom boom boom boom
> ✓ OK

> ⚠ ...and they all go marching down
> to the ground
> to get out
> of the rain.
>
> boom boom boom boom boom boom boom boom
> ✓ OK

If you're unfamiliar with this song, it simply recounts the story of a bunch of ants. The littlest one apparently has some sort of attention issues (but we love him anyway). During each verse, the little one gets distracted by something that rhymes with the verse number. The song typically has ten verses, but I'm just doing two for the demo.

Thinking about structure

Before you look at the code, think about the structure of the song, "The Ants Go Marching." Like many songs, it has two parts. The *chorus* is a phrase repeated many times throughout the song. The song has several *verses*, which are similar to each other, but not quite identical.

Think about the song sheet passed around the campfire. (I'm getting hungry for a S'more.) The chorus is usually listed only one time, and each verse is listed. Sometimes, you have a section somewhere on the song sheet that looks like the following:

Verse 1

Chorus

Verse 2

Chorus

Musicians call this a *road map,* and that's a great name for it. A road map is a high-level view of how you progress through the song. In the road map, you don't worry about the details of the particular verse or chorus. The road map shows the big picture, and you can look at each verse or chorus for the details.

Building the antsFunction.html program

Take a look at the code for antsFunction.html and see how it reminds you of the song sheet for "The Ants Go Marching":

```
<script type = "text/javascript">
  //<![CDATA[
  //from antsFunction.html

  function chorus() {
    var text = "...and they all go marching down\n";
    text += "to the ground \n";
    text += "to get out \n";
    text += "of the rain. \n";
    text += " \n";
    text += "boom boom boom boom boom boom boom boom \n";
    alert(text);
  } // end chorus

  function verse1(){
    var text = "The ants go marching 1 by 1 hurrah, hurrah \n";
    text += "The ants go marching 1 by 1 hurrah, hurrah \n";
    text += "The ants go marching 1 by 1 \n";
    text += " The little one stops to suck his thumb \n";
    alert(text);
  } // end verse1

  function verse2(){
    var text = "The ants go marching 2 by 2 hurrah, hurrah \n";
    text += "The ants go marching 2 by 2 hurrah, hurrah \n";
    text += "The ants go marching 2 by 2 \n";
    text += " The little one stops to tie his shoe \n";
    alert(text);
  } // end verse2

  //main code
  verse1();
  chorus();
  verse2();
  chorus();

  //]]>
</script>
```

The program code breaks the parts of the song into the same pieces a song sheet does. Here are some interesting features of antsFunction.html:

✦ **I created a function called `chorus()`.** Functions are simply collections of code lines with a name.

✦ **All the code for the chorus goes into this function.** Anything I want as part of printing the chorus goes into the `chorus()` function. Later, when I want to print the chorus, I can just call the `chorus()` function and it will perform the code I stored there.

✦ **Each verse has a function, too.** I broke the code for each verse into its own function.

✦ **The main code is a road map.** When all the details are delegated to the functions, the main part of the code just controls the order in which the functions are called.

✦ **Details are hidden in the functions.** The main code handles the big picture. The details (how to print the chorus or verses) are hidden inside the functions.

Passing Data to and from Functions

Functions are logically separated from the main program. This separation is a good thing because it prevents certain kinds of errors. However, sometimes you want to send information to a function. You may also want a function to return some type of value. The `antsParam.html` page rewrites the "The Ants Go Marching" song in a way that takes advantage of function input and output.

```
<script type = "text/javascript">
//<![CDATA[
//from antsParam.html
function chorus() {
  var text = "...and they all go marching down\n";
  text += "to the ground \n";
  text += "to get out \n";
  text += "of the rain. \n";
  text += " \n";
  text += "boom boom boom boom boom boom boom boom \n";
  return text;
} // end chorus

function verse(verseNum){
  var distraction = "";
  if (verseNum == 1){
    distraction = "suck his thumb.";
  } else if (verseNum == 2){
    distraction = "tie his shoe.";
  } else {
    distraction = "I have no idea.";
  }

  var text = "The ants go marching ";
  text += verseNum + " by " + verseNum + " hurrah, hurrah \n";
  text += "The ants go marching ";
  text += verseNum + " by " + verseNum + " hurrah, hurrah \n";
```

```
        text += "The ants go marching ";
        text += verseNum + " by " + verseNum;
        text += " the little one stops to ";
        text += distraction;
        return text;
    } // end verse

    //main code
    alert(verse(1));
    alert(chorus());
    alert(verse(2));
    alert(chorus());

    //]]>
</script>
```

I don't provide a figure of this program because it looks just like ants Function.html to the user. One advantage of functions is that I can improve the underlying behavior of a program without imposing a change in the user's experience.

This code incorporates a couple important new ideas. (The following list is just the overview; the specifics are coming in the following sections.)

✦ **These functions return a value.** The functions no longer do their own alerts. Instead, they create a value and return it to the main program.

✦ **Only one verse function exists.** Because the verses are all pretty similar, using only one verse function makes sense. This improved function needs to know what verse it's working on to handle the differences.

Examining the main code

The main code has been changed in one significant way. In the last program, the main code called the functions, which did all the work. This time, the functions don't actually output anything themselves. Instead, they collect information and pass it back to the main program. Inside the main code, each function is treated like a variable.

You've seen this behavior. The prompt() method returns a value. Now the chorus() and verse() methods return values. You can do anything you want to this value, including storing it to a variable, printing it, or comparing it to some other value.

Separating the creation of data from its use as I've done here is a good idea. That way, you have more flexibility. After a function creates some information, you can print it to the screen, store it on a Web page, put it in a database, or whatever.

Looking at the chorus

The chorus of "The Ants Go Marching" song program has been changed to return a value. Take another look at the chorus() function to see what I mean.

```
function chorus() {
  var text = "...and they all go marching down\n";
  text += "to the ground \n";
  text += "to get out \n";
  text += "of the rain. \n";
  text += " \n";
  text += "boom boom boom boom boom boom boom boom \n";
  return text;
} // end chorus
```

Here's what changed:

+ **The purpose of the function has changed.** The function is no longer designed to output some value to the screen. Instead, it now provides text to the main program, which can do whatever it wants with the results.

+ **There's a variable called `text`.** This variable contains all the text to be sent to the main program. (It contained all the text in the last program, but it's even more important now.)

+ **The `text` variable is concatenated over several lines.** I used string concatenation to build a complex value. Note the use of new lines (\n) to force carriage returns.

+ **The `return` statement sends `text` to the main program.** When you want a function to return some value, simply use return followed by a value or variable. Note that return should be the last line of the function.

Handling the verses

The verse() function is quite interesting:

+ It can print more than one verse.

+ It takes input to determine which verse to print.

+ It modifies the verse based on the input.

+ It returns a value, just like chorus().

To make the verse so versatile (get it? verse-atile!), it must take input from the primary program and return output.

Passing data to the verse () function

The verse() function is always called with a value inside the parentheses. For example, the main program sets verse(1) to call the first verse, and verse(2) to invoke the second. The value inside the parentheses is called an *argument*.

The verse function must be designed to accept an argument (because I call it using values inside the parentheses). Look at the first line to see how.

```
function verse(verseNum){
```

In the function definition, I include a variable name. Inside the function, this variable is known as a *parameter*. (Don't get hung up on the terminology. People often use the terms parameter and argument interchangeably.) The important idea is that whenever the verse() function is called, it automatically has a variable called verseNum. Whatever argument you send to the verse() function from the main program will become the value of the variable verseNum inside the function.

You can define a function with as many parameters as you want. Each parameter gives you the opportunity to send a piece of information to the function.

Determining the distraction

If you know the verse number, you can determine what distracts "the little one" in the song. You can determine the distraction in a couple ways, but a simple if-else if structure is sufficient for this example.

```
var distraction = "";
if (verseNum == 1){
  distraction = "suck his thumb.";
} else if (verseNum == 2){
  distraction = "tie his shoe.";
} else {
  distraction = "I have no idea.";
}
```

I initialized the variable distraction to be empty. If verseNum is 1, set distraction to "suck his thumb." If verseNum is 2, distraction should be "tie his shoe". Any other value for verseNum is treated as an error by the else clause.

If you're an experienced coder, you may be yelling at this code. It still isn't optimal. Fortunately, in the section "Building a basic array" later in this chapter, I show an even better solution for handling this particular situation with arrays.

By the time this code segment is complete, verseNum and distraction both contain a legitimate value.

Creating the text

When you know these variables, it's pretty easy to construct the output text:

```
var text = "The ants go marching ";
text += verseNum + " by " + verseNum + " hurrah, hurrah \n";
text += "The ants go marching ";
text += verseNum + " by " + verseNum + " hurrah, hurrah \n";
```

Book IV Chapter 4

Functions, Arrays, and Objects

```
      text += "The ants go marching ";
      text += verseNum + " by " + verseNum;
      text += " the little one stops to ";
      text += distraction;
      return text;
   } // end verse1
```

A whole lotta' concatenating is going on, but it's essentially the same code as the original `verse()` function. This one's just a lot more flexible because it can handle any verse. (Well, if the function has been preloaded to understand how to handle the `verseNum`.)

Managing Scope

A function is much like an independent mini-program. Any variable you create inside a function has meaning only inside that function. When the function is finished executing, its variables disappear! This setup is actually a really good thing. A major program will have hundreds of variables, and they can be difficult to keep track of. You can reuse a variable name without knowing it or have a value changed inadvertently. When you break your code into functions, each function has its own independent set of variables. You don't have to worry about whether the variables will cause problems elsewhere.

Introducing local and global variables

You can also define variables at the main (script) level. These variables are *global* variables. A global variable is available at the main level and inside each function. A *local* variable (one defined inside a function) has meaning only inside the function. The concept of local versus global functions is sometimes referred to as *scope*.

Local variables are kind of like local police. Local police have a limited geographical jurisdiction, but they're very useful within that space. They know the neighborhood. Sometimes, you encounter situations that cross local jurisdictions. This situation is the kind that requires a state trooper or the FBI. Local variables are local cops, and global variables are the FBI.

Generally, try to make as many of your variables local as possible. The only time you really need a global variable is when you want some information to be used in multiple functions.

Examining variable scope

To understand the implications of variable scope, take a look at `scope.html`:

```
<script type = "text/javascript">
  //<![CDATA[
  //from scope.html
  var globalVar = "I'm global!";
```

```
function myFunction(){
  var localVar = "I'm local";
  console.log(localVar);
}

myFunction();

//]]>
</script>
```

This program defines two variables. In the main code, globalVar is defined, and localVar is defined inside a function. If you run the program in debug mode while watching the variables, you can see how they behave. Figure 4-2 shows what the program looks like early in the run.

localVar doesn't have meaning until the function is called, so it remains undefined until the computer gets to that part of the code. Step ahead a few lines, and you see that localVar has a value, as shown in Figure 4-3.

Be sure to use Step Into rather than Step Over on the "remote control" toolbar for this example. When Step Over encounters a function, it runs the entire function as one line. If you want to look into the function and see what's happening inside it (as you do here), use Step Into.

globalVar still has a value (it's an FBI agent), and so does localVar because it's inside the function.

**Book IV
Chapter 4**

**Functions, Arrays,
and Objects**

Figure 4-2:
globalVar is
defined, but
localVar
is not.

![Screenshot of scope.html in Mozilla Firefox with Firebug debugger showing globalVar and localVar watch variables]

If you move a few more steps, `localVar` no longer has a value when the function ends (see Figure 4-4).

Figure 4-3:
localVar
has a value
because I'm
inside the
function.

Figure 4-4:
Once again,
localVar has
no meaning.

Variable scope is a good thing because it means you have to keep track of only global variables and the variables defined inside your current function. The other advantage of scope is the ability to reuse a variable name. You can have ten different functions all using the same variable name, and they won't interfere with each other because they're entirely different variables.

Building a Basic Array

If functions are groups of code lines with a name, *arrays* are groups of variables with a name. Arrays are similar to functions because they're used to manage complexity. An array is a special kind of variable. Use an array whenever you want to work with a list of similar data types.

The following code shows a basic demonstration of arrays:

```
<script type = "text/javascript">
  //<![CDATA[
  //from genres.html

  //creating an empty array
  var genre = new Array(5);

  //storing data in the array
  genre[0] = "flight simulation";
  genre[1] = "first-person shooters";
  genre[2] = "driving";
  genre[3] = "action";
  genre[4] = "strategy";

  //returning data from the array
  alert ("I like " + genre[4] + " games.");

  //]]>
</script>
```

The variable `genre` is a special variable because it contains many values. Essentially, it's a list of genres. The `new array(5)` construct creates space in memory for five variables, all named genre.

Accessing array data

After you specify an array, you can work with the individual elements using square-bracket syntax. An integer identifies each element of the array. The index usually begins with zero.

```
genre[0] = "flight simulation";
```

The preceding code assigns the text value `"flight simulation"` to the genre array variable at position 0.

Most languages require all array elements to be the same type. JavaScript is very forgiving. You can combine all kinds of stuff in a JavaScript array. This flexibility can sometimes be useful, but be aware that this trick doesn't work in all languages. Generally, I try to keep all the members of an array the same type.

After you store the data in the array, you can use the same square-bracket syntax to read the information.

The line

```
alert ("I like " + genre[4] + " games.");
```

finds element 4 of the `genre` array and includes it in an output message.

Figure 4-5 shows a run of `genre.html`.

Figure 4-5:
This data came from an array.

Using arrays with for loops

The main reason to use arrays is convenience. When you have a lot of information in an array, you can write code to work with the data quickly. Whenever you have an array of data, you commonly want to do something with each element in the array. Take a look at `games.html` to see how you can do so:

```
<script type = "text/javascript">
  //<![CDATA[
  //from games.html

  //pre-loading an array
  var gameList = new Array("Flight Gear", "Sauerbraten", "Future Pinball",
    "Racer", "TORCS", "Orbiter", "Step Mania", "NetHack",
    "Marathon", "Crimson Fields");

  var text = "";
  for (i = 0; i < gameList.length; i++){
    text += "I love " + gameList[i] + "\n";
  } // end for loop
  alert(text);

  //]]>
</script>
```

Notice several things in this code:

✦ **The array called `gameList`.** This array contains the names of some of my favorite freeware games.

✦ **The array is preloaded with values.** If you provide a list of values when creating an array, JavaScript simply preloads the array with the values you indicate. You don't need to specify the size of the array if you pre-load it.

✦ **A `for` loop steps through the array.** Arrays and `for` loops are natural companions. The `for` loop steps through each element of the array.

✦ **The array's length is used in the `for` loop condition.** Rather than specifying the value 10, I used the array's `length` property in my `for` loop. This practice is good because the loop automatically adjusts to the size of the array when I add or remove elements.

✦ **Do something with each element.** Because i goes from 0 to 9 (the array indices), I can easily print each value of the array. In this example, I simply add to an output string.

✦ **Note the newline characters.** The `\n` combination is a special character that tells JavaScript to add a carriage return, such as pressing the Enter key. Figure 4-6 shows a run of `games.html`.

Figure 4-6:
Now I
have a list
of games.
Arrays and
loops
are fun!

> The page at http://localhost says:
>
> I love Flight Gear
> I love Sauerbraten
> I love Future Pinball
> I love Racer
> I love TORCS
> I love Orbiter
> I love Step Mania
> I love NetHack
> I love Marathon
> I love Crimson Fields
>
> ✓ OK

If you want to completely ruin your productivity, Google some of these game names. They're absolutely incredible, and every one of them is free. It's hard to beat that. See, even if you don't learn how to program in this book, you get something good from it!

Revisiting the ants song

If you read the earlier sections, you probably just got that marching ant song out of your head. Sorry. Take a look at the following variation, which uses arrays and loops to simplify the code even more.

```
<script type = "text/javascript">
  //<![CDATA[
  //from antsArray.html

  var distractionList = new Array("", "suck his thumb", "tie his shoe");
```

```
function chorus() {
  var text = "...and they all go marching down\n";
  text += "to the ground \n";
  text += "to get out \n";
  text += "of the rain. \n";
  text += " \n";
  text += "boom boom boom boom boom boom boom boom \n";
  return text;
} // end chorus

function verse(verseNum){
  //pull distraction from array
  var distraction = distractionList[verseNum];

  var text = "The ants go marching ";
  text += verseNum + " by " + verseNum + " hurrah, hurrah \n";
  text += "The ants go marching ";
  text += verseNum + " by " + verseNum + " hurrah, hurrah \n";
  text += "The ants go marching ";
  text += verseNum + " by " + verseNum;
  text += " the little one stops to ";
  text += distraction;
  return text;
} // end verse

//main code is now a loop
for (verseNum = 1; verseNum < distractionList.length; verseNum++){
  alert(verse(verseNum));
  alert(chorus());
} // end for loop

//]]>
</script>
```

This code is just a little different from the `antsParam` program shown in the section of this chapter called "Passing Data to and from Functions."

✦ **It has an array called `distractionList`.** This array is (despite the misleading name) a list of distractions. I made the first one (element zero) blank so that the verse numbers would line up properly.

✦ **The `verse()` function looks up a distraction.** Because distractions are now in an array, you can use the `verseNum` as an index to loop up a particular distraction. Compare this function to the `verse()` function in `antsParam`. This program can be found in the section "Passing data to and from Functions." Although arrays require a little more planning than code structures, they can highly improve the readability of your code.

✦ **The main program is in a loop.** I step through each element of the `distractionList` array, printing the appropriate verse and chorus.

✦ **The `chorus()` function remains unchanged.** You don't need to change `chorus()`.

Working with Two-Dimension Arrays

Arrays are useful when working with lists of data. Sometimes, you encounter data that's best imagined in a table. For example, what if you want to build a distance calculator that determines the distance between two cities? The original data might look like Table 4-1.

Table 4-1	Distance between Major Cities			
	0) Indianapolis	*1) New York*	*2) Tokyo*	*3) London*
0) Indianapolis	0	648	6476	4000
1) New York	648	0	6760	3470
2) Tokyo	6476	6760	0	5956
3) London	4000	3470	5956	0

Think about how you would use Table 4-1 to figure out a distance. If you wanted to travel from New York to London, for example, you'd pick the New York row and the London column and figure out where they intersect. The data in that cell is the distance (3,470 miles).

When you look up information in any kind of a table, you're actually working with a *two-dimensional data structure* — a fancy term, but it just means table. If you want to look something up in a table, you need two indices, one to determine the row and another to determine the column.

If this concept is difficult to grasp, think of the old game Battleship. The playing field is a grid of squares. You announce I-5, meaning column I, row 5, and the opponent looks in that grid to discover that you've sunk his battleship. In programming, you typically use integers for both indices, but otherwise, it's exactly the same as Battleship. Any time you have two-dimensional data, you access it with two indices.

Often, we call the indices *row* and *column* to help you think of the structure as a table. Sometimes, other names more clearly describe how the behavior works. Take a look at Figure 4-7, and you see that the distance.html program asks for two cities and returns a distance according to the data table.

Yep, you can have three, four, or more dimension arrays in programming, but don't worry about that yet. (It may make your head explode.) Most of the time, one or two dimensions are all you need.

This program is a touch longer than some of the others, so I break it into parts in the following sections for easy digestion. Be sure to look at the program in its entirety on the CD-ROM.

Figure 4-7:
It's a *Tale of Two Cities.* You even get the distance between them!

Setting up the arrays

The key to this program is the data organization. The first step is to set up two arrays.

```
<script type = "text/javascript">
//<![CDATA[
//from distance.html

//cityName has the names of the cities
cityName = new Array("Indianapolis", "New York", "Tokyo", "London");

//create a 2-dimension array of distances
distance = new Array (
  new Array (0, 648, 6476, 4000),
  new Array (648, 0, 6760, 3470),
  new Array (6476, 6760, 0, 5956),
  new Array (4000, 3470, 5956, 0)
);
```

The first array is an ordinary single-dimension array of city names. I've been careful to always keep the cities in the same order, so whenever I refer to city 0, I'm talking about Indianapolis (my hometown), New York is always going to be at position 1, and so on.

You have to be careful in your data design that you always keep things in the same order. Be sure to organize your data on paper before you type it into the computer, so you'll understand what value goes where.

The `cityNames` array has two jobs. First, it reminds me what order all the cities will be in, and, second, it gives me an easy way to get a city name when I know an index. For example, I know that `cityName[2]` will always be `"Tokyo"`.

The distance array is very interesting. If you squint at it a little bit, it looks a lot like Table 4-1, shown earlier in this chapter. That's because it *is* Table 4-1, just in a slightly different format.

distance is an array. JavaScript arrays can hold just about everything, including other arrays! That's what distance does. It holds an array of rows. Each element of the distance array is another (unnamed) array holding all the data for that row. If you want to extract information from the array, you need two pieces of information. First, you need the row. Then because the row is an array, you need the column number within that array. So, distance[1][3] means go to row one ("New York") of distance. Within that row go to element 3 ("London") and return the resulting value (3470). Cool, huh?

Getting a city

The program requires that you ask for two cities. You want the user to enter a city number, not a name, and you want to ask this question twice. Sounds like a good time for a function.

```
function getCity(){
  // presents a list of cities and gets a number corresponding to
  // the city name
  var theCity = "";   //will hold the city number

  var cityMenu = "Please choose a city by typing a number: \n";
  cityMenu += "0) Indianapolis \n";
  cityMenu += "1) New York \n";
  cityMenu += "2) Tokyo \n";
  cityMenu += "3) London \n";

  theCity = prompt(cityMenu);
  return theCity;
} // end getCity
```

The getCity() function prints a little menu of city choices and asks for some input. It then returns that input.

You can improve getCity() in all kinds of ways. For one thing, maybe it should repeat until you get a valid number so that users can't type the city name or do something else crazy. I'll leave it simple for now. If you want to find out how user interface elements help the user submit only valid input, skip ahead to Chapter 5 of this minibook.

Creating a main ( ) function

The main() function handles most of the code for the program.

```
function main(){
  var output = "";
  var from = getCity();
  var to = getCity();
  var result = distance[from][to];
```

```
    output = "The distance from " + cityName[from];
    output += " to " + cityName[to];
    output += " is " + result + " miles.";
    alert(output);
} // end main

main();
```

The `main()` function controls traffic. Here's what you do:

1. **Create an `output` variable.**

   The point of this function is to create some text output describing the distance. I begin by creating a variable called `output` and setting its initial value to empty.

2. **Get the city of origin.**

   Fortunately, you have a great function called `getCity()` that handles all the details of getting a city in the right format. Call this function and assign its value to the new variable `from`.

3. **Get the destination city.**

   That `getCity()` function sure is handy. Use it again to get the city number you'll call `to`.

4. **Get the distance.**

   Because you know two indices, and you know they're in the right format, you can simply look them up in the table. Look up `distance[from][to]` and store it in the variable `result`.

5. **Output the response.**

   Use concatenation to build a suitable response string and send it to the user.

6. **Get city names from the `cityNames` array.**

   The program uses numeric indices for the cities, but they don't mean anything to the user. Use the `cityNames` array to retrieve the two city names for the output.

7. **Run the `main()` function.**

   Only one line of code doesn't appear in a function. That line calls the `main()` function and starts the whole thing.

I didn't actually write the program in the order I showed it to you in the preceding steps. Sometimes it makes more sense to go "inside out." I actually created the data structure first (as an ordinary table on paper) and then constructed the `main()` function. This approach made it obvious that I needed a `getCity()` function and gave me some clues about how `getCity` should work. (In other words, it should present a list of cities and prompt for a numerical input.)

Creating Your Own Objects

So far you've used a lot of wonderful objects in JavaScript. However, that's just the beginning. It turns out you can build your own objects too, and these objects can be very powerful and flexible. Objects typically have two important components: *properties* and *methods*. A *property* is like a variable associated with an object. It describes the object. A method is like a function associated with an object. It describes things the object can do. If functions allow you to put code segments together and arrays allow you to put variables together, objects allow you to put both code segments and variables (and functions and arrays) in the same large construct.

Building a basic object

JavaScript makes it trivially easy to build an object. Because a variable can contain any value, you can simply start treating a variable like an object and it becomes one.

Figure 4-8 shows a critter that has a property.

Figure 4-8:
This alert box is actually using an object.

The page at http://localhost says:

the critter's name is Milo

OK

Take a look at the following code:

```
//from basicObject.html
//create the critter
var critter = new Object();

//add some properties
critter.name = "Milo";
critter.age = 5;

//view property values
alert("the critter's name is " + critter.name);
```

The way it works is not difficult to follow:

1. **Create a new `Object`.**

JavaScript has a built-in object called `Object`. Make a variable with the `new Object()` syntax, and you'll build yourself a shiny, new standard object.

2. **Add properties to the object.**

   A property is a subvariable. It's nothing more than a variable attached to a specific object. When you assign a value to `critter.name`, for example, you're specifying that `critter` has a property called `name` and you're also giving it a starting value.

3. **An object can have any number of properties.**

   Just keep adding properties. This allows you to group a number of variables into one larger object.

4. **Each property can contain any type of data.**

   Unlike arrays where it's common for all the elements to contain exactly the same type of data, each property can have a different type.

5. **Use the dot syntax to view or change a property.**

   If the `critter` object has a name property, you can use `critter.name` as a variable. Like other variables, you can change the value by assigning a new value to `city.name` or you can read the content of the property.

If you're used to a stricter object-oriented language, such as Java, you'll find JavaScript's easy-going attitude quite strange and maybe a bit sloppy. Other languages do have a lot more rules about how objects are made and used, but JavaScript's approach has its charms. Don't get too tied up in the differences. The way JavaScript handles objects is powerful and refreshing.

Adding methods to an object

Objects have other characteristics besides properties. They can also have *methods*. A method is simply a function attached to an object. To see what I'm talking about, take a look at this example:

```
//create the critter
//from addingMethods.html
var critter = new Object();

//add some properties
critter.name = "Milo";
critter.age = 5;

//create a method
critter.talk = function(){
  msg = "Hi! My name is " + this.name;
  msg += " and I'm " + this.age;
  alert(msg);
}; // end method

// call the talk method
critter.talk();
```

This example extends the `critter` object described in the last section. In addition to properties, the new critter has a `talk()` method. If a property describes a characteristic of an object, a method describes something the object can do. Figure 4-9 illustrates the critter showing off its `talk()` method:

Figure 4-9:
Now the
critter can
talk!

> **The page at http://localhost says:** ☐ ✕
>
> ⚠️ Hi! My name is Alpha and I'm 1
>
>   ✓ OK

Here's how it works:

1. Build an object with whatever properties you need.

   Begin by building an object and giving it some properties.

2. Define a method much like a property.

   In fact, methods *are* properties in JavaScript, but don't worry too much about that; it'll make your head explode.

3. You can assign a prebuilt function to a method.

   If you created a function that you want to use as a method, you can simply assign it.

4. You can also create an anonymous function.

   More often, you'll want to create your method right away. You can create a function immediately with the `function(){` syntax.

5. The `this` keyword refers to the current object.

   Inside the function, you may want to access the properties of the object. `this.name` refers to the `name` property of the current object.

6. You can then refer to the method directly.

   After you define an object with a method, you can invoke it. For example, if the `critter` object has a `talk` method, use `critter.talk()` to invoke this method.

Building a reusable object

These objects are nice, but what if you want to build several objects with the same definition? JavaScript supports an idea called a *constructor,* which allows you to define an object pattern and reuse it.

Here's an example:

```
//building a constructor
//from constructor.html
function Critter(lName, lAge){
  this.name = lName;
  this.age = lAge;
  this.talk = function(){
    msg = "Hi! My name is " + this.name;
    msg += " and I'm " + this.age;
```

```
   alert(msg);
 } // end talk method
} // end Critter class def

function main(){
  //build two critters
  critterA = new Critter("Alpha", 1);

  critterB = new Critter("Beta", 2);
  critterB.name = "Charlie";
  critterB.age = 3;

  //have 'em talk
  critterA.talk();
  critterB.talk();

} // end main
main();
```

This example involves creating a *class* (a pattern for generating objects) and reusing that definition to build two different critters. First, look over how the class definition works:

✦ **Build an ordinary function:** JavaScript classes are defined as extensions of a function. The function name will also be the class name. Note that the name of a class function normally begins with an uppercase letter. When a function is used in this way to describe an object, the function is called the object's *constructor.* The constructor can take parameters if you wish, but it normally does not return any values. In my particular example, I add parameters for name and age.

✦ **Use this to define properties:** Add any properties you want to include, including default values. Note that you can change the values of these later if you wish. Each property should begin with `this` and a period. If you want your object to have a color property, you'd say something like `this.color = "blue"`. My example uses the local parameters to define the properties. This is a very common practice because it's an easy way to preload important properties.

✦ **Use this to define any methods you want:** If you want your object to have methods, define them using the `this` operator followed by the `function(){` keyword. You can add as many functions as you wish.

The way JavaScript defines and uses objects is easy but a little nonstandard. Most other languages that support object-oriented programming (OOP) do it in a different way than the technique described here. Some would argue that JavaScript is not a true OOP language, as it doesn't support a feature called *inheritance*, but instead uses a feature called *prototyping*. The difference isn't all that critical because most uses of OOP in JavaScript are very simple objects like the ones described here. Just appreciate that this introduction to object-oriented programming is very cursory, but enough to get you started.

Using your shiny new objects

After you define a class, you can reuse it. Look again at the main function to see how I use my newly minted `Critter` class:

```
function main(){
  //build two critters

  critterA = new Critter("Alpha", 1);

  critterB = new Critter("Beta", 2);
  critterB.name = "Charlie";
  critterB.age = 3;

  //have 'em talk
  critterA.talk();
  critterB.talk();

} // end main
main();
```

After you define a class, you can use it as a new data type. This is a very powerful capability. Here's how it works:

✦ **Be sure you have access to the class:** A class isn't useful unless JavaScript knows about it. In this example, the class is defined within the code.

✦ **Create an instance of the class with the new keyword:** The new keyword means you want to make a particular critter based on the definition. Normally, you assign this to a variable. My constructor expects the name and age to be supplied, so it automatically creates a critter with the given name and age.

✦ **Modify the class properties as you wish:** You can change the values of any of the class properties. In my example, I change the name and age of the second critter just to show how it's done.

✦ **Call class methods:** Because the `critter` class has a `talk()` method, you can use it whenever you want the critter to talk.

Introducing JSON

JavaScript objects and arrays are incredibly flexible. In fact, they are so well known for their power and ease of use that a special data format called JavaScript Object Notation (JSON) has been adopted by many other languages.

JSON is mainly used as a way to store complex data (especially multidimension arrays) and pass the data from program to program. JSON is essentially another way of describing complex data in a JavaScript object format. When you describe data in JSON, you generally do not need a constructor because the data is used to determine the structure of the class.

JSON data is becoming a very important part of Web programming, because it allows an easy mechanism for transporting data between programs and programming languages.

Storing data in JSON format

To see how JSON works, look at this simple code fragment:

```
var critter = {
  "name": "George",
  "age": 10
};
```

This code describes a critter. The critter has two properties, a name and an age. The critter looks much like an array, but rather than using a numeric index like most arrays, the critter has string values to serve as indices. It is in fact an object.

You can refer to the individual elements with a variation of array syntax, like this:

```
alert(critter["name"]);
```

You can also use what's called *dot* notation (as used in objects) like this:

```
alert(critter.age);
```

Both notations work the same way. Most of the built-in JavaScript objects use dot notation, but either is acceptable.

The reason JavaScript arrays are so useful is that they are in fact objects. When you create an array in JavaScript, you are building an object with numeric property names. This is why you can use either array or object syntax for managing JSON object properties.

Look at `jsonDistance.html` on the Web site to see the code from this section in action. I don't show a screenshot here because all the interesting work happens in the code.

To store data in JSON notation:

1. **Create the variable.**

You can use the `var` statement like you do any variable.

2. **Contain the content within braces ({}).**

This is the same mechanism you use to create a preloaded array (as described earlier in this chapter).

3. **Designate a key.**

For the critter, I want the properties to be named "name" and "age" rather than numeric indices. For each property, I begin with the property name. The key can be a string or an integer.

4. **Follow the key with a colon (:).**

5. **Create the value associated with that key.**

   You can then associate any type of value you want with the key. In this case, I associate the value George with the key name.

6. **Separate each name/value pair with a comma (,).**

   You can add as many name value pairs as you wish.

If you're familiar with other languages, you might think a JSON structure similar to a hash table or associative array. JavaScript does use JSON structures the way these other structures are used, but it isn't quite accurate to say JSON is either a hash or an associative array. It's simply an object. However, if you want to think of it as one of these things, I won't tell anybody.

Building a more complex JSON structure

JSON is convenient because it can be used to handle quite complex data structures. For example, look at the following (oddly familiar) data structure written in JSON format:

```
var distance = {
  "Indianapolis" :
    { "Indianapolis": 0,
      "New York": 648,
      "Tokyo": 6476,
      "London": 4000 },

  "New York" :
    { "Indianapolis": 648,
      "New York": 0,
      "Tokyo": 6760,
      "London": 3470 },

  "Tokyo" :
    { "Indianapolis": 6476,
      "New York": 6760,
      "Tokyo". 0,
      "London": 5956 },

  "London" :
    { "Indianapolis": 4000,
      "New York": 3470,
      "Tokyo": 5956,
      "London": 0 },
};
```

This data structure is another way of representing the distance data used to describe two-dimension arrays. This is another two-dimension array, but it is a little different than the one previously described.

✦ **distance is a JSON object:** The entire data structure is stored in a single variable. This variable is a JSON object with name/value pairs.

✦ **The distance object has four keys:** These correspond to the four rows of the original chart.

✦ **The keys are city names:** The original 2D array used numeric indices, which are convenient but a bit artificial. In the JSON structure, the indices are actual city names.

✦ **The value of each entry is another JSON object:** The value of a JSON element can be anything, including another JSON object. Very complex relationships can be summarized in a single variable.

✦ **Each row is summarized as a JSON object:** For example, the value associated with "Indianapolis" is a list of distances from Indianapolis to the various cities.

✦ **The entire declaration is one "line" of code:** Although it is placed on several lines in the editor (for clarity) the entire definition is really just one line of code.

Setting up the data in this way seems a bit tedious, but it's very easy to work with. The city names are used directly to extract data, so you can find the distance between two cities with array-like syntax:

```
alert(distance["Indianapolis"]["London"]);
```

If you prefer, you can use the dot syntax:

```
alert(distance.Indianapolis.Tokyo);
```

You can even go with some kind of hybrid:

```
alert(distance["London"].Tokyo);
```

JSON has a number of important advantages as a data format:

✦ **Self-documenting:** Even if you see the data structure on its own without any code around it, you can tell what it means.

✦ **The use of strings as indices makes the code more readable:** It's much easier to understand distance["Indianapolis"]["London"] than distance[0][3].

✦ **JSON data can be stored and transported as text:** This turns out to have profound implications for Web programming, especially in AJAX (the techniques described in minibook 7).

✦ **JSON can describe complex relationships:** The example shown here is a simple two-dimension array, but the JSON format can be used to describe much more complex relationships including complete databases.

✦ **Many languages support JSON format:** Many Web languages now offer direct support for JSON. The most important of these is PHP, which is frequently used with JavaScript in AJAX applications.

✦ **JSON is more compact than XML:** Another data format called XML is frequently used to transmit complex data. However, JSON is more compact and less "wordy" than XML.

✦ **JavaScript can read JSON natively:** Some kinds of data need to be translated before they can be used. As soon as your JavaScript program has access to JSON data, it can be used directly.

You might wonder whether you can embed methods in JSON objects. The answer is yes, but this isn't usually done when you're using JSON to transport information. In minibook VII about AJAX, you see that methods are often added to JSON objects to serve as *callback functions*, but that usage won't make sense until you learn more about events.

**Book IV
Chapter 4**

Functions, Arrays,
and Objects

Chapter 5: Talking to the Page

In This Chapter

✔ **Introducing the Document Object Model**

✔ **Responding to form events**

✔ **Connecting a button to a function**

✔ **Retrieving data from text fields**

✔ **Changing text in text fields**

✔ **Sending data to the page**

✔ **Working with other text-related form elements**

*J*avaScript is fun and all, but it lives in Web browsers for a reason: to let you change Web pages. The best thing about JavaScript is how it helps you control the page. You can use JavaScript to read useful information from the user and to change the page on the fly.

In the first few chapters of this minibook, I concentrate on JavaScript without worrying about the HTML. The HTML code in those programs was unimportant, so I didn't include it in the code listings. This chapter is about how to integrate code with HTML, so now I incorporate the HTML as well as the JavaScript segments. Sometimes I still print code in separate blocks, so (as always) try to look at the code in its natural habitat, through your browser.

Understanding the Document Object Model

JavaScript programs usually live in the context of a Web page. The contents of the page are available to the JavaScript programs through a mechanism called the *Document Object Model* (DOM).

The DOM is a special set of complex variables that encapsulates the entire contents of the Web page. You can use JavaScript to read from the DOM and determine the status of an element. You can also modify a DOM variable and change the page from within JavaScript code.

Navigating the DOM

The easiest way to get a feel for the DOM is to load a page in Firefox and look at the Firebug window's DOM tab. I do just that in Figure 5-1.

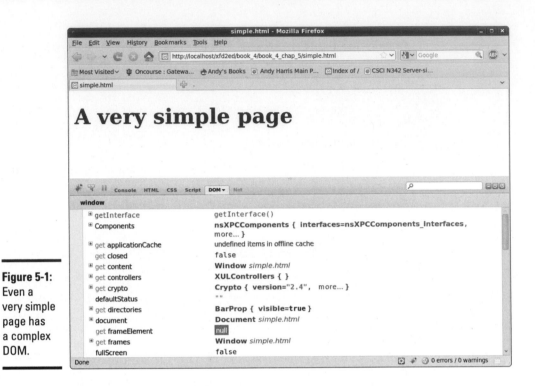

Figure 5-1:
Even a
very simple
page has
a complex
DOM.

When you look over the DOM of a simple page, you can easily get over-whelmed. You'll see a lot of variables listed. Technically, these variables are all elements of a special object called `window`. The `window` object has a huge number of subobjects, all listed in the DOM view. Table 5-1 describes a few important `window` variables.

Table 5-1   **Primary DOM Objects**

Variable	Description	Notes
`document`	Represents XHTML page	Most commonly scripted element
`location`	Describes current URL	Change `location.href` to move to a new page
`history`	A list of recently visited pages	Access this to view previous pages
`status`	The browser status bar	Change this to set a message in the status bar

Changing DOM properties with Firebug

To illustrate the power of the DOM, try this experiment in Firefox:

1. **Load any page.**

   It doesn't matter what page you work with. For this example, I use `simple.html`, a very basic page with only an `<h1>` header.

2. **Enable the Firebug extension.**

   You can play with the DOM in many ways, but the Firebug extension is one of the easiest and most powerful tools for experimentation.

3. **Enable the DOM tab.**

   You see a list of all the top-level variables.

4. **Scroll down until you see the `status` element.**

   When you find the `status` element, double-click it.

5. **Type a message to yourself in the resulting dialog box and press Enter.**

6. **Look at the bottom of the browser.**

   The status bar at the bottom of the browser window should now contain your message.

7. **Experiment.**

   Play around with the various elements in the DOM list. You can modify many of them. Try changing `window.location.href` to any URL and watch what happens. Don't worry; you can't permanently break anything here.

Examining the document object

If the `window` object is powerful, its offspring, the `document`, is even more amazing. (If you're unfamiliar with the `window` object, see the section "Navigating the DOM," earlier in this chapter.)

Once again, the best way to get a feel for this thing is to do some exploring:

1. **Reload `simple.html`.**

   If your previous experiments caused things to get really weird, you may have to restart Firefox. Be sure the Firebug extension displays the DOM tab.

2. **Find the `document` object.**

   It's usually the second object in the `window` list. When you select this object, it expands, showing a huge number of child elements.

3. **Look for the `document.body`.**

Somewhere in the `document` you'll see the `body`. Select this object to see what you discover.

4. **Find the `document.body.style`.**

   The `document` object has a `body` object, which has a style. Will it never end?

5. **Look through the style elements.**

   Some styles will be unfamiliar, but keep going, and you'll probably see some old friends.

6. **Double-click `backgroundColor`.**

   Each CSS `style` attribute has a matching (but not quite identical) counterpart in the DOM. Wow. Type a new color and see what happens.

7. **Marvel at your cleverness.**

   You can navigate the DOM to make all kinds of changes in the page. If you can manipulate something here, you can write code to do it, too.

If you're lost here, Figure 5-2 shows me modifying the `backgroundColor` of the style of the body of the document. A figure can't really do this justice, though. You have to experiment for yourself. But don't be overwhelmed. You don't really need to understand all these details, just know they exist.

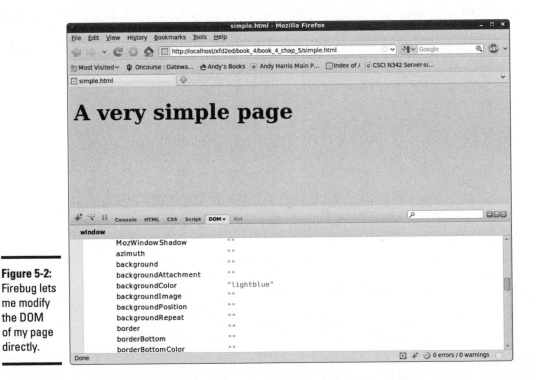

Figure 5-2:
Firebug lets me modify the DOM of my page directly.

Messing with the DOM through Firebug is kind of cool, and it helps you see how the page is organized, but it doesn't always work. Don't worry if you can't make the firebug DOM business work. You see in the next section it's actually easier to write code that changes the DOM than it is to change it through Firebug. The Firebug DOM tool is mainly used to look over your DOM to see how the page is currently organized in memory.

Harnessing the DOM through JavaScript

Sure, using Firebug to trick out your Web page is geeky and all, but why should you care? The whole purpose of the DOM is to provide JavaScript magical access to all the inner workings of your page.

Getting the blues, JavaScript-style

It all gets fun when you start to write JavaScript code to access the DOM. Take a look at `blue.html` in Figure 5-3.

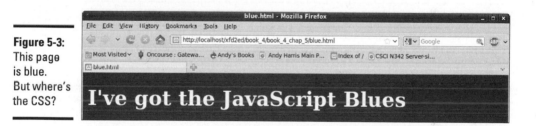

Figure 5-3: This page is blue. But where's the CSS?

The page has white text on a blue background, but there's no CSS! Instead, it has a small script that changes the DOM directly, controlling the page colors through code.

```
<!DOCTYPE html PUBLIC "-//W3C//DTD XHTML 1.0 Strict//EN"
"http://www.w3.org/TR/xhtml1/DTD/xhtml1-strict.dtd">
<html lang="EN" dir="ltr" xmlns="http://www.w3.org/1999/xhtml">
  <head>
    <meta http-equiv="content-type" content="text/xml; charset=utf-8" />
    <title>blue.html</title>

  </head>

  <body>
    <h1>I've got the JavaScript Blues</h1>
    <script type = "text/javascript">
      //<![CDATA[

      // use javascript to set the colors
      document.body.style.color = "white";
      document.body.style.backgroundColor = "blue";

      //]]>
    </script>
  </body>
</html>
```

Shouldn't it be background-color?

If you've dug through the DOM style elements, you'll notice some interesting things. Many of the element names are familiar but not quite identical. `background-color` becomes `backgroundColor` and `font-weight` becomes `fontWeight`. CSS uses dashes to indicate word breaks, and the DOM combines words and uses capitalization for clarity. You'll find all your old favorite CSS elements, but the names change according to this very predictable formula. Still, if you're ever confused, just use the Firebug DOM inspector to look over various style elements.

Writing JavaScript code to change colors

The page shown in Figure 5-3 is pretty simple, but it has a few features not found in Chapters 1 through 4 of this minibook.

+ **It has no CSS.** A form of CSS is dynamically created through the code.

+ **The script is in the body.** I can't place this particular script in the header because it refers to the body.

When the browser first sees the script, there must be a body for the text to change. If I put the script in the head, no body exists when the browser reads the code, so it gets confused. If I place the script in the body, there is a body, so the script can change it. (It's really okay if you don't get this discussion. This example is probably the only time you'll see this trick because I show a better way in the next example.)

+ **Use a DOM reference to change the style colors.** That long "trail of breadcrumbs" syntax takes you all the way from the document through the body to the style and finally the color. It's tedious but thorough.

+ **Set the foreground color to white.** You can change the color property to any valid CSS color value (a color name or a hex value). It's just like CSS, because you are affecting the CSS.

+ **Set the background color to blue.** Again, this adjustment is just like setting CSS.

Managing Button Events

Of course, there's no good reason to write code like `blue.html`, which I discuss in the section "Harnessing the DOM through JavaScript," earlier in this chapter. You will find that it's just as easy to build CSS as it is to write JavaScript. The advantage comes when you use the DOM dynamically to change the page's behavior after it has finished loading.

Figure 5-4 shows a page called `"backgroundColors.html"`.

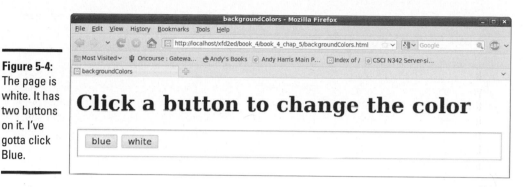

Figure 5-4:
The page is
white. It has
two buttons
on it. I've
gotta click
Blue.

The page is set up with the default white background color. It has two buttons on it, which should change the body's background color. Click the Blue button, and you see that it works, as verified in Figure 5-5.

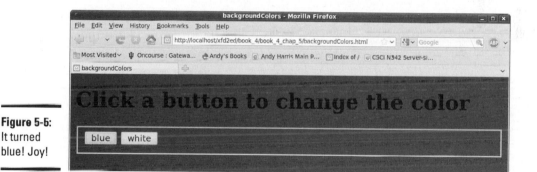

Figure 5-5:
It turned
blue! Joy!

Some really exciting things just happened.

✦ **The page has a form.** For more information on form elements, refer to Book I, Chapter 7.

✦ **The button does something.** Plain-old XHTML forms don't really do anything. You've got to write some kind of programming code to accomplish a task. This program does it.

✦ **The page has a `setColor()` function.** The page has a function that takes a color name and applies it to the background style.

✦ **Both buttons pass information to `setColor`.** Both of the buttons call the `setColor()` function, but they each pass a different color value. That's how the program knows what color to use when changing the background.

Take a look at the code:

```
<!DOCTYPE html PUBLIC "-//W3C//DTD XHTML 1.0 Strict//EN"
"http://www.w3.org/TR/xhtml1/DTD/xhtml1-strict.dtd">
<html lang="EN" dir="ltr" xmlns="http://www.w3.org/1999/xhtml">
  <head>
    <meta http-equiv="content-type" content="text/xml; charset=utf-8" />
    <title>backgroundColors</title>
    <script type = "text/javascript">
      //<![CDATA[
      // from backgroundColors

      function changeColor(color){
        document.body.style.backgroundColor = color;
      } // end changeColor

      //]]>
    </script>
  </head>

  <body>
    <h1>Click a button to change the color</h1>
    <form action = "">
      <fieldset>
        <input type = "button"
               value = "blue"
               onclick = "changeColor('blue')"/>

        <input type = "button"
               value = "white"
               onclick = "changeColor('white')" />
      </fieldset>

    </form>
  </body>
</html>
```

Most Web pages actually treat the XHTML page as the user interface and the JavaScript as the event-manipulation code that goes underneath. It makes sense, then, to look at the HTML code that acts as the playground first:

✦ **It contains a form.** Note that the form's `action` attribute is still empty. You don't mess with that attribute until you work with the server in Book V.

✦ **The form has a `fieldset`.** The `input` elements need to be inside something, and a `fieldset` seems like a pretty natural choice.

✦ **The page has two buttons.** The two buttons on the page are nothing new, but they've never done anything before.

✦ **The buttons both have `onclick` attributes.** This special attribute can accept one line of JavaScript code. Usually, that line calls a function, as I do in this example.

✦ **Each button calls the same function but with a different parameter.** Both buttons call `changeColor()`, but one sends the value `"blue"` and the other `"white"`.

✦ **Presumably, `changeColor` changes a color.** That's exactly what it will do. In fact, it changes the background color.

Generally, I write the XHTML code before the script. As you can see, the form provides all kinds of useful information that can help me make the script. Specifically, I need to write a function called `changeColor()`, and this function should take a color name as a parameter and change the background to the indicated color. With that kind of help, the function is half written!

Embedding quotes within quotes

Take a careful look at the `onclick` lines in the code in the preceding section. You may not have noticed one important issue:

`onclick` is an XHTML parameter, and its value must be encased in quotes. The parameter happens to be a function call, which sends a string value. String values must also be in quotes. This setup can become confusing if you use double quotes everywhere because the browser has no way to know the quotes are nested.

```
onclick = "changeColor("white")" />
```

XHTML thinks the `onclick` parameter contains the value `"changeColor("` and it will have no idea what `white")"` is.

Fortunately, JavaScript has an easy fix for this problem. If you want to embed a quote inside another quote, just switch to single quotes. The line is written with the parameter inside single quotes:

```
onclick = "changeColor('white')" />
```

Writing the changeColor function

The `changeColor()` function is pretty easy to write.

```
<script type = "text/javascript">
  //<![CDATA[
  // from backgroundColors

  function changeColor(color){
    document.body.style.backgroundColor = color;
  } // end changeColor

  //]]>
</script>
```

It goes in the header area as normal. It's simply a function accepting one parameter called `color`. The body's `backgroundColor` property is set to `color`.

I can write JavaScript in the header that refers to the body because the header code is all in a function. The function is read before the body is in place, but it isn't activated until the user clicks the button. By the time the user activates the code by clicking on the button, there is a body, and there's no problem.

Managing Text Input and Output

Perhaps the most intriguing application of the DOM is the ability to let the user communicate with the program through the Web page, without all those annoying dialog boxes. Figure 5-6 shows a page with a Web form containing two textboxes and a button.

Figure 5-6: I've typed a name into the top textbox.

When you click the button, something exciting happens, demonstrated by Figure 5-7.

Clearly, form-based input and output is preferable to the constant interruption of dialog boxes.

Introducing event-driven programming

Graphic user interfaces usually use a technique called *event-driven programming*. The idea is simple.

1. Create a user interface.

In Web pages, the user interface is usually built of XHTML and CSS.

2. Identify events the program should respond to.

If you have a button, users will click it. (If you want to guarantee they click it, put the text "Launch the Missiles" on the button. I don't know why, but it always works.) Buttons almost always have events. Some other elements do, too.

3. **Write a function to respond to each event.**

   For each event you want to test, write a function that does whatever needs to happen.

4. **Get information from form elements.**

   Now you're accessing the contents of form elements to get information from the user. You need a mechanism for getting information from a text field and other form elements.

5. **Use form elements for output.**

   For this simple example, I also use form elements for output. The output goes in a second textbox, even though I don't intend the user to type any text there.

**Book IV
Chapter 5**

Talking to the Page

Figure 5-7:
I got a greeting! With no alert box!

Creating the XHTML form

The first step in building a program that can manage text input and output is to create the XHTML framework. Here's the XHTML code:

```
<title>textBoxes.html</title>

<link rel = "stylesheet"
      type = "text/css"
      href = "textBoxes.css" />

</head>
```

```
<body>
  <h1>Text Box Input and Output</h1>
  <form action = "">
    <fieldset>
      <label>Type your name: </label>
      <input type = "text"
             id = "txtName" />

      <input type = "button"
             value = "click me"
             onclick = "sayHi()"/>

      <input type = "text"
             id = "txtOutput" />
    </fieldset>
  </form>

</body>
</html>
```

As you look over the code, note a few important ideas:

✦ **The page uses external CSS.** The CSS style is nice, but it's not important in the discussion here. It stays safely encapsulated in its own file. Of course, you're welcome to look it over or change it.

✦ **Most of the page is a form.** All form elements must be inside a form.

✦ **A `fieldset` is used to contain form elements.** input elements need to be inside some sort of block-level element, and a `fieldset` is a natural choice.

✦ **There's a text field named `txtName`.** This text field contains the name. I begin with the phrase txt to remind myself that this field is a textbox.

✦ **The second element is a button.** You don't need to give the button an ID (as it won't be referred to in code), but it does have an `onclick()` event.

✦ **The button's `onclick` event refers to a (yet undefined) function.** In this example, it's named `"sayHi()"`.

✦ **A second textbox contains the greeting.** This second textbox is called `txtOutput` because it's the text field meant for output.

After you set up the HTML page, the function becomes pretty easy to write because you've already identified all the major constructs. You know you need a function called `sayHi()`, and this function reads text from the `txtName` field and writes to the `txtOutput` field.

Using GetElementById to get access to the page

XHTML is one thing, and JavaScript is another. You need some way to turn an HTML form element into something JavaScript can read. The magical `getElementById()` method does exactly that. First, look at the first two lines of the `sayHi()` function (defined in the header as usual).

```
function sayHi(){
  var txtName = document.getElementById("txtName");
  var txtOutput = document.getElementById("txtOutput");
```

You can extract every element created in your Web page by digging through the DOM. In the old days, this approach is how we used to access form elements. It was ugly and tedious. Modern browsers have the wonderful `getElementById()` function instead. This beauty searches through the DOM and returns a reference to an object with the requested ID.

A *reference* is simply an indicator where the specified object is in memory. You can store a reference in a variable. Manipulating this variable manipulates the object it represents. If you want, you can think of it as making the textbox into a variable.

Note that I call the variable `txtName`, just like the original textbox. This variable refers to the text field from the form, not the value of that text field. Once I have a reference to the text field object, I can use its methods and properties to extract data from it and send new values to it.

Manipulating the text fields

Once you have access to the text fields, you can manipulate the values of these fields with the `value` property:

```
var name = txtName.value;
txtOutput.value = "Hi there, " + name + "!"
```

Text fields (and, in fact, all input fields) have a `value` property. You can read this value as an ordinary string variable. You can also write to this property, and the text field will be updated on the fly.

This code handles the data input and output:

1. **Create a variable for the name.**

This is an ordinary string variable.

2. **Copy the value of the textbox into the variable.**

Now that you have a variable representing the textbox, you can access its `value` property to get the value typed in by the user.

3. **Create a message for the user.**

Use ordinary string concatenation.

4. **Send the message to the `output` textbox.**

You can also write text to the `value` property, which changes the contents of the text field on the screen.

Text fields always return string values (like prompts do). If you want to pull a numeric value from a text field, you may have to convert it with the parseInt() or parseFloat() functions.

Writing to the Document

Form elements are great for getting input from the user, but they're not ideal for output. Placing the output in an editable field really doesn't make much sense. Changing the Web document is a much better approach.

The DOM supports exactly such a technique. Most XHTML elements feature an innerHTML property. This property describes the HTML code inside the element. In most cases, it can be read from and written to.

So what are the exceptions? Single-element tags (like <img> and <input>) don't contain any HTML, so obviously reading or changing their inner HTML doesn't make sense. Table elements can often be read from but not changed directly.

Figure 5-8 shows a program with a basic form.

Figure 5-8:
Wait, there's no output text field!

This form doesn't have a form element for the output. Enter a name and click the button, and you see the results in Figure 5-9.

Amazingly enough, this page can make changes to itself dynamically. It isn't simply changing the values of form fields, but changing the HTML.

Preparing the HTML framework

To see how the page changes itself dynamically, begin by looking at the XHTML body for innerHTML.html:

```
<body>
  <h1>Inner HTML Demo</h1>
  <form action = "">
    <fieldset>
      <label>Please type your name</label>
      <input type = "text"
             id = "txtName" />
      <button type = "button"
              onclick = "sayHi()">
        Click Me
      </button>
    </fieldset>
  </form>

  <div id = "divOutput">
    Watch this space.
  </div>
</body>
```

Figure 5-9:
The page has changed itself.

The code body has a couple of interesting features:

✦ **The program has a form.** The form is pretty standard. It has a text field for input and a button, but no output elements.

✦ **The button will call a `sayHi()` function.** The page requires a function with this name. Presumably, it says hi somehow.

✦ **There's a div for output.** A `div` element in the main body is designated for output.

✦ **The div has an ID.** The `id` attribute is often used for CSS styling, but the DOM can also use it. Any HTML elements that will be dynamically scripted should have an `id` field.

Writing the JavaScript

The JavaScript code for modifying `innerHTML` isn't very hard:

```
<script type = "text/javascript">
  //<![CDATA[
  //from innerHTML.html

  function sayHi(){
    txtName = document.getElementById("txtName");
    divOutput = document.getElementById("divOutput");

    name = txtName.value;

    divOutput.innerHTML = "<em>" + name +  "<\/em>";
    divOutput.innerHTML += " is a very nice name.";
  }
  //]]>
</script>
```

The first step (as usual with Web forms) is to extract data from the input elements. Note that I can create a variable representation of any DOM element, not just form elements. The `divOutput` variable is a JavaScript representation of the DOM div.

Finding your innerHTML

Like form elements, divs have other interesting properties you can modify. The `innerHTML` property allows you to change the HTML code displayed by the div. You can put any valid XHTML code you want inside the `innerHTML` property, even HTML tags. Be sure that you still follow the XHTML rules so that your code will be valid.

Even with the `CDATA` element in place, validators get confused by forward slashes (like the one in the `</em>` tag). Whenever you want to use a `/` character in JavaScript strings, precede it with a backslash (`<\/em>`). A backslash helps the validator understand that you intend to place a slash character at the next position.

Working with Other Text Elements

When you know how to work with text fields, you've mastered about half of the form elements. Several other form elements work exactly like text fields, including these:

+ **Password fields** obscure the user's input with asterisks, but preserve the text.

+ **Hidden fields** allow you to store information in a page without revealing it to the user. (They're used a little bit in client-side coding, but almost never in JavaScript.)

+ **Text areas** are a special variation of textboxes designed to handle multiple lines of input.

Figure 5-10 is a page with all these elements available on the same form.

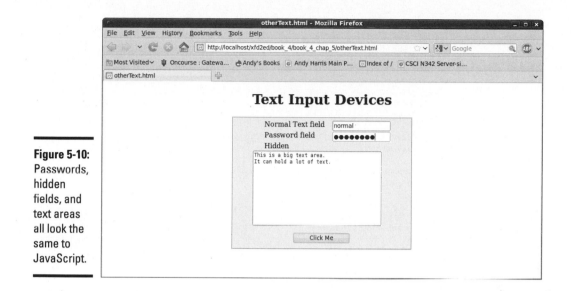

Figure 5-10:
Passwords,
hidden
fields, and
text areas
all look the
same to
JavaScript.

When the user clicks the button, the contents of all the fields (even the password and hidden fields) appear on the bottom of the page, as shown in Figure 5-11.

Figure 5-11:
Now you
can see
what was in
everything.

Building the form

Here's the XHTML (`otherText.html`) that generates the form shown in Figures 5-10 and 5-11:

```
<body>
  <h1>Text Input Devices</h1>
  <form action = "">
    <fieldset>
      <label>Normal Text field</label>
      <input type = "text"
             id = "txtNormal" />
      <label>Password field</label>
      <input type = "password"
             id = "pwd" />
      <label>Hidden</label>
      <input type = "hidden"
             id = "hidden"
             value = "I can't tell you" />
      <textarea id = "txtArea"
                rows = "10"
                cols = "40">
This is a big text area.
It can hold a lot of text.
      </textarea>
      <button type = "button"
              onclick = "processForm()">
        Click Me
      </button>
    </fieldset>
  </form>

  <div id = "output">

  </div>
</body>
```

The code may be familiar to you if you read about form elements in Book I, Chapter 7. A few things are worth noting for this example:

✦ **An ordinary text field appears, just for comparison purposes.** It has an `id` so that it can be identified in the JavaScript.

✦ **The next field is a password field.** Passwords display asterisks, but store the actual text that was entered. This password has an `id` of `pwd`.

✦ **The hidden field is a bit strange.** You can use hidden fields to store information on the page without displaying that information to the user. Unlike the other kinds of text fields, the user can't modify a hidden field. (She usually doesn't even know it's there.) This hidden field has an `id` of `secret` and a value (`"I can't tell you"`).

✦ **The text area has a different format.** The `input` elements are all single-tag elements, but the `textarea` is designed to contain a large amount of text, so it has beginning and end tags. The text area's `id` is `txtArea`.

✦ **A button starts all the fun.** As usual, most of the elements just sit there gathering data, but the button has an `onclick` event associated with it, which calls a function.

✦ **External CSS gussies it all up.** The page has some minimal CSS to clean it up. The CSS isn't central to this discussion, so I don't reproduce it. Note that the page will potentially have a dl on it, so I have a CSS style for it, even though it doesn't appear by default.

The password and hidden fields seem secure, but they aren't. Anybody who views the page source will be able to read the value of a hidden field, and passwords transmit their information in the clear. You really shouldn't be using Web technology (especially this kind) to transport nuclear launch codes or the secret to your special sauce. (Hmmm, maybe the secret sauce recipe *is* the launch code — sounds like a bad spy movie.)

When I create a text field, I often suspend my rules on indentation because the text field preserves everything inside it, including any indentation.

Writing the function

After you build the form, all you need is a function. Here's the good news: JavaScript treats all these elements in exactly the same way! The way you handle a password, hidden field, or text area is identical to the technique for a regular text field (described under "Managing Text Input and Output," earlier in this chapter). Here's the code:

```
<script type = "text/javascript">
//<![CDATA[

// from otherText.html
function processForm(){
  //grab input from form
  var txtNormal = document.getElementById("txtNormal");
  var pwd = document.getElementById("pwd");
  var hidden = document.getElementById("hidden");
  var txtArea = document.getElementById("txtArea");

  var normal = txtNormal.value;
  var password = pwd.value;
  var secret = hidden.value;
  var bigText = txtArea.value;

  //create output
  var result = ""
  result += "<dl> \n";
  result += "  <dt>normal<\/dt> \n";
  result += "  <dd>" + normal + "<\/dd> \n";
  result += " \n";
  result += "  <dt>password<\/dt> \n";
  result += "  <dd>" + password + "<\/dd> \n";
  result += " \n";
  result += "  <dt>secret<\/dt> \n";
  result += "  <dd>" + secret + "<\/dt> \n";
  result += "   \n";
  result += "  <dt>big text<\/dt> \n";
  result += "  <dd>" + bigText + "<\/dt> \n";
  result += "<\/dl> \n";

  var output = document.getElementById("output");
  output.innerHTML = result;

} // end function
```

The function is a bit longer than the others in this chapter, but it follows exactly the same pattern: It extracts data from the fields, constructs a string for output, and writes that output to the `innerHTML` attribute of a div in the page.

The code has nothing new, but it still has a few features you should consider:

✦ **Create a variable for each form element.** Use the `document.get ElementById` mechanism.

✦ **Create a string variable containing the contents of each element.** Don't forget: The `getElementById` trick returns an object. You need to extract the `value` property to see what's inside the object.

✦ **Make a big string variable to manage the output.** When output gets long and messy like this one, concatenate a big variable and then just output it in one swoop.

✦ **HTML is your friend.** This output is a bit complex, but `innerHTML` is HTML, so you can use any HTML styles you want to format your code. The `return` string is actually a complete definition list. Whatever is inside the textbox is (in this case) reproduced as HTML text, so if I want carriage returns or formatting, I have to add them with code.

✦ **Don't forget to escape the slashes.** The validator gets confused by ending tags, so add the backslash character to any ending tags occurring in JavaScript string variables. In other words, `</dl>` becomes `<\/dl>`.

✦ **Newline characters (\n) clean up the output.** If I were writing an ordinary definition list in HTML, I'd put each line on a new line. I try to make my programs write code just like I do, so I add newline characters everywhere I'd add a carriage return in ordinary HTML.

Understanding generated source

When you run the program in the preceding section, your JavaScript code actually changes the page it lives on. The code that doesn't come from your server (but is created by your program) is sometimes called *generated source*. The generated code technique is powerful, but it can have a significant problem. Try this experiment to see what I mean:

1. **Reload the page.**

You want to view it without the form contents showing so that you can view the source. Everything will be as expected; the source code shows exactly what you wrote.

2. **Click the Click Me button.**

Your function runs, and the page changes. You clearly added HTML to the `output` div, because you can see the output right on the screen.

3. **View the source again.**

You'll be amazed. The `output` div is empty, even though you can clearly see that it has changed.

4. **Check generated code.**

Using the HTML validator extension or the W3 validator (described in Book I, Chapter 2) doesn't check for errors in your generated code. You have to check it yourself, but it's hard to see the code!

Here's what's going on: The `view source` command (on most browsers) doesn't actually view the source of the page as it currently stands. It goes back to the server and retrieves the page but displays it as source rather than rendered output. As a result, the `view source` command isn't useful for telling you how the page has changed dynamically. Likewise, the page validators check the page as it occurs on the server without taking into account things that may have happened dynamically.

Figure 5-12 illustrates this problem.

Clearly there is content in the output div...   ...but the content div is empty in the source viewer.

Figure 5-12: The ordinary view source command isn't showing the contents of the div!

When you build regular Web pages, this approach isn't a problem because regular Web pages don't change. Dynamically generated pages can change on the fly, and the browser doesn't expect that. If you made a mistake in the HTML, you can't simply view the source to see what you did wrong in the code generated by your script. Fortunately, Firefox plugins give you two easy solutions:

- ✦ **The Web developer toolbar:** This toolbar has a wonderful tool called `view generated source` available on the `view source` menu. It allows you to view the source code of the current page in its current state, including any code dynamically generated by your JavaScript.

- ✦ **The Firebug window:** Open this window when a page is open and browse (with the HTML tab) around your page. Firebug gives you an accurate view of the page contents even when they're changed dynamically, which can be extremely useful.

These tools keep you sane when you're trying to figure out why your generated code isn't acting right. (I wish I'd had them years ago. . . .)

Figure 5-13 shows the Firebug toolbar with the dynamically generated contents showing.

Figure 5-13: Firebug shows the current status of the page, even if it's dynamically modified.

Chapter 6: Getting Valid Input

In This Chapter

🖊 **Extracting data from drop-down lists**

🖊 **Working with multiple-selection lists**

🖊 **Getting data from check boxes and radio groups**

🖊 **Validating input with regular expressions**

🖊 **Using character, boundary, and repetition operators**

🖊 **Using pattern memory**

Getting input from the user is always nice, but sometimes users make mistakes. Whenever you can, you want to make the user's job easier and prevent certain kinds of mistakes.

Fortunately, you can take advantage of several tools designed exactly for that purpose. In this chapter, you discover two main strategies for improving user input: specialized input elements and pattern-matching. Together, these tools can help ensure that the data the user enters is useful and valid.

Getting Input from a Drop-Down List

The most obvious way to ensure that the user enters something valid is to supply him with valid choices. The drop-down list is an obvious and easy way to do this, as you can see from Figure 6-1.

The list-box approach has a lot of advantages over text field input:

✦ The user can input with the mouse, which is faster and easier than typing.

✦ You shouldn't have any spelling errors because the user didn't type the response.

✦ The user knows all the answers available because they're listed.

✦ You can be sure the user gives you a valid answer because you supplied the possible responses.

✦ User responses can be mapped to more complex values — for example, you can show the user Red and have the list box return the hex value #FF0000.

Figure 6-1:
The user
selects from
a predefined
list of valid
choices.

If you want to know how to build a list box with the XHTML `select` object, refer to Book I, Chapter 7.

Building the form

When you're creating a predefined list of choices, create the HTML form first because it defines all the elements you'll need for the function. The code is a standard form:

```
<body>
  <form action = "">
    <h1>Please select a color</h1>
    <fieldset>
      <select id = "selColor">
        <option value = "#FFFFFF">White</option>
        <option value = "#FF0000">Red</option>
        <option value = "#FFCC00">Orange</option>
        <option value = "#FFFF00">Yellow</option>
        <option value = "#00FF00">Green</option>
        <option value = "#0000FF">Blue</option>
        <option value = "#663366">Indigo</option>
        <option value = "#FF00FF">Violet</option>
      </select>

      <input type = "button"
             value = "change color"
             onclick = "changeColor()" />
```

```
      </fieldset>
    </form>

  </body>
</html>
```

The `select` object's default behavior is to provide a drop-down list. The first element on the list is displayed, but when the user clicks the list, the other options appear.

A `select` object that the code refers to should have an `id` field.

In this and most examples in this chapter, I add CSS styling to clean up each form. Be sure to look over the styles if you want to see how I did it. Note also that I'm only showing the HTML right now. The entire code listing also includes JavaScript code, which I describe in the next section.

The other element in the form is a button. When the user clicks the button, the `changeColor()` function is triggered.

Because the only element in this form is the `select` object, you may want to change the background color immediately without requiring a button click. You can do so by adding an event handler directly onto the `select` object:

```
<select id = "selColor"
        onchange = "changeColor()">
```

The event handler causes the `changeColor()` function to be triggered as soon as the user changes the `select` object's value. Typically, you'll forego the user clicking a button only when the `select` is the only element in the form. If the form includes several elements, processing doesn't usually happen until the user signals she's ready by clicking a button.

Reading the list box

Fortunately, standard drop-down lists are quite easy to read. Here's the JavaScript code:

```
<script type = "text/javascript">
  //<![CDATA[
  // from dropdownList.html

  function changeColor(){
    var selColor = document.getElementById("selColor");
    var color = selColor.value;
    document.body.style.backgroundColor = color;
  } // end function
  //]]>
</script>
```

As you can see, the process for reading the `select` object is much like working with a text-style field:

✦ **Create a variable to represent the `select` object.** The `document.getElementById()` trick works here just like it does for text fields.

✦ **Extract the `value` property of the `select` object.** The `value` property of the `select` object reflects the `value` of the currently selected `option`. So, if the user has chosen Yellow, the value of `selColor` is `"#FFFF00"`.

✦ **Set the document's background color.** Use the DOM mechanism to set the body's background color to the chosen value.

Managing Multiple Selections

You can use the `select` object in a more powerful way than the method I describe in the preceding section. Figure 6-2 shows a page with a multiple-selection list box.

To make multiple selection work, you have to make a few changes to both the HTML and the JavaScript code.

Figure 6-2: You can pick multiple choices from this list.

Coding a multiple selection select object

You modify the `select` code in two ways to make multiple selections:

✦ **Indicate multiple selections are allowed.** By default, `select` boxes have only one value. You'll need to set a switch to tell the browser to allow more than one item to be selected.

✦ **Make the mode a multiline select.** The standard drop-down behavior doesn't make sense when you want multiple selections, because the user needs to see all the options at once. Most browsers automatically switch into a multiline mode, but you should control the process directly.

The XHTML code for `multiSelect.html` is similar to the `dropdownList` page, described in the preceding section, but note a couple of changes.

```
<body>
  <h1>Multiple Selections</h1>
  <form action = "">
    <fieldset>
      <label>
        Select the language(s) you know.
        (ctrl-click to select multiple lines)
      </label>
      <select id = "selLanguage"
              multiple = "multiple"
              size = "10">
      <option value = "XHTML">XHTML</option>
      <option value = "CSS">CSS</option>
      <option value = "JavaScript">JavaScript</option>
      <option value = "PHP">PHP</option>
      <option value = "MySQL">MySQL</option>
      <option value = "Java">Java</option>
      <option value = "VB.NET">VB.NET</option>
      <option value = "Python">Python</option>
      <option value = "Flash">Flash</option>
      <option value = "Perl">perl</option>
      </select>
      <button type = "button"
              onclick = "showChoices()">
        Submit
      </button>
    </fieldset>
  </form>

  <div id = "output">

  </div>
</body>
</html>
```

The code isn't shocking, but it does have some important features:

✦ **Call the `select` object `selLanguage`.** As usual, the form elements need an `id` attribute so that you can read it in the JavaScript.

✦ **Add the `multiple` attribute to your `select` object.** This attribute tells the browser to accept multiple inputs using Shift+click (for contiguous selections) or Ctrl+click (for more precise selection).

✦ **Set the `size` to 10.** The size indicates the number of lines to be displayed. I set the size to 10 because my list has ten options.

✦ **Make a button.** With multiple selection, you probably won't want to trigger the action until the user has finished making selections. A separate button is the easiest way to make sure the code is triggered when you want it to happen.

✦ **Create an `output` div.** This code holds the response.

Writing the JavaScript code

The JavaScript code for reading a multiple-selection list box is a bit different than the standard selection code described in the section "Reading the list box" earlier in this chapter. The `value` property usually returns one value, but a multiple-selection list box often returns more than one result.

The key is to recognize that a list of `option` objects inside a `select` object is really a kind of array, not just one value. You can look more closely at the list of objects to see which ones are selected, which is essentially what the `showChoices()` function does:

```
<script type = "text/javascript">
//<![CDATA[
//from multi-select.html
function showChoices(){
  //retrieve data
  var selLanguage = document.getElementById("selLanguage");

  //set up output string
  var result = "<h2>Your Languages<\/h2>";
  result += "<ul> \n";

  //step through options
  for (i = 0; i < selLanguage.length; i++){
    //examine current option
    currentOption = selLanguage[i];

    //print it if it has been selected
    if (currentOption.selected == true){
      result += "  <li>" + currentOption.value + "<\/li> \n";
    } // end if
  } // end for loop

  //finish off the list and print it out
  result += "<\/ul> \n";

  output = document.getElementById("output");
  output.innerHTML = result;
} // end showChoices
//]]>
</script>
```

At first, the code seems intimidating, but if you break it down, it's not too tricky.

1. **Create a variable to represent the entire `select` object.**

   The standard `document.getElementById()` technique works fine.

   ```
   var selLanguage = document.getElementById("selLanguage");
   ```

2. **Create a string variable to hold the output.**

   When you're building complex HTML output, working with a string variable is much easier than directly writing code to the element.

   ```
   var result = "<h2>Your Languages<\/h2>";
   ```

3. **Build an unordered list to display the results.**

   An unordered list is a good way to spit out the results, so I create one in my `result` variable.

   ```
   result += "<ul> \n";
   ```

4. **Step through `selLanguage` as if it were an array.**

   Use a `for` loop to examine the list box line by line. Note that `selLanguage` has a `length` property like an array.

   ```
   for (i = 0; i < selLanguage.length; i++){
   ```

5. **Assign the current element to a temporary variable.**

   The `currentOption` variable holds a reference to the each `option` element in the original `select` object as the loop progresses.

   ```
   currentOption = selLanguage[i];
   ```

6. **Check to see whether the current element has been selected.**

   The object `currentOption` has a `selected` property that tells you whether the object has been highlighted by the user. `selected` is a Boolean property, so it's either true or false.

   ```
   if (currentOption.selected == true){
   ```

7. **If the element has been selected, add an entry to the output list.**

   If the user has highlighted this object, create an entry in the unordered list housed in the `result` variable.

   ```
   result += "  <li>" + currentOption.value + "<\/li> \n";
   ```

8. **Close up the list.**

   Once the loop has finished cycling through all the objects, you can close up the unordered list you've been building.

   ```
   result += "<\/ul> \n";
   ```

9. **Print results to the `output` div.**

   The `output` div's `innerHTML` property is a perfect place to print the unordered list.

   ```
   output = document.getElementById("output");
   output.innerHTML = result;
   ```

Something strange is going on here. The options of a select box act like an array. An unordered list is a lot like an array. Bingo! They *are* arrays, just in different forms. You can think of any listed data as an array. Sometimes you organize the data like a list (for display), sometimes like an array (for storage in memory), and sometimes it's a select group (for user input). Now you're starting to think like a programmer!

Check, Please: Reading Check Boxes

Check boxes fulfill another useful data input function. They're useful any time you have Boolean data. If some value can be true or false, a check box is a good tool. Figure 6-3 illustrates a page that responds to check boxes.

Check boxes are independent of each other. Although they're often found in groups, any check box can be checked or unchecked regardless of the status of its neighbors.

Building the check box page

To build the check box page shown in Figure 6-3, start by looking at the HTML:

```
<body>
  <h1>What do you want on your pizza?</h1>
  <form action = "">
    <fieldset>
      <input type = "checkbox"
             id = "chkPepperoni"
             value = "pepperoni" />
      <label>Pepperoni</label>

      <input type = "checkbox"
             id = "chkMushroom"
             value = "mushrooms" />
      <label>Mushrooms</label>

      <input type = "checkbox"
             id = "chkSausage"
             value = "sausage" />
      <label>Sausage</label>

      <button type = "button"
              onclick = "order()">
        Order Pizza
      </button>
    </fieldset>
  </form>
  <h2>Your order:</h2>
  <div id = "output">

  </div>
</body>
```

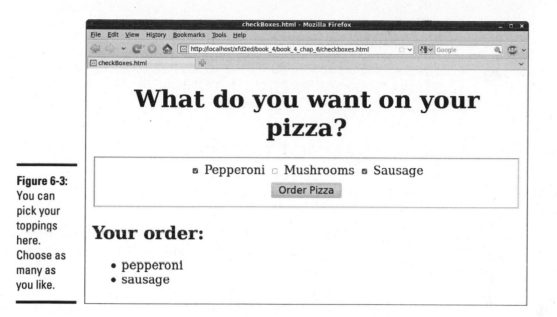

Figure 6-3:
You can
pick your
toppings
here.
Choose as
many as
you like.

Each check box is an individual input element. Note that check box values aren't displayed. Instead, a label (or similar text) is usually placed after the check box. A button calls an order() function.

Responding to the check boxes

Check boxes don't require a lot of care and feeding. Once you extract it, the check box has two critical properties:

✦ You can use the value property to store a value associated with the check box (just like you do with text fields in Chapter 5 of this minibook).

✦ The checked property is a Boolean value, indicating whether the check box is checked or not.

The code for the order() function shows how it's done:

```
<script type = "text/javascript">
  //<![CDATA[
  //from checkBoxes.html

  function order(){
    //get variables
    var chkPepperoni = document.getElementById("chkPepperoni");
    var chkMushroom = document.getElementById("chkMushroom");
    var chkSausage = document.getElementById("chkSausage");

    var output = document.getElementById("output");
    var result = "<ul> \n";

    if (chkPepperoni.checked){
      result += "<li>" + chkPepperoni.value + "<\/li> \n";
```

```
      } // end if

      if (chkMushroom.checked){
        result += "<li>" + chkMushroom.value + "<\/li> \n";
      } // end if

      if (chkSausage.checked){
        result += "<li>" + chkSausage.value + "<\/li> \n";
      } // end if

      result += "<\/ul> \n"
      output.innerHTML = result;
    } // end function

    //]]>
  </script>
```

For each check box:

1. **Determine whether the check box is checked.**

Use the `checked` property as a condition.

2. **If so, return the `value` property associated with the check box.**

Often, in practice, the `value` property is left out. The important thing is whether the check box is checked. If `chkMushroom` is checked, the user obviously wants mushrooms, so you may not need to explicitly store that data in the check box itself.

Working with Radio Buttons

Radio button groups appear pretty simple, but they're more complex than they seem. Figure 6-4 shows a page using radio button selection.

Figure 6-4:
One and only one member of a radio group can be selected at one time.

The most important thing to remember about radio buttons is that, like wildebeests and power-walkers, they must be in groups. Each group of radio buttons has only one button active. The group should be set up so that one button is always active.

You specify the radio button group in the XHTML code. Each element of the group can have an `id` (although the IDs aren't really necessary in this application). What's more important here is the `name` attribute. Look over the code, and you'll notice something interesting. All the radio buttons have the same name!

```
<body>
  <h1>With what weapon will you fight the dragon?</h1>
  <form action = "">
    <fieldset>
      <input type = "radio"
             name = "weapon"
             id = "radSpoon"
             value = "spoon"
             checked = "checked" />
      <label>Spoon</label>

      <input type = "radio"
             name = "weapon"
             id = "radFlower"
             value = "flower" />
      <label>Flower</label>

      <input type = "radio"
             name = "weapon"
             id = "radNoodle"
             value = "wet noodle" />
      <label>Wet Noodle</label>
      <button type = "button"
              onclick = "fight()">
        fight the dragon
      </button>
    </fieldset>
  </form>
  <div id = "output">

  </div>
</body>
</html>
```

Using a `name` attribute when everything else has an `id` seems a little odd, but you do it for a good reason. The `name` attribute is used to indicate the *group* of radio buttons. Because all the buttons in this group have the same name, they're related, and only one of them will be selected.

The browser recognizes this behavior and automatically unselects the other buttons in the group whenever one is selected.

I added a label to describe what each radio button means.

You need to preset one of the radio buttons to true with the `checked = "checked"` attribute. If you fail to do so, you have to add code to account for the possibility that there is no answer at all.

Interpreting radio buttons

Getting information from a group of radio buttons requires a slightly different technique than most of the form elements. Unlike the `select` object, there is no container object that can return a simple value. You also can't just go through every radio button on the page because you may have more than one group. (Imagine a page with a multiple-choice test.)

This issue is where the `name` attribute comes in. Although `ids` must be unique, multiple elements on a page can have the same `name`. If they do, you can treat these elements as an array.

Look over the code to see how it works:

```
<script type = "text/javascript">
  //<![CDATA[
  // from radioGroup.html
  function fight(){

    var weapon = document.getElementsByName("weapon");

    for (i = 0; i < weapon.length; i++){
      currentWeapon = weapon[i];

      if (currentWeapon.checked){
        var selectedWeapon = currentWeapon.value;
      } // end if

    } // end for

    var output = document.getElementById("output");
    var response = "<h2>You defeated the dragon with a ";
    response += selectedWeapon + "<\/h2> \n";
    output.innerHTML = response;
  } // end function

  //]]>
</script>
```

This code looks much like all the other code in this chapter, but it has a sneaky difference:

✦ **It uses `getElementsByName` to retrieve an array of elements with this name.** Now that you're comfortable with `getElementById`, I throw a monkey wrench in the works. Note that it's plural — `getElementsByName` — because this tool is used to extract an array of elements. It returns an array of elements. (In this case, all the radio buttons in the `weapon` group.)

✦ **It treats the result as an array.** The resulting variable (weapon in this example) is an array. As usual, the most common thing to do with arrays is process them with loops. Use a `for` loop to step through each element in the array.

✦ **Assign each element of the array to `currentWeapon`.** This variable holds a reference to the current radio button.

✦ **Check to see whether the current weapon is checked.** The `checked` property indicates whether any radio button is checked.

✦ **If so, retain the value of the radio button.** If a radio button is checked, its value is the current value of the group, so store it in a variable for later use.

✦ **Output the results.** You can now process the results as you would with data from any other resource.

Working with Regular Expressions

Having the right kinds of form elements can be helpful, but things can still go wrong. Sometimes, you have to let the user type things, and that information must be in a particular format. As an example, take a look at Figure 6-5.

Figure 6-5:
This page is a mess. No username plus an invalid e-mail and phone number.

A mechanism that checks whether input from a form is in the correct format would be great. This program implements such a feature, checking whether there is content in every field and ensuring the e-mail address and phone number are formatted correctly. You can create this kind of testing feature with string functions, but it can be really messy. Imagine how many `if` statements and string methods it would take to enforce the following rules on this page:

+ **An entry must appear in each field.** This one is reasonably easy — just check for non-null values.

+ **The e-mail must be in a valid format.** That is, it must consist of a few characters, an "at" sign (@), a few more characters, a period, and a domain name of two to four characters. That format would be a real pain to check for.

+ **The phone number must also be in a valid format.** Phone numbers can appear in multiple formats, but assume that you require an area code in parentheses, followed by an optional space, followed by three digits, a dash, and four digits. All digits must be numeric.

Although you can enforce these rules, it would be extremely difficult to do so using ordinary string manipulation tools.

JavaScript strings have a `match` method, which helps find a substring inside a larger string. This tool is good, but we're not simply looking for specific text, but patterns of text. For example, we want to know whether something's an e-mail address (text, an @, more text, a period, and two to four more characters).

Imagine how difficult that code would be to write; then take a look at the code for the `validate.html` page:

```
<script type = "text/javascript">
  function validate(){
    // get inputs
    name = document.getElementById("txtName").value;
    email = document.getElementById("txtEmail").value;
    phone = document.getElementById("txtPhone").value;

    //create an empty error message
    errors = "";

    //check name - It simply needs to exist
    if (name == ""){
      errors += "please supply a name \n";
    } // end if

    //check email
    emailRE = /^.+@.+\..{2,4}$/;
    if (email.match(emailRE)){
```

```
    //console.log("email match");
    //do nothing.
  } else {
    //console.log("email not a match");
    errors += "please check email address \n";
  } // end if

  //check phone number
  phoneRE = /^\(\d{3}\) *\d{3}-\d{4}$/;
  if (phone.match(phoneRE)){
    //console.log("phone matches");
    //do nothing
  } else {
    //console.log("phone problem");
    errors += "please check phone #\n";
  } // end phone if

  //check for errors
  if (errors == ""){
    alert ("now processing data");
    //process the form
  } else {
    alert(errors);
  } // end if

} // end function
```

I only show the JavaScript code here to save space. Look on the CD-ROM to see how the HTML and CSS are written.

The code isn't really all that difficult!

+ **It extracts data from the form.** It does so in the usual way.

+ **The validation is a series of nested if statements.** Look at the overall structure. The if statements go three layers deep.

+ **The name check is very simple.** The only way it can go wrong is to have no name.

+ **Don't check anything else if the name is wrong.** If the name isn't right, you don't need to check the other things.

+ **Build a regular expression.** This verification seems pretty simple until you look at the line that contains the emailRE = /^.+@.+\..{2,4}$/; business. It looks like a cursing cartoonist in there. That weird-looking text is a *regular expression* and the key to this program. For now, just accept it as a magic incantation. I explain it in a moment, but focus on the big picture here.

+ **Match the regular expression against the e-mail address.** The next line checks to see whether the e-mail address is a match to the regular expression. The result is true if the expression matches an e-mail address or null if it doesn't.

✦ **Check the phone number.** Once again, the phone number check is simple except the match business, which is just as mysterious: `/^\(\d{3}\) *\d{3}-\d{4}$/` (seriously, who makes this stuff up?). That's another regular expression.

✦ **If everything worked, process the form.** Usually, at this point, you call some sort of function to finish handling the form processing.

Frequently, you do validation in JavaScript before you pass information to a program on the server. This way, your server program already knows the data is valid by the time it gets there.

Introducing regular expressions

Of course, the secret of this program is to decode the mystical expressions used in the `match` statements. They aren't really strings at all, but very powerful text-manipulation techniques called *regular expression parsing*. Regular expressions have migrated from the Unix world into many programming languages, including JavaScript.

A *regular expression* is a powerful mini-language for searching and replacing text patterns. Essentially, what it does is allow you to search for complex patterns and expressions. It's a weird-looking language, but it has a certain charm once you know how to read the arcane-looking expressions.

Regular expressions are normally used with the string `match()` method in JavaScript, but you can also use them with the `replace()` method and a few other places.

Table 6-1 summarizes the main operators in JavaScript regular expressions.

Table 6-1	Regular Expression Operators in JavaScript			
Operator	*Description*	*Sample Pattern*	*Matches*	*Doesn't Match*
. (period)	Any single character except newline	.	E	\n
^	Beginning of string	^a	Apple	Banana
$	End of string	a$	Banana	Apple
[characters]	Any of a list of characters in braces	[abcABC]	A	D

Operator	Description	Sample Pattern	Matches	Doesn't Match
[char range]	Any character in the range	[a-zA-Z]	F	9
\d	Any single numerical digit	\d\d\d-\d\d\d\d	123-4567	The-thing
\b	A word boundary	\bthe\b	The	Theater
+	One or more occurrences of the previous character	\d+	1234	Text
*	Zero or more occurrences of the previous character	[a-zA-Z]d*	B17, g	7
{digit}	Repeat preceding character *digit* times	\d{3}-\d{4}	123-4567	999-99-9999
{min, max}	Repeat preceding character at least *min* but not more than *max* times	.{2,4}	Ca, com, info	water-melon
(pattern segment)	Store results in pattern memory returned with code	^(.).*\1$	gig, wallow	Bobby

Don't memorize this table! I explain in the rest of this chapter exactly how regular expressions work. Keep Table 6-1 handy as a reference.

To see how regular expressions work, take a look at regex.html in Figure 6-6.

The top textbox accepts a regular expression, and the second text field contains text to examine. You can practice the examples in the following sections to see how regular expressions work. They're really quite useful after you get the hang of them. While you walk through the examples, try them out in this tester. (I include it on the CD-ROM for you, but I don't reproduce the code here.)

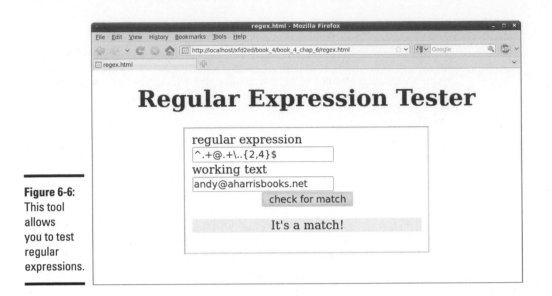

Figure 6-6:
This tool
allows
you to test
regular
expressions.

Using characters in regular expressions

The main thing you do with a regular expression is search for text. Say that you work for the bigCorp company, and you ask for employee e-mail addresses. You can make a form that accepts only e-mail addresses with the term *bigCorp* in them by using the following code:

```
if (email.match(/bigCorp/)){
  alert("match");
} else {
  alert("no match");
} // end if
```

The text in the `match()` method is enclosed in slashes (/) rather than quote symbols because the expression isn't technically a string; it's a regular expression. The slashes help the interpreter realize this special kind of text requires additional processing.

If you forget and enclose a regular expression inside quotes, it will still work most of the time. JavaScript tries to convert string values into regular expressions when it needs to. However, if you've ever watched a science fiction movie, you know it's generally not best to trust computers. Use the slash characters to explicitly coerce the text into regular expression format. I'm not saying your computer will take over the world if you don't, but you never can tell. . . .

This match is the simplest type. I'm simply looking for the existence of the needle (bigCorp) in a haystack (the e-mail address stored in `email`). If *bigCorp* is found anywhere in the text, the match is true, and I can do what I want (usually process the form on the server). More often, you want to trap for an error and remind the user what needs to be fixed.

Marking the beginning and end of the line

You may want to improve the search, because what you really want are addresses that end with `bigCorp.com`. You can put a special character inside the match string to indicate where the end of the line should be:

```
if (email.match(/bigCorp.com$/)){
  alert("match");
} else {
  alert("no match");
} // end if
```

The dollar sign at the end of the match string indicates that this part of the text should occur at the end of the search string, so `andy@bigCorp.com` is a match, but not *bigCorp.com announces a new Website*.

If you're an ace with regular expressions, you know this example has a minor problem, but it's pretty picky. I explain it in the upcoming "Working with special characters" section. For now, just appreciate that you can include the end of the string as a search parameter.

Likewise, you can use the caret character (^) to indicate the beginning of a string.

If you want to ensure that a text field contains only the phrase *oogie boogie* (and why wouldn't you?), you can tack on the beginning and ending markers. The code `/^oogie boogie$/` is a true match only if nothing else appears in the phrase.

Working with special characters

In addition to ordinary text, you can use a bunch of special character symbols for more flexible matching:

✦ **Matching a character with the period:** The most powerful character is the period (.), which represents a single character. Any single character except the newline (\n) matches against the period. A character that matches any character may seem silly, but it's actually quite powerful. The expression `/b.g/` matches *big, bag,* and *bug.* In fact, it matches any phrase that contains *b* followed by any single character and then *g,* so *bxg, b g,* and *b9g* are also matches.

✦ **Using a character class:** You can specify a list of characters in square braces, and JavaScript matches if any one of those characters matches. This list of characters is sometimes called a *character class.* For example, `/b[aeiou]g/` matches on *bag, beg, big, bog,* or *bug.* This method is a really quick way to check a lot of potential matches.

You can also specify a character class with a range. `[a-zA-Z]` checks all the letters.

✦ **Specifying digits:** One of the most common tricks is to look for numbers. The special character \d represents a number (0–9). You can check for a U.S. phone number (without the area code — yet) using a pattern that looks for three digits, a dash, and four digits: /\d\d\d-\d\d\d\d/.

✦ **Marking punctuation characters:** You can tell that regular expressions use a lot of funky characters, such as periods and braces. What if you're searching for one of these characters? Just use a backslash to indicate that you're looking for the actual character and not using it as a modifier. For example, the e-mail address would be better searched with bigCorp\.com because it specifies there must be a period. If you don't use the backslash, the regular expression tool interprets the period as "any character" and allows something like *bigCorpucom*. Use the backslash trick for most punctuation, such as parentheses, braces, periods, and slashes.

If you want to include an area code with parentheses, just use backslashes to indicate the parentheses: /\(\d\d\d\) \d\d\d-\d\d\d\d/. And if you want to ensure the only thing in the sample is the phone number, just add the boundary characters: /^\(\d\d\d\) \d\d\d \d\d\d\d$/.

✦ **Finding word boundaries:** Sometimes you want to know whether something is a word. Say that you're searching for *the,* but you don't want a false positive on *breathe* or *theater*. The \b character means "the edge of a word," so /\bthe\b/ matches *the* but not words containing "the" inside them.

Conducting repetition operations

All the character modifiers refer to one particular character at a time, but sometimes you want to deal with several characters at once. Several operators can help you with this process.

✦ **Finding one or more elements:** The plus sign (+) indicates "one or more" of the preceding character, so the pattern /ab+c/ matches on *abc, abbbbbbc,* or *abbbbbbbc,* but not on *ac* (there must be at least one b) or on *afc* (it's gotta be b).

✦ **Matching zero or more elements:** The asterisk means "zero or more" of the preceding character. So /I'm .* happy/ matches on *I'm happy* (zero occurrences of any character between *I'm* and *happy*). It also matches on *I'm not happy* (because characters appear in between).

The .* combination is especially useful, because you can use it to improve matches like e-mail addresses: /^.*@bigCorp\.com$/ does a pretty good job of matching e-mail addresses in a fictional company.

✦ **Specifying the number of matches:** You can use braces ({}) to indicate the specific number of times the preceding character should be repeated. For example, you can rewrite a phone number pattern as /\

(\d{3}\) *\d{3}-\d{4}/. This structure means "three digits in parentheses, followed by any number of spaces (zero or more), and then three digits, a dash, and four digits. Using this pattern, you can tell whether the user has entered the phone number in a valid format.

You can also specify a minimum and maximum number of matches, so / [aeiou]{1, 3}/ means "at least one and no more than three vowels."

Now you can improve the e-mail pattern so that it includes any number of characters, an @ sign, and ends with a period and two to four letters: /^.+@.+\..{2,4}$/.

Working with pattern memory

Sometimes you want to remember a piece of your pattern and reuse it. You can use parentheses to group a chunk of the pattern and remember it. For example, /(foo){2}/ doesn't match on *foo*, but it does on *foofoo*. It's the entire segment that's repeated twice.

You can also refer to a stored pattern later in the expression. The pattern /^(.).*\1$/ matches any word or phrase that begins and ends with the same character. The \1 symbol represents the first pattern in the string; \2 represents the second, and so on.

After you've finished a pattern match, the remembered patterns are still available in special variables. The variable $1 is the first; $2 is the second, and so on. You can use this trick to look for HTML tags and report what tag was found: Match ^<(.*)>.*<\/\1>$ and then print $1 to see what the tag was.

There's much more to discover about regular expressions, but this basic overview should give you enough to write some powerful and useful patterns.

Chapter 7: Animating Your Pages

In This Chapter

- ✓ Moving an object on the screen
- ✓ Responding to keyboard input
- ✓ Reading mouse input
- ✓ Running code repeatedly
- ✓ Bouncing off the walls
- ✓ Swapping images
- ✓ Preloading image files
- ✓ Reusing code
- ✓ Using external script files

*J*avaScript has a serious side, but it can be a lot of fun, too. You can easily use JavaScript to make things move, animate, and wiggle. In this chapter, you find out how to make your pages dance. Even if you aren't interested in animation, you can discover important ideas about how to design your pages and code more efficiently.

Making Things Move

You may think you need Flash or Java to put animation in your pages, but that's not the only way. You can use JavaScript to create some pretty interesting motion effects. Take a look at Figure 7-1.

Because this chapter is about animation, most of the pages feature motion. You really must see these pages in your browser to get the effect because a static screen shot can't really do any of these programs justice.

The general structure of this page provides a foundation for other kinds of animation:

- ✦ **The HTML is pretty simple.** The page really doesn't require much HTML code. It's a couple of divs and some buttons.

- ✦ **The ball is in a special div called `sprite`.** Game developers call the little images that move around on the screen *sprites,* so I use the same term.

Figure 7-1:
Click the
buttons
and the ball
moves.

+ **The `sprite` div has a local style.** JavaScript animation requires a locally defined style.

+ **The `sprite` div has absolute positioning.** Because I'll be moving this thing around on the screen, it makes sense that it's absolutely positioned.

+ **The code and CSS are as modular as possible.** Things can get a little complicated when you start animating things, so throughout this chapter, I simplify as much as I can. The CSS styles are defined externally, and the JavaScript code is also imported.

+ **Code is designed to be reused.** Many programs in this chapter are very similar to each other. To save effort, I've designed things so that I don't have to rewrite code if possible.

Looking over the HTML

The HTML code for this program provides the basic foundation:

```
<!DOCTYPE html PUBLIC "-//W3C//DTD XHTML 1.0 Strict//EN"
"http://www.w3.org/TR/xhtml1/DTD/xhtml1-strict.dtd">
<html lang="EN" dir="ltr" xmlns="http://www.w3.org/1999/xhtml">
  <head>
    <meta http-equiv="content-type" content="text/xml; charset=utf-8" />
    <title>movement.html</title>

    <link rel = "stylesheet"
```

```
            type = "text/css"
            href = "movement.css" />

    <script type = "text/javascript"
            src = "movement.js">
    </script>
  </head>

  <body onload = "init()">
    <h1>Click buttons to move ball</h1>
    <div id = "surface">
      <div id = "sprite"
           style = "position: absolute;
           top: 100px;
           left: 100px;
           height: 25px;
           width: 25px;" >
        <img src = "ball.gif"
             alt = "ball" />
      </div>
    </div>
    <form action = ""
          id = "controls">
      <fieldset>
        <button type = "button"
                onclick = "moveSprite(-5, 0)">
          left
        </button>
        <button type = "button"
                onclick = "moveSprite(5, 0)">
          right
        </button>
      </fieldset>
    </form>
    <p id = "output">
      x = 100, y = 100
    </p>
  </body>
</html>
```

You should notice a few interesting things about this code:

+ **It has an external style sheet.** Most of the CSS (the stuff that defines the surface and the forms) is moved off-stage into an external style sheet. You have to define some CSS locally, but anything that can be moved away is in another file.

```
      <link rel = "stylesheet"
            type = "text/css"
            href = "movement.css" />
```

+ **The JavaScript is also outsourced.** The script tag has a src attribute, which you can use to load JavaScript code from an external file. The browser loads the specified file and reads it as if it were directly in the code. (*Note:* External scripts still require a </script> tag.) This program gets its scripts from a file called movement.js.

```
      <script type = "text/javascript"
              src = "movement.js">
      </script>
```

✦ **The `body` tag calls a method.** In animation (and other advanced JavaScript), you commonly have some code you want to run right away. The body has an `onload` event. You can feed it the name of a function (just like you do with a button's `onclick` event). In this case, I want the function called `init()` to run as soon as the body finishes loading into the computer's memory.

```
<body onload = "init()">
```

✦ **The yellow box is a div called `surface`.** It isn't absolutely necessary, but when you have something moving around on the screen, you want some kind of boundary so that the user knows where she can move.

✦ **A `sprite` div appears inside `surface`.** This sprite is the thing that actually moves around.

```
<div id = "sprite"
     style = "position: absolute;
     top: 100px;
     left: 100px;
     height: 25px;
     width: 25px;" >
  <img src = "ball.gif"
       alt = "ball" />
</div>
```

✦ **The `sprite` div has a local style.** Your code can change only styles that have been defined locally. The `sprite` div has a local style specifying absolute position, left, and top properties.

✦ **It has buttons in a form.** This particular program uses form buttons to discern the user's intent. Those buttons are in a form.

```
<button type = "button"
        onclick = "moveSprite(-5, 0)">
  left
</button>
```

✦ **Each button calls the `moveSprite()` method.** The `moveSprite()` method is defined in the `movement.js` file. It accepts two parameters: `dx` determines how much the sprite should move in the *x* (side to side) axis, and `dy` controls how much the sprite will move in the *y* (vertical) axis.

Getting an overview of the JavaScript

The following programming concepts improve programmer efficiency, which is good when the JavaScript code becomes more complex:

✦ **Move code to an external file.** As with CSS code, when the JavaScript starts to get complex, it's a good idea to move it to its own file, so it's easier to manage.

✦ **Encapsulate code in functions.** Rather than writing a long, complicated function, try to break the code into smaller functions that solve individual problems. If you design these functions well, your code is easier to write, understand, and recycle.

✦ **Create a few global variables.** You can reuse a few key variables throughout your code. Create global variables for these key items, but don't make anything global that doesn't need to be.

✦ **Define constants for clarity.** Sometimes having a few key values stored in special variables is handy. I've created some constants to help me track the boundary of the visual surface.

Creating global variables

The first part of this document simply defines the global variables I use throughout the program:

```
//movement.js
//global variables
var sprite;
var x, y;      //position variables

//constants
var MIN_X = 15;
var MAX_X = 365;
var MIN_Y = 05;
var MAX_Y = 435;
```

The movement program has three main global variables:

✦ **sprite** represents the div that moves around on the screen.

✦ **x** is the x (horizontal) position of the sprite.

✦ **y** is the y (vertical) position of the sprite.

You don't need to give values to global variables right away, but you should define them outside any functions so that their values are available to all functions. (See Chapter 4 in this minibook for more about functions and variable scope.)

In computer graphics, the y axis works differently than it does in math. Zero is the top of the screen, and y values increase as you move down the page. (This increase happens because video memory models the top-to-bottom pattern of most display devices.)

This program also features some special *constants*. A constant is a variable (usually global) whose value isn't intended to change as the program runs. Constants are almost always used to add clarity.

Through experimentation, I found that the ball's x value should never be smaller than 15 or larger than 365. By defining special constants with these values, I can make it clear what these values represent. (See the section called "Checking the boundaries" later in this chapter to see how this feature really works.)

Traditionally, you put constants entirely in uppercase letters. Many languages have special modifiers for creating constants, but JavaScript doesn't. If you want something to be a constant, just make a variable with an uppercase name and treat it as a constant. (Don't change it during the run of the program.)

Initializing

The `init()` function is small but mighty:

```
function init(){
  sprite = document.getElementById("sprite");
} // end init
```

It does a simple but important job: loading up the `sprite` div and storing it into a variable named `sprite`. Because `sprite` is a global variable, all other functions have access to the `sprite` variable and are able to manipulate it.

You often use the `init()` function to initialize key variables in your programs. You also can use this function to set up more advanced event handlers, as you see in the animation sections of this chapter.

Moving the sprite

Of course, the most interesting function in the program is the one that moves sprites around the screen. Take a look at the following code, which I break down for you:

```
function moveSprite(dx, dy){
  var surface = document.getElementById("surface");

  x = parseInt(sprite.style.left);
  y = parseInt(sprite.style.top);

  x += dx;
  y += dy;

  checkBounds();

  // move ball to new position
  sprite.style.left = x + "px";
  sprite.style.top = y + "px";

  //describe position
  var output = document.getElementById("output");
  output.innerHTML = "x: " + x + ", y: " + y;
} // end MoveSprite
```

The function works essentially by determining how much the sprite should be moved in x and y and then manipulating the `left` and `top` properties of its style. Here's what happens:

1. **Accept dx and dy as parameters.**

   The function expects two parameters: dx stands for delta-x, and dy is delta-y. (You can read them *difference in x* and *difference in y* if you prefer, but I like sounding like a NASA scientist.) These parameters tell how much the sprite should move in each dimension.

   ```
   function moveSprite(dx, dy){
   ```

   You may wonder why I'm working with dx and dy when this object moves only horizontally. See, I'm thinking ahead. I'm going to reuse this function in the next few programs, which I discuss in the upcoming sections. Even though I don't need to move vertically yet, I will as I continue programming, so I built the capability in.

2. **Get a reference to the surface.**

   Use the normal document.getElementById trick to extract the sprite from the page. Be sure the sprite you're animating has absolute position with top and left properties defined in a local style.

   ```
   var surface = document.getElementById("surface");
   ```

3. **Extract the sprite's x and y parameters.**

   The horizontal position is stored in the left property. CSS styles are stored as strings and include a measurement. For example, the original left value of the sprite is 100px. For the program, you need only the numeric part. The parseInt() function pulls out only the numeric part of the left property and turns it into an integer, which is then stored in x. Do the same thing to get the y value.

   ```
   x = parseInt(sprite.style.left);
   y = parseInt(sprite.style.top);
   ```

4. **Increment x and y.**

   Now that you have the x and y properties stored as integer variables, you can do math on them. It isn't complicated math. Just add dx to x and dy to y. This syntax allows you to move the object as many pixels as the user wants in both x and y axes.

   ```
   x += dx;
   y += dy;
   ```

5. **Check boundaries.**

   If you have young children, you know this rule: Once you have something that can move, it will get out of bounds. If you let your sprite move, it will leave the space you've designated. Checking the boundaries isn't difficult, but it's another task, so I'm just calling a function here. I describe checkBounds() in the next section, but basically it just checks to see whether the sprite is leaving the surface and adjusts its position to stay in bounds.

   ```
   checkBounds();
   ```

6. Move the ball.

Changing the x and y properties doesn't really move the sprite. To do that, you need to convert the integers back into the CSS format. If x is 120, you need to set left to 120px. Just concatenate "px" to the end of each variable.

```
// move ball to new position
sprite.style.left = x + "px";
sprite.style.top = y + "px";
```

7. Print the position.

For debugging purposes, I like to know exactly where the x and y positions are, so I just made a string and printed it to an output panel.

```
//describe position
var output = document.getElementById("output");
output.innerHTML = "x: " + x + ", y: " + y;
```

Checking the boundaries

You can respond in a number of ways when an object leaves the playing area. I'm going with wrapping, one of the simplest techniques. If something leaves the rightmost border, simply have it jump all the way to the left.

The code handles all four borders:

```
function checkBounds(){
  //wrap
  if (x > MAX_X){
    x = MIN_X;
  } // end if
  if (x < MIN_X){
    x = MAX_X;
  } // end if
  if (y > MAX_Y){
    y = MIN_Y;
  } // end if
  if (y < MIN_Y){
    y = MAX_Y;
  } // end if
} // end function
```

The checkBounds() function depends on the constants, which helps in a couple of ways. When you look at the code, you can easily see what's going on:

```
if (x > MAX_X){
  x = MIN_X;
} // end if
```

If x is larger than the maximum value for x, set it to the minimum value. You almost can't write it any more clearly than this. If the size of the playing surface changes, you simply change the values of the constants.

Shouldn't you just get size values from the surface?

In a perfect world, I would extract the position values from the playing surface itself. Unfortunately, JavaScript/DOM is not a perfect animation framework. Because I'm using absolute positioning, the position of the sprite isn't attached to the surface (as it should be) but to the main screen. It's a little annoying, but some experimentation can help you find the right values.

Remember, when you start using absolute positioning on a page, you're pretty much commit-

ted to it. If you're using animation like the one described in this section, you'll probably want to use absolute positioning everywhere or do some other tricks to make sure that the sprite stays where you want it to go without overwriting other parts of the page. Regardless, using constants keeps the code easy to read and maintain, even if you have to hack a little bit to find the specific values you need.

You probably wonder how I came up with the actual values for the constants. In some languages, you can come up with nice mathematical tricks to predict exactly what the largest and smallest values should be. In JavaScript, it's a little tricky because the environment just isn't that precise.

I chose a simple but effective technique. I temporarily took out the check-bounds() call and just took a look at the output to see what the values of x and y were. I looked to see how large x should be before the sprite wraps and wrote down the value on paper. Likewise, I found the largest and smallest values for y.

Once I knew these values, I simply placed them in constants. I don't really care that the maximum value for x is 365. I just want to know that x doesn't go past the MAX_X value when I'm messing around with it.

If the size of my playing surface changes, I just change the constants, and everything works out fine.

Reading Input from the Keyboard

You can use JavaScript to read directly from the keyboard. This trick is useful in several situations, but it's especially handy in animation and simple gaming applications.

Figure 7-2 shows a program with a moving ball.

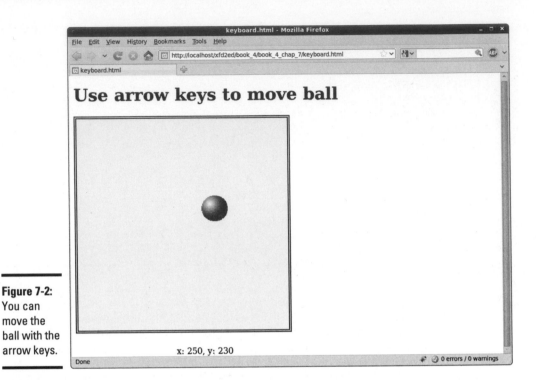

Figure 7-2:
You can
move the
ball with the
arrow keys.

The `keyboard.html` page has no buttons because the keyboard arrows are used to manage all the input.

You know what I'm going to say. Look this thing over in your browser because it just doesn't have any charm unless you run it and mash on some arrow keys.

Building the keyboard page

The keyboard page is very much like the movement page.

```
<!DOCTYPE html PUBLIC "-//W3C//DTD XHTML 1.0 Strict//EN"
"http://www.w3.org/TR/xhtml1/DTD/xhtml1-strict.dtd">
<html lang="EN" dir="ltr" xmlns="http://www.w3.org/1999/xhtml">
  <head>
    <meta http-equiv="content-type" content="text/xml; charset=utf-8" />
    <title>keyboard.html</title>

    <link rel = "stylesheet"
          type = "text/css"
          href = "keyboard.css" />

    <script type = "text/javascript"
          src = "movement.js">
    </script>
    <script type = "text/javascript"
```

```
              src = "keyboard.js">
      </script>

   </head>

   <body onload = "init()">
     <h1>Use arrow keys to move ball</h1>

     <div id = "surface">
       <div id = "sprite"
            style = "position: absolute;
            top: 100px;
            left: 100px;
            height: 25px;
            width: 25px;" >
         <img src = "ball.gif"
              alt = "ball" />
       </div>
     </div>

     <p id = "output">
       x = 100, y = 100
     </p>
   </body>
</html>
```

The preceding code is when it really pays off to build reusable code. I basically copied the `movement.html` page with a couple of important changes:

✦ **Import the `movement.js` script.** This page uses the same functions as
the `movement.html` page, so just reimport the script.

✦ **Add another script specific to reading the keyboard.** You need a
couple of modifications, which are housed in a second script file called
`keyboard.js`.

✦ **Keep the rest of the page similar.** You still call `init()` when the body
loads, and you still want the same visual design, except for the buttons.
The `surface` and `sprite` divs are identical to the `movement.html`
design.

✦ **Take out the form.** This page responds to the keyboard, so you no
longer need a form.

This program begins with the `movement.js` script. As far as the browser is
concerned, that entire script file has been loaded before the `keyboard.js`
script appears. The basic foundation is already in place from `movement`.
The `keyboard` script just handles the modifications to make keyboard
support work.

Overwriting the init() function

Working with a keyboard still requires some initialization. I need a little
more work in the `init()` function, so I make a new version to replace the
version created in `movement.js`.

```
//assumes movement.js

function init(){
  sprite = document.getElementById("sprite");
  document.onkeydown = keyListener;
} // end init
```

The order in which you import scripts matters. If you duplicate a function, the browser interprets only the last script read.

Setting up an event handler

In my `init()` function, I still want to initialize the sprite (as I did in `movement.js`, described in the "Moving the sprite" section earlier in this chapter). When you want to read the keyboard, you need to tap into the browser's *event-handling* facility. Browsers provide basic support for page-based events (such as `body.onload` and `button.onclick`), but they also provide a lower level support for more fundamental input, such as keyboard and mouse input.

If you want to read this lower level input, you need to specify a function that will respond to the input.

```
document.onkeydown = keyListener;
```

This line specifies that a special function called `keyListener` is called whenever the user presses a key. Keep a couple of things in mind when you create this type of event handler:

✦ **It should be called in `init()`.** You'll probably want keyboard handling to be available immediately, so setting up event handlers in the `init()` function is common.

✦ **The function is called as if it were a variable.** This syntax is slightly different than typically used in JavaScript. When you create function handlers in HTML, you simply feed a string that represents the function name complete with parameters (`button onclick = "do Something()"`). When you call a function within JavaScript (as opposed to calling the function in HTML), the function name is actually much like a variable, so it doesn't require quotes.

If you want to know the truth, functions *are* variables in JavaScript. Next time somebody tells you JavaScript is a toy language, mention that it supports automatic dereferencing of function pointers and treats functions like first-class citizens. Then run away before they ask you what that means. (That's what I do. . . .)

✦ **You need to create a function with the specified name.** If you've got this code in `init`, the browser calls a function called `keyListener()` whenever a key is pressed. (You can call the function something else, but `keyListener()` is a pretty good name for it.)

Responding to keystrokes

After you've set up an event-handler, you need to write the function to respond to keystrokes. Fortunately, this task turns out to be pretty easy.

```
function keyListener(e){
  // if e doesn't already exist, we're in IE so make it

  if (!e){
    e = window.event;
  } // end IE-specific code

  //left
  if (e.keyCode == 37){
    moveSprite(-10, 0);
  } // end if

  //up
  if (e.keyCode == 38){
    moveSprite(0, -10);
  } // end if

  //right
  if (e.keyCode == 39){
    moveSprite(10, 0);
  } // end if

  //down
  if (e.keyCode == 40){
    moveSprite(0, 10);
  } // end if

} // end keyListener
```

The `keyListener()` function is a good example of an *event handler*. These functions are used to determine what events have happened in the system, and to respond to those events. Here's how to build this one:

✦ **Event functions have event objects.** Just knowing that an event has occurred isn't enough. You need to know which key has been pressed. Fortunately, the browsers all have an event object available to tell you what's happened.

✦ **Many browsers pass the event as a parameter.** When you create an event function, the browser automatically assigns a special parameter to the function. This parameter (normally called e) represents the event. Just make the function with a parameter called e, and most browsers create e automatically.

```
function keyListener(e){
```

✦ **Internet Explorer needs a little more help.** Internet Explorer doesn't automatically create an event object for you, so you need to specifically create it.

```
// if e doesn't already exist, we're in IE so make it

if (!e){
  e = window.event;
} // end IE-specific code
```

✦ **You can use e to figure out which key was pressed.** The e object has some nifty properties, including `keyCode`. This property returns a number that tells you which key was pressed.

Do a quick search on *JavaScript event object* to discover other kinds of event tricks. I show the most critical features here, but this section is just an introduction to the many interesting things you can do with events.

✦ **Compare to known keycodes.** You can figure out the keycodes of any keys on your keyboard and use basic `if` statements to respond appropriately. See the next section to discover what code is attached to your favorite keys on the keyboard.

```
//left
if (e.keyCode == 37){
  moveSprite(-10, 0);
} // end if
```

✦ **Call appropriate variations of moveSprite.** If the user presses the left arrow, move the sprite to the left. You can use the `moveSprite()` function defined in `movement.js` (in the "Moving the sprite" section of this chapter) for this task.

Deciphering the mystery of key codes

Of course, the big mystery of a keyboard handler is where all those funky key numbers came from. How did I know that the left arrow is keycode 37, for example? It's pretty simple, really. I just wrote a program to tell me. Figure 7-3 shows `readKeys.html` in action.

Run `readKeys` and press a few keys. You can then easily determine what keycode is related to which key on the keyboard. You may also want to look over this code if you're a little confused; because all the code is in one place, it may be a bit easier to read than the movement examples.

If you use a notebook or international keyboard, be aware that some of the key codes may be nonstandard, especially numeric keypad keys. Try to stick to standard keys if you want to ensure that your program works on all keyboards.

Figure 7-3: This program reads the keyboard and reports the key codes.

Following the Mouse

You can also create an event-handler that reads the mouse. Figure 7-4 shows such a program.

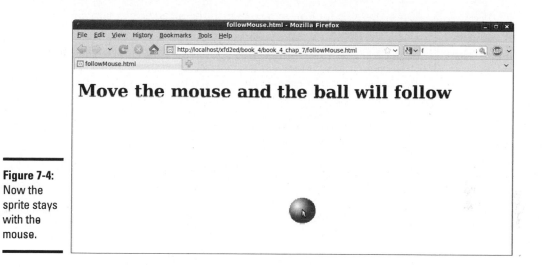

Figure 7-4: Now the sprite stays with the mouse.

The mouse-following effect is actually quite an easy effect once you know how to read the keyboard because it works in almost exactly the same way as the keyboard approach.

Looking over the HTML

The code for `followMouse.html` is simple enough that I kept it in one file:

```
<!DOCTYPE html PUBLIC "-//W3C//DTD XHTML 1.0 Strict//EN"
"http://www.w3.org/TR/xhtml1/DTD/xhtml1-strict.dtd">
<html lang="EN" dir="ltr" xmlns="http://www.w3.org/1999/xhtml">
  <head>
    <meta http-equiv="content-type" content="text/xml; charset=utf-8" />
    <title>followMouse.html</title>
    <script type = "text/javascript">
      var sprite;

      function init(){
        sprite = document.getElementById("sprite");
        document.onmousemove = mouseListener;
      } // end init

      function mouseListener(e){
        if (!e){
          e = window.event;
        } // end IE catch

        //get width and height
        height = parseInt(sprite.style.height);
        width = parseInt(sprite.style.width);
```

```
        //move center of sprite to mouse
        x = e.pageX - (width/2);
        y = e.pageY - (height/2);

        sprite.style.left = x + "px";
        sprite.style.top = y + "px";
      } // end function
    </script>
  </head>

  <body onload = "init()">
    <h1>Move the mouse and the ball will follow</h1>
    <div id = "sprite"
         style = "position: absolute;
                  left: 100px;
                  top: 100px;
                  width: 50px;
                  height: 50px;">
      <img src = "ball.gif"
           alt = "ball" />
    </div>
  </body>
</html>
```

The HTML page is simple. This time I'm letting the mouse take up the entire page. No borders are necessary because the sprite isn't able to leave the page. (If the mouse leaves the page, it no longer sends event messages.)

Just create a sprite with an image as normal and be sure to call `init()` when the body loads.

Initializing the code

The initialization is also pretty straightforward:

1. Create a global variable for the sprite.

Define the `sprite` variable outside any functions so that it is available to all of them.

```
var sprite;
```

2. Build the sprite in `init()`.

The `init()` function is a great place to create the sprite.

```
function init(){
    sprite = document.getElementById("sprite");
    document.onmousemove = mouseListener;
```

3. Set up an event handler in `init()` for mouse motion.

This time, you're trapping for mouse events, so call this one `mouseListener`.

```
document.onmousemove = mouseListener;
```

Building the mouse listener

The mouse listener works much like a keyboard listener. It examines the event object to determine the mouse's current position and then uses that value to place the sprite:

1. **Get the event object.**

   Use the cross-platform technique to get the event object.

   ```
   function mouseListener(e){
     if (!e){
       e = window.event;
     } // end IE catch
   ```

2. **Determine the sprite's width and height.**

   The `top` and `left` properties point to the sprite's top-left corner. Placing the mouse in the center of the sprite looks more natural. To calculate the center, you need the height and width. Don't forget to add these values to the local style for the sprite.

   ```
   //get width and height
   height = parseInt(sprite.style.height);
   width = parseInt(sprite.style.width);
   ```

3. **Use `e.pageX` and `e.pageY` to get the mouse position.**

   These properties return the current position of the mouse.

4. **Determine x and y under the mouse cursor.**

   Subtract half of the sprite's width from the mouse's x (`e.pageX`) so that the sprite's horizontal position is centered on the mouse. Repeat with the y position.

   ```
   //move center of sprite to mouse
   x = e.pageX - (width/2);
   y = e.pageY - (height/2);
   ```

5. **Move the mouse to the new x and y coordinates.**

   Use the conversion techniques to move the sprite to the new position.

   ```
   sprite.style.left = x + "px";
   sprite.style.top = y + "px";
   ```

 Another fun effect is to have the sprite influenced by the mouse. Don't make it follow the mouse directly, but check to see where the mouse is in relationship with the sprite. Have the sprite move up if the mouse is above the sprite, for example.

Creating Automatic Motion

You can make a sprite move automatically by attaching a special timer to the object. Figure 7-5 shows the ball moving autonomously across the page.

**Book IV
Chapter 7**

Animating Your Pages

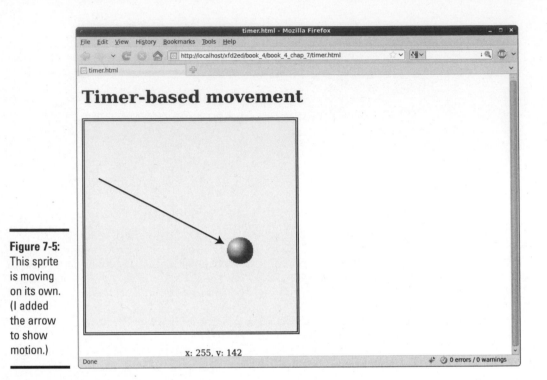

Figure 7-5:
This sprite
is moving
on its own.
(I added
the arrow
to show
motion.)

`Timer.html` is surprisingly simple because it borrows almost everything from other code.

```
<!DOCTYPE html PUBLIC "-//W3C//DTD XHTML 1.0 Strict//EN"
"http://www.w3.org/TR/xhtml1/DTD/xhtml1-strict.dtd">
<html lang="EN" dir="ltr" xmlns="http://www.w3.org/1999/xhtml">
  <head>
    <meta http-equiv="content-type" content="text/xml; charset=utf-8" />
    <title>timer.html</title>

    <link rel = "stylesheet"
          type = "text/css"
          href = "keyboard.css" />

    <script type = "text/javascript"
            src = "movement.js">
    </script>

    <script type = "text/javascript">
      function init(){
        sprite = document.getElementById("sprite");
        setInterval("moveSprite(5, 3)", 100);
      } // end init

    </script>
  </head>

  <body onload = "init()">
```

```
<h1>Timer-based movement</h1>

<div id = "surface">
  <div id = "sprite"
       style = "position: absolute;
       top: 100px;
       left: 100px;
       height: 25px;
       width: 25px;" >
    <img src = "ball.gif"
         alt = "ball" />
  </div>
</div>

<p id = "output">
  x = 100, y = 100
</p>
  </body>
</html>
```

The HTML and CSS are exactly the same as the button.html code. Most of the JavaScript comes from movement.js. The only thing that's really new is a tiny but critical change in the init() method.

Creating a setInterval() call

JavaScript contains a very useful function called setInterval. This thing takes two parameters:

✦ **A function call.** Create a string containing a function call including any of its parameters.

✦ **A time interval in milliseconds.** You can specify an interval in 1000ths of a second. If the interval is 500, the given function is called twice per second, 50 milliseconds is 20 times per second, and so on.

You can set the interval at whatever speed you want, but that doesn't guarantee things will work that fast. If you put complex code in a function and tell the browser to execute it 1,000 times a second, it probably won't be able to keep up (especially if the user has a slower machine than you do).

The browser will call the specified function at the specified interval. Put any code that you want repeated inside the given function.

Don't put anything in an interval function that doesn't have to go there. Because this code happens several times per second, it's called a *critical path,* and any wasteful processing here can severely slow down the entire program. Try to make the code in an interval function as clean as possible. (That's why I created the sprite as a global variable. I didn't want to re-create the sprite 20 times per second, making my program impossible for slower browsers to handle.)

Automatically moving objects are a great place to play with other kinds of boundary detection. If you want to see how to make something bounce when it hits the edge, look at `bounce.html` and `bounce.js` on the CD-ROM.

Building Image-Swapping Animation

The other kind of animation you can do involves rapidly changing an image. Look at Figure 7-6 to see one frame of an animated figure.

Figure 7-6:
This sprite is
kicking!

Animation is never that easy to show in a still screen shot, so Figure 7-7 shows the sequence of images used to build the kicking sprite.

Figure 7-7:
I used this
series of
images to
build the
animation.

You can use any series of images you want. I got these images from a site called Reiner's Tilesets (`http://reinerstileset.4players.de/englisch.htm`). It includes a huge number of sprites, each with several animations. These animations are called Freya.

(I include all the Freya images in a Zip file on the Web site and CD-ROM if you want to try this yourself.)

This page might lag when you try to run it from a server because the animation starts immediately and the images may take some time to download. I'm going to live with this for now to keep the example simple. Look at the upcoming "Preloading Your Images" section to see how to prevent this problem.

Preparing the images

You can build your own images, or you can get them from a site like Reiner's. In any case, here are a few things to keep in mind when building image animations:

+ **Keep them small.** Larger images take a long time to download and don't swap as smoothly as small ones. My images are 128 by 128 pixels, which is a good size.

+ **Consider adding transparency.** The images from Reiner have a brown background. I changed the background to transparent using my favorite graphics editor (Gimp).

+ **Change the file format.** The images came in .bmp format, which is inefficient and doesn't support transparency. I saved them as .gif images to make them smaller and enable the background transparency.

+ **Consider changing the names.** I renamed the images to make the names simpler and to eliminate spaces from the filenames. I called the images kick00.gif to kick12.gif.

+ **Put animation images in a subdirectory.** With ordinary page images, I often find a subdirectory to be unhelpful. When you start building animations, you can easily have a lot of little images running around. A large number of small files is a good place for a subdirectory.

Building the page

The code for animation just uses variations of techniques described throughout this chapter: a setInterval function and some DOM coding.

```
<!DOCTYPE html PUBLIC "-//W3C//DTD XHTML 1.0 Strict//EN"
"http://www.w3.org/TR/xhtml1/DTD/xhtml1-strict.dtd">
<html lang="EN" dir="ltr" xmlns="http://www.w3.org/1999/xhtml">
  <head>
    <meta http-equiv="content-type" content="text/xml; charset=utf-8" />
    <title>imageSwap.html</title>
    <script type = "text/javascript">
      //<![CDATA[
      var imgList = new Array (
        "freya/kick00.gif",
        "freya/kick01.gif",
        "freya/kick02.gif",
        "freya/kick03.gif",
        "freya/kick04.gif",
        "freya/kick05.gif",
        "freya/kick06.gif",
        "freya/kick07.gif",
        "freya/kick08.gif",
        "freya/kick09.gif",
```

```
          "freya/kick10.gif",
          "freya/kick11.gif",
          "freya/kick12.gif"
        );

      var frame = 0;
      var spriteImage

      function init(){
        setInterval("animate()", 100);
        spriteImage = document.getElementById("image");
      } // end init

      function animate(){
        frame += 1;
        if (frame >= imgList.length){
          frame = 0;
        } // end if
        spriteImage.src = imgList[frame];
      }
      //]]>
    </script>
  </head>

  <body onload = "init()">
    <div id = "sprite">
      <img id = "image"
           src = "freya/kick00.gif"
           alt = "kicking sprite" />
    </div>
  </body>
</html>
```

The HTML is incredibly simple:

1. **Set up the body with an `init()` method.**

As usual, the body's `onload` event calls an `init()` method to start things up.

2. **Create a `sprite` div.**

Build a div named `sprite`. Because you aren't changing the position of this div (yet), you don't need to worry about the local style.

3. **Name the `img`.**

In this program, you animate the `img` inside the div, so you need to give it an `id`.

Building the global variables

The JavaScript code isn't too difficult, but it requires a little bit of thought.

1. **Create an array of image names.**

You have a list of images to work with. The easiest way to support several related images is with an array of image names. Each element of the array is the filename of an image. Put them in the order you want the animation frames to appear.

```
var imgList = new Array (
  "freya/kick00.gif",
  "freya/kick01.gif",
  "freya/kick02.gif",
  "freya/kick03.gif",
  "freya/kick04.gif",
  "freya/kick05.gif",
  "freya/kick06.gif",
  "freya/kick07.gif",
  "freya/kick08.gif",
  "freya/kick09.gif",
  "freya/kick10.gif",
  "freya/kick11.gif",
  "freya/kick12.gif"
);
```

2. **Build a `frame` variable to hold the current frame number.**

   Because this animation has 12 frames, the `frame` variable goes from 0 to 11.

   ```
   var frame = 0;
   ```

3. **Set up `spriteImage` to reference to the `img` tag inside the `sprite` tag.**

   ```
   var spriteImage
   ```

Setting up the interval

The `init()` function attaches the `spriteImage` variable to the image object and sets up the `animate()` method to run ten times per second.

```
function init(){
  setInterval("animate()", 100);
  spriteImage = document.getElementById("image");
} // end init
```

Animating the sprite

The actual animation happens in the (you guessed it . . .) `animate()` function. The function is straightforward:

1. **Increment frame.**

   Add one to the frame variable.

   ```
   frame += 1;
   ```

2. **Check for bounds.**

   Any time you change a variable, you should consider whether it may go out of bounds. I'm using `frame` as an index in the `imgList` array, so I check to see that `frame` is always less than the length of `imgList`.

   ```
   if (frame >= imgList.length){
     frame = 0;
   } // end if
   ```

3. **Reset `frame`, if necessary.**

   If the frame counter gets too high, reset it to zero and start the animation over.

4. **Copy the image filename over from the array to the `src` property of the `spriteImage` object.**

   This step causes the given file to display.

   ```
   spriteImage.src = imgList[frame];
   ```

JavaScript is not an ideal animation framework, but it will do. You do get some delays on the first pass while the images load. (Making the images smaller and in the GIF or PNG formats will help with this issue.) Most browsers store images locally, so the images animate smoothly after the first pass.

If you want smoother animation, you can either preload the images or combine all the frames into a single image and simply change what part of the image is displayed.

Even if you don't like animation, these techniques can be useful. You can use the `setInterval()` technique for any kind of repetitive code you want, including the dynamic display of menus or other page elements. In fact, before CSS became the preferred technique, most dynamic menus used JavaScript animation.

Preloading Your Images

The image-swapping trick is pretty cool, but it has one problem: It takes some time for all those images to download from the server, but the animation starts immediately. The animation starting before the images are all available can cause the initial animation to look jerky. It would be great if there was some way to preload the images and not start the animation until they were all available.

Yep, there is a way to do that. Take a look at this code:

```
<!DOCTYPE html PUBLIC "-//W3C//DTD XHTML 1.0 Strict//EN"
"http://www.w3.org/TR/xhtml1/DTD/xhtml1-strict.dtd">
<html lang="EN" dir="ltr" xmlns="http://www.w3.org/1999/
   xhtml">
  <head>
    <meta http-equiv="content-type" content="text/xml;
    charset=utf-8" />
    <title>preload.html</title>
    <script type = "text/javascript">
      //<![CDATA[
      var imgFiles = new Array (
        "freya/kick00.gif",        "freya/kick01.gif",
```

```
            "freya/kick02.gif",
            "freya/kick03.gif",
            "freya/kick04.gif",
            "freya/kick05.gif",
            "freya/kick06.gif",
            "freya/kick07.gif",
            "freya/kick08.gif",
            "freya/kick09.gif",
            "freya/kick10.gif",
            "freya/kick11.gif",
            "freya/kick12.gif"
        );

        var frame = 0;
        var spriteImage
        var images = new Array(12);

        function init(){
          setInterval("animate()", 100);
          spriteImage = document.getElementById("image");
          loadImages();
        } // end init

        function animate(){
          frame += 1;
          if (frame >= images.length){
            frame = 0;
          } // end if
          spriteImage.src = images[frame].src;
        } // end animate

        function loadImages(){
          //preloads all the images for faster display.
          for (i=0; i < images.length; i++){
            images[i] = new Image();
            images[i].src = imgFiles[i];
          } // end for loop
        } // end loadImages

        //]]>
      </script>
  </head>

  <body onload = "init()">
    <div id = "sprite">
      <img id = "image"
           src = "freya/kick00.gif"
           alt = "kicking sprite" />
    </div>
  </body>
</html>
```

Here's how you preload images:

1. **Change the array name to imgFiles.**

   This is a subtle but important distinction. The array doesn't represent actual images, but the filenames of the images. You create another array to hold the actual image data.

2. **Create an array of images.**

   JavaScript has a data type designed specifically for holding image data. The images array holds the actual image data (not just filenames, but the actual pictures). The images array should be global.

3. **Create a function to populate the images array.**

   The loadImages() function creates the array of image data. Call load-Images() from init().

4. **Build a loop that steps through each element of the imgFiles array.**

   You build an image object to correspond to each filename, so the length of the two arrays needs to be the same.

5. **Build a new image object for each filename.**

   Use the new Image() construct to build an image object representing the image data associated with a particular file.

6. **Attach that image object to the images array.**

   This array contains all the image data.

7. **Modify animate() to read from the images array.**

   The animate() function reads from the images() array. Because the image data has been preloaded into the array, it should display more smoothly.

 Preloading images doesn't make the animation faster. It just delays the animation until all the images are loaded into the cache, making it appear smoother. Some browsers will still play the animation before the cache has finished loading, but the technique still has benefits.

Movement and swapping

Finally, you can combine motion effects with image swapping to have an image move around on the screen with animated motion. Figure 7-8 tries to show this effect (I added the arrow just so you can see how the movement works, but you need to use a browser to really see it).

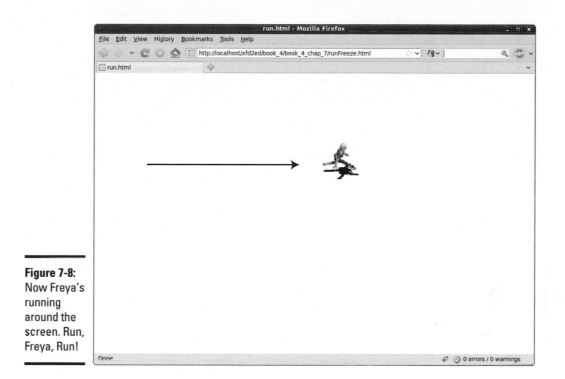

Figure 7-8:
Now Freya's running around the screen. Run, Freya, Run!

Making this program requires nothing at all new. It's just a combination of the techniques used throughout this chapter. Figure 7-9 shows the list of images used to make Freya run.

Figure 7-9:
These are the running images from Reiner's Tilesets.

The HTML is (as usual) pretty minimal here:

```
<!DOCTYPE html PUBLIC "-//W3C//DTD XHTML 1.0 Strict//EN"
"http://www.w3.org/TR/xhtml1/DTD/xhtml1-strict.dtd">
<html lang="EN" dir="ltr" xmlns="http://www.w3.org/1999/xhtml">
  <head>
    <meta http-equiv="content-type" content="text/xml; charset=utf-8" />
```

```
      <title>run.html</title>
      <script type = "text/javascript"
              src = "run.js">
      </script>
   </head>

   <body onload = "init()">
     <div id = "sprite"
          style = "position: absolute;
                   top: 100px;
                   left: 100px;">
       <img src = "freya/run0.gif"
            id = "image"
            alt = "running image" />
     </div>
   </body>
</html>
```

When you want to create a moving image-swap animation:

1. Import the script.

You can build the script locally (as I did in the last example), but any time the script gets complex, it may be better in an external file.

2. Call an `init()` method.

Most animation requires an `init()` method called from `body.onload()`, and this one is no exception.

3. Name the sprite.

The sprite is a div that moves, so it needs absolute position, top, and left all defined as local styles.

4. Name the image.

You also animate the image inside the sprite. The only property you change here is the `src`, so no local styles are necessary.

Building the code

The JavaScript code is familiar because all the elements can be borrowed from previous programs. Here's the code in its entirety:

```
//run.js

var frame = 0;
var images = new Array(8);
var sprite;
var spriteImage;
var MAX_X = 500;

function init(){
  sprite = document.getElementById("sprite");
  spriteImage = document.getElementById("image");
  loadImages()
```

```
      setInterval("animate()", 100);
} // end init

function loadImages(){
  //pre-loads images into an array
  //make temporary array of image file names
  var imgList = new Array(
    "freya/run0.gif",
    "freya/run1.gif",
    "freya/run2.gif",
    "freya/run3.gif",
    "freya/run4.gif",
    "freya/run5.gif",
    "freya/run6.gif",
    "freya/run7.gif"
  );

  //create the array of image objects used in the
  //rest of the program
  for(i = 0; i < images.length; i++){
    images[i] = new Image();
    images[i].src = imgList[i];
  } // end for loop
} // end loadImages

function animate(){
  updateImage();
  updatePosition();
} // end animate

function updateImage(){
  frame++;
  if (frame >= images.length){
    frame = 0;
  } // end if
  spriteImage.src = images[frame].src;
} // end updateImage

function updatePosition(){
  sprite = document.getElementById("sprite");
  var x = parseInt(sprite.style.left);
  x += 10;
  if (x > MAX_X){
    x = 0;
  } // end if
  sprite.style.left = x + "px";
} // end function
```

Defining global variables

You have a few global variables in this code:

+ **frame** is the frame number. It is an integer from 0 to 11, which serves as the index for the imgList array.

+ **imgList** is an array of filenames with the animation images.

+ **sprite** is the div that moves around the screen.

✦ **spriteImage** is the img element of sprite and the image that is swapped.

✦ **MAX_X** is a constant holding the maximum value of X. In this program, I'm only moving in one direction, so the only boundary I'm worried about is MAX_X. If the sprite moved in other directions, I'd add some other constants for the other boundary conditions.

Initializing your data

The init() function performs its normal tasks: setting up sprite variables and calling the animate() function on an interval.

```
function init(){
  sprite = document.getElementById("sprite");
  spriteImage = document.getElementById("image");
  loadImages();

  setInterval("animate()", 100);
} // end init
```

When you move and swap images, sometimes you have to adjust the animation interval and the distance traveled each frame so that the animation looks right. Otherwise, the sprite may seem to skate rather than run.

Preloading the images

I take advantage of the preloading trick described in the previous section to make my images load properly. The loadImages() method does this job:

```
function loadImages(){
  //pre-loads images into an array
  //make temporary array of image file names
  var imgList = new Array(
    "freya/run0.gif",
    "freya/run1.gif",
    "freya/run2.gif",
    "freya/run3.gif",
    "freya/run4.gif",
    "freya/run5.gif",
    "freya/run6.gif",
    "freya/run7.gif"
  );

  //create the array of image objects used in the
  //rest of the program
  for(i = 0; i < images.length; i++){
    images[i] = new Image();
    images[i].src = imgList[i];
  } // end for loop
} // end loadImages
```

This function works just like its counterpart in the `preload.html` program described earlier in this chapter.

Animating and updating the image

I really have two kinds of animation happening at once, so in the grand tradition of encapsulation, the `animate()` function passes off its job to two other functions:

```
function animate(){
  updateImage();
  updatePosition();
} // end animate
```

The `updateImage()` function handles the image-swapping duties:

```
function updateImage(){
  frame++;
  if (frame >= images.length){
    frame = 0;
  } // end if
  spriteImage.src = images[frame].src;
} // end updateImage
```

Moving the sprite

The sprite is moved in the `updatePosition()` function:

```
function updatePosition(){
  sprite = document.getElementById("sprite");
  var x = parseInt(sprite.style.left);
  x += 10;
  if (x > MAX_X){
    x = 0;
  } // end if
  sprite.style.left = x + "px";
} // end function
```

I know what you're thinking: You can use this stuff to make a really cool game. It's true. You can make games with JavaScript, but you eventually run into JavaScript's design limitations. JavaScript-based games have a bright future, with advances like the canvas tag, integrated audio, and faster JavaScript engines coming in the newest browsers. However, JavaScript is not yet an ideal game programming platform.

I prefer Flash and Python as languages to learn game development. Now that you mention it, I've written other Wiley books on exactly these topics. Check out *Beginning Flash Game Programming For Dummies* and *Game Programming: The L Line* (for Python development).

Book V

Server-Side Programming with PHP

The 5th Wave   By Rich Tennant

"Okay, I think I forgot to mention this, but we now have a Web management function that automatically alerts us when there's a broken link on The Aquarium's Web site."

Contents at a Glance

Chapter 1: Getting Started on the Server

In This Chapter

✔ Introducing server-side programming

✔ Testing your installation

✔ Inspecting `phpinfo()`

✔ Writing XHTML with embedded PHP

✔ Understanding various types of quotation

✔ Managing concatenation and interpolation

✔ Using heredocs to simplify coding

*W*elcome to the server-side programming portion of the book. In this minibook, you discover all the basics of PHP and how you can use PHP to make your pages dynamic and relevant in today's Internet.

In this chapter, you read about getting your server set up and ready to go. I walk you through the process as painlessly as possible, and by the end, you'll be up and running, and ready to serve up your own Web pages in a test environment. (I talk about making them available to the rest of the world in Book VIII.)

Introducing Server-Side Programming

I begin with an introduction to server-side programming. This is a bit different than the client-side programming you may have done in JavaScript.

Programming on the server

Server-side programming is what you use to create pages dynamically on the server before sending them to the client. Whereas client-side programming is executed on the client's machine, server-side programming all happens on the server before the Web page is even sent to the user.

Client-side programming (as done in JavaScript) does most of the work on the individual user's machine. This has advantages because those machines have doohickeys, like mice and graphics cards. Client-side programs can be interactive in real time.

The client has a big problem, though. Programs written on the client usually have a form of forced amnesia (no long-term memory). For security reasons, client-side applications can't store information in files and can't interact with other programs on the computer. Also, you never know exactly what kind of setup the user has, so you can't really be sure whether your program will work.

This is where server-side programming comes in. In a pure server-side programming environment, all the action happens on the Web server. The user thinks she's asking for a Web page like normal, but the address really goes to a computer program. The program does some magic and produces a Web page. The user sees a Web page, perhaps never knowing this wasn't a regular Web page, but a page that was produced instead by a program.

A program running on a Web server has some really nice advantages, such as

✦ **A server-side program can access the local file system.** Asking a server program to load and save files on the server is no problem at all.

✦ **A server-side program can call external programs.** This is a very big deal because many Web applications are really about working with data. Database programs are very important to modern Web development. See Book VI for much more on this.

✦ **All the user sees is ordinary XHTML.** You can set up your program to do whatever you want, but the output is regular XHTML. You don't have to worry about what browser the user has, or whether he has a Mac, or what browser version he's using. Any browser that can display XHTML can be used with PHP.

Serving your programs

When using a browser to retrieve Web pages, you send a request to a server. The server then looks at the extension (.html, .php, .js, and so on) of your requested file and decides what to do. If the server sees .html or .js, it says, "Cool. Nothing doing here. Just gotta send her back as is." When the server sees .php, it says, "Oh, boy. They need PHP to build something here."

The server takes the page and hollers for PHP to come along and construct the requested Web page on the fly. PHP goes through and looks at the programmer's blue print and then constructs the working page out of XHTML.

The server then takes that page from PHP and sends back plain XHTML to the client for the browser to display to the user.

When you write PHP programs, a Web server must process the form before the browser can see it. To test your PHP programs, you need to have a Web server available and place the file in a specific place on your computer for the server to serve it. You can't run a PHP file directly from your desktop.

It must be placed in a special place — often, the `htdocs` or `public_html` directory under the server.

Picking a language

There are all sorts of different ways to go about dynamically creating Web pages with server-side programming. Back in the day when the Internet was still in diapers, people used things like Perl and CGI scripting to handle all their server-side programming. Eventually, people placed more and more demand on their Web sites, and soon these technologies just weren't enough.

The prevalent languages today are

✦ **ASP.NET:** Microsoft's contender

✦ **Java:** The heavyweight offering from Sun Microsystems

✦ **PHP:** The popular language described in this minibook

ASP.NET

ASP.NET is event-driven, compiled, and object-oriented. ASP.NET replaced the '90s language ASP in 2002. Microsoft repurposed it for use with the .NET framework to facilitate cross-compatibility with its desktop applications (apps) and integration into Visual Studio (although you can write ASP.NET apps from any text editor). ASP.NET runs on Microsoft's Internet Information Services (IIS) Web server, which isn't free. I don't recommend it for cost-conscious users.

Java

Java has been a strong contender for a long time now. The language is indeed named after coffee. If you work for a banking company or insurance company, or need to build the next eBay or Amazon.com, you might want to consider using Java. However, Java can consume a lot of time, and it's hard to figure out. You may have to write up to 16 lines of code to do in Java what could take a mere 4 lines of code in PHP. Java is absolutely free, as is the Apache Tomcat Web server that It uses to serve its Web components. Java was originally created to write desktop applications and is still very good at doing that. If you're comfortable with C/C++, you'll be very comfortable with Java because it's very similar. It's fully object-oriented, and it's compiled. Java is powerful, but it can be challenging for beginners. It'd be a great second language to work with.

PHP

PHP was born from a collection of modifications for Perl and has boomed ever since (in a way, replacing Perl, which was once considered the duct tape and bubble gum that held the Internet together).

Compile versus interpret?

What's the difference between an interpreted language and a compiled language? A *compiled* language is compiled one time into a more computer-friendly format for faster processing when called by the computer. Compiled languages are typically very fast but not very flexible. *Interpreted* languages have to be interpreted on the spot by the server *every time* they're called, which is slower but provides more flexibility. With blazing fast servers these days, interpreted languages can normally stand under the load, and the ability to handle changes without recompiling can be an advantage in the fast-paced world of Web development.

PHP works great for your server-side Web development purposes. *MediaWiki* (the engine that was written to run the popular Internet encyclopedia Wikipedia) runs on PHP, as do many other popular large-, medium-, and small-scale Web sites. PHP is a solid, easy-to-learn, well-established language (it's 13 years old). PHP can be object-oriented or procedural (you can take your pick!). PHP is interpreted rather than compiled.

Installing Your Web Server

For PHP to work usefully, you have to have some other things installed on your computer, such as

✦ **A Web server:** This special program enables a computer to process files and send them to Web browsers. I use Apache because it's free and powerful, and works very well with PHP.

✦ **A database backend:** Modern Web sites rely heavily on data, so a program that can manage your data needs is very important. I use MySQL (a free and powerful tool) for this. Book VI is entirely dedicated to creating data with MySQL and some related tools.

✦ **A programming language:** Server-side programming relies on a language. I use PHP because it works great, and it's free.

There are two main ways to work with a Web server:

✦ **Install your own, using the free XAMPP software.** Download from www. apachefriends.org/en/xampp.html. Book VIII, Chapter 1 has complete instructions on installing XAMPP.

✦ **Work on a remote server that somebody has already set up.** Freehostia (www.freehostia.com) is one example that has everything you need for free.

Please check out Book VIII, Chapter 1 for complete information on both techniques. After you have your machine set up or you have an account somewhere with PHP access, come back here. I'll wait.

Inspecting phpinfo ( )

Using your shiny new server is really quite simple, but a lot of beginners can get confused at this point.

One thing you have to remember is that anything you want the server to serve must be located in the server's file structure. If you have a PHP file on your Desktop and you want to view it in your browser, it won't work because it isn't in your server. Although, yes, technically it might be on the same *machine* as your server (if you're using XAMPP), it is not *in* the server.

So, to serve a file from the server, it must be located in the htdocs directory of your server install. If you've installed XAMPP, go to the folder where you installed XAMPP (probably either c:/xampp or c:/Program Files/xampp) and locate the htdocs directory. This is where you'll put all your PHP files. Make note of it now.

If you're using a remote server, you'll need to use your hosts file management tools or FTP (both described in Book VIII, Chapter 1) to transfer the file. Normally, you can place your files anywhere on the remote file system.

To get the hang of placing your files in the correct place and accessing them, create a test file that will display all your PHP, Apache, and MySQL settings.

To test everything, make the PHP version of the famous "Hello World!" program. Follow these steps to make your first PHP program:

1. **Open a text editor to create a new file.**

   PHP files are essentially plain text files, just like XHTML and JavaScript. You can use the same editors to create them.

2. **Build a standard Web page.**

   Generally, your PHP pages start out as standard Web pages, using your basic XHTML template. However, start with a simpler example, so you can begin with an empty text file.

3. **Add a PHP reference.**

   Write a tag to indicate PHP. The starting tag looks like <?php, and the ending tag looks like ?>. As far as XHTML is concerned, all the PHP code is embedded in a single XHTML tag.

4. **Write a single line of PHP code.**

You'll learn a lot more PHP soon, but one command is especially useful for testing your configuration to see how it works. Type the line **phpinfo();**. This powerful command supplies a huge amount of diagnostic information.

5. **Save the file to your server.**

   A PHP file can't be stored just anywhere. You need to place it under an accessible directory of your Web server. If you're running XAMPP, that's the htdocs directory of your xampp directory. If you're running a remote server, you'll need to move the file to that server, either with your host's file transfer mechanism, an FTP program, or automatically through your editor. (See the nearby sidebar "Picking a PHP editor" for information on remote editing in Komodo.)

6. **Preview your page in the browser.**

   Use your Web browser to look at the resulting page. Note that you cannot simply load the file through the file menu or drag it to your browser. If you have XAMPP installed, you need to refer to the file as http://localhost/fileName.php. If the file is on a remote server, use the full address of the file on that server: for example, http://myhost.freehostia.com/fileName.php.

Your code from Steps 3 and 4 should look like this:

```
<?php
    phpinfo();
?>
```

Hmm. Only three lines of code, and it doesn't seem to do much. There's precious little HTML code there. Run it through the browser, though, and you'll see the page shown in Figure 1-1.

If you see the actual PHP code rather than the results shown in Figure 1-1, you probably didn't refer to the page correctly. Please check the following:

✦ **Is the file in the right place?** Your file must be in htdocs or on a remote server (or in a subdirectory of these places).

✦ **Did you use the .php extension?** The server won't invoke PHP unless the filename has a .php extension.

✦ **Did you refer to the file correctly?** If the URL in the address bar reads file://, then you bypassed the server, and PHP was not activated. Your address must begin with http://. Either use http://localhost (for a locally stored file in XAMPP) or the URL of your remote hosting service.

This phpinfo page of Figure 1-1 is critical in inspecting your server configuration. It displays all the different settings for your server, describing what version of PHP is running and what modules are active. This can be very useful information.

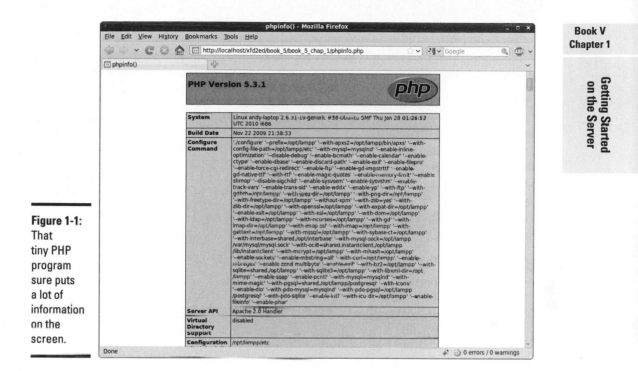

Figure 1-1:
That
tiny PHP
program
sure puts
a lot of
information
on the
screen.

You generally should not have a page with all the phpinfo() information running on a live server because it tells the bad guys information they might use to do mischief.

Picking a PHP editor

In the previous edition of this book, I recommend using Aptana for PHP editing. If you already use Aptana for your other Web editing, you may also enjoy using it for PHP. However, Aptana has changed, and PHP support is no longer built into the standard version of Aptana. If you want to have PHP support (syntax completions and the like), you need to install a plugin. Choose My Studio from the Window menu, click the Plugins tab, find the PHP plugin, and then click Get It. I've heard reports of the installation not working, but it worked fine for me.

I honestly prefer using Komodo Edit (also mentioned in Book I, Chapter 3) for PHP editing. It's a little simpler than Aptana, and it still has all the important features like syntax completion and highlighting built in with no plugins needed.

Komodo has another feature that can be a lifesaver for PHP programmers. If you're working on a remote Web server, you can set up a connection to that server (choose Edit⇨ Preferences⇨Servers). Then you can use the Save Remotely command to save the file to the server directly. That way, you can use all the features of Komodo without a local installation of Apache or PHP, and without having to implement an extra file transfer step.

This `test.php` program shows one of the most interesting things about PHP. The program itself is just a few lines long, but when you run it, the result is a complex Web page. Take a look at the source of the Web page, and you'll see a lot of code that you didn't write. That's the magic of PHP. You write a program, and it creates a Web page for you.

Don't panic if you don't understand the first thing in the page that gets produced with the `phpinfo()` command. It contains many details about how PHP is configured on your server, which may not mean much now. If you have trouble with PHP and ask me for help, though, it's the first thing I'll ask you for. As you get more experienced, you'll be able to learn a lot from this page.

The basic flow of PHP programming works like this:

1. You build a standard page, and you include PHP code inside it.

2. When the server recognizes the PHP code, it calls the PHP interpreter and passes that code to it.

PHP programs are almost always designed to create HTML code, which gets passed back to the user. The user will never see PHP code, because it will get translated to HTML/XHTML before it gets to the browser.

By default, Apache will load `index.html` or `index.php` automatically if you type a directory path into the Web browser. There's already a program in `htdocs` called `index.php`. Rename it `index.php.off`. Now, if you navigate to `http://localhost/`, you'll see a list of directories and files your server can run, including `test.php`. When you have a live site, you'll typically name one file `index.html` or `index.php` so the user doesn't have to type the entire filename. See Book VIII, Chapter 1 for more information on how to set up your server to make it easiest to use.

Building XHTML with PHP

In PHP, you aren't actually printing anything to the user. Instead, you're building an HTML document that will be sent to the browser, which will interpret the HTML and then print *that* (the HTML) to the user. Therefore, all your code gets interpreted twice: first on the server to generate the HTML and then on the user's machine to generate the output display.

If you've used XHTML, CSS, and JavaScript, you might have been frustrated because all these environments run on the client, and you have no control of the client environment. You don't know what browser the user will have, and thus you don't know exactly how XHTML, CSS, and JavaScript will run there. When you program in PHP, you're working on a machine (the server) that you actually control. You know exactly what the server's capabilities are because (in many cases) you configured it yourself.

It's still not a perfect situation, though, because your PHP code will generate XHTML/CSS pages (sometimes even with JavaScript), and those pages still have to contend with the wide array of client environments.

The first program you ever write in any language is invariably the `"Hello World!"` program or some variant thereof. Follow these steps:

1. Create a new PHP file in your editor.

I prefer using Komodo Edit because it already supports PHP, but if you add the PHP plugin to Aptana, that's a great choice, too. (Read about these two programs in the earlier sidebar, "Picking a PHP editor.")

If you're using some other text editor, just open a plain text file however you normally do that (often File➪New) and be sure to save it under `htdocs` with a `.php` extension. If you're using a remote server, transfer your file to that server before testing.

2. Create your standard XHTML page.

PHP code is usually embedded into the context of an HTML page. Begin with your standard XHTML template. (See Book I, Chapter 2 for a refresher on XHTML.)

3. Enter the following code in the body:

```
<?php
print "<h1>Hello World!</h1>";
?>
```

Depending on your installation of Apache, you may be able to use the shorter `<? ?>` version of the PHP directive (instead of `<?php ?>`). However, nearly all installations support the `<?php ?>` version, so that's probably the safest way to go.

Note that you're not just writing text, but creating an XHTML tag. PHP creates XHTML. That's a really important idea.

4. Save the file.

Remember to save directly into `htdocs` or a subdirectory of `htdocs`. If you're using a remote server, save remotely to that server (with Komodo) or save it locally and transfer it to the server to view it.

5. View the file in a Web browser, as shown in Figure 1-2.

The address of a Web page begins with the `http://` protocol and then the server name. If the page is on the local machine, the server name is `localhost`, which corresponds directly to your `htdocs` directory. If you have a file named `thing.php` in the `htdocs` directory, the address would be `http://localhost/thing.php`. Likewise, if it's in a subdirectory of `htdocs` called `project`, the address would be `http://localhost/project/thing.php`. If the page is on a remote server, the address will include the server's name, like this:

```
http://www.myserver.com/thing.php
```

Figure 1-2:
The "Hello
World!"
program
example.

So, what is it that you've done here? You've figured out how to use the `print` statement. This allows you to spit out any text you want to the user.

Note that each line ends with a semicolon (`;`), just like JavaScript code. PHP is pretty fussy about semicolons, and if you forget, you're likely to get a really strange error that can be hard to figure out.

Coding with Quotation Marks

There are many different ways to use `print`. The following are all legal ways to print text, but they have subtle differences:

```
print ("<p>Hello World!</p>");
print ("<p>Hello World!<br />
Hello Computer!</p>");
print '<p><a href="http://www.google.com">Hello Google!</a></p>';
```

Any way you cut it, you have to have some form of quotations around text that you want printed. However, PHP is usually used to write XHTML code, and XHTML code contains a lot of quote marks itself. All those quotations can lead to headaches.

What if you want to print double quotation marks inside a `print` statement surrounded by double quotation marks? You *escape* them (you tell PHP to treat them as literal characters, rather than the end of the string) with a backslash, like this:

```
print "<a href=\"link.html\">A Link</a>";
```

This can get tedious, so a better solution is discussed in the "Generating output with heredocs" section, later in this chapter.

This backslash technique works only with text encased inside double quotes. Single quotes tell PHP to take everything inside the quotes exactly as is. Double quotes give PHP permission to analyze the text for special characters, like escaped quotes (and variables, which you learn about in the next section of this chapter). Single quotes do not allow for this behavior, which is why they are rarely used in PHP programming.

echo or print?

echo is another way to generate your code for the browser. In almost all circumstances, you use echo exactly like you use print. Everyone knows what print does, but echo sounds like I should be making some sort of dolphin noise.

The difference is that print returns a value, and echo doesn't. print can be used as part of a complex expression, and echo can't. It really just comes down to the fact that print is more dynamic, whereas echo is slightly (and I'm talking very slightly here) faster.

I prefer print because there's nothing that echo can do that print can't.

To see a more detailed discussion, go here: www.faqts.com/knowledge_base/view.phtml/aid/1/fid/40.

Working with Variables PHP-Style

Variables are extremely important in any programming language and no less so in PHP.

A variable in PHP always begins with a $.

A PHP variable can be named almost anything. There are some reserved words that you can't name a variable (like print, which already has a meaning in PHP), so if your program isn't working and you can't figure out why, try changing some variable names or looking at the reserved words list (in the online help at http://www.php.net) to find out whether your variable name is one of these illegal words.

PHP is very forgiving about the type of data in a variable. When you create a variable, you simply put content in it. PHP automatically makes the variable whatever type it needs. This is called *loose typing*. The same variable can hold numeric data, text, or other more complicated kinds of data. PHP determines the type of data in a variable on the fly by examining the context.

Even though PHP is cavalier about data types, it's important to understand that data is still stored in one of several standard formats based on its type. PHP supports several forms of integers and floating-point numbers. PHP also has great support for text data. Programmers usually don't say "text," but call text data *string* data. This is because the internal data representation of text reminded the early programmers of beads on a string. You rarely have to worry about what type of information you're using in PHP, but you do need to know that PHP is quietly converting data into formats that it can use.

Escape sequences

In the first section of this chapter, "Creating Your First PHP Program," you see that you can escape double quotation marks with a back-slash. Quotation marks aren't the only thing you can escape, though. You can give a whole host of other special escape directives to PHP.

The most common ones are

✔ \t: Creates a tab in the resulting HTML

✔ \n: Creates a new line in the resulting HTML

✔ \$: Creates a dollar sign in the resulting HTML

✔ \": Creates a double quote in the resulting HTML

✔ \': Creates a single quote in the resulting HTML

✔ \\: Creates a backslash in the resulting HTML

PHP can take care of this for you automatically if you're receiving these values from a form. To read more, go here: `http://us3.php.net/types.string`.

Concatenation

Concatenation is the process of joining smaller strings to form a larger string. (See Book IV, Chapter 1 for a description of concatenation as it's applied in JavaScript.) PHP uses the period (.) symbol to concatenate two string values. The following example code returns the phrase oogieboogie:

```
$word = "oogie ";
$dance = "boogie";

Print $word . $dance
```

If you already know some JavaScript or another language, most of the ideas transfer, but details can trip you up. JavaScript uses the + sign for concatenation, and PHP uses the period. These are annoying details, but with practice, you'll be able to keep it straight.

When PHP sees a period, it treats the values on either side of the period as strings (text) and concatenates (joins) them. If PHP sees a plus sign, it treats the values on either side of the plus sign as numbers and attempts to perform mathematical addition on them. The operation helps PHP figure out what type of data it's working with.

The following program illustrates the difference between concatenation and addition (see Figure 1-3 for the output):

```
<?php
    $output = "World!";
    print "<p>Hello " . $output . "</p>";
    print "<p>" . $output + 5 . "</p>";
?>
```

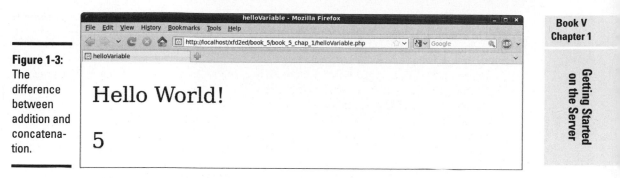

Figure 1-3:
The
difference
between
addition and
concatena-
tion.

The previous code takes the variable output with the value World and concatenates it to Hello when printed. Next, it adds the variable output to the number 5. When PHP sees the plus sign, it interprets the values on either side of it as numbers. Because output has no logical numerical value, PHP assigns it the value of 0, which it adds to 5, resulting in the output of <p>5</p> being sent to the browser.

Interpolating variables into text

If you have a bunch of text to print with variables thrown in, it can get a little tedious to use concatenation to add in the variables. Luckily, you don't have to!

With PHP, you can include the variables as follows (see Figure 1-4 for the output):

```
<!DOCTYPE html
PUBLIC "-//W3C//DTD XHTML 1.0 Strict//EN"
"http://www.w3.org/TR/xhtml1/DTD/xhtml1-strict.dtd">

<html xmlns="http://www.w3.org/1999/xhtml" xml:lang="en" lang="en">

<head>
<title>helloInterpolation</title>
</head>
<body>

<?php
  $firstName = "John";
  $lastName = "Doe";

  print "<p>Hello $firstName $lastName!</p>";
?>

</body>
</html>
```

Figure 1-4:
The
variables
print without
having to do
concatena-
tions.

```
                                    helloInterpolation - Mozilla Firefox                    _ □ x
 File  Edit  View  History  Bookmarks  Tools  Help

   ◄ ▸  ▾  C  🗙  🏠  [ 🔲 http://localhost/xfd2ed/book_5/book_5_chap_1/helloInterpolation.php  ] ▾ 🔍▾  Google     🔍  ABP ▾
 🔲 helloInterpolation            ➕
```

Hello John Doe!

This process is called *interpolation*. Because all PHP variables begin with quotes, you can freely put variables right inside your string values, and when PHP sees a variable, it will automatically replace that variable with its value.

Interpolation works only with double-quoted strings because double quotes indicate PHP should process the string before passing it to the user.

Building XHTML Output

The output of a PHP program is usually an XHTML page. As far as PHP is concerned, XHTML is just string data, so your PHP program often has to do a lot of string manipulation. You'll often be writing long chunks of text (XHTML code) with several variables (generated by your PHP program) interspersed throughout the code. This type of text (XHTML output) will often stretch over several lines, requires carriage returns to be preserved, and often contains special characters like quotes and <> symbols. The ordinary quote symbols are a little tedious if you want to use them to build a Web page. Here's an example.

Say you wanted to create a program which could take the value of the $name and $address variables and put them into a table like this:

```
<table style = "border: 1px solid black">
   <tr>
     <td>name</td>
     <td>John</td>
   </tr>
   <tr>
     <td>address</td>
     <td>123 Main St.</td>
   </tr>
</table>
```

There are a few ways to combine the PHP and XHTML code as shown in the following sections.

Using double quote interpolation

Using regular double quotes, the code would look something like this:

```
$name = "John";
$address = "123 Main St.";
$output = "";
$output .= "<table style = \"border: 1px solid black\"> \n";
$output .= "   <tr> \n";
$output .= "     <td>name</td> \n";
$output .= "     <td>$name</td> \n";
$output .- "   </tr> \n";
$output .= "   <tr> \n";
$output .- "     <td>address</td> \n";
$output .= "     <td>$address</td> \n";
$output .= "   </tr> \n";
$output .= "</table> \n";

print $output
```

However, using quotes to generate XHTML output is inconvenient for the following reasons:

✦ **The $output variable must be initialized.** Before adding anything to the $output variable, give it an initial null value.

✦ **You must repeatedly concatenate data onto the $output variable.** The .= operator allows me to append something to a string variable.

✦ **All quotes must be escaped.** Because double quotes indicate the end of the string, all internal double quotes must be preceded with the backslash (\).

✦ **Every line must end with a newline (\n) sequence.** PHP creates XHTML source code. Your PHP-derived code should look as good as what you write by hand, so you need to preserve carriage returns. This means you need to end each line with a newline.

✦ **The XHTML syntax is buried inside PHP syntax.** The example shows PHP code creating HTML code. Each line contains code from two languages interspersed. This can be disconcerting to a beginning programmer.

Generating output with heredocs

PHP uses a clever solution called heredocs to resolve all these issues. A *heredoc* is simply a type of multiline quote, usually beginning and ending with the word HERE.

The best way to understand heredocs is to see one in action, so here's the same example written as a heredoc:

```
<?
$name = "John";
$address = "123 Main St.";
print <<<HERE
```

```
<table style = "border: 1px solid black">
  <tr>
    <td>name</td>
    <td>$name</td>
  </tr>
  <tr>
    <td>address</td>
    <td>$address</td>
  </tr>
</table>
HERE;
?>
```

Figure 1-5 illustrates this code in action.

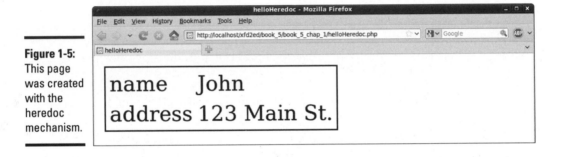

Figure 1-5:
This page
was created
with the
heredoc
mechanism.

Heredocs have some great advantages:

+ **All carriage returns are preserved.** There's no need to put in any new-line characters. Whatever carriage returns are in the original text will stay in the output.

+ **Heredocs preserve quote symbols.** There's also no need to escape your quotes because the double quote is not the end-of-string character for a heredoc.

+ **Variable interpolation is supported.** You can use variable names in a heredoc, just like you do for an ordinary quoted string.

+ **The contents of a heredoc feel like ordinary XHTML.** When you're working inside a heredoc, you can temporarily put your mind in XHTML mode, but with the ability to interpolate variables.

The following are some things to keep in mind about heredocs:

+ A heredoc is opened with three less-than symbols (<<<) followed by a heredoc symbol that will act as a "superquote" (instead of single or double quotation marks, you make your own custom quotation mark from any value that you want).

✦ A heredoc symbol can be denoted by almost any text, but HERE is the most common delimiter (thus, heredoc). You can make absolutely anything you want serve as a heredoc symbol. You probably should just stick to HERE because that's what other programmers are expecting.

✦ You need only one semicolon for the whole heredoc. Technically, the entire heredoc counts as one line. That means that the only semicolon you need is after the closing symbol.

✦ A heredoc must be closed with the same word it was opened with.

✦ The closing word for the heredoc must be on its own line.

✦ You can't indent the closing word for the heredoc; there can't be any spaces or tabs preceding the closing word.

By far, the most common problem with heredocs is indenting the closing token. The HERE (or whatever other symbol you're using) must be flush with the left margin of your editor, or PHP won't recognize it. This usually means PHP interprets the rest of your program as part of a big string and never finishes executing it.

Heredocs have one disadvantage: They tend to mess up your formatting because you have to indent heredocs differently than the rest of the code.

When writing a heredoc, don't put a semicolon after the first <<<HERE. Also, don't forget that the last HERE; can't have any whitespace before it — it must be alone on a new line without any spaces preceding it. An editor that understands the heredoc rules will highlight all the code inside the heredoc and save you lots of grief. Komodo does this automatically, as does Aptana (if you've installed the PHP plugin). Notepad++ also has this feature.

Switching from PHP to XHTML

There's one more way to combine PHP and XHTML code. The server treats a PHP document mainly as an XHTML document. Any code not inside the `<?php ?>` symbols is treated as XHTML, and anything inside the PHP symbols is interpreted as PHP.

This means you can switch in and out of PHP, like the following example:

```
<?php
    $name = "John";
    $address = "123 Main St.";
    // switch 'out' of PHP temporarily
?>
<table style = "border: 1px solid black">
  <tr>
    <td>name</td>
    <td><?php print $name; ?></td>
  </tr>
  <tr>
    <td>address</td>
    <td><?php print $address; ?></td>
```

```
   </tr>
</table>
<?php
   //I'm back in PHP
?>
```

This option (switching back and forth) is generally used when you have a lot of XHTML code with only a few simple PHP variables. I prefer the heredoc approach, but feel free to experiment and find out what system works for you.

Printing shortcut

When switching in and out of PHP, if you have just one variable you want to print, depending upon your server setup, you may be able to do print the variable like this:

```
<?= $name ?>
```

You don't have to actually write `print` when using this technique. Note that this trick doesn't work if you have to type **php** after the question mark in the opening PHP tag.

Chapter 2: PHP and XHTML Forms

In This Chapter

- ✔ Understanding the relationship between XHTML and PHP
- ✔ Using the `date()` function
- ✔ Formatting date and time information
- ✔ Creating XHTML forms designed to work with PHP
- ✔ Choosing between `get` and `post` data transmission
- ✔ Retrieving data from your XHTML forms
- ✔ Working with XHTML form elements

*P*HP is almost never used on its own. PHP is usually used in tight conjunction with XHTML. Many languages have features for creating input forms and user interfaces, but with PHP, the entire user experience is based on XHTML. The user never really sees any PHP. Most of the input to PHP programs comes from XHTML forms, and the output of a PHP program is an XHTML page.

In this chapter, you discover how to integrate PHP and XHTML. You explore how PHP code is embedded into XHTML pages, how XHTML forms can be written so they will send information to a PHP program, how to write a PHP program to read that data, and how to send an XHTML response back to the user.

Exploring the Relationship between PHP and XHTML

PHP is a different language than XHTML, but the two are very closely related. It may be best to think of PHP as an extension that allows you to do things you cannot do easily in XHTML. See Figure 2-1 for an example.

Every time you run `getTime.php`, it generates the current date and time and returns these values to the user. This would not be possible in ordinary XHTML because the date and time (by definition) always change. While you could make this page using JavaScript, the PHP approach is useful for demonstrating how PHP works. First, take a look at the PHP code:

```
<!DOCTYPE html PUBLIC "-//W3C//DTD XHTML 1.0 Strict//EN"
"http://www.w3.org/TR/xhtml1/DTD/xhtml1-strict.dtd">
<html lang="EN" dir="ltr" xmlns="http://www.w3.org/1999/xhtml">
  <head>
```

```
        <meta http-equiv="content-type" content="text/xml; charset=utf-8" />
        <title>showDate.php</title>
    </head>


    <body>
    <h1>Getting the Time, PHP Style</h1>
    <?php

print "        <h2>Date: ";
print date("m-d");
print "</h2> \n";

print "        <h2>Time: ";
print date("h:i");
print "</h2>";

    ?>

    </body>
</html>
```

Figure 2-1:
This program gives me the current date and time.

Getting the Time, PHP Style

Date: 03-12

Time: 03:14

Embedding PHP inside XHTML

The PHP code has some interesting characteristics:

✦ **It's structured mainly as an XHTML document.** The `doctype` definition, document heading, and initial H1 heading are all ordinary XHTML.
Begin your page as you do any XHTML document. A PHP page can have
as much XHTML code as you wish. (You might have no PHP at all!) The
only thing the PHP designation does is inform the server that PHP code
may be embedded into the document.

✦ **PHP code is embedded into the page.** You can switch from XHTML to
PHP with the `<?php` tag. Signify the end of the PHP code with the `?>`
symbol.

✦ **The PHP code creates XHTML.** PHP is usually used to create XHTML
code. In effect, PHP takes over and prints out the part of the page that
can't be created in static XHTML. The result of a PHP fragment is usually
XHTML code.

✦ **The `date()` function returns the current date with a specific format.**
The format string indicates how the date should be displayed. (See the
sidebar "Exploring the date() format function," in this chapter, for more
information about date formatting.)

✦ **The result of the PHP code will be an XHTML document.** When the
PHP code is finished, it will be replaced by XHTML code.

Viewing the results

If you view `showDate.php` in your browser, you won't see the PHP code.
Instead, you'll see an XHTML page. It's even more interesting when you use
your browser to view the page source. Here's what you'll see:

```
<!DOCTYPE html PUBLIC "-//W3C//DTD XHTML 1.0 Strict//EN"
"http://www.w3.org/TR/xhtml1/DTD/xhtml1-strict.dtd">
<html lang="EN" dir="ltr" xmlns="http://www.w3.org/1999/xhtml">
  <head>
    <meta http-equiv="content-type" content="text/xml; charset=utf-8" />
    <title>showDate.php</title>
  </head>

  <body>
    <h1>Getting the Time, PHP Style</h1>
    <h2>Date: 02-13</h2>
    <h2>Time: 10:02</h2>
  </body>
</html>
```

The remarkable thing is what you don't see. When you look at the source
of `showDate.php` in your browser, the PHP is completely gone! This is one
of the most important points about PHP: The browser never sees any of the
PHP. The PHP code is converted completely to XHTML before anything is
sent to the browser. This means that you don't need to worry about
whether a user's browser understands PHP. Because the user never sees
your PHP code (even if he views the XHTML source), PHP code will work on
any browser.

Exploring the date() format function

The `showDate.php` program takes advantage of one of PHP's many interesting and powerful functions to display the date. The PHP `date()` function returns the current date. Generally, you'll pass the `date()` function a special format string that indicates how you want the date to be formatted. Characters in the date string indicate a special code. Here are a few of the characters and their meanings:

✔ `d`: day of the month (numeric)

✔ `D`: three character abbreviation of weekday (`Wed`)

✔ `m`: month (numeric)

✔ `M`: three-character abbreviation of month (`Feb`)

✔ `F`: text representation of month (`February`)

✔ `y`: two-digit representation of the year (`08`)

✔ `Y`: four-digit representation of the year (`2008`)

✔ `h`: hour (12 hours)

✔ `H`: hour (24 hours)

✔ `i`: minutes

✔ `s`: seconds

You can embed standard punctuation in the format as well, so `d/m/y` will include the slashes between each part of the date. There are many more symbols available. Check the PHP documentation at `http://us3.php.net/manual/en/function.date.php` for more information about date and time formatting.

Sending Data to a PHP Program

You can send data to a PHP program from an HTML form. For an example of this technique, see `askName.html` in Figure 2-2.

Figure 2-2:
This XHTML page has a simple form.

XHTML forms (described fully in Book I, Chapter 7) allow the user to enter data onto a Web page. However, XHTML cannot respond to a form on its own. You need some sort of program to respond to the form. Book IV describes how to use JavaScript to respond to forms, but you can also write PHP code to handle form-based input. When the user submits the form, the `askName.html` disappears completely from the browser and is replaced with `greetUser.php`, as shown in Figure 2-3.

Figure 2-3:
This program uses the entry from the previous form.

The greetUser.php program retrieves the data from the previous page (askName.html, in this case) and returns an appropriate greeting.

Creating a form for PHP processing

The askName.html program is a standard XHTML form, but it has a couple of special features which make it suitable for PHP processing. (See Book I, Chapter 7 for more information about how to build XHTML forms.) Here is the XHTML code:

```
<!DOCTYPE html PUBLIC "-//W3C//DTD XHTML 1.0 Strict//EN"
"http://www.w3.org/TR/xhtml1/DTD/xhtml1-strict.dtd">
<html lang="EN" dir="ltr" xmlns="http://www.w3.org/1999/xhtml">
  <head>
    <meta http-equiv="content-type" content="text/xml; charset=utf-8" />
    <title>askName.html</title>
  </head>

  <body>
    <form action = "greetUser.php"
          method = "get">
      <fieldset>
        <label>Please enter your name</label>
        <input type = "text"
               name = "userName" />
        <button type = "submit">
          submit
        </button>
      </fieldset>

    </form>
  </body>
</html>
```

To build a form designed to work with PHP, there are a few special steps to take:

1. **Write an XHTML page as the framework.**

This page is a regular XHTML page. Begin with the same XHTML framework you use for building your standard XHTML pages. You can use CSS styles, if you wish (but I'm leaving them out of this simple example).

Normally, you can create an XHTML document anywhere you want, but this is so when your page will be working with PHP. This page is meant to be paired with a PHP document. PHP documents will run only if they are in a server's file space, so you should save your XHTML document under htdocs to be sure it will call the PHP form correctly.

2. **Set the form's `action` property to point to a PHP program.**

The form element has an attribute called `action`. The `action` attribute is used to determine which program should receive the data transmitted by the form. I want this data to be processed by a program called greet User.php, so I set greetUser.php as the `action`:

```
<form action = "greetUser.php"
      method = "get">
```

3. **Set the form's `method` attribute to get.**

The `method` attribute indicates how the form data will be sent to the server. For now, use the `get` method. See the section "Choosing the Method of Your Madness," later in this chapter, for information on the various methods available:

```
<form action = "greetUser.php"
      method = "get">
```

4. **Add any input elements your form needs.**

The point of a form is to get information from the user and send it to a program on the server. Devise a form to ask whatever questions you want from the server. My form is as simple as possible, with one text field, but you can use any XHTML form elements you want:

```
<form action = "greetUser.php"
      method = "get">
  <fieldset>
    <label>Please enter your name</label>
    <input type = "text"
           name = "userName" />
    <button type = "submit">
      submit
    </button>
  </fieldset>
```

5. **Give each element a `name` attribute.**

If you want a form element to be passed to the server, you must give it a name attribute. *Note:* This is a different attribute than id, which is used in client-side processing.

```
<input type = "text"
       name = "userName" />
```

The name attribute will be used by the PHP program to extract the information from the form.

A form element can have both a name and an ID, if you wish. The `name` attribute will be used primarily by server-side programs, and the `id` attribute is mainly used for CSS and JavaScript. The name and ID can (and probably should) have the same value.

6. **Add a submit button to the page.**

   The most important difference between a client-side form and a form destined for processing on the server is the button. A special submit button packages all the data in the form and passes it to the program indicated in the `action` property. Submit buttons can be created in two forms:

   ```
   <input type = "submit" value = "click me"/>
   ```

   or

   ```
   <button type = "submit">click me</button>
   ```

   Specify `submit` as the button's `type` attribute to ensure the button sends the data to the server.

   If your form has a submit button and a blank `action` attribute, the current page will be reloaded.

Receiving data in PHP

PHP code is usually a two-step process. First, you create an XHTML form, and then you send that form to a PHP program for processing. Be sure to read the previous section on "Creating a form for PHP processing" because now I show you how to read that form with a PHP program.

The XHTML form in the last section pointed to a program named greet User.php. This tells the server to go to the same directory that contained the original XHTML document (askName.html) and look for a program named greetUser.php in that directory. Because greetUser is a PHP program, the server passes it through PHP, which will extract data from the form. The program then creates a greeting using data that came from the form. Look over all the code for greetUser.php before I explain it in more detail:

```
<!DOCTYPE html PUBLIC "-//W3C//DTD XHTML 1.0 Strict//EN"
"http://www.w3.org/TR/xhtml1/DTD/xhtml1-strict.dtd">
<html lang="EN" dir="ltr" xmlns="http://www.w3.org/1999/xhtml">
  <head>
    <meta http-equiv="content-type" content="text/xml; charset=utf-8" />
    <title>greetUser.php</title>
  </head>

  <body>
    <?php
    $userName = $_REQUEST["userName"];
    print "<h1>Hi, $userName!</h1>"
    ?>

  </body>
</html>
```

greetUser.php is not a complex program, but it shows the most common use of PHP: retrieving data from a form. Here's how you build it:

1. **Build a new PHP program.**

   This program should be in the same directory as askName.html, which should be somewhere the server can find (usually under the htdocs or public_html directory).

2. **Start with ordinary XHTML.**

   PHP programs are usually wrapped inside ordinary XHTML, so begin the document as if it were plain XHTML. Use whatever CSS styling and ordinary HTML tags you want. (I'm keeping this example as simple as possible, although I'd normally add some CSS styles to make the output less boring.)

3. **Add a PHP segment.**

   Somewhere in the page, you'll need to switch to PHP syntax so that you can extract the data from the form. Use the <?php symbol to indicate the beginning of your PHP code:

   ```
   <?php
   $userName = $_REQUEST["userName"];
   print "<h1>Hi, $userName!</h1>";
   ?>
   ```

4. **Extract the username variable.**

   PHP stores all the data sent to the form inside a special variable called $_REQUEST. This object contains a list of all the form elements in the page that triggered this program. In this case, I want to extract the value of the userName field and store it in a PHP variable called $userName:

   ```
   $userName = $_REQUEST["userName"];
   ```

   See the upcoming section "Getting data from the form" for more information on the $_REQUEST object and some of the other tools that are available for retrieving information.

5. **Print the greeting.**

   Now, your PHP program has a variable containing the user's name, so you can print a greeting to the user. Remember that all output of a PHP program is XHTML code, so be sure to embed your output in a suitable XHTML tag. I'm putting the greeting inside a level-one heading:

   ```
   print "<h1>Hi, $userName!</h1>";
   ```

The greetUser.php script is not meant to be run directly. It relies on askName.html. If you provide a direct link to greetUser.php, the program will run, but it will not be sent the username, so it will not work as expected. Do not place links to your PHP scripts unless you designed them to work without input.

Choosing the Method of Your Madness

The key to server-side processing is adding `method` and `action` properties to your XHTML form. You have two primary choices for the `method` property:

✦ **get:** The `get` method gathers the information in your form and appends it to the URL. The PHP program extracts form data from the address. The contents of the form are visible for anyone to see.

✦ **post:** The `post` method passes the data to the server through a mechanism called *environment variables*. This mechanism makes the form elements slightly more secure because they aren't displayed in public as they are with the `get` method.

Using get to send data

The `get` method is easy to understand. View `getRequest.php` after it has been called from `askName.html` in Figure 2-4. Pay careful attention to the URL in the address bar.

Figure 2-4:
The address
has been
modified!

http://localhost/xfd2ed/book_5/book_5_chap_2/greetUser.php?userName=

The address sent to the PHP program has additional material appended:

```
http://localhost/xfd/ar/xfd5.3_AR_AH/greetUser.php?userName=Andy%20Harris
```

Most of this address is the (admittedly convoluted) address of the page on my test server. The interesting part is the section after `greetUser.php`:

```
greetUser.php?userName=Andy%20Harris
```

This line shows exactly how the `get` method passes information to the program on the server:

✦ **The URL is extracted from the form `action` property.** When the submit button is activated, the browser automatically creates a special URL beginning with the `action` property of the form. The default address is the same directory as the original XHTML file.

✦ **A question mark indicates form data is on the way.** The browser appends a question mark to the URL to indicate form data follows.

✦ **Each field/value pair is listed.** The question mark is followed by each field name and its associated value in the following format:

```
URL?field1=value1&field2=value2
```

✦ **An equal sign (=) follows each field name.** Each field name is separated by the value of that field with an equal sign (and no spaces).

✦ **The field value is listed immediately after the equal sign.** The value of each field follows the equal sign.

✦ **Spaces are converted to hexadecimal symbols.** `get` data is transmitted through the URL, and URLS are not allowed to have spaces or other special characters in them. The browser will automatically convert all spaces in field names or values to the `%20` symbol. Other special characters (like ampersands and equal signs) are also automatically converted to special symbols.

Sometimes, the spaces are converted to + signs, rather than `%20`. It isn't really that important because the conversion is done automatically. Just know that URLs can't contain spaces.

✦ **An ampersand (&) is used to add a new field name/value pair.** This particular example (the URL created by `askName.html`) has only one name/value pair. If the form had more elements, they would all be separated by ampersands.

You don't have to do any of the URL formatting. It automatically happens when the user clicks the submit button. You'll also never have to decode all this, as PHP will do it for you.

If you understand how the `get` method works, you can take advantage of it to send data to programs without the original form. For example, take a look at this address:

```
http://www.google.com/search?q=dramatic%20chipmunk
```

If you type this code into your browser's location bar, you'll get the Google search results for a classic five-second video. (If you haven't seen this video, it's worth viewing.) If you know a particular server-side program (like Google's search engine) uses the `get` protocol, and you know which fields are needed (q stands for the query in Google's program), you can send a request to a program as if that request came from a form.

You can also write a link with a preloaded search query in it:

```
<a href = "http://www.google.com/search/q=dramatic%20chipmunk">
  Google search for the dramatic chipmunk
</a>
```

How did I know how to write the Google query?

You might wonder how I knew what fields the Google engine expects. If the program uses `get`, just use the intended form to make a search and look at the resulting URL. Some testing and experience told me that only the `q` field is absolutely necessary.

This trick (bypassing the form) could be considered rude by some because it circumvents safety features that may be built into the form. Still, it can be helpful for certain very public features, like preloaded Google searches, or looking up weather data for a particular location through a hard-coded link.

If a user clicks the resulting link, he would get the current Google search for the dramatic chipmunk video. (Really, it's a prairie dog, but "dramatic chipmunk" just sounds better.)

Of course, if you can send requests to a program without using the intended form, others can do the same to you. You can never be 100 percent sure that people are sending requests from your forms. This can cause some problems. Look at the next section for a technique to minimize this problem by reading only data sent via the `post` method.

Using the post method to transmit form data

The `get` method is easy to understand because it sends all data directly in the URL. This makes it easy to see what's going on, but there are some downsides to using `get`:

+ **The resulting URL can be very messy.** Addresses on the Web can already be difficult without the added details of a `get` request. A form with several fields can make the URL so long that it's virtually impossible to follow.

+ **All form information is user-readable.** The `get` method displays form data in the URL, where it can easily be read by the user. This may not be desired, especially when the form sends potentially sensitive data.

+ **The amount of information that can be passed is limited.** The Apache server (in its default form) won't accept URLs longer than 4,000 characters. If you have a form with many fields or with fields that contain a lot of data, you will easily exceed this limit.

The answer to the limitations of the `get` method is another form of data transmission: the `post` methodHere's how it works:

✦ **You specify that the form's method will be post.** You create the
   XHTML form in exactly the same way. The only difference is the form
   method attribute. Set it to post:

```
<form action = "greetUser.php"
      method = "post">
```

✦ **Data is gathered and encoded, just like it is in the get method.** When
   the user clicks the submit button, the data is encoded in a format similar
   to the get request, but it's not attached to the URL.

✦ **The form data is sent directly to the server.** The PHP program can still
   retrieve the data (usually through a mechanism called *environment variables*) even though the data is not encoded on the URL. Again, you won't be
   responsible for the details of extracting the data. PHP makes it pretty easy.

The post method is often preferable to get because

✦ **The URL is not polluted with form data.** The data is no longer passed
   through the URL, so the resulting URL is a lot cleaner than one generated by the get method.

✦ **The data is not visible to the user.** Because the data isn't presented in
   the URL, it's slightly more secure than get data.

✦ **There is no practical size limit.** The size of the URL isn't a limiting
   factor. If your page will be sending a large amount of data, the post
   method is preferred.

With all these advantages, you might wonder why anybody uses get at all.
Really, there are two good reasons. The get approach allows you to embed
requests in URLs (which can't be done with post). Also, get is sometimes a
better choice for debugging because it's easier to see what's being passed to
the server.

Getting data from the form

PHP includes a number of special built-in variables that give you access to
loads of information. Each variable is stored as an associative array; see
Chapter 5 of this minibook for more on associative arrays. These special
variables are available anywhere in your PHP code, so they're called *superglobals*. Here's a few of the most important ones:

✦ **$_GET:** A list of variables sent to this program through the get method

✦ **$_POST:** A list of variables sent to this program through the post
   method

✦ **$_REQUEST:** A combination of $_GET and $_POST

Can't I just have automatic access to form variables?

The earliest forms of PHP had a feature called *register_globals* that automatically did the $_REQUEST extraction for you. If your program comes from a userName field, the program will "magically" just have a $user-Name variable preloaded with the value of that field. Although this was a very convenient option, evildoers soon learned how to take advantage of this behavior to cause all kinds of headaches. Convenient as it may be, the register_globals feature is now turned off on most servers and isn't even available on the next version of PHP. The $_REQUEST approach is safer and not much harder. If you want even more control of how information is passed to your programs, investigate the filter_input() functions that are in the latest versions of PHP. They are not quite complete (as of this writing), but by the time PHP6 rolls around, they'll probably become an even better way to extract data from forms.

You can use these variables to look up information posted in the form. For example, the askName.html page contains a field called userName. When the user views this page, it sends a request to greetUser.php via the get method. greetUser.php can then check its $_GET variable to see whether a field named userName exists:

```
$userName = $_GET["userName"];
```

This line checks all the data sent via get, looks for a field named userName, and copies the contents of that field to the variable $userName.

If you want to retrieve a value sent through the post method, use this variation:

```
$userName = $_POST["userName"];
```

If you don't care whether the data was sent via get or post, use $_REQUEST:

```
$userName = $_REQUES["userName"];
```

The $_REQUEST superglobal grabs data from both get and post requests, so it works, no matter how the form was encoded. Many programmers use the $_REQUEST technique because then they don't have to worry about the encoding mechanism.

If you don't like the idea of somebody accessing your data without a form, use $_POST in your PHP program. If data is encoded in the URL, your program ignores it because you're only responding to post data, and data encoded in the URL is (by definition) get data.

This solution is far from foolproof. There's nothing to prevent a bad guy from writing his own form using the post method and passing data to your program that way. You can never be 100 percent safe.

Retrieving Data from Other Form Elements

It's just as easy to get data from drop-down lists and radio buttons as it is to get data from text fields. In PHP (unlike JavaScript), you use exactly the same technique to extract data from any type of form element.

Building a form with complex elements

For an example of a more complex form, look over monty.html in Figure 2-5. This program is a tribute to my favorite movie of all time. (You might just have to rent this movie if you're really going to call yourself a programmer. It's part of the culture.)

Figure 2-5:
The Monty Python quiz features a drop-down list, radio buttons, and check boxes (and a newt).

The XHTML form poses the questions. (Check out Book I, Chapter 7 for a refresher on XHTML forms, if you need it.) Here's the code:

```
<!DOCTYPE html PUBLIC "-//W3C//DTD XHTML 1.0 Strict//EN"
"http://www.w3.org/TR/xhtml1/DTD/xhtml1-strict.dtd">
<html lang="EN" dir="ltr" xmlns="http://www.w3.org/1999/xhtml">
  <head>
    <meta http-equiv="content-type" content="text/xml; charset=utf-8" />
    <title>monty.html</title>
    <link rel = "stylesheet"
          type = "text/css"
          href = "monty.css" />
  </head>

  <body>
    <h1>Monty Python Quiz</h1>
    <form action = "monty.php"
          method = "post">
      <fieldset>
        <p>
          <label>What is your name?</label>
          <select name = "name">

            <option value = "Roger">
              Roger the shrubber
            </option>
            <option value = "Arthur">
              Arthur, King of the Britons
            </option>
            <option value = "Tim">
              Tim the Enchanter
            </option>
          </select>
        </p>

        <p>
          <label>What is your quest?</label>
          <span>
            <input type = "radio"
                   name = "quest"
                   value = "herring" />

            To chop down the mightiest tree in the forest
            with a herring
          </span>
          <span>
            <input type = "radio"
                   name = "quest"
                   value = "grail" />

            I seek the holy grail.
          </span>
          <span>
            <input type = "radio"
                   name = "quest"
                   value = "shrubbery" />
            I'm looking for a shrubbery.
          </span>
        </p>

        <p>
```

```
            <label>How can you tell she's a witch?</label>
            <span>
              <input type = "checkbox"
                     name = "nose"
                     value = "nose"/>
              She's got a witch nose.
            </span>
            <span>
              <input type = "checkbox"
                     name = "hat"
                     value = "hat"/>
              She has a witch hat.
            </span>
            <span>
              <input type = "checkbox"
                     name = "newt"
                     value = "newt" />
              She turned me into a newt.
            </span>
          </p>
            <button type = "submit">
              Submit
            </button>
        </fieldset>
      </form>
    </body>
</html>
```

There's nothing too crazy about this code. Please note the following features:

+ **The `action` attribute is set to `monty.php`.** This page (`monty.html`) will send data to `monty.php`, which should be in the same directory on the same server.

+ **The `method` attribute is set to `post`.** All data on this page will be passed to the server via the `post` method.

+ **Each form element has a `name` attribute.** The `name` attributes will be used to extract the data in the PHP program.

+ **All the radio buttons have the same `name` value.** The way you get radio buttons to work together is to give them all the same `name`. And although they all have the same name, each has a different value. When the PHP program receives the request, it will get only the value of the selected radio button.

+ **Each check box has an individual name.** Check boxes are a little bit different. Each check box has its own name, but the value is sent to the server only if the check box is checked.

I don't cover text areas, passwords fields, or hidden fields here because to PHP, they are just like text boxes. Retrieve data from these elements just like you do for text fields.

Responding to a complex form

The `monty.php` program is designed to respond to `monty.html`. You can see it respond when I submit the form in `monty.html`, as shown in Figure 2-6.

REMEMBER

It's no coincidence that `monty.html` uses `monty.css` and calls `monty.php`. I deliberately gave these files similar names so it will be easy to see how they fit together.

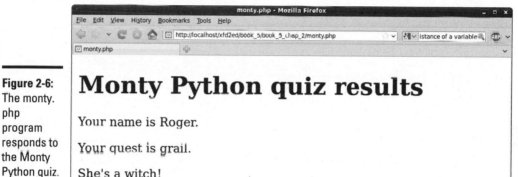

Figure 2-6: The monty. php program responds to the Monty Python quiz.

This program works like most PHP programs: It loads data from the form into variables and assembles output based on those variables. Here's the PHP code:

```
<!DOCTYPE html PUBLIC "-//W3C//DTD XHTML 1.0 Strict//EN"
"http://www.w3.org/TR/xhtml1/DTD/xhtml1-strict.dtd">
<html lang="EN" dir="ltr" xmlns="http://www.w3.org/1999/xhtml">
  <head>
    <meta http-equiv="content-type" content="text/xml; charset=utf-8" />
    <title>monty.php</title>
    <!-- Meant to run from monty.html -->
  </head>

  <body>
    <h1>Monty Python quiz results</h1>
    <?php
      //gather the variables
      $name = $_REQUEST["name"];
      $quest = $_REQUEST["quest"];
      //don't worry about check boxes yet; they may not exist

      //send some output
      $reply = <<< HERE
  <p>
    Your name is $name.
  </p>

  <p>
    Your quest is $quest.
  </p>
```

```
HERE;
     print $reply;

     //determine if she's a witch
     $witch = false;

     //See if check boxes exist
     if(isset($_REQUEST["nose"])){
       $witch = true;
     }
     if(isset($_REQUEST["hat"])){
       $witch = true;
     }
     if(isset($_REQUEST["newt"])){
       $witch = true;
     }

     if ($witch == true){
       print "<p>She's a witch!</p> \n";
     } // end if
   ?>

  </body>
</html>
```

If you want to respond to a form with multiple types of data, here's how it's done:

1. **Begin with the XHTML form.**

Be sure you know the names of all the fields in the form because your PHP program will need this information.

2. **Embed your PHP inside an XHTML framework.**

Use your standard XHTML framework as the starting point for your PHP documents, too. The results of your PHP code should still be standards-compliant XHTML. Use the `<?php` and `?>` symbols to indicate the presence of PHP code.

3. **Create a variable for each form element.**

Use the `$_REQUEST` technique described in the "Receiving data in PHP" section of this chapter to extract form data and store it in local variables:

```
//gather the variables
$name = $_REQUEST["name"];
$quest = $_REQUEST["quest"];
```

Don't worry about the check boxes yet. Later on, you'll determine whether they exist. You don't really care about their values.

4. **Build your output in a heredoc.**

PHP programming almost always involves constructing an XHTML document influenced by the variables that were extracted from the previous form. The heredoc method (described in Chapter 1 of this minibook) is an ideal method for packaging output:

```
         //send some output
         $reply = <<< HERE
<p>
   Your name is $name.
</p>

<p>
   Your quest is $quest.
</p>

HERE;
       print $reply;
```

5. **Check for the existence of each check box.**

   Check boxes are the one exception to the "treat all form elements the same way" rule of PHP. The important part of a check box isn't really its value. What you really need to know is whether the check box is checked. Here's how it works: If the check box is checked, a name and value are passed to the PHP program. If the check box is not checked, it's like the variable never existed:

   a. *Create a variable called* $witch *set to* false. Assume innocent until proven guilty in *this* witch hunt.

   Each check box, if checked, would be proof that she's a witch. The isset() function is used to determine whether a particular variable exists. This function returns true if the variable exists and false if it doesn't.

   b. *Check each check box variable.*

   If it exists, the corresponding check box was checked, so she must be a witch (and she must weigh the same as a duck — you've *really* got to watch this movie).

   After testing for the existence of all the check boxes, the $witch variable will still be false if none of the check boxes were checked. If any combination of check boxes is checked, $witch will be true:

```
//determine if she's a witch
$witch = false;

//See if check boxes exist
if(isset($_REQUEST["nose"])){
  $witch = true;
}
if(isset($_REQUEST["hat"])){
  $witch = true;
}
if(isset($_REQUEST["newt"])){
  $witch = true;
}

if ($witch == true){
  print "<p>She's a witch!</p> \n";
} // end if
```

Chapter 3: Control Structures

In This Chapter

✔ Getting used to conditions

✔ Using if, else if, and else

✔ Using switch structures

✔ Working with while and for loops

✔ Using comparison operators

C omputer programs are most interesting when they appear to make decisions. PHP has many of the same decision-making structures as JavaScript, so if you've already looked over Chapters 2 and 3 of Book IV, you will find this chapter very familiar. In any case, take a look at conditions to see the key to making the computer branch and loop.

Introducing Conditions (Again)

Computer programs make decisions. That's part of what makes them interesting. But all the decisions a computer seems to make were already determined by the programmer. The computer's decision-making power is all based on an idea called a *condition*. This little gem is an expression that can be evaluated as true or false. (That sounds profound. I wonder if it will be on the mid-term?)

Conditions can be comparisons of one variable to another, they can be Boolean (true or false) variables, or they can be functions that return a true or false value.

 If this talk of conditions is sounding like déjà vu, you've probably read about conditions in Book IV, Chapters 2 and 3. You'll find a lot of the same ideas here; after all, conditions (and branches and loops, and lots of other stuff) are bigger than one programming language. Even though this mini-book covers a different language, you'll see coverage of the same kinds of things. If you haven't read that minibook already, you might want to look it over first so you can see how programming remains the same even when the language changes.

Building the Classic if Statement

The if statement is the powerhouse of computer programming. Take a look at Figure 3-1 to see it in action. This program might be familiar if you read Book IV already. It rolls a standard six-sided die, and then displays that die on the screen.

When it rolls a six, it displays an elaborate multimedia event, as shown in Figure 3-2. (Okay, it just says *Holy Guacamole! That's a six!*)

This program is much like the duece.html program in Book IV, Chapter 2. I'm talking about exactly the same topic, and do all the same things here as in that program. However, PHP and JavaScript are a little different, and that's part of the game of programming. Appreciate the concepts that flow between languages while noting those details that are different.

Figure 3-1:
This program rolls a die. Try it again.

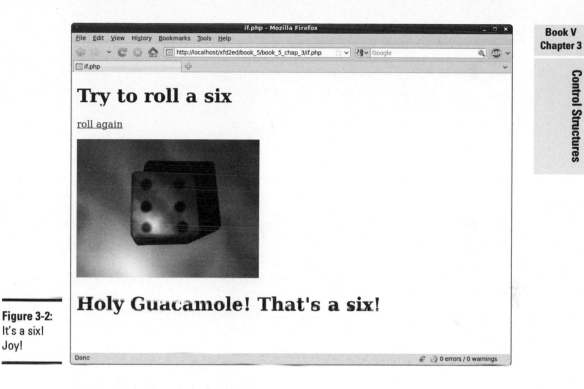

Figure 3-2:
It's a six!
Joy!

Rolling dice the PHP way

PHP has a random number generator, which works a little differently than the one in JavaScript. The PHP version is actually easier for dice.

```
$variable = rand(a, b);
```

This code creates a random integer between a and b (inclusive), so if you want a random 1–6 die, you can use a statement like this:

```
$die = rand(1,6);
```

It doesn't get a lot easier than that.

Checking your six

The code for the if.php program rolls a die, displays an image, and celebrates the joyous occasion of a six.

```
<!DOCTYPE html PUBLIC "-//W3C//DTD XHTML 1.0 Strict//EN" "http://www.w3.org/TR/
    xhtml1/DTD/xhtml1-strict.dtd">

<html xmlns="http://www.w3.org/1999/xhtml" xml:lang="en">
<head>
  <title>if.php</title>
  <meta http-equiv="Content-Type" content="text/html;charset=UTF-8" />
</head>

<body>
  <h1>Try to roll a six</h1>
  <p>
    <a href = "if.php">roll again</a>
  </p>

  <?php

  $roll = rand(1,6);

  print <<<HERE
  <p>
    <img src = "images/die$roll.jpg"
         alt = "$roll" />
  </p>
HERE;

  if ($roll == 6){
    print("<h1>Holy Guacamole! That's a six!</h1>\n");
  } // end if
  ?>
</body>
</html>
```

The process is eerily familiar:

1. Begin with a standard XHTML template.

As always, PHP is encased in XHTML. There's no need to switch to PHP until you get to the part that HTML can't do: that is, rolling dice and responding to the roll.

2. Add a link to let the user roll again.

Add a link that returns to the same page. When the user clicks the link, the server refreshes the page and rolls a new number.

3. Roll the `rand()` function to roll a die. Put the result in a variable called `$roll`.

4. Print out a graphic by creating the appropriate `<img>` tag.

I preloaded a bunch of die images into a directory called images. Each image is carefully named `die1.jpg` through `die6.jpg`. To display an image in PHP, just print out a standard img tag. The URL is created by interpolating the variable $roll into the image name. Don't forget that XHTML requires an alt attribute for the img tag. I just use the $roll value as the alt. That way, the die roll will be known even if the image doesn't work.

5. **Check whether the die is a six.**

   This is where the condition comes in. Use the if statement to see whether the value of $roll is 6. If so, print out a message.

WARNING!

The == (two equal sign) means "is equal to." A single equal sign means assignment. If you use the single equal sign in a condition, the code may not crash, but it probably won't do what you intended.

The else clause is used when you want to do one thing if a condition is true and something else if the condition is false. The highLow.php program shown in Figure 3-3 handles this kind of situation.

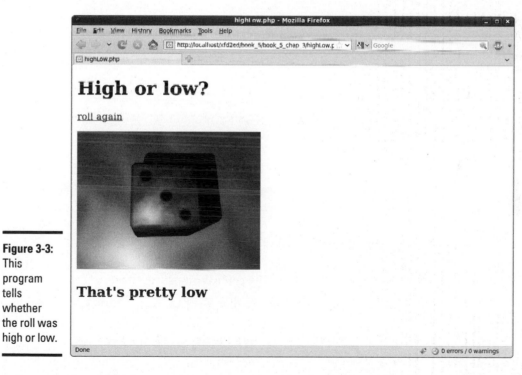

Figure 3-3:
This program tells whether the roll was high or low.

The code is very similar to the if.php program.

The bold code shows the only part of the program that's new.

```
<!DOCTYPE html PUBLIC "-//W3C//DTD XHTML 1.0 Strict//EN" "http://www.w3.org/TR/
    xhtml1/DTD/xhtml1-strict.dtd">
<html xmlns="http://www.w3.org/1999/xhtml" xml:lang="en">

<head>

  <title>highLow.php</title>

  <meta http-equiv="Content-Type" content="text/html;charset=UTF-8" />

</head>

<body>
  <h1>High or low?</h1>
  <p>
    <a href = "highLow.php">roll again</a>
  </p>

  <?php
  $roll = rand(1,6);

  print <<<HERE
  <p>
    <img src = "images/die$roll.jpg"
         alt = "$roll" />
  </p>
HERE;

  if ($roll > 3){
    print "<h2>You rolled a high one</h2>\n";
  } else {
    print "<h2>That's pretty low</h2> \n";
  } // end if

  ?>

</body>
</html>
```

Most of the code for this program is the same as the previous code example, but the condition is slightly different:

✦ **Now the condition is an inequality.** I now use the greater-than symbol (>) to compare the roll to the value 3. You can use any of the comparison operators in Table 3-1. If `$roll` is higher than 3, the condition will evaluate as true, and the first batch of code will run.

✦ **Add an `else` clause.**

The `else` clause is special because it handles the situation when the condition is false. All it does is set up another block of code.

✦ **Include code for the false condition.**

The code between `else` and the ending brace for `if` ending brace will run only if the condition is evaluated false.

Understanding comparison operators

PHP uses the same comparison operators as JavaScript (and many other languages based on C). Table 3-1 summarizes these operators.

Table 3-1	Comparison Operators
Comparison	*Discussion*
A == B	True if A is equal to B
A !- B	True if A is not equal to B
A < B	True if A is less than B (if they are numeric) or earlier in the alphabet (for strings)
A > B	True if A is larger than B (numeric) or later in the alphabet (string)
A >= B	A is larger than or equal to B
A<= B	A is less than or equal to B

Note that PHP determines the variable type dynamically, so comparisons between numeric and string values may cause problems. It's best to explicitly force variables to the type you want if you're not sure. For example, if you want to ensure that the variable $a is an integer before you compare it to the value 4, you could use this condition:

```
(integer)$a == 4
```

This will force the variable $a to be read as an integer. You can also use this technique (called *typecasting*) to force a variable to other types: `float`, `string`, or `boolean`.

Taking the middle road

Another variation of the `if` structure allows you to check multiple conditions. As an example, look at the `highMidLow.php` page featured in Figure 3-4.

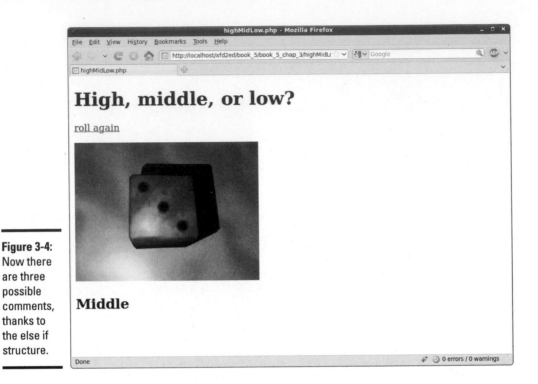

Figure 3-4:
Now there are three possible comments, thanks to the else if structure.

If the roll is 1 or 2, the program reports Low. If the roll is 3 or 4, it says Middle; and if it's 5 or 6, the result is High. This if has three branches. See how it works; you can add as many branches as you wish.

```
<!DOCTYPE html PUBLIC "-//W3C//DTD XHTML 1.0 Strict//EN" "http://www.w3.org/TR/
    xhtml1/DTD/xhtml1-strict.dtd">

<html xmlns="http://www.w3.org/1999/xhtml" xml:lang="en">

<head>
  <title>highMidLow.php</title>
  <meta http-equiv="Content-Type" content="text/html;charset=UTF-8" />
</head>

<body>
  <h1>High, middle, or low?</h1>
  <p>
    <a href = "highMidLow.php">roll again</a>
  </p>

  <?php
  $roll = rand(1,6);
  print <<<HERE
  <p>
    <img src = "images/die$roll.jpg"
         alt = "$roll" />
  </p>
```

```
HERE;

  if ($roll > 4){
    print "<h2>High!</h2>\n";
  } else if ($roll <= 2){
    print "<h2>Low</h2>\n";
  } else {
    print "<h2>Middle</h2> \n";
  } // end if

  ?>

</body>
</html>
```

The `if` statement is the only part of this program that's new. It's not terribly shocking.

1. **Begin with a standard condition.**

   Check whether the roll is greater than 4. If so, say `High`. If the first condition is true, the computer evaluates the code in the first section and then skips the rest of the `while` loop.

2. **Add a second condition.**

   The `else if` section allows me to add a second condition. This second condition (`roll <= 2`) Is evaluated only if the first condition is false. If this condition is true, the code inside this block will be executed (printing the value `Low`). You can add as many `else if` sections as you want. As soon as one is found to be true, the code block associated with that condition executes, and the program leaves the whole else system.

3. **Include an `else` clause to catch stragglers.**

   If none of the previous conditions are true, the code associated with the `else` clause operates. In this case, the roll is lower than 4 and higher than 2, so report that it's in the `Middle`.

Building a program that makes its own form

An especially important application of the `if` structure is unique to server-side programming. Up to now, many of your PHP programs required two separate files: an HTML page to get information from the user and a PHP program to respond to that code. Wouldn't it be great if the PHP program could determine whether it had the data or not? If it has data, it will process it. If not, it just produces a form to handle the data. That would be pretty awesome, and that's exactly what you can do with the help of the `if` statement. Figure 3-5 shows the first pass of `ownForm.php`.

Figure 3-5:
On the
first pass,
ownForm.
php
produces an
HTML form.

The interesting thing happens when the user submits the form. The program calls itself! This time, though, ownForm recognizes that the user has sent some data and processes that information, giving the result shown in Figure 3-6.

Figure 3-6:
Now the
same
program
processes
the data!

This program doesn't really require anything new, just a repurposing of some tools you already know. Take a look at the following code:

```
<!DOCTYPE html PUBLIC "-//W3C//DTD XHTML 1.0 Strict//EN" "http://www.w3.org/TR/
    xhtml1/DTD/xhtml1-strict.dtd">
<html xmlns="http://www.w3.org/1999/xhtml" xml:lang="en">
<head>
  <title>ownForm.php</title>
  <meta http-equiv="Content-Type" content="text/html;charset=UTF-8" />
</head>
<body>
<?php
if (isset($_REQUEST["userName"])){
  $userName = $_REQUEST["userName"];
  print "<h1>Hi, $userName</h1>\n";
} else {
  print <<<HERE
  <form action = ""
        method = "post">
    <fieldset>
      <label>Name</label>
```

```
        <input type = "text"
             name = "userName">
        <button type = "submit">
           submit
        </button>
     </fieldset>
   </form>
HERE;
} // end if


?>
</body>
</html>
```

Making a program "do its own stunts" like this is pretty easy. The key is using an `if` statement. However, begin by thinking about the behavior. In this example, the program revolves around the `$userName` variable. If this variable has a value, it can be processed. If the variable has not been set yet, the user needs to see a form so she can enter the data.

1. **Check for the existence of a key variable.**

   Use the `isset()` function to determine whether the variable in question has been set. Check the `$_REQUEST` or one of the other superglobals (`$_POST` or `$_GET`) to determine whether the form has already been submitted. You need to check the existence of only one variable, even if the form has dozens.

2. **If the variable exists, process the form.**

   If the variable exists, extract all the variables from the form and carry on with your processing.

3. **If the variable does not exist, build the form.**

   If the variable does not exist, you need to make the form that will ask the user for that variable (and any others you need). Note that the action attribute of the form element should be null (`""`). This tells the server to re-call the same program.

Making a switch

Often, you will run across a situation where you have one expression that can have many possible values. You can always use the `if - elseif` structure to manage this situation, but PHP supplies another interesting option, shown in Figure 3-7.

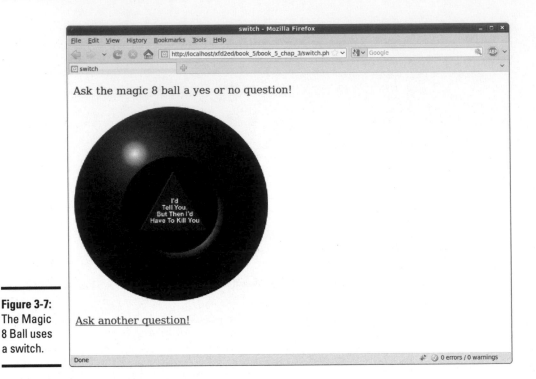

Figure 3-7:
The Magic
8 Ball uses
a switch.

The code for this program uses the `switch` structure. Take a look at how it's done:

```
<!DOCTYPE html PUBLIC "-//W3C//DTD XHTML 1.0 Strict//EN""http://www.w3.org/TR/
xhtml1/DTD/xhtml1-strict.dtd">
<html xmlns="http://www.w3.org/1999/xhtml" xml:lang="en" lang="en">
<head>
<title>switch.php</title>
</head>
<body>
<p>Ask the magic 8 ball a yes or no question!</p>

<?php

$yourNumber = rand(1,8);

switch($yourNumber){
  case 1:
    print "<p><img src=\"images/8ball1.png\" alt = \"fat chance\" /></p>";
    break;
  case 2:
    print "<p><img src=\"images/8ball2.png\" alt = \"Yes\" /></p> ";
    break;
  case 3:
    print "<p><img src=\"images/8ball3.png\" alt = \"PhD\" /></p>";
    break;
```

```
case 4:
  print "<p><img src=\"images/8ball4.png\" alt = \"You didn't say please\" /></
  p>";
  break;
case 5:
  print "<p><img src=\"images/8ball5.png\" alt = \"tell, then kill\" /></p>";
  break;
case 6:
  print "<p><img src=\"images/8ball6.png\" alt = \"Why trust me?\" /></p>";
  break;
case 7:
  print "<p><img src=\"images/8ball7.png\" alt = \"Ask your mother\" /></p>";
  break;
case 8:
  print "<p><img src=\"images/8ball8.png\" alt = \"The answer is in the
  question\" /></p>";
  break;
  default:
  print "<p>An error has occurred. Please try again, or contact support@
  somesite.com for assistance. Error code: 8BIC:$yourNumber</p>";
}

?>

<p>
  <a href="switch.php">Ask another question!</a>
</p>
</body>
</html>
```

The main (in fact nearly only) feature of this code is the switch statement. Here's how it works:

1. Begin with the switch statement.

This indicates that you will be building a switch structure.

2. Put the expression in parentheses.

Following the switch statement is a pair of parentheses. Put the expression (usually a variable) you wish to evaluate inside the parentheses. In this case, I'm checking the value of the variable $yourNumber.

3. Encase the entire switch in braces.

Use squiggle braces to indicate the entire case. As in most blocking structures, use indentation to help you remember how the structure is organized.

4. Establish the first case.

Put the first value you want to check for. In this situation, I'm looking for the value 1. Note that the type of data matters, so be sure you're comparing against the same type of data you think the variable will contain. Use a colon (:) to indicate the end of the case. This is one of the rare situations where you do not use a semicolon or brace at the end of a line.

5. **Write code that should happen if the expression matches the case.**

   If the expression matches the case (for example, if $yourNumber is equal to 1), the code you write here will execute.

6. **End the code with the `break` statement.**

   When you use an `if-else if` structure to work with multiple conditions, the interpreter jumps out of the system as soon as it encounters the first true condition. Switches work differently. Unless you specify (with the `break` statement), code will continue to evaluate even when one of the expressions is matched. You almost always need the `break` statement.

7. **Use the `default` clause to handle any unexpected behavior.**

   The `default` section of the `switch` structure is used to handle any situation that wasn't covered by one of the previously defined cases. It's a good idea to always include a `default` clause.

It may seem odd to have a `default` clause in this example. After all, I know how the `rand()` function works, and I know that I'll get values only between 1 and 8. It shouldn't be possible to have a value that isn't covered by one of the cases, yet I have a `default` clause in place for exactly that eventuality. Even though something *shouldn't* ever happen, sometimes it does. At the very least, I want a nice piece of code to explain what happened and send some kind of error message. If it's an important problem, I may have the code quietly e-mail me a message letting me know what went wrong.

You might wonder whether the switch is necessary at all. I could have used the interpolation tricks shown in the dice example to get the necessary images. However, remember that XHTML requires all images to have `alt` tags. With dice, the value of the roll is a perfectly acceptable `alt` value. The Magic 8 Ball needs to return text if the image doesn't work properly. I used a switch to ensure that I have the appropriate `alt` text available. (Extra points if you think an array would be an even better way to handle this situation.)

Looping with for

Sometimes you want to repeat something. PHP (like most languages) supports a number of looping constructs. Begin with the humble but lovable `for` loop, as shown in Figure 3-8.

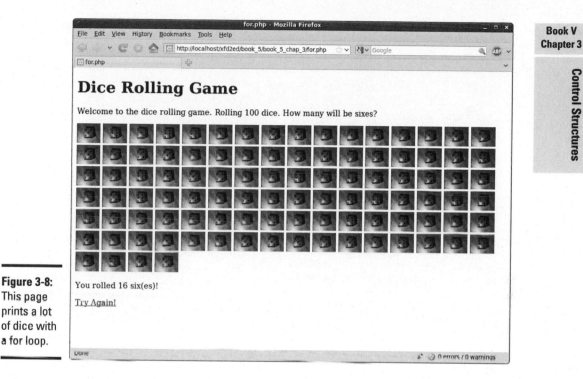

Figure 3-8:
This page
prints a lot
of dice with
a for loop.

As you can see, Figure 3-8 prints a *lot* of dice. In fact, it prints 100 dice. This would be tedious to do by hand, but that's exactly the kind of stuff computers are so good at.

The following code explains all:

```
<!DOCTYPE html
PUBLIC "-//W3C//DTD XHTML 1.0 Strict//EN"
"http://www.w3.org/TR/xhtml1/DTD/xhtml1-strict.dtd">
<html xmlns="http://www.w3.org/1999/xhtml" xml:lang="en" lang="en">
<head>
<title>for.php</title>
<style type="text/css">
  img{
    height: 40px;
    width: 50px;
  }
</style>
</head>
<body>
<h1>Dice Rolling Game</h1>
<p>Welcome to the dice rolling game. Rolling 100 dice. How many will be sixes?</
    p>
<p>
```

```php
<?php
$sixCount = 0;

for ($i = 0; $i < 100; $i++){
  $userNumber = rand(1,6);
  print <<< HERE
    <img src="images/die$userNumber.jpg"
         alt = "$userNumber" />
HERE;

  if($userNumber == 6){
    $sixCount++;
  } // end if
} // end for
print "</p><p>You rolled $sixCount six(es)!</p>";
?>

<p><a href="for.php">Try Again!</a></p>

</body>
</html>
```

Most of the code is plain-old HTML. Note the lone `print` statement responsible for printing out dice. That `print` statement (and a few supporting characters) are repeated 100 times. `for` loops are extremely powerful ways to get a lot of work done.

1. Begin with the `for` keyword.

This keyword indicates the beginning of the `for` structure.

```
for ($i = 0; $i < 100; $i++){
```

2. Add an initializer.

`for` loops usually center around a specific integer variable, sometimes called the *sentry variable*. The first part of the `for` loop sets up the initial value of that variable. Often, the variable is initialized to 0 or 1.

```
for ($i = 0; $i < 100; $i++){
```

3. Add a condition.

The loop will continue as long as the condition is true and will exit as soon as the condition is evaluated as false. Normally, the condition will check whether if the variable is larger than some value.

```
for ($i = 0; $i < 100; $i++){
```

4. Add a modifier.

Every time through the loop, you need to do something to change the value of the sentry. Normally, you add 1 to the sentry variable.

```
for ($i = 0; $i < 100; $i++){
```

5. **Encase the body of the loop in braces.**

The code that will be repeated is placed inside braces({ }). As usual, indent all code inside braces so you understand that you're inside a structure.

for loops are first described in Book IV, Chapter 3. Please look to that chapter for more details on for loops, including how to build a loop that counts backward and counts by fives. I don't repeat that material here because for loops work exactly the same in PHP and JavaScript.

This particular program has a few other features that make it suitable for printing out 100 dice.

✦ **It uses $i as a counting variable.** When the sentry variable's name isn't important, $i is often used. $i will vary from 0 to 99, giving 100 iterations of the loop.

✦ **Each time through the loop, roll a die.** The familiar rand() function is used to roll a random die value between 1 and 6. Because this code is inside the loop, it is repeated.

```
$userNumber = rand(1,6);
```

✦ **Print out an image related to the die roll.** I use interpolation to determine which image to display. Note that I used CSS to resize my image files to a smaller size.

```
print <<< HERE
  <img src="images/die$userNumber.jpg"
       alt - "$userNumber" />
HERE;
```

✦ **Check whether you rolled a 6.** For some strange reason, my obsession with sixes continues. If the roll is a 6, add 1 to the $sixCount variable. By the end of the loop, this will contain the total number of sixes rolled.

```
if($userNumber == 6){
    $sixCount++;
} // end if
```

✦ **Print the value of $sixCount.** After the loop is completed, report how many sixes were rolled.

```
print "</p><p>You rolled $sixCount six(es)!</p>";
```

Looping with while

The while loop is the other primary way of repeating code. Figure 3-9 shows a variation of the die rolling game.

Figure 3-9:
This time,
the program
continues
until it
gets a 6.

while loops are much like for loops. They require the same thought:

✦ **A sentry variable:** This special variable controls access to the loop. Unlike the int usually used in for loops, the sentry of a while loop can be any type.

✦ **Initialization:** Set the initial value of the sentry variable before the loop begins. Do not rely on default settings (because you don't know what they will be) but set this value yourself.

✦ **A condition:** The while statement requires a condition. This condition controls access to the loop. As long as the condition is true, the loop continues. As soon as the condition is evaluated as false, the loop will exit.

✦ **A modifier:** You must somehow modify the value of the sentry variable. It's important that the modification statement happen somewhere inside the loop. In a for loop, you almost always add or subtract to modify a variable. In a while loop, any kind of assignment statement can be used to modify the variable.

for loops are a little safer than while loops because the structure of the for loop requires you to think about initialization, condition, and modification. All three features are built into the for statement. The while statement requires only the condition. This might make you think that you don't need the other parts, but that would be dangerous. In any kind of loop, you need to initialize the sentry variable and modify its value. With the `while` loop, you're responsible for adding these features yourself. Failure to do so will cause endless loops, or loops that never happen. See much more about this in Book IV, Chapter 3.

Take a look at the following code for the `while.php` program to see how it works:

```
<!DOCTYPE html
PUBLIC "-//W3C//DTD XHTML 1.0 Strict//EN"
"http://www.w3.org/TR/xhtml1/DTD/xhtml1-strict.dtd">
<html xmlns="http://www.w3.org/1999/xhtml" xml:lang="en" lang="en">
<head>
<title>while.php</title>
<style type="text/css">
img {
  height: 40px;
  width: 50px;
}
</style>
</head>
<body>
<h1>Dice Rolling Game 2</h1>
<p>Welcome to the dice rolling game. See how many rolls it takes to get a six!
    </p>
<div id = "output">
<?php
$userNumber = 999;
$counter = 0;
while ($userNumber != 6){
  $userNumber = rand(1,6);
  print "<img src=\"images/die$userNumber.jpg\" alt = \"$userNumber\" />";
  $counter++;
}
print "<p>It took $counter tries to get a six.</p>";
?>
</div>

<p><a href="while.php">Try Again!</a></p>
</body>
</html>
```

Can I use a debugger for PHP?

In Book IV, you can see how to use the firebug debugger to check your code. This is especially handy for the logic errors that tend to occur when you're writing `while` loops. It would be great if there was a similar facility for PHP code. Unfortunately, PHP debuggers are relatively rare and can be difficult to install and use. That's because PHP is not an interactive language, but it processes code in batch mode on the server.

Firebug is a client-side application, and it doesn't ever see the PHP code. The best way to debug PHP is with good-old `print` statements. If something doesn't work correctly, print out the sentry variable before, inside, and after the loop to see whether you can find the pattern. One reason why people are switching to AJAX (see Book VII) is that much of the logic is done on the client side, where it's easier to debug.

This example illustrates how subtle while loops can be. All the key elements are there, but they don't all *look* like part of the while loop.

1. Initialize $userNumber.

For this loop, $userNumber will be the sentry variable. The initialization needs to guarantee that the loop runs exactly once. Because the condition will be ($userNumber != 6), I need to give $userNumber a value that clearly isn't 6. 999 will do the job, and it's wild enough to be clearly out of range. Although the initialization step appears in the code before the while loop, it's often best to start with your condition and then back up a line to initialize because the initialization step depends on the condition.

2. Set up the condition.

Think about what should cause the loop to continue or quit. Remember that the condition explains when the loop continues. It's often easier to think about what causes the loop to exit. That's fine; just reverse it. For example, I want the loop to quit when $userNumber is equal to 6, so I'll have it continue as long as $userNumber != 6.

3. Modify the sentry.

This one is tricky. In this particular example, modify the sentry variable by getting a new random number: $userNumber = rand(1,6). Often in a while loop, the modification step is intrinsic to the problem you're solving. Sometimes you get the new value from the user, sometimes you get it from a file or database, or sometimes you just add (just like a for loop). The key here is to ensure you have a statement that modifies the sentry variable and that the condition can trigger. For example, using $userNumber = rand(1,5) would result in an endless loop because $userNumber could never be 6.

while loops can cause a lot of problems because they may cause logic errors. That is, the *syntax* (structure and spelling of the code) may be fine, but the program still doesn't operate properly. Almost always, the problem can be resolved by thinking about those three parts of a well-behaved loop: Initialize the sentry, create a meaningful condition, and modify the sentry appropriately. See Book IV, Chapter 3 for more on while loops.

Chapter 4: Working with Arrays

In This Chapter

⊾ **Creating one-dimensional arrays**

⊾ **Making the most of multidimensional arrays**

⊾ **Using foreach loops to simplify array management**

⊾ **Breaking a string into an array**

In time, arrays will become one of the most important tools in your tool-box. They can be a bit hard to grasp for beginners, but don't let that stop you. Arrays are awesome because they allow you to quickly apply the same instructions to a large number of items.

In PHP, an *array* is a variable that holds multiple values that are mapped to keys. Think of a golfing scorecard. You have several scores, one for each hole on the golf course. The hole number is the key, and the score for that hole is the value. Keys are usually numeric, but values can be any type. You can have an array of strings, numbers, or even objects. Any time you're thinking about a list of things, an array is the natural way to represent this list.

Using One-Dimensional Arrays

The most basic array is a *one-dimensional array,* which is basically just one container with slots. Each slot has only one variable in it. In this section, you find out how to create this type of array and fill it.

Creating an array

Array creation is pretty simple. First, you need to create a variable and then tell PHP that you want that variable to be an array:

```
$theVar = array();
```

Now, $theVar is an array. However, it's an empty array waiting for you to come along and fill it.

Technically, you can skip the variable creation step. It's still a good idea to explicitly define an array because it helps you remember the element is an array, and there are a few special cases (such as passing an array into a function) where the definition really matters.

Filling an array

An array is a container, so it's a lot more fun if you put something in it. You can refer to an array element by adding an *index* (an integer) representing which element of the array you're talking about.

Say I have the following array:

```
$spanish = array();
$spanish[1] = "uno";
$spanish[2] = "dos";
```

What I did here is to add two elements to the array. Essentially, I said that element 1 is uno, and element 2 is dos.

PHP has another interesting trick available. Take a look at the next line:

```
$spanish[] = "tres";
```

This seems a little odd because I didn't specify an index. PHP is pretty helpful. If you don't specify an index, it looks at the largest index already used in the array and places the new value at the next spot. So, the value tres will be placed in element 3 of the array.

PHP is somewhat notorious for its array mechanism. Depending on how you look at it, PHP is far more forgiving or far sloppier than most languages when it comes to arrays. For example, you don't have to specify the length of an array. PHP just makes the array whatever size seems to work. In fact, you don't even have to explicitly create the array. When you start using an array, PHP automatically just makes it if it isn't already there. Although this is pretty easy, I've seen enough science fiction movies to know what can happen when we let computers make all the decisions for us.

Viewing the elements of an array

You can access the elements of an array in exactly the same way you created them. Array elements are just variables; the only difference is the numeric index. Here's one way to print out the elements of the array:

```
print <<< HERE
One: $spanish[1] <br />
Two: $spanish[2] <br />
Three: $spanish[3] <br />

HERE;
```

I can simply print out the array elements like any ordinary variable. Just remember to add the index.

Another great way to print out arrays is particularly useful for debugging. Take a look at this variation:

```
print "<pre> \n";
print_r($spanish);
print "</pre> \n";
```

The `print_r()` function is a special debugging function. It allows you to pass an entire array, and it prints out the array in an easy-to-read format. It's best to put the output of the `print_r()` function inside a `<pre>` element so that the output is preserved.

Of course, the results of the `print_r()` function mean something to you, but your users don't care about arrays. This is only a debugging tool. Typically, you'll use some other techniques for displaying arrays to your users.

To see what all the code in `basicArray.php` looks like, take a look at Figure 4-1.

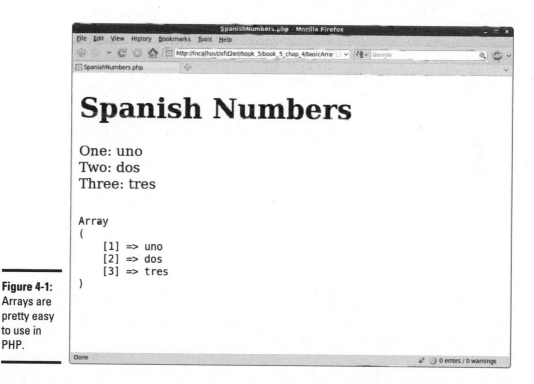

Figure 4-1:
Arrays are
pretty easy
to use in
PHP.

Preloading an array

Sometimes you'll know the elements that go into an array right away. In those cases, you can use a special version of the `array()` function to make this work. Take a look at this code.

```
$english = array("zero", "one", "two", "three");

print "<pre> \n";
print_r($english);
print "<pre> \n";
```

This simple program allows you to load up the value of the array in one swoop. Note that I started with zero. Computers tend to start counting at zero, so if you don't specify indices, the first element will be zero-indexed.

I use the `print_r()` function to quickly see the contents of the array. The preloaded array is shown in Figure 4-2.

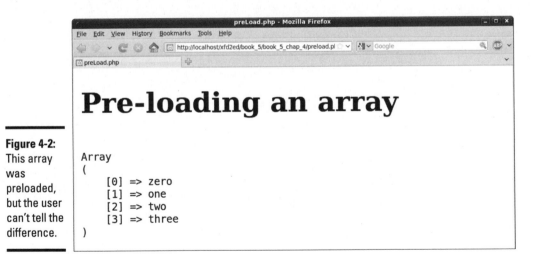

Figure 4-2:
This array was preloaded, but the user can't tell the difference.

Using Loops with Arrays

Arrays and loops are like peanut butter and jelly; they just go together. When you start to use arrays, eventually, you'll want to go through each element in the array and do something with it. The `for` loop is the perfect way to do this.

Look at the `loopingArrays.php` code to see how I step through an array with a couple of variations of the `for` loop.

```
<!DOCTYPE html PUBLIC "-//W3C//DTD XHTML 1.0 Strict//EN" "http://www.w3.org/TR/
    xhtml1/DTD/xhtml1-strict.dtd">
<html xmlns="http://www.w3.org/1999/xhtml" xml:lang="en">
<head>
  <title>loopingArrays.php</title>
  <meta http-equiv="Content-Type" content="text/html;charset=UTF-8" />
</head>
<body>
  <h1>Looping through arrays.</h1>
<div>
<?php
//first make an array of mini-book names
$books = array("Creating the XHTML Foundation",
               "Styling with CSS",
               "Using Positional CSS for Layout",
               "Client-Side Programming with JavaScript",
               "Server-Side Programming with PHP",
               "Databases with MySQL",
               "Into the Future with AJAX",
               "Moving From Pages to Web Sites");


//just print them out with a loop
print "<p> \n";
for ($i = 0; $i < sizeof($books);$i++){
  print $books[$i] . "<br />\n";
} // end for
print "</p> \n";

//use the foreach mechanism to simplify printing out the elements
print "<p> \n";
foreach ($books as $book){
  print $book . " <br />\n";
} // end foreach
print "</p> \n";

?>
</div>

</body>
</html>
```

The relationship between arrays and loops isn't hard to see:

1. **Create your array.**

   This example uses an array of minibook titles in a charming and lovable book on Web development. Note that I preloaded the array. There's no problem with the fact that the array statement (while a single line of logic) actually takes up several lines in the editor.

2. **Build a `for` loop to step through the array.**

   The loop needs to happen once for each element in the array; in this case, that's eight times. Set up a loop that repeats eight times. It will start at 0 and end at 8.

3. **Use the `sizeof()` function to determine the ending point.**

Because you know that this array has eight elements, you could just set the condition to `$i < 8`. The `sizeof()` function is preferred because it will work even if the array size changes. Also, it's easier to understand what I meant. `sizeof($books)` means "the size of the `$books` array." The number 8 could mean anything.

4. **Print out each element.**

Inside the loop, I simply print out the current element of the array, which will be `$books[$i]`. Don't forget to add a `<br />` tag if you want a line break in the HTML output. Add the `\n` to keep the HTML source code looking nice.

Simplifying loops with foreach

The relationship between loops and arrays is so close that many languages provide a special version of the `for` loop just for arrays. Take a look at this code fragment to see how cool it is:

```
//use the foreach mechanism to simplify printing out the elements
print "<p> \n";
foreach ($books as $book){
  print $book . " <br />\n";
} // end foreach
print "</p> \n";
```

The `foreach` loop is a special version of the `for` loop that simplifies working with arrays. Here's how it works.

1. **Use the `foreach` keyword to begin the loop.**

This tells PHP that you're working with the `foreach` variation.

2. **The first parameter is the array name.**

The `foreach` loop is designed to work with an array, so the first parameter is the array you want to step through.

3. **Create a variable to hold each element of the array.**

On each pass through the loop, the `$book` variable will hold the current element of the `$books` array. Most of the time, you use a loop for an array because you want to deal with each element of the array. Using a `foreach` loop makes this easier.

4. Use the $book variable inside the loop.

The $book variable is ready to go. The nice thing about using foreach is you don't have to worry about indices. The $book variable always contains the current element of the array.

You can see the results of both of these loops in Figure 4-3. To the user, there's no difference. Both are simply text when it comes to output.

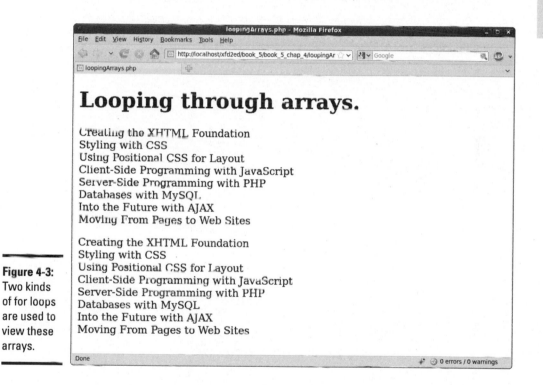

Figure 4-3: Two kinds of for loops are used to view these arrays.

Arrays and HTML

Arrays are great because they're used to hold lists of data in your programming language. Of course, HTML already has other ways of working with lists. The <ul> and <ol> tags are both used for visual representations of lists, and the <select> object is used to let the user choose from a list. It's very common to build these HTML structures from arrays. Figure 4-4 illustrates exactly how this is done.

The code for the page is not too different than the previous examples. It just adds some HTML formatting:

```
<!DOCTYPE html PUBLIC "-//W3C//DTD XHTML 1.0 Strict//EN" "http://www.w3.org/TR/
    xhtml1/DTD/xhtml1-strict.dtd">
<html xmlns="http://www.w3.org/1999/xhtml" xml:lang="en">
<head>
  <title>arrayHTML.php</title>
  <meta http-equiv="Content-Type" content="text/html;charset=UTF-8" />
</head>
<body>
  <h1>Arrays are useful in HTML</h1>
<div>

<?php
//first make an array of mini-book names
$books = array("Creating the XHTML Foundation",
               "Styling with CSS",
               "Using Positional CSS for Layout",
               "Client-Side Programming with JavaScript",
               "Server-Side Programming with PHP",
               "Databases with MySQL",
               "Into the Future with AJAX",
               "Moving From Pages to Web Sites");

//make the array into a numbered list
print "<ol>\n";
```

```
foreach ($books as $book){
  print "  <li>$book</li> \n";
} // end foreach
print "</ol>\n";

//make the array into a select object
print "<select name = \"book\"> \n";
foreach ($books as $book){
  print "  <option value = \"$book\">$book</option> \n";
} // end foreach
print "</select> \n";

?>
</div>

</body>
</html>
```

It's a relatively simple matter to build HTML output based on arrays. To
create an ordered list or unordered list, just use a `foreach` loop but add
HTML formatting to convert the array to a list formatted in HTML:

```
//make the array into a numbered list
print "<ol>\n";
foreach ($books as $book){
  print "  <li>$book</li> \n";
} // end foreach
print "</ol>\n";
```

Likewise, if you want to allow the user to choose an element from an array,
it's pretty easy to set up a `<select>` structure that displays the elements of
an array.

```
//make the array into a select object
print "<select name = \"book\"> \n";
foreach ($books as $book){
  print "  <option value = \"$book\">$book</option> \n";
} // end foreach
print "</select> \n";
```

Introducing Associative Arrays

You can use string values as keys. For example, you might create an array
like this:

```
$myStuff = array();
$myStuff["name"] = "andy";
$myStuff["email"] = "andy@aharrisbooks.net";

Print $myStuff["name"];
```

Associative arrays are different than normal (numeric-indexed) arrays in some subtle but important ways:

+ **The order is undefined.** Regular arrays are always sorted based on the numeric index. You don't know what order an associative array will be because the keys aren't numeric.

+ **You must specify a key.** If you're building a numeric-indexed array, PHP can always guess what key should be next. This isn't possible with an associative array.

+ **Associative arrays are best for name-value pairs.** Associative arrays are used when you want to work with data that comes in name/value pairs. This comes up a lot in PHP and XHTML. XHTML attributes are often in this format, as are CSS rules and form input elements.

+ **Some of PHP's most important values are associative arrays.** The $_REQUEST variable (described in Chapter 3 of this minibook) is an important associative array. So are $_GET, $_POST, and several others.

Make sure to include quotation marks if you're using a string as an array index. It will probably work if you don't, but it's bad programming practice and may not work in the future.

Using foreach with associative arrays

It's very common to have a large associative array that you want to evaluate. For example, PHP includes a very useful array called $_SERVER that gives you information about your server configuration (things like your hostname, PHP version, and lots of other useful stuff). The following code snippet (from serverInput.php) runs through the entire $_SERVER array and prints each key/value pair:

```php
<?php
print "<dl> \n";

foreach ($_SERVER as $key => $value){
  print <<<HERE
  <dt>$key</dt>
  <dd>$value</dd>

HERE;
} // end foreach
print "</dl> \n";
?>
```

You can see this program running on my work server in Figure 4-5.

Figure 4-5:
This variable
stores
data in an
associative
array.

Here's how it works:

1. **Begin the `foreach` loop as normal.**

   The associative form of the `foreach` loop begins just like the
   regular one:

   ```
   foreach ($_SERVER as $key => $value){
   ```

2. **Identify the associative array.**

   The first parameter is the array name:

   ```
   foreach ($_SERVER as $key => $value){
   ```

3. **Create a variable for the key.**

   Each element of an associative array has a key and a value. I put the key
   in a variable named $key:

   ```
   foreach ($_SERVER as $key => $value){
   ```

4. **Use the => symbol to indicate the associative relationship.**

   This symbol helps PHP recognize you're talking about an associative array lookup:

   ```
   foreach ($_SERVER as $key => $value){
   ```

5. **Assign the value of the element to a variable.**

   The $value variable holds the current value of the array item:

   ```
   foreach ($_SERVER as $key => $value){
   ```

6. **Use the variables inside your loop.**

   Each time PHP goes through the loop, it pulls another element from the array, puts that element's key in the $key array, and puts the associated value in $value. You can then use these variables inside the loop however you wish. I used a definition list because it's a natural way to display key-value pairs. A list of definitions is keys and values.

   ```
   print <<<HERE
     <dt>$key</dt>
     <dd>$value</dd>

   HERE;
   ```

The $_SERVER variable is extremely useful for checking your environment, but you shouldn't make a program that displays this kind of information available on a publicly accessible server. Doing so gives the bad guys information they could use to cause you headaches. Use it for testing and debugging, and then remove it. I have this example disabled on my site, but you can still look at the source code if you wish.

Introducing Multidimensional Arrays

Arrays in PHP can hold anything, even other arrays. This turns out to be an extremely useful function. A *multidimensional array* is an array that holds arrays. Multidimensional arrays are used when your data is arranged in some sort of tabular form.

We're going on a trip

Some uses for these are to group things or to use as lookup tables. See Book IV, Chapter 4 for one possible use of lookup tables — using multidimensional arrays to hold the distances between cities. You can do exactly the same thing with PHP. Even though the syntax is somewhat different, the concept is exactly the same. Figure 4-6 is an HTML page that lets the user choose what city she is traveling from and to.

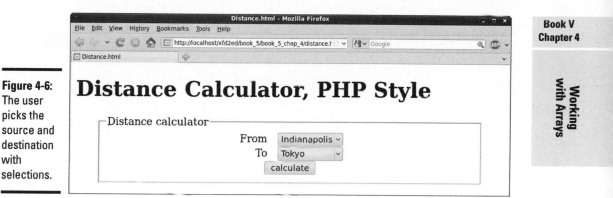

Figure 4-6:
The user
picks the
source and
destination
with
selections.

The following code shows the basic HTML form:

```
<!DOCTYPE html PUBLIC "-//W3C//DTD XHTML 1.0 Strict//EN" "http://www.w3.org/TR/
    xhtml1/DTD/xhtml1-strict.dtd">
<html xmlns="http://www.w3.org/1999/xhtml" xml:lang="en">
<head>
    <title>Distance.html</title>
<style type="text/css">
form {
  width: 600px;
  margin: auto;
}

label {
  width: 250px;
  float: left;
  clear: left;
  text-align: right;
  margin-right: 1em;
}

select {
  float: left;
}

button {
  display: block;
  clear: both;
  margin: auto;
}

</style>
  <meta http-equiv="Content-Type" content="text/html;charset=UTF-8" />
</head>
<body>
  <h1>Distance Calculator, PHP Style</h1>
  <form action = "distance.php"
        method = "post">
    <fieldset>
      <legend>Distance calculator</legend>
      <label>From</label>
      <select name = "from">
        <option value="0">Indianapolis</option>
```

```
      <option value="1">New York</option>
      <option value="2">Tokyo</option>
      <option value="3">London</option>
  </select>
      <label>To</label>
  <select name = "to">
      <option value="0">Indianapolis</option>
      <option value="1">New York</option>
      <option value="2">Tokyo</option>
      <option value="3">London</option>
  </select>

  <button type = "submit">
      calculate
  </button>
  </fieldset>
</form>

</body>
</html>
```

There's nothing unfamiliar about this form:

1. **Set the form's action to `distance.php`.**

   That's the program that will actually calculate the distance. Use the `post` method, as usual.

2. **Create a `select` object to determine where the user is leaving.**

   This form element will be called `from` because it represents the city the user is coming from. Note that the value is an integer that will relate to the various city numbers (0 for Indianapolis, and so on).

3. **Create a second `select` object for the destination.**

   The second selection is much like the first, but it has the name `to`.

4. **Use CSS for beautification.**

   A little CSS can go a long way to make this page look nicer.

Looking up the distance

When the user submits the form, she is rewarded with the display shown in Figure 4-7.

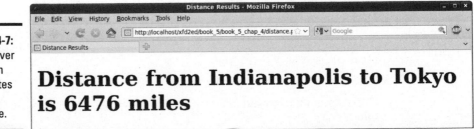

Figure 4-7:
This clever program calculates the distance.

Distance from Indianapolis to Tokyo is 6476 miles

Of course, you could calculate the distance between cities with `if` statements, switches, and the like, but this kind of problem is really a *lookup table*. That means that the best way to solve it without a computer is to build a table. To use the table, you would use the row to indicate the source and the column to designate the destination, and then see where they cross for a result. It's very easy to get the computer to do exactly the same thing by using a two-dimension array, as shown in the following code:

```
<!DOCTYPE html PUBLIC "-//W3C//DTD XHTML 1.0 Strict//EN" "http://www.w3.org/TR/
    xhtml1/DTD/xhtml1-strict.dtd">
<html xmlns="http://www.w3.org/1999/xhtml" xml:lang="en">
<head>
  <title>Distance Results</title>
  <meta http-equiv="Content-Type" content="text/html;charset=UTF-8" />
</head>
<body>
<?php

$cityName = array("Indianapolis", "New York", "Tokyo", "London");

//get variables from form
$from = $_REQUEST["from"];
$to = $_REQUEST["to"];

$distance = array(
  array(0, 648, 6476, 4000),
  array(648, 0, 6760, 3470),
  array(6476, 6760, 0, 5956),
  array(4000, 3470, 5956, 0));

$result = $distance[$from][$to];

print "<h1>Distance from $cityName[$from] to $cityName[$to] is $result miles</
    h1>\n";

?>
</body>
</html>
```

The two-dimension array simplifies things greatly. Take a look at how the program calculates the result:

1. **Create a standard array to handle city names.**

   The cities all have numbers, so I use an array to help attach the names to the numbers. It's important that this array is in the correct order, so city 0 is Indianapolis throughout.

2. **Retrieve `to` and `from` data from the form.**

   These values were sent by the previous form, so get the data and place them in variables.

3. **Build a 2D array to hold the distance data.**

   The distance is stored in a table. A 2D array is a perfect way to hold this data.

4. **Look up the distance in the `distance` array.**

   A 2D array requires two indices. The first indicates the row, and the second indicates the column.

5. **Print out the result.**

   After you get the data, it's pretty easy to print out.

Breaking a String into an Array

Many times, it can be useful to break a string into an array, especially when reading input from a file.

Here are the two different ways of doing this:

✦ **explode:** explode takes one parameter as a delimiter and splits the string into an array based upon that one parameter.

✦ **preg_split:** If you require regular expressions, using preg_split is the way to go. split allows you to take complicated chunks of text, look for multiple different delimiters stored in a regular expression, and break it into an array based on the delimiters you specify.

explode works well with comma-separated value (CSV) files and the like, where all the parameters you wish to break the text on are the same. preg_split works better for when there are many different parameters that you wish to break the text on or when the parameter you're looking for is complex.

Creating arrays with explode

Array creation with explode is very straightforward:

```
explode(" ", $theString);
```

The first value is the parameter on which you're splitting up the string. The second value is the string you would like to split into an array. In this example, the string would be split up on each space. You can put anything you want as the split parameter.

So, if you have the string that you want to store each word as a value in, enter the following code (see Figure 4-8 for the output):

```
<!DOCTYPE html
PUBLIC "-//W3C//DTD XHTML 1.0 Strict//EN"
"http://www.w3.org/TR/xhtml1/DTD/xhtml1-strict.dtd">
<html xmlns="http://www.w3.org/1999/xhtml" xml:lang="en" lang="en">
```

```
<head>
<title>explode.php</title>
</head>
<body>
<h1>Using explode</h1>
<?php
$theString = "PARC (Palo Alto Research Center) was one of the single most
    important hubs of invention for modern computing";

$theArray = explode(" ", $theString);
print "<pre> \n";
print_r($theArray);
print "</pre> \n";
?>
</body>
</html>
```

Figure 4-8:
A string
exploded
into an
array.

The delimiter can be anything you want. If you're dealing with a CSV file,
where each value is separated by a comma, your explode method might
look like this:

```
$theArray = explode(",", $theString);
```

Creating arrays with preg_split

preg_split is a bit more complicated. split uses regular expressions to split a string into an array, which can make it a bit slower than explode.

split looks exactly like explode, but instead of one character inside quotations, you can cram all the characters you want to split on into brackets inside the quotations, or you can use a complicated regular expression to determine how the values will split.

If you need a refresher on regular expressions, check Book IV, Chapter 6. Regular expressions work the same in JavaScript and in PHP because both languages derived their regular expression tools from the older language perl. (The preg part of preg_split stands for "perl regular expression.")

An instance where you'd want to use preg_split instead of explode could be when processing an e-mail address. A basic e-mail address has dots (.) and an at sign (@). So, to split on both of these, you could do the following (see Figure 4-9 for the output):

```
<!DOCTYPE html
PUBLIC "-//W3C//DTD XHTML 1.0 Strict//EN"
"http://www.w3.org/TR/xhtml1/DTD/xhtml1-strict.dtd">
<html xmlns="http://www.w3.org/1999/xhtml" xml:lang="en" lang="en">
<head>
<title>split</title>
</head>
<body>
<h1>Using preg_split</h1>
<?php
$theString = "joe@somebody.net";
$theArray = preg_split("/[@\.]/", $theString);
print "<pre>\n";
print_r($theArray);
print "</pre>\n";

?>
</body>
</html>
```

Recall that regular expressions are encased in the slash character, and the square braces indicate one of a number of options. I want to split on either the at sign or the period. Remember to specify the period with \ . because an ordinary period means "any character."

preg_split works well for timestamps, e-mail addresses, and other things where there's more than just one unique delimiter that you wish to split the string on.

Figure 4-9:
The e-mail
address
split into an
array.

Earlier versions of PHP had a function called `split`. It was much like the `preg_split` function, but it used a different regular expression syntax. Hardly anybody used it, and it will not be in PHP6 and later. Use `explode` for simple patterns and `preg_split` when you need the power of regular expressions.

Chapter 5: Using Functions and Session Variables

In This Chapter

✓ Creating functions to manage your code's complexity

✓ Enhancing your code by using functions

✓ Working with variable scope

✓ Getting familiar with session variables

✓ Incorporating session variables into your code

*P*HP programs are used to solve interesting problems, which can get quite complex. In this chapter, you explore ways to manage this complexity. You discover how to build functions to encapsulate your code. You also learn how to use session variables to make your programs keep track of their values, even when the program is called many times.

Creating Your Own Functions

It won't take long before your code starts to get complex. Functions are used to manage this complexity. As an example, take a look at Figure 5-1.

Rolling dice the old-fashioned way

Before I show you how to improve your code with functions, look at a program that doesn't use functions so you have something to compare with.

The following `rollDice.php` program creates five random numbers and displays a graphic for each die:

```
<!DOCTYPE html PUBLIC "-//W3C//DTD XHTML 1.0 Strict//EN"
"http://www.w3.org/TR/xhtml1/DTD/xhtml1-strict.dtd">
<html lang="EN" dir="ltr" xmlns="http://www.w3.org/1999/xhtml">
  <head>
    <meta http-equiv="content-type" content="text/xml; charset=utf-8" />
    <title>rollDice1.php</title>
  </head>

  <body>
    <h1>RollDice 1</h1>
    <h2>Uses Sequential Programming</h2>
    <div>
    <?php
```

```
$roll = rand(1,6);
$image = "die$roll.jpg";
print <<< HERE
    <img src = "$image"
        alt = "roll: $roll" />

HERE;

$roll = rand(1,6);
$image = "die$roll.jpg";
print <<< HERE
    <img src = "$image"
        alt = "roll: $roll" />

HERE;

$roll = rand(1,6);
$image = "die$roll.jpg";
print <<< HERE
    <img src = "$image"
        alt = "roll: $roll" />

HERE;

$roll = rand(1,6);
$image = "die$roll.jpg";
print <<< HERE
    <img src = "$image"
        alt = "roll: $roll" />

HERE;

$roll = rand(1,6);
$image = "die$roll.jpg";
print <<< HERE
    <img src = "$image"
        alt = "roll: $roll" />

HERE;
    ?>
    </div>
  </body>
</html>
```

Here are some interesting features of this code:

✦ **The built-in `rand()` function rolls a random number.** Whenever possible, try to find functions that can help you. The `rand()` function produces a random integer. If you use two parameters, the resulting number will be in the given range. To roll a standard six-sided die, use `rand(1,6)`:

```
$roll = rand(1,6);
```

✦ **I created an image for each possible roll.** To make this program more visually appealing, I created an image for each possible die roll. The images are called `die1.jpg`, `die2.jpg`, and so on. All these images are stored in the same directory as the PHP program.

✦ **The img tag is created based on the die roll.** After I have a die roll, it's easy to create an image based on that roll:

```
    $image = "die$roll.jpg";
    print <<< HERE
<img src = "$image"
        alt = "roll: $roll" />

HERE;
```

✦ **The die-rolling code is repeated five times.** If you can roll one die, you can easily roll five. It's as easy as copying and pasting the code. This seems pretty easy, but it leads to problems. What if I want to change the way I roll the dice? If so, I'll have to change the code five times. What if I want to roll 100 dice? The program will quickly become unwieldy. In general, if you find yourself copying and pasting code, you can improve the code by adding a function.

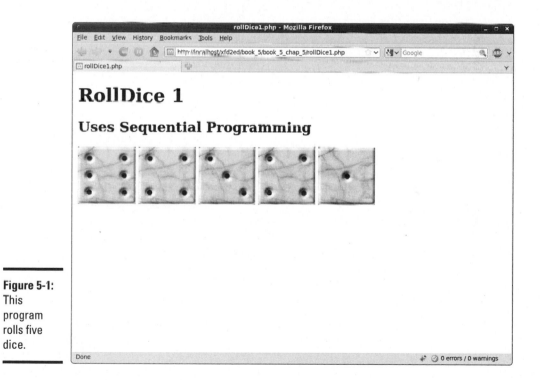

Figure 5-1:
This program rolls five dice.

Improving code with functions

Functions are predefined code fragments. After you define a function, you can use it as many times as you wish. As you can see in the following code, the outward appearance of this program is identical to `rollDice1.php`, but the internal organization is quite different:

```
<!DOCTYPE html PUBLIC "-//W3C//DTD XHTML 1.0 Strict//EN"
"http://www.w3.org/TR/xhtml1/DTD/xhtml1-strict.dtd">
<html lang="EN" dir="ltr" xmlns="http://www.w3.org/1999/xhtml">
  <head>
    <meta http-equiv="content-type" content="text/xml; charset=utf-8" />
    <title>rollDice2.php</title>
  </head>

  <body>
    <h1>RollDice 2</h1>
    <h2>Uses Functions</h2>
    <?php

function rollDie(){
  $roll = rand(1,6);
  $image = "die$roll.jpg";
  print <<< HERE
    <img src = "$image"
         alt = "roll: $roll" />

HERE;
} // end rollDie

for ($i = 0; $i < 5; $i++){
  rollDie();
} // end for loop

    ?>

  </body>
</html>
```

Here's how things have changed in this version:

1. Use the `function` keyword to define a function.

The `function` keyword indicates that a function definition will follow. The code inside the definition won't be run immediately, but instead, PHP will "remember" the code inside the function definition and play it back on demand:

```
function rollDie(){
```

2. Give the function a name.

The function name should indicate what the function does. I call my function `rollDie()` because that's what it does (rolls a die):

```
function rollDie(){
```

3. Specify arguments with parentheses.

You can send *arguments* (special variables for your function to work
with) by indicating them in the parentheses. This function doesn't need
arguments, so I leave the parentheses empty:

```
function rollDie(){
```

TIP

For more information on functions, arguments, and the `return` statement, turn to Book IV, Chapter 4. Functions in PHP act almost exactly
like their cousins in JavaScript.

4. Begin the function definition with a left brace ({).

The left brace is used to indicate the beginning of the function code.

5. Indent the code that makes up your function.

Use indentation to indicate which code is part of your function. In this
case, the function generates the random number and prints an image tag
based on that random number:

```
function rollDie(){
  $roll = rand(1,6);
  $image = "die$roll.jpg";
  print <<< HERE
    <img src = "$image"
         alt = "roll: $roll" />

HERE;
} // end rollDie
```

6. Denote the end of the function with a right brace (}).

7. Call the function by referring to it.

After the function is defined, you can use it in your code as if it were
built into PHP. In this example, I call the function inside a loop:

```
for ($i = 0; $i < 5; $i++){
  rollDie();
} // end for loop
```

Because the code is defined in a function, it's a simple matter to run it as
many times as I want. Functions also make your code easier to read because
the details of rolling the dice are hidden in the function.

Managing variable scope

Two kinds of scope are in PHP: global and local.

If you define a variable outside a function, it has the potential to be used
inside any function. If you define a variable inside a function, you can access it
only from inside the function in which it was created. See Book IV, Chapter 4
for more on variable scope.

Naming functions and variables

It can be hard to come up with a good naming scheme for your variables and functions. Doing so is very important because when you come back to your program, if you haven't named your functions and variables consistently, you'll have a hard time understanding what you wrote. Here are two common naming schemes to make this simple: using underscores (_) between words or camel-casing.

Using underscores is as straightforward as separating_each_word_with_an_underscore. It's readable, but it's ugly and can cause the variable names to get awfully lengthy.

The method I prefer and use throughout this book is *camel-casing*, where each new word after the first word gets capitalized just LikeThis. It takes up less space than the underscore method and makes reading the code quicker — and after you get used to it, you won't even notice it anymore.

Tons of naming schemes are out there, and even if you don't use either of these, picking one and being consistent is important. Searching for *naming variables* in Google returns more than one million hits, so plenty of resources are available.

So, if you have a variable that you want to access and modify from within the function, you either need to pass it through the parentheses or access it with the global modifier.

The following code will print hello world! only once:

```php
<?php
$output = "<p>hello world!</p>";

function helloWorld(){
    global $output;

    print $output;
}

function helloWorld2(){
    print $output;
}

helloWorld();
helloWorld2();
?>
```

I left the global keyword off in the helloWorld2() function, so it didn't print at all because inside the function, the local variable $output is undefined. By putting the global keyword on in the helloWorld() function, I let it know I was referring to a global variable defined outside the function.

PHP defaults to local inside functions because it doesn't want you to accidentally access or overwrite other variables throughout the program. For more information about global and local scoping, check out `http://us3.php.net/global`.

Returning data from functions

At the end of the function, you can tell the function to return one (and only one) thing. The `return` statement should be the last statement of your function. The `return` statement isn't required, but it can be handy.

The `getName()` function in the following code example will return `world` to be used by the program. The program will print it once and store the text in a variable to be printed multiple times later, as shown in the following code and Figure 5-2:

```
<!DOCTYPE html
PUBLIC "-//W3C//DTD XHTML 1.0 Strict//EN"
"http://www.w3.org/TR/xhtml1/DTD/xhtml1-strict.dtd">
<html xmlns="http://www.w3.org/1999/xhtml" xml:lang="en" lang="en">
<head>
<title>helloFunction</title>
</head>
<body>

<?php
function getName(){
    return "World";
}

print "<h1>Hello, " . getName() . "!</h1>";

$name = getName();

print <<<HERE
<p>$name, welcome to our site. We are so very happy to have you here.</p>
<p>If you would like to contact us, $name, just use the form on the contact
    page.</p>
HERE;
?>

</body>
</html>
```

Figure 5-2:
An example
of a function
with a return
statement.

```
                    helloFunction - Mozilla Firefox                    _ □ ×
File  Edit  View  History  Bookmarks  Tools  Help
  ←  ▾  ⟳  ⊗  ⌂  ☒ http://localhost/xfd2ed/book_5/book_5_chap_5/helloFunction.php  ☆ ▾  ◆▾ Google      🔍 ◉ ▾
  ☒ helloFunction            ✚
```

Hello, World!

World, welcome to our site. We are so very happy to have you here.

If you would like to contact us World, just use the form on the contact page.

TIP

The example in Figure 5-2 is admittedly contrived. This function could easily be replaced by a variable, but the program that uses the function doesn't know that the function has only one line. Later on, I could make the function much more complicated (maybe pulling the name from a database or session variable). This points out a very important feature of functions that return values: they can feel like variables when you use them.

Managing Persistence with Session Variables

Server-side programming is very handy, but it has one major flaw. Every connection to the server is an entirely different transaction. Sometimes, you'll want to reuse a variable between several calls of the program. As an example, take a look at `rollDice3.php` in Figure 5-3.

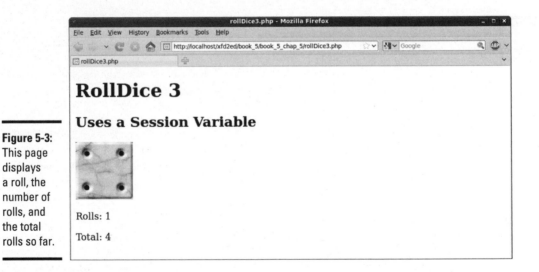

Figure 5-3:
This page
displays
a roll, the
number of
rolls, and
the total
rolls so far.

The interesting feature of `rollDice3.php` happens when you reload the page. Take a look at Figure 5-4. This is still `rollDice3.php`, after I refreshed the browser a few times. Take a look at the total. It increases with each roll.

The `rollDice3.php` program is interesting because it defies normal server-side programming behavior. In a normal PHP program, every time you refresh the browser, the program starts over from scratch. Every variable starts out new.

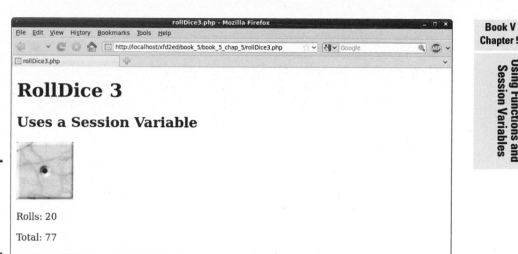

Figure 5-4:
The count
and total
values keep
on growing.

Understanding session variables

The `rollDice3.php` program acts differently. It has a mechanism for keeping track of the total rolls and number of visits to the page.

When a visitor accesses your Web site, she's automatically assigned a unique session id. The session id is either stored in a cookie or in the URL. *Sessions* allow you to keep track of things for that specific user during her time on your site and during future visits if she's not cleared her cache or deleted her cookies.

Any mundane hacker can sniff out your session ids if you allow them to be stored in the URL. To keep this from happening, use the `session.use_only_cookies` directive in your PHP configuration file. This may be inconvenient to users who don't want you to have a cookie stored on their machine, but it's necessary if you're storing anything sensitive in their session.

Sessions are great because they are like a big box that the user carries around with him that you can just throw stuff into. Even if the user comes back to the site multiple times, the variables stored in the session retain their values. If you have hundreds of users accessing your site at the same time, each one will still have access to only their own versions of the variable.

Here's the code for `rollDice3.php`:

```php
<?php
  session_start();
?>
```

```
<!DOCTYPE html PUBLIC "-//W3C//DTD XHTML 1.0 Strict//EN"
"http://www.w3.org/TR/xhtml1/DTD/xhtml1-strict.dtd">
<html lang="EN" dir="ltr" xmlns="http://www.w3.org/1999/xhtml">
  <head>
    <meta http-equiv="content-type" content="text/xml; charset=utf-8" />
    <title>rollDice3.php</title>
  </head>

  <body>
    <h1>RollDice 3</h1>
    <h2>Uses a Session Variable</h2>

    <?php

function init(){
  global $count;
  global $total;

  //increment count if it exists
  if (isset($_SESSION["count"])){
    $count = $_SESSION["count"];
    $count++;
    $_SESSION["count"] = $count;
  } else {
    //if count doesn't exist, this is our first pass,
    //so initialize both session variables
    $_SESSION["count"] = 1;
    $_SESSION["total"] = 0;
    $count = 1;
  } // end if
} // end init

function rollDie(){
  global $total;

  $roll = rand(1,6);
  $image = "die$roll.jpg";
  print <<< HERE
    <img src = "$image"
         alt = "roll: $roll" />

HERE;
  $total = $_SESSION["total"];
  $total += $roll;
  $_SESSION["total"] = $total;

} // end rollDie


init();
rollDie();

print "    <p>Rolls: $count</p> \n";
print "    <p>Total: $total</p> \n";

    ?>
  </body>
</html>
```

This program rolls a die, but it uses session variables to keep track of the number of rolls and total value rolled. The session variable is updated every time the same user (using the same browser) visits the site.

Adding session variables to your code

Here's how to incorporate sessions into your programs:

1. **Begin your code with a call to `session_start()`.**

   If you want to use session variables, your code must begin with a `session_start()` call, even before the DOCTYPE definition. I put a tiny `<?php ?>` block at the beginning of the program to enable sessions:

   ```php
   <?php
     session_start();
   ?>
   ```

2. **Check for the existence of the session variables.**

   Like form variables, session variables may or may not exist when the program is executed. If this is the first pass through the program, the session variables may not have been created yet. The `init()` function checks whether the `count` session variable exists. If so, it will increment the counter; if not, it will initialize the sessions. `$_SESSION` is a super-global array (much like `$_REQUEST`).

   ```php
   if (isset($_SESSION["count"])){
   ```

3. **Load session variables from the `$_SESSION` superglobal.**

   Create a local variable and extract the current value from the `$_SESSION` associative array:

   ```php
   $count = $_SESSION["count"];
   ```

   Note that this line may trigger an error if you haven't already initialized the variable. Some PHP configurations are set up to automatically assign 0 to a nonexistent session variable, and some trigger an error.

4. **Increment the counter.**

   The `$count` variable is now an ordinary variable, so you can add a value to it in the ordinary way:

   ```php
   $count++;
   ```

5. **Store the value back into the `$_SESSION` superglobal.**

   You can manipulate the local variable, but if you want to use the value the next time the program runs for this user, you need to store the value back into the session after you change it.

   For example, the following code loads the variable `$count` from the session, adds 1 to it, and stores it back into the session:

   ```php
   $count = $_SESSION["count"];
   $count++;
   $_SESSION["count"] = $count;
   ```

6. **Initialize the session variables if they do not exist.**

Sometimes you need access to a session variable, but that session doesn't already exist. Usually, this will happen on the first pass of a program meant to run multiple times. It will also happen if the user jumps straight into a program without going through the appropriate prior programs (say you have got a system with three PHP programs and the user uses a bookmark to jump straight to program 3 without going to program 1, which sets up the sessions). In these situations, you'll either want to pass an error message or quietly create new session variables. In my example, I simply create a new session if it doesn't already exist. It's an easy matter of assigning values to the $_SESSION superglobal:

```
//if count doesn't exist, this is our first pass,

//so initialize both session variables

$_SESSION["count"] = 1;

$_SESSION["total"] = 0;

$count = 1;
```

If you want to reset your sessions for testing purposes, you can write a quick program to set the variables to 0, or you can use the Web Developer toolbar: Cookies⇔Clear Session Cookies. Note that the session data itself isn't stored in the cookie. The cookie just contains a reference number so the server can look up the session data in a file stored on the server.

Sessions and security

The session mechanism is powerful and easy to use. It isn't quite foolproof, though. Sessions are automatically handled through a browser mechanism called *cookies.* Cookies aren't inherently good or evil, but they've gotten a bad reputation because some programs use them maliciously. You'll occasionally run across a user who's turned off cookies, but this is not a major problem because PHP can automatically use other options when cookies are not available. There's rarely a need to work with cookies directly in PHP because sessions are a higher-level abstraction of the cookie concept.

Like all data passed through the HTTP protocol, session and cookie information is passed entirely in the clear. A person with evil intent can capture your session information and use it to do bad things.

Generally, you should stay away from sensitive information (credit card data, Social Security numbers, and so on) unless you're extremely comfortable with security measures. If you must pass potentially sensitive data in your PHP program, investigate a technology called TLS (Transport Layer Security), which automatically encrypts all data transferred through your site. TLS replaces the older SSL technology and is available as a free plugin to Apache servers.

Chapter 6: Working with Files and Directories

In This Chapter

✔ Saving to text files

✔ Reading from text files

✔ Reading a file as an array

✔ Parsing delimited text data

✔ Working with file and directory functions

*A*n important part of any programming language is file manipulations. Whether you need to create a comma-separated value (CSV) file or generate a dynamic list of files in a directory, or just need a semi-permanent place to log records on the server, file manipulation functions are an indispensable part of your PHP toolbox.

Text File Manipulation

Work with text files is split into two basic categories: writing and reading. Writing and reading come down to six basic functions. See the following bullet list for a brief explanation of the six basic file functions. Each function has an entire subsection in the following "Writing text to files" and "Reading from the file" sections:

✦ fopen(): Stores a connection to a file you specify in a variable you specify

✦ fwrite(): Writes text you specify to a file you specify

✦ fclose(): Closes the connection to a file you specify that you created with fopen()

✦ fgets(): Reads a line from a file you specify

✦ feof(): Checks whether you have hit the end of a file you specify during a file read

✦ file(): Puts the entire contents of a file you specify into an array

Writing text to files

This section details the functions needed to access and write to a file, such as how to request access to a file from PHP with the `fopen()` function, write to the file using the `fwrite()` function, and let PHP know you are done with the file with the `fclose()` function.

fopen()

To do any file manipulations, you must tell PHP about the file you would like to manipulate and tell PHP how you would like to manipulate that file.

The `fopen()` function has two required parameters that you must pass to it: the path to the file and the type of file manipulation you would like to perform (the *mode*).

The `fopen()` function returns a connection to the requested file if it's successful. (The connection is called a *pointer* — see the "Official file manipulation terminology" sidebar for more information.) If there is an error, the `fopen()` function returns `False`. Whatever the `fopen()` function returns (the connection or `False`), it should be assigned to a variable (a *stream*).

Here is an example of the `fopen()` function; see the section "Storing data in a CSV file" later in this chapter for an example of the `fopen()` function in action:

```
$fileConnection = fopen($theFile, $theMode);
```

In the preceding example, the file connection returned by the `fopen()` function is assigned to the variable `$fileConnection`. The variable `$theFile` would contain the path to a file; for example, both `C:\\xampp\\htdocs\\inc\\info.txt` and `/inc/log.txt` are valid file paths. The file must be in a place the server can access, meaning that you can put the file anywhere you could put a PHP page for the server to serve.

 Although possible, you probably shouldn't try to connect to a file in the My Documents folder or its equivalent on your operating system. You'll need the actual file path, which can be quite convoluted. It's also not necessary for the files you open to be in the htdocs directory. This could be useful if you want to access a file that will not be available except through your program. Use a relative reference if the file will be in the same directory as your program, or use an absolute reference if it will be somewhere else on your system. If you move your program to a remote server, you can only access files that reside on that server.

Official file manipulation terminology

If you look at the documentation for `fopen()`, or any of the file manipulation functions, you will see some funny terminology. To keep things simple, I decided to use more recognizable, easily understandable terms. I wanted you to know that I switched things up a little bit to give you a quick primer to help you out if you did happen to look at the official documentation or talk to a more seasoned programmer who might use the official terms.

According to the official online PHP documentation, the `fopen()` function *returns a file pointer, and binds a named resource to a stream.*

What this means is that when you use the `fopen()` function, it opens a file (much like you would do if you opened the file in Notepad) and returns a pointer to that file.

It's as if you had put your mouse arrow at the beginning of the file and clicked there to create the little blinky-line cursor telling Notepad where you are focusing (where you would like to begin editing the text). The pointer is PHP's focus on the file.

With the `fopen()` function, PHP's focus is *bound to a stream,* which means that it is attached to a variable. When you use the `fopen()` function, you associate the file with a variable of your choosing. This variable is how PHP keeps track of the location of the file and keeps track of where PHP's cursor is in the file. Normally, when you think of a stream, you might think of a one-way flow. But, in this case, the stream can either be read into the program character by character, line by line, or you can move the cursor around to any point in the file that you want. So, rather than being just a one-way flow, the stream is really an open connection to a file.

See `http://us.php.net/manual/en/function.fopen.php` for more detail on the `fopen()` function.

The variable `$theMode` would contain one of the values from the following list:

✦ `r`: Grants read-only access to the file

✦ `w`: Grants write access to the file

Be careful, though, because if you specify this mode (`w`) for the `fopen()` function and use the `fwrite()` function, you will completely overwrite anything that may have been in the file. Don't use `w` if there's anything in the file you want to keep.

✦ `a`: Grants the right to append text to the file. When you specify this mode for the `fopen()` function and use the `fwrite()` function, the `fwrite()` function appends whatever text you specify to the end of the existing file.

✦ `r+` or `w+`: Grants read and write access to the file. I don't talk about `r+` and `w+` in this book, except to say that they're a special way of accessing the file. This special file access mode is called *random access.* This allows you to simultaneously read and write to the file. If you require this type of access, you probably should be using something more simple and powerful, like relational databases.

fwrite ( )

After you open a file with the `fopen()` function and assign the file connection to a variable (see the "fopen( )" section, earlier in this chapter, for more information), you can use the file in your PHP code. You can either read from the file, or you can write to the file with the `fwrite()` function.

Depending on what mode you specify when you opened the file with the `fopen()` function, the `fwrite()` function will either overwrite the entire contents of the file (if you used the w mode) or it will append the text you specify to the end of the file (if you used the a mode).

The `fwrite()` function has two required parameters you must pass to it: the connection to the file that was established by the `fopen()` function and the text you wish to write to the file. The `fwrite()` function returns the number of bytes written to the file on success and `False` on failure.

Here is an example of the `fwrite()` function (see the section "Storing data in a CSV file" later in this chapter for an example of the `fwrite()` function in action):

```
$writeResults = fwrite($fileConnection, $text);
```

The `fwrite()` function can also be written `fputs()`. `fwrite()` and `fputs()` both do the exact same thing. `fputs()` is just a different way of writing `fwrite()` `fputs()` is referred to as an *alias* of `fwrite()`.

fclose ( )

After you finish working with the file, closing the file connection is important.

To close the connection to a file you've been working with, you must pass the connection to the file you wish to close to the `fclose()` function. The `fclose()` function will return `True` if it is successful in closing the connection to the file and `False` if it is not successful in closing the connection to the file.

Here is an example of the `fclose()` function:

```
fclose($fileConnection);
```

Writing a basic text file

Often, you'll want to do something as simple as record information from a form into a text file. Figure 6-1 illustrates a simple program that responds to a form and passes the input to a text form.

contact form

first name	Linus
last name	Torvalds
email	linus@linux.org
phone	444-4444
	submit

Figure 6-1:
Here's a standard form that asks for some contact information.

I didn't reproduce the code for this form here because it's basic XHTML. Of course, it's available on the book's companion CD-ROM and Web site, and I encourage you to look it over there.

I'm being attacked by robots!

The basic HTML form shown here is fine, but you'll find that when you start putting forms on the Web, you'll eventually get attacked by robot spam programs using your form to post (often inappropriate) content through your form.

The best solution to this is a technique called CAPTCHA, which is a mechanism for determining whether a form is submitted by a human or a computer. When you fill out forms online and have to type random words or letters from a weird image, you're using a form of CAPTCHA.

You can implement a very simple form of CAPTCHA by converting your form to a PHP page. Create a simple math problem and store the answer in a session variable. Ask the user to solve the problem and submit the response as part of the form. Have your program check the user's answer against the session.

Although this will not prevent a concerted attack, it is good enough for basic protection.

When the user enters contact data into this form, it will be passed to a program that reads the data, prints out a response, and stores the information in a text file. The output of the program is shown in Figure 6-2.

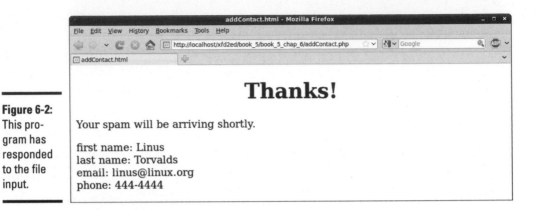

Figure 6-2:
This program has responded to the file input.

The more interesting behavior of the program is not visible to the user. The program opens a file for output and prints the contents of the form to the end of that file. Here are the contents of the data file after a few entries:

```
first: Andy
last: Harris
email: andy@aharrisbooks.net
phone: 111-1111

first: Bill
last: Gates
email: bill@Microsoft.com
phone: 222-2222

first: Steve
last: Jobs
email: steve@apple.com
phone: 333-3333

first: Linus
last: Torvalds
email: linus@linux.org
phone: 444-4444
```

The program to handle this input is not complicated. It essentially grabs data from the form, opens up a data file for output, and appends that data to anything already in the file. Here's the code for addContact.php:

```
<!DOCTYPE html PUBLIC "-//W3C//DTD XHTML 1.0 Strict//EN" "http://www.w3.org/TR/
    xhtml1/DTD/xhtml1-strict.dtd">
<html xmlns="http://www.w3.org/1999/xhtml" xml:lang="en">
<head>
  <title>addContact.html</title>
  <meta http-equiv="Content-Type" content="text/html;charset=UTF-8" />
```

```
    <link rel = "stylesheet"
          type = "text/css"
          href = "contact.css" />
</head>

<body>
<?php

//read data from form
$lName = $_REQUEST["lName"];
$fName = $_REQUEST["fName"];
$email = $_REQUEST["email"];
$phone = $_REQUEST["phone"];

//print form results to user

print <<< HERE
<h1>Thanks!</h1>

<p>
  Your spam will be arriving shortly.
</p>

<p>
first name: $fName <br />
last name: $lName <br />
email: $email <br />
phone: $phone
</p>

HERE;

//generate output for text file

$output = <<< HERE
first: $fName
last: $lName
email: $email
phone: $phone


HERE;

//open file for output
$fp = fopen("contacts.txt", "a");

//write to the file
fwrite($fp, $output);
fclose($fp);

?>

</body>
</html>
```

The process is straightforward:

1. Read data from the incoming form.

Just use the $_REQUEST mechanism to read variables from the form.

2. **Report what you're doing.**

   Let users know that something happened. As a minimum, report the contents of the data and tell them that their data has been saved. This is important because the file manipulation will be invisible to the user.

3. **Create a variable for output.**

   In this simple example, I print nearly the same values to the text file that I reported to the user. The text file does not have HTML formatting because it's intended to be read with a plain text editor.

4. **Open the file in append mode.**

   You might have hundreds of entries. Using *append mode* ensures that each entry goes at the end of the file, rather than overwriting the previous contents.

5. **Write the data to the file.**

   Using the `fwrite()` or `fputs()` function writes the data to the file.

6. **Close the file.**

   Don't forget to close the file with the `fclose()` function.

The file extension you use implies a lot about how the data is stored. If you store data in a file with an `.txt` extension, the user will assume it can be read by a plain text editor. The `.dat` extension implies some kind of formatted data, and `.csv` implies comma-separated values (explained later in this chapter). You can use any extension you want, but be aware you will confuse the user if you give a text file an extension like `.pdf` or `.doc`.

A note about file permissions

Your programs will be loading and storing files, so you need to know a little about how this works. If you're using a Windows-based server, you will probably have no problems because Windows has a very simplistic file permission system. However, your program will probably be housed on a Unix-like system eventually, so you need to understand a bit about how file permission works on these systems. In the Unix/Linux world, each file has an owner, and that owner can designate who can do what with a file. Typically, if your program creates a file, it can write to it and read from it, but this isn't always the case. If you get a file-access error when testing these programs, it's likely that the operating system is confused about who the file's owner is and what can be done to the file. You should be able to change the ownership of a file and its permissions through the file management system of your server or your FTP client (see Book VIII for more about these tools). Begin by trying to set the permission of your data file to 777 (all permissions for all users). If you cannot do this, you may need to change ownership to yourself. Try right-clicking the filename in your tool and looking for a Properties dialog box for these options.

Reading from the file

If you can write data to a file, it would make sense that you could read from that file as well. The showContacts.php program displayed in Figure 6-3 pulls the data saved in the previous program and displays it to the screen.

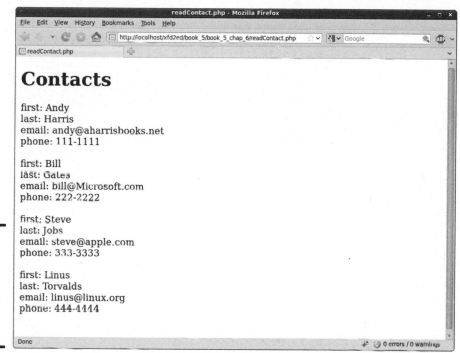

Figure 6-3:
This program reads the text file and displays it onscreen.

It is not difficult to write a program to read a text file. Here's the code:

```
<!DOCTYPE html PUBLIC "-//W3C//DTD XHTML 1.0 Strict//EN" "http://www.w3.org/TR/
    xhtml1/DTD/xhtml1-strict.dtd">
<html xmlns="http://www.w3.org/1999/xhtml" xml:lang="en">
<head>
  <title>readContact.php</title>
</head>
<body>
<h1>Contacts</h1>
<div>
<?php

//open up the contact file
$fp = fopen("contacts.txt", "r") or die("error");

//print a line at a time
while (!feof($fp)){
  $line = fgets($fp);
  print "$line <br />";
}
```

```
//close the file
fclose($fp);

?>
</div>

</body>
</html>
```

The procedure is similar to writing the file, but it uses a `for` loop.

1. Open the file in read mode.

Open the file just as you do when you write to it, but use the `r` designator to open the file for read mode. Now you can use the `fgets()` function on the file.

2. Create a `while` loop for reading the data.

Typically, you'll read a file one line at a time. You'll create a `while` loop to control the action.

3. Check for the end of the file with `feof()`.

You want the loop to continue as long as there are more lines in the file. The `feof()` function returns the value `true` if you are at the end of the file, and `false` if there are more lines to read. You want to continue as long as `feof()` returns false.

4. Read the next line with the `fgets()` function.

This function reads the next line from the file and passes that line into a variable (in this case, `$line`).

5. Print out the line.

With the contents of the current line in a variable, you can do whatever you want with it. In this case, I'll simply print it out, but you could format the contents, search for a particular value, or whatever else you want.

Why not just link to the file?

If this program just prints out the contents of a text file, you might wonder why it's necessary at all. After all, you could just supply a link to the text file. For this trivial example, that might be true, but the process of reading the file gives you many other options. For example, you might want to add improved CSS formatting.

You might also want to filter the contents: for example, only matching the lines that relate to a particular entry. Finally, you may want to do more than print the contents of a file — say, e-mail them or transfer them to another format. When you read the contents into memory, you can do anything to them.

Using Delimited Data

This basic mechanism for storing data is great for small amounts of data, but it will quickly become unwieldy if you're working with a lot of information. If you're expecting hundreds or thousands of people to read your forms, you'll need a more organized way to store the data. You can see how to use relational databases for this type of task in Book VI, but for now, another compromise is fine for simpler data tasks. You can store data in a very basic text format that can be easily read by spreadsheets and databases. This has the advantage of imposing some structure on the data and is still very easy to manage.

The basic plan is to format the data in a way that it can be read back into variables. Generally, you store all of the data for one form on a single line, and you separate the values on that line with a *delimiter,* which is simply some character intended to separate data points. Spreadsheets have used this format for many years as a basic way to transport data. In the spreadsheet world, this type of file is called a CSV (for *comma-separated values*) file. However, the delimiter doesn't need to be a comma. It can be nearly any character. I typically use a tab character or the pipe (|) symbol because they are unlikely to appear in the data I'm trying to save and load.

Storing data in a CSV file

Here's how you store data in a CSV file:

1. **You can use the same HTML form.**

   The data is gathered in the same way regardless of the storage mechanism. I did make a new page called addContactCSV.html, but the only difference between this file and the addContact.html page is the action property. I have the two pages send the data to different PHP programs, but everything else is the same.

2. **Read the data as normal.**

   In your PHP program, you begin by pulling data from the previous form.

   ```
   //read data from form
   $lName = $_REQUEST["lName"];
   $fName = $_REQUEST["fName"];
   $email = $_REQUEST["email"];
   $phone = $_REQUEST["phone"];
   ```

3. **Store all the data in a single tab-separated line.**

   Concatenate a large string containing all the data from the form. Place a delimiter (I used the tab symbol \t) between variables, and a newline (\n) at the end.

   ```
   //generate output for text file
   $output = $fName . "\t";
   $output .= $lName . "\t";
   $output .= $email . "\t";
   $output .= $phone . "\n";
   ```

4. **Open a file in append mode.**

   This time, I name the file contacts.csv to help myself remember that the contact form is now stored in a CSV format.

5. **Write the data to the file.**

   The fwrite() function does this job with ease.

6. **Close the file.**

   This part (like most of the program) is identical to the earlier version of the code.

Here's the code for addContactCSV.php in its entirety:

```
<!DOCTYPE html PUBLIC "-//W3C//DTD XHTML 1.0 Strict//EN" "http://www.w3.org/TR/
    xhtml1/DTD/xhtml1-strict.dtd">
<html xmlns="http://www.w3.org/1999/xhtml" xml:lang="en">
<head>
  <title>addContactCSV.php</title>
  <meta http-equiv="Content-Type" content="text/html;charset=UTF-8" />
  <link rel = "stylesheet"
        type = "text/css"
        href = "contact.css" />
</head>

<body>
<?php

//read data from form
$lName = $_REQUEST["lName"];
$fName = $_REQUEST["fName"];
$email = $_REQUEST["email"];
$phone = $_REQUEST["phone"];

//print form results to user

print <<< HERE
<h1>Thanks!</h1>

<p>
  Your spam will be arriving shortly.
</p>

<p>
first name: $fName <br />
last name: $lName <br />
email: $email <br />
phone: $phone
</p>

HERE;
```

```
//generate output for text file
$output = $fName . "\t";
$output .= $lName . "\t";
$output .= $email . "\t";
$output .= $phone . "\n";

//open file for output
$fp = fopen("contacts.csv", "a");

//write to the file
fwrite($fp, $output);
fclose($fp);

?>

</body>
</html>
```

As you can see, this is not a terribly difficult way to store data.

Viewing CSV data directly

If you look at the resulting file in a plain text editor, it looks like Figure 6-4.

Figure 6-4:
The data is
separated by
tab charac-
ters and
each entry
is on its
own line.

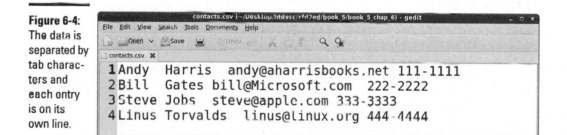

Of course, CSV data isn't meant to be read as plain text. On most operating systems, the `.csv` file extension is automatically linked to the default
spreadsheet program. If you double-click the file, it will open in your spreadsheet, which will look something like Figure 6-5.

This is an easy way to store large amounts of data because you can use
the spreadsheet to manipulate the data. Of course, relational databases
(described in Book VI) are even better, but this is a very easy approach for
relatively simple data sets. I've built many data entry systems by using this
general approach.

Figure 6-5:
Most
spread-
sheets
can read
CSV data
directly.

Reading the CSV data in PHP

Of course, you may also want to read in the CSV data yourself. It's not too difficult to do. The following code for `readContactCSV.php`:

```
<!DOCTYPE html PUBLIC "-//W3C//DTD XHTML 1.0 Strict//EN" "http://www.w3.org/TR/
    xhtml1/DTD/xhtml1-strict.dtd">
<html xmlns="http://www.w3.org/1999/xhtml" xml:lang="en">
<head>
  <title>readContactCSV.php</title>
</head>
<body>
<h1>Contacts</h1>
<div>
<?php

print <<< HERE

<table border = "1">
  <tr>
    <th>First</th>
    <th>Last</th>
    <th>email</th>
    <th>phone</th>
  </tr>
```

```
HERE;

$data = file("contacts.csv");
foreach ($data as $line){
  $lineArray = explode("\t", $line);

  list($fName, $lName, $email, $phone) = $lineArray;
  print <<< HERE
    <tr>
      <td>$fName</td>
      <td>$lName</td>
      <td>$email</td>
      <td>$phone</td>
    </tr>

HERE;
} // end foreach

//print the bottom of the table
print "</table> \n";

?>
</div>

</body>
</html>
```

Figure 6-6 shows this program in action.

Figure 6-6:
This program creates an HTML table from the data in the file.

In this program, I read the contents of a CSV file and display it in an HTML table. It's not terribly different than reading any other text file, but there are some new twists.

1. **Print the table heading.**

   It's easiest to manually print out the table heading with the field names, because I know what they'll be. A simple heredoc will do the job.

   ```
   print <<< HERE

   <table border = "1">
     <tr>
       <th>First</th>
       <th>Last</th>
       <th>email</th>
       <th>phone</th>
     </tr>

   HERE;
   ```

2. **Load the data into an array.**

   PHP has a marvelous tool called `file`. This function takes a filename as its only input. It then opens that file and places all the contents in an array, placing each line in its own element of the array. There's no need to make a file pointer, or to open or close the file. In this example, I load all the contents of `contacts.csv` into an array called `$data`.

   ```
   $data = file("contacts.csv");
   ```

3. **Use a `foreach` loop to step through the contents.**

   Now I can walk through the contents of the file with a simple `foreach` loop. I place the current line in a variable called (wait for it . . .) `$line`.

   ```
   foreach ($data as $line){
   ```

4. **Explode each line into its own array.**

   You have got to love a function with a violent name, especially when it's really useful. Use the `explode` command to separate the line into its component parts. For this example, I break on the tab (`\t`) character because that's the delimiter I used when storing the file.

   ```
   $lineArray = explode("\t", $line);
   ```

5. **Use the `list()` function to store each element of the array into its own variable.**

   I could just use the array, but I think it's easier to pass the data back to the same variable names I used when creating the program. The `list()` construct does exactly that. Feed it a bunch of variable names and assign an array to it, and now each element of the array will be assigned to the corresponding variable.

   ```
   list($fName, $lName, $email, $phone) = $lineArray;
   ```

6. **Print the variables in an HTML table row.**

   All the variables fit well in an HTML table, so just print out the current row of the table.

   ```
   print <<< HERE
     <tr>
   ```

```
        <td>$fName</td>
        <td>$lName</td>
        <td>$email</td>
        <td>$phone</td>
    </tr>

HERE;
```

7. **Clean up your playthings.**

    There's a little housekeeping to do. Finish the loop and close up the HTML table. There's no need to close the file because that was automatically done by the file() function.

```
    } // end foreach

    //print the bottom of the table
    print "</table> \n";
```

These shortcuts — the file() function and list() — make it very easy to work with CSV data. That's one reason this type of data is popular for basic data problems.

The list() construct works only on numerically indexed arrays and assumes that the array index begins at 0. If you want to use the list() function with associative arrays, surround the array variable with the array_values() function. Technically, list() is not a function but a language construct. (See http://us3.php.net/list for more information on the list() function.)

The file() function is appealing, but it isn't perfect for every situation. It's great as long as the file size is relatively small, but if you try to load in a very large file, you will run into memory limitations. The "line at a time" approach used in readContact.php doesn't have this problem because there's only a small amount of data in memory at any given time.

Escaping with HTML entities

If you're planning on displaying the user's input to the screen, escape all the special characters before saving the user's input to a file or sending it to the browser. Otherwise, some malicious user could use some simple CSS and HTML to really mess up your page. Remember: Paranoia is your friend. The simplest way to guard against this is to use the html entities() function:

```
$userInput =
    htmlentities($userInput);
```

This function converts any HTML characters the user may have entered into the character's HTML entities equivalent. That is, if the user entered <div>, it'd be converted to <div>. When you display it back to the page, instead of creating a new HTML div, the browser will simply output the literal string <div> to the user.

If, for some reason, you want to decode these entities, use the html_entity_decode() function. This works exactly like its html entities() counterpart, just in reverse.

Working with File and Directory Functions

Sometimes, you may need PHP to work with files in a directory. Say you have a reporting tool for a client. Each week, you generate a new report for the client and place it in a directory. You don't want to have to alter the page each time you do this, so instead, make a page that automatically generates a list of all the report files for the client to select from. This is the kind of thing you can do with functions like opendir() and readdir().

opendir()

Using the opendir() function, you can create a variable (technically speaking, this type of variable is called a *handle*) that allows you to work with a particular directory.

The opendir() function takes one parameter: the path to the directory you want to work with. The opendir() function returns a directory handle (kind of like a connection to the directory) on success and False on failure.

Here is an example of the opendir() function (see the "Generating the list of file links" section to see the opendir() function in action). This function stores a directory handle to the C:\xampp\htdocs\XFD\xfd5.7 directory in the $directoryHandle variable:

```
$directoryHandle = opendir("C:\xampp\htdocs\XFD\xfd5.7");
```

readdir()

After you open the directory with the opendir() function, you have a cursor pointed at the first file. At this point, you can read the filenames one by one with a while loop. To do this, use the readdir() function.

The readdir() function takes one parameter; the variable containing the directory handle created with the opendir() function. The readdir() function returns the name of a file currently being focused on by the cursor on success and False on failure.

Here is an example of the readdir() function. This function iterates through each file in the directory specified by $dp and assigns the filename of the current file to a new index in $fileArray array:

```
while($currentFile !== false){
    $currentFile = readDir($dp);
    $filesArray[] = $currentFile;
}
```

The actual readdir() function itself is readdir($dp). For more on the readdir() function, see the official PHP online documentation at http://us.php.net/function.readdir.

In some circumstances, the readdir() function might return non-Boolean values which evaluate to False, such as 0 or "". When testing the return value of the readdir() function, use === or !==, instead of == or !=, to accommodate these special cases.

chdir()

If you want to create a file in a directory other than the directory that the PHP page creating the file is in, you need to change directories. You change directories in PHP with the chdir() function.

If you want to be absolutely sure that you're in the right directory before writing the file, you can use an if statement with the getcwd() function. This is usually a bit of overkill, but it can be helpful.

The chdir() function takes one parameter: the path to the directory you wish to work with. The chdir() function returns True on success and False on failure.

Here is an example of the chdir(). This function changes to the C:\ xampp\htdocs\XFD\xfd5.6 directory:

```
chdir("C:\xampp\htdocs\XFD\xfd5.6");
```

When you change to a directory; you're then free to write to it with the fwrite() function. See the "fwrite()" section, earlier in this chapter.

Generating the list of file links

Using the opendir() and readdir() functions, you can generate a list of links to the files in a directory.

Take a look at the PHP code for the file links list example; see Figure 6-7 for the HTML generated by this example:

```
<!DOCTYPE html
PUBLIC "-//W3C//DTD XHTML 1.0 Strict//EN"
"http://www.w3.org/TR/xhtml1/DTD/xhtml1-strict.dtd">
<html xmlns="http://www.w3.org/1999/xhtml" xml:lang="en" lang="en">
<head>
<meta http-equiv="Content-Type" content="text/html;charset=utf-8" />
<title>fileList.php</title>
</head>
<body>
<ul>
<?php
$dp = opendir(".");
$currentFile = "";

while($currentFile !== false){
  $currentFile = readDir($dp);
  $filesArray[] = $currentFile;
} // end while
```

```
//sort the array in alpha order
sort($filesArray);

$output = "";
foreach($filesArray as $aFile){
  $output .= "  <li><a href=\"$aFile\">$aFile</a></li> \n";
} // end foreach

print "$output";
?>
</ul>
</body>
</html>
```

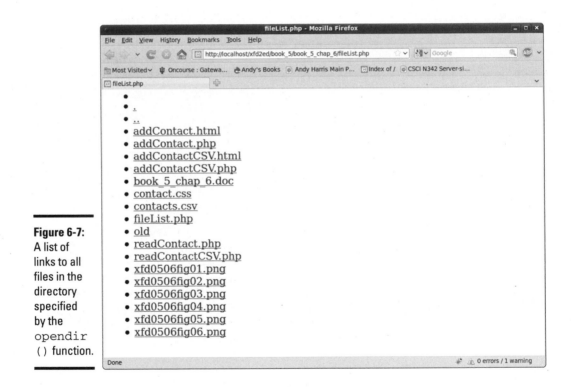

Figure 6-7:
A list of links to all files in the directory specified by the `opendir()` function.

Here's how the `fileList.php` program performs its magic:

1. **Open a directory pointer to the current directory.**

In all major operating systems, the period (`.`) character indicates the current directory.

```
$dp = opendir(".");
```

2. Build a loop that repeats until there are no files left.

The special `!==` comparison is used to prevent rare problems, such as files named `false`. (Yes, believe it or not, that sometimes happens.)

```
while($currentFile !== false){
```

3. Read the next file from the directory pointer.

The `readDir()` function reads the next file in and stores it to a variable (`$currentFile`).

```
$currentFile = readDir($dp);
```

4. Append the current file to an array.

If you simply assign a file to an array without an index, PHP places the element in the next available space.

```
$filesArray[] = $currentFile;
```

5. Sort the array.

The files won't be in any particular order in the array, so use the `sort()` function.

```
sort($filesArray);
```

6. Print each element of the array.

I use an unordered list of links to display each file. Make it a link so that the user can click the file to view it directly.

```
foreach($filesArray as $aFile){
  $output .= "  <li><a href=\"$aFile\">$aFile</a></li> \n";
} // end foreach
```

On a Windows server, you have to escape the backslashes in the file path. You do this by adding a backslash before the backslashes in the file path. (For example, you would write `C:\\xampp\\htdocs\\XFD\\xfd5.7\\` instead of `C:\xampp\htdocs\XFD\xfd5.7\`.) On a Unix server, you don't have to do this because file paths use slashes (/) instead of backslashes (\).

If you want just one particular file type, you can use regular expressions to filter the files. If I had wanted only the `.txt` and `.dat` files from the directory, I could have run the files array through this filter to weed out the unwanted file types:

```
$filesArray = preg_grep("/txt$|dat$/", $filesArray);
```

For more on regular expressions, check Book IV, Chapter 6 as well as Chapter 4 of this book.

Chapter 7: Connecting to a MySQL Database

In This Chapter

✔ Building the connection string

✔ Sending queries to a database

✔ Retrieving data results

✔ Formatting data output

✔ Allowing user queries

✔ Cleaning user-submitted data requests

Data has become the prominent feature of the Web. As you build more sophisticated sites using XHTML and CSS, you will eventually feel the need to incorporate data into your Web sites. You can do a certain amount of data work with the basic data structures built into PHP. Increasingly, Web sites turn to relational database management systems (RDBMSs) to handle their data needs. A *RDBMS* is a special program which accepts requests, processes data, and returns results.

This chapter assumes you have a database available and also that you have some basic knowledge of how SQL (Structured Query Language; the language of databases) works. If you're unfamiliar with these topics, please look over Book VI, which describes using data in detail.

Retrieving Data from a Database

PHP programmers frequently use MySQL as their preferred data back end for a number of good reasons:

✦ **MySQL is open source and free.** Like PHP, MySQL is open source, so PHP and MySQL can be used together (with Apache) to build a very powerful low-cost data solution.

✦ **MySQL is very powerful.** MySQL's capability as a data program has improved steadily, and it is now nearly as capable as commercial tools costing thousands of dollars. (And it is better than many that cost hundreds of dollars.)

✦ **PHP has built-in support for MySQL.** PHP includes a number of functions specifically designed to help programmers maintain MySQL databases.

✦ **You probably already have MySQL.** If you installed XAMPP, you probably already have an installation of MySQL ready to go. Check Book VIII, Chapter 1 for installation details.

✦ **MySQL was designed with remote control in mind.** MySQL is meant to be managed from some other program (like the code you write in PHP). It's not designed with a user interface (like Access has), but it's designed from the beginning to be controlled through a programming language like PHP.

Before diving into details, here's an overview of how you get information to and from a MySQL database:

1. Establish a connection.

Before you can work with a database, you must establish a relationship between your PHP program and the database. This process involves identifying where the database is and passing it a username and password.

2. Formulate a query.

Most of the time, you'll have some sort of query or request you want to pass to the database. For example, you may want to see all the data in a particular table, or you may want to update a record. In either case, you use SQL to prepare a request to pass to the database.

3. Submit the query.

After you build the query, you pass it (through the connection) to the database. Assuming that the query is properly formatted, the database processes the request and returns a result.

4. Process the result.

The database returns a special variable containing the results of your query. You'll generally need to pick through this complex variable to find all the data it contains. For example, it can contain hundreds of records. (For more on records, see the upcoming section "Processing the results.")

5. Display output to the user.

Most of the time, you'll process the query results and convert them to some sort of XHTML display that the user can view.

As an example, take a look at `contact.php` in Figure 7-1.

Figure 7-1:
This program gets all the contact data from a database.

The contact.php program contains none of the actual contact information. All the data was extracted from a database. Here's an overview of the code:

```
<!DOCTYPE html PUBLIC "-//W3C//DTD XHTML 1.0 Strict//EN"
"http://www.w3.org/TR/xhtml1/DTD/xhtml1-strict.dtd">
<html lang="EN" dir="ltr" xmlns="http://www.w3.org/1999/xhtml">
  <head>
    <meta http-equiv="content-type" content="text/xml; charset=utf-8" />
    <title>showContact.php</title>
  </head>

  <body>
  <p>
  <?php

$conn = mysql_connect("localhost","user","password") or die(mysql_error());
mysql_select_db("xfd");

$sql = "SELECT * FROM contact";
$result = mysql_query($sql, $conn) or die(mysql_error());

while($row = mysql_fetch_assoc($result)){
  foreach ($row as $name => $value){
    print "$name: $value <br />\n";
  } // end foreach
  print "<br /> \n";
} // end while

  ?>
  </p>
  </body>
</html>
```

If you want to try this program at home, begin by running the `build ContactAutoIncrement.sql` script (available in Book VI, Chapter 2) in your copy of MySQL. This will ensure you have the database created. See Book VI, Chapter 2 if you need more information on creating databases.

Understanding data connections

The key to all database work is the connection. Database connections remind me of the pneumatic tubes at some bank drive-through locations. There's a little container you can stick your request into. You press a button, and the container shoots through a tube to the teller, who processes your request and sends you the results back through the tube.

In data programming, the connection is like that tube: It's the pipeline between your program (your car) and the data (the bank). To establish a data connection, you need to know four things:

+ **The hostname (where the server is):** Often, the data server will be housed on the same physical machine as the Web server and PHP program. In these cases, you can use `localhost` as the server name. Test servers using XAMPP almost always use `localhost` connections. If you're working in a production environment, you may need to ask your service provider for the server address of your database.

+ **Your database username:** Database programs should always have some type of security enabled. (See Book VI, Chapter 1 for information on setting up database users and passwords.) Your program needs to know the username it should use for accessing the data. (I often create a special username simply for my programs. Book VI, Chapter 1 outlines this process.)

When you first install MySQL through XAMPP, it allows root access with no password. These settings allow anybody to do anything with your data. Obviously, that's not a good solution, security-wise. Be sure to set up at least one username and password combination for your database. If you're using an online hosting service, you probably don't have root access. In this case, you typically have a new user created for each database you build. Book VI explains all.

+ **A password for the database:** The username isn't secure without a password. Your PHP program also needs a password. This is established when you create the database.

If you're going to make your source code available (as I do on the companion CD and Web site), be sure to change the username and password so people can't use this information to hack your live data.

+ **The database name:** A single installation of MySQL can have many databases available. You'll typically have a separate database designed for each project you build. MySQL needs to know which particular database houses the information you're seeking.

Building a connection

The data connection is created with the mysql_connect() function. Here's how to do it:

1. **Create a variable to house the connection.**

   When you build a connection, a special variable is created to house information about that variable. I usually call my connection $conn:

   ```
   $conn = mysql_connect("localhost","user","password") or die(mysql_error());
   ```

2. **Invoke the mysql_connect() function.**

   This function (usually built into PHP) attempts to build a connection to the database given all the connection information:

   ```
   $conn = mysql_connect("localhost","user","password") or die(mysql_error());
   ```

3. **Pass the hostname, username, and password to mysql_connect().**

   These three values are required parameters of the mysql_connect() function:

   ```
   $conn = mysql_connect("localhost","user","password") or die(mysql_error());
   ```

   You'll need to supply your own username and password. My values here are just samples.

4. **Prepare for a graceful crash.**

   It's very possible that something will go wrong when you attempt a data connection. The or die() clause tells PHP what to do if something goes wrong while making the connection:

   ```
   $conn = mysql_connect("localhost","user","password") or die(mysql_error());
   ```

   How many times in your life have you heard that phrase? "Prepare for a graceful crash." You've got to love programming.

5. **Invoke mysql_error() if something goes wrong.**

   If there's a problem with the MySQL connection, the error message will come from MySQL, not PHP. To ensure that you see the MySQL error, use the mysql_error() function. If you made a mistake (like misspelling the username), MySQL will report this error to PHP. Use mysql_error() to print out the last error from MySQL:

   ```
   $conn = mysql_connect("localhost","user","password") or die(mysql_error());
   ```

6. **Specify the particular database.**

   After you're connected to the server, you need to specify which database on the server will be used for your transaction. I'm using a database called xfd for all the examples in this book. The mysql_select_db() function is used to handle this task:

   ```
   mysql_select_db("xfd");
   ```

Passing a query to the database

The reason for connecting to a database is to retrieve data from it (or to add or modify data, but the basic approach is always the same). In any case, you need to pass instructions to the database in SQL. (If you're unfamiliar with SQL, read Book VI, Chapter 1.)

Your PHP program usually constructs an SQL statement in a string variable and then passes this value to the database. For this basic example, I specify the entire query. See the section "Processing the input," later in this chapter, for some warnings about how to incorporate user information in data queries.

The showContact.php program simply asks for a list of all the values in the contact table of the xfd database. The SQL query for displaying all the data in a table looks like this:

```
SELECT * FROM contact;
```

To use an SQL statement, package it into a string variable, like this:

```
$sql = "SELECT * FROM contact";
```

Note that you don't need to include the semicolon inside the string variable. You can call the variable anything you wish, but it's commonly called $sql. SQL queries can get complex, so if the SQL requires more than one line, you may want to encase it in a heredoc. (See Chapter 2 of this minibook for information on using heredocs.)

Pass the request to the database using the msql_query() function:

```
$result = mysql_query($sql, $conn) or die(mysql_error());
```

The mysql_query() function has a lot going on. Here's how you put it together:

1. **Create a variable to house the results.**

   When the query is finished, it will send results back to the program. The $result variable will hold that data:

   ```
   $result = mysql_query($sql, $conn) or die(mysql_error());
   ```

2. **Invoke mysql_query().**

   This function passes the query to the database:

   ```
   $result = mysql_query($sql, $conn) or die(mysql_error());
   ```

3. **Send the query to the database.**

   The first parameter is the query. Normally, this is stored in a variable called $sql:

   ```
   $result = mysql_query($sql, $conn) or die(mysql_error());
   ```

4. **Specify the connection.**

The second parameter is the connection object created when you ran `mysql_connect()`. If you leave out the connection object, PHP uses the last MySQL connection that was created:

```
$result = mysql_query($sql, $conn) or die(mysql_error());
```

5. **Handle errors.**

If there's an error in your SQL request, MySQL will send back an error message. Prepare for this with the `or die()` clause (just like you used for `mysql_connect()`):

```
$result = mysql_query($sql, $conn) or die(mysql_error());
```

6. **Return the MySQL error if there was a problem.**

If something went wrong in the SQL code, have your program reply with the MySQL error so you'll at least know what went wrong:

```
$result = mysql_query($sql, $conn) or die(mysql_error());
```

Processing the results

The results of an SQL query are usually data tables, which are a complex data structure. The next step when you work with a database is to get all the appropriate information from the `$request` object and display it in an XHTML output for the user to understand.

This process is a little involved because SQL results are normally composed of two-dimensional data. A query result typically consists of multiple *records* (information about a specific entity — sometimes also called a *row*). Each record consists of a number of *fields* (specific data about the current record).

I'm tossing a bunch of database terms at you here. Databases deserve (and have) a minibook of their own. If nothing in this chapter makes sense to you, build your own copy of the `contact` database following the instructions in Book VI and then come back here to have your program present that data through your Web site.

The `$request` variable has a lot of data packed into it. You get that data out by using a pair of nested loops:

1. **The outer loop extracts a record at a time.**

The first job is to get each record out of the request, one at a time.

2. **Use another loop to extract each field from the record.**

After you have a record, you need to extract each field from the record.

Here's all the code for this segment; I explain it in detail in the following sections:

```
while($row = mysql_fetch_assoc($result)){
  foreach ($row as $name => $value){
    print "$name: $value <br />\n";
  } // end foreach
  print "<br /> \n";
} // end while
```

Extracting the rows

The first task is to break the $result object into a series of variables that each represent one record (or row). Here's the line that does the job:

```
while($row = mysql_fetch_assoc($result)){
```

To break a result into its constituent rows, follow these steps:

1. **Begin a while loop.**

   This code will continue as long as more rows are available in the $result object:

   ```
   while($row = mysql_fetch_assoc($result)){
   ```

2. **Extract the next row as an associative array.**

   Every time through the loop, you'll extract the next row from the result. There are several functions available for this task, but I use mysql_fetch_assoc() because I think it's easiest to understand (see the sidebar "MySQL fetch options" for some other options and when you might choose them):

   ```
   while($row = mysql_fetch_assoc($result)){
   ```

3. **Pass the resulting object to a variable called $row.**

   The output of mysql_fetch_assoc is an array (specifically, an associative array). Copy that value to a variable called $row:

   ```
   while($row = mysql_fetch_assoc($result)){
   ```

4. **Continue as long as there are more rows to retrieve.**

   mysql_fetch_assoc() has an important side effect. In addition to extracting an associative array from $result, the function returns the value false if no more records are left. Because I'm using this statement inside a condition, the loop will continue as long as another row is available. When no rows are left, the assignment will evaluate to false, and the loop will exit.

   ```
   while($row = mysql_fetch_assoc($result)){
   ```

MySQL fetch options

You can extract data from a MySQL result in four different ways:

✔ `mysql_fetch_row()` creates an ordinary (numeric index) array from the current row.

✔ `mysql_fetch_assoc()` creates an associative array from the current row, with the field name as the key and field value as the value in each key/value pair.

✔ `mysql_fetch_array()` can be used to get numeric or associative arrays, based on a parameter.

✔ `mysql_fetch_object()` returns a PHP object corresponding to the current row. Each field in the row is a property of the object.

In general, the `mysql_fetch_assoc()` provides the best combination of ease-of-use and information. Use `mysql_fetch_array()` when you don't need the field names: for example, you're using an XHTML table for output, and you're getting the field names from the `mysql_fetch_field()` function. The `mysql_fetch_object()` technique is useful if you're going to build a complete object based on a query row, but that's beyond the scope of this book.

Extracting fields from a row

Each time you go through the `while` loop described in the previous section, you'll have a variable called `$row`. This will be an associative array containing all the field names and values from the current form. If you know a field name, you can access it directly. For example, I know the `contact` table has a field named `company`, so you can use an associative array lookup to see the current company name:

```
print $row["company"];
```

This will print the company name of the current record.

More often, you will want to print out all the information in the row, so you can use the special form of `foreach()` loop used with associative arrays:

```
foreach ($row as $name => $value){
```

Here's how it works:

1. **Set up the `foreach` loop.**

   This form of `for` loop automatically loads variables with members of the array:

   ```
   foreach ($row as $name => $value){
   ```

2. **Analyze the $row array.**

   The $row variable contains an associative array, so it's a perfect candidate for this type of loop:

   ```
   foreach ($row as $name => $value){
   ```

3. **Assign each key to $name.**

   On each pass of the loop, assign the current key of the array (which will contain the current field name) to the variable $name:

   ```
   foreach ($row as $name => $value){
   ```

4. **Indicate the relationship between $name and $value with the => operator.**

   This indicates that $name is the key and that $value is the value in this relationship:

   ```
   foreach ($row as $name => $value){
   ```

5. **Assign the value to $value.**

   The value of the current element will be placed in the $value variable:

   ```
   foreach ($row as $name => $value){
   ```

When you use a foreach loop with an associative array, you assign each element to two variables because each element in an associative array has a name and a value. Check Chapter 4 of this minibook for more information about associative arrays and the foreach loop.

Inside this loop, you'll have the name of the current field in a variable called $name and its value in a variable called $value. This loop will continue for each field in the current record.

Printing the data

For this simple example, I'm using the simplest way I can think of to print out the contents:

```
print "$name: $value <br />\n";
```

This line simply prints out the current field name, followed by a colon and the current field value. Because this simple line is inside the complex nested loops, it ends up printing the name and value of every field in the query result. Here's the whole chunk of code again:

```
while($row = mysql_fetch_assoc($result)){
  foreach ($row as $name => $value){
    print "$name: $value <br />\n";
  } // end foreach
  print "<br /> \n";
} // end while
```

The result isn't the most elegant formatting on the Internet, but it gets the job done, and it's easy to understand. Note I added a `<br />` tag at the end of each line, so each field will appear on its own line of XHTML output. I also added a final `<br />` at the end of each `for` loop. This will cause a line break between each record so that the records are separated.

Improving the Output Format

Using `<br />` tags for output is a pretty crude expedient. It's fine for a basic test, but `<br />` tags are usually a sign of sloppy XHTML coding. Take a look at this variation called `contactDL.php` in Figure 7-2.

Figure 7-2: Now, the output of the query is in a nice definition list.

Building definition lists

Definition lists are designed for name/value pairs, so they're often a good choice for data in associative arrays. It's not too difficult to convert the basic data result program (shown in the following code) into a form that uses definition lists:

```
<!DOCTYPE html PUBLIC "-//W3C//DTD XHTML 1.0 Strict//EN"
"http://www.w3.org/TR/xhtml1/DTD/xhtml1-strict.dtd">
<html lang="EN" dir="ltr" xmlns="http://www.w3.org/1999/xhtml">
```

```html
<head>
  <meta http-equiv="content-type" content="text/xml; charset=utf-8" />
  <title>contactDL.php</title>
  <style type = "text/css">
    dt {
       float: left;
       width: 7em;
       font-weight: bold;
       clear: left;
    }

    dd {
       float: left;
    }

    dl {
       float: left;
       clear: left;
    }

  </style>
</head>

<body>
<?php

$conn = mysql_connect("localhost","user","password") or die(mysql_error());
mysql_select_db("xfd");

$sql = "SELECT * FROM contact";
$result = mysql_query($sql, $conn) or die(mysql_error());


while($row = mysql_fetch_assoc($result)){
  print "    <dl> \n";
  foreach ($row as $name => $value){
    print "        <dt>$name</dt> \n";
    print "        <dd>$value</dd> \n";
  } // end foreach
  print "    </dl> \n";
} // end while

  ?>
  </body>
</html>
```

The general design is copied from `contact.html`, with the following changes:

1. Add CSS styling for the definition list.

Definition lists are great for this kind of data, but the default style is pretty boring. I added some float styles to make the data display better. (See Book III, Chapter 1 for how to use floating styles.)

2. Put each record in its own definition list.

The `while` loop executes once per record, so begin the definition list at the beginning of the `while` loop. The `</dl>` tag goes at the end of the `while` loop. Each pass of the `while` loop creates a new definition list.

3. **Display the field names as `<dt>` elements.**

The field name maps pretty well to the concept of a definition term, so put each $name value in a `<dt></dt>` pair.

4. **Place the values inside `<dd>` tags.**

The values will be displayed as definition data. Now, you have the contents of the data set up in a form that can be easily modified with CSS.

Using XHTML tables for output

The basic unit of structure in SQL is called a *table* because it's usually displayed in a tabular format. XHTML also has a table structure, which is ideal for outputting SQL data. Figure 7-3 shows `contactTable.php`, which displays the `contact` information inside an XHTML table.

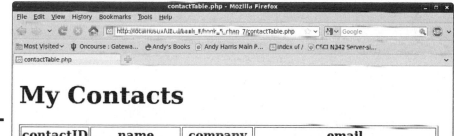

Figure 7-3:
The contact information displayed in an XHTML table.

Tables are a very common way to output SQL results. There's one big difference between table output and the techniques that have been shown elsewhere in this chapter. In a table, you have a separate row containing field names. Here's the code:

```
<!DOCTYPE html PUBLIC "-//W3C//DTD XHTML 1.0 Strict//EN"
"http://www.w3.org/TR/xhtml1/DTD/xhtml1-strict.dtd">
<html lang="EN" dir="ltr" xmlns="http://www.w3.org/1999/xhtml">
  <head>
    <meta http-equiv="content-type" content="text/xml; charset=utf-8" />
    <title>contactTable.php</title>
    <style type = "text/css">
      table, th, td {
        border: 1px solid black;
      }
    </style>
  </head>
```

```
<body>
  <h1>My Contacts</h1>
  <?php
$conn = mysql_connect("localhost", "user", "password");
mysql_select_db("xfd");
$sql = "SELECT * FROM contact";
$result = mysql_query($sql, $conn);

print "  <table> \n";

//get field names first
print "      <tr> \n";
while ($field = mysql_fetch_field($result)){
  print "        <th>$field->name</th> \n";
} // end while
print "      </tr> \n";

while ($row = mysql_fetch_assoc($result)){
  print "      <tr> \n";
  foreach ($row as $name => $value){
    print "        <td>$value</td> \n";
  } // end foreach
  print "      </tr> \n";

} // end while loop

print "    </table> \n";

  ?>
  </body>
</html>
```

TIP

You might be confused that I'm using a table here, seeing as how I argue pretty strongly against use of tables for page layout in the HTML and CSS minibooks. Tables aren't evil: they just aren't designed to be a page layout mechanism. Tables, however, *are* designed to display tabular data, and the result of a data query is pretty much the definition of tabular data. You can (and should) still use CSS for specific layout details of the table. Tables are fine when used to present data, which is what I'm doing here.

This code is still very similar to the basic contact.php program. It extracts data from the database exactly the same way. The main difference is how field names are treated. The field names will go in table headings, and only the values are printed from each row. To make this work, follow these steps:

1. **Build a normal MySQL connection.**

   Begin with the standard connection. Don't worry about formatting until you're reasonably certain that you can read data from the database.

2. **Print the table tag before extracting any results.**

   All the query data will be displayed inside the table, so print the table tag before you start printing anything that should go inside the table.

3. **Print the table header row first.**

The table headers must be printed before you can worry about the other data:

```
//get field names first
print "      <tr> \n";
while ($field = mysql_fetch_field($result)){
  print "        <th>$field->name</th> \n";
} // end while
print "      </tr> \n";
```

4. **Extract metadata from the result set with `mysql_fetch_field()`.**

After you get a result from a data query, you can learn a lot about the data by using the `mysql_fetch_field()` function:

```
while ($field = mysql_fetch_field($result)){
```

This function (`mysql_fetch_field()`) extracts the next field object from the result and passes it to a variable called `$field`. It returns `false` if there are no more fields in the result, so it can be used in a `while` loop, like `mysql_fetch_assoc()`.

5. **Print the field's name.**

The field is an object, so you can extract various elements from it easily. In this case, I'm interested in the field name. `$field->name` yields the name of the current field. (See the nearby sidebar, "More about metadata," for more information about information you can extract from field objects.)

```
        print "        <th>$field->name</th> \n";
```

6. **Print each row's data as a table row.**

Each row of the data result maps to a table row. Use the preceding variation of nested loops to build your table rows.

7. **Finish off the table.**

The `table` tag must be completed. Don't forget to print `</table>` when you're done printing out all the table information.

8. **Clean up your XHTML.**

Check your code in a browser. Make sure it looks right, but don't stop there. Check with a validator to make sure that your program produces valid XHTML code. View the source and ensure that the indentation and white space are adequate. Even though a program produced this code, it needs to be XHTML code you can be proud of.

More about metadata

You can find out all sorts of information about the table you're querying with the `mysql_fetch_field()` function.

This function returns an object that has the following properties:

✔ `table`: The name of the table the field (column) belongs to.

✔ `name`: The field's name.

✔ `type`: The field's datatype.

✔ `primary_key`: If the field is a primary key, will return a 1.

✔ `unique_key`: If the field is a unique key, will return a 1.

✔ `max_length`: The field's maximum length.

✔ `def`: The field's default value (if any).

✔ `not_null`: If the field can't be NULL, will return a 1.

✔ `multiple_key`: If the field is a non-unique key, will return a 1.

✔ `numeric`: If the field is numeric, will return a 1.

✔ `blob`: If the field is a `blob`, will return a 1.

✔ `unsigned`: If the field is unsigned, will return a 1.

✔ `zerofill`: If the field is zero-filled, will return a 1.

You'll probably end up using `table`, `name`, `type`, `primary_key`, and `max_length` the most. Refer to any of these values using object-oriented syntax, so if you have a field named `$field`, get its name by using `$field->name`.

Allowing User Interaction

If you have a large database, you probably want to allow users to search the database. For example, the form in Figure 7-4 allows the user to search the My Contacts database.

Figure 7-4: The user can check for any value in any field.

Here are a couple of interesting things about the form in Figure 7-4:

✦ **The search value can be anything.** The first field is an ordinary text field. The user can type absolutely anything here, so you should expect some surprises.

✦ **The user selects a field with a drop-down menu.** You don't expect the user to know exactly what field names you are using in your database. Whenever possible, supply this type of information in a format that's easier for the user and less prone to error.

✦ **This form is built to fill in a query.** The back-end program (search. php) will be constructing a query from data gathered from this form. The point of the form is to request two pieces of information from the user: a field to search in and a value to look for in that field. search. php will use the data gleaned from this form to construct and submit that query to the database.

✦ **The user doesn't know SQL.** Even if the user does know SQL, don't let him use it. The SQL query should always be built on the server side. Get enough information to build an SQL query, but don't send a query to the PHP. Doing so exposes your database to significant abuse, such as the SQL injection attack described later in this chapter.

✦ **The form uses the post mechanism.** From the XHTML perspective, it isn't important whether the form uses get or post, but when you're using forms to construct SQL queries, using post is a bit safer because it makes the bad guys work a little bit harder to spoof your site and send bogus requests to your database.

Building an XHTML search form

This is what the XHTML code for search.html looks like:

```
<!DOCTYPE html PUBLIC "-//W3C//DTD XHTML 1.0 Strict//EN"
"http://www.w3.org/TR/xhtml1/DTD/xhtml1-strict.dtd">
<html lang="EN" dir="ltr" xmlns="http://www.w3.org/1999/xhtml">
  <head>
    <meta http-equiv="content-type" content="text/xml; charset=utf-8" />
    <title>search.html</title>
    <link rel = "stylesheet"
          type = "text/css"
          href = "search.css" />
  </head>

  <body>
    <h1>Search my contacts</h1>

    <form action = "search.php"
          method = "post">
      <fieldset>

        <label>Search for</label>
        <input type = "text"
               name = "srchVal" />
```

```
      <label>in</label>
      <select name = "srchField">
        <option value = "contactID">ID</option>
        <option value = "name">contact name</option>
        <option value = "company">company name</option>
        <option value = "email">email address</option>
      </select>

      <button type = "submit">submit request</button>
    </fieldset>

  </form>
 </body>
</html>
```

This is really a pretty basic form. The interesting stuff happens in the search.php program that's triggered when the user submits this form.

Responding to the search request

When the user submits search.html, a page like Figure 7-5 appears, created by search.php.

Figure 7-5:
The program searches the database according to the parameters in search.html.

The search.php program isn't really terribly different from contactTable.php. It takes an SQL query, sends it to a database, and returns the result as an XHTML table. The only new idea is how the SQL query is built. Rather than preloading the entire query into a string variable, as I did in all other examples in this chapter, I used input from the form to inform the query. As usual, I provide the code in its entirety here, and then I point out specific features. Look at the big picture first:

```
<!DOCTYPE html PUBLIC "-//W3C//DTD XHTML 1.0 Strict//EN"
"http://www.w3.org/TR/xhtml1/DTD/xhtml1-strict.dtd">
<html lang="EN" dir="ltr" xmlns="http://www.w3.org/1999/xhtml">
  <head>
    <meta http-equiv="content-type" content="text/xml; charset=utf-8" />
    <title>search.php</title>
    <style type = "text/css">
      table, th, td {
        border: 1px solid black;
      }
```

```
        </style>
    </head>

    <body>
        <h1>My Contacts</h1>
        <?php

$sql = processInput();
printResults($sql);

function processInput(){
    //extract information from previous form and build a safe query
    $srchVal = $_POST["srchVal"];
    $srchField = $_POST["srchField"];
    $srchVal = mysql_real_escape_string($srchVal);
    $srchField = mysql_real_escape_string($srchField);

    $sql = "SELECT * FROM contact WHERE $srchField LIKE '%$srchVal%'";
    return $sql;

} // end processInput

function printResults($sql){
    $conn = mysql_connect("localhost", "user", "password");
    mysql_select_db("xfd");

    $result = mysql_query($sql, $conn);

    print "  <table> \n";

    //get field names first
    print "      <tr> \n";
    while ($field = mysql_fetch_field($result)){
        print "         <th>$field->name</th> \n";
    } // end while
    print "      </tr> \n";

    while ($row = mysql_fetch_assoc($result)){
        print "      <tr> \n";
        foreach ($row as $name => $value){
            print "         <td>$value</td> \n";
        } // end foreach
        $count++;
        print "      </tr> \n";

    } // end while loop

    print "   </table> \n";
} // end printResults
?>
    </body>
</html>
```

Breaking the code into functions

This code is complex enough to deserve functions. The program has two
main jobs, so it's not surprising that a function is designated to perform
each major task. Here's the main section of the PHP code:

```
$sql = processInput();
printResults($sql);
```

This code fragment nicely summarizes the entire program (as well-designed main code ought to do). Here's the overview:

1. **Designate a variable called `$sql` to hold a query.**

   The central data for this program is the SQL query.

2. **Create the query with `processInput()`.**

   The job of `processInput()` is to get the data from the `search.html` form and create a safe, properly formatted query, which will be passed to the `$sql` variable.

3. **Process the query with the `printResults()` function.**

   This function will process the query and format the output as an XHTML table.

Processing the input

The `processInput()` function does just what it says — processes input:

```
function processInput(){
    //extract information from previous form and build a safe query
    $srchVal = $_POST["srchVal"];
    $srchField = $_POST["srchField"];

    $conn = mysql_connect("localhost", "user", "password");
    $srchVal = mysql_real_escape_string($srchVal, $conn);
    $srchField = mysql_real_escape_string($srchField, $conn);

    $sql = "SELECT * FROM contact WHERE $srchField LIKE '%$srchVal%'";
    return $sql;

} // end processInput
```

It works by doing several small but important tasks:

1. **Retrieve values from the form.**

   The key values for this program are `$srchVal` and `$srchField`. They both come from the previous form. Note that I use `$_POST` rather than `$_REQUEST`: post requests are mildly harder to hack than get, and I really don't want anybody spamming my database:

   ```
   $srchVal = $_POST["srchVal"];
   $srchField = $_POST["srchField"];
   ```

2. **Filter each field with `mysql_real_escape_string()`.**

   You never want to use input from a form without passing it through a security check. It's quite easy for a bad guy to post additional text in the query that could cause you a lot of headaches. This bit of nastiness is commonly called a *SQL injection attack.* Fortunately, PHP provides a very useful function for preventing this sort of malice. The `mysql_real_escape_string()` function processes a string and strips out any potentially dangerous characters, effectively minimizing the risks of SQL injection ickiness.

The second parameter of `mysql_real_escape_string()` is the name of the data connection, so I make a connection and pass it as a parameter:

```
$conn = mysql_connect("localhost", "xfd", "xfdaio");
$srchVal = mysql_real_escape_string($srchVal, $conn);
$srchField = mysql_real_escape_string($srchField, $conn);
```

For more on database security and preventing SQL injection attacks, a good place to start is this document in the PHP online manual:

```
http://us3.php.net/manual/en/security.database.sql-injection.php
```

3. **Embed the cleaned-up strings in the `$sql` variable.**

   Now, you can build the query comfortably. Note that a LIKE clause is more likely to provide the kinds of results your user is expecting. Also, don't forget that SQL often requires single quotes (see Book VI, Chapter 2 for more on building LIKE clauses):

   ```
   $sql = "SELECT * FROM contact WHERE $srchField LIKE '%$srchVal%'";
   ```

4. **Return the final `$sql` variable.**

   The query is now ready to be sent back to the main code segment, which will pass it on to the next function:

   ```
   return $sql;
   ```

Generating the output

Now that query is complete, the job of `printResults()` is quite easy. The following code is really just a copy of the `contactTable.php` code packaged into a function:

```
function printResults($sql){
  $conn = mysql_connect("localhost", "user", "password");
  mysql_select_db("xfd");

  $result = mysql_query($sql, $conn);

  print "  <table> \n";

  //get field names first
  print "      <tr> \n";
  while ($field = mysql_fetch_field($result)){
    print "          <th>$field->name</th> \n";
  } // end while
  print "      </tr> \n";

  while ($row = mysql_fetch_assoc($result)){
    print "      <tr> \n";
    foreach ($row as $name => $value){
      print "          <td>$value</td> \n";
    } // end foreach
    $count++;
    print "      </tr> \n";

  } // end while loop

  print "  </table> \n";
} // end printResults
```

There's only one twist here: SQL is now a parameter. This function won't create the $sql variable itself. Instead, it accepts $sql as a parameter. I took out the line that created $sql as a hard-coded query because now I want to implement the query created by processInput(). Otherwise, the code in this function is a direct copy of contactTable.php.

Book VI

Managing Data with MySQL

Well-defined data is the central element in most commercial Web sites.

Contents at a Glance

Chapter 1: Getting Started with Data

Most programs and Web sites are really about data. Data drives the Internet, so you really need to understand how data works and how to manage it well if you want to build high-powered, modern Web sites.

The trend in Web development is to have a bunch of specialized languages that work together. XHTML describes page content, CSS manages visual layout, JavaScript adds client-side interactivity, and PHP adds server-side capabilities. You're probably not surprised when I tell you that yet another language, SQL (Structured Query Language), specializes in working with data.

In this minibook, you discover how to manage data. Specifically, you find out how to create databases, add data, create queries to retrieve data, and create complex data models to solve real-world problems. In this chapter, I show you some tools that automate the process of creating a data structure and adding data to it. In later chapters in this minibook, I show how to control the process directly through SQL.

Examining the Basic Structure of Data

Data has been an important part of programming since computing began. Many languages have special features for working with data, but through the years, a few key ideas have evolved. A system called *relational data modeling* has become the primary method for data management, and a standard language for this model, called SQL (Structured Query Language), has been developed.

SQL has two major components:

+ *Data Definition Language* (DDL) is a subset of SQL that helps you create and maintain databases. You use DDL to build your databases and add data to them.

+ *Data Query Language* (DQL) is used to pull data out of a database after it's been placed there. Generally, your user input is converted to queries to get information from an existing database.

The easiest way to understand data is to simply look at some. The following table contains some basic contact information:

Name	Company	E-mail
Bill Gates	Microsoft	bill@msBob.com
Steve Jobs	Apple	steve@rememberNewton.com
Linus Torvalds	Linux Foundation	linus@gnuWho.org
Andy Harris	Wiley Press	andy@aharrisBooks.net

Note: All these e-mail addresses are completely made up (except mine). Bill Gates hasn't given me his actual e-mail address. He doesn't answer my calls, either. . . . (sniff).

It's very common to think of data in the form of tables. In fact, the fancy official database programmer name for this structure is *table*. A table (in database terms) is just a two-dimensional representation of data. Of course, some fancy computer-science words describe what's in a table:

+ **Each row is a *record*.** A record describes a discrete entity. In this table, each record is a person in an e-mail directory.

+ **A record is made of *fields*.** All the records in this table have three fields: name, company, and e-mail. Fields are a lot like variables in programming languages; they can have a type and a value. Sometimes, fields are also called *columns*.

+ **A collection of records is a *table*.** All records in a table have the same field definitions but can have different values in the fields.

✦ **A bunch of tables makes a *database*.** Real-world data doesn't usually fit well in one table. Often, you'll make several different tables that work together to describe complex information. The database is an aggregate of a bunch of tables. Normally, you restrict access to a database through a user and password system.

Determining the fields in a record

If you want to create a database, you need to think about what entity you're describing and what fields that entity contains. In the table in the preceding section, I'm describing e-mail contacts. Each contact requires three pieces of information:

✦ **Name:** Gives the name of the contact, in 50 characters or less

✦ **Company:** Describes which company the contact is associated with, in 30 characters or less

✦ **E-mail:** Lists the e-mail address of the contact, in 50 characters or less

Whenever you define a record, begin by thinking about what the table represents and then think of the details associated with that entity. The topic of the table (the kind of thing the table represents) is the record. The fields are the details of that record.

Before you send me e-mails about my horrible data design, know that I'm deliberately simplifying this first example. Sure, it should have separate fields for first and last name, and it should also have a primary key. I talk about these items later in this minibook, as well as in the section "Defining a primary key," later in this chapter. If you know about these items already, you probably don't need to read this section. For the rest of you, you should start with a simple data model, and I promise to add all those goodies soon.

Introducing SQL data types

Each record contains a number of fields, which are much like variables in ordinary languages. Unlike scripting languages, such as JavaScript and PHP (which tend to be freewheeling about data types), databases are particular about the type of data that goes in a record.

Table 1-1 illustrates several key data types in MySQL (the variant of SQL used in this book).

Table 1-1	MySQL Data Types	
Data Type	*Description*	*Notes*
INT (INTEGER)	Positive or negative integer (no decimal point)	Ranges from about −2 billion to 2 billion. Use BIGINT for larger integers.
DOUBLE	Double-precision floating point	Holds decimal numbers in scientific notation. Use for extremely large or extremely small values.
DATE	Date stored in YYYY-MM-DD format	Can be displayed in various formats.
TIME	Time stored in HH:MM:SS format	Can be displayed in various formats.
CHAR(*length*)	Fixed-length text	Always same length. Shorter text is padded with spaces. Longer text is truncated.
VARCHAR(*length*)	variable-length text	Still fixed length, but trailing spaces are trimmed. Limit 256 characters.
TEXT	Longer text	Up to 64,000 (roughly) characters. Use LONGTEXT for more space.
BLOB	Binary data	Up to 64K of binary data. LONGBLOB for more space.

I list only the most commonly used data types in Table 1-1. These data types handle most situations, but check the documentation of your database package if you need some other type of data.

Specifying the length of a record

Data types are especially important when you're defining a database. Relational databases have an important structural rule: Each record in a table must take up the same amount of memory. This rule seems arbitrary, but it's actually very useful.

Imagine that you're looking up somebody's name in a phone book, but you're required to go one entry at a time. If you're looking for Aaron Adams, things will be pretty good, but what if you're looking for Zebulon Zoom? This sequential search would be really slow because you'd have to go all the way through the phone book to find Zebulon. Even knowing that Zeb was in record number 5,379 wouldn't help much because you don't know exactly when one record ends and another begins.

If your name is really Zebulon Zoom, you have a very cool name — a good sign in the open-source world, where names like Linus and Guido are really popular. I figure the only reason I'm not famous is my name is too boring. I'm thinking about switching to a dolphin name or something. (Hi, my name is "Andy Squeeeeeeek! Click Click Harris.")

Relational databases solve this problem by forcing each record to be the same length. Just for the sake of argument, imagine that every record takes exactly 100 bytes. You would then be able to figure out where each record is on the disk by multiplying the length of each record by the desired record's index. (Record 0 would be at byte 0, record 1 is at 100, record 342 is at 34200, and so on.) This mechanism allows the computer to keep track of where all the records are and jump immediately to a specific record, even if hundreds or thousands of records are in the system.

**Book VI
Chapter 1**

**Getting Started
with Data**

My description here is actually a major simplification of what's going on, but the foundation is correct. You should really investigate more sophisticated database and data structures classes or books if you want more information. It's pretty cool stuff.

The length of the record is important because the data types of a record's fields determine its size. *Numeric data* (integers and floating-point values) have a fixed size in the computer's memory. Strings (as used in other programming languages) typically have *dynamic length*. That is, the amount of memory used depends on the length of the text. In a database application, you rarely have dynamic length text. Instead, you generally determine the number of characters for each text field.

Defining a primary key

When you turn the contact data into an actual database, you generally add one more important field. Each table should have one field that acts as a *primary key*. A primary key is a special field that's

+ **Unique:** You can't have two records in a table with the same primary key.

+ **Guaranteed:** Every record in the table has a value in the primary key.

Primary key fields are often (though not always) integers because you can easily build a system for generating a new unique value. (Find the largest key in the current database and add one.)

In this book, each table has a primary key. They are usually numeric and are usually the first field in a record definition. I also end each key field with the letters ID to help me remember it's a primary key.

Primary keys are useful because they allow the database system to keep a Table of Contents for quick access to the table. When you build multitable data structures, you can see how you can use keys to link tables together.

Defining the table structure

When you want to build a table, you begin with a definition of the *structure* of the table. What are the field names? What is each field's type? If it's text, how many characters will you specify?

The definition for the e-mail contacts table may look like this:

Field Name	Type	Length (Bytes)
ContactID	INTEGER	11
Name	VARCHAR	50
Company	VARCHAR	30
E-mail	VARCHAR	50

Look over the table definition, and you'll notice some important ideas:

✦ **There's now a contactID field.** This field serves as the primary key. It's an INTEGER field.

✦ **INTEGERs are automatically assigned a length.** It isn't necessary to specify the size of an INTEGER field (as all INTEGERs are exactly 11 bytes long in MySQL).

✦ **The text fields are all VARCHARs.** This particular table consists of a lot of text. The text fields are all stored as VARCHAR types.

✦ **Each VARCHAR has a specified length.** Figuring out the best length can be something of an art form. If you make the field too short, you aren't able to squeeze in all the data you want. If you make it too long, you waste space.

VARCHAR isn't quite variable length. The length is fixed, but extra spaces are added. Imagine that I had a VARCHAR(10) field called `userName`. If I enter the name 'Andy', the field contains 'Andy   ' (that is, 'Andy' followed by six spaces). If I enter the value 'Rumplestiltskin', the field contains the value `"Rumplestil"` (the first 10 characters of 'Rumplestiltskin').

The difference between CHAR and VARCHAR is what happens to shorter words. When you return the value of a CHAR field, all the padding spaces are included. A VARCHAR automatically lops off any trailing spaces.

In practice, programmers rarely use CHAR because VARCHAR provides the behavior you almost always want.

Introducing MySQL

Programs that work with SQL are usually called relational database management systems (RDBMS). A number of popular RDBMSs are available:

Book VI
Chapter 1

Getting Started
with Data

+ **Oracle** is the big player. Many high-end commercial applications use the advanced features of Oracle. It's powerful, but the price tag makes it primarily useful for large organizations.

+ **MS SQL Server** is Microsoft's entry in the high-end database market. It's usually featured in Microsoft-based systems integrated with .NET programming languages and the Microsoft IIS server. It can also be quite expensive.

+ **MS Access** is the entry-level database system installed with most versions of Microsoft Office. While Access is a good tool for playing with data design, it has some well-documented problems handling the large number of requests typical of a Web-based data tool.

+ **MySQL** is an open-source database that has made a big splash in the open-source world. While it's not quite as robust as Oracle or SQL Server, it's getting closer all the time. The latest version has features and capabilities that once belonged only to expensive proprietary systems.

+ **SQLite** is another open-source database that's really showing some promise. This program is very small and fast, so it works well in places you wouldn't expect to see a full-fledged database (think cellphones and PDAs).

The great news is that almost all of these databases work in the same general way. They all read fairly similar dialects of the SQL language. No matter which database you choose, the basic operation is roughly the same.

Why use MySQL?

This book focuses on MySQL because this program is

+ **Very accessible:** If you've already installed XAMPP (see Book VIII), you already have access to MySQL. Many hosting accounts also have MySQL access built in.

+ **Easy to use:** You can use MySQL from the command line or from a special program. Most people manipulate SQL through a program called phpMyAdmin (introduced in the section "Setting Up phpMyAdmin," later in this chapter). This program provides a graphical interface to do most of the critical tasks.

✦ **Reasonably typical:** MySQL supports all the basic SQL features and a few enhancements. If you understand MySQL, you'll be able to switch to another RDBMS pretty easily.

✦ **Very powerful:** MySQL is powerful enough to handle typical Web server data processing for a small to mid-size company. Some extremely large corporations even use it.

✦ **Integrated with XAMPP and PHP:** PHP has built-in support for MySQL, so you can easily write PHP programs that work with MySQL databases.

✦ **Free and open source**: MySQL is available at no cost, which makes it quite an attractive alternative. MySQL offers other advantages of open-source software. Because the code is freely available, you can learn exactly how it works. The open-source nature of the tool also means there are likely to be add-ons or variations, because it's easy for developers to modify open-source tools.

Understanding the three-tier architecture

Modern Web programming often uses what's called the *three-tiered architecture,* as shown in Table 1-2.

Table 1-2	The Three-Tiered Architecture		
Tier	*Platform (software)*	*Content*	*Language*
Client	Web browser (Firefox)	Web page	XHTML/CSS/JS
Server	Web server (Apache)	Business rules and logic	PHP (or other similar language)
Data	Data server (MySQL)	Data content	SQL (through MySQL or another data server)

The user talks to the system through a Web browser, which manages XHTML code. CSS and JavaScript may also be at the user tier, but everything is handled through the browser. The user then makes a request of the server, which is sometimes passed through a server-side language like PHP. This program then receives a request and processes it, returning HTML back to the client. Many requests involve data, which brings the third (data) tier into play. The Web server can package up a request to the data server through SQL. The data server manages the data and prepares a response to the Web server, which then makes HTML output back for the user.

Figure 1-1 provides an overview of the three-tier system.

Client
(browser)

HTML results

HTML Form

PHP program

Server

SQL results

PHP program

SQL Code

Database

Figure 1-1:
An overview
of the three-
tier data
modol.

Practicing with MySQL

MySQL is a server, so it must be installed on a computer in order to work. To
practice with MySQL, you have a few options:

✦ **Run your own copy of MySQL from the command line.** If you have
MySQL installed on your own machine, you can go to the command
line and execute the program directly. This task isn't difficult, but it is
tedious.

✦ **Use phpMyAdmin to interact with your own copy of MySQL.** This solution is often the best. phpMyAdmin is a set of PHP programs that allows
you to access and manipulate your database through your Web browser.
If you've set up XAMPP, you've got everything you need. (See Book VIII
for more information about XAMPP.) You can also install MySQL and
phpMyAdmin without XAMPP, but you should really avoid the headaches of manual configuration, if you can. In this chapter, I do all MySQL
through phpMyAdmin, but I show other alternatives in Book V
(where you can connect to MySQL through PHP) and Chapter 2 of this
minibook.

✦ **Run MySQL from your hosting site.** If you're using Freehostia or some
other hosting service, you generally access MySQL through phpMyAdmin.

Setting Up phpMyAdmin

By far the most common way to interact with MySQL is through phpMyAdmin. If you've installed XAMPP, you already have phpMyAdmin. Here's how you use it to get to MySQL:

1. **Turn on MySQL with the XAMPP Control Panel, shown in Figure 1-2.**

You also need Apache running (because XAMPP runs through the server). You don't need to run MySQL or Apache as a service, but you must have them both running.

Figure 1-2:
I've turned on Apache and MySQL in the XAMPP control panel using the buttons.

2. **Go to the XAMPP main directory in your browser.**

If you used the default installation, you can just point your browser to `http://localhost/xampp`. It should look like Figure 1-3.

Don't just go through the regular file system to find the XAMPP directory. You must use the `localhost` mechanism so that the PHP code in phpMyAdmin is activated.

3. **Find phpMyAdmin in the Tools section of the menu.**

The phpMyAdmin page looks like Figure 1-4.

4. **Create a new database.**

Type the name for your database in the indicated text field. I call my database `xfd`. (*Xhtml For Dummies* — get it?)

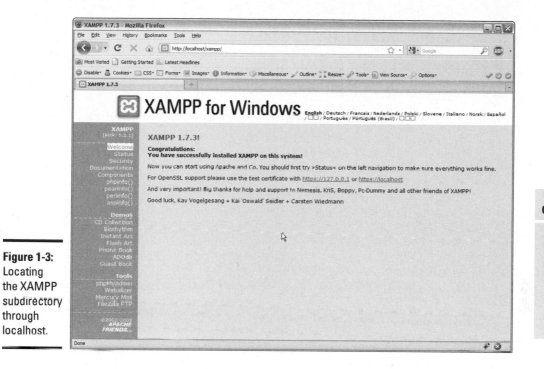

Figure 1-3:
Locating
the XAMPP
subdirectory
through
localhost.

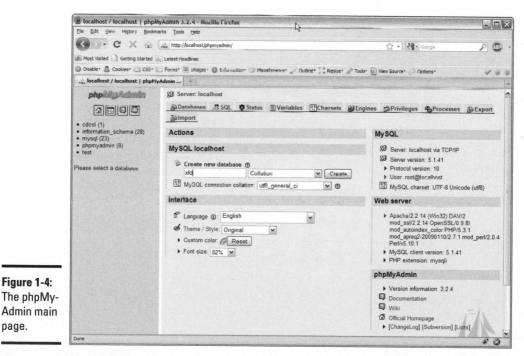

Figure 1-4:
The phpMy-
Admin main
page.

Changing the root password

MySQL is a powerful system, which means it can cause a lot of damage in the wrong hands. Unfortunately, the default installation of MySQL has a security loophole you could drive an aircraft carrier through. The default user is called root and has no password whatsoever. Although you don't have to worry about any pesky passwords, the KGB can also get to your data without passwords.

This section is a bit technical, and it's pretty important if you're running your own data server with XAMPP. But if you're using an online service like Freehostia, you won't have to worry about the data security problems described in this section. You can skip on to the section called "Using php-MyAdmin on a remote server." Still, you'll eventually need this stuff, so don't tear these pages out of the book or anything.

Believe me, the bad guys know that root is the most powerful account on MySQL and that it has no password by default. They're glad to use that information to do you harm (or worse, to do harm in your name). Obviously, giving the root account a password is a very good idea. Fortunately, it's not difficult to do:

1. **Log into phpMyAdmin as normal.**

The main screen looks like Figure 1-5. Note the scary warning of gloom at the bottom. You're about to fix that problem.

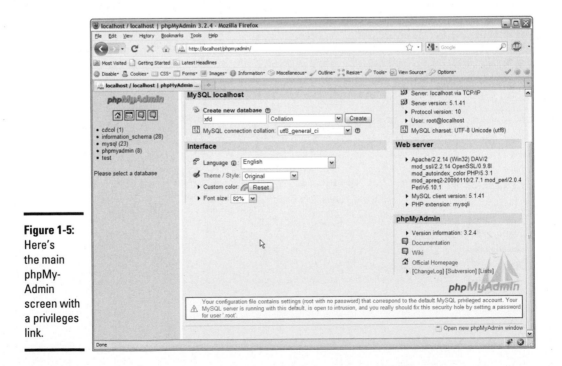

Figure 1-5: Here's the main phpMy-Admin screen with a privileges link.

2. Click the Privileges link to modify user privileges.

The new screen looks something like Figure 1-6.

3. Edit the root user.

Chances are good that you have only one user, called root (and maybe another called pma which is the phpMyAdmin user). The root account's `Password` field says No. You'll be adding a password to the root user. The icon at the right allows you to edit this record. (Hover your mouse over the small icon to see ToolTips if you can't find it.) The edit screen looks like Figure 1-7.

4. Examine the awesome power of the root administrator.

Even if you don't know what all these things are, root can clearly do lots of things, and you shouldn't let this power go unchecked. (Consult any James Bond movie for more information on what happens with unfettered power.) You're still going to let root do all these things, but you're going to set a password so that only you can be root on this system. Scroll down a bit on the page until you see the segment that looks like Figure 1-8.

Book VI Chapter 1

Getting Started with Data

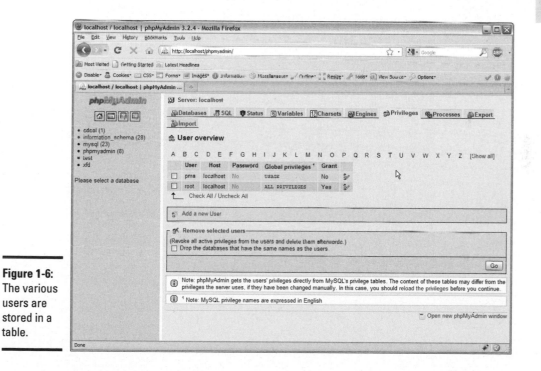

Figure 1-6: The various users are stored in a table.

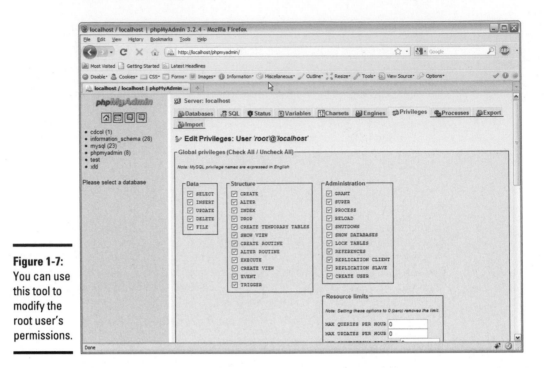

Figure 1-7:
You can use
this tool to
modify the
root user's
permissions.

Figure 1-8:
This area
is where
you add the
password.

5. **Assign a password.**

   Simply enter the password in the Password box, and then reenter it in the next box. Be sure that you type the same password twice. Follow all your typical password rules (six or more characters long, no spaces, case-sensitive).

6. **Hit the Go button.**

   If all went well, the password changes.

7. **Recoil in horror.**

   Try to go back to the phpMyAdmin home (with the little house icon), and something awful happens, as shown in Figure 1-9.

Don't panic about the error in Figure 1-9. Believe it or not, this error is good. Up to now, phpMyAdmin was logging into your database as root without a password (just like the baddies were going to do). Now, phpMyAdmin is trying to do the same thing (log in as root without a password), but it can't because now root has a password.

What you have to do is tell phpMyAdmin that you just locked the door, and give it the key. (Well, the password, but I was enjoying my metaphor.)

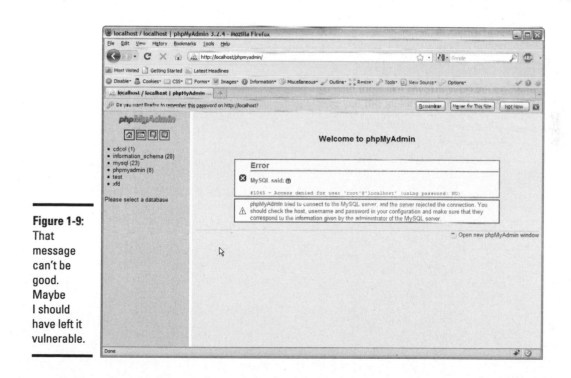

Figure 1-9:
That message can't be good. Maybe I should have left it vulnerable.

1. Find the phpMyAdmin configuration file.

You have to let phpMyAdmin know that you've changed the password. Look for a file in your phpMyAdmin directory called `config.inc.php`. (If you used the default XAMPP installation under Windows, the file is in `C:\Program Files\xampp\phpMyAdmin\config.inc.php`.)

2. Find the root password setting.

Using the text editor's search function, I found it on line 70, but it may be someplace else in your editor. In Notepad++, it looks like Figure 1-10.

3. Change the root setting to reflect your password.

Enter your root password. For example, if your new password is myPassword, change the line so that it looks like

```
$cfg['Servers'][$i]['password']        = 'myPassword';     // MySQL password
```

Of course, myPassword is just an example. It's really a bad password. Put your actual password in its place.

4. Save the `config.inc.php` file.

Save the configuration file and return to phpMyAdmin. You may need to set the file's permissions to 644 if you're on a Mac or Linux machine.

Figure 1-10:
Here's the username and configuration information.

```
10    */
11    $i = 0;
12
13    /*
14     * First server
15     */
16    $i++;
17
18    /* Authentication type and info */
19    $cfg['Servers'][$i]['auth_type']      = 'config';
20    $cfg['Servers'][$i]['user']           = 'root';
21    $cfg['Servers'][$i]['password']       = 'myPassword';  //I changed this line
22    $cfg['Servers'][$i]['AllowNoPassword'] = true;
23
24    /* Server parameters */
25    $cfg['Servers'][$i]['host']           = 'localhost';
26    $cfg['Servers'][$i]['connect_type']   = 'tcp';
27    $cfg['Servers'][$i]['compress']       = false;
28
29    /* Select mysqli if your server has it */
30    $cfg['Servers'][$i]['extension'] = 'mysqli';
31
32    /* User for advanced features */
33    $cfg['Servers'][$i]['controluser'] = 'pma';
34    $cfg['Servers'][$i]['controlpass'] = '';
35
36    /* Advanced phpMyAdmin features */
37    $cfg['Servers'][$i]['pmadb']          = 'phpmyadmin';
38    $cfg['Servers'][$i]['bookmarktable']  = 'pma_bookmark';
39    $cfg['Servers'][$i]['relation']       = 'pma_relation';
40    $cfg['Servers'][$i]['table_info']     = 'pma_table_info';
41    $cfg['Servers'][$i]['table_coords']   = 'pma_table_coords';
42    $cfg['Servers'][$i]['pdf_pages']      = 'pma_pdf_pages';
43    $cfg['Servers'][$i]['column_info']    = 'pma_column_info';
44    $cfg['Servers'][$i]['history']        = 'pma_history';
```

5. **Try getting into phpMyAdmin again.**

   This time, you don't get the error, and nobody is able to get into your database without your password. You shouldn't have to worry about this issue again, but whenever you connect to this database, you do need to supply the username and password.

Adding a user

Changing the root password is the absolute minimum security measure, but it's not the only one. You can add various virtual users to your system to protect it further.

You're able to log into your own copy of MySQL (and phpMyAdmin) as root because you're the root owner. (If not, then refer to the preceding section.) It's your database, so you should be allowed to do anything with it.

You probably don't want your programs logging in as root because that can allow malicious code to sneak into your system and do mischief. You're better off setting up a different user for each database and allowing that user access only to the tables within that database.

I'm really not kidding about the danger here. A user with root access can get into your database and do anything, including creating more users or changing the root password so that you can no longer get into your own database! You generally shouldn't write any PHP programs that use root. Instead, have a special user for that database. If the bad guys get in as anything but root, they can't blow up everything.

Fortunately, creating new users with phpMyAdmin isn't a difficult procedure:

1. **Log into phpMyAdmin with root access.**

   If you're running XAMPP on your own server, you'll automatically log in as root.

2. **Activate the Privileges tab to view user privileges.**

3. **Add a new user using the Add a New User link on the Privileges page.**

4. **Fill in user information on the new user page (see Figure 1-11).**

   Be sure to add a username and password. Typically, you use `local host` as the host.

5. Create a database, if it doesn't already exist.

If you haven't already made a database for this project, you can do so automatically with the Create Table Automatically radio button.

6. Do not assign global privileges.

Only the root user should have global privileges. You want this user to have the ability to work only within a specific database.

7. Create the user by clicking the Go button.

You see a new screen like Figure 1-12 (you need to scroll down a bit to see this part of the page).

8. Specify the user's database.

Select the database in the drop-down list. This user (xfd) will have access only to tables in the xfd database. Note that you probably don't have many databases on your system when you start out.

9. Apply most privileges.

You generally want your programs to do nearly everything within their own database so that you can apply almost all privileges (for now, anyway). I typically select all privileges except Grant, which lets the user allow access to other users. Figure 1-13 shows the Privileges page.

Figure 1-11: Here's the new xfd user being created.

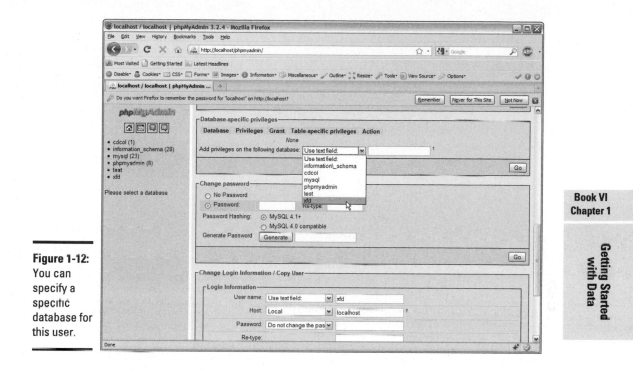

Book VI
Chapter 1

Getting Started
with Data

Figure 1-12:
You can
specify a
specific
database for
this user.

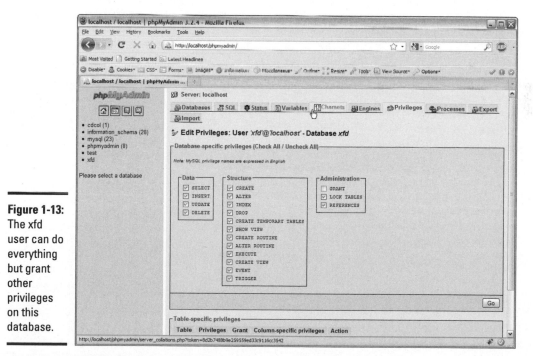

Figure 1-13:
The xfd
user can do
everything
but grant
other
privileges
on this
database.

As you're starting out, your programs have access to one database and are able to do plenty with it. As your data gets more critical, you'll probably want to create more restrictive user accounts so that those programs that should only be reading your data don't have the ability to modify or delete records. This change makes it more difficult for the bad guys to mess up your day.

Your database users won't usually be people. This idea is hard, particularly if you haven't used PHP or another server-side language yet. The database users are usually programs you have written that access the database in your name.

Using phpMyAdmin on a remote server

If you're working on some remote system with your service provider, the mechanism for managing and creating your databases may be a bit different. Each host has its own quirks, but they're all pretty similar. As an example, here's how I connect to the system on Freehostia at `http://freehostia.com` (where I post the example pages for this book):

1. **Log onto your service provider using the server login.**

You usually see some sort of control panel with the various tools you have as an administrator. These tools often look like Figure 1-14.

Figure 1-14:
The Free Hostia site shows a number of useful adminis-tration tools.

2. **Locate your database settings.**

Not all free hosting services provide database access, but some (like Free Hostia — at least, as of this writing) do have free MySQL access. You usually can access some sort of tool for managing your databases. (You'll probably have a limited number of databases available on free servers, but more with commercial accounts.) Figure 1-15 shows the database administration tool in Free Hostia.

3. **Create a database according to the rules enforced by your system.**

Sometimes, you can create the database within phpMyAdmin (as I did in the last section), but more often, you need to use a special tool like the one shown in Figure 1-15 to create your databases. Free Hostia imposes a couple of limits: The database name begins with the system username, and it can't be more than 16 characters long.

**Book VI
Chapter 1**

**Getting Started
with Data**

Don't freak out if your screen looks a little different than Figure 1-15. Different hosting companies have slightly different rules and systems, so things won't be just like this, but they'll probably be similar. If you get stuck, be sure to look at the hosting service's Help system. You can also contact the support system. They're usually glad to help, but they're (understandably) much more helpful if you've paid for the hosting service. Even the free hosting systems offer some online support, but if you're going to be serious, paying for online support is a good deal.

Figure 1-15:
The database administration tool lets me create or edit databases.

4. **Create a password for this database.**

You probably need a password (and sometimes another username) for your databases to prevent unauthorized access to your data. Because the database is a different server than the Web server, it has its own security system. On Free Hostia, I must enter a password, and the system automatically creates a MySQL username with the same name as the database. Keep track of this information because you need it later when you write a program to work with this data.

5. **Use phpMyAdmin to add tables to your database.**

Once you've defined the database, you can usually use phpMyAdmin to manipulate the data. With Free Hostia, you can simply click a database name to log into phpMyAdmin as the administrator of that database. Figure 1-16 shows the new database in phpMyAdmin, ready for action.

Typically, a remote server doesn't give you root access, so you don't have to mess around with the whole root password mess described in the "Changing the root password" section of this chapter. Instead, you often either have one password you always use in phpMyAdmin or you have a different user and password for each database.

Figure 1-16:
Now I can access the database in phpMy-Admin.

Making a Database with phpMyAdmin

When you've got a database, you can build a table. When you've defined a table, you can add data. When you've got data, you can look at it. Begin by building a table to handle the contact data described in the first section of this chapter, "Examining the Basic Structure of Data":

1. Be sure you're logged into phpMyAdmin.

The phpMyAdmin page should look something like Figure 1-17, with your database name available in the left column.

2. Activate the database by clicking the database name in the left column.

If the database is empty, an Add Table page, shown in Figure 1-18, appears.

3. Create a new table using the phpMyAdmin tool.

Now that you have a database, add the contacts table to it. The contacts database has four fields, so type a 4 into the box and let 'er rip. A form like Figure 1-19 appears.

4. Enter the field information.

Type the field names into the grid to create the table. It should look like Figure 1-20.

Book VI
Chapter 1

Getting Started
with Data

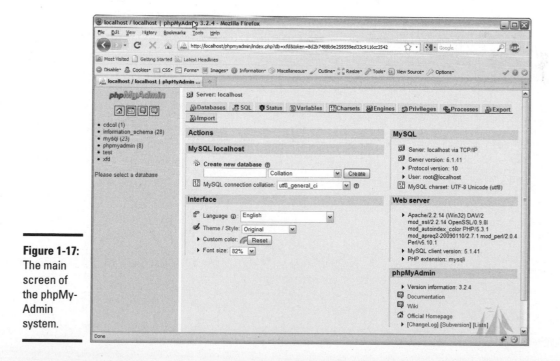

Figure 1-17:
The main screen of the phpMy-Admin system.

Figure 1-18:
Type a
table name
to begin
adding a
table.

Figure 1-19:
Creating the
contacts
table.

In Figure 1-20, you can't see it, but you can select the index of contactID as a primary key. Be sure to add this indicator. Also set the collation of the entire table to `ascii_general_ci`.

5. **Click the Save button and watch the results.**

   phpMyAdmin automatically writes some SQL code for you and executes it. Figure 1-21 shows the code and the new table.

   Now, the left panel indicates that you're in the `xfd` database, which has a table called Contact.

After you define a table, you can add data. Click Contact in the left column, and you see the screen for managing the contact table, as shown in Figure 1-22.

You can add data with the Insert tab, which gives a form like Figure 1-23, based on your table design.

After you add the record, choose Insert Another Row and click the Go button. Repeat until you've added all the contacts you want in your database.

After you add all the records you want to the database, you can use the Browse tab to see all the data in the table. Figure 1-24 shows my table after I added all my contacts to it and browsed.

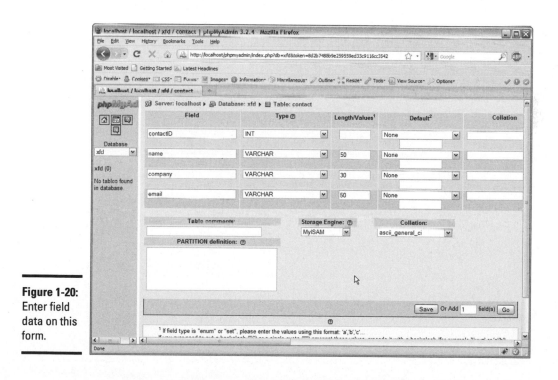

Figure 1-20:
Enter field
data on this
form.

Figure 1-21:
phpMy-
Admin
created this
mysterious
code and
built a table.

Figure 1-22:
I've added
the fields.

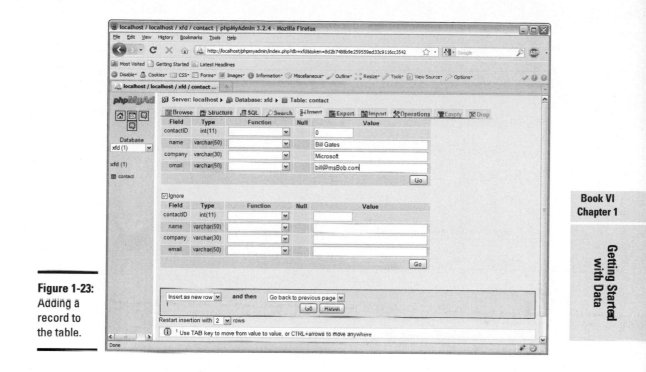

Figure 1-23:
Adding a
record to
the table.

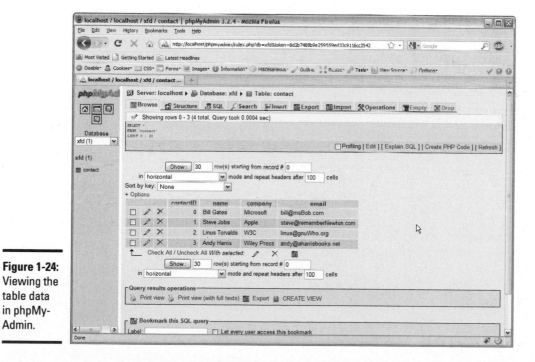

Figure 1-24:
Viewing the
table data
in phpMy-
Admin.

Chapter 2: Managing Data with SQL

In This Chapter

✓ **Working with SQL script files**

✓ **Using** `AUTO_INCREMENT` **to build primary key values**

✓ **Selecting a subset of fields**

✓ **Displaying a subset of records**

✓ **Modifying your data**

✓ **Deleting records**

✓ **Exporting your data**

*A*lthough we tend to think of the Internet as a series of interconnected documents, the Web is increasingly about data. The HTML and XHTML languages are still used to manage Web documents, but the SQL (Structured Query Language) — the language of data — is becoming increasingly central. In this chapter, you discover how SQL is used to define a data structure, add data to a database, and modify that data.

Writing SQL Code by Hand

Although you can use phpMyAdmin to build databases, all it really does is write and execute SQL code for you. You should know how to write SQL code yourself for many reasons:

✦ **It's pretty easy.** SQL isn't terribly difficult (at least, to begin with — things do get involved later).Writing the code in SQL is probably easier for you to write than to creating the code in phpMyAdmin.

✦ **You need to write code in your programs.** You probably run your database from within PHP programs. You need to be able to write SQL commands from within your PHP code, and phpMyAdmin doesn't help much with that job.

✦ **You can't trust computers.** You should understand any code that has your name on it, even if you use a tool like phpMyAdmin to write the code. If your program breaks, you have to fix it eventually, so you really should know how it works.

✦ **SQL scripts are portable.** Moving an entire data structure to a new server is difficult, but if you have a script that creates and populates the database, that script is just an ASCII file. You can easily move a complete database (including the data) to a new machine.

✦ **SQL scripts allow you to quickly rebuild a corrupted database.** As you're testing your system, you'll commonly make mistakes that can harm your data structure. It's very nice to have a script that you can use to quickly reset your data to some standard test state.

Understanding SQL syntax rules

SQL is a language (like XHTML, JavaScript, CSS, and PHP), so it has its own syntax rules. The rules and traditions of SQL are a bit unique because this language has a different purpose than more traditional programming languages:

✦ **Keywords are in uppercase.** Officially, SQL is not case-sensitive, but the tradition is to make all reserved words in uppercase and the names of all your custom elements camel-case (described in Book V, Chapter 6). Some variations of SQL are case-sensitive, so you're safest assuming that they all are.

✦ **One statement can take up more than one line in the editor.** SQL statements aren't usually difficult, but they can get long. Having one statement take up many lines in the editor is common.

✦ **Logical lines end with semicolons.** Like PHP and JavaScript, each statement in SQL ends with a semicolon.

✦ **White space is ignored.** DBMS systems don't pay attention to spaces and carriage returns, so you can (and should) use these tools to help you clarify your code meaning.

✦ **Single quotes are used for text values.** MySQL generally uses single quotes to denote text values, rather than the double quotes used in other languages. If you really want to enclose a single quote in your text, backslash it.

Examining the buildContact.sql script

Take a look at the following code:

```
-- buildContact.sql

DROP TABLE IF EXISTS contact;

CREATE TABLE contact (
  contactID int PRIMARY KEY,
  name VARCHAR(50),
  company VARCHAR(30),
  email VARCHAR(50)
);
```

```
INSERT INTO contact VALUES
   (0, 'Bill Gates', 'Microsoft', 'bill@msBob.com');
INSERT INTO contact VALUES
   (1, 'Steve Jobs', 'Apple', 'steve@rememberNewton.com');
INSERT INTO contact VALUES
   (2, 'Linus Torvalds', 'Linux Foundation', 'linus@gnuWho.org');
INSERT INTO contact VALUES
   (3, 'Andy Harris', 'Wiley Press', 'andy@aharrisBooks.net');

SELECT * FROM contact;
```

This powerful code is written in SQL. I explain each segment in more detail throughout the section, but here's an overview:

1. **Delete the contact table, if it already exists.**

   This script completely rebuilds the contact table, so if it already exists, it is temporarily deleted to avoid duplication.

2. **Create a new table named** contact.

   As you can see, the table creation syntax is spare but pretty straightforward. Each field name is followed by its type and length (at least, in the case of VARCHARs).

3. **Add values to the table by using the** INSERT **command.**

   Use a new INSERT statement for each record.

4. **View the table data using the** SELECT **command.**

   This command displays the content of the table.

Dropping a table

It may seem odd to begin creating a table by deleting it, but there's actually a good reason. As you experiment with a data structure, you'll often find yourself building and rebuilding the tables.

The line

```
DROP TABLE IF EXISTS contact
```

means, "Look at the current database and see whether the table contact appears in it. If so, delete it." This syntax ensures that you start over fresh as you are rebuilding the table in the succeeding lines. Typical SQL scripts begin by deleting any tables that will be overwritten to avoid confusion.

Creating a table

You create a table with the (aptly named) CREATE TABLE command. The specific table creation statement for the contact table looks like the following:

```
CREATE TABLE contact (
```

```
    contactID int PRIMARY KEY,
    name VARCHAR(50),
    company VARCHAR(30),
    email VARCHAR(50)
);
```

Creating a table involves several smaller tasks:

1. **Specify the table name.**

   The CREATE TABLE statement requires a table name. Specify the table name. Table names (like variables and filenames) should generally not contain spaces or punctuation without good reason.

2. **Begin the field definition with a parenthesis.**

   The left parenthesis indicates the beginning of the field list. You traditionally list one field per line, indented as in regular code, although that format isn't required.

3. **Begin each field with its name.**

   Every field has a name and a type. Begin with the field name, which should also be one word.

4. **Indicate the field type.**

   The field type immediately follows the field name (with no punctuation).

5. **Indicate field length, if necessary.**

   If the field is a VARCHAR or CHAR field, specify its length within parentheses. You can specify the length of numeric types, but I don't recommend it because MySQL automatically determines the length of numeric fields.

6. **Add special modifiers.**

   Some fields have special modifiers. For now, note that the primary key is indicated on the contactID field.

7. **End the field definition with a comma.**

   The comma character indicates the end of a field definition.

8. **End the table definition with a closing parenthesis and a semicolon.**

   Close the parenthesis that started the table definition and end the entire statement with a semicolon.

Adding records to the table

You add data to the table with the INSERT command. The way this command works isn't too surprising:

```
INSERT INTO contact VALUES
    (0, 'Bill Gates', 'Microsoft', 'bill@msBob.com');
```

Follow these steps:

1. **Begin with the** `INSERT` **keyword.**

   Use `INSERT` to clarify that this instruction is a data insertion command.

2. **Specify the table you want to add data to.**

   In my example, I have only one table, so use `INTO contact` to specify that's where the table goes.

3. **(Optional) Specify field names.**

   You can specify a list of field names, but this step is unnecessary if you add data to all fields in their standard order. (Normally, you don't bother with field names.)

4. **Use the** `VALUES` **keyword to indicate that a list of field values is coming.**

5. **Enclose the values within parentheses.**

   Use parentheses to enclose the list of data values.

6. **Put all values in the right order.**

   Place values in exactly the same order the fields were designated.

7. **Place text values within single quotes.**

   MySQL uses single quotes to specify text values.

8. **End the statement with a semicolon, as you do with all SQL commands.**

9. **Repeat with other data.**

   Add as many `INSERT` commands as you want to populate the data table.

Viewing the sample data

Once you've created and populated a table, you'll want to look it over. SQL provides the `SELECT` command for this purpose. `SELECT` is amazingly powerful, but its basic form is simplicity itself:

```
SELECT * FROM contact;
```

This command simply returns all fields of all records from your database.

Running a Script with phpMyAdmin

phpMyAdmin provides terrific features for working with SQL scripts. You can write your script directly in phpMyAdmin, or you can use any text editor.

Aptana Studio is fine for editing SQL files, but it doesn't have built-in SQL support, such as syntax checking and coloring. You can download a plugin to add these features (search for eclipse SQL plugins); use another editor like Notepad++ or Komodo Edit, which both support syntax coloring for SQL; or just do without syntax coloring in Aptana.

If you've written a script in some other editor, you'll need to save it as a text file and import it into phpMyAdmin.

To run a script in phpMyAdmin, follow these steps:

1. **Connect to phpMyAdmin.**

   Be sure that you're logged in and connected to the system.

2. **Navigate to the correct database.**

   Typically, you use a drop-down list to the left of the main screen to pick the database. (If you haven't created a database, see the instructions in Chapter 1 of this minibook.) Figure 2-1 shows the main phpMyAdmin screen with the xfd database enabled.

3. **Activate the SQL pop-up window.**

   You can do so by clicking the small SQL icon in the left-hand navigation menu. The resulting window looks like Figure 2-2.

Figure 2-1:
The xfd database is created and ready to go.

![Screenshot of phpMyAdmin 3.2.4 in Mozilla Firefox showing the localhost/localhost/xfd database with the contact table listed under the Structure tab.]

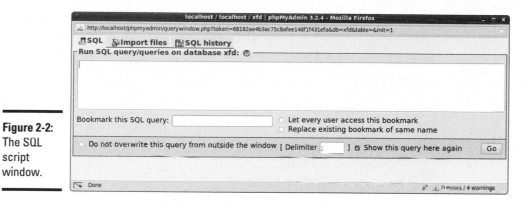

**Book VI
Chapter 2**

**Managing Data
with SQL**

Figure 2-2:
The SQL
script
window.

4. (Optional) Type your SQL code directly into this dialog box.

This shortcut is good for making quick queries about your data, but generally you create and initialize data with prewritten scripts.

5. Move to the Import Files tab.

In this tab, you can upload the file directly into the MySQL server. Figure 2-3 shows the resulting page. Use the Browse button to locate your file and the Go button to load it into MySQL.

If you've already created the contact database by following the instructions in Chapter 1 of this minibook, you may be nervous that you'll overwrite the data. You will, but for this stage in the process, that's exactly what you want. The point of a script is to help you build a database and rebuild it quickly. After you have meaningful data in the table, you won't be rebuilding it so often, but during the test and creation stage, this skill is critical.

6. Examine your handiwork.

Look back at the phpMyAdmin page, and you see something like Figure 2-4. It shows your script and, if you ended with a SELECT statement, an output of your table. (Later versions of phpMyAdmin display only the last statement in the script, but all are executed.)

Figure 2-3:
Importing an
externally
defined SQL
script.

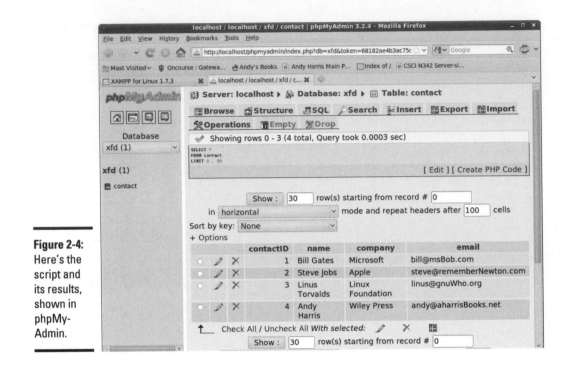

Figure 2-4:
Here's the
script and
its results,
shown in
phpMy-
Admin.

Using AUTO_INCREMENT for Primary Keys

Primary keys are important because you use them as a standard index for the table. The job of a primary key is to uniquely identify each record in the table. Remember that a primary key has a few important characteristics:

✦ **It must exist.** Every record must have a primary key.

✦ **It must be unique.** Two records in the same table can't have the same key.

✦ **It must not be null.** There must be a value in each key.

When you initially create a table, you have all the values in front of you, but what if you want to add a field later? Somehow, you have to ensure that the primary key in every record is unique.

Over the years, database developers have discovered that integer values are especially handy as primary keys. The great thing about integers is that you can always find a unique one. Just look for the largest index in your table and add one.

Fortunately, MySQL (like most database packages) has a wonderful feature for automatically generating unique integer indices.

Latin-Swedish?

phpMyAdmin is a wonderful tool, but it does have one strange quirk. When you look over your table design, you may find that the `collation` is set to `latin1_swedish_ci`. This syntax refers to the native character set used by the internal data structure. Nothing is terribly harmful about this set (Swedish is a wonderful language), but I don't want to incorrectly imply that my database is written in Swedish.

Fortunately, it's an easy fix. In phpMyAdmin, go to the Operations tab and look for Table Options. You can then set your collation to whatever you want. I typically use `latin1_general_ci` as it works fine for American English, which is the language used in most of my data sets. (See the MySQL documentation about internationalization if you're working in a language that needs the collation feature.)

I've only run into this problem with phpMyAdmin. If you create your database directly from the MySQL interpreter or from within PHP programs, the collation issue doesn't seem to be a problem.

Take a look at this variation of the `buildContact.sql` script:

```
-- buildContactAutoIncrement.sql

DROP TABLE IF EXISTS contact;

CREATE TABLE contact (
  contactID int PRIMARY KEY AUTO_INCREMENT,
  name VARCHAR(50),
  company VARCHAR(30),
  email VARCHAR(50)
);

INSERT INTO contact VALUES
  (null, 'Bill Gates', 'Microsoft', 'bill@msBob.com');
INSERT INTO contact VALUES
  (null, 'Steve Jobs', 'Apple', 'steve@rememberNewton.com');
INSERT INTO contact VALUES
  (null, 'Linus Torvalds', 'Linux Foundation', 'linus@gnuWho.org');
INSERT INTO contact VALUES
  (null, 'Andy Harris', 'Wiley Press', 'andy@aharrisBooks.net');

SELECT * FROM contact;
```

Here are the changes in this script:

✦ **Add the AUTO_INCREMENT tag to the primary key definition.** This tag indicates that the MySQL system will automatically generate a unique integer for this field. You can apply the AUTO_INCREMENT tag to any field, but you most commonly apply it to primary keys.

✦ **Replace index values with** null. When you define a table with AUTO_INCREMENT, you should no longer specify values in the affected field.

Instead, just place the value `null`. When the SQL interpreter sees the value `null` on an `AUTO_INCREMENT` field, it automatically finds the next largest integer.

TIP

You may wonder why I'm entering the value `null` when I said primary keys should never be null. Well, I'm not really making them null. The `null` value is simply a signal to the interpreter: "Hey, this field is AUTO_INCREMENT, and I want you to find a value for it."

Selecting Data from Your Tables

Creating a database is great, but the real point of a database is to extract information from it. SQL provides an incredibly powerful command for retrieving data from the database. The basic form looks as follows:

```
SELECT * FROM contact;
```

The easiest way to practice SQL commands is to use phpMyAdmin. Figure 2-5 shows phpMyAdmin with the SQL tab open.

Figure 2-5:
You can easily test queries in phpMy-Admin.

Note that you can enter SQL code in multiple places. If you're working with a particular table, you can invoke that table's SQL tab (as I do in Figure 2-5). You can also always enter SQL code into your system with the SQL button on the main phpMyAdmin panel (on the left panel of all phpMyAdmin screens).

If you have a particular table currently active, the SQL dialog box shows you the fields of the current table, which can be handy when you write SQL queries.

Try the `SELECT * FROM contact;` code in the SQL dialog box, and you see the results shown in Figure 2-6.

Selecting only a few fields

As databases get more complex, you'll often find that you don't want everything. Sometimes, you only want to see a few fields at a time. You can replace the * characters with field names. For example, if you want to see only the names and e-mail addresses, use this variation of the SELECT statement:

```
SELECT name, email FROM contact;
```

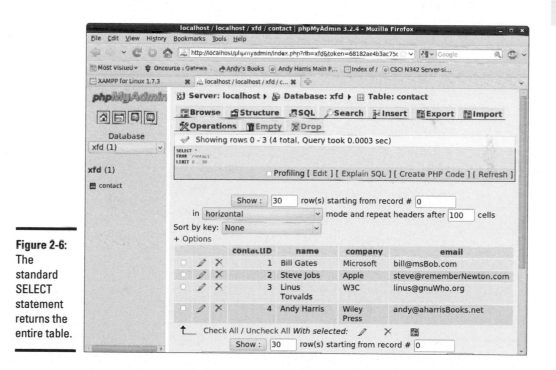

Figure 2-6:
The standard SELECT statement returns the entire table.

Only the columns you specify appear, as you can see in Figure 2-7.

Here's another really nice trick you can do with fields. You can give each column a new virtual field name:

```
SELECT
  name as 'Person',
  email as 'Address'
FROM contact;
```

This code also selects only two columns, but this time, it attaches the special labels Person and Address to the columns. You can see this result in Figure 2-8.

TIP

The capability to add a virtual name for each column doesn't seem like a big deal now, but it becomes handy when your database contains multiple tables. For example, you may have a table named `pet` and another table named `owner` that both have a `name` field. The virtual title feature helps keep you (and your users) from being confused.

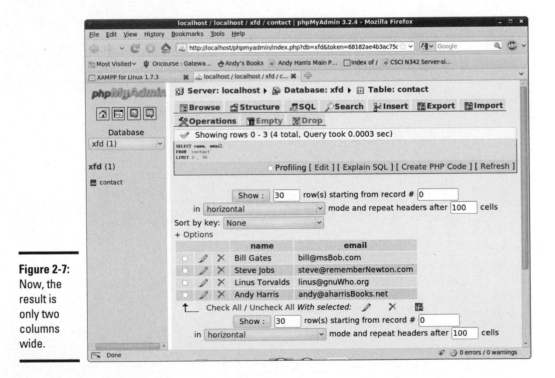

Figure 2-7:
Now, the result is only two columns wide.

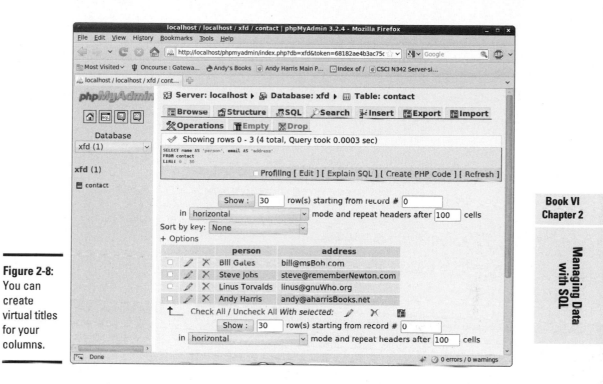

Figure 2-8:
You can
create
virtual titles
for your
columns.

Selecting a subset of records

One of the most important jobs in data work is returning a smaller set of the
database that meets some kind of criterion. For example, what if you want to
dash off a quick e-mail to Steve Jobs? Use this query:

```
SELECT *
FROM contact
WHERE
  name = 'Steve Jobs';
```

This query has a few key features:

✦ **It selects all fields.** This query selects all the fields (for now).

✦ **A** WHERE **clause appears.** The WHERE clause allows you to specify
a condition.

✦ **It has a condition.** SQL supports conditions, much like ordinary programming languages. MySQL returns only the records that match this
condition.

✦ **The condition begins with a field name.** SQL conditions usually compare a field to a value (or to another field).

✦ **Conditions use single equal signs.** You can easily get confused on this detail because SQL uses the single equal sign (=) in conditions, whereas most programming languages use double equals (==) for the same purpose.

✦ **All text values must be within single quotes.** I'm looking for an exact match on the text string 'Steve Jobs'.

✦ **It assumes that searches are case-sensitive.** Different databases have different behavior when it comes to case-sensitivity in SELECT statements, but you're safest assuming that case matters.

Figure 2-9 shows the result of this query.

SQL is pretty picky about the entire text string. The following query doesn't return any results in the contact database:

```
SELECT *
FROM contact
WHERE
  name = 'Steve';
```

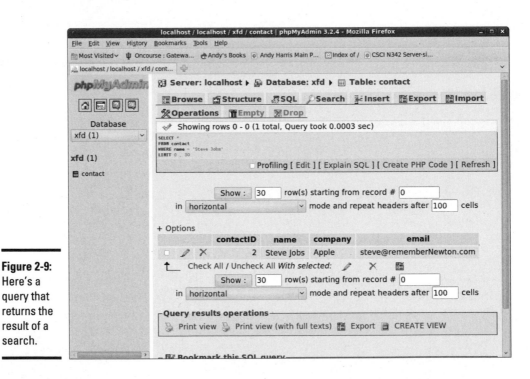

Figure 2-9: Here's a query that returns the result of a search.

The contact table doesn't have any records with a name field containing Steve (unless you added some records when I wasn't looking). Steve Jobs is not the same as Steve, so this query returns no results.

Searching with partial information

Of course, sometimes all you have is partial information. Take a look at the following variation to see how it works:

```
SELECT *
FROM contact
WHERE
  company LIKE 'W%';
```

This query looks at the company field and returns any records with a company field beginning with W. Figure 2-10 shows how it works.

The LIKE clause is pretty straightforward:

✦ **The keyword** LIKE **indicates a partial match is coming.** It's still the SELECT statement, but now it has the LIKE keyword to indicate an exact match isn't necessary.

Figure 2-10: This query returns companies that begin with W.

+ **The search text is still within single quotes, just like the ordinary** SELECT **statement.**

+ **The percent sign (%) indicates a wildcard value.** A search string of `'W%'` looks for W followed by any number of characters.

+ **Any text followed by % indicates that you're searching the beginning of the field.** So, if you're looking for people named Steve, you can write SELECT * FROM contact WHERE name LIKE 'Steve%';.

Searching for the ending value of a field

Likewise, you can find fields that end with a particular value. Say that you want to send an e-mail to everyone in your contact book with a .com address. This query does the trick:

```
SELECT *
FROM contact
WHERE
  email LIKE '%.com';
```

Figure 2-11 shows the results of this query.

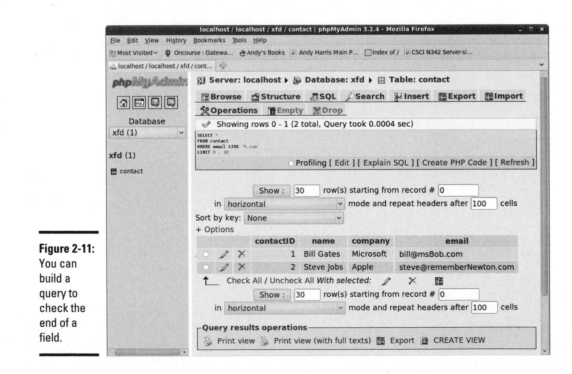

Figure 2-11: You can build a query to check the end of a field.

Searching for any text in a field

One more variant of the LIKE clause allows you to find a phrase anywhere in the field. Say that you remember somebody in your database writes books, and you decide to search for e-mail addresses containing the phrase book:

```
SELECT *
FROM contact
WHERE
  email LIKE '%book%';
```

The search phrase has percent signs at the beginning and the end, so if the phrase "book" occurs anywhere in the specified field, you get a match. And what do you know? Figure 2-12 shows this query matches on the record of a humble, yet lovable author!

Searching with regular expressions

If you know how to use regular expressions, you know how great they can be when you need a more involved search. MySQL has a special form of the SELECT keyword that supports regular expressions:

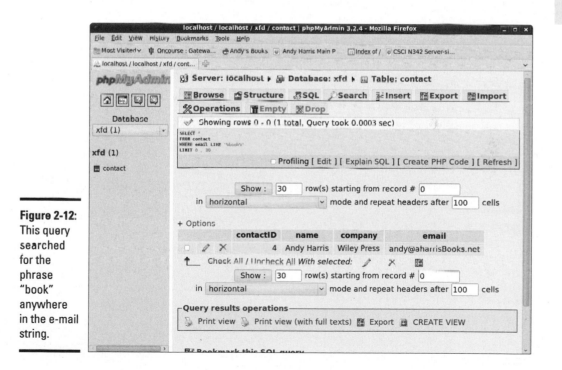

Figure 2-12:
This query searched for the phrase "book" anywhere in the e-mail string.

```
SELECT *
FROM contact
WHERE
    company REGEXP '^.{3}$';
```

The REGEXP keyword lets you search using powerful regular expressions. (Refer to Book IV, Chapter 6 for more information on regular expressions.) This particular expression checks for a company field with exactly three letters. In this table, it returns only one value, shown in Figure 2-13.

Unfortunately, not all database programs support the REGEXP feature, but MySQL does, and it's really powerful if you understand the (admittedly arcane) syntax of regular expressions.

Sorting your responses

You can specify the order of your query results with the ORDER BY clause. It works like this:

```
SELECT *
FROM contact
ORDER BY email;
```

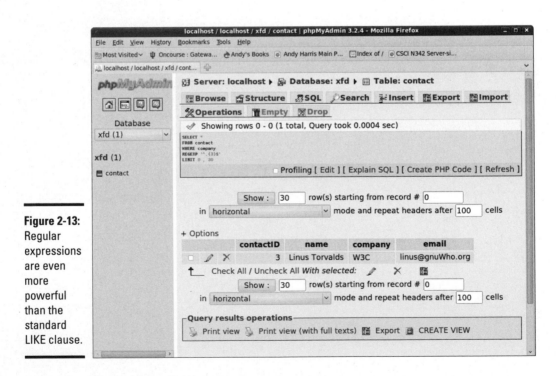

Figure 2-13: Regular expressions are even more powerful than the standard LIKE clause.

The ORDER BY directive allows you to specify a field to sort by. In this case, I want the records displayed in alphabetical order by e-mail address. Figure 2-14 shows how it looks.

By default, records are sorted in ascending order. Numeric fields are sorted from smallest to largest, and text fields are sorted in standard alphabetic order.

Well, not quite standard alphabetic order . . . SQL isn't as smart as a librarian, who has special rules about skipping "the" and so on. SQL simply looks at the ASCII values of the characters for sorting purposes.

You can also invert the order:

```
SELECT *
FROM contact
ORDER BY email DESC;
```

Inverting the order causes the records to be produced in reverse alphabetic order by e-mail address. DESC stands for descending order. ASC stands for ascending order, but because it's the default, it isn't usually specified.

Figure 2-14:
Now, the
result is
sorted
by e-mail
address.

[Screenshot: localhost / localhost / xfd / contact | phpMyAdmin 3.2.4 - Mozilla Firefox showing a contact table with the following records sorted by email:]

	contactID	name	company	email ▲
4	Andy Harris	Wiley Press	andy@aharrisBooks.net
1	Bill Gates	Microsoft	bill@msBob.com
3	Linus Torvalds	W3C	linus@gnuWho.org
2	Steve Jobs	Apple	steve@rememberNewton.com

Editing Records

Of course, the purpose of a database is to manage data. Sometimes, you want to edit data after it's already in the table. SQL includes handy commands for this task: UPDATE and DELETE. The UPDATE command modifies the value of an existing record, and the DELETE command removes a record altogether.

Updating a record

Say that you decide to modify Bill Gates's address to reinforce a recent marketing triumph. The following SQL code does the trick:

```
UPDATE contact
SET email = 'bill@vistaRocks.com'
WHERE name = 'Bill Gates';
```

The UPDATE command has a few parts:

✦ **The** UPDATE **command.** This indicates which table you will modify.

✦ **The** SET **command.** This indicates a new assignment.

✦ **Assign a new value to a field.** This uses a standard programming-style assignment statement to attach a new value to the indicated field. You can modify more than one field at a time. Just separate the field = value pairs with commas.

✦ **Specify a** WHERE **clause.** You don't want this change to happen to all the records in your database. You want to change only the e-mail address in records where the name is Bill Gates. Use the WHERE clause to specify which records you intend to update.

More than one person in your database may be named Bill Gates. Names aren't guaranteed to be unique, so they aren't really the best search criteria. This situation is actually a very good reason to use primary keys. A better version of this update looks as follows:

```
UPDATE contact
SET email = 'bill@vistaRocks.com'
WHERE contactID = 1;
```

The contactID is guaranteed to be unique and present, so it makes an ideal search criterion. Whenever possible, UPDATE (and DROP) commands should use primary key searches so that you don't accidentally change or delete the wrong record.

Deleting a record

Sometimes, you need to delete records. SQL has a command for this eventuality, and it's pretty easy to use:

```
DELETE FROM contact
WHERE contactID = 1;
```

The preceding line deletes the entire record with a `contactID` of 1.

Be very careful with the `DELETE` command, as it is destructive. Be absolutely sure that you have a `WHERE` clause, or you may delete all the records in your table with one quick command! Likewise, be sure that you understand the `WHERE` clause so that you aren't surprised by what gets deleted. You're better off running an ordinary `SELECT` using the `WHERE` clause before you `DELETE`, just to be sure that you know exactly what you're deleting. Generally, you should `DELETE` based on only a primary key so that you don't produce any collateral damage.

Exporting Your Data and Structure

After you've built a wonderful data structure, you probably will want to export it for a number of reasons:

+ **You want a backup.** Just in case something goes wrong!

+ **You want to move to a production server.** It's smart to work on a local (offline) server while you figure things out, but eventually you'll need to move to a live server. Moving the actual database files is tricky, but you can easily move a script.

+ **You want to perform data analysis.** You may want to put your data in a spreadsheet for further analysis or in a comma-separated text file to be read by programs without SQL access.

+ **You want to document the table structure.** The structure of a data set is extremely important when you start writing programs using that structure. Having the table structure available in a word-processing or PDF format can be very useful.

MySQL (and thus phpMyAdmin) has some really nice tools for exporting your data in a number of formats.

Figure 2-15 shows an overview of the Export tab, showing some of the features.

The different styles of output are used for different purposes:

+ **CSV (comma-separated value) format:** A plain ASCII comma-separated format. Each record is stored on its own line, and each field is separated by a comma. CSV is nice because it's universal. Most spreadsheet programs can read CSV data natively, and it's very easy to write a program to read CSV data, even if your server doesn't support MySQL. If you want to back up your data to move to another server, CSV is a good choice. Figure 2-16 shows some of the options for creating a CSV file.

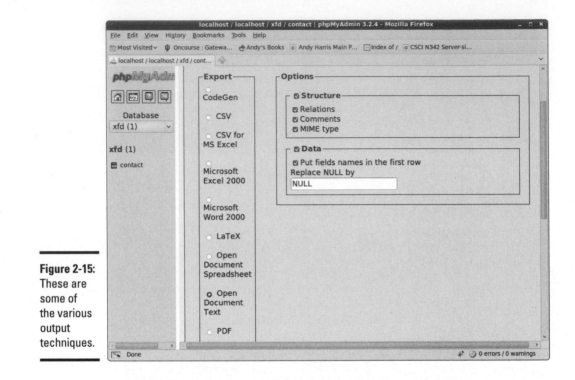

Figure 2-15:
These are
some of
the various
output
techniques.

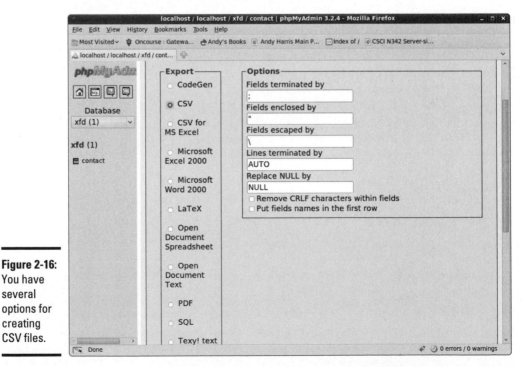

Figure 2-16:
You have
several
options for
creating
CSV files.

The data file created using the specified options looks like the following:

```
'contactID','name','company','email'
'1','Bill Gates','Microsoft','bill@msBob.com'
'2','Steve Jobs','Apple','steve@rememberNewton.com'
'3','Linus Torvalds','Linux Foundation','linus@gnuWho.org'
'4','Andy Harris','Wiley Press','andy@aharrisBooks.net'
```

The CSV format often uses commas and single quotes, so if these characters appear in your data, you may encounter problems. Be sure to test your data and use some of the other delimiters if you have problems.

✦ **MS Excel and Open Document Spreadsheet:** These are the two currently supported spreadsheet formats. Exporting your data using one of these formats gives you a spreadsheet file that you can easily manipulate, which is handy when you want to do charts or data analysis based on your data. Figure 2-17 shows an Excel document featuring the contact table.

✦ **Word-processing formats:** Several formats are available to create documentation for your project. Figure 2-18 shows a document created with this feature. Typically, you use these formats to describe your format of the data and the current contents. LaTeX and PDF are special formats used for printing.

**Book VI
Chapter 2**

**Managing Data
with SQL**

Figure 2-17:
This Excel
spreadsheet
was
automatically
created.

	A	B	C	D	E
1	contactID	name	company	email	
2	1	Bill Gates	Microsoft	bill@msBob.com	
3	2	Steve Jobs	Apple	steve@rememberNewton.com	
4	3	Linus Torvalds	W3C	linus@gnuWho.org	
5	4	Andy Harris	Wiley Press	andy@aharrisBooks.net	

Figure 2-18: Word-processing, PDF, and LaTeX formats are great for documentation.

Exporting SQL code

One of the neatest tricks is to have phpMyAdmin build an entire SQL script for re-creating your database. Figure 2-19 shows the available options.

The resulting code is as follows:

```
-- phpMyAdmin SQL Dump
-- version 2.9.2
-- http://www.phpmyadmin.net
--
-- Host: localhost
-- Generation Time: Dec 08, 2007 at 12:15 PM
-- Server version: 5.0.33
-- PHP Version: 5.2.1
--
-- Database: 'xfd'
--


-- --------------------------------------------------------


--
-- Table structure for table 'contact'
--

CREATE TABLE 'contact' (
  'contactID' int(11) NOT NULL auto_increment,
  'name' varchar(50) collate latin1_general_ci default NULL,
  'company' varchar(30) collate latin1_general_ci default NULL,
```

```
'email' varchar(50) collate latin1_general_ci default NULL,
PRIMARY KEY  ('contactID')
) ENGINE=MyISAM  DEFAULT CHARSET=latin1 COLLATE=latin1_general_ci AUTO_
    INCREMENT=5 ;


--
-- Dumping data for table 'contact'
--

INSERT INTO 'contact' VALUES (1, 'Bill Gates', 'Microsoft', 'bill@msBob.com');
INSERT INTO 'contact' VALUES (2, 'Steve Jobs', 'Apple', 'steve@rememberNewton.
    com');
INSERT INTO 'contact' VALUES (3, 'Linus Torvalds', 'W3C', 'linus@gnuWho.org');
INSERT INTO 'contact' VALUES (4, 'Andy Harris', 'Wiley Press', 'andy@
    aharrisBooks.net');
```

You can see that phpMyAdmin made a pretty decent script that you can use to re-create this database. You can easily use this script to rebuild the database if it gets corrupted or to copy the data structure to a different implementation of MySQL.

Generally, you use this feature for both purposes. Copy your data structure and data every once in a while (just in case Godzilla attacks your server or something).

Book VI
Chapter 2

Managing Data
with SQL

Figure 2-19:
You can specify several options for outputting your SQL code.

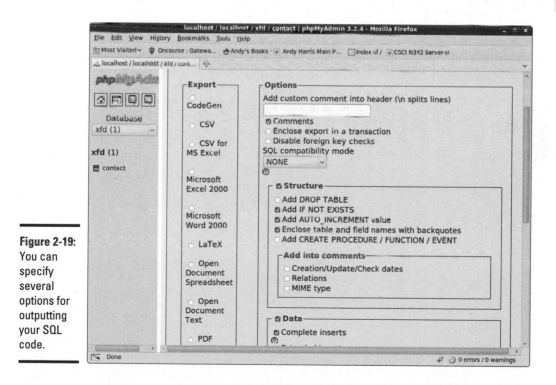

Typically, you build your data on one server and want to migrate it to another server. The easiest way to do so is by building the database on one server. You can then export the script for building the SQL file and load it into the second server.

Creating XML data

One more approach to saving data is through XML. phpMyAdmin creates a standard form of XML encapsulating the data. The XML output looks like this:

```
<?xml version="1.0" encoding="utf-8" ?>
<!--
-
- phpMyAdmin XML Dump
- version 2.9.2
- http://www.phpmyadmin.net
-
- Host: localhost
- Generation Time: Dec 08, 2007 at 08:16 PM
- Server version: 5.0.33
- PHP Version: 5.2.1
-->

<!--
- Database: 'xfd'
-->
<xfd>
   <!-- Table contact -->
     <contact>
         <contactID>1</contactID>
         <name>Bill Gates</name>
         <company>Microsoft</company>
         <email>bill@msBob.com</email>
     </contact>
     <contact>
         <contactID>2</contactID>
         <name>Steve Jobs</name>
         <company>Apple</company>
         <email>steve@rememberNewton.com</email>
     </contact>
     <contact>
         <contactID>3</contactID>
         <name>Linus Torvalds</name>
         <company>W3C</company>
         <email>linus@gnuWho.org</email>
     </contact>
     <contact>
         <contactID>4</contactID>
         <name>Andy Harris</name>
         <company>Wiley Press</company>
         <email>andy@aharrisBooks.net</email>
     </contact>
</xfd>
```

XML is commonly used as a common data language, especially in AJAX applications.

Chapter 3: Normalizing Your Data

In This Chapter

✔ Understanding why single-table databases are inadequate

✔ Recognizing common data anomalies

✔ Creating entity-relationship diagrams

✔ Using MySQL Workbench to create data diagrams

✔ Understanding the first three normal forms

✔ Defining data relationships

Databases can be deceptive. Even though databases are pretty easy to create, beginners usually run into problems as soon as they start working with actual data.

Computer scientists (particularly a gentleman named E. F. Codd in the 1970s) have studied potential data problems and defined techniques for organizing data. This scheme is called *data normalization*. In this chapter, you discover why single-table databases rarely work for real-world data and how to create a well-defined data structure according to basic normalization rules.

On the CD-ROM, I include a script called `buildHero.sql` that builds all the tables in this chapter. Feel free to load that script into your MySQL environment to see all these tables for yourself.

Recognizing Problems with Single-Table Data

Packing everything you've got into a single table is tempting. Although you can do it pretty easily (especially with SQL), and it seems like a good solution, things can go wrong pretty quickly.

Table 3-1 shows a seemingly simple database describing some superheroes.

Table 3-1		A Sample Database			
Name	*Powers*	*Villain*	*Plot*	*Mission*	*Age*
The Plumber	Sewer snake of doom, unclogging, ability to withstand smells	Septic Slime Master	Overcome Chicago with slime	Stop the Septic Slime	37
Binary Boy	Hexidecimation beam, obfuscation	Octal	Eliminate the numerals 8 and 9	Make the world safe for binary representation	19
The Janitor	Mighty Mop	Septic Slim Master	Overcome New York with slime	Stop the Septic Slime	41

It seems that not much can go wrong here because the database is only three records and six fields. The data is simple, and there isn't that much of it. Still, a lot of trouble is lurking just under the surface. The following sections outline potential problems.

The identity crisis

What's Table 3-1 about? At first, it seems to be about superheroes, but some of the information isn't about the superhero as much as things related to the superhero, such as villains and missions. This issue may not seem like a big deal, but it causes all kinds of practical problems later on. A table should be about only one thing. When it tries to be about more than that, it can't do its job as well.

Every time a beginner (and, often, an advanced data developer) creates a table, the table usually contains fields that don't belong there. You have to break things up into multiple tables so that each table is really about only one thing. The process for doing so solves a bunch of other problems, as well.

The listed powers

Take a look at the powers field. Each superhero can have more than one power. Some heroes have tons of powers. The problem is, how do you handle a situation where one field can have a lot of values? You frequently see the following solutions:

+ **One large text field:** That's what I did in this case. I built a massive (255 character) VARCHAR field and hoped it would be enough. The user just has to type all the possible skills.

+ **Multiple fields:** Sometimes, a data designer just makes a bunch of fields, such as power1, power2, and so on.

Both these solutions have the same general flaw. You never know how much room to designate because you never know exactly how many items will be in the list. Say that you choose the large text field approach. You may have a really clever hero with a lot of powers, so you fill up the entire field with a list of powers. What happens if your hero learns one more power? Should you delete something just to make things fit? Should you abbreviate?

If you choose to have multiple power fields, the problem doesn't go away. You still have to determine how many skills the hero can have. If you designate ten skill fields and one of your heroes learns an eleventh power, you've got a problem.

The obvious solution is to provide far more room than anybody needs. If it's a text field, make it huge; and if it's multiple fields, make hundreds of them. Both solutions are wasteful. Remember, a database can often have hundreds or thousands of records, and each one has to be the same size. If you make your record definition bigger than it needs to be, this waste is multiplied hundreds or thousands of times.

You may argue that this is not the 1970s. Processor power and storage space are really cheap today, so why am I worrying about saving a few bytes here and there? Well, cheap is still not free. Programmers tend to be working with much larger data sets than they did in the early days, so efficiency still matters. And here's another important change. Today, data is much more likely to be transmitted over the Internet. The big deal today isn't really processor or storage efficiency. Today's problem is transmission efficiency, which comes down to the same principle: Don't store unnecessary data.

When databases have listed fields, you tend to see other problems. If the field doesn't have enough room for all the data, people will start abbreviating. If you're looking for a hero with invisibility, you can't simply search for "invisibility" in the powers field because it may be "inv," "in," or "invis" (or even "can't see"). If you desperately need an invisible hero, the search can be frustrating, and you may miss a result because you didn't guess all the possible abbreviations.

If the database uses the listed fields model, you have another problem. Now, your search has to look through all ten (or hundreds of) power fields because you don't know which one holds the "invisible" power. This problem makes your search queries far more complicated than they would have been otherwise.

Another so-called solution you sometimes see is to have a whole bunch of Boolean fields: Invisibility, Super-speed, X-ray vision, and so on. This fix solves part of the problem because Boolean data is small. It's still troublesome, though, because now the data developer has to anticipate every possible power. You may have an other field, but it then reintroduces the problem of listed fields.

Listed fields are a nightmare.

Repetition and reliability

Another common problem with data comes with repetition. If you allow data to be repeated in your database, you can have some really challenging side effects. Refer to Table 3-1, earlier in this chapter, and get ready to answer some questions about it. . . .

What is the Slime Master's evil plot?

This question seems simple enough, but Table 3-1 provides an ambiguous response. If you look at the first row (The Plumber), the plot is Overcome Chicago with slime. If you look at The Janitor, you see that the plot is to Overcome New York with slime. Which is it? Presumably, it's the same plot, but in one part of the database, New York is the target, and elsewhere, it's Chicago. From the database, you can't really tell which is correct or if it could be both. I was required to type in the plot in two different records. It's supposed to be the same plot, but I typed it differently. Now, the data has a conflict, and you don't know which record to trust.

Is it possible the plots were supposed to be different? Sure, but you don't want to leave that assumption to chance. The point of data design is to ask exactly these questions and to design your data scheme to reinforce the rules of your organization.

Here's a related question. What if you needed to get urgent information to any hero fighting the Septic Slime Master? You'd probably write a query like

```
SELECT * FROM hero WHERE villain = 'Septic Slime Master'
```

That query is a pretty reasonable request, but it wouldn't work. The villain in The Janitor record is the Septic *Slim* Master. Somebody mistyped something in the database, and now The Janitor doesn't know how to defeat the Slime Master.

If your database allows duplication, this type of mistake will happen all the time.

In general, you don't want to enter anything into a database more than once. If you have a way to enter the Septic Slime Master one time, that should eliminate this type of problem.

Fields that change

Another kind of problem is evident in the Age field. (See, even superheroes have a mandatory retirement age.) Age is a good example of a field that shouldn't really be in a database because it changes all the time. If you have age in your database, how are you going to account for people getting older? Do you update the age on each hero's birthday? (If so, you need to store that birthday, and you need to run a script every day to see whether it's somebody's birthday.) You could just age everybody once a year, but this solution doesn't seem like a good option, either.

Whenever possible, you want to avoid fields that change regularly and instead use a formula to generate the appropriate results when you need them.

Deletion problems

Another kind of problem is lurking right under the surface. Say that you have to fire the Binary Boy. (With him, everything is black and white. You just can't compromise with him.) You delete his record, and then you want to assign another hero to fight Octal. When you delete Binary Boy, you also delete all the information about Octal and his nefarious scheme.

In a related problem, what if you encounter a new villain and you haven't yet assigned a hero to this villain? The current data design doesn't allow you to add villains without heroes. You have to make up a fake hero, and that just doesn't seem right.

Introducing Entity-Relationship Diagrams

You can solve all the problems with the database shown in Table 3-1 by breaking the single table into a series of smaller, more specialized tables.

The typical way of working with data design is to use a concept called an *Entity-Relationship (ER) diagram.* This form of diagram usually includes the following:

✦ **Entities:** Typically, a table is an entity, but you see other kinds of entities, too. An entity is usually drawn as a box with each field listed inside.

✦ **Relationships:** Relationships are drawn as lines between the boxes. As you find out about various forms of relationships, I show you the particular symbols used to describe these relationship types.

Using MySQL Workbench to draw ER diagrams

You can create ER diagrams with anything (I typically use a whiteboard), but some very nice free software can help. One particularly nice program is called MySQL Workbench. This software has a number of really handy features:

✦ **Visual representation of database design:** MySQL Workbench allows you to define a table easily and then see how it looks in ER form. You can create several tables and manipulate them visually to see how they relate.

✦ **An understanding of ER rules:** MySQL Workbench is not simply a drawing program. It's specialized for drawing ER diagrams, so it creates a standard design for each table and relationship. Other data administrators can understand the ER diagrams you create with this tool.

✦ **Integration with MySQL:** Once you've created a data design you like, you can have MySQL Workbench create a MySQL script to create the databases you've defined. In fact, you can even have Workbench look at an existing MySQL database and create an ER diagram from it.

Creating a table definition in Workbench

Creating your tables in MySQL Workbench is a fairly easy task:

1. **Create a new model.**

   Choose File➪New to create a new model. Figure 3-1 shows the MySQL Workbench main screen.

Figure 3-1:
MySQL
Workbench
main
screen.

2. Create a new table.

Use the Add Table icon to create a new table. A new dialog box opens at the bottom of the screen, allowing you to change the table name. You see a new table form like the one in Figure 3-2. Change the table name to **'hero'** but leave the other values blank for now.

Figure 3-2:
Now your model has a table in it.

3. Edit the columns.

Select the Columns tab at the bottom of the screen to edit the table's fields. You can add field names and types here. Create a table that looks like the hero table shown in Figure 3-3. You can use the tab key to add a new field.

4. Make a diagram of the table.

So far, MySQL Workbench seems a lot like phpMyAdmin. The most useful feature of Workbench is the way it lets you view your tables in diagram form. You can view tables in a couple of ways, but the easiest way is to select `Create Diagram from Catalog Objects` from the `Model` menu. When you do so, you'll see a screen, as shown in Figure 3-4.

The diagram doesn't show the *contents* of the table, just the design. In fact, MySQL workbench doesn't really care that much about what is in the database. The key idea here is how the data is organized. This matters because you will be creating several tables to manage your superheroes.

5. **Extract the code.**

   If you want, you can see the SQL code used to create the table you just designed. Simply right-click the table and choose Copy SQL to Clipboard. The CREATE statement for this table is copied to the Clipboard, and you can paste it to your script. Here's the code created by Workbench:

```
CREATE  TABLE IF NOT EXISTS 'mydb''.'hero' (
  'heroID' INT NOT NULL ,
  'name' VARCHAR(50) NULL ,
  'birthdate' DATE NULL ,
  'missionID' INT NULL ,
  PRIMARY KEY ('heroID') )
ENGINE = InnoDB
```

**Book VI
Chapter 3**

**Normalizing
Your Data**

This is great and all...

But how do I work with an actual database? MySQL Workbench is used to help you design and understand complex databases. So far, you've been working in a local system that isn't attached to a particular database. This is actually a pretty good way to work. Eventually, though, you'll be settled on a design, and you'll want to build a real database from the model. MySQL Workbench has a number of tools to help you with this. First, use the Database — Manage Connections dialog box to create a connection to your database. Then you can use the Forward Engineering option to commit your design to the database or the Reverse Engineering option to extract a database you've already created and build a diagram from it.

While these options can be handy, they aren't really critical. To be honest, I don't generally use the code engineering features in MySQL Workbench. In fact, I (like a lot of data developers) do most of my initial data design on a white board and then make cleaner versions of the design with tools like MySQL Workbench. I'm showing you the tool here because it may be helpful to you, and it produces prettier artwork than my white board scribblings.

The hard work is organizing the data. It's pretty easy to convert a diagram to SQL code. Use a tool like MySQL to see how your data fits together. Then if you want, you can either let it build the code for you or simply use it as a starting place to build the code by hand.

As you've seen with other languages, visual tools can help you build code, but they don't absolve you of responsibility. If the code has your name on it, you need to understand how it works. That's most easily done when you write it by hand.

Introducing Normalization

Trying to cram all your data into a single table usually causes problems. The process for solving these problems is called *data normalization.* Normalization is really a set of rules. When your database follows the first rule, it's said to be in *first normal form.* For this introductory book, you get to the third normal form, which is suitable for most applications.

First normal form

The official definitions of the normal forms sound like the offspring of a lawyer and a mathematician. Here's an official definition of the first normal form:

```
A table is in first normal form if and only if it represents a relation. It does
    not allow nulls or duplicate rows.
```

Yeah, whatever.

Here's what it means in practical terms:

```
Eliminate listed fields.
```

A database is in first normal form if

+ **It has no repeating fields.** Take any data that would be in a repeating field and make it into a new table.

+ **It has a primary key.** Add a primary key to each table. (Some would argue that this requirement isn't necessarily part of first normal form, but it'll be necessary in the next step, anyway.)

In a practical sense, the first normal form means getting rid of listed fields and making a new table to contain powers. You'll need to go back to the model view to create a new table and then create the diagram again. Figure 3-5 shows an ER diagram of the data in first normal form.

A couple of things happen here:

1. **Make a new table called** power.

   This table contains nothing but a key and the power name.

2. **Take the** power **field away from the** hero **table.**

   The hero table no longer has a power field.

3. **Add a primary key to both tables.**

   Both tables now have an integer primary key. Looking over my tables, there are no longer any listed fields, so I'm in first normal form.

Figure 3-5:
Now I have two tables.

All this is well and good, but the user really wants this data connected, so how do you join it back together? For that answer, see Chapter 4 of this minibook.

Second normal form

The official terminology for the second normal form is just as baffling as the first normal form:

```
A table is in second normal form (2NF) only if it is in 1NF and all nonkey fields
    are dependant entirely on the entire candidate key, not just part of it.
```

Huh? You've gotta love these computer scientists.

In practical terms, second normal form is pretty easy, too. It really means

Eliminate repetition.

Look at all those places where you've got duplicated data and create new tables to take care of them.

In the hero data (shown in Table 3-1, earlier in this chapter), you can eliminate a lot of problems by breaking the hero data into three tables. Figure 3-6 illustrates one way to break up the data.

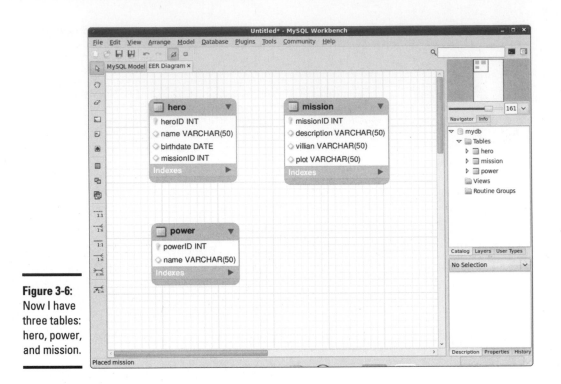

Figure 3-6:
Now I have
three tables:
hero, power,
and mission.

Many of the problems in the badHero design happen because apparently more than one hero can be on a particular mission, and thus the mission data gets repeated. By separating mission data into another table, I've guaranteed that the data for a mission is entered only once.

Note that each table has a primary key, and none of them has listed fields. The same data won't ever be entered twice. The solution is looking pretty good!

Notice that everything related to the mission has been moved to the mission table. I added one field to the hero table, which contains an integer. This field is called a *foreign key reference*. You can find out much more about how foreign key references work in Chapter 4 of this minibook.

Third normal form

The third normal form adds one more requirement. Here is the official definition:

```
A table is in 3NF if it is in 2NF and has no transitive dependencies on the
    candidate key.
```

Wow! These definitions get better and better. Once again, it's really a lot easier than it sounds:

```
Ensure functional dependency.
```

In other words, check each field of each table and ensure that it really describes what the table is about. For example, is the plot related to the mission or the hero? What about the villain?

The tricky thing about functional dependency is that you often don't really know how the data is supposed to be connected. Only the person who uses the data really knows how it's supposed to work. (Often, they don't know, either, when you ask them.) You have to work with the client to figure out exactly what the *business rules* (the rules that describe how the data really works) are. You can't really tell from the data itself.

The good news is that, for simple structures like the hero data, you're often already in third normal form by the time you get to second normal form. Still, you should check.

Once a database is in third normal form, you've reduced the possibility of several kinds of anomalies, so your data is far more reliable than it was in the past. Several other forms of normalization exist, but third normal form is enough for most applications.

Identifying Relationships in Your Data

After you normalize the data (see the preceding section), you've created the entities (tables). Now, you need to investigate the relationships among these entities.

Three main types of data relationships exist (and of these, only two are common):

+ **One-to-one relationship:** Each element of table A is related to exactly one element of table B. This type of relationship isn't common because if a one-to-one relationship exists between two tables, the information can be combined safely into one table.

+ **One-to-many relationship:** For each element of table A, there could be many possible elements in table B. The relationship between mission and hero is a one-to-many relationship, as each mission can have many heroes, but each hero has only one mission. (My heroes have attention issues and can't multitask very well.) Note that hero and mission are not a one-to-many relationship, but a many-to-one. The order matters.

+ **Many-to-many relationship:** This type of relationship happens when an element of A may have many values from B, and B may also have many values of A. Usually, listed fields turn out to be many-to-many relationships. In the hero data, the relationship between hero and power is a many-to-many relationship because each hero can have many powers, and each power can belong to multiple heroes.

You can use an ER tool to diagram the various relationship types. Figure 3-7 shows this addition to the `hero` design.

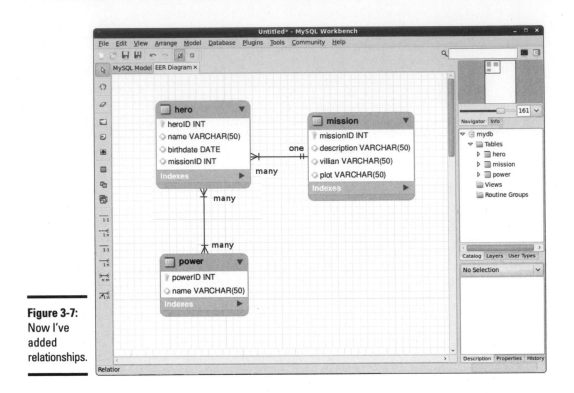

Figure 3-7:
Now I've
added
relationships.

Note that MySQL Workbench doesn't actually allow you to draw many-to-many joins. I drew that into Figure 3-7 to illustrate the point. In the next chapter, I show how to emulate many-to-many relationships with a special trick called a *link table.* ER diagrams use special symbols to represent different kinds of relationships. The line between tables indicates a *join,* or relationship, but the type of join is indicated by the markings on the ends of the lines. In general, the crow's feet or filled-in circle indicate many, and the double lines indicate one.

ER diagrams get much more complex than the simple ones I show here, but for this introduction, the one and many symbols are enough to get you started.

Chapter 4: Putting Data Together with Joins

Single tables aren't sufficient for most data. If you understand the rules of data normalization (see Chapter 3 of this minibook), you know how to break your data into a series of smaller tables. The question remains, though: How do you recombine all these broken-up tables to make something the user can actually use?

In this chapter, you discover several techniques for combining the data in your tables to create useful results.

I wrote a quick PHP script to help me with most of the figures in this chapter. Each SQL query I intend to look at is stored in a separate SQL file, and I can load up the file and look at it with the PHP code. Feel free to look over the code for showQuery on the CD-ROM. If you want to run this code yourself, be sure to change the username and password to reflect your data settings. Use queryDemo.html to see all the queries in action. I also include a script called buildHero.sql that creates a database with all the tables and views I mention in this chapter. Feel free to load that script into your database so that you can play along at home.

Calculating Virtual Fields

Part of data normalization means that you eliminate fields that can be calculated. In the hero database described in Chapter 3 of this minibook, data normalization meant that you don't store the hero's age, but his or her birthday instead (see Chapter 3 of this minibook). Of course, if you really want the age, you should be able to find some way to calculate it. SQL includes support for calculating results right in the query.

Begin by looking over the improved hero table in Figure 4-1.

Figure 4-1:
The hero
table after
normali-
zation.

The original idea for the database, introduced in Table 3-1 in Chapter 3 of this minibook, was to keep track of each hero's age. This idea was bad because the age changes every year. Instead, I stored the hero's birthday. But what if you really do want the age?

Introducing SQL Functions

It turns out SQL supports a number of useful functions that you can use to manipulate data. Table 4-1 shows especially useful MySQL functions. Many more functions are available, but these functions are the most frequently used.

Table 4-1	Useful MySQL Functions
Function	*Description*
CONCAT(A, B)	Concatenates two string results. Can be used to create a single entry from two or more fields. For example, combine firstName and lastName fields.
FORMAT(X, D)	Formats the number X to the number of digits D.
CURRDATE(), CURRTIME()	Returns the current date or time.

Function	Description
NOW()	Returns the current date and time.
MONTH(), DAY(), YEAR(), WEEK(), WEEKDAY()	Extracts the particular value from a date value.
HOUR(), MINUTE(), SECOND()	Extracts the particular value from a time value.
DATEDIFF(A, B)	Frequently used to find the time difference between two events (age).
SUBTIMES(A, B)	Determines the difference between two times.
FROMDAYS(INT)	Converts an integer number of days into a date value.

Typically, you use a programming language, such as PHP, to manage what the user sees, and programming languages tend to have a much richer set of functions than the database. Still, it's often useful to do certain kinds of functionality at the database level.

Knowing when to calculate virtual fields

You calculate data in these situations:

✦ **You need to create a single field from multiple text fields.** You might need to combine first, middle, and last name fields to create a single name value. You can also combine all the elements of an address to create a single output.

✦ **You want to do a mathematical operation on your data.** Imagine that you're writing a database for a vegetable market, and you want to calculate the value from the costPerPound field plus the poundsPurchased field. You can include the mathematical operation in your query.

✦ **You need to convert data.** Perhaps you stored weight information in pounds, and you want a query to return data in kilograms.

✦ **You want to do date calculations.** Often, you need to calculate ages from specific days. Date calculations are especially useful on the data side because databases and other languages often have different date formats.

Calculating Date Values

The birthday value is stored in the hero table, but what you really want to know is the hero's age. It's very common to have a date stored in a database. You often need to calculate the time from that date to the current date in years, or perhaps in years and months. Functions can help you do these calculations.

Begin by looking at a simple function that tells you the current date and time, as I do in Figure 4-2.

now

Query

    SELECT NOW();

Result

NOW()
2010-05-18 16:39:32

Figure 4-2:
The NOW()
function
returns the
current date
and time.

The current date and time by themselves aren't that important, but you can combine this information with other functions, described in the following sections, to do some very interesting things.

Using DATEDIFF to determine age

The NOW() function is very handy when you combine it with the DATEDIFF() function, as shown in Figure 4-3.

This query calculates the difference between the current date, NOW(), and each hero's birthday. The DATEDIFF() function works by converting both dates into integers. It can then subtract the two integers, giving you the result in number of days.

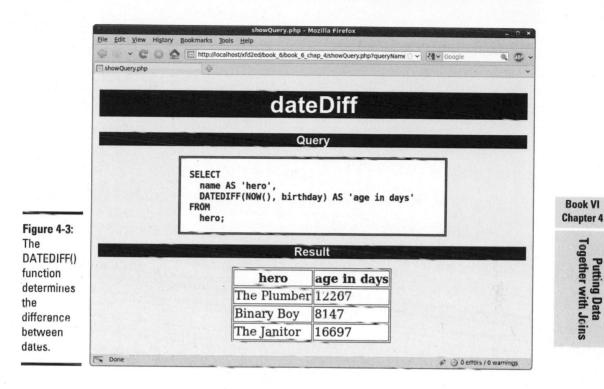

Book VI
Chapter 4

Putting Data
Together with Joins

Figure 4-3:
The
DATEDIFF()
function
determines
the
difference
between
dates.

You normally name the fields you calculate because, otherwise, the formula used to calculate the results becomes the virtual field's name. The user doesn't care about the formula, so use the AS feature to give the virtual field a more useful name.

Adding a calculation to get years

Of course, most people don't think about age in terms of days. Age (unless you're talking about fruit flies or something) is typically measured in years. One simple solution is to divide the age in days by 365 (the number of days in a year). Figure 4-4 shows this type of query.

This code is almost like the query shown in Figure 4-3, except it uses a mathematical operator. You can use most of the math operators in queries to do quick conversions. Now, the age is specified in years, but the decimal part is a bit odd. Normally, you either go with entire year measurements or work with months, weeks, and days.

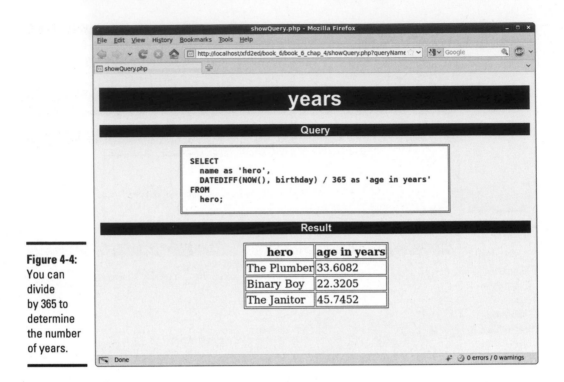

Converting the days integer into a date

The YEAR() function extracts only the years from a date, and the MONTH() function pulls out the months, but both these functions require a date value. The DATEDIFF() function creates an integer. Somehow, you need to convert the integer value produced by DATEDIFF() back into a date value. (For more on this function, see the section "Using DATEDIFF to determine age," earlier in this chapter.)

Figure 4-5 is another version of a query that expresses age in terms of years and months.

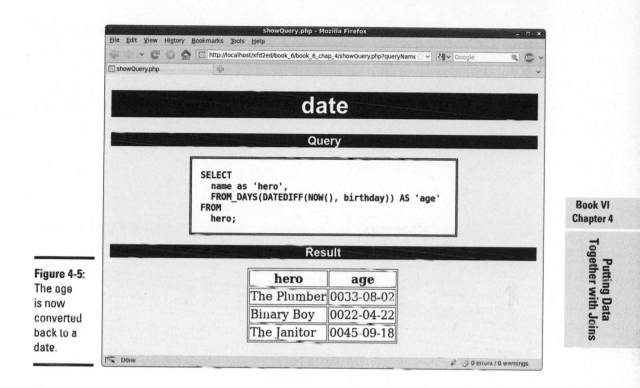

Figure 4-5:
The age
is now
converted
back to a
date.

This query takes the DATEDIFF() value and converts it back to a date. The actual date is useful, but it has some strange formatting. If you look carefully at the dates, you'll see that they have the age of each hero, but it's coded as if it were a particular date in the ancient world.

Using YEAR() and MONTH() to get readable values

After you've determined the age in days, you can use the YEAR() and MONTH() functions to pull out the hero's age in a more readable way, as illustrated by Figure 4-6.

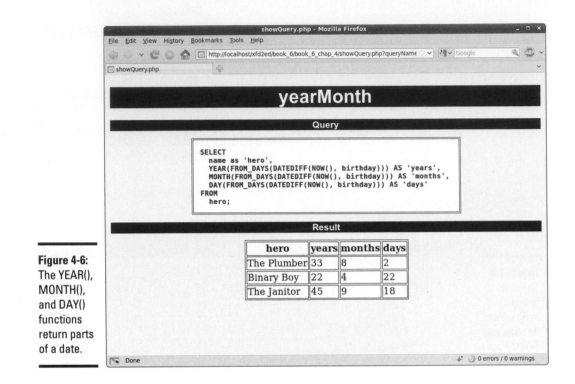

Figure 4-6:
The YEAR(),
MONTH(),
and DAY()
functions
return parts
of a date.

The query is beginning to look complex, but it's producing some really nice output. Still, it's kind of awkward to have separate fields for year, month, and day.

Concatenating to make one field

If you have year, month, and day values, it would be nice to combine some of this information to get a custom field, as you can see in Figure 4-7.

There's no way I'm writing that every time. . . .

I know what you're thinking. All this fancy function stuff is well and good, but there's no stinkin' way you're going to do all those function gymnastics every time you want to extract an age out of the database. Here's the good news: You don't have to. It's okay that the queries are getting a little tricky because you'll write code to do all the work for you. You write it only once, and then your code does all the heavy lifting. Generally, you write PHP code to manage each query inside a function. Once you've tested it, you run that function and off you go. . . . You can also use a little gem called the view, described in the "Creating a View" section. Views allow you to store complex queries right in your database.

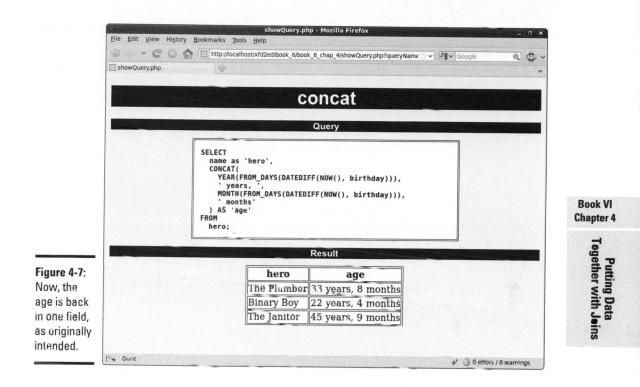

Figure 4-7:
Now, the
age is back
in one field,
as originally
intended.

This query uses the CONCAT() function to combine calculations and literal values to make exactly the output the user is expecting. Even though the birthday is the stored value, the output can be the age.

Creating a View

The query that converts a birthday into a formatted age is admittedly complex. Normally, you'll have this query predefined in your PHP code so that you don't have to think about it anymore. If you have MySQL 5.0 or later, though, you have access to a wonderful tool called the VIEW. A *view* is something like a virtual table.

The best way to understand a view is to see a sample of it in action. Take a look at this SQL code:

```
CREATE VIEW heroAgeView AS
  SELECT
    name as 'hero',
    CONCAT(
      YEAR(FROM_DAYS(DATEDIFF(NOW(), birthday))),
      ' years, ',
      MONTH(FROM_DAYS(DATEDIFF(NOW(), birthday))),
      ' months'
    ) AS 'age'
  FROM
    hero;
```

So what if I'm stuck with MySQL 4.0?

Views are so great that it's hard to imagine working with data without them. However, your hosting service may not have MySQL 5.0 or later installed, which means you aren't able to use views. All is not lost. You can handle this issue in two ways.

The most common approach is to store all the queries you're likely to need (the ones that would be views) as strings in your PHP code. Execute the query from PHP, and you've essentially

executed the view. This method is how most programmers did it before views were available in MySQL.

Another approach is to create a new table called something like `storeQuery` in your database. Put the text of all your views inside this table, and then you can extract the view code from the database and execute it using a second pass at the data server.

If you look closely, it's exactly the same query used to generate the age from the birth date, just with a `CREATE VIEW` statement added. When you run this code, nothing overt happens, but the database stores the query as a view called `heroView`. Figure 4-8 shows the cool part.

hero	age
The Plumber	33 years, 8 months
Binary Boy	22 years, 4 months
The Janitor	45 years, 9 months

```
SELECT * FROM heroAgeView;
```

Figure 4-8: This simple query hides a lot of complexity.

This code doesn't look really fancy, but look at the output. It's just like you had a table with all the information you wanted, but now the data is guaranteed to be in a decent format.

After you create a view, you can use it in subsequent SELECT statements as if it were a table! Here are a couple of important things to know about views:

✦ **They aren't stored in the database.** The view isn't really data; it's just a predefined query. It looks and feels like a table, but it's created in real time from the tables.

✦ **You can't write to a view.** Because views don't contain data (they reflect data from other tables), you can't write directly to them. You don't use the INSERT or UPDATE commands on views, as you do ordinary tables.

✦ **They're a relatively new feature of MySQL.** Useful as they are, views weren't added to MySQL until Version 5.0. If your server uses an earlier version, you'll have to do some workarounds, described in the sidebar "So what if I'm stuck with MySQL 4.0?"

✦ **You can treat views as tables in** SELECT **statements.** You can build SELECT statements using views as if they were regular tables.

Book VI
Chapter 4

Putting Data Together with Joins

Some database packages make it appear as though you can update a view, but that's really an illusion. Such programs reverse-engineer views to update each table. This approach is far from foolproof, and you should probably avoid it.

Using an Inner Join to Combine Tables

When I normalized the hero database in Chapter 3 of this minibook, I broke it up into several tables. Take a quick look at the hero table in Figure 4-9.

You probably noticed that most of the mission information is now gone from this table, except one important field. The missionID field is an integer field that contains the primary key of the mission table. A *foreign key* is a field that contains the primary key of another table. Foreign keys are used to reconnect tables that have been broken apart by normalization.

Look at the mission table in Figure 4-10, and the relationship between the mission and hero tables begins to make sense.

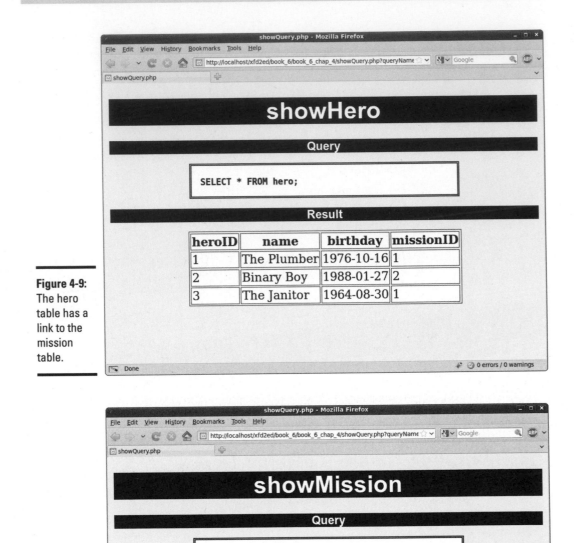

Figure 4-9: The hero table has a link to the mission table.

Figure 4-10: The mission table handles mission data but has no link to the hero.

The mission table doesn't have a link back to the hero. It can't. because any mission can be connected to any number of heroes, and you can't have a listed field.

Building a Cartesian join and an inner join

Compare the hero and mission tables, and you see how they fit together. The `missionID` field in the hero table identifies which mission the hero is on. None of the actual mission data is in the `hero` field, just a link to which mission the player is on.

Creating a query with both tables, as in Figure 4-11, is tempting. This query appears to join the tables, but it obviously isn't doing the right thing. You have only three heroes and two missions, yet this query returns six rows! What's happened here is called a *Cartesian join*. It's a combination of all the possible values of hero and mission, which is obviously not what you want.

You don't really want all these values to appear; you want to see only the ones where the hero table's `missionID` matches up to the `missionID` field in the mission table. In other words, you want a query that says only return rows where the two values of `missionID` are the same. That query may look like Figure 4-12. It's almost identical to the last query, except this time, a `WHERE` clause indicates that the foreign key and primary key should match up.

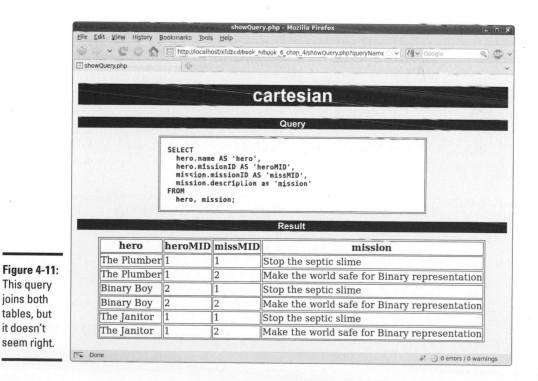

Figure 4-11: This query joins both tables, but it doesn't seem right.

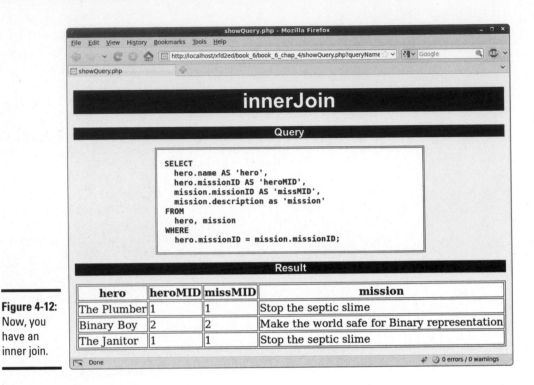

Figure 4-12:
Now, you
have an
inner join.

This particular setup (using a foreign key reference to join up two tables) is
called an *inner join*. Sometimes, you see the syntax like

```
SELECT
  hero.name AS 'hero',
  hero.missionID AS 'heroMID',
  mission.missionID AS 'missMID',
  mission.description as 'mission'
FROM
  hero INNER JOIN mission
ON
  hero.missionID = mission.missionID;
```

Some of Microsoft's database offerings prefer this syntax, but it really does
the same thing: join up two tables.

Enforcing one-to-many relationships

Whenever your ER diagram indicates a many-to-one (or one-to-many) relationship, you generally use an inner join (see the preceding section). Here's how you do it:

1. **Start with the ER diagram.**

No way are you going to get this right in your head! Make a diagram. Use a tool like MySQL Workbench, some other software, pencil and paper, lipstick on a mirror, whatever. You need a sketch.

2. **Identify one-to-many relationships.**

You may have to talk with people who use the data to determine which relationships are one-to-many. In the hero data, a hero can have only one mission, but each mission can have many heroes. Thus, the hero is the many side, and the mission is the one side.

3. **Find the primary key of the one table and the many table.**

Every table should have a primary key. (You'll sometimes see advanced alternatives like multifield keys, but wait until you're a bit more advanced for that stuff.)

4. **Make a foreign key reference to the one table in the many table.**

Add a field to the table on the many side of the relationship that contains only the key to the table on the one side.

You don't need a foreign key in the table on the one side of the relationship. This concept confuses most beginners. You don't need (or want) a link back to the many table because you don't know how many links you'll need. Multiple links would be a listed field, which is exactly what you're trying to avoid.

If the preceding steps are hard for you to understand, think back to the hero example. Each hero (according to the business rules) can be on only one mission. Thus, it makes sense to put a link to the mission in the hero table because you have only one mission. Each mission can be related to many heroes, so if you try to link missions to heroes, you have listed fields in the mission table, violating the first normal form. (For information on the types of normal forms, see Chapter 3 of this minibook.) Figure 4-13 shows how it works in action. The result of this join looks a lot like the original intention of the database, but now it's normalized.

Figure 4-13: Here's a nice join of the hero and mission tables.

Counting the advantages of inner joins

Even though the table in Figure 4-13 contains everything in the original non-normalized data set (except for the repeated field — that's coming up soon), the new version is considerably better for several reasons:

✦ **No data is repeated.** The plot is stored only one time in the database. Even though it may appear several times in this output, each value is stored only once.

✦ **Searching is much more efficient.** Because the data is stored only one time, you no longer have to worry about spelling and typing errors. If the entry is wrong, it is universally wrong, and you can repair it in only one place.

✦ **The data is organized correctly.** Although the user can't see it from this output, the tables are now separated so that each type of data goes where it belongs.

✦ **The output still looks like what the user wants.** Users don't care about the third normal form. (For more on normalization, see Chapter 3 of this minibook.) They just want to get to their data. This table gives them a query that returns the data they're looking for, even though the underlying data structure has changed dramatically.

Building a view to encapsulate the join

The inner join query is so useful, it's a dandy place for a view. I created a view from it:

```
CREATE VIEW heroMissionView AS
  SELECT
    hero.name AS 'hero',
    mission.description AS 'mission',
    mission.villain AS 'villian',
    mission.plot AS 'plot'
  FROM hero, mission
  WHERE
    hero.missionID = mission.missionID;
```

Having a view means that you don't have to re-create the query each time. You can treat the view as a virtual table for new queries:

```
SELECT * FROM heroMissionView;
```

Managing Many-to-Many Joins

Inner joins are a perfect way to implement one-to-many relationships. If you look at ER diagrams, you often see many-to-many relationships, too. Of course, you also need to model them. Here's the secret: You can't really do it. It's true. The relational data model doesn't really have a good way to do many-to-many joins. Instead, you fake it out. It isn't hard, but it's a little bit sneaky.

You use many-to-many joins to handle listed data, such as the relationship between hero and power. Each hero can have any number of powers, and each power can belong to any number of heroes (see the table in Figure 4-14).

The inner join was easy because you just put a foreign key reference to the one side of the relationship in the many table. (See the section "Using an Inner Join to Combine Tables," earlier in this chapter.) In a many-to-many join, there is no "one" side, so where do you put the reference? Leave it to computer scientists to come up with a sneaky solution.

First, review the hero table in Figure 4-14.

Figure 4-14:
The hero table has no reference to powers.

Note that this table contains no reference to powers. Now, look at the power table in Figure 4-15. You see a lot of powers, but no reference to heroes.

Figure 4-15:
The power table has no reference to heroes.

Here's the tricky part. Take a look at a new table in Figure 4-16.

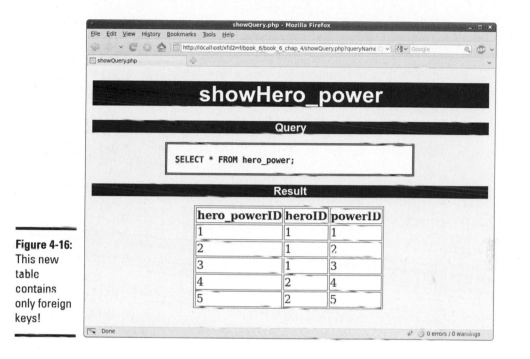

Figure 4-16:
This new
table
contains
only foreign
keys!

The results of this query may surprise you. The new table contains nothing but foreign keys. It doesn't make a lot of sense on its own, yet it represents one of the most important ideas in data.

Understanding link tables

The hero_power table shown in Figure 4-16 is a brand new table, and it's admittedly an odd little duck:

✦ **It contains no data of its own.** Very little appears inside the table.

✦ **It isn't about an entity.** All the tables shown earlier in this chapter are about entities in your data. This one isn't.

✦ **It's about a relationship.** This table is actually about relationships between hero and power. Each entry of this table is a link between hero and power.

✦ **It contains two foreign key references.** Each record in this table links an entry in the hero table with one in the power table.

✦ **It has a many-to-one join with each of the other two tables.** This table has a many-to-one relationship with the hero table. Each record of hero_power connects to one record of hero. Likewise, each record of hero_power connects to one record of power.

✦ **The two many-to-one joins create a many-to-many join.** Here's the magical part: By creating a table with two many-to-one joins, you create a many-to-many join between the original tables!

✦ **This type of structure is called a *link table*.** Link tables are used to create many-to-many relationships between entities.

Using link tables to make many-to-many joins

Figure 4-17 displays a full-blown ER diagram of the hero data.

Figure 4-17: Here's the ER diagram of the hero data.

Link tables aren't really useful on their own because they contain no actual data. Generally, you use a link table inside a query or view:

```
SELECT
  hero.name AS 'hero',
  power.name AS 'power'
FROM
  hero, power, hero_power
```

```
WHERE
  hero.heroID = hero_power.heroID
AND
  power.powerID = hero_power.powerID;
```

Here are some thoughts about this type of query:

✦ **It combines three tables.** That complexity seems scary at first, but it's really fine. The point of this query is to use the hero_power table to identify relationships between hero and power. Note that the FROM clause lists all three tables.

✦ **The** WHERE **clause has two links.** The first part of the WHERE clause links up the hero_power table with the hero table with an inner join. The second part links up the power table with another inner join.

✦ **You can use another** AND **clause to further limit the results.** Of course, you can still add other parts to the AND clause to make the results solve a particular problem, but I leave that alone for now.

Figure 4-18 shows the result of this query. Now, you have results you can use.

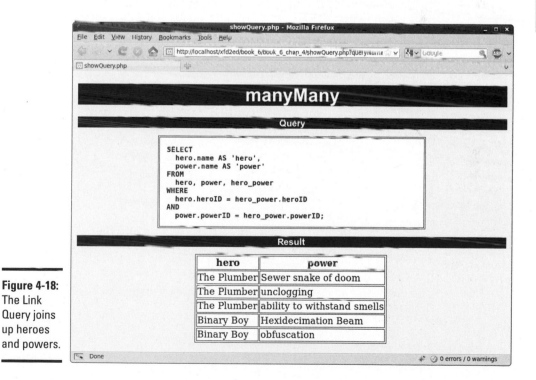

Figure 4-18:
The Link Query joins up heroes and powers.

Once again, this query is an obvious place for a view:

```
CREATE VIEW heroPowerView AS
  SELECT
    hero.name AS 'hero',
    power.name AS 'power'
  FROM
    hero, power, hero_power
  WHERE
    hero.heroID = hero_power.heroID
  AND
    power.powerID = hero_power.powerID;
```

Typically, you won't do your results exactly like this view. Instead, you display information for, say, Binary Boy, and you want a list of his powers. It isn't necessary to say Binary Boy three times, so you tend to use two queries (both from views, if possible) to simplify the task. For example, look at these two queries:

```
SELECT * FROM heroMissionView WHERE hero = 'binary boy';
SELECT power FROM heroPowerView WHERE hero = 'binary boy';
```

The combination of these queries gives you enough data to describe everything in the original table. Typically, you attach all this data together in your PHP code. Figure 4-19 shows a PHP page using both queries to build a complete picture of Binary Boy.

Figure 4-19: Use two different queries to get the formatting you want.

hero	Binary Boy
mission	Make the world safe for Binary representation
villian	Octal
plot	Eliminate the numerals 8 and 9
powers	• Hexidecimation Beam • obfuscation

showDetails.php - Mozilla Firefox

File Edit View History Bookmarks Tools Help

http://localhost/xfd2ed/book_6/book_6_chap_4/showDetails.php

The code is standard PHP data access, except it makes two passes to the database:

```
<!DOCTYPE html PUBLIC
"-//W3C//DTD XHTML 1.0 Strict//EN"
"http://www.w3.org/TR/xhtml1/DTD/xhtml1-strict.dtd">
<html lang = "EN" xml:lang = "EN" dir = "ltr">
```

```
<head>
<meta http-equiv="content-type" content="text/xml; charset=iso-8859-1" />
<title>showDetails.php</title>
<style type = "text/css">
  dt {
    float: left;
    width: 4em;
    clear: left;
  }

  dd {
    float: left;
    width: 20em;
  }
</style>

</head>

<body>
<?php
//connect
$conn = mysql_connect("localhost", "xfd", "password");
//change this password and username to work on your system
mysql_select_db("xfd");

//get most information for requested hero
$hero = "binary boy";
$query = <<<HERE
SELECT
  *
FROM
  heroMissionView
WHERE
  hero = '$hero'
HERE;

print "<dl> \n";
$result = mysql_query($query, $conn);
$row = mysql_fetch_assoc($result);
foreach ($row as $field => $value){
  print <<<HERE
  <dt>$field</dt>
  <dd>$value</dd>

HERE;
} // end foreach
print " <dt>powers</dt> \n";
print " <dd> \n";
print "   <ul> \n";

//create another query to grab the powers
$query = <<<HERE
SELECT
  power
FROM
  heroPowerView
WHERE hero = '$hero'
HERE;
```

```
//put powers in an unordered list
$result = mysql_query($query, $conn);
while ($row = mysql_fetch_assoc($result)){
  foreach ($row as $field => $value){
    print "    <li>$value</li> \n";
  } // end foreach
}  // end while loop
print "   </ul> \n";
print "</dd> \n";
print "</dl> \n";
?>
</body>
</html>
```

Refer to Book V to read more on PHP and how it's used to access databases.

Book VII

Into the Future with AJAX

The 5th Wave   By Rich Tennant

"Evidently he died of natural causes following a marathon session animating everything on his personal Web site. And no, Morganstern — the irony isn't lost on me."

Contents at a Glance

Chapter 1: AJAX Essentials

In This Chapter

✔ **Understanding AJAX**

✔ **Using JavaScript to manage HTTP requests**

✔ **Creating an XMLHttpRequest object**

✔ **Building a synchronous AJAX request**

✔ **Retrieving data from an AJAX request**

✔ **Managing asynchronous AJAX requests**

*I*f you've been following the Web trends, you've no doubt heard of AJAX. This technology has generated a lot of interest. Depending on who you listen to, it's either going to change the Internet or it's a lot of overblown hype. In this chapter, I show you what AJAX really is, how to use it, and how to use a particular AJAX library to supercharge your Web pages.

The first thing is to figure out exactly what AJAX is and what it isn't. It isn't:

✦ **A programming language:** It isn't one more language to learn along with the many others you encounter.

✦ **New:** Most of the technology used in AJAX isn't really all that new; it's the way the technology is being used that's different.

✦ **Remarkably different:** For the most part, AJAX is about the same things you'll see in the rest of this book: building compliant Web pages that interact with the user.

So you have to be wondering why people are so excited about AJAX. It's a relatively simple thing, but it has the potential to change the way people think about Internet development. Here's what it really is:

✦ **Direct control of client-server communication:** Rather than the automatic communication between client and server that happens with Web forms and server-side programs, AJAX is about managing this relationship more directly.

✦ **Use of the XMLHttpRequest object:** This is a special object that's been built into the DOM of all major browsers for some time, but it wasn't used heavily. The real innovation of AJAX was finding creative (and perhaps unintentional) uses for this heretofore virtually unknown utility.

+ **A closer relationship between client-side and server-side programming:** Up to now, client-side programs (usually JavaScript) did their own thing, and server-side programs (PHP) operated without too much knowledge of each other. AJAX helps these two types of programming work together better.

+ **A series of libraries that facilitate this communication:** AJAX isn't that hard, but it does have a lot of details. Several great libraries have sprung up to simplify using AJAX technologies. You can find AJAX libraries for both client-side languages, like JavaScript, and server-side languages, like PHP.

Perhaps you're making an online purchase with a shopping-cart mechanism.

In a typical (pre-AJAX) system, an entire Web page is downloaded to the user's computer. There may be a limited amount of JavaScript-based interactivity, but anything that requires a data request needs to be sent back to the server. For example, if you're on a shopping site and you want more information about that fur-lined fishbowl you've had your eye on, you might click the More Information button. This causes a request to be sent to the server, which builds an entirely new Web page for you containing your new request.

Every time you make a request, the system builds a whole new page on the fly. The client and server have a long-distance relationship.

In the old days when you wanted to manage your Web site's content, you had to refresh each Web page — time-consuming to say the least. But with AJAX, you can update the content on a page without refreshing the page. Instead of the server sending an entire page response just to update a few words on the page, the server *just sends the words you want to update and nothing else.*

If you're using an AJAX-enabled shopping cart, you might still click the fishbowl image. An AJAX request goes to the server and gets information about the fishbowl, which is immediately placed on the current page, without requiring a complete page refresh.

AJAX technology allows you to send a request to the server, which can then change just a small part of the page. With AJAX, you can have a whole bunch of smaller requests happening all the time, rather than a few big ones that rebuild the page in large, distracting flurries of activity.

To the user, this makes the Web page look more like traditional applications. This is the big appeal of AJAX: It allows Web applications to act more like desktop applications, even if these Web applications have complicated features like remote database access.

Google's Gmail was the first major application to use AJAX, and it blew people away because it felt so much like a regular application inside a Web browser.

AJAX Spelled Out

Technical people love snappy acronyms. Nothing is more intoxicating than inventing a term. AJAX is one term that has taken on a life of its own. Like many computing acronyms, it may be fun to say, but it doesn't really mean much. AJAX stands for Asynchronous JavaScript And XML. Truthfully, these terms were probably chosen to make a pronounceable acronym rather than for their accuracy or relevance to how AJAX works.

A is for asynchronous

An *asynchronous* transaction (at least in AJAX terms) is one in which more than one thing can happen at once. For example, you can make an AJAX call process a request while the rest of your form is being processed. AJAX requests do not absolutely have to be asynchronous, but they usually are.

When it comes to Web design, *asynchronous* means that you can independently send and receive as many different requests as you want. Data may start transmitting at any time without having any effect on other data transmissions. You could have a form that saves each field to the database as soon as it's filled out, or perhaps a series of drop-down lists that generate the next drop-down list based on the value you just selected. (It's okay if this doesn't make sense right now. It's not an important part of understanding AJAX, but vowels are always nice in an acronym.)

In this chapter, I show you how to do both synchronous and asynchronous versions of AJAX.

Book VII
Chapter 1

AJAX Essentials

J is for JavaScript

If you want to make an AJAX call, you simply write some JavaScript code that simulates a form. You can then access a special object hidden in the DOM (the `XMLHttpRequest` object) and use its methods to send that request to the user. Your program acts like a form, even if there was no form there. In that sense, when you're writing AJAX code, you're really using JavaScript. Of course, you can also use any other client-side programming language that can speak with the DOM, including Flash and (to a lesser extent) Java. JavaScript is the dominant technology, so it's in the acronym.

A lot of times, you also use JavaScript to decode the response from the AJAX request.

A is for . . . and?

I think it's a stretch to use *And* in an acronym, but AJX just isn't as cool as AJAX. They didn't ask me.

And X is for . . . data

The *X* is for *XML,* which is one way to send the data back and forth from the server. Because the object you're using is the XMLHttpRequest object, it makes sense that it requests XML. It can do that, but it can also get any kind of text data. You can use AJAX to retrieve all kinds of things:

✦ **Plain old text:** Sometimes you just want to grab some text from the server. Maybe you have a text file with a daily quote in it or something.

✦ **Formatted HTML:** You can have text stored on the server as a snippet of HTML/XHTML code and use AJAX to load this page snippet into your browser. This gives you a powerful way to build a page from a series of smaller segments. You can use this to reuse parts of your page (say, headings or menus) without duplicating them on the server.

✦ **XML data:** XML is a great way to pass data around. (That's what it was invented for.) You might send a request to a program that goes to a database, makes a request, and returns the result as XML.

✦ **JSON data:** A new standard called JSON (JavaScript Object Notation) is emerging as an alternative to XML for formatted data transfer. It has some interesting advantages. You might have already built JSON objects in Book IV, Chapter 4. You can read in a text file already formatted as a JavaScript object.

Making a Basic AJAX Connection

AJAX uses some pretty technical parts of the Web in ways that may be unfamiliar to you. Read through the rest of this chapter so that you know what AJAX is doing, but don't get bogged down in the details. *Nobody does it by hand!* (Except people who write AJAX libraries or books about using AJAX.) In Chapter 2 of this minibook, I show a library that does all the work for you. If all these details are making you misty-eyed, just skip ahead to the next chapter and come back here when you're ready to see how all the magic works.

The basicAJax.html program shown in Figure 1-1 illustrates AJAX at work.

Figure 1-1:
Click the
button and
you'll see
some AJAX
magic.

When the user clicks the link, the small pop-up shown in Figure 1-2 appears.

Figure 1-2:
This text
came from
the server.

If you don't get the joke, you need to go rent *Monty Python and the Holy Grail.*
It's part of the geek culture. Trust me. In fact, you should really own a copy.

It's very easy to make JavaScript pop up a dialog box, but the interesting
thing here is where that text comes from. The data is stored on a text file on
the server. Without AJAX, you don't have an easy way to get data from the
server without reloading the entire page.

You might claim that HTML frames allow you to pull data from the server, but frames have been deprecated in XHTML because they cause a lot of other problems. You can use a frame to load data from the server, but you can't do all the other cool things with frame-based data that you can with AJAX. Even if frames were allowed, AJAX is a much better solution most of the time.

You won't be able to run this example straight from the CD-ROM. Like PHP, AJAX requires a server to work properly. If you want to run this program, put it in a subdirectory of your server and run it through localhost as you do for PHP programs.

This particular example uses a couple of shortcuts to make it easier to understand:

✦ **The program isn't fully asynchronous.** The program pauses while it retrieves data. As a user, you probably won't even notice this, but as you'll see, this can have a serious drawback. But the synchronous approach is a bit simpler, so I start with this example and then extend it to make the asynchronous version.

✦ **This example isn't completely cross-browser-compatible.** The AJAX technique I use in this program works fine for IE 7 and all versions of Firefox (and most other standards-compliant browsers). It does not work correctly in IE 6 and earlier. I recommend that you use jQuery or another library (described in Chapter 2 of this minibook) for cross-browser compatibility.

Look over the following code, and you'll find it reasonable enough:

```
<!DOCTYPE html PUBLIC
"-//W3C//DTD XHTML 1.0 Strict//EN"
"http://www.w3.org/TR/xhtml1/DTD/xhtml1-strict.dtd">
<html lang = "EN" xml:lang = "EN" dir = "ltr">
<head>
<meta http-equiv="content-type" content="text/xml; charset=utf-8" />

<title>Basic AJAX</title>
<script type = "text/javascript">
//<![CDATA[

function getAJAX(){
  var request = new XMLHttpRequest();
  request.open("GET", "beast.txt", false);
  request.send(null);

  if (request.status == 200){
    //we got a response
    alert(request.responseText);
  } else {
    //something went wrong
    alert("Error- " + request.status + ": " + request.statusText);
  } // end if
} // end function
//]]>
```

```
</script>

</head>

<body>
<h1>Basic AJAX</h1>

<form action = "">
  <p>
    <button type = "button"
            onclick = "getAJAX()">
      Summon the vicious beast of Caerbannog
    </button>
  </p>
</form>


</body>
</html>
```

Throughout this chapter, I explain exactly how to build an AJAX-enabled Web page by hand. It's good to know how this works, but almost nobody does it this way in the real world. Read this chapter to get the basic understanding, but don't worry if the details are a little foggy. The other chapters in this minibook describe a powerful library that greatly simplifies AJAX programming. Feel free to skip ahead if this chapter is too technical. Just come back when you're ready.

Building the HTML form

You don't absolutely need an HTML form for AJAX, but I have a simple one here. Note that the form is not attached to the server in any way.

```
<form action = "">
  <p>
    <button type = "button"
            onclick = "getAJAX()">
      Summon the vicious beast of Caerbannog
    </button>
  </p>
</form>
```

This page is set up like a client-side (JavaScript) interaction. The form has an empty action element. The code uses a button (not a submit element), and the button is attached to a JavaScript function called getAJAX().

All you really need is some kind of structure that can trigger a JavaScript function.

AJAX isn't a complex technology, but it does draw on several other technologies. You may need to look over the JavaScript chapters in Book IV if this material is unfamiliar to you. Although these examples don't require PHP, they do involve server-side responses like PHP does, so AJAX is usually studied by people who are already familiar with both JavaScript and PHP as well as the foundational XHTML and CSS environments.

Creating an XMLHttpRequest object

The key to AJAX is a special object called XMLHttpRequest. All the major browsers have it, and knowing how to use it in code is what makes AJAX work. It's pretty easy to create:

```
var request = new XMLHttpRequest();
```

Internet Explorer 5 and 6 had an entirely different way of invoking the XMLHttpRequest object that involved a technology called ActiveX. If you want to support these older browsers, use one of the libraries that I mention in Chapter 2 of this minibook. I've decided not to worry about them in this introductory chapter.

This line makes an instance of the XMLHttpRequest object. You use methods and properties of this object to control a request to the server.

AJAX is really nothing more than HTTP, the protocol that your browser and server quietly use all the time to communicate with each other. You can think of an AJAX request like this: Imagine that you have a basket with a balloon tied to the handle and a long string. As you walk around the city, you can release the basket under a particular window and let it rise. The window (server) puts something in the basket, and you can then wind the string to bring the basket back down and retrieve the contents. The various characteristics of the XMLHttpRequest object are described in Table 1-1.

Table 1-1   Useful Members of the XMLHttpRequest Object

Member	Description	Basket Analogy
open(protocol, URL, synchronization)	Opens a connection to the indicated file on the server.	Stand under a particular window.
send(parameters)	Initiates the transaction with given parameters (or null).	Release the basket but hang on to the string.
status	Returns the HTTP status code returned by the server (200 is success).	Check for error codes ("window closed," "balloon popped," "string broken," or "everything's great").
statusText	Text form of HTTP status.	Text form of status code.
responseText	Text of the transaction's response.	Get the contents of the basket.

Member	Description	Basket Analogy
readyState	Describes the current status of the transaction (4 is complete).	Is the basket empty, going up, coming down, or here and ready to get contents?
onReadyStateChange	Event handler. Attach a function to this para-meter, and when the ready State changes, the function will be called automatically.	What should I do when the state of the basket changes? For example, should I do something when I've gotten the basket back?

Don't worry about all the details in Table 1-1. I describe these things as you need them in the text. Also, some of these elements only pertain to asynchronous connections, so you won't always need them all.

Opening a connection to the server

The XMLHttpRequest object has several useful methods. One of the most important is the open() method:

```
request.open("GET", "beast.txt", false);
```

The open() method opens a connection to the server. As far as the server is concerned, this connection is identical to the connection made when the user clicks a link or submits a form. The open() method takes the following three parameters:

✦ **Request method:** The request method describes how the server should process the request. The values are identical to the form method values described in Book V, Chapter 3. Typical values are GET and POST.

✦ **A file or program name:** The second parameter is the name of a file or program on the server. This is usually a program or file in the same directory as the current page.

✦ **A synchronization trigger:** AJAX can be done in synchronous or asynchronous mode. (Yeah, I know, then it would just be JAX, but stay with me here.) The synchronous form is easier to understand, so I use it first. The next example (and all the others in this book) uses the asynchronous approach.

For this example, I use the GET mechanism to load a file called beast.txt from the server in synchronized mode.

Sending the request and parameters

After you've opened a request, you need to pass that request to the server. The `send()` method performs this task. It also provides you with a mechanism for sending data to the server. This only makes sense if the request is going to a PHP program (or some other program on the server). Because I'm just requesting a regular text document, I send the value null to the server: Chapter 6 of this minibook describes how to work with other kinds of data.

```
request.send(null);
```

This is a synchronous connection, so the program pauses here until the server sends the requested file. If the server never responds, the page will hang. (This is exactly why you usually use asynchronous connections.) Because this is just a test program, assume that everything will work okay and motor on.

Returning to the basket analogy, the `send()` method releases the basket, which floats up to the window. In a synchronous connection, you assume that the basket is filled and comes down automatically. The next step doesn't happen until the basket is back on earth. (But if something went wrong, the next step may *never* happen, because the basket will never come back.)

Checking the status

The next line of code doesn't happen until the server passes some sort of response. Any HTTP request is followed by a numeric code. Normally, your browser checks these codes automatically, and you don't see them. Occasionally, you run across an HTTP error code, like 404 (file not found) or 500 (internal server error). If the server was able to respond to the request, it passes a status code of 200.

The `XMLHttpRequest` object has a property called `status` that returns the HTTP status code. If the status is 200, everything went fine and you can proceed. If the status is some other value, some type of error occurred.

Make sure that the status of the request is successful before you run the code that depends on the request. (Don't get anything out of the basket unless the entire process worked.)

You can check for all the various status codes if you want, but for this simple example, I'm just ensuring that the status is 200:

```
if (request.status == 200){
  //we got a response
  alert(request.responseText);
} else {
  //something went wrong
  alert("Error- " + request.status + ": " + request.statusText);
} // end if
```

Fun with HTTP response codes

Just like the post office stamping success/error messages on your envelope, the server sends back status messages with your request. You can see all the possible status codes on the World Wide Web Consortium's Web site at `www.w3.org/Protocols/rfc2616/rfc2616-sec10.html`, but the important ones to get you started are as follows:

✔ `200 = OK`: This is a success code. Everything went okay, and your response has been returned.

✔ `400 = Bad Request`: This is a client error code. It means that something went wrong on the user side. The request was poorly formed and couldn't be understood.

✔ `404 = Not Found`: This is a client error code. The page the user requested doesn't exist or couldn't be found.

✔ `408 = Request Timeout`: This is a client error code. The server gave up on waiting for the user's computer to finish making its request.

✔ `500 = Internal Server Error`: This is a server error code. It means that the server had an error and couldn't fill the request.

The `request.status` property contains the server response. If this value is 200, I want to do something with the results. In this case, I simply display the text in an alert box. If the request is anything but 200, I use the `statusText` property to determine what went wrong and pass that information to the user in an alert.

The `status` property is like looking at the basket after it returns. It might have the requested data in it, or it might have some sort of note. ("Sorry, the window was closed. I couldn't fulfill your request.") There's not much point in processing the data if it didn't return successfully.

Of course, I could do a lot more with the data. If it's already formatted as HTML code, I can use the `innerHTML` DOM tricks described in Book IV to display the code on any part of my page. It might also be some other type of formatted data (XML or JSON) that I can manipulate with JavaScript and do whatever I want with.

All Together Now — Making the Connection Asynchronous

The synchronous AJAX connection described in the previous section is easy to understand, but it has one major drawback: The client's page stops processing while waiting for a response from the server. This doesn't seem like a big problem, but it is. If aliens attack the Web server, it won't make the connection, and the rest of the page will never be activated. The user's browser will hang indefinitely. In most cases, the user will have to shut down the browser process by pressing Ctrl+Alt+Delete (or the similar procedure on other OSs). Obviously, it would be best to prevent this kind of error.

That's why most AJAX calls use the asynchronous technique. Here's the big difference: When you send an asynchronous request, the client keeps on processing the rest of the page. When the request is complete, an event handler processes the event. If the server goes down, the browser will not hang (although the page probably won't do what you want).

In other words, the readyState property is like looking at the basket's progress. The basket could be sitting there empty because you haven't begun the process. It could be going up to the window, being filled, coming back down, or it could be down and ready to use. You're only concerned with the last state, because that means the data is ready.

I didn't include a figure of the asynchronous version, because to the user, it looks exactly the same as the synchronous connection. Be sure to put this code on your own server and check it out for yourself.

The asynchronous version looks exactly the same on the front end, but the code is structured a little differently:

```
<!DOCTYPE html PUBLIC
"-//W3C//DTD XHTML 1.0 Strict//EN"
"http://www.w3.org/TR/xhtml1/DTD/xhtml1-strict.dtd">
<html lang = "EN" xml:lang = "EN" dir = "ltr">
<head>
<meta http-equiv="content-type" content="text/xml; charset=utf-8" />

<title>asynch.html</title>
<script type = "text/javascript">
//<![CDATA[

var request;  //make request a global variable

function getAJAX(){
  request = new XMLHttpRequest();
  request.open("GET", "beast.txt");
  request.onreadystatechange = checkData;
  request.send(null);
} // end function

function checkData(){
  if (request.readyState == 4) {
    // if state is finished
    if (request.status == 200) {
      // and if attempt was successful
      alert(request.responseText);
    } // end if
  } // end if
} // end checkData
```

```
//]]>

</script>

</head>

<body>
<h1>Asynchronous AJAX transmission</h1>
<form action = "">
  <p>
    <button type = "button"
            onclick = "getAJAX()">
      Summon the beast of Caerbannogh
    </button>
  </p>
</form>
</body>
</html>
```

Setting up the program

The general setup of this program is just like the earlier AJAX example. The HTML is a simple button that calls the getAJAX() function.

The JavaScript code now has two functions. The getAJAX() function sets up the request, but a separate function (checkData()) responds to the request. In an asynchronous AJAX model, you typically separate the request and the response in different functions.

Note that in the JavaScript code, I made the XMLHttpRequest object (request) a global variable by declaring it outside any functions. I generally avoid making global variables, but it makes sense in this case because I have two different functions that require the request object.

Building the getAJAX() function

The getAJAX() function sets up and executes the communication with the server:

```
function getAJAX(){
  request = now XMLHttpRequest();
  request.open("GET", "beast.txt");
  request.onreadystatechange = checkData;
  request.send(null);
} // end function
```

The code in this function is pretty straightforward:

1. Create the request object.

The request object is created exactly as it was in the first example in the section "Creating an XMLHttpRequest object," earlier in this chapter.

2. **Call `request`'s `open()` method to open a connection.**

   Note that this time I left the synchronous parameter out, which creates the (default) asynchronous connection.

3. **Assign an event handler to catch responses.**

   You can use event handlers much like the ones in the DOM. In this particular case, I'm telling the `request` object to call a function called `checkData` whenever the state of the request changes.

   You can't easily send a parameter to a function when you call it using this particular mechanism. That's why I made `request` a global variable.

4. **Send the request.**

   As before, the `send()` method begins the process. Because this is now an asynchronous connection, the rest of the page continues to process. As soon as the request's state changes (hopefully because a successful transfer has occurred), the `checkData` function is activated.

Ready, set, ready state!

The `readyState` property of the `request` object indicates the ready state of the request. It has five possible values:

- 0 = Uninitialized: The `request` object has been created, but the `open()` method hasn't been called on.

- 1 = Loading: The `request` object has been created, the `open()` method has been called, but the `send()` method hasn't been called.

- 2 = Loaded: The `request` object has been created, the `open()` method has been called, the `send()` method has been called, but the response isn't yet available from the server.

- 3 = Interactive: The `request` object has been created, the `open()` method has

been called, the `send()` method has been called, the response has started trickling back from the server, but not everything has been received yet.

- 4 = Completed: The `request` object has been created, the `open()` method has been called, the `send()` method has been called, the response has been fully received, and the `request` object is finished with all its request/response tasks.

Each time the `readyState` property of the request changes, the function you map to `readyStateChanged` is called. In a typical AJAX program, this happens four times per transaction. There's no point in reading the data until the transaction is completed, which will happen when `readyState` is equal to 4.

Reading the response

Of course, you now need a function to handle the response when it comes back from the server. This works by checking the *ready state* of the response. Any HTTP request has a ready state, which is a simple integer value that describes what state the request is currently in. You find many ready states, but the only one you're concerned with is 4, meaning that the request is finished and ready to process.

The basic strategy for checking a response is to check the ready state in the aptly named `request.readyState` property. If the ready state is 4, check the status code to ensure that no error exists. If the ready state is 4 and the status is 200, you're in business, so you can process the form. Here's the code:

```
function checkData(){
  if (request.readyState == 4) {
    // if state is finished
    if (request.status == 200) {
      // and if attempt was successful
      alert(request.responseText);
    } // end if
  } // end if
} // end checkData
```

Once again, you can do anything you want with the text you receive. I'm just printing it, but the data can be incorporated into the page or processed in any way you want.

Chapter 2: Improving JavaScript and AJAX with jQuery

In This Chapter

- ✔ Downloading and including the jQuery library
- ✔ Making an AJAX request with jQuery
- ✔ Using component selectors
- ✔ Adding events to components
- ✔ Creating a simple content management system with jQuery

*J*avaScript has amazing capabilities. It's useful on its own, and when you add AJAX, it becomes incredibly powerful. However, JavaScript can be tedious. You have a lot to remember, and it can be a real pain to handle multiplatform issues. Some tasks (like AJAX) are a bit complex and require a lot of steps. Regardless of the task, you always have browser-compatibility issues to deal with.

For these reasons, Web programmers began to compile commonly used functions into reusable libraries. These libraries became more powerful over time, and some of them have now become fundamental to Web development.

As these libraries became more powerful, they not only added AJAX capabilities, but many of them also added features to JavaScript/DOM programming that were once available only in traditional programming languages. Many of these libraries allow a new visual aesthetic as well as enhanced technical capabilities. In fact, most applications considered part of the Web 2.0 revolution are based in part on one of these libraries.

A number of very powerful JavaScript/AJAX libraries are available. All make basic JavaScript easier, and each has its own learning curve. No library writes code for you, but a good library can handle some of the drudgery and let you work instead on the creative aspects of your program. JavaScript libraries can let you work at a higher level than plain JavaScript, writing more elaborate pages in less time.

What is Web 2.0?

I'm almost reluctant to mention the term *Web 2.0* here, because it isn't really a very useful description. People describe Web 2.0 — if such a thing really exists — in three main ways:

✔ Some talk about Web 2.0 as a design paradigm (lots of white space, simple color schemes, rounded corners). I believe the visual trends will evolve to something else and that other aspects of the Web 2.0 sensibility will have a longer-lasting impact.

✔ The technical aspects of Web 2.0 (heavy use of AJAX and libraries to make Web programming more like traditional programming) are more important than the visual aspects. These technologies make it possible to build Web applications in much the same way that desktop applications are now created.

✔ I personally think the most important emerging model of the Web is the change in the communication paradigm. Web 2.0 is no longer about a top-down broadcast model of communication, but more of a conversation among users of a site or system. While the visual and technical aspects are important, the changing relationship between producers and users of information is perhaps more profound.

The design and communication aspects are fascinating, but this book focuses on the technical aspects. When you work in Web 2.0 technologies, decide for yourself how you will express the technology visually and socially. I can't wait to see what you produce.

Several important JavaScript/AJAX libraries are available. Here are a few of the most prominent:

✦ **DOJO:** A very powerful library that includes a series of user interface widgets (like those in Visual Basic and Java) as well as AJAX features.

✦ **MochiKit:** A nice lower-level set of JavaScript functions to improve JavaScript programming. It makes JavaScript act much more like the Python language, with an interactive interpreter.

✦ **Prototype:** One of the first AJAX libraries to become popular. It includes great support for AJAX and extensions for user interface objects (through the scriptaculous extension).

✦ **Yahoo User Interface (YUI):** This is used by Yahoo! for all its AJAX applications. Yahoo! has released this impressive library as open source.

✦ **jQuery:** This has emerged as one of the more popular JavaScript and AJAX libraries. It is the library emphasized in this book.

Introducing jQuery

This book focuses on the jQuery library. While many outstanding AJAX/ JavaScript libraries are available, jQuery has quickly become one of the most prominent. The following are some reasons for the popularity of jQuery:

✦ **It's a powerful library.** The jQuery system is incredibly powerful. It can do all kinds of impressive things to make your JavaScript easier to write.

✦ **It's lightweight.** You need to include a reference to your library in every file that needs it. The entire jQuery library fits in 55K, which is smaller than many image files. It won't have a significant impact on download speed.

✦ **It supports a flexible selection mechanism.** jQuery greatly simplifies and expands the `document.getElementById` mechanism that's central to DOM manipulation.

✦ **It has great animation support.** You can use jQuery to make elements appear and fade, move and slide.

✦ **It makes AJAX queries trivial.** You'll be shocked at how easy AJAX is with jQuery.

✦ **It has an enhanced event mechanism.** JavaScript has very limited support for events. jQuery adds a very powerful tool for adding event handlers to nearly any element.

✦ **It provides cross-platform support.** The jQuery library tries to manage browser-compatibility issues for you, so you don't have to stress so much about exactly which browser is being used.

✦ **It supports user interface widgets.** jQuery comes with a powerful user interface library, including tools HTML doesn't have, like drag-and-drop controls, sliders, and date pickers.

✦ **It's highly extensible.** jQuery has a plug-in library that supports all kinds of optional features, including new widgets and tools like audio integration, image galleries, menus, and much more.

✦ **It introduces powerful new programming ideas.** jQuery is a great tool for learning about some really interesting ideas like functional programming and chainable objects. I explain these as you encounter them, mainly in Chapter 4 of this minibook.

✦ **It's free and open source.** It's available under an open-source license, which means it costs nothing to use, and you can look it over and change it if you wish.

✦ **It's reasonably typical.** If you choose to use a different AJAX library, you can still transfer the ideas you learned in jQuery.

Installing jQuery

The jQuery library is easy to install and use. Follow these steps:

1. **Go to http://jquery.com.**

2. **Download the current version.**

   As of this writing, the most current version is 1.4.2.

 You may be able to choose from a number of versions of the file. I recommend the minimized version for actual use. To make this file as small as possible, every unnecessary character (including spaces and carriage returns) was removed. This file is very compact but difficult to read. Download the nonminimized version if you want to actually read the code, but it's generally better to include the minimized version in your programs.

3. **Store the resulting `.js` file to your working directory.**

   `jQuery-1.4.2.min.js` is the current file.

To incorporate the library in your pages, simply link to it as an external JavaScript file:

```
<script type = "text/javascript"
        src = "jquery-1.4.2.min.js"></script>
```

 Be sure to include the preceding code before you write or include other code that refers to jQuery.

Importing jQuery from Google

 Easy as it is to add jQuery support, you have another great way to add jQuery (and other AJAX library) support to your pages without downloading anything. Google has a publicly available version of several important libraries (including jQuery) that you can download from its servers.

This has a couple of interesting advantages:

✦ **You don't have to install any libraries.** All the library files stay on the Google server.

✦ **The library is automatically updated.** You always have access to the latest version of the library without making any changes to your code.

✦ **The library may load faster.** The first time one of your pages reads the library from Google's servers, you have to wait for the full download, but then the library is stored in a *cache* (a form of browser memory) so that subsequent requests are essentially immediate.

Here's how you do it:

```
<script type = "text/javacript"
        src="http://www.google.com/jsapi"></script>
<script type = "text/javacript">
  //<[CDATA[
  // Load jQuery
  google.load("jquery", "1");

  //your code here

  //]]>
</script>
```

Essentially, loading jQuery from Google is a two-step process:

1. **Load the Google API from Google.**

   Use the first `<script>` tag to refer to the Google AJAX API server. This gives you access to the `google.load()` function.

2. **Invoke `google.load()` to load jQuery.**

   - The first parameter is the name of the library you want to load.

   - The second parameter is the version number. If you leave this parameter blank, you get the latest version. If you specify a number, Google gives you the latest variation of that version. In my example, I want the latest variation of version 1, but not version 2. While version 2 doesn't exist yet, I expect it to have major changes, and I don't want any surprises.

Book VII
Chapter 2

Improving
JavaScript and
AJAX with jQuery

Note that you don't need to install any files locally to use the Google approach.

All these options for managing jQuery can be dizzying. Use whichever technique works best for you. I prefer using the local code rather than the Google solution because I find it easier, and this method works even if I'm offline. For smaller projects (like the demonstrations in this chapter), I don't like the overhead of the Aptana solution or the online requirement of Google. In this chapter, I simply refer to a local copy of the jQuery file.

Your First jQuery App

As an introduction to jQuery, build an application that you can already create in JavaScript/DOM. This introduces you to some powerful features of jQuery. Figure 2-1 illustrates the `change.html` page at work, but the interesting stuff (as usual) is under the hood.

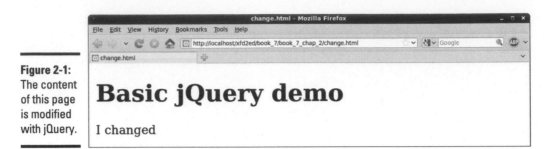

Figure 2-1:
The content
of this page
is modified
with jQuery.

Setting up the page

At first, the jQuery app doesn't look much different than any other HTML/
JavaScript code you've already written, but the JavaScript code is a bit
different:

```
<!DOCTYPE html PUBLIC "-//W3C//DTD XHTML 1.0 Strict//EN"
"http://www.w3.org/TR/xhtml1/DTD/xhtml1-strict.dtd">
<html lang="EN" dir="ltr" xmlns="http://www.w3.org/1999/
    xhtml">
<head>
  <meta http-equiv="content-type" content="text/xml;
  charset=utf-8" />

  <title>change.html</title>
  <script type = "text/javascript"
          src = "jquery-1.4.2.min.js"></script>

  <script type = "text/javascript">
    //<![CDATA[
    function changeMe(){
      $("#output").html("I changed");
    }

    //]]>
  </script>
</head>
<body onload = "changeMe()">
        <h1>Basic jQuery demo</h1>
    <div id = "output">
      Did this change?
    </div>
</body>
</html>
```

If you're already knowledgeable about jQuery, you may be horrified at my
use of `body onload` in this example. jQuery provides a wonderful alternative to the onload mechanism, but I want to introduce only one big, new
idea at a time. The next example illustrates the jQuery alternative to `body
onload` and explains why it is such an improvement.

The basic features of changeme.html are utterly unsurprising:

✦ **The HTML has a div named output.** This div initially says, "Did this change?" The code should change the content to something else.

✦ **The HTML calls a function called changeMe() when the body finishes loading.** This is a mechanism used frequently in DOM programming, although you see a new way to call an initial function in the next section.

✦ **There is a reference to the jQuery library.** Any page that uses jQuery must load it using one of the mechanisms described earlier in this chapter.

✦ **The changeMe() function looks really crazy.** When you run the program, you can tell what it does. The code gets a reference to the output div and changes its innerHTML property to reflect a new value ("I've changed."). However, the syntax is really new. All that functionality got packed into one line of (funky-looking) code.

Meet the jQuery node object

The secret behind jQuery's power is the underlying data model. jQuery has a unique way of looking at the DOM that's more powerful than the standard object model. Understanding the way this works is the key to powerful programming with jQuery.

The jQuery *node* is a special object that adds a lot of functionality to the ordinary DOM element. Any element on the Web page (any link, div, heading, or whatever) can be defined as a jQuery node. You can also make a list of jQuery nodes based on tag types, so you can have a jQuery object that stores a list of all the paragraphs on the page or all the objects with a particular class name. The jQuery object has very useful methods like html(), which is used to change the innerHTML property of an element.

The jQuery node is based on the basic DOM node, so it can be created from any DOM element. However, it also adds significant new features. This is a good example of the object-oriented philosophy.

Creating a jQuery object

You have many ways to create a jQuery object, but the simplest is through the special $() function. You can place an identifier (very similar to CSS identifiers) inside the function to build a jQuery object based on an element. For example,

```
var jQoutput = $("#output");
```

creates a variable called `jQoutput`, which contains a jQuery object based on the `output` element. It's similar to the following:

```
var DOMoutput = document.getElementById("output");
```

The jQuery approach is a little cleaner, and it doesn't get a reference to a DOM object (as the `getElementById` technique does), but it makes a new jQuery object that is based on the DOM element. Don't worry if this is a little hard to understand. It gets easier as you get used to it.

Enjoying your new jQuery node object

Because `jQoutput` is a jQuery object, it has some powerful methods. For example, you can change the content of the object with the `html()` method. The following two lines are equivalent:

```
jQoutput.html("I've changed"); //jQuery version
DOMoutput.innerHTML = "I've changed"; //ordinary JS / DOM
```

jQuery doesn't require you to create variables for each object, so the code in the `changeMe()` function can look like this:

```
//build a variable and then modify it
var jQoutput = $("#output");
jQoutput.html("I've changed");
```

Or you can shorten it like this:

```
        $("#output").html("I've changed");
```

This last version is how the program is actually written. It's very common to refer to an object with the `$()` mechanism and immediately perform a method on that object as I've done here.

Creating an Initialization Function

Many pages require an initialization function. This is a function that's run early to set up the rest of the page. The `body onload` mechanism is frequently used in DOM/JavaScript to make pages load as soon as the document has begun loading. This technique is described in Book IV, Chapter 7. While `body onload` does this job well, a couple of problems exist with the traditional technique:

✦ **It requires making a change to the HTML.** The JavaScript code should be completely separated from HTML. You shouldn't have to change your HTML to make it work with JavaScript.

✦ **The timing still isn't quite right.** The code specified in `body unload` doesn't execute until after the entire page is displayed. It would be better if the code was registered *after* the DOM is loaded but *before* the page displays.

Using $(document).ready()

JQuery has a great alternative to `body onload` that overcomes these shortcomings. Take a look at the code for `ready.html` to see how it works:

```
<!DOCTYPE html PUBLIC "-//W3C//DTD XHTML 1.0 Strict//EN"
"http://www.w3.org/TR/xhtml1/DTD/xhtml1-strict.dtd">
<html lang="EN" dir="ltr" xmlns="http://www.w3.org/1999/
    xhtml">
<head>
  <meta http-equiv="content-type" content="text/xml;
   charset=utf-8" />

  <title>ready.html</title>
  <script type = "text/javascript"
          src = "jquery-1.4.2.min.js"></script>

  <script type = "text/javascript">
    //<![CDATA[
    $(document).ready(changeMe);

    function changeMe(){
      $("#output").html("I've changed");
    }

    //]]>
  </script>
</head>
<body>
    <h1>Using the document.ready mechanism</h1>
    <div id = "output">
      Did this change?
    </div>
</body>
</html>
```

This code is much like `change.html`, but it uses the jQuery technique for running initialization code:

✦ **The body tag no longer has an `onload` attribute.** This is a common feature of jQuery programming. The HTML no longer has direct links to the JavaScript because jQuery lets the JavaScript code attach itself to the Web page.

✦ **The initialization function is created with the `$(document).ready()` function.** This technique tells the browser to execute a function when the DOM has finished loading (so that it has access to all elements of the form) but before the page is displayed (so that any effects of the form appear instantaneous to the user).

✦ **`$(document)` makes a jQuery object from the whole document.** The entire document can be turned into a jQuery object by specifying `document` inside the `$()` function. Note that you don't use quotation marks in this case.

✦ **The function specified is automatically run.** In this particular case, I want to run the `changeMe()` function, so I place it in the parameter of the `ready()` method. Note that I'm referring to `changeMe` as a variable, so it has no quotation marks or parentheses. (Look at Book IV, Chapter 7 for more discussion of referring to functions as variables.)

You see several other places (particularly in event handling) where jQuery expects a function as a parameter. Such a function is frequently referred to as a *callback* function, because it's called after some sort of event has occurred. You also see callback functions that respond to keyboard events, mouse motion, and the completion of an AJAX request.

Alternatives to document.ready

You sometimes see a couple of shortcuts, because it's so common to run initialization code. You can shorten

```
$(document).ready(changeMe);
```

to the following code:

```
$(changeMe);
```

If this code is not defined inside a function and `changeMe` is a function defined on the page, jQuery automatically runs the function directly just like the `document.ready` approach.

You can also create an anonymous function directly:

```
$(document).ready(function(){
  $("#output").html("I changed");
});
```

I think this method is cumbersome, but you frequently see jQuery code using this technique. Personally, I tend to create a function called `init()` and call it with a line like this:

```
$(init);
```

I think this technique is simple and easy to understand but you may encounter the other variations as you examine code on the Web.

Investigating the jQuery Object

The jQuery object is interesting because it is easy to create from a variety of DOM elements, and because it adds wonderful, new features to these elements.

Changing the style of an element

If you can dynamically change the CSS of an element, you can do quite a lot to it. jQuery makes this process quite easy. After you have a jQuery object, you can use the css method to add or change any CSS attributes of the object. Take a look at styleElements.html, shown in Figure 2-2, as an example.

Figure 2-2:
All the styles here are applied dynamically by jQuery functions.

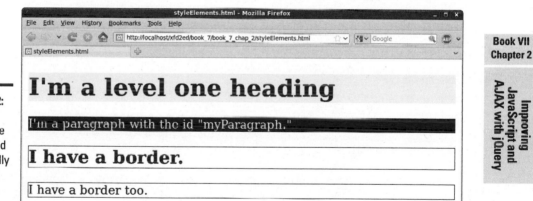

The code displays a terseness common to jQuery code:

```
<!DOCTYPE html PUBLIC "-//W3C//DTD XHTML 1.0 Strict//EN"
"http://www.w3.org/TR/xhtml1/DTD/xhtml1-strict.dtd">
<html lang="EN" dir="ltr" xmlns="http://www.w3.org/1999/
    xhtml">
<head>
  <meta http-equiv="content-type" content="text/xml;
    charset=utf-8" />
  <script type = "text/javascript"
          src = "jquery-1.4.2.min.js"></script>
```

```
<script type = "text/javascript">
  //<![CDATA[
  $(init);

  function init(){
    $("h1").css("backgroundColor", "yellow");

    $("#myParagraph").css({"backgroundColor":"black",
                           "color":"white"});

    $(".bordered").css("border", "1px solid black");
  }
  //]]>
</script>
<title>styleElements.html</title>
</head>
<body>
    <h1>I'm a level one heading</h1>
    <p id = "myParagraph">
      I'm a paragraph with the id "myParagraph."
    </p>

    <h2 class = "bordered">
      I have a border.
    </h2>

    <p class = "bordered">
      I have a border too.
    </p>
</body>
</html>
```

You find a few interesting things in this program. First, take a look at the HTML:

✦ **It contains an h1 tag.** I'm aware that's not too exciting, but I use it to show how to target elements by DOM type.

✦ **There's a paragraph with the ID myParagraph.** This will be used to illustrate how to target an element by ID.

✦ **There are two elements with the class bordered.** You have no easy way in ordinary DOM work to apply code to all elements of a particular class, but jQuery makes it easy.

✦ **Several elements have custom CSS, but no CSS is defined.** The jQuery code changes all the CSS dynamically.

The init() function is identified as the function to be run when the document is ready. In this function, I use the powerful CSS method to change each element's CSS dynamically. I come back to the CSS in a moment, but first notice how the various elements are targeted.

Selecting jQuery objects

jQuery gives you several alternatives for creating jQuery objects from the DOM elements. In general, you use the same rules to select objects in jQuery as you do in CSS:

+ **DOM elements are targeted as is.** You can include any DOM element inside the $("") mechanism to target all similar elements. For example, use $("h1") to refer to all h1 objects or $("p") to refer to all paragraphs.

+ **Use the # identifier to target a particular ID.** This works exactly the same as in CSS. If you have an element with the ID myThing, use the code $("#myThing").

+ **Use the . identifier to target members of a class.** Again, this is the same mechanism that you use in CSS, so all elements with the class bordered attached to them can be modified with the code $(".bordered").

+ **You can even use complex identifiers.** You can even use complex CSS identifiers like $("li img");. This identifier only targets images inside a list item.

These selection methods (all borrowed from familiar CSS notation) add incredible flexibility to your code. You can now easily select elements in your JavaScript code according to the same rules you use to identify elements in CSS.

Modifying the style

After you've identified an object or a set of objects, you can apply jQuery methods. One very powerful and easy method is the style() method. The basic form of this method takes two parameters: a style rule and value.

For example, to make the background color of all h1 objects yellow, I use the following code:

```
$("h1").css("backgroundColor", "yellow");
```

If you apply a style rule to a collection of objects (like all h1 objects or all objects with the bordered class), the same rule is instantly applied to all the objects.

A more powerful variation of the style rule exists that allows you to apply several CSS styles at once. It takes a single object in JSON notation as its argument:

```
$("#myParagraph").css({"backgroundColor":"black",
                       "color":"white"});
```

This example uses a JSON object defined as a series of rule/value pairs. If you need a refresher on how JSON objects work, look at Book IV, Chapter 4.

Adding Events to Objects

The jQuery library adds another extremely powerful capability to JavaScript. It allows you to easily attach events to any jQuery object. As an example, take a look at hover.html, as shown in Figure 2-3.

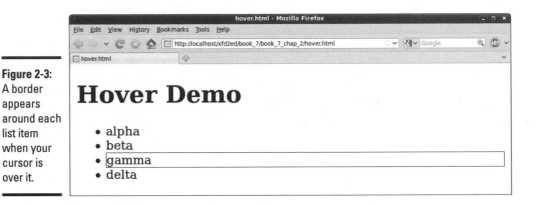

Figure 2-3: A border appears around each list item when your cursor is over it.

When you move your cursor over any list item, a border appears around the item. This would be a difficult effect to achieve in ordinary DOM/JavaScript, but it's pretty easy to manage in jQuery.

Adding a hover event

Look at the code to see how it works:

```
<!DOCTYPE html PUBLIC "-//W3C//DTD XHTML 1.0 Strict//EN"
"http://www.w3.org/TR/xhtml1/DTD/xhtml1-strict.dtd">
<html lang="EN" dir="ltr" xmlns="http://www.w3.org/1999/
    xhtml">
<head>
  <meta http-equiv="content-type" content="text/xml;
  charset=utf-8" />

  <script type = "text/javascript"
          src = "jquery-1.4.2.min.js"></script>

  <script type = "text/javascript">
    //<![CDATA[
    $(init);
```

```
    function init(){
      $("li").hover(border, noBorder);
    } // end init

    function border(){
      $(this).css("border", "1px solid black");
    }

    function noBorder(){
      $(this).css("border", "0px none black");
    }

    //]]>
  </script>

  <title>hover.html</title>
</head>
<body>
  <h1>Hover Demo</h1>
    <ul>
      <li>alpha</li>
      <li>beta</li>
      <li>gamma</li>
      <li>delta</li>
    </ul>
</body>
</html>
```

The HTML couldn't be simpler. It's simply an unordered list. The JavaScript isn't much more complex. It consists of three one-line functions:

+ **`init()` is called when the document is ready.** It makes jQuery objects of all list items and attaches the `hover` event to them. The `hover()` function accepts two parameters:

  • The first is a function to be called when the cursor hovers over the object.

  • The second is a function to be called when the cursor leaves the object.

+ **`border()` draws a border around the current element.** The `$(this)` identifier is used to specify the current object. In this example, I use the `css` function to draw a border around the object.

+ **`noBorder()` is a function that is very similar to the `border()` function, but it removes a border from the current object.**

In this example, I used three different functions. Many jQuery programmers prefer to use anonymous functions (sometimes called *lambda* functions) to enclose the entire functionality in one long line:

```
$("li").hover(
  function(){
    $(this).css("border", "1px solid black");
  },
  function(){
    $(this).css("border", "0px none black");
  }
);
```

Note that this is still technically a single line of code. Instead of referencing two functions that have already been created, I build the functions immediately where they are needed. Each function definition is a parameter to the `hover()` method.

If you're a computer scientist, you might argue that this is not a perfect example of a lambda function, and you would be correct. The important thing is to notice that some ideas of functional programming (such as lambda functions) are creeping into mainstream AJAX programming, and that's an exciting development. If you just mutter "lambda" and then walk away, people will assume that you're some kind of geeky computer scientist. What could be more fun than that?

Although I'm perfectly comfortable with anonymous functions, I often find the named-function approach easier to read, so I tend to use complete named functions more often.

Changing classes on the fly

jQuery supports another wonderful feature. You can define a CSS style and then add or remove that style from an element dynamically. Figure 2-4 shows a page that can dynamically modify the border of any list item.

Figure 2-4: Click list items, and their borders toggle on and off.

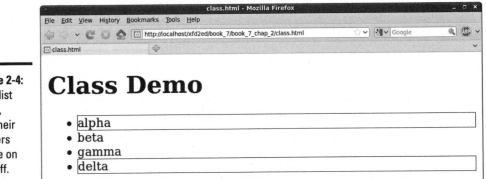

JQuery events

jQuery supports a number of other events. Any jQuery node can read any of the following events:

✔ Change: The content of the element changes.

✔ Click: The user clicks the element.

✔ DblClick: The user double-clicks the element.

✔ Focus: The user has selected the element.

✔ Keydown: The user presses a key while the element has the focus.

✔ Hover: The cursor is over the element; a second function is called when the cursor leaves the element.

✔ MouseDown: A mouse button is clicked over the element.

✔ Select: The user has selected text in a text-style input.

The code shows how easy this kind of feature is to add:

```
<!DOCTYPE html PUBLIC "-//W3C//DTD XHTML 1.0 Strict//EN"
"http://www.w3.org/TR/xhtml1/DTD/xhtml1-strict.dtd">
<html lang="EN" dir="ltr" xmlns="http://www.w3.org/1999/
    xhtml">
<head>
  <meta http-equiv="content-type" content="text/xml;
  charset=utf-8" />
  <style type = "text/css">
    .bordered {
      border: 1px solid black;
    }
  </style>
  <script type = "text/javascript"
        src = "jquery-1.4.2.min.js"></script>

  <script type = "text/javascript">
  //<![CDATA[
  $(init);

  function init(){
    $("li").click(toggleBorder);
  } // end init

  function toggleBorder(){
    $(this).toggleClass("bordered");
  }
  //]]>
</script>

<title>class.html</title>
```

```
</head>
<body>
<h1>Class Demo</h1>
    <ul>
      <li>alpha</li>
      <li>beta</li>
      <li>gamma</li>
      <li>delta</li>
    </ul>

</body>
</html>
```

Here's how to make this program:

1. **Begin with a basic HTML page.**

   All the interesting stuff happens in CSS and JavaScript, so the actual contents of the page aren't that critical.

2. **Create a class you want to add and remove.**

   I build a CSS class called `bordered` that simply draws a border around the element. Of course, you can make a much more sophisticated CSS class with all kinds of formatting if you prefer.

3. **Link an `init()` method.**

   As you're beginning to see, most jQuery applications require some sort of initialization. I normally call the first function `init()`.

4. **Call the `toggleBorder()` function whenever the user clicks a list item.**

   The `init()` method simply sets up an event handler. Whenever a list item receives the click event (that is, it is clicked) the `toggleBorder()` function should be activated. The `toggleBorder()` function, well, toggles the border.

   jQuery has several methods for manipulating the class of an element:

   - `addClass()` assigns a class to the element.

   - `removeClass()` removes a class definition from an element.

   - `toggleClass()` switches the class (adds it if it isn't currently attached or removes it otherwise).

Making an AJAX Request with jQuery

The primary purpose of an AJAX library like jQuery is to simplify AJAX requests. It's hard to believe how easy this can be with jQuery. Figure 2-5 shows `ajax.html`, a page with a basic AJAX query.

Figure 2-5:
The text file
is requested
with an
AJAX call.

Including a text file with AJAX

This program is very similar in function to the `asynch.html` program
described in Chapter 1 of this minibook, but the code is much cleaner:

```
<!DOCTYPE html PUBLIC "-//W3C//DTD XHTML 1.0 Strict//EN"
"http://www.w3.org/TR/xhtml1/DTD/xhtml1-strict.dtd">
<html lang="EN" dir="ltr" xmlns="http://www.w3.org/1999/
   xhtml">
  <head>
    <meta http-equiv="content-type" content="text/xml;
  charset=utf-8" />
    <title>ajax.html</title>
    <script type = "text/javascript"
           src = "jquery-1.4.2.min.js"></script>

    <script type = "text/javascript">
      //<![CDATA[
      $(document).ready(getAJAX);

      function getAJAX(){
        $("#output").load("hello.txt");
      }
      //]]>
    </script>

  </head>

  <body>
    <div id = "output"></div>
  </body>
</html>
```

**Book VII
Chapter 2**

**Improving
JavaScript and
AJAX with jQuery**

The HTML is very clean (as you should be expecting from jQuery examples).
It simply creates an empty div called `output`.

The JavaScript code isn't much more complex. A standard `$(document).
ready` function calls the `getAJAX()` function as soon as the document is
ready. The `getAJAX()` function simply creates a jQuery node based on the
output div and loads the `hello.txt` file through a basic AJAX request.

This example does use AJAX, so if it isn't working, you might need to remember some details about how AJAX works. A program using AJAX should be run through a Web server, not just from a local file. Also, the file being read should be on the same server as the program making the AJAX request.

The `load()` mechanism described here is suitable for a basic situation where you want to load a plain-text or HTML code snippet into your pages. You read about much more sophisticated AJAX techniques in Chapter 6 of this minibook.

Building a poor man's CMS with AJAX

AJAX and jQuery can be a very useful way to build efficient Web sites, even without server-side programming. Frequently a Web site is based on a series of smaller elements that can be swapped and reused. You can use AJAX to build a framework that allows easy reuse and modification of Web content.

As an example, take a look at `cmsAJAX`, shown in Figure 2-6.

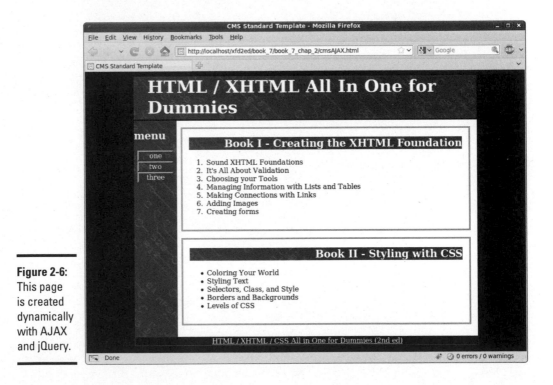

Figure 2-6:
This page is created dynamically with AJAX and jQuery.

While nothing is all that shocking about the page from the user's perspective, a look at the code can show some surprises:

```
<!DOCTYPE html PUBLIC "-//W3C//DTD XHTML 1.0 Strict//EN"
"http://www.w3.org/TR/xhtml1/DTD/xhtml1-strict.dtd">
<html lang="EN" dir="ltr" xmlns="http://www.w3.org/1999/
   xhtml">
  <head>
    <meta http-equiv="content-type" content="text/xml;
    charset=utf-8" />
    <title>CMS Standard Template</title>
    <link rel = "stylesheet"
          type = "text/css"
          href = "cmsStd.css" />
    <script type = "text/javascript"
            src = "jquery-1.4.2.min.js"></script>
    <script type = "text/javascript">
      //<![CDATA[
      $(init);

      function init(){
        $("#heading").load("head.html"),
        $("#menu").load("menu.html");
        $("#content1").load("story1.html");
        $("#content2").load("story2.html");
        $("#footer").load("footer.html");
      };
      //]]>
    </script>
  </head>

  <body>
    <div id = "all">
      <!-- This div centers a fixed-width layout -->
      <div id = "heading">
      </div><!-- end heading div -->

      <div id = "menu">
      </div> <!-- end menu div -->

      <div class = "content"
           id = "content1">
      </div> <!-- end content div -->

      <div class = "content"
           id = "content2">
      </div> <!-- end content div -->

      <div id = "footer">
      </div> <!-- end footer div -->
```

```
    </div> <!-- end all div -->
  </body>
</html>
```

Look over the code, and you can see these interesting features:

✦ **The page has no content!** All the divs are empty. None of the text shown in the screen shot is present in this document, but all is pulled from smaller files dynamically.

✦ **The page consists of empty named divs.** Rather than any particular content, the page consists of placeholders with IDs.

✦ **It uses jQuery.** The jQuery library is used to vastly simplify loading data through AJAX calls.

✦ **All contents are in separate files.** Look through the directory, and you can see very simple HTML files that contain small parts of the page. For example, story1.html looks like this:

```
<h2>Book I - Creating the XHTML Foundation</h3>

<ol>
  <li>Sound XHTML Foundations</li>
  <li>It's All About Validation</li>
  <li>Choosing your Tools</li>
  <li>Managing Information with Lists and Tables</li>
  <li>Making Connections with Links</li>
  <li>Adding Images</li>
  <li>Creating forms</li>

</ul>
```

✦ **The init() method runs on document.ready.** When the document is ready, the page runs the init() method.

✦ **The init() method uses AJAX calls to dynamically load content.** It's nothing more than a series of jQuery load() methods.

This approach may seem like a lot of work, but it has some very interesting characteristics:

✦ If you're building a large site with several pages, you usually want to design the visual appearance once and reuse the same general template repeatedly.

✦ Also, you'll probably have some elements (such as the menu and heading) which that will be consistent over several pages. You could simply create a default document and copy and paste it for each page, but this approach gets messy. What happens if you have created 100 pages according to a template and then need to add something to the menu or change the header? You need to make the change on 100 different pages.

The advantage of the template-style approach is code reuse. Just like the use of an external style allows you to multiply a style sheet across hundreds of documents, designing a template without content allows you to store code snippets in smaller files and reuse them. All 100 pages point to the same menu file, so if you want to change the menu, you change one file and everything changes with it.

Here's how you use this sort of approach:

1. **Create a single template for your entire site.**

   Build basic HTML and CSS to manage the overall look and feel for your entire site. Don't worry about content yet. Just build placeholders for all the components of your page. Be sure to give each element an ID and write the CSS to get things positioned as you want.

2. **Add jQuery support.**

   Make a link to the jQuery library, and make a default `init()` method. Put in code to handle populating those parts of the page that will always be consistent. (I use the template shown here exactly as it is.)

3. **Duplicate the template.**

   After you have a sense of how the template will work, make a copy for each page of your site.

4. **Customize each page by changing the `init()` function.**

   The only part of the template that changes is the `init()` function. All your pages will be identical, except they have customized `init()` functions that load different content.

5. **Load custom content into the divs with AJAX.**

   Use the `init()` function to load content into each div. Build more content as small files to create new pages.

This is a great way to manage content, but it isn't quite a full-blown content-management system. Even AJAX can't quite allow you to *store* content on the Web. More complex content management systems also use databases rather than files to handle content. You'll need some sort of server-side programming (like PHP, covered throughout Book V) and usually a database (like mySQL, covered in Book VI) to handle this sort of work. Content-management systems and complex site design are covered in Book VIII.

Chapter 3: Animating jQuery

In This Chapter

✔ Hiding and showing elements with jQuery

✔ Fading elements in and out

✔ Adding a callback function to a transition

✔ Element animation

✔ Object chaining

✔ Using selection filters

✔ Adding and removing elements

The jQuery library simplifies a lot of JavaScript coding. One of its best features is how it adds features that would be difficult to achieve in ordinary JavaScript and DOM programming. This chapter teaches you to shake and bake your programs by identifying specific objects, moving them around, and making them appear, slide, and fade.

Playing Hide and Seek

To get it all started, take a look at hideShow.html shown in Figure 3-1.

The hideShow program looks simple at first, but it does some quite interesting things. All of the level-two headings are actually buttons, so when you click them, interesting things happen:

✦ **The show button displays a previously hidden element.** Figure 3-2 demonstrates the revealed content.

✦ **The hide button hides the content.** The behavior of the hide button is pretty obvious. If the content is showing, it disappears instantly.

✦ **The toggle button swaps the visibility of the content.** If the content is currently visible, it is hidden. If it is hidden, it appears.

✦ **The slide down button makes the content transition in.** The slide down transition acts like a window shade being pulled down to make the content visible through a basic animation.

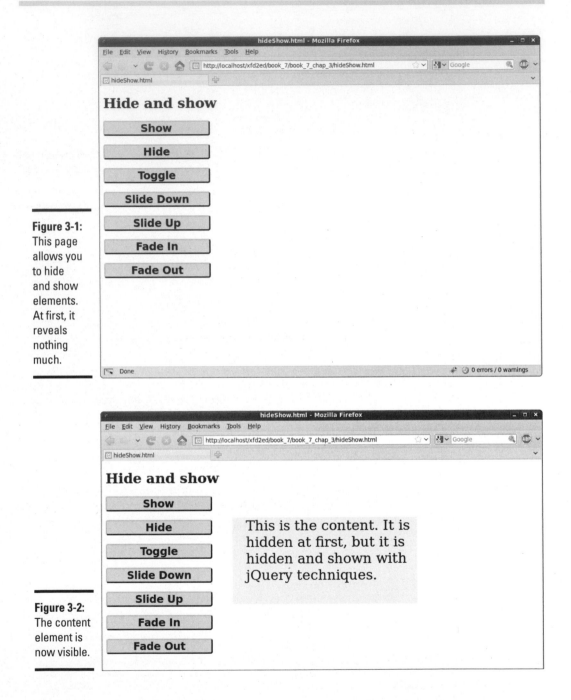

Figure 3-1:
This page
allows you
to hide
and show
elements.
At first, it
reveals
nothing
much.

Figure 3-2:
The content
element is
now visible.

- ✦ **The `slide up` button transitions the content out.** This animation looks like a window shade being pulled up to hide the content.

- ✦ **The speed of the animation can be controlled** It's possible to adjust how quickly the transition animation plays. This example plays the slide down animation slowly, and the slide up animation more quickly. It's possible to specify exactly how long the transition takes in milliseconds (1/1000ths of a second).

- ✦ **The `fade in` button allows the element to dissolve into visibility.** This looks much like a fade effect used in video. As in the sliding animations, the speed of the animation can be controlled.

- ✦ **The `fade out` button fades the element to the background color.** This technique gradually modifies the opacity of the element so that it eventually disappears.

You can adjust how quickly the transition animation plays. You can specify exactly how long the transition takes in milliseconds ($\frac{1}{1000}$ of a second). Also, any transition can have a callback function attached.

Of course, this example relies on animation, which you can't see in a static book. Be sure to look at this and all other example pages on my Web site: www.aharrisbooks.net. Better yet, install them on your own machine and play around with my code until they make sense to you.

The animations shown in this example are useful when you want to selectively hide and display parts of your page:

- ✦ **Menus are one obvious use.** You might choose to store your menu structure as a series of nested lists and only display parts of the menu when the parent is activated.

- ✦ **Small teaser sentences expand to show more information when the user clicks or hovers over them.** This technique is commonly used on blog and news sites to let users preview a large number of topics, kind of like a text-based thumbnail image.

Getting transition support

The jQuery library has built-in support for transitions that make these effects pretty easy to produce. Look over the entire program before digging into the details:

```
<!DOCTYPE html PUBLIC "-//W3C//DTD XHTML 1.0 Strict//EN"
"http://www.w3.org/TR/xhtml1/DTD/xhtml1-strict.dtd">
<html lang="EN" dir="ltr" xmlns="http://www.w3.org/1999/
    xhtml">
<head>
  <meta http-equiv="content-type" content="text/xml;
  charset=utf-8" />
  <style type = "text/css">
```

```
#content {
  width: 400px;
  height: 200px;
  font-size: 200%;
  padding-left:1em;
  background-color: yellow;
  position: absolute;
  left: 300px;
  top: 100px;
}
h2 {
  width: 10em;
  border: 3px outset black;
  background-color: lightgray;
  text-align: center;
  font-family: sans-serif;
  /* corners for compliant browsers */
  -moz-border-radius: 5px;
  -webkit-border-radius: 5px;
}
</style>

<script type = "text/javascript"
        src = "jquery-1.4.2.min.js"></script>
<script type = "text/javascript">
  //<![CDATA[
  $(init);
  function init(){
    //styleContent();
    $("#content").hide();
    $("#show").click(showContent);
    $("#hide").click(hideContent);
    $("#toggle").click(toggleContent);
    $("#slideDown").click(slideDown);
    $("#slideUp").click(slideUp);
    $("#fadeIn").click(fadeIn);
    $("#fadeOut").click(fadeOut);
  } // end init

  function showContent(){
    $("#content").show();
  } // end showContent
  function hideContent(){
    $("#content").hide();
  } // end hideContent

  function toggleContent(){
    $("#content").toggle();
  } // end toggleContent

  function slideDown(){
    $("#content").slideDown("medium");
  } // end slideDown
```

```
      function slideUp(){
        $("#content").slideUp(500);
      } // end slideUp

      function fadeIn(){
        $("#content").fadeIn("slow", present);
      } // end fadeIn

      function fadeOut(){
        $("#content").fadeOut("fast");
      } // end fadeOut.

      function present(){
        alert("I'm here");
      } // end present
      //]]>
  </script>
  <title>hideShow.html</title>
</head>

<body>
  <h1>Hide and show</h1>
  <h2 id = "show">Show</h2>
  <h2 id = "hide">Hide</h2>
  <h2 id = "toggle">Toggle</h2>
  <h2 id = "slideDown">Slide Down</h2>
  <h2 id = "slideUp">Slide Up</h2>
  <h2 id = "fadeIn">Fade In</h2>
  <h2 id = "fadeOut">Fade Out</h2>

  <p id = "content">
    This is the content. It is hidden at first, but it is
   hidden and shown with jQuery techniques.
  </p>

</body>
</html>
```

This example may look long and complicated when you view it all at once, but it really isn't hard to understand when you break it into pieces.

Writing the HTML and CSS foundation

The HTML used in this example is minimal, as is common in jQuery development:

+ A single level-one heading

+ A series of level-two headings

+ A paragraph

Well rounded

I used some sneaky CSS tricks to make the h2 elements look like buttons. First, I made them gray (like most buttons are). I also gave them an outset border to make them appear in 3D. Finally, I added the experimental `border-radius` element to get rounded corners. Unfortunately, `border-radius` is not an official CSS element yet. I added the experimental versions supported by Firefox, Safari, and Chrome, but the corners will not be rounded in any form of IE.

The level-two headings will be used as buttons in this example. I use a CSS style to make the h2 tags look more like buttons (adding a border and background color). I added an ID attribute to every button so that I can add jQuery events later.

If I wanted the h2 elements to look and act like buttons, why didn't I just make them with button tags in the first place? In this example, I wanted to focus on the jQuery and keep the HTML as simple as possible. jQuery helps make *any* element act like a button easily, so that's what I did. Users don't expect h2 elements to be clickable, so you need to do some styling (as I did) to help them understand that the element can be clicked. For comparison purposes, the other two examples in this chapter use actual HTML buttons.

The other interesting part of the HTML is the content div. In this example, the actual content isn't really important, but I did add some CSS to make the content easy to see when it pops up.

The most critical part of the HTML from a programming perspective is the inclusion of the ID attribute. This makes it easy for a jQuery script to manipulate the component, making it hide and reappear in various ways. Note that the HTML and CSS do nothing to hide the content. It will be hidden (and revealed) entirely through jQuery code.

Initializing the page

The initialization sequence simply sets the stage and assigns a series of event handlers:

```
$(init);

function init(){
  //styleContent();
  $("#content").hide();
  $("#show").click(showContent);
  $("#hide").click(hideContent);
  $("#toggle").click(toggleContent);
```

```
$("#slideDown").click(slideDown);
$("#slideUp").click(slideUp);
$("#fadeIn").click(fadeIn);
$("#fadeOut").click(fadeOut);
} // end init
```

The pattern for working with jQuery should be familiar:

1. **Set up an initialization function.**

   Use the `$(document).ready()` mechanism (described in Chapter 2 of this minibook) or this cleaner shortcut to specify an initialization function.

2. **Hide the `content` div.**

   When the user first encounters the page, the `content` div should be hidden.

3. **Attach event handlers to each h2 button.**

   This program is a series of small functions. The `init()` function attaches each function to the corresponding button. Note how I carefully named the functions and buttons to make all the connections easy to understand.

Hiding and showing the content

All the effects on this page are based on hiding and showing the `content` div. The `hide()` and `show()` methods illustrate how jQuery animation works:

```
function showContent(){
  $("#content").show();
} // end showContent

function hideContent(){
  $("#content").hide();
} // end hideContent
```

Each of these functions works in the same basic manner:

✦ **Identifies the `content` div:** Creates a jQuery node based on the `content` div.

✦ **Hides or shows the node:** The jQuery object has built-in methods for hiding and showing.

The hide and show methods act instantly. If the element is currently visible, the `show()` method has no effect. Likewise, `hide()` has no effect on an element that's already hidden.

Toggling visibility

In addition to `hide()` and `show()`, the jQuery object supports a `toggle()` method. This method takes a look at the current status of the element and changes it. If the element is currently hidden, it becomes visible. If it's currently visible, it is hidden. The `toggleContent()` function illustrates how to use this method:

```
function toggleContent(){
  $("#content").toggle();
} // end toggleContent
```

Sliding an element

jQuery supports effects that allow you to animate the appearance and disappearance of your element. The general approach is very similar to `hide()` and `show()`, but you find one additional twist:

```
function slideDown(){
  $("#content").slideDown("medium");
} // end slideDown

function slideUp(){
  $("#content").slideUp(500);
} // end slideUp
```

The `slideDown()` method makes an element appear like a window shade being pulled down. The `slideUp()` method makes an element disappear in a similar manner.

These functions take a speed parameter that indicates how quickly the animation occurs. If you omit the speed parameter, the default value is medium. The speed can be these string values:

✦ Fast

✦ Medium

✦ Slow

✦ A numeric value in milliseconds ($\frac{1}{1000}$ of a second; the value 500 means 500 milliseconds, or half a second)

The `show()`, `hide()`, and `toggle()` methods also accept a speed parameter. In these functions, the object shrinks and grows at the indicated speed.

A `slideToggle()` function is also available that toggles the visibility of the element, but using the sliding animation technique.

Fading an element in and out

A third type of "now you see it" animation is provided by the `fade` methods. These techniques adjust the opacity of the element. The code should look quite familiar by now:

```
function fadeIn(){
  $("#content").fadeIn("slow", present);
} // end fadeIn

function fadeOut(){
  $("#content").fadeOut("fast");
} // end fadeOut.

function present(){
  alert("I'm here");
} // end present
```

`fadeIn()` and `fadeout()` work just like the `hide()` and `slide()` techniques. The fading techniques adjust the opacity of the element and then remove it, rather than dynamically changing the size of the element as the slide and show techniques do.

I've added one more element to the `fadeIn()` function. If you supply the `fadeIn()` method (or indeed any of the animation methods described in this section) with a function name as a second parameter, that function is called upon completion of the animation. When you click the fade-in button, the `content` div slowly fades in, and then when it is completely visible, the `present()` function gets called. This function doesn't do a lot in this example but simply pops up an alert, but it could be used to handle some sort of instructions after the element is visible. A function used in this way is a callback function.

If the element is already visible, the callback method is triggered immediately.

Book VII
Chapter 3

Animating jQuery

Changing Position with jQuery

The `jQuery` library also has interesting features for changing any of an element's characteristics, including its position. The `animate.html` page featured in Figure 3-3 illustrates a number of interesting animation techniques.

You know what I'm going to say, right? This program moves things around. You can't see that in a book. Be sure to look at the actual page. Trust me, it's a lot more fun than it looks in this screen shot.

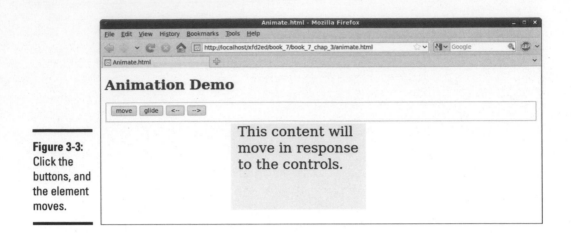

Figure 3-3:
Click the
buttons, and
the element
moves.

This page illustrates how to move a jQuery element by modifying its CSS. It also illustrates an important jQuery technique called *object chaining* and a very useful animation method that allows you to create smooth motion over time. As usual, look over the entire code first; I break it into sections for more careful review.

```
<!DOCTYPE html PUBLIC "-//W3C//DTD XHTML 1.0 Strict//EN"
"http://www.w3.org/TR/xhtml1/DTD/xhtml1-strict.dtd">
<html lang="EN" dir="ltr" xmlns="http://www.w3.org/1999/
    xhtml">
<head>
  <meta http-equiv="content-type" content="text/xml;
  charset=utf-8" />

  <style type = "text/css">
  #content {
    width: 300px;
    height: 200px;
    font-size: 200%;
    background-color: yellow;
    position: absolute;
    left: 300px;
    top: 100px;
    padding-left: .5em;
  }
  </style>

  <script type = "text/javascript"
          src = "jquery-1.4.2.min.js"></script>

  <script type = "text/javascript">
    //<![CDATA[
    $(init);
```

```
function init(){
  $("#move").click(move);
  $("#glide").click(glide);
  $("#left").click(left);
  $("#right").click(right);
} // end init

function move(){
  $("#content").css("left", "50px")
  .css("top", "100px");
} // end move

function glide(){
  //move to initial spot
  $("#content").css("left", "50px")
  .css("top", "100px");

  //slide to new spot
  $("#content").animate({
    "left": "400px",
    "top": "200px"
  }, 2000);
} // end glide

function left(){
  $("#content").animate({"left": "-=10px"}, 100);
} // end left

function right(){
  $("#content").animate({"left": "+=10px"}, 100);
} // end left
//]]>
</script>

<title>Animate.html</title>
</head>
<body>
<h1>Animation Demo</h1>
<form action = "">
  <fieldset>
    <button type = "button"
            id = "move">
      move
    </button>
    <button type = "button"
            id = "glide">
      glide
    </button>

    <button type = "button"
            id = "left">
      &lt;--
    </button>
```

**Book VII
Chapter 3**

Animating jQuery

```
        <button type = "button"
                id = "right">
         -->
        </button>

  </fieldset>
</form>

<p id = "content">
  This content will move in response to the controls.
</p>
</body>
</html>
```

Creating the framework

The HTML always forms the foundation. This page is similar to the hide Show page, but I decided to use a real form with buttons as the control panel. Buttons are not difficult to use, but they are a little more tedious to code because they must be inside a form element as well as a block-level element, and they require more coding to produce than h2 elements.

Note that I used < in one of the button captions. This HTML attribute displays the less-than symbol. Had I used the actual symbol (<), the browser would have thought I was beginning a new HTML tag and would have been confused.

The buttons all have id attributes, but I didn't attach functions to them with the onclick attribute. After you're using jQuery, it makes sense to commit to a jQuery approach and use the jQuery event techniques.

The only other important HTML element is the content div. Once again, this element is simply a placeholder, but I added CSS styling to make it obvious when it moves around. This element must be set to be absolutely positioned, because the position will be changed dynamically in the code.

Setting up the events

The initialization is all about setting up the event handlers for the various buttons. An init() function is called when the document is ready. That function contains function pointers for the various events, directing traffic to the right functions when a button is pressed:

```
function init(){
```

```
$("#move").click(move);
$("#glide").click(glide);
$("#left").click(left);
$("#right").click(right);
} // end init
```

As usual, naming conventions makes it easy to see what's going on.

Don't go chaining . . . okay, do it all you want

The move function isn't really that radical. All it does is use the css() method described in Book VII, Chapter 2 to alter the position of the element. After all, position is just a CSS attribute, right? Well, it's a little more complex than that.

The position of an element is actually stored in *two* attributes, top and left.

Your first attempt at a move function would probably look like this:

```
function move(){
  $("#content").css("left", "50px");
  $("#content").css("top", "100px");
} // end move
```

While this approach certainly works, it has a subtle problem. It moves the element in two separate steps. While most browsers are fast enough to avoid making this an issue, jQuery supports a really neat feature called *node chaining* that allows you to combine many jQuery steps into a single line.

Almost all jQuery methods return a jQuery object as a side effect. So, the line

```
$("#content").text("changed");
```

not only changes the text of the content node but also makes a new node. You can attach that node to a variable like this if you want:

```
var newNode = $("#content").text("changed");
```

However, what most jQuery programmers do is simply attach new functionality onto the end of the previously defined node, like this:

```
$("#content").text("changed").click(hiThere);
```

Easing on down

The jQuery `animation()` method supports one more option: *easing.* The term refers to the relative speed of the animation throughout its lifespan. If you watch the animations on the `animate.html` page carefully, you can see that the motion begins slowly, builds speed, and slows again at the end. This provides a natural-feeling animation. By default, jQuery animations use what's called a `swing` easing style (slow on the ends and fast in the middle, like a child on a swing). If you want to have a more consistent speed, you can specify "linear" as the fourth parameter, and the animation works at a constant speed. You can also install plugins for more advanced easing techniques.

This new line takes the node created by $("#content") and changes its text value. It then takes this new node (the one with changed text) and adds a click event to it, calling the hiThere() function when the content element is clicked. In this way, you build an ever-more complex node by *chaining* nodes on top of each other.

These node chains can be hard to read, because they can result in a lot of code on one physical line. JavaScript doesn't care about carriage returns, though, because it uses the semicolon to determine the end of a logical line. You can change the complex chained line so that it fits on several lines of the text editor like this:

```
$("#content")
.text("changed")
.click(hiThere);
```

Note that only the last line has a semicolon, because it's all one line of *logic* even though it occurs on three lines in the editor.

Building the move() function with chaining

Object chaining makes it easy to build the move() function so that it shifts the content's left and top properties simultaneously:

```
function move(){
  $("#content").css("left", "50px")
  .css("top", "100px");
} // end move
```

This function uses the css() method to change the left property to 50px. The resulting object is given a second css() method call to change the top property to 100px. The top and left elements are changed at the same time as far as the user is concerned.

Building time-based animation with animate ( )

Using the css method is a great way to move an element around on the
screen, but the motion is instantaneous. jQuery supports a powerful method
called animate() that allows you to change any DOM characteristics over
a specified span of time. The glide button on animate.html smoothly
moves the content div from (50, 100) to (400, 200) over 2 seconds:

```
function glide(){
  //move to initial spot
  $("#content").css("left", "50px")
  .css("top", "100px");

  //slide to new spot
  $("#content").animate({
    "left": "400px",
    "top": "200px"
  }, 2000);
} // end glide
```

The function begins by moving the element immediately to its initial spot
with chained css() methods. It then uses the animate() method to control the animation. This method can have up to three parameters:

✦ **A JSON object describing attributes to animate:** The first parameter is
 an object in JSON notation describing name/value attribute pairs. In this
 example, I'm telling jQuery to change the left attribute from its current value to 400px, and the top value to 200px. Any numeric value that
 you can change through the DOM can be included in this JSON object.
 Instead of a numerical value, you can use "hide," "show," or "toggle" to
 specify an action. Review Book IV, Chapter 4 for more details on JSON
 objects.

✦ **A speed attribute:** The speed parameter is defined in the same way
 as the speed for fade and slide animations. You find three predefined
 speeds: slow, medium, and fast. You can also indicate speed in milliseconds; for example, 2000 means two seconds.

✦ **A callback function:** This optional parameter describes a function to be
 called when the animation is complete. The use of callback functions is
 described earlier in this chapter in the section "Fading an element in
 and out."

Move a little bit: Relative motion

You can also use the animation mechanism to move an object relative to its
current position. The arrow buttons and their associated functions perform
this task:

```
function left(){
  $("#content").animate({"left": "-=10px"}, 100);
} // end left

function right(){
  $("#content").animate({"left": "+=10px"}, 100);
} // end left
```

These functions also use the `animate()` method, but you see a small difference in the position parameters. The += and −= modifiers indicate that I want to add to or subtract from (respectively) the value rather than indicating an absolute position. Of course, you can add as many parameters to the JSON object as you want, but these are a good start.

Note that because I'm moving a small amount (10 pixels), I want the motion to be relatively quick. Each motion lasts 100 milliseconds, or ¹⁄₁₀ of a second.

Modifying Elements on the Fly

The jQuery library supports a third major way of modifying the page: the ability to add and remove contents dynamically. This is a powerful way to work with a page. The key to this feature is another of jQuery's most capable tools — its flexible selection engine. You can also use numerous attributes to modify nodes. The `changeContent.html` page, shown in Figure 3-4, demonstrates some of the power of these tools.

Figure 3-4: The default state of change-Content is a little dull.

Of course, the buttons allow the user to make changes to the page dynamically. Clicking the Add Text button adds more text to the content area, as you can see in Figure 3-5.

✦ The `clone` button is interesting, because it allows you to make a copy of an element and place it somewhere else in the document hierarchy. Clicking the `clone` button a few times can give you a page like that shown in Figure 3-6.

✦ The `wrap in div` button lets you wrap an HTML element around any existing element. The `wrap in div` button puts a div (with a red border) around every cloned element. You can click this button multiple times to add multiple wrappings to any element. Figure 3-7 shows what happens after I wrap a few times.

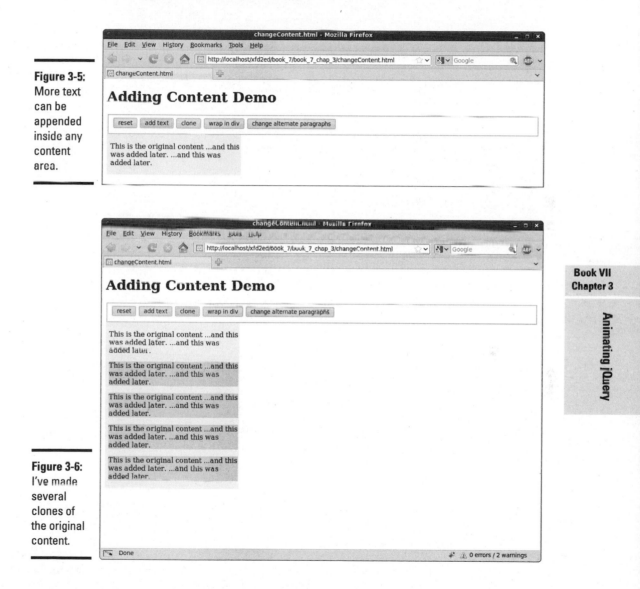

Figure 3-5:
More text can be appended inside any content area.

Figure 3-6:
I've made several clones of the original content.

Figure 3-7:
Now you
see a red-
bordered div
around all
the cloned
elements.

✦ The `change alternate paragraphs` button increases readability;
sometimes you want to be able to alternate styles of lists and tables.
jQuery has an easy way to select every other element in a group and
give it a style. The `change alternate paragraphs` button activates
some code that turns all odd-numbered paragraphs into white text with
a green background. Look at Figure 3-8 for a demonstration.

✦ The reset button resets all the changes you made with the other buttons.

The code for `changeDocument.html` seems complex, but it follows the
same general patterns you've seen in jQuery programming. As always, look
over the entire code first and then read how it breaks down:

```
<!DOCTYPE html PUBLIC "-//W3C//DTD XHTML 1.0 Strict//EN"
"http://www.w3.org/TR/xhtml1/DTD/xhtml1-strict.dtd">
<html lang="EN" dir="ltr" xmlns="http://www.w3.org/1999/
    xhtml">
<head>
  <meta http-equiv="content-type" content="text/xml;
    charset=utf-8" />

  <style type = "text/css">
  #content {
    width: 300px;
```

```
    background-color: yellow;
    left: 300px;
    top: 100px;
    padding-left: .5em;
    border: 0px none black;
}

div {
    border: 2px solid red;
    padding: 3px;
}
</style>

<script type = "text/javascript"
        src = "jquery-1.4.2.min.js"></script>

<script type = "text/javascript">
  //<![CDATA[
  $(init);

  function init(){
    $("#reset").click(reset);
    $("#addText").click(addText);
    $("#wrap").click(wrap);
    $("#clone").click(clone);
    $("#oddGreen").click(oddGreen);
  } // end init

  function reset(){
    //remove all but the original content
    $("p:gt(0)").remove();
    $("div:not(#content)").remove();
    //reset the text of the original content
    $("#content").html("<p>This is the original content</
p>");
  } // end reset

  function addText(){
    $("p:first").append(" ...and this was added later.");
  } // end addContent

  function wrap(){
    $("p:gt(0)").wrap("<div></div>");
  } // end wrap

  function clone(){
   $("p:first").clone()
   .insertAfter("p:last")
   .css("backgroundColor", "lightblue");
  } // end clone

  function oddGreen(){
```

**Book VII
Chapter 3**

Animating jQuery

```
                //turn alternate (odd numbered) paragraph elements
        green
          $("p:odd").css("backgroundColor", "green")
          .css("color", "white");
        } // end oddGreen
        //]]>
      </script>
      <title>changeContent.html</title>
  </head>
  <body>
    <h1>Adding Content Demo</h1>
    <form action = "">
      <fieldset>
        <button type = "button"
                id = "reset">
          reset
        </button>

        <button type = "button"
                id = "addText">
          add text
        </button>

        <button type = "button"
                id = "clone">
          clone
        </button>

        <button type = "button"
                id = "wrap">
          wrap in div
        </button>

        <button type = "button"
                id = "oddGreen">
          change alternate paragraphs
        </button>
      </fieldset>
    </form>

    <div id = "content">
      <p>
        This is the original content
      </p>
    </div>
  </body>
</html>
```

Admittedly you see a lot of code here, but when you consider how much functionality this page has, it really isn't too bad. Look at it in smaller pieces, and it all makes sense.

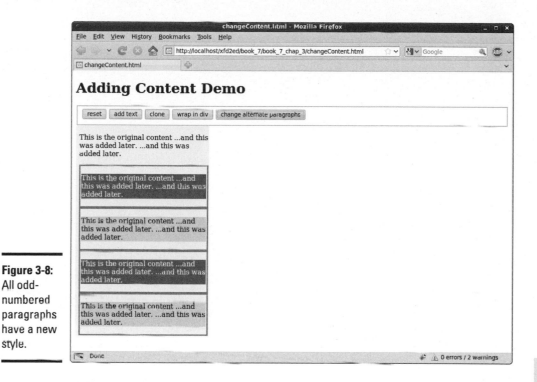

Figure 3-8:
All odd-
numbered
paragraphs
have a new
style.

Building the basic page

As usual, begin by inspecting the HTML. The basic code for this page sets up
the playground:

1. **Create a form with buttons.**

   This form will become the control panel. Add a button for each function
   you want to add. Make sure that each button has an ID, but you don't
   need to specify an `onclick` function, because the `init()` function
   takes care of that.

2. **Build a prototype `content` div.**

   Build a div called `content`, and add a paragraph to the div.

Be careful with your initial HTML structure. The manipulation and selection
tricks you experiment with in this chapter rely on a thorough understanding of the beginning page structure. Be sure that you understand exactly
how the page is set up so that you understand how to manipulate it. If your
standard XHTML page (before any JavaScript/jQuery code is added) doesn't
validate, it's unlikely your code will work as expected.

Initializing the code

The initialization section is pretty straightforward. Set up an `init()` function, and use it to assign event handlers to all the buttons:

```
$(init);

function init(){
  $("#reset").click(reset);
  $("#addText").click(addText);
  $("#wrap").click(wrap);
  $("#clone").click(clone);
  $("#oddGreen").click(oddGreen);
} // end init
```

Adding text

It's pretty easy to add text to a component. The `append()` method attaches text to the end of a jQuery node. Table 3-1 shows a number of other methods for adding text to a node.

Table 3-1	Methods That Add Text to a Node
Method	*Description*
`append(text)`	Adds the text (or HTML) to the end of the selected element(s)
`prepend(text)`	Adds the content at the beginning of the selected element(s)
`insertAfter(text)`	Adds the text after the selected element (outside the element)
`insertBefore(text)`	Adds the text before the selected element (outside the element)

More methods are available, but these are the ones I find most useful. Be sure to check out the official documentation at `http://docs.jquery.com` to see the other options.

```
function addText(){
  $("p:first").append(" ...and this was added later.");
} // end addContent
```

The `append()` method adds text to the end of the element, but inside the element (rather than after the end of the element). In this example, the text will become part of the paragraph contained inside the content div. The more interesting part of this code is the selector. It could read like this:

```
$("p").append(" ...and this was added later.");
```

That would add the text to the end of the paragraph. The default text has only one paragraph, so that makes lots of sense. If there are more paragraphs (and there will be), the p selector can select them all, adding the text to all the paragraphs simultaneously. By specifying p:first, I'm using a special *filter* to determine exactly which paragraph should be affected.

Many of the examples on this page use jQuery filters, so I describe them elsewhere in the following sections. For now, note that p:first means the first paragraph. Of course, you also see p:last and many more. Read on. . . .

Attack of the clones

You can *clone* (copy) anything you can identify as a jQuery node. This makes a copy of the node without changing the original. The cloned node isn't immediately visible on the screen. You need to place it somewhere, usually with an append(), prepend(), insertBefore(), or insertAfter() method.

Take a look at the clone() function to see how it works:

```
function clone(){
  $("p:first").clone()
  .insertAfter("p:last")
  .css("backgroundColor", "lightblue");
} // end clone
```

1. **Select the first paragraph.**

   The first paragraph is the one I want to copy. (In the beginning, only one exists, but that will change soon.)

2. **Use the clone() method to make a copy.**

   Now you've made a copy, but it still isn't visible. Use chaining to do some interesting things to this copy.

3. **Add the new element to the page after the last paragraph.**

   The p:last identifier is the last paragraph, so insertAfter ("p:last") means put the new paragraph after the last paragraph available in the document.

4. Change the CSS.

Just for grins, chain the `css()` method onto the new element and change the background color to light blue. This just reinforces the fact that you can continue adding commands to a node through chaining.

Note that the paragraphs are inside `content`. Of course, I could have put them elsewhere with careful use of selectors, but I put them where I want them.

It's hard to keep track of changes to the page because a standard `view source` command shows you the *original* source code, not the code that's been changed by your jQuery magic. jQuery changes the HTML of your page in memory but doesn't change the text file that contains your page. If your page is not doing what you expect, you need to look at the script-generated source code to see what's really going on.

Firefox plugins are the key to headache-free debugging. The Web developer toolbar has a wonderful feature called View Generated Source (available on the View Source menu) that shows the page source as it currently exists in memory. If you prefer the firebug extension, its Inspect mode also inspects the page as it currently is displayed. Both tools are described in Book I, Chapter 3.

Note that the content of the first paragraph is cloned with its current content and style information copied to the new element. If you clone the paragraph and then add content to it and clone it again, the first clone will have the default text and the second clone will contain the additional text. If you modify the CSS style of an element and then clone it, the clone will also inherit any of the style characteristics of the original node.

It's a wrap

Sometimes you want to embed an object inside another element (or two). For example, the `wrap` button on the `changeContent` page surrounds each cloned paragraph with a `<div></div>` pair. I've defined the `div` tag in my CSS to include a red border. Repeatedly clicking the `wrap` button surrounds all cloned paragraphs with red borders. This would be a very tedious effect to achieve in ordinary DOM and JavaScript, but jQuery makes it pretty easy to do:

```
function wrap(){
  $("p:gt(0)").wrap("<div></div>");
} // end wrap
```

The `wrap` method is pretty easy to understand. If you feed it any container tag, it wraps that container around the selected node. You can also use multiple elements, so if you wanted to enclose a paragraph in a single item list, you could do something like this:

```
$("p").wrap("<ul><li></li></ul>");
```

The resulting code would surround each paragraph with an unordered list and list item.

Returning to the `wrap` function, I've decided not to wrap every paragraph with a div, just the ones that have been cloned. (Mainly I'm doing this so that I can show you some other cool selection filters.) The `p:gt(0)` selector means to select all paragraphs with an index greater than 0. In other words, ignore the first paragraph, but apply the following methods to all other paragraphs. You also find these filters:

+ **Less-than** (`:lt`) isolates elements before a certain index.

+ **Equals** (`:eq`) isolates an element with a certain index.

Alternating styles

It's a common effect to alternate background colors on long lists or tables of data, but this can be a tedious effect to achieve in ordinary CSS and JavaScript. Not surprisingly, jQuery selectors make this a pretty easy job:

```
function oddGreen(){
  //turn alternate (odd numbered) paragraph elements
green
  $("p:odd").css("backgroundColor", "green")
  .css("color", "white");
} // end oddGreen
```

The `:odd` selector only chooses elements with an odd index and returns a jQuery node that can be further manipulated with chaining. Of course, you also see an `:even` selector for handling the even-numbered nodes. The rest of this code is simply CSS styling.

Resetting the page

You need to be able to restore the page to its pristine state. A quick jQuery function can easily do the trick:

```
function reset(){
  //remove all but the original content
  $("p:gt(0)").remove();
  $("div:not(#content)").remove();
  //reset the text of the original content
  $("#content").html("<p>This is the original content</
p>");
} // end reset
```

This function reviews many of the jQuery and selection tricks shown in this chapter:

1. **Remove all but the first paragraph.**

Any paragraph with an index greater than 0 is a clone, so it needs to go away. The remove() method removes all jQuery nodes associated with the current selector.

2. **Remove all divs but the original content.**

I could have used the :gt selector again, but instead I use another interesting selector — :not. This removes every div that isn't the primary content div. This removes all divs added through the wrap function.

3. **Reset the original content div to its default text.**

Set the default text back to its original status so that the page is reset.

All I really need here is the last line of code. Changing the HTML of the content div replaces the current contents with whatever is included, so the first two lines aren't entirely necessary in this particular context. Still, it's useful to know how to remove elements when you need to do so.

More fun with selectors and filters

The jQuery selectors and filters are really fun and powerful. Table 3-2 describes a few more filters and indicates how they might be used.

Note that this is a representative list. Be sure to check out the official documentation at http://docs.jquery.com for a more complete list of filters.

Table 3-2	Selected jQuery filters
Filter	**Description**
:header	Any header tag (h1, h2, h3).
:animated	Any element that is currently being animated.
:contains(text)	Any element that contains the indicated text.
:empty	The element is empty.
:parent	This element contains some other element.
:attribute=value	The element has an attribute with the specified value.

Chapter 4: Using the jQuery User Interface Toolkit

In This Chapter

↙ **Exploring the jQuery UI**

↙ **Installing the UI and templates**

↙ **Adding datepickers, dialog boxes, and icons**

↙ **Dragging and dropping**

↙ **Working with scroll bars**

↙ **Building a sorting mechanism**

↙ **Creating an accordion page**

↙ **Building a tab-based interface**

The jQuery library is an incredible tool for simplifying JavaScript programming. It's so popular and powerful that developers began adding new features to make it even more useful. Among the most important of these is a framework called jQuery UI (User Interface), sometimes also called the UI toolkit. That's what this chapter's all about.

What the jQuery User Interface Brings to the Table

This tool adds some very welcome features to Web development, including new visual elements (widgets), a uniform icon set, and a mechanism for easily generating attractive CSS styles:

✦ **New user interface elements:** As a modern user interface tool, HTML is missing some important tools. Most modern visual languages include built-in support for such devices as scroll bars, dedicated datepickers, and multiple tab tools. jQuery UI adds these features and more.

✦ **Advanced user interaction:** The jQuery widgets allow new and exciting ways for the user to interact with your page. With the UI toolkit, you can easily let users make selections by dragging and dropping elements, and expand and contract parts of the page.

✦ **Flexible theme templates:** jQuery UI includes a template mechanism that controls the visual look and feel of your elements. You can choose from dozens of prebuilt themes or use a tool to build your own particular look. You can reuse this template library to manage the look of your other page elements, too (not just the ones defined by the library).

✦ **A complete icon library:** The jQuery UI has a library of icons for use in your Web development. It has arrows, buttons, and plenty of other doo-dads that can be easily changed to fit your template.

✦ **A very clean, modern look:** It's very easy to build forward-looking visual designs with jQuery UI. It supports rounded corners and plenty of special visual effects.

✦ **The power of jQuery:** Because jQuery UI is an extension of jQuery, it adds on to the incredible features of the jQuery language.

✦ **Open-source values:** The jQuery UI (like jQuery itself) is an open-source project with a very active community. This means the library is free to use and can be modified to suit your needs.

The jQuery toolkit is pretty exciting. The best way to get an overview of it is to see an example online. The jQuery Web site (`http://jqueryui.com`) is a great place to get the latest information about jQuery.

It's a theme park

One of the coolest tools in jQuery UI is a concept called a *theme,* which is simply a visual rule-set. The theme is essentially a complex CSS document designed to be used with the UI library.

Using the themeRoller to get an overview of jQuery

The jQuery Web site also features a marvelous tool called the *themeRoller.* The themeRoller allows you to select and modify themes, so it's a great place to preview how themes work, as well as see the key features of the UI extension. Figure 4-1 shows this Web page, which demonstrates many of the great features of jQuery UI.

Before you use themeRoller to change themes, use it to get acquainted with the UI elements. Several useful tools are visible in Figure 4-1:

✦ **Accordion:** The upper-middle segment of the page has three segments (section 1, section 2, and section 3). By clicking a section heading, the user can expand that section and collapse the others.

✦ **Slider:** Sliders (or scroll bars) are an essential user interface element. They allow the user to choose a numeric value with an easy visual tool. jQuery sliders can be adjusted in many ways to allow easy and error-free input.

Figure 4-1: The themeRoller lets you review many jQuery UI elements and modify their look.

✦ **Datepicker:** It's very difficult to ensure that users enter dates properly. The datepicker control automatically pops up a calendar into the page and lets the user manipulate the calendar to pick a date. It's a phenomenally useful tool.

✦ **Tabs:** It's common to have a mechanism for hiding and showing parts of your page. The accordion technique is one way to do so, but tabs are another very popular technique. This mechanism allows you to build a very powerful multitab document without much work.

Scrolling down the page, you see even more interesting tools. Figure 4-2 shows some of these widgets in action.

These widgets demonstrate even more of the power of the jQuery UI library:

✦ **Progress bar:** It's always best to design your code so that little delay exists, but if part of your program is taking some time, a progress bar is a great reminder that something is happening.

✦ **Dialog:** The `open dialog` button pops up what appears to be a dialog box. It acts much like the JavaScript alert, but it's much nicer looking, and it has features that make it much more advanced. In Figure 4-2, the dialog has a clever title: Dialog Title.

✦ **Formatting tools:** The jQuery UI includes special tools for setting apart certain parts of your page as warnings, as highlighted text, or with added shadows and transparency. If you look carefully at Figure 4-2, you'll see several examples of special formatting, including the red alert box, drop shadows, and the UI-highlight style.

✦ **Icons:** jQuery UI ships with a large collection of icons that you can use on your page. Hover over each of the icons on the themeRoller to see a description of the icon. These can be easily used to allow various user interactions.

This is just a quick preview of the visual elements. Read more about how to implement the various elements in Chapter 5 of this minibook after you understand the basics of how to install and work with jQuery UI in this chapter.

Look at the left column on the themeRoller page. If you click the gallery tab (yep, it's using a jQuery UI tab interface), you can see a list of prebuilt themes. Figure 4-3 shows the themeRoller page with an entirely different theme in place.

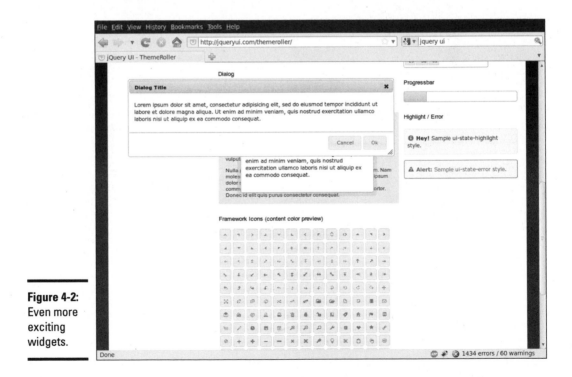

Figure 4-2:
Even more exciting widgets.

Figure 4-3:
Now
themeRoller
is using
the Le Frog
theme.

The built-in themes are pretty impressive, but of course, you can make your own. While you're always free to edit the CSS manually, the whole point of the themeRoller application is to make this process easier.

If you go back to the Roll Your Own tab, you can see an accordion selection that you can use to pick various theme options. You can change fonts, add rounded corners, pick various color schemes, and much more. You can mess around with these options all you want and create your own visual style. You can then save that theme and use it in your own projects.

The themes and widgets are obvious features of the jQuery user interface library, but they aren't the only features. In addition to these more visible tools, jQuery UI adds a number of new behaviors to jQuery nodes. These new behaviors (drag and drop, resize, and more) are used to add functionality to a Web page, which is quite difficult to achieve in more traditional programming.

The themeRoller example

themeRoller is a great example for a number of reasons. It offers a pretty good overview of the jQuery UI library, but it's also a great example of where the Web is going. It's not really a Web page as much as an application that happens to be written in Web technologies. Notice that the functionality of the page (the ability to change styles dynamically) uses many jQuery and jQuery UI tricks: tabs, accordions, dialog boxes, and so on. This kind of programming is almost certainly the direction Web development is heading, and may indeed be the primary form of application in the future. Certainly it appears that applications using this style of user interface and AJAX for data communication and storage are going to be important for some time to come.

Wanna drag? Making components draggable

The basic idea of this program is completely consistent with the jQuery concepts described in Chapters 2 and 3 of this minibook. The page has very simple HTML code. An initialization function creates a special jQuery node and gives it functionality. That's all there is to it.

Your first building example is a simple application that allows the user to pick up a page element and move it with the mouse. While you do this with JavaScript and DOM in Book IV, Chapter 7, you'll find it's quite easy to get the same effect with jQuery UI. Figure 4-4 shows this page in action.

Figure 4-4:
The user can simply drag the box anywhere on the page.

This example is a good starting place, because it's pretty easy. Often, the hardest part of jQuery UI applications is attaching to the library. After that's done (and it's not *that* hard) the rest of the programming is ridiculously easy. Take a look at the code, and you can see what I'm talking about:

```
<!DOCTYPE html PUBLIC "-//W3C//DTD XHTML 1.0 Strict//EN"
"http://www.w3.org/TR/xhtml1/DTD/xhtml1-strict.dtd">
<html lang="EN" dir="ltr" xmlns="http://www.w3.org/1999/
   xhtml">
<head>
  <meta http-equiv="content-type" content="text/xml;
   charset=utf-8" />
  <style type - "text/css">
  #dragMe {
    width: 100px;
    height: 100px;
    border: 1px solid blue;
    text-align: center;
  }

  </style>
  <script type = "text/javascript"
          src = "js/jquery-1.4.2.min.js"></script>
  <script type = "text/javascript"
          src = "js/jquery-ui-1.8.1.custom.min.js"></script>
  <script type = "text/javascript">
    $(init);
    function init(){
      $("#dragMe").draggable();
    }
  </script>
  <title>drag.html</title>
</head>

<body>
  <h1>Drag Demo</h1>
  <div id = "dragMe">
    Drag me
  </div>

</body>
</html>
```

Downloading the library

Writing jQuery UI code isn't difficult, but getting the right parts of the library can be a bit confusing. The jQuery UI library is much larger than the standard jQuery package, so you may not want to include the entire thing if you don't need it.

Previous versions of jQuery UI allowed you to download the entire package but stored each of the various elements in a separate JavaScript file. It was common to have a half-dozen different script tags active just to get the various elements in place. Worse, some dependency issues existed, so you needed to make sure that you had certain packages installed before you used other packages. This made a simple library quite complex to actually use.

Fortunately, the latest versions of the jQuery UI make this process quite a bit simpler:

1. **Pick (or create) your theme.**

   Use the themeRoller site to pick a starting place from the template library. You can then customize your theme exactly to make whatever you want (changing colors, fonts, and other elements).

2. **Download the theme.**

   The themeRoller has a download button. Click this when you're ready to download your theme.

3. **Pick the elements you want.**

   When you're first starting on a project, you'll probably pick all the elements. If you find that the page is loading too slowly, you might build a smaller version that contains only those elements you need. For now, pick everything.

4. **Download the file.**

   After you've chosen the elements you want, you can download them in a zip file.

5. **Install the contents of the zip file to your working directory.**

   The zip file contains a number of files and directories. Place the entire contents of the `css` and `js` directories in the directory where your Web pages will be (often the `public_html` or `htdocs` directory). You do not need to copy the development-bundle directory or the `index.html` page.

6. **If you install multiple themes, copy only the theme information from additional themes.**

   All themes use the same JavaScript. Only the CSS (and related image files) changes. If you want to have multiple themes in your project, simply copy the CSS contents. Each theme will be a different subdirectory of the main CSS directory.

7. **Link to the CSS files.**

   Use the standard link technique to link to the CSS files created by jQuery UI. You can also link to your own CSS files or use internal CSS in addition to the custom CSS. Be sure that you get the path right. Normally, the path looks something like `css/themeName/jquery-ui-1.8.1.custom.css`.

8. **Link to the JavaScript files.**

   The jQuery UI toolkit also installs two JavaScript files: the standard jQuery library and the jQuery UI library. By default, both of these files are installed in the `js` directory.

If something isn't working right, check your file paths again. Almost always, when the jQuery UI stuff isn't working right, it's because you haven't linked to all the right files. Also, note that the CSS files created by jQuery UI also include images. Make sure that your theme has an associated images directory, or your project may not work correctly.

Writing the program

Here's how you go about putting the program together:

1. **Create a basic HTML document.**

The standard document doesn't have to be anything special. I created one div with the ID dragMe. That's the div I want to make draggable (but of course you can apply dragging functionality to anything you can select with jQuery).

2. **Add the standard jQuery library.**

The first script tag imports the standard jQuery library. The UI library requires jQuery to be loaded first.

3. **Add a link to the jQuery UI library.**

A second script tag imports the jQuery UI library. (See the following section on downloading and installing jQuery for details on how to obtain this library.)

4. **Create an initialization function.**

Use the standard jQuery techniques to build an initialization function for your page (as usual, I call mine init()).

5. **Build a draggable node.**

Use standard jQuery selection techniques to isolate the element(s) you want to make draggable. Use the draggable() method to make the element draggable.

6. **Test your application.**

Believe it or not, that's all there is to it. As long as everything's set up properly, your element will be draggable! The user can drag it with the mouse and place it anywhere on the screen.

Resizing on a Theme

The next example demonstrates two important ideas in the jQuery UI package:

✦ **It shows an element that is resizable.** The user can drag on the bottom or right border to change the size of the element. Making an element resizable is very similar to making it draggable.

**Book VII
Chapter 4**

Using the jQuery
User Interface
Toolkit

✦ **It shows the use of a theme.** Take a look at Figure 4-5 to see what's going on.

You can see from Figure 4-5 that the page has a definite visual style. The elements have distinctive fonts and backgrounds, and the headers are in a particular visual style. While there's nothing earth-shattering about this (after all, it's just CSS), the exciting thing is that these styles are defined by the theme. The theme can easily be changed to another theme (created by hand or via themeRoller), and the visual look of all these elements will reflect the new theme.

Themes provide a further level of abstraction to your Web sites that make changing the overall visual style much easier.

Figure 4-6 shows the page after the `resize me` element has changed sizes, and you can see that the rest of the page reformats itself to fit the newly resized element.

Figure 4-5:
The size of this lovely element can be changed by the user.

**Book VII
Chapter 4**

**Using the jQuery
User Interface
Toolkit**

Figure 4-6:
When the element is resized, the rest of the page adjusts.

The following code reveals that most of the interesting stuff is really CSS coding, and the resizing is really just more jQuery UI magic:

```
<!DOCTYPE html PUBLIC "-//W3C//DTD XHTML 1.0 Strict//EN"
"http://www.w3.org/TR/xhtml1/DTD/xhtml1-strict.dtd">
<html lang="EN" dir="ltr" xmlns="http://www.w3.org/1999/
    xhtml">
<head>
  <meta http-equiv="content-type" content="text/xml;
  charset=utf-8" />
  <link rel = "stylesheet"
        type = "text/css"
        href = "css/ui-lightness/jquery-ui-1.8.1.custom.css"
  />

  <style type = "text/css">
  h1 {
    text-align: center;
  }
```

```
#resizeMe {
  width: 300px;
  height: 300px;
  text-align: center;
}

#sample {
  width: 200px;
  height: 200px;
  margin: 1em;
}

</style>
<script type = "text/javascript"
        src = "js/jquery-1.4.2.min.js"></script>
<script type = "text/javascript"
        src = "js/jquery-ui-1.8.1.custom.min.js"></script>
<script type = "text/javascript">
  //<![CDATA[
  $(init);
  function init(){
    $("#resizeMe").resizable();
    themify();
  } // end init

  function themify(){
    //add theme-based CSS to the elements
    $("div").addClass("ui-widget")
    .addClass("ui-widget-content")
    .addClass("ui-corner-all");
    $(":header").addClass("ui-widget-header")
    .addClass("ui-corner-all");
    $("#resizeMe").append('<span class = "ui-icon ui-icon-
  star"></span>');

  }
  //]]>
</script>
<title>resize.html</title>
</head>

<body>
  <h1>Resize Demo</h1>
  <div id = "resizeMe">
    <h2>Resize me</h2>
    <p>
      Drag the right or bottom to resize.
    </p>

  </div>

  <div id = "sample">
    <h2>Sample Widget</h2>
```

```
<p>
   This is made to look like a widget
   with the theme css code.
</p>

</div>


</body>
</html>
```

Examining the HTML and standard CSS

As usual, the HTML is the foundation of the entire page. It's very clean as usual, and it shows the general structure of the page. The HTML consists of only three primary elements: a heading and two divs. Each div contains its own level-two heading and a paragraph. The divs are given IDs to make them easier to style.

I also included a basic CSS section to handle the general layout of the page. I wanted the widgets to have specified beginning sizes, so I used ordinary CSS to get this effect.

Importing the files

Book VII
Chapter 4

Using the jQuery User Interface Toolkit

jQuery applications require importation of JavaScript code libraries. In this application (and most jQuery UI applications), I import three files:

✦ **The main jQuery library:** This file is the essential jQuery base library. It is imported as described in Chapter 2 of this minibook, as an ordinary JavaScript file.

✦ **The jQuery UI library:** This file is also a standard JavaScript library. Earlier in this chapter, I describe how to obtain a custom version of this file.

✦ **The theme CSS file:** When you create a theme with themeRoller, you are provided with a CSS file. This file is your theme. Because this is a CSS file rather than JavaScript code, use the `link` tag to attach it to your page.

Not all jQuery UI examples require a theme, but most do. As you see in the following example, themes provide some other really great effects too, so it's worth it to include a theme CSS file whenever you want to use jQuery UI.

Making a resizable element

Surprisingly, the easiest part of the project is making the `resizable` element have the resizable behavior. It's a pretty standard jQuery UI trick:

```
$(init);
function init(){
  $("#resizeMe").resizable();
  themify();
} // end init
```

1. **Begin with an initialization function.**

   Like all good jQuery code, this example begins with standard initialization.

2. **Make an element resizable.**

   Identify the `resizeMe` div as a jQuery node, and use the `resizable()` method to make it resizable. That's all there is to it.

3. **Call a second function to add theming to the elements.**

   While the resizable method doesn't require use of jQuery themes, the themes do improve the look of the element.

Adding themes to your elements

The jQuery theme tool makes it quite easy to decorate your elements through CSS. The great thing about jQuery themes is that they are *semantic,* that is, you specify the general purpose of the element and then let the theme apply the appropriate specific CSS. You can use the themeRoller application to easily create new themes or modify existing ones. In this way, you can create a very sophisticated look and feel for your site and write very little CSS on your own. It's a very powerful mechanism.

Many of the jQuery interface elements (such as the accordion and tab tools described elsewhere in this chapter) automatically use the current CSS theme. Of course you can also apply them to any of your own elements to get a consistent look.

Themes are simply CSS classes. To apply a CSS theme to an element, you can just add a special class to the object.

For example, you can make a paragraph look like the current definition of the ui-widget by adding this code to it:

```
<div class = "ui-widget">
My div now looks like a widget
</div>
```

Of course, adding classes into the HTML violates one of the principles of semantic design (that is, separating the content from the layout), so it's better (and more efficient) to do the work in JavaScript with jQuery:

```
function themify(){
```

```
//add theme-based CSS to the elements
$("div").addClass("ui-widget")
.addClass("ui-widget-content")
.addClass("ui-corner-all");
$(":header").addClass("ui-widget-header")
.addClass("ui-corner-all");
$("#resizeMe")
.append('<span class = "ui-icon ui-icon-star"></
span>');
}
```

The `themify` function adds all the themes to the elements on my page, applying the pretty jQuery theme to it. I use jQuery tricks to simplify the process:

1. **Identify all divs with jQuery.**

I want all the divs on my page to be styled like widgets, so I use jQuery to identify all div elements.

2. **Add the `ui-widget` class to all divs.**

This class is defined in the theme. All jQuery themes have this class defined, but the specifics (colors, font sizes, and so on) vary by theme. In this way, you can swap out a theme to change the appearance, and the code still works. The `ui-widget` class defines an element as a widget.

3. **Add `ui-widget-content` as well.**

The divs need to have two classes attached, so I use chaining to specify that divs should also be members of the `ui-widget-content` class. This class indicates that the contents of the widget (and not just the class itself) should be styled.

4. **Specify rounded corners.**

Rounded corners have become a standard of the Web 2.0 visual design. This effect is extremely easy to achieve with jQuery — just add the `ui-corner-all` class to any element you want to have rounded corners.

Rounded corners use CSS3, which is not yet supported by all browsers. Your page will not show rounded corners in most versions of IE, but the page will still work fine otherwise.

5. **Make all headlines conform to the widget-header style.**

The jQuery themes include a nice headline style. You can easily make all heading tags (h1 to h6) follow this theme. Use the `:header` filter to identify all headings, and apply the `ui-widget-header` and `ui-corner-all` classes to these headers.

The jQuery UI package supports a number of interesting classes, which are described in Table 4-1.

Book VII
Chapter 4

Using the jQuery
User Interface
Toolkit

Table 4-1	CSS Classes Defined by jQuery UI	
Class	*Used On*	*Description*
ui-widget	Outer container of widget	Makes element look like a widget.
ui-widget-header	Heading element	Applies distinctive heading appearance.
ui-widget-content	Widget	Applies widget content style to element and children.
ui-state-default	Clickable elements	Displays standard (unclicked) state.
ui-state-hover	Clickable elements	Displays hover state.
ui-state-focus	Clickable elements	Displays focus state when element has keyboard focus.
ui-state-active	Clickable elements	Displays active state when mouse is clicked on element.
ui-state-highlight	Any widget or element	Specifies that an element is currently highlighted.
ui-state-error	Any widget or element	Specifies that an element contains an error or warning message.
ui-state-error text	Text element	Allows error highlighting without changing other elements (mainly used in form validation).
ui-state-disabled	Any widget or element	Demonstrates that a widget is currently disabled.
ui-corner-all, ui-corner-tl (etc)	Any widget or element	Adds current corner size to an element. Specify specific corners with tl, tr, bl, br, top, bottom, left, right.
ui-widget-shadow	Any widget	Applies shadow effect to a widget.

A few other classes are defined in UI themes, but these are the most commonly used. Refer to the current jQuery UI documentation for more details.

Adding an icon

Note the small start that appears inside the resizeMe element in Figure 4-6. This element is an example of a jQuery UI icon. All jQuery themes support a standard set of icons, which are small (16px square) images. The icon set includes standard icons for arrows as well as images commonly used in menus and toolbars (save and load, new file, and so on). Some jQuery UI elements use icons automatically, but you can also add them directly. To use an icon in your programs, follow these steps:

1. **Include a jQuery UI theme.**

   The icons are part of the theme package. Include the CSS style sheet that corresponds with the theme (as you've already done in this example).

2. **Be sure that the images are accessible.**

   When you download a theme package, it includes a directory of images. The images included in this directory are used to create custom backgrounds as well as icons. The CSS file expects a directory called images to be in the same directory as the CSS. This directory should contain several images that begin with ui-icons. These images contain all the necessary icons. If the icon image files are not available, the icons will not display. (Of course, you can edit these images in your graphics tool to customize them if you want.)

3. **Create a span where you want the icon to appear.**

   Place an empty span element wherever you want the icon to appear in the HTML. You can place the span directly in the HTML if you want, or you can add it through jQuery. I prefer to add UI elements through jQuery to keep the HTML as pristine as possible.

4. **Attach the ui-icon class to the span.**

   This tells jQuery to treat the span as an icon. The contents of the span will be hidden, and the span will be resized to hold a 16-pixel square icon image.

5. **Attach a second class to identify the specific icon.**

   Look at the themeRoller page to see the available icons. When you hover over an icon on this page, you can see the class name associated with the icon.

You can add the code directly in your HTML like this:

```
<p id = "myPara">
  This is my text
  <span class = "ui-icon ui-icon-star"></span>
</p>
```

Or, you can use jQuery to add the appropriate code to your element:

```
$("#myPara").append('<span class = "ui-icon ui-icon-star">
  </span>');
```

Dragging, Dropping, and Calling Back

JQuery elements look good, but they also have interesting functionality. Most jQuery UI objects have the ability to respond to specialized events. As an example, look over the dragDrop.html page shown in Figure 4-7.

When you drop an element onto the target, the color and content of the target change, as shown in Figure 4-8.

Figure 4-7: The page has a group of draggable elements and a target.

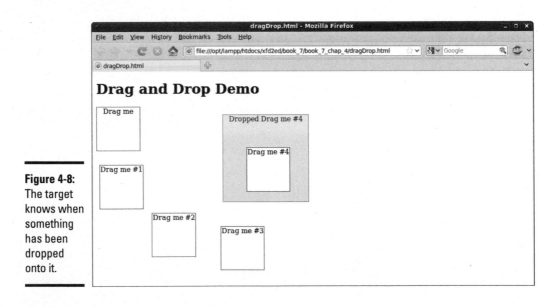

Figure 4-8: The target knows when something has been dropped onto it.

Another interesting aspect of this program is the inclusion of several draggable elements. This program demonstrates how jQuery simplifies working with a number of elements.

Take a look at the entire program before you see the smaller segments:

```
<!DOCTYPE html PUBLIC "-//W3C//DTD XHTML 1.0 Strict//EN"
"http://www.w3.org/TR/xhtml1/DTD/xhtml1-strict.dtd">
<html lang="EN" dir="ltr" xmlns="http://www.w3.org/1999/
    xhtml">
<head>
  <meta http-equiv="content-type" content="text/xml;
    charset=utf-8" />
  <link rel = "stylesheet"
        type = "text/css"
        href = "css/ui-lightness/jquery-ui-1.8.1.custom.css" />
  <style type = "text/css">
  .dragMe {
    width: 100px;
    height: 100px;
    border: 1px solid blue;
    text-align: center;
    background-color: white;
    position: absolute;
    z-index: 100;
  }
  #target {
    width: 200px;
    height: 200px;
    border: 1px solid red;
    text-align: center;
    position: absolute;
    left: 300px;
    top: 100px;
    z-index: 0;
  }
  </style>
  <script type = "text/javascript"
          src = "js/jquery-1.4.2.min.js"></script>
  <script type = "text/javascript"
          src = "js/jquery-ui-1.8.1.custom.min.js"></script>
  <script type = "text/javascript">
    $(init);

    function init(){
      // make some clones of dragMe
      cloneDragMe();

      //make all drag me elements draggable
      $(".dragMe").draggable();
```

Book VII
Chapter 4

Using the jQuery
User Interface
Toolkit

```
        //set target as droppable
        $("#target").droppable();

        //bind events to target
        $("#target").bind("drop", changeTarget);
        $("#target").bind("dropout", resetTarget);

    } // end init

    function cloneDragMe(){
       for (i = 1; i <=4; i++){
          zValue = (101 + i) + "";
          yPos = 100 + (i * 20) + "px";

          $("div:first").clone()
          .insertAfter("div:first")
          .css("top", yPos)
          .css("zIndex", zValue)
          .append(" #" + i);
       } // end for loop
    } // end cloneDragMe

    function changeTarget(event, ui){
       $("#target").addClass("ui-state-highlight")
       .html("Dropped ")
       .append(ui.draggable.text());
    } // end changeTarget

    function resetTarget(event, ui){
        $("#target").removeClass("ui-state-highlight")
        .html("Drop on me");
    } // end reset

  </script>
  <title>dragDrop.html</title>
</head>

<body>
  <h1>Drag and Drop Demo</h1>
  <div class = "dragMe">
    Drag me
  </div>
  <div id = "target">
    Drop on me
  </div>
</body>
</html>
```

Building the basic page

As typical with jQuery, the HTML code is simple. It's very striking that you only see a single dragMe element. It turns out to be simpler to build a single element in HTML and use jQuery and JavaScript to make as many copies as you need. You also see a single `target` element. I added basic CSS to make the element easy to see (borders) and set them as absolute positioned so that I could control the initial position.

Note that I attached an ID to `target` (because there will be a single target on the page) and made `dragMe` a class (because I want to be able to have several draggable elements on the page).

Initializing the page

The initialization is a bit more elaborate than some of the earlier examples in this chapter, but it still isn't too difficult to follow. The main addition is the ability to respond to some specialty events:

```
$(init);

function init(){
  // make some clones of dragMe
  cloneDragMe();

  //make all drag me elements draggable
  $(".dragMe").draggable();

  //set target as droppable
  $("#target").droppable();

  //bind events to target
  $("#target").bind("drop", changeTarget);
  $("#target").bind("dropout", resetTarget);

} // end init
```

The steps here aren't hard to follow:

1. **Make copies of the `dragme` element.**

This part isn't critical (in fact, I added it after testing with a single element). However, if you want to have multiple copies of the draggable element, use a method to encapsulate the process.

2. **Make all `dragme` elements draggable.**

Use the jQuery `draggable()` method on all elements with the `dragMe` class.

3. **Establish the target as a droppable element.**

The `droppable()` method sets up an element so that it can receive events when a draggable element is dropped on it. Note that making something droppable doesn't have any particular effect on its own. The interesting thing comes when you bind events to the element.

4. **Bind a `drop` event to the target.**

   Droppable elements can have events attached to them just like any jQuery object. However, the mechanism for attaching an event to a user interface object is a little bit different than the standard jQuery event mechanism (which involves a custom function for each event). Use the `bind` method to specify a function to be called when a particular event occurs. When the user drops a node that has been made draggable onto the target element, this triggers the `drop` event, so call the `change Target()` function.

5. **Bind a `dropout` event to the target as well.**

   You can bind another event to occur when the user removes all draggable elements from the target. This event is called `dropout`, and I've told the program to call the `resetTarget()` function when this event is triggered.

You often see programmers using shortcuts for this process. Sometimes, the functions are defined anonymously in the `bind` call, or sometimes the event functions are attached as a JSON object directly in the `droppable()` method assignment. Feel free to use these techniques if you are comfortable with them. I've chosen the technique used here because I think it is the clearest model to understand.

Handling the drop

When the user drags a `dragMe` element and drops it on the target, the target's background color changes and the program reports the text of the element that was dragged. The code is easy:

```
function changeTarget(event, ui){
  $("#target").addClass("ui-state-highlight")
  .html("Dropped ")
  .append(ui.draggable.text());
} // end changeTarget
```

Here's how to put this together:

1. **Create a function to correspond to the `drop` event.**

   The `drop` event is bound to a function called `changeTarget`, so I need to create such a function.

2. **Include two parameters.**

   Bound event functions require two parameters. The first is an object that encapsulates the event (much like the one in regular DOM programming) and a second element called `ui`, which encapsulates information about the user interface. You can use the `ui` object to determine which draggable element was dropped onto the target.

3. **Highlight the target.**

It's a good idea to signal that the target's state has changed. You can change the CSS directly (with jQuery) or use jQuery theming to apply a predefined highlight class. I chose to use the jQuery theme technique to simply add the `ui-state-highlight` class to the `target` object.

4. **Change the text to indicate the new status.**

Normally you should do something to indicate what was dropped. (If it's a shopping application, you should add the element to an array so that you can remember what the user wants to purchase, for example.) In this example, I simply change the text of the target to indicate that the element has been dropped.

5. **Use `ui.draggable` to get access to the element that was dropped.**

The `ui` object contains information about the user interface. `ui.draggable` is a link to the draggable element that triggered the current function. It's a jQuery element, so you can use whatever jQuery methods you want on it. In this case, I extract the text from the draggable element and append it to the end of the target's text.

Beauty school dropout events

Another function is used to handle the dropout condition, which occurs when draggable elements are no longer dropped on the target. I bind the resetTarget function to this event:

```
function resetTarget(event, ui){
    $("#target").removeClass("ui-state-highlight")
    .html("Drop on me");
} // end reset
```

All you have to do is this:

1. **Remove the highlight class from the target.**

One great thing about using the theme classes is how easy they are to remove. Remove the highlight class, and the target reverts to its original appearance.

2. **Reset the HTML text.**

Now that the target is empty, reset its HTML so that it prompts the user to drop a new element.

Cloning the elements

You can simply run the program as it is (with a single copy of the `dragMe` class), but more often, drag and drop is used with a number of elements. For

Book VII
Chapter 4

Using the jQuery
User Interface
Toolkit

example, you might allow users to drag various icons from your catalog to a shopping cart.

The basic jQuery library provides all the functionality necessary to make as many copies of an element as you want. Copying an element is a simple matter of using the jQuery `clone()` method.

The more elaborate code is used to ensure that the various elements display properly:

```
function cloneDragMe(){
  for (i = 1; i <=4; i++){
    zValue = (101 + i) + "";
    yPos = 100 + (i * 20) + "px";

    $("div:first").clone()
    .insertAfter("div:first")
    .css("top", yPos)
    .css("zIndex", zValue)
    .append(" #" + i);
  } // end for loop
} // end cloneDragMe
```

Here are the steps:

1. Create a `for` loop.

Anytime you're doing something repetitive, a `for` loop is a likely tool. In this case, I want to make four clones numbered 1 through 4, so I have a variable named i that can vary from 1 to 4.

2. Create a `zValue` for the element.

The CSS `zIndex` property is used to indicate the overlapping of elements. Higher values appear to be closer to the user. I give each element a zOrder of over 100 to ensure that it appears over the target. (If you don't specify the `zIndex`, dragged elements might go under the target and become invisible.) The `zValue` variable is mapped to the `zIndex`.

3. Determine the y position of the element.

I want each successive copy of the `dragMe` element to be a bit lower than the previous one. Multiplying i by 20 ensures that each element is separated from the previous one by 20 pixels. Add 100 pixels to move the new stack of elements near the original.

4. Make a clone of the first element.

Use the `clone()` method to make a clone of the first div. (Use the `:first` filter to specify which div you want to copy.)

5. **Remember to insert the newly cloned element.**

   The cloned element exists only in memory until it is somehow added to the page. I chose to add the element right after the first element.

6. **Set the top of the element with the yPos variable.**

   Use the `yPos` variable you calculated earlier to set the vertical position of the newly minted element. Use the `css()` method to apply the `yPos` variable to the element's `left` CSS rule.

7. **Set the zIndex.**

   Like the y position, the `zValue` variable you created is mapped to a CSS value. In this case, `zValue` is mapped to the `zIndex` property.

8. **Add the index to the element's text.**

   Use the `append()` method to add the value of `I` to the element's HTML. This way you can tell which element is which.

Chapter 5: Improving Usability with jQuery

In This Chapter

✔ Working with scroll bars

✔ Building a sorting mechanism

✔ Managing selectable items

✔ Using the dialog tool

✔ Creating an accordion page

✔ Building a tab-based interface

The jQuery UI adds some really great capabilities to your Web pages. Some of the most interesting tools are *widgets,* which are user interface elements not supplied in standard HTML. Some of these elements supplement HTML by providing easier input options. For example, it can be quite difficult to get the user to enter a date in a predictable manner. The datepicker widget provides an easy-to-use calendar for picking dates. The interface is easy for the programmer to add and makes it hard for the user to enter the date incorrectly. Another important class of tools provided by the jQuery UI helps manage complex pages by hiding content until it is needed.

Multi-element Designs

Handling page complexity has been a constant issue in Web development. As a page gets longer and more complex, navigating the page becomes more difficult. The early versions of HTML had few solutions to this problem. The use of frames was popular for a time, because it allows the programmer to place navigation information in one frame and content in another. However, frames added additional usability problems and have fallen from favor. Dynamic HTML and AJAX seem like perfect replacement technologies, but they can be difficult to implement, especially in a reliable cross-browser manner.

The jQuery UI provides two incredible tools for managing larger pages:

✦ The accordion tool allows you to create a large page but display only smaller parts of it at a time.

✦ The tabs tool allows you to easily turn a large page into a page with a tab menu.

These tools are incredibly easy to use, and they add tremendously to your page development options. Both of these tools automate and simplify the DOM and AJAX work it takes to build a large page with dynamic content.

Playing the accordion widget

Some of the most powerful jQuery tools are actually the easiest to use. The accordion widget has become an extremely popular part of the jQuery UI toolset. Take a look at `accordion.html` in Figure 5-1 to see how it works.

When you look at Figure 5-1, you see headings for the first three minibooks of this book. The details for the first minibook are available, but the other books' details are hidden. If you click the heading for Book II, Book I is minimized and Book II is now expanded, as you can see Figure 5-2.

This marvelous effect allows the user to focus on a particular part of a larger context while seeing the overall outline. It's called an *accordion* because the various pieces expand and contract to allow the user to focus on a part without losing place of its position in the whole. Collapsible content has become an important usability tool made popular by the system bar in Mac OS and other popular usability tools.

Figure 5-1: This page shows the first minibook outline of a familiar-sounding book.

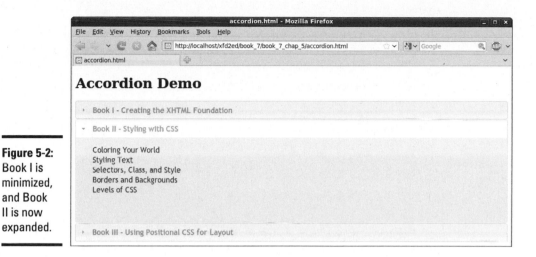

Figure 5-2:
Book I is
minimized,
and Book
II is now
expanded.

The accordion effect is strikingly easy to achieve with
    jQuery:

```
<!DOCTYPE html PUBLIC "-//W3C//DTD XHTML 1.0
    Strict//EN"
"http://www.w3.org/TR/xhtml1/DTD/xhtml1-strict.dtd">
<html lang="EN" dir="ltr" xmlns="http://www.w3.org/1999/
    xhtml">
<head>
  <meta http-equiv="content-type" content="text/xml;
    charset=utf-8" />
  <link rel = "stylesheet"
        type = "text/css"
        href = "css/ui-lightness/jquery-ui-1.8.1.custom.css"
  />

  <script type = "text/javascript"
          src = "js/jquery-1.4.2.min.js"></script>
  <script type = "text/javascript"
          src = "js/jquery-ui-1.8.1.custom.min.js"></script>
  <script type = "text/javascript">
    //<![CDATA[

    $(init);

    function init(){
      $("#accordion").accordion();
    }
    //]]>
    </script>

  <title>accordion.html</title>
</head>
<body>
<h1>Accordion Demo</h1>
```

```
<div id = "accordion">
  <h2><a href = "#">Book I - Creating the XHTML Foundation</
    a></h2>
  <ol>
    <li>Sound XHTML Foundations</li>
    <li>It's All About Validation</li>
    <li>Choosing your Tools</li>
    <li>Managing Information with Lists and Tables</li>
    <li>Making Connections with Links</li>
    <li>Adding Images</li>
    <li>Creating forms</li>
  </ol>

  <h2><a href = "#">Book II - Styling with CSS</a></h2>
  <ol>
    <li>Coloring Your World</li>
    <li>Styling Text</li>
    <li>Selectors, Class, and Style</li>
    <li>Borders and Backgrounds</li>
    <li>Levels of CSS</li>
  </ol>

  <h2><a href = "#">Book III - Using Positional CSS for
    Layout</a></h2>
  <ol>
    <li>Fun with the Fabulous Float</li>
    <li>Building Floating Page Layouts</li>
    <li>Styling Lists and Menus</li>
    <li>Using alternative Positioning</li>
  </ol>
</div>
</body>
</html>
```

As you can see by looking over the code, it's mainly just HTML. The effect is really easy to accomplish:

1. **Import all the usual suspects.**

   You need to import the jQuery and jQuery UI JavaScript files, and a theme CSS file. (See Book VII, Chapter 4 if you need a refresher on this process.) You also need to make sure that the CSS has access to the images directory with icons and backgrounds, because it will use some of these images automatically.

2. **Build your HTML page as normal.**

   Build an HTML page as you would normally do. Pay attention to the sections that you want to collapse. There should normally be a heading tag for each element, all at the same level (Level 2 headings in my case).

3. **Create a div that contains the entire collapsible content.**

   Put all the collapsible content in a single div with an ID. You'll be turning this div into an accordion jQuery element.

4. **Add an anchor around each heading you want to specify as collapsible.**

   Place an empty anchor tag (`<a href = "#"></a>`) around each heading that you want to use as a collapsible heading. The # sign indicates that the anchor will call the same page and is used as a placeholder by the jQuery UI engine. You can add the anchor directly in the HTML or through jQuery code.

5. **Create a jQuery `init()` function.**

   Use the normal techniques to build a jQuery initializer as shown in Chapter 3 of this minibook.

6. **Apply the `accordion()` method to the div.**

   Use jQuery to identify the div that contains collapsible content and apply `accordion()` to it:

   ```
   function init(){
     $("#accordion").accordion();
   }
   ```

Building a tabbed interface

Another important technique in Web development is the use of a tabbed interface. This allows the user to change the contents of a segment by selecting one of a series of tabs. Figure 5-3 shows an example.

Figure 5-3: This is another way to look at that hauntingly familiar table of contents.

In a tabbed interface, only one element is visible at a time, but the tabs are all visible. The tabbed interface is a little more predictable than the accordion, because the tabs (unlike the accordion's headings) stay in the same place. The tabs change colors to indicate which tab is currently highlighted, and they also change state (normally by changing color) to indicate that they are being hovered over. When you click another tab, the main content area of the widget is replaced with the corresponding content. Figure 5-4 shows what happens when the user clicks the book 3 tab.

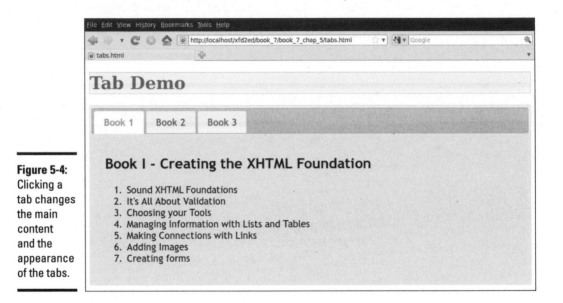

Figure 5-4: Clicking a tab changes the main content and the appearance of the tabs.

Like the accordion, the tab effect is incredibly easy to achieve. Look over the code:

```
<!DOCTYPE html PUBLIC "-//W3C//DTD XHTML 1.0 Strict//EN"
"http://www.w3.org/TR/xhtml1/DTD/xhtml1-strict.dtd">
<html lang="EN" dir="ltr" xmlns="http://www.w3.org/1999/
    xhtml">
<head>
  <meta http-equiv="content-type" content="text/xml;
    charset=utf-8" />
  <link rel = "stylesheet"
        type = "text/css"
        href = "css/ui-lightness/jquery-ui-1.8.1.custom.css"
  />

  <script type = "text/javascript"
        src = "js/jquery-1.4.2.min.js"></script>
  <script type = "text/javascript"
        src = "js/jquery-ui-1.8.1.custom.min.js"></script>
```

```
<script type = "text/javascript">
  //<![CDATA[

  $(init);

  function init(){
    $("#tabs").tabs();
  }
  //]]>
  </script>

<title>tabs.html</title>
</head>
<body>
<h1 class = "ui-state-default">Tab Demo</h1>

<div id = "tabs">
  <ul>
    <li><a href = "#book1">Book 1</a></li>
    <li><a href = "#book2">Book 2</a></li>
    <li><a href = "#book3">Book 3</a></li>
  </ul>

  <div id - "book1">
    <h2>Book I - Creating the XHTML Foundation</h2>
    <ol>
      <li>Sound XHTML Foundations</li>
      <li>It's All About Validation</li>
      <li>Choosing your Tools</li>
      <li>Managing Information with Lists and Tables</li>
      <li>Making Connections with Links</li>
      <li>Adding Images</li>
      <li>Creating Forms</li>
    </ol>
  </div>

  <div id = "book2">
    <h2>Book II - Styling with CSS</h2>
    <ol>
      <li>Coloring Your World</li>
      <li>Styling Text</li>
      <li>Selectors, Class, and Style</li>
      <li>Borders and Backgrounds</li>
      <li>Levels of CSS</li>
    </ol>
  </div>

  <div id = "book3">
    <h2>Book III - Using Positional CSS for Layout</h2>
    <ol>
      <li>Fun with the Fabulous Float</li>
      <li>Building Floating Page Layouts</li>
      <li>Styling Lists and Menus</li>
```

```
        <li>Using alternative Positioning</li>
      </ol>
    </div>
  </div>
</body>
</html>
```

The mechanism for building a tab-based interface is very similar to the one for accordions:

1. **Add all the appropriate files.**

   Like most jQuery UI effects, you need jQuery, jQuery UI, and a theme CSS file. You also need access to the images directory for the theme's background graphics.

2. **Build HTML as normal.**

   If you're building a well-organized Web page anyway, you're already pretty close.

3. **Build a div that contains all the tabbed data.**

   This is the element that you'll be doing the jQuery magic on.

4. **Place main content areas in named divs.**

   Each piece of content that will be displayed as a page should be placed in a div with a descriptive ID. Each of these divs should be placed in the tab div. (See my code for organization if you're confused.)

5. **Add a list of local links to the content.**

   Build a menu of links. Place this at the top of the tabbed div. Each link should be a local link to one of the divs. For example, my index looks like this:

   ```
   <ul>
     <li><a href = "#book1">Book 1</a></li>
     <li><a href = "#book2">Book 2</a></li>
     <li><a href = "#book3">Book 3</a></li>
   </ul>
   ```

6. **Build an `init()` function as usual.**

   Use the normal jQuery techniques.

7. **Call the `tabs()` method on the main div.**

   Incredibly, one line of jQuery code does all the work.

Using tabs with AJAX

You have an even easier way to work with the jQuery tab interface. Rather than placing all your code in a single file, place the HTML code for each panel in a separate HTML file. You can then use a simplified form of the tab mechanism to automatically import the various code snippets through AJAX calls. Look at the AJAXtabs.html code for an example:

```
<!DOCTYPE html PUBLIC "-//W3C//DTD XHTML 1.0 Strict//EN"
"http://www.w3.org/TR/xhtml1/DTD/xhtml1-strict.dtd">
<html lang="EN" dir="ltr" xmlns="http://www.w3.org/1999/
    xhtml">
<head>
  <meta http-equiv="content-type" content="text/xml;
  charset=utf-8" />
  <link rel = "stylesheet"
        type = "text/css"
        href = "css/ui-lightness/jquery-ui-1.8.1.custom.css"
  />

  <script type = "text/javascript"
          src = "js/jquery-1.4.2.min.js"></script>
  <script type = "text/javascript"
          src = "js/jquery-ui-1.8.1.custom.min.js"></script>
  <script type = "text/javascript">
    //<![CDATA[

    $(init);

    function init(){
      $("#tabs").tabs();
    }
    //]]>
    </script>

  <title>AJAXtabs.html</title>
</head>
<body>
  <h1>AJAX tabs</h1>
  <div id = "tabs">
      <ul>
        <li><a href = "book1.html">Book 1</a></li>
        <li><a href = "book2.html">Book 2</a></li>
        <li><a href = "book3.html">Book 3</a></li>
      </ul>
  </div>
</body>
</html>
```

**Book VII
Chapter 5**

**Improving Usability
with jQuery**

Note: I didn't provide a screen shot for the AJAXtabs.html page, because it looks exactly like tabs.html, shown in Figure 5-4.

This version of the code doesn't contain any of the actual content! Instead, jQuery builds the tab structure and then uses the links to make AJAX requests to load the content. As a default, it finds the content specified by the first tab (`chap1.html`) and loads it into the display area. Here's what `book1.html` contains:

```
<!DOCTYPE html PUBLIC "-//W3C//DTD XHTML 1.0 Strict//EN"
"http://www.w3.org/TR/xhtml1/DTD/xhtml1-strict.dtd">
<html lang="EN" dir="ltr" xmlns="http://www.w3.org/1999/
   xhtml">
<head>
  <meta http-equiv="content-type" content="text/xml;
    charset=utf-8" />
  <link rel = "stylesheet"
        type = "text/css"
        href = "css/ui-lightness/jquery-ui-1.8.1.custom.css"
   />

  <script type = "text/javascript"
          src = "js/jquery-1.4.2.min.js"></script>
  <script type = "text/javascript"
          src = "js/jquery-ui-1.8.1.custom.min.js"></script>
  <script type = "text/javascript">
    //<![CDATA[

    $(init);

    function init(){
      $("#tabs").tabs();
    }
    //]]>
    </script>

  <title>AJAXtabs.html</title>
</head>
<body>
  <h1>AJAX tabs</h1>
  <div id = "tabs">
      <ul>
        <li><a href = "book1.html">Book 1</a></li>
        <li><a href = "book2.html">Book 2</a></li>
        <li><a href = "book3.html">Book 3</a></li>
      </ul>
  </div>
</body>
</html>
```

As you can see, `book1.html` is simply a code snippet. It doesn't need all the complete trappings of a Web page (like the doctype or header) because it's meant to be pulled in as part of a larger page. The AJAX trick is a marvelous technique because it allows you to build a modular system quite easily. You can build these code pages separately and include them easily into a larger page. This is a good foundation for a content-management system.

Improving Usability

While the UI widgets are good looking and fun, another important aspect is how they can improve usability. Web pages are often used to get information from users. Certain kinds of information can be very difficult for the user to enter correctly. The jQuery UI elements include a number of tools to help you with this specific problem. The UItools.html page, shown in Figure 5-5, illustrates some of these techniques.

Figure 5-5:
The UItools page uses a tabbed interface to demonstrate many input tools.

A lot is going on in this page, but the tabbed interface really cleans it up and lets the user concentrate on one idea at a time. Using the tabbed interface can really simplify your user's life.

This page is a bit long because it has a number of sections. I demonstrate the code in chunks to make it easier to manage. Be sure to look on the Web site for the complete code.

Here's the main HTML code so that you can see the general structure of the page:

```
<h1>UI tools</h1>
<div id = "tabs">
  <ul>
    <li><a href = "#datePickerTab">datePicker</a></li>
    <li><a href = "#sliderTab">slider</a></li>
    <li><a href = "#selectableTab">selectable</a></li>
    <li><a href = "#sortableTab">sortable</a></li>
    <li><a href = "#dialogTab">dialog</a></li>
  </ul>
```

You see a main div named tabs. This contains a list of links to the various divs that will contain the demonstrations. I describe each of these divs in the section that demonstrates it. The page also imports jQuery, jQuery UI, and the theme CSS. The init() method contains most of the jQuery code:

```
$(init);

function init(){
  $("h1").addClass("ui-widget-header");

  $("#tabs").tabs();
  $("#datePicker").datepicker();

  $("#slider").slider()
  .bind("slide", reportSlider);

  $("#selectable").selectable();

  $("#sortable").sortable();

  $("#dialog").dialog();

  //initially close dialog
  $("#dialog").dialog("close");

} // end init
```

The init section initializes the various components. The details of the init() function are described in each section as they are used.

Most of these special widgets require the standard jquery link, jqueryui, and one of the templates to be installed. Many of the widgets use features from the template library. Of course, you can start with a default template and tune it up later. You just have to have a template available to see all the effects.

Playing the dating game

Imagine that you're writing a program that requires a birth date. Getting date information from the user can be an especially messy problem, because so many variations exist. Users might use numbers for the month, month names, or abbreviations. Some people use month/day/year, and others use day/month/year. They may enter the year as two or four characters. (That silly Y2K thing hasn't really died yet. I still have the bunker in the backyard.) Worse, it's really hard to pick a date without a calendar in front of you.

The datepicker dialog box is one of the coolest elements in the entire jQuery UI library. When you add datepicker() functionality to a textbox, that textbox becomes a datepicker. When the user selects the date box, a calendar automatically pops up, as shown in Figure 5-6.

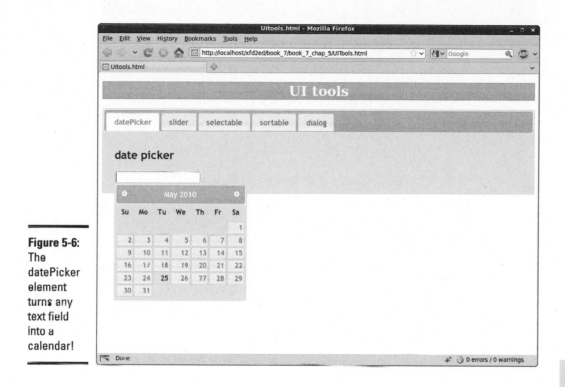

Figure 5-6:
The
datePicker
element
turns any
text field
into a
calendar!

The user can select a date on the calendar, and it will be placed in the text-box in a standard format. You have no better way to get date input from the user. Building a datepicker can't be much easier:

1. **Begin with a jQuery UI page.**

You need jQuery, jQuery UI, and a theme to use the datepicker.

2. **Build a form with a text field.**

Any standard text input element will do. Be sure to give the element an ID so that you can refer to it in JavaScript:

```
<div id = "datePickerTab">
  <h2>date picker</h2>
  <input type = "text"
         id = "datePicker" />
</div>
```

3. **Isolate the text input element with jQuery.**

Build a standard jQuery node from the input element.

4. **Add the `datepicker()` functionality.**

   Use the `datePicker()` method to convert the text node into a dat-epicker. This is usually done in some type of `init()` function. The rest is automatic!

   ```
   $("#datePicker").datepicker();
   ```

5. **Retrieve data from the form element in the normal way.**

   When the user has selected the date, it is placed in the text field auto-matically. As far as your program is concerned, the text field is still an ordinary text field. Retrieve the data in the ordinary way.

The datepicker is a powerful tool with a large number of additional options. Look at the jQuery UI documentation to see how to use it to select date ranges, produce specific date formats, and much more.

Picking numbers with the slider

Numeric input is another significant usability problem. When you want users to enter numeric information, it can be quite difficult to ensure that the data really is a number and that it's in the range you want. Traditional program-mers often use *sliders* (sometimes called *scroll bars*) to simplify accepting numeric input. Figure 5-7 shows a slider.

Figure 5-7:
The user can choose a number with the mouse using a slider.

The slider is (like many jQuery UI objects) very easy to set up. Here's the rel-evant chunk of HTML code:

```
<div id = "sliderTab">
  <h2>slider</h2>
  <div id = "slider"></div>
  <div id = "slideOutput">0</div>
</div>
```

The Slider tab is a basic div. It contains two other divs:

✦ The `slider` div is actually empty. It will be replaced by the slider element when the jQuery is activated.

✦ The other div (`slideOutput`) in this section will be used to output the current value of the slider.

Create the slider element in the `init()` function with some predictable jQuery code:

```
$("#slider").slider();
```

The `slider()` method turns any jQuery element into a slider, replacing the contents with a visual slider.

Note that you can add a JSON object as a parameter to set up the slider with various options. See `rgbSlider.html` on this book's Web site (www. aharrisbooks.net/xfd_2ed/ or www.dummies.com/go/htmlxhtml andcssaiofd) for an example of sliders with customization.

You can set up a callback method to be called whenever the slider is moved. In my example, I chained this to the code that created the slider in the first place:

```
$("#slider").slider()
.bind("slide", reportSlider);
```

Use the `bind` method to bind the `reportSlider` function (described next) to the `slide` event.

The `reportSlider()` function reads the slider's value and reports it in an output div:

```
function reportSlider(){
  var sliderVal = $("#slider").slider("value");
  $("#slideOutput").html(sliderVal);
} // end reportSlider
```

To read the value of a slider, identify the jQuery node and invoke its `slider()` method again. This time, pass the single word `value`, and you get the value of the slider. You can pass the resulting value to a variable as I did and then do anything you want with that variable.

Selectable elements

You may have a situation where you want the user to choose from a list of elements. The selectable widget is a great way to create this functionality from an ordinary list. The user can drag or Ctrl+click items to select them. Special CSS classes are automatically applied to indicate that the item is being considered for selecting or selected. Figure 5-8 illustrates the selection in process.

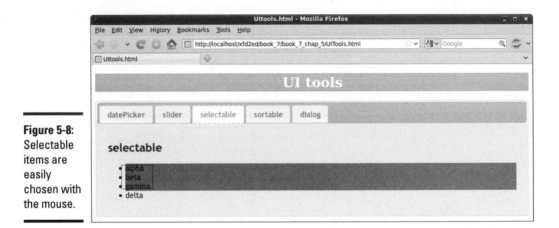

Figure 5-8:
Selectable
items are
easily
chosen with
the mouse.

Follow these steps to make a selectable element:

1. Begin with an unordered list.

Build a standard unordered list in your HTML. Give the ul an ID so that it can be identified as a jQuery node:

```
<div id = "selectableTab">
  <h2>selectable</h2>
  <ul id = "selectable">
    <li>alpha</li>
    <li>beta</li>
    <li>gamma</li>
    <li>delta</li>
  </ul>
</div>
```

2. Add CSS classes for selecting and selected states.

If you want the selectable items to change appearance when the items are being selected or have been selected, add CSS classes as shown. Some special classes (ui-selecting and ui-selected) are predefined and will be added to the elements at the appropriate times:

```
<style type = "text/css">
  h1 {
    text-align: center;
  }

  #selectable .ui-selecting {
    background-color: gray;
  }
  #selectable .ui-selected {
    background-color: black;
    color: white;
  }
</style>
```

3. **In the `init()` function, specify the list as a selectable node.**

   Use the standard jQuery syntax: `selectable()`.

   ```
   $("#selectable").selectable();
   ```

The `ui-selected` class is attached to all elements when they have been selected. Be sure to add some kind of CSS to this class, or you won't be able to tell that items have been selected.

If you want to do something with all the items that have been selected, just create a jQuery group of elements with the `ui-selected` class:

```
var selectedItems = $(".ui-selected");
```

Building a sortable list

Sometimes you want the user to be able to change the order of a list. This is easily done with the `sortable` widget. Figure 5-9 shows the sortable list in its default configuration.

**Book VII
Chapter 5**

**Improving Usability
with jQuery**

Figure 5-9:
This looks
like an
ordinary list.

The user can grab members of the list and change their order, as shown in Figure 5-10.

Making a sortable list is really easy. Follow these steps:

1. Build a regular list.

Sortable elements are usually lists. The list is a regular list, but with an ID:

```
<div id = "sortableTab">
  <h2>sortable</h2>
  <ul id = "sortable">
    <li>alpha</li>
    <li>beta</li>
    <li>gamma</li>
    <li>delta</li>
  </ul>
</div>
```

2. Turn it into a sortable node.

Add the following code to the init() method:

```
$("#sortable").sortable();
```

Creating a custom dialog box

JavaScript supplies a few dialog boxes (the alert and prompt dialog boxes), but these are quite ugly and relatively inflexible. The jQuery UI includes a technique for turning any div into a virtual dialog box. The dialog box follows the theme and is resizable and movable. Figure 5-11 shows a dialog box.

Figure 5-10: The user can drag the elements into a different order.

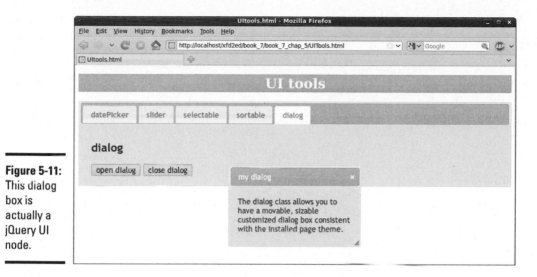

Figure 5-11:
This dialog box is actually a jQuery UI node.

Building the dialog box is not difficult, but you need to be able to turn it on and off with code, or it will not act like a proper dialog (which mimics a window in the operating system):

**Book VII
Chapter 5**

Improving Usability with jQuery

1. **Create the div you intend to use as a dialog box.**

   Create a div and give it an ID so that you can turn it into a dialog box node. Add the `title` attribute, and the title shows up in the dialog box's title bar.

   ```
   <div id = "dialog"
        title = "my dialog">
     <p>
        The dialog class allows you to have a
   movable, sizable
        customized dialog box consistent with the
   installed
        page theme.
     </p>
   </div>
   ```

2. **Turn the div into a dialog box.**

   Use the `dialog()` method to turn the div into a jQuery dialog box node in the `init()` function:

   ```
   $("#dialog").dialog();
   ```

3. **Hide the dialog box by default.**

   Usually you don't want the dialog box visible until some sort of event happens. In this particular example, I don't want the dialog box to appear until the user clicks a button. I put some code to close the dialog box in the `init()` function so that the dialog box will not appear until it is summoned.

4. Close the dialog box.

To close a dialog box, refer to the dialog box node and call the `dialog()` method on it again. This time, send the single value `"close"` as a parameter, and the dialog box will immediately close:

```
//initially close dialog
$("#dialog").dialog("close");
```

5. The x automatically closes the dialog box.

The dialog box has a small x that looks like the Close Window icon on most windowing systems. The user can close the dialog box by clicking this icon.

6. You can open and close the dialog box with code.

My Open Dialog and Close Dialog buttons call functions that control the behavior of the dialog box. For example, here is the function attached to the Open Dialog button:

```
function openDialog(){
  $("#dialog").dialog("open");
} // end openDialog
```

Chapter 6: Working with AJAX Data

In This Chapter

✔ Understanding the advantages of server-side programming

✔ Getting to know PHP

✔ Writing a form for standard PHP processing

✔ Building virtual forms with AJAX

✔ Submitting interactive AJAX requests

✔ Working with XML data

✔ Responding to JSON data

AJAX and jQuery are incredibly useful, but perhaps the most important use of AJAX is to serve as a conduit between the Web page and programs written on the server. In this chapter, you get an overview of how programming works on the Web server and how AJAX changes the relationship between client-side and server-side programming. You read about the main forms of data sent from the server, and you see how to interpret this data with jQuery and JavaScript.

Sending Requests AJAX Style

AJAX work in other parts of this book involves importing a preformatted HTML file. That's a great use of AJAX, but the really exciting aspect of AJAX is how it tightens the relationship between the client and server. Figure 6-1 shows a page called AJAXtest.html, which uses a JavaScript function to call a PHP program and incorporates the results into the same page.

Figure 6-1:
This page
gets data
from PHP
with no
form!

Sending the data

The AJAX version of this program is interesting because it has no form. Normally an HTML page that makes a request of a PHP document has a form, and the form requests the PHP page. This page has no form, but a JavaScript function creates a "virtual form" and passes this form data to a PHP page. Normally the result of a PHP program is a completely new page, but in this example the results of the PHP program are integrated directly onto the original HTML page. Begin by looking over the HTML/JavaScript code:

```
<!DOCTYPE html PUBLIC "-//W3C//DTD XHTML 1.0 Strict//EN"
"http://www.w3.org/TR/xhtml1/DTD/xhtml1-strict.dtd">
<html lang="EN" dir="ltr" xmlns="http://www.w3.org/1999/
   xhtml">
<head>
  <meta http-equiv="content-type" content="text/xml;
  charset=utf-8" />

  <script type = "text/javascript"
          src = "jquery-1.3.2.min.js"></script>

  <script type = "text/javascript">
    //<![CDATA[

    $(init);

    function init(){
      $.get("simpleGreet.php", { "userName": "Andy" },
    processResult);
    }

    function processResult(data, textStatus){
      $("#output").html(data);
    }
    //]]>
    </script>

  <title>AJAXTest.html</title>
</head>
<body>
```

```
<h1>AJAX Test</h1>

<div id = "output">
 This is the default output
</div>

</body>
</html>
```

This program uses a jQuery function to simulate a form. It generates its own virtual form and passes it directly to the PHP program. The PHP program then processes the form data and produces text results, which are available for JavaScript to handle directly. In essence, JavaScript and jQuery are directly managing the server request (rather than allowing the browser to do it automatically) so that the programmer has more control over the process.

Here's how it works:

1 **Begin with an XHTML framework.**

   As always, XHTML forms the spine of any Web program. The XHTML here is quite simple — a heading and a div for output. Note that this example does not include a form.

2. **Include the jQuery library.**

   You can do AJAX without jQuery, but you don't have much reason to do that. The jQuery library makes life much easier and manages cross-browser issues to boot. You can also incorporate the jQuery UI and a theme if you choose, but they aren't absolutely necessary.

3. **Initialize as usual.**

   As soon as this program runs, it's going to get data from the server. (In the next example, I show you how to make this process more interactive.) Set up an init() function in the normal way to handle immediate execution after the page has loaded.

4. **Use the .get() function to set up an AJAX call.**

   jQuery has a number of interesting AJAX functions. The .ajax function is a very powerful tool for managing all kinds of AJAX requests, but jQuery also includes a number of utility functions that simplify particular kinds of requests. The get() function used here sets up a request that looks to the server just like a form submitted with the get method. (Yep, there's also a post() function that acts like a post form.)

5. **Indicate the program to receive the request.**

   Typically your AJAX requests will specify a program that should respond to the request. I'm using greetUser.php.

6. **Pass form data as a JSON object.**

   Encapsulate all the data you want to send to the program as a JSON object. (Check out Book IV, Chapter 4 for a refresher on JSON.) Typically this will be a series of name/value pairs. In this example, I'm simply indicating a field named userName with the value "Andy".

7. **Specify a callback function.**

   Normally you want to do something with the results of an AJAX call. Use a callback function to indicate which function should execute when the AJAX call is completed. In this example, I call the processResult function as soon as the server has finished returning the form data.

Simplifying PHP for AJAX

One of the nice things about AJAX is how it simplifies your server-side programming. Most PHP programs create an entire page every time. (Check out nameForm.html and greetUser.php on the Web site to compare a more typical HTML/PHP solution.) That's a lot of overhead, building an entire XHTML page every pass. A lot of material is repeated. However, because you're using AJAX, the PHP result doesn't have to create an entire Web page. The PHP can simply create a small snippet of HTML.

Take a look at simpleGreet.php and you can see that it's very stripped down:

```php
<?php
$userName = $_REQUEST["userName"];
print "<p>Hi, $userName!</p> ";
?>
```

This is a lot simpler than most PHP programs. All it needs to do is grab the username and print it back out. The JavaScript function takes care of making the code go in the right place. When you're using AJAX, the HTML page stays on the client, and JavaScript makes smaller calls to the server. The PHP is simpler, and the code transmission is generally smaller, because there's less repeated structural information.

Back in the HTML, I need a function to process the results of the AJAX request after it has returned from the server. The processResult() function has been designated as the callback function, so take another look at that function:

```javascript
function processResult(data, textStatus){
  $("#output").html(data);
}
```

This function is pretty simple with jQuery:

1. **Accept two parameters.**

   AJAX callback functions always accept two parameters. The first is a string that contains whatever output was sent by the server (in this case, the greeting from processResult.php). The second parameter contains the text version of the HTTP status result. The status is useful for testing in case the AJAX request was unsuccessful.

2. **Identify an output area.**

   Just make a jQuery node from the output div.

3. **Pass the data to the output.**

   You sometimes do more elaborate work with AJAX results, but for now, the results are plain HTML that you can just copy straight to the div.

Building a Multipass Application

The most common use of AJAX is to build an application that hides the relationship between the client and the server. For example, look at the multiPass.html page shown in Figure 6-2. This seems to be an ordinary HTML page. It features a drop-down list that contains hero names. However, that list of names comes directly from a database, which can't be read directly in HTML/JavaScript. When the user selects a hero from the list, the page is automatically updated to display details about that hero. Again, this data comes directly from the database. Figure 6-3 shows the page after a hero has been selected.

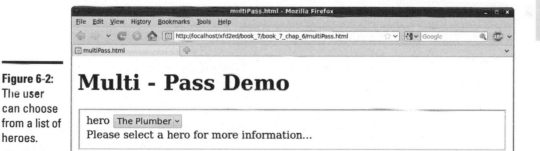

Figure 6-2:
The user can choose from a list of heroes.

Figure 6-3:
Hero data
is automa-
tically
updated
from the
database.

It's certainly possible to get this behavior from PHP alone, but it's interesting to see an HTML/JavaScript page that can access data from a database. Of
course, some PHP is happening, but AJAX manages the process. Take a look
at the code for multiPass.html to see what's happening:

```
<!DOCTYPE html PUBLIC "-//W3C//DTD XHTML 1.0 Strict//EN"
    "http://www.w3.org/TR/xhtml1/DTD/xhtml1-strict.dtd">
<html xmlns="http://www.w3.org/1999/xhtml" xml:lang="en">
<head>
  <title>multiPass.html</title>
  <meta http-equiv="Content-Type" content="text/
   html;charset=UTF-8" />
  <script type = "text/javascript"
          src = "jquery-1.4.2.min.js"></script>
  <script type = "text/javascript">
  //<![CDATA[
  $(init);

  function init(){
    //load up list from database
    $("#heroList").load("loadList.php");
  } // end init

  function showHero(){

    //pass a hero id, retrieve all data about that hero
    heroID = $("#heroList").val();
    $("#output").load("showHero.php", {"heroID": heroID});
  } // end showHero


  //]]>
  </script>

</head>
<body>
  <h1>Multi - Pass Demo</h1>
```

```
      <form action = "">
        <fieldset>
          <label>hero</label>
          <select id = "heroList"
                  onchange = "showHero()">
          </select>


          <div id = "output">
             Please select a hero for more information...
          </div>
        </fieldset>
      </form>
    </body>
    </html>
```

Setting up the HTML framework

As always, the HTML page provides the central skeleton of the page. This site is reasonably simple, because it sets up some empty areas that will be filled in with AJAX requests later:

1. Import jQuery.

The jQuery library makes AJAX really simple, so begin by importing the library. Check out Chapter 2 of this minibook if you need a refresher on importing jQuery. You can also include the jQuery UI modules if you want, but it isn't necessary for this simple example.

2. Build a simple form.

The page has a form, but this form is designed more for client-side interaction than server-side. Note that the form has a null action. That's because the form won't be directly contacting the PHP program. Let AJAX functions do that.

3. Don't add a button.

Traditional forms almost always have buttons (either standard buttons in client-side coding or submit buttons for server-side). While you can still include buttons, one of the goals of AJAX is to simplify user interaction. The page will update as soon as the user selects a new hero, so you don't need a button.

4. Create an empty <select> object.

Build an HTML select element that will contain all the hero names, but don't fill it yet. The hero names should come from the database. Give the select object an id property so that it can be manipulated through the code.

5. Apply an onchange event to the select object.

When the user chooses a new hero, call a JavaScript function to retrieve data about that hero.

Book VII
Chapter 6

Working with AJAX Data

6. Build a div for output.

Create a placeholder for the output. Give it an id so that you can refer to it later in code.

Note that `multiPass.html` will not validate as valid XHTML strict. That's because the `select` tag is empty. That error is really not a problem, because you're going to fill the `select` element with data through AJAX calls. Validators are really meant to read standard HTML/XHTML code. They check the code directly as it comes off the server, without running any JavaScript or PHP. The original code is invalid because it has an empty select tag, but as soon as the AJAX runs, the select tag will have data in it, and will be valid. The validator isn't smart enough to check the second pass, but it is correct.

At this point, you're doing some work that's a little more sophisticated than the validator was expecting, so it's okay that you got an error. As with spelling and grammar checkers, advanced users take the validator as a guideline and know that it's occasionally acceptable to ignore warnings.

Loading the select element

The first task is to load the select element from the database. This should be done as soon as the page is loaded, so the code will go in a standard `init()` function:

1. Write an initialization function.

Use the standard jQuery technique for this. I just use the `$(init)` paradigm because I think it's easiest.

2. Build a jQuery node based on the `select` object.

Use jQuery selection techniques to build a jQuery node.

3. Invoke the jQuery `load()` method.

This method allows you to specify a server-side file to activate. Many AJAX examples in this book use plain HTML files, but in this case you call a PHP program.

The `load()` method works just like `get()` (used earlier in this chapter), but it's a bit easier to use `load()` when the purpose of the AJAX call is to populate some element on your Web page (as is the case here).

4. Call `loadList.php`.

When you call a PHP program, you won't be loading in the text of the program. Instead, you're asking that program to do whatever it does (in this case, get a list of hero names and `heroID`s) and place the *results* of the program in the current element's contents. In this situation, the PHP program does a database lookup and returns the `<option>` elements needed to flesh out the `select` object.

Writing the loadList.php program

Of course, you need to have a PHP program on the server to do the work. AJAX makes PHP programming a lot simpler than the older techniques, because each PHP program typically solves only one small problem, rather than having to build entire pages. The `loadList.php` program is a great example:

```php
<?php

//connect to database
$db = mysql_connect("localhost", "username", "password") or
    die(mysql_error);
mysql_select_db("xfd");

//build an option element for each hero
$query = "SELECT * FROM hero";
$result = mysql_query($query);
while ($row = mysql_fetch_assoc($result)){
  print <<< HERE
    <option value = "$row[heroID]">$row[name]</option>

HERE;
} // end while

?>
```

The code for `loadList.php` is typical of PHP programs using AJAX. It's small and focused and does a simple job cleanly. (I tend to think of PHP programs in AJAX more like external functions than complete programs.) The key to this particular program is understanding the output I'm trying to create. Recall that this example has an empty `select` element on the form. I want the program to add the following (bold) source code to the page:

```html
 <select id="heroList" onchange="showHero()">
    <option value="1">The Plumber</option>
    <option value="2">Binary Boy</option>
    <option value="3">The Janitor</option>
</select>
```

It should go to the database and find all the records in the hero table. It should then assign `heroID` to the `value` attribute of each option, and should display each hero's name. After you know what you want to create, it isn't difficult to pull off:

1. **Make a database connection.**

In this example, PHP is used mainly for connecting to the database. It's not surprising that the first task is to make a data connection. Build a connection to your database using the techniques outlined in Book V, Chapter 7.

2. **Create a query to get data from the database.**

   The option elements I want to build need the heroID and name fields from the hero database. It's easiest to just use a SELECT * FROM hero; query to get all the data I need.

3. **Apply the query to the database.**

   Pass the query to the database and store the results in the $result variable.

4. **Cycle through each record.**

   Use the mysql_fetch_assoc() technique described in Book V, Chapter 7.

5. **Build an <option> element based on the current record.**

   Because each record is stored as an associative array, it's easy to build an option element using fields from the current record.

6. **Print the results.**

   Whatever you print from the PHP program becomes the contents of the jQuery element that called the load() method. In this case, the <option> elements are placed in the <select> object (where all good option elements live).

Responding to selections

After the page has initialized, the select object contains a list of the heroes. When the user selects a hero, the showHero() function is called by the select element's onchange event.

The showHero() function is another AJAX function. It gathers the details needed to trigger another PHP program. This time, the PHP program needs a parameter. The showHero() function simulates a form with a data element in it, and then passes that data to the PHP through the AJAX load() method:

```
function showHero(){
    //pass a hero id, retrieve all data about that hero
    heroID = $("#heroList").val();
    $("#output").load("showHero.php", {"heroID": heroID});
} // end showHero
```

If the user has selected a hero, you have the hero's heroID as the value of the select object. You can use this data to bundle a request to a PHP program. That program uses the heroID to build a query and return data about the requested hero:

1. **Extract the heroID from the select element.**

   You're building a JSON object which will act as a virtual form, so you need access to all the data you want to send to the server. The only information the PHP program needs is a `heroID`, so use the jQuery `val()` method to extract the value from the select element.

2. Use the `load()` method to update the output element.

Once again, use the exceptionally handy `load()` method to invoke an AJAX request. This time, load the results of `showHero.php`.

3. Pass form data to the server.

The `showHero.php` program thinks it's getting information from a form. In AJAX, the easiest way to simulate a form is to put all the data that would have been in the form in a JSON object. In this case, only one data element needs to be passed: `{"heroID": heroID}`. This sends a field called `heroID` that contains the contents of the JavaScript variable `heroID`. See Book IV, Chapter 4 if you need a refresher on the JSON format.

The virtual form technique is a common AJAX idiom. It's important because it overcomes a serious usability limitation of ordinary HTML. In old-school programming, the primary way to invoke a server-side program was through an HTML form submission. With AJAX, you can respond to any JavaScript event (like the `onchange` event used in this example) and use JavaScript code to create any kind of fake form you want. You can use variables that come from one or more forms, or you can send data from JavaScript variables. AJAX lets you use JavaScript to control precisely what data gets sent to the server and when that data gets sent. This improves the user experience (as in this example). It's also commonly used to allow form validation in JavaScript before passing the data to the server.

Writing the showHero.php script

The `showHero.php` script is a simple PHP program that has a single task: After being given a `heroID`, pass a query to the database based on that key, and return an HTML snippet based on the query. The code is a standard database access script:

```php
<?php

//get heroID
$heroID = $_REQUEST['heroID'];

//connect to db
$heroID = mysql_real_escape_string($heroID);

$db = mysql_connect("localhost", "userName", "password") or
    die(mysql_error);
mysql_select_db("xfd");
//extract query
$query = "SELECT * FROM hero WHERE heroID = $heroID";
$result = mysql_query($query);
while ($row = mysql_fetch_assoc($result)){
```

```
    foreach ($row as $name => $value){
      print "$name: $value <br />";
    }
} // end while

?>
```

As far as the `showQuery.php` program is concerned, it got a request from an ordinary form. Its job is to produce HTML output based on that input:

1. **Get the `$heroID` value from the form.**

   Use the standard `$_REQUEST` mechanism to extract data from the form. (It doesn't matter to the PHP program that this isn't a normal form.)

2. **Sanitize the `$heroID` variable.**

   Any form variable that can be used in an SQL query should be sanitized to prevent SQL injection attacks. See Book V, Chapter 7 for more information on the use of `mysql_real_escape_string()`.

3. **Build an SQL query.**

   You only want data from the hero identified by `$heroID`, so build a query that selects a single record.

4. **Print each field name and value.**

   Of course, you can make more sophisticated output, but it's best to start with something simple and clean.

Working with XML Data

Server-side work normally involves storage of data, because that's one thing that's easy to do on the server and difficult to do on the client. Data can be stored in many ways:

✦ In plain-text files

✦ In HTML

✦ In XHTML

✦ In XML

✦ In a relational database

The database approach is most common because it's incredibly powerful and flexible. Normally programmers use a PHP program to request information from a Web page, and then use this information to prepare a request for the database in a special language called SQL (Structured Query Language). The data request is passed to the database management system, which returns some kind of result set to the PHP program. The PHP program then typically builds an HTML page and passes the page back to the browser.

The process can be easier when you use AJAX, because the PHP program doesn't have to create an entire Web page. All that really needs to be passed back to the JavaScript program is the results of the data query. The examples in this chapter have created XHTML snippets as their output, but you often want to make your server-side programs a little more generic so that the data can be used in a number of different ways. Normally, the data is returned using a special data format so that the JavaScript program can easily manage the data.

Review of XML

The XML format has become an important tool for encapsulating data for transfer between the client and the server. You're already familiar with XML, because XHTML is simply HTML following the stricter XML standard.

XML is much more than XHTML. XML can actually be used to store any kind of data. For example, take a look at the following file (pets.xml):

```
<?xml version="1.0" encoding="utf-8"?>
<pets>
  <pet>
    <animal>cat</animal>
    <name>Lucy</name>
    <breed>American Shorthair</breed>
    <note>She raised me</note>
  </pet>
  <pet>
    <animal>cat</animal>
    <name>Homer</name>
    <breed>unknown</breed>
    <note>Named after a world-famous bassoonist</note>
  </pet>
  <pet>
    <animal>dog</animal>
    <name>Muchacha</name>
    <breed>mutt</breed>
    <note>One of the ugliest dogs I've ever met</note>
  </pet>
</pets>
```

If you look over pets.xml, you can see that it looks a lot like HTML. HTML/XHTML tags are very specific (only a few are legal), but XML tags can be anything, as long as they follow a few simple (but familiar) rules:

1. Begin with a doctype.

Formal XML declarations often have doctypes as complex as the XHTML doctype definition, but basic XML data typically uses a much simpler definition:

```
<?xml version="1.0" encoding="utf-8"?>
```

Anytime you make your own XML format (as I'm doing in this example), you can use this generic doctype.

2. **Create a container for all elements.**

The entire structure must have one container tag. I'm using `pets` as my container. If you don't have a single container, your programs will often have trouble reading the XML data.

3. **Build your basic data nodes.**

In my simple example, each pet is contained inside a `pet` node. Each pet has the same data elements (but that is not a requirement).

Tags are case sensitive. Be consistent in your tag names. Use camel-case and single words for each element.

4. **Add attributes as needed.**

You can add attributes to your XML elements just like the ones in XHTML. As in XHTML, attributes are name/value pairs separated by an equals sign (=), and the value must always be encased in quotes.

5. **Nest elements as you do in XHTML.**

Be careful to carefully nest elements inside each other like you do with XHTML.

You can get an XML file in a number of ways:

✦ Most databases can export data in XML format.

✦ More often, a PHP program reads data from a database and creates a long string of XML for output.

For this simple introduction, I just wrote the XML file in a text editor and saved it as a file.

You manipulate XML in the same way with JavaScript, whether it comes directly from a file or is passed from a PHP program.

Manipulating XML with jQuery

XML data is actually familiar, because you can use the tools you used to work with XHTML. Better, the jQuery functions normally used to extract elements from an XHTML page work on XML data with few changes. All the standard jQuery selectors and tools can be used to manage an XML file in the same way that they manage parts of an HTML page.

The `readXML.html` page featured in Figure 6-4 shows a JavaScript/jQuery program that reads the `pets.xml` file and does something interesting with the data.

In this case, it extracts all the pet names and puts them in an unordered list. Here's the code:

```
<!DOCTYPE html PUBLIC "-//W3C//DTD XHTML 1.0 Strict//EN"
"http://www.w3.org/TR/xhtml1/DTD/xhtml1-strict.dtd">
<html lang="EN" dir="ltr" xmlns="http://www.w3.org/1999/
  xhtml">
<head>
  <meta http-equiv="content-type" content="text/xml;
  charset=utf-8" />

  <script type = "text/javascript"
         src = "jquery-1.4.2.min.js"></script>

  <script type = "text/javascript">
    //<![CDATA[

  $(init);

  function init(){
    $.get("pets.xml", processResult);
  } // end init

  function processResult(data, textStatus){
    //clear the output
    $("#output").html("");
    //find the pet nodes...
    $(data).find("pet").each(printPetName);
  } // end processResult

  function printPetName(){
    //isolate the name text of the current node
    thePet = $(this).find("name").text();

    //add list item elements around it
    thePet = "<li>" + thePet + "<\/li>";

    //add item to the list
```

```
    $("#output").append(thePet);
    } // end printPetName
    //]]>
    </script>

  <title>readXML.html</title>
</head>
<body>
<h1>Reading XML</h1>

<ul id = "output">
 <li>This is the default output</li>
</ul>

</body>
</html>
```

Creating the HTML

Like most jQuery programs, this page begins with a basic HTML framework. This one is especially simple: a heading and a list. The list has an ID (so that it can be recognized through jQuery easily) and a single element (that will be replaced by data from the XML file).

Retrieving the data

The init() function sets up an AJAX request:

```
$(init);

function init(){
   $.get("pets.xml", processResult);
} // end init
```

This function uses the get() function to request data:

1. **Use the jQuery get() mechanism to set up the request.**

   Because I'm just requesting a static file (as opposed to a PHP program), the get() function is the best AJAX tool to use for setting up the request.

2. **Specify the file or program.**

   Normally you call a PHP program to retrieve data, but for this example, I pull data straight from the pets.xml file because it's simpler and it doesn't really matter how the XML was generated. The get() mechanism can be used to retrieve plain text, HTML, or XML data. My program will be expecting XML data, so I should be calling an XML file or a program that produces XML output.

3. Set up a callback function.

When the AJAX is complete, specify a function to call. My example calls the `processResult` function after the AJAX transmission is complete.

Processing the results

The `processResult()` function accepts two parameters: `data` and `textStatus`:

```
function processResult(data, textStatus){
  //clear the output
  $("#output").html("");
  //find the pet nodes...
  $(data).find("pet").each(printPetName);
} // end processResult
```

The `processResult()` function does a few simple tasks:

1. Clear the output ul.

The `output` element is an unordered list. Use its `html()` method to clear the default list item.

2. Make a jQuery node from the data.

The data (passed as a parameter) can be turned into a jQuery node. Use `$(data)` for this process.

3. Find each pet node.

Use the `find()` method to identify the `pet` nodes within the data.

4. Specify a command to operate on each element.

Use the `each()` method to specify that you want to apply a function separately to each of the `pet` elements. Essentially, this creates a loop that calls the function once per element.

The each mechanism is an example of a concept called an *iterator,* which is a fundamental component of *functional programming.* (Drop *those* little gems to sound like a hero at your next computer science function. You're welcome.)

5. Run the `printPetName` function once for each element.

The `printPetName` is a callback function.

Printing the pet name

The `printPetName` function is called once for each `pet` element in the XML data. Within the function, the `$(this)` element refers to the current element as a jQuery node:

```
function printPetName(){
  //isolate the name text of the current node
  thePet = $(this).find("name").text();

  //add list item elements around it
  thePet = "<li>" + thePet + "</li>";

  //add item to the list
  $("#output").append(thePet);
} // end printPetName
```

1. **Retrieve the pet's name.**

   Use the find() method to find the name element of the current pet node.

2. **Pull the text from the node.**

   The name is still a jQuery object. To find the actual text, use the text() method.

3. **Turn the text into a list item.**

   I just used string concatenation to convert the plain text of the pet name into a list item.

4. **Append the pet name list item to the list.**

   The append() method is perfect for this task.

Of course, you can do more complex things with the data, but it's just a matter of using jQuery to extract the data you want and then turning it into HTML output.

Working with JSON Data

XML has been considered the standard way of working with data in AJAX (in fact, the X in AJAX stands for XML). The truth is, another format is actually becoming more popular. While XML is easy for humans (and computer programs) to read, it's a little bit verbose. All those ending tags can get a bit tedious and can add unnecessarily to the file size of the data block. While XML is not difficult to work with on the client, it does take some getting used to. AJAX programmers are beginning to turn to JSON as a data transfer mechanism. JSON is nothing more than the JavaScript object notation described in Book IV, Chapter 4 and used throughout this minibook.

Knowing JSON's pros

JSON has a number of very interesting advantages:

✦ **Data is sent in plain text.** Like XML, JSON data can be sent in a plain-text format that's easy to transmit, read, and interpret.

✦ **The data is already usable.** Client programs are usually written in JavaScript. Because the data is already in a JavaScript format, it is ready to use immediately, without the manipulation required by XML.

✦ **The data is a bit more compact than XML.** JavaScript notation doesn't have ending tags, so it's a bit smaller. It can also be written to save even more space (at the cost of some readability) if needed.

✦ **Lots of languages can use it.** Any language can send JSON data as a long string of text. You can then apply the JavaScript `eval()` function on the JSON data to turn it into a variable.

✦ **PHP now has native support for JSON.** PHP version 5.2 and later supports the `json_encode()` and `json_decode()` functions, which convert PHP arrays (even very complex ones) into JSON objects and back.

✦ **jQuery has a `getJSON()` method.** This method works like the `get()` or `post()` methods, but it's optimized to receive a JSON value.

If a program uses the `eval()` function to turn a result string into a JSON object, there's a potential security hazard: Any code in the string is treated as JavaScript code, so bad guys could sneak some ugly code in there. Be sure that you trust whoever you're getting JSON data from.

The `pet` data described in `pets.xml` looks like this when it's organized as a JSON variable:

```
{
  "Lucy": { "animal": "Cat",
            "breed": "American Shorthair",
            "note": "She raised me"},
  "Homer": { "animal": "Cat",
             "breed": "unknown",
             "note": "Named after a world-famous bassoonist"},
  "Muchacha": { "animal": "Dog",
            "breed": "mutt",
            "note": "One of the ugliest dogs I've ever met"}
}
```

Note a couple of things:

✦ The data is a bit more compact in JSON format than it is in XML.

✦ You don't need an overarching variable type (like `pets` in the XML data) because the entire entity is one variable (most likely called `pets`).

JSON takes advantages of JavaScript's flexibility when it comes to objects:

✦ **An object is encased in braces: { }.** The main object is denoted by a pair of braces.

✦ **The object consists of key/value pairs.** In my data, I used the animal name as the node key. Note that the key is a string value.

✦ **The contents of a node can be another node.** Each animal contains another JSON object, holding the data about that animal. JSON nodes can be nested (like XML nodes), giving the potential for complex data structures.

✦ **The entire element is one big variable.** JavaScript can see the entire element as one big JavaScript object that can be stored in a single variable. This makes it quite easy to work with JSON objects on the client.

Reading JSON data with jQuery

As you might expect, jQuery has some features for simplifying the (already easy) process of managing JSON data.

Figure 6-5 shows `readJSON.html`, a program that reads JSON data and returns the results in a nice format.

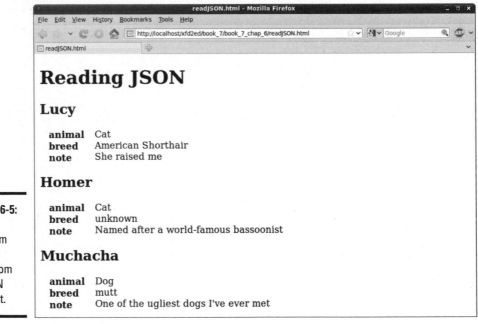

Figure 6-5:
This program got the data from a JSON request.

Here's the complete code of `readJSON.html`:

```
<!DOCTYPE html PUBLIC "-//W3C//DTD XHTML 1.0 Strict//EN"
"http://www.w3.org/TR/xhtml1/DTD/xhtml1-strict.dtd">
<html lang="EN" dir="ltr" xmlns="http://www.w3.org/1999/
    xhtml">
<head>
```

```
<meta http-equiv="content-type" content="text/xml;
  charset=utf-8" />
<style type = "text/css">
  dt {
     font-weight: bold;
     float: left;
     width: 5em;
     margin-left: 1em;
     clear: left;
  }
</style>
<script type = "text/javascript"
        src = "jquery-1.4.2.min.js"></script>

<script type = "text/javascript">
  //<![CDATA[

  $(init);

  function init(){
    $.getJSON("pets.json", processResult);
  } // end init

  function processResult(data){
    $("#output").text("");
    for(petName in data){
      var pet = data[petName];
      $("#output").append("<h2>" + petName + "<h2>");
      $("#output").append("<dl>");
      for (detail in pet){
        $("#output").append("  <dt>" + detail + "<\/dt>");
        $("#output").append("  <dd>" + pet[detail] + "<\/
  dd>");
      } // end for
      $("#output").append("<\/dl>");

    } // end for
  } // end processResults

  //]]>
  </script>

  <title>readJSON.html</title>
</head>
<body>
<h1>Reading JSON</h1>

<div id = "output">
 This is the default output
</div>

</body>
</html>
```

Managing the framework

The foundation of this program is the standard XTML and CSS. Here are the details:

1. Build a basic XHTML page.

Much of the work will happen in JavaScript, so an h1 and an output div are all you really need.

2. Put default text in the output div.

Put some kind of text in the output div. If the AJAX doesn't work, you'll see this text. If the AJAX does work, the contents of the output div will be replaced by a definition list.

3. Add CSS for a definition list.

I print out each pet's information as a definition list, but I don't like the default formatting for <dl>. I add my own CSS to tighten up the appearance of the definitions. (I like the <dt> and <dd> on the same line of output.)

Retrieving the JSON data

The jQuery library has a special AJAX function for retrieving JSON data. The getJSON() function makes an AJAX call and expects JSON data in return:

```
$(init);

function init(){
  $.getJSON("pets.json", processResult);
} // end init
```

It isn't difficult to get JSON data with jQuery:

1. Set up the standard init() function.

In this example, I'm pulling the JSON data in as soon as the page has finished loading.

2. Use the getJSON() function.

This tool gets JSON data from the server.

3. Pull data from pets.json.

Normally you make a request to a PHP program, which does some kind of database request and returns the results as a JSON object. For this simple example, I'm just grabbing data from a JSON file I wrote with a text editor, so I don't have to write a PHP program. The client-side processing is identical whether the data came from a straight file or a program.

4. Specify a callback function.

Like most AJAX methods, `getJSON()` allows you to specify a callback function that is triggered when the data has finished transferring to the client.

Processing the results

The data returned by a JSON request is already in a valid JavaScript format, so all you need is some `for` loops to extract the data. Here's the process:

```
function processResult(data){
  $("#output").text("");
  for(petName in data){
    var pet = data[petName];
    $("#output").append("<h2>" + petName + "<h2>");
    $("#output").append("<dl>");
    for (detail in pet){
      $("#output").append("  <dt>" + detail + "<\/dt>");
      $("#output").append("  <dd>" + pet[detail] +
        "<\/dd>");
    } // end for
    $("#output").append("<\/dl>");

  } // end for
} // end processResults
```

1. Create the callback function.

This function expects a `data` parameter (like most AJAX requests). In this case, the `data` object contains a complete JSON object encapsulating all the data from the request.

2. Clear the output.

I replace the output with a series of definition lists. Of course, you can format the output however you wish.

```
$("#output").text("");
```

3. Step through each `petName` in the list.

This special form of the `for` loop finds each element in a list. In this case, it gets each pet name found in the data element:

```
for(petName in data){
```

4. Extract the pet as a variable.

The special form of `for` loop doesn't retrieve the actual pets but rather the key associated with each pet. Use that pet name to find a pet and make it into a variable using an array lookup:

```
var pet = data[petName];
```

5. Build a heading with the pet's name.

Surround the pet name with <h2> tags to make a heading and append this to the output:

```
$("#output").append("<h2>" + petName + "<h2>");
```

6. Create a definition list for each pet.

Begin the list with a <dl> tag. Of course, you can use whichever formatting you prefer, but I like the definition list for this kind of name/value data:

```
$("#output").append("<dl>");
```

7. Get the detail names from the pet.

The pet is itself a JSON object, so use another for loop to extract each of its detail names (animal, breed, note):

```
for (detail in pet){
```

8. Set the detail name as the definition term.

Surround each detail name with a <dt></dt> pair. (Don't forget to escape the slash character to avoid an XHTML validation warning.)

```
$("#output").append("  <dt>" + detail + "<\/dt>");
```

9. Surround the definition value with <dd></dd>.

This provides appropriate formatting to the definition value:

```
$("#output").append("  <dd>" + pet[detail] + "<\/dd>");
```

10. Close the definition list.

After the inner for loop is complete, you're done describing one pet, so close the definition list:

```
$("#output").append("  <dd>" + pet[detail] + "</dd>");
```

Book VIII

Moving from Pages to Sites

The 5th Wave   By Rich Tennant

"Look into my Web site, Ms. Carruthers. Look deep into its rotating spiral, spinning, spinning, pulling you deeper into its vortex, deeper...deeper..."

Contents at a Glance

Chapter 1: Managing Your Servers

*W*eb pages are a complex undertaking. The basic Web page itself isn't too overwhelming, but Web pages are unique because they have meaning only in the context of the Internet — a vastly new undertaking with unique rules.

Depending where you are on your Web development journey, you may need to understand the entire architecture, or you may be satisfied with a smaller part. Still, you should have a basic idea of how the Internet works and how the various technologies described in this book fit in.

Understanding Clients and Servers

A person using the Web is a *client*. You can also think of the user's computer or browser as the client. Clients on the Internet have certain characteristics:

✦ **Clients are controlled by individual users.** You have no control over what kind of connection or computer the user has. It may not even be a computer but may be instead a cellphone or (I'm not kidding) refrigerator.

✦ **Clients have temporary connections.** Clients typically don't have permanent connections to the Internet. Even if a machine is on a permanent network, most machines used as clients have temporarily assigned addresses that can change.

✦ **Clients might have wonderful resources.** Client machines may have multimedia capabilities, a mouse, and real-time interactivity with the user.

✦ **Clients are limited.** Web browsers and other client-side software are often limited so that programs accessed over the Internet can't make major changes to the local file system. For this reason, most client programs operate in a sort of "sandbox" to prevent malicious coding.

✦ **Clients can be turned off without penalty.** It doesn't really cause anybody else a problem if you turn off your computer. Generally, client machines can be turned off or moved without any problems.

Servers are the machines that typically host Web pages. They have a much different set of characteristics:

✦ **Servers are controlled by server administrators.** A server administrator is responsible for ensuring that all data on the server is secure.

✦ **Servers have permanent connections.** The purpose of a server is to accept requests from clients. For this reason, a server needs to have an IP number permanently assigned to it.

✦ **Servers usually have names, too.** To make things easier for users, server administrators usually register domain names to make their servers easier to find.

✦ **Servers can access other programs.** Web servers often talk to other programs or computers (especially data servers).

✦ **Servers must be reliable.** If a Web server stops working, anybody trying to reach the pages on that server is out of luck. This is why Web servers frequently run Unix or Linux because these operating systems tend to be especially stable.

✦ **Servers must have specialized software.** The element that truly makes a computer a server is the presence of Web server software. Although several options are available, only two dominate the market: Apache and Microsoft IIS.

Parts of a client-side development system

A development system is made up of several components. If you're programming on the client (using XHTML, CSS, and JavaScript), you need the following tools:

✦ **Web browsers:** You need at least a couple of browsers so that you can see how your programs behave in different ones. Firefox is especially useful for Web developers because of its numerous available extensions.

✦ **Browser extensions:** Consider adding extensions to Firefox to improve your editing experience. Web Developer, Firebug, and HTML Validator are extremely helpful.

✦ **Text editor:** Almost all Web development happens with plain-text files. A standard text editor should be part of your standard toolkit. I prefer

Notepad++ for Windows and prefer VI or Emacs for other operating systems.

✦ **Integrated Development Environment:** Komodo Edit and Aptana Studio are specialized text editors with added features for Web programming. They understand all the main Web languages and have syntax help, code coloring, and preview features. Using one of these tools can be extremely helpful (both are free.)

For client-side development, you don't necessarily need access to a server. You can test all your programs directly on your own machine with no other preparation. Of course, you'll eventually want a server so that you can show your pages to everyone.

The client-side development tools listed here are described in more detail in Book I, Chapter 3.

Parts of a server-side system

When you start working on the server side (with PHP, MySQL, and AJAX), you need a somewhat more complex setup. In addition to everything you need for client-side development, you also need these items:

✦ **A Web server:** This piece of software allows users to request Web pages from your machine. You must either sign on to a hosting service and use its server or install your own. (I show you both techniques in this chapter.) By far the most common server in use is Apache. Web server software usually runs all the time in the background because you never know when a request will come in.

✦ **A server-side language:** Various languages can be connected to Web servers to allow server-side functionality. PHP is the language I chose in this book because it has an excellent combination of power, speed, price (free), and functionality. PHP needs to be installed on the server machine, and the Web server has to be configured to recognize it. See Book VI, Chapter 1 for a review of other server-side languages.

✦ **A data server:** Many of your programs work with data, and they need some sort of application to deal with that data. The most common data server in the open-source world is MySQL. This data package is free, powerful, and flexible. The data server is also running in the background all the time. You have to configure PHP to know that it has access to MySQL.

✦ **A mail server:** If your programs send and receive e-mail, you need some sort of e-mail server. The most popular e-mail server in the Windows world is Mercury Mail, and Sendmail is popular in the world of Unix and Linux. You probably won't bother with this item on a home server, but you should know about it when you're using a remote host.

✦ **An FTP server:** Sometimes, you want the ability to send files to your server remotely. The FTP server allows this capability. Again, you probably don't need this item for your own machine, but you definitely should know about it when you use a remote host.

✦ **phpMyAdmin:** There's a command-line interface to MySQL, but it's limited and awkward. The easiest way to access your MySQL databases is to use the phpMyAdmin program. Because it's a series of PHP programs, it requires a complete installation of PHP, MySQL, and Apache (but, normally, you install all these things together anyway).

Creating Your Own Server with XAMPP

If the requirements for a Web hosting solution seem intimidating, that's because they are. It's much more difficult to set up a working server system by hand than it is to start programming with it.

I don't recommend setting up your own system by hand. It's simply not worth the frustration, because very good options are available.

XAMPP is an absolutely wonderful open-source tool. It has the following packages built in:

✦ **Apache:** The standard Web server and the cornerstone of the package

✦ **PHP:** Configured and ready to start with Apache and MySQL

✦ **MySQL:** Also configured to work with Apache and PHP

✦ **phpMyAdmin:** A data management tool that's ready to run

✦ **Mercury Mail:** A mail server

✦ **FileZilla FTP server:** An FTP server

✦ **PHP libraries:** A number of useful PHP add-ons, including GD (graphics support), Ming (Flash support), and more

✦ **Additional languages:** Perl, another extremely popular scripting and server language, and SQLite, another useful database package

✦ **Control and configuration tools:** A Control Panel that allows you to easily turn various components on and off

This list is a description of the Windows version. The Mac and Linux versions have all the same types of software, but the specific packages vary.

Considering the incredible amount of power in this system, the download is remarkably small. The installer is only 34MB. A copy is included on the CD-ROM that accompanies this book.

XAMPP installation is pretty painless: Simply download the installer and respond to all the default values.

If you use Vista or Windows 7, you may want to change where the package is installed because the program files directory causes problems for some users.

Running XAMPP

After you install XAMPP, you can manage your new tools with the XAMPP Control Panel. Figure 1-1 shows this program in action.

Figure 1-1:
XAMPP
Control
Panel
allows
you to turn
features on
and off.

Some components of XAMPP (PHP, for example) run only when they're needed. Some other components (Apache and MySQL) are meant to run constantly in the background. Before you start working with your server, you need to ensure that it's turned on.

You can choose to run Apache and MySQL as a service, which means that the program is always running in the background. This arrangement is convenient, but it slightly reduces the performance of your machine. I generally turn Apache on and off as I need it and leave MySQL running as a service because I have a number of other programs that work with MySQL.

Leaving server programs open on your machine constitutes a security hazard. Be sure to take adequate security precautions. See the section "Setting the security level," later in this chapter, for information on setting up your security features.

Testing your XAMPP configuration

Ensure that Apache and MySQL are running, and then open your Web browser. Set the address to `http://localhost`, and you see a screen like the one shown in Figure 1-2.

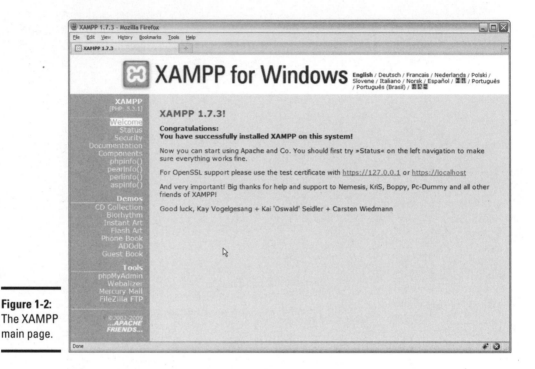

Figure 1-2:
The XAMPP
main page.

This page indicates that XAMPP is installed and working. Feel free to experiment with the various items in the Demos section. Even though you may not know yet what they do, you should know what some of their capabilities are.

Adding your own files

Of course, the point of having a Web server is to put your own files in it. Use your file management tool to find the XAMPP directory in your file system. Right under the XAMPP directory is the `htdocs` folder, the primary Web directory. Apache serves only files that are in this directory or under it. (That way, you don't have to worry about your love letters being distributed over the Internet.)

All the files you want Apache to serve must be in `htdocs` or in a subdirectory of it.

When you specified `http://localhost` as the address in your browser, you were telling the browser to look on your local machine in the main `htdocs` directory. You didn't specify a particular file to load. If Apache isn't given a filename and it sees the file named `index.html` or `index.php`, it displays that file, instead. So, in the default `htdocs` directory, the `index.php` program is immediately being called. Although this program displays the XAMPP welcome page, you don't usually want that to happen.

Rename `index.php` to `index.php.old` or something similar. It's still there if you want it, but now there's no index page, and Apache simply gives you a list of files and folders in the current directory. Figure 1-3 shows my `localhost` directory as I see it through the browser.

Index of /

Name	Last modified	Size	Description
index.off.html	20-Dec-2009 00:00	44	
index.off.php	20-Dec-2009 00:00	256	
practice.php	25-Jan-2010 14.42	138	
xampp/	20-Dec-2009 00:00	-	

Apache/2.2.14 (Win32) DAV/2 mod_ssl/2.2.14 OpenSSL/0.9.8l mod_autoindex_color PHP/5.3.1 mod_apreq2-20090110/2.7.1 mod_perl/2.0.4 Perl/v5.10.1 Server at localhost Port 80

Figure 1-3:
After disabling index.php, I can see a list of files and directories.

You typically don't want users to see this ugly index in a production server, but I prefer it in a development environment so that I can see exactly what's on my server. After everything is ready to go, I put together `index.html` or `index.php` pages to generate more professional directories.

Generally, you want to have subdirectories to all your main projects. I added a few others for my own use, including `xfd`, which contains all the code for this book.

If you want to display the XAMPP welcome screen after you remove the `index.php` program, simply point your browser to `http://localhost/xampp`.

Setting the security level

When you have a Web server and a data server running, you create some major security holes. You should take a few precautions to ensure that you're reasonably safe:

✦ **Treat your server only as a local asset.** Don't run a home installation of Apache as a production server. Use it only for testing purposes. Use a remote host for the actual deployment of your files. It's prepared for all the security headaches.

✦ **Run a firewall.** You should run, at an absolute minimum, the Windows firewall that comes with all recent versions of Windows (or the equivalent for your OS). You might also consider an open-source or commercial firewall. Block incoming access to all ports by default and open them only when needed. There's no real need to allow incoming access to your Web server. You only need to run it in localhost mode.

The ports XAMPP uses for various tools are listed on the security screen shown in Figure 1-4.

✦ **Run basic security checks.** The XAMPP package has a handy security screen. Figure 1-4 shows the essential security measures. I've already adjusted my security level, so you'll probably have a few more "red lights" than I do. Click the security link at the bottom of the page for some easy-to-use security utilities.

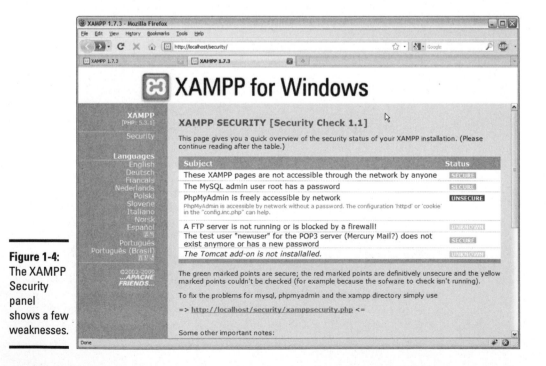

Figure 1-4:
The XAMPP Security panel shows a few weaknesses.

✦ **Change the MySQL root password.** If you haven't already done so, use the security link to change the MySQL root password, as shown in Figure 1-5. (I show an alternative way to change the password in Book VI, Chapter 1.)

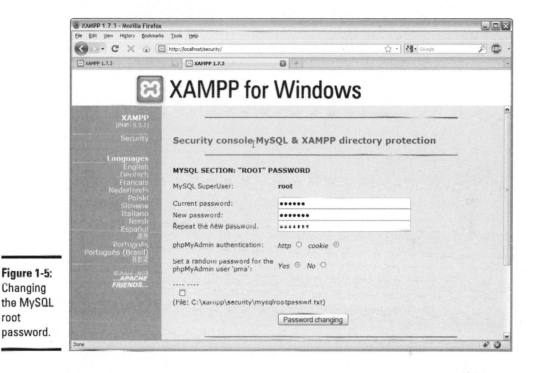

Figure 1-5:
Changing the MySQL root password.

✦ **Add an XAMPP Directory password.** Type a password into the lower half of the security form to protect your xampp directory from unauthorized access. When you try to go to the xampp directory, you're prompted for this password.

Security is always a compromise. When you add security, you often introduce limits in functionality. For example, if you changed the root password for MySQL, some of the examples (and phpMyAdmin) may not work any more because they're assuming that the password is blank. You often have to tweak. See Chapter 1 in Book VI for a complete discussion of password issues in MySQL and phpMyAdmin.

Compromising between functionality and security

You may be shocked that my example still has a couple of security holes. It's true, but it's not quite as bad as it looks:

✦ **The firewall is the first line of defense.** If your firewall blocks external access to your servers, the only real danger your system faces is from yourself. Begin with a solid firewall and ensure that you don't allow access to port 80 (Apache) or port 3306 (MySQL) unless you're absolutely sure that you have the appropriate security measures in place.

✦ **I left phpMyAdmin open.** phpMyAdmin needs root access to the MySQL database, so if anybody can get to phpMyAdmin through the Web server, they can get to my data and do anything to it. Because my firewall is blocking port 80 access, you can't get to phpMyAdmin from anything other than localhost access, and it's not really a problem.

✦ **I'm not running a mail or FTP server on this machine.** The security system isn't sure whether my FTP or mail system is secure, but because I'm not running them, it isn't really a problem.

Choosing a Web Host

Creating a local server is useful for development purposes because you can test your programs on a server you control, and you don't need a live connection to the Internet.

However, you should avoid running a production server on your own computer, if you can. A typical home connection doesn't have the guaranteed IP number you need. Besides, you probably signed an agreement with your broadband provider that you won't run a public Web server from your account.

This situation isn't really a problem, because thousands of Web hosting services are available that let you easily host your files. You should consider an external Web host for these reasons:

✦ **The host, not you, handles the security headaches.** This reason alone is sufficient. Security isn't difficult, but it's a never-ending problem (because the bad guys keep finding new loopholes).

✦ **The remote server is always up.** Or, at least, it should be. The dedicated Web server isn't doing anything other than serving Web pages. Your Web pages are available, even if your computer is turned off or doing something else.

✦ **A dedicated server has a permanent IP address.** Unlike most home connections, a dedicated server has an IP address permanently assigned to it. You can easily connect a domain name to a permanent server so that users can easily connect.

✦ **Ancillary services usually exist.** Many remote hosting services offer other services, like databases, FTP, and e-mail hosting.

✦ **The price can be quite reasonable.** Hosting is a competitive market, which means that some good deals are available. Decent hosting is available for free, and improved services are extremely reasonable.

You can find a number of free hosting services at sites like `http://free-webhosts.com`.

Finding a hosting service

When looking for a hosting service, ask yourself these questions:

+ **Does the service have limitations on the types of pages you can host?** Some servers are strictly for personal use, and some allow commercial sites. Some have bandwidth restrictions and close your site if you draw too many requests.

+ **How much space are you given?** Ordinary Web pages and databases don't require a huge amount of space, but if you do a lot of work with images, audio, and video files, your space needs will increase dramatically.

+ **Is advertising forced on you?** Many free hosting services make money by forcing advertisements on your pages. This practice can create a problem because you might not always want to associate your page with the company being advertised. (A page for a day care center probably should not have advertisements for dating services, for example.)

+ **Which scripting languages (if any) are supported?** Look for PHP support.

+ **Does the host offer prebuilt scripts?** Many hosts offer a series of pre-built and preinstalled scripts. These can often include content management systems, message boards, and other extremely useful tools. If you know that you're going to need Moodle, for example (a course management tool for teachers), you can look for hosting services that have it built in. (If a tool you want isn't there, make sure you have FTP access so you can install it yourself.)

+ **Does the host provide access to a database?** Is phpMyAdmin support provided? How many databases do you get? What is the size limit?

+ **What sort of Control Panel does the service provide?** Does it allow easy access to all the features you need?

+ **What type of file management is used?** For example, determine how you upload files to the system. Most services use browser-based uploading. This system is fine for small projects, but it's quite inconvenient if you have a large number of files you want to transfer. Look for FTP support to handle this.

+ **Does the host have an inactivity policy?** Many free hosting services automatically shut down your site if you don't do anything with it (usually after 30 to 90 days of inactivity). Be sure you know about this policy.

+ **Do you have assurances that the server will remain online?** Are backups available? What sort of support is available? Note that these services are much more likely on a paid server.

✦ **How easily can you upgrade if you want?** Does a particular hosting plan meet your needs without being too expensive?

✦ **Does the service offer you a subdomain, and can you register your own?** You may also want to redirect a domain that you didn't get through the service. (See the section "Naming Your Site," later in this chapter, for information on domain names.)

✦ **What kind of support is available?** Most hosting services have some kind of support mechanism with e-mail or ticket systems. Some hosts offer live chat, and some have telephone support. Talking to a real human in real time can be extremely helpful, and this is often worth paying for.

Connecting to a hosting service

The sample pages for this book are hosted on Freehostia.com, an excellent, free hosting service. You can find many great hosting services, but the rest of the examples in this chapter use Freehostia. I chose this service for the examples because

✦ **Its free account is terrific.** At the time of this writing, the features of the free account at Freehostia are as good as they are at many paid accounts.

✦ **The pages have no forced advertising.** Freehostia doesn't place any ads on your pages (a major selling point for me).

✦ **PHP, phpMyAdmin, and MySQL are supported — all on the free account.** Often, you have to upgrade to a paid service to get these features.

✦ **You get enough space to start with.** The free account comes with 250MB of space. This amount is fine for ordinary Web pages, PHP, and database needs. You need more, though, if you do a lot of image or video hosting.

✦ **You can have a subdomain for free.** Even if your site doesn't have a domain name, you can choose a subdomain so that your site has a recognizable address, like `http://myStuff.freehostia.com`.

✦ **It has a good list of script installers.** It comes with a nice batch of scripts that you can install effortlessly.

✦ **The upgrade policy is reasonable.** Freehostia makes money on commercial Web hosting. It offers an excellent free service that, ideally, gets you hooked so that you then upgrade to a commercial plan. It has a number of good upgrade packages for various sizes of businesses.

✦ **You get a nice batch of extras.** The free service comes with FTP and e-mail support and also a MySQL database.

✦ **Customer support is excellent.** Most free hosting services offer no customer support. Freehostia provides good support, even to the free services. (I asked a couple of questions before anyone there knew that I was writing this book, and I was impressed with the speed and reliability of the responses.)

Choose whichever hosting service works for you. If you find a free hosting service that you really like, upgrade to a paid service. Hosting is a reasonably cheap commodity, and a quality hosting service is well worth the investment.

Managing a Remote Site

Obviously, having a hosting service isn't much fun if you don't have pages there. Fortunately, there are a lot of ways to work with your new site.

Using Web-based file tools

Most of the time, your host has some sort of Control Panel that looks like the one shown in Figure 1-6.

Figure 1-6: This Control Panel allows you to manage your site remotely.

There's usually some sort of file management tool that might look like the one shown in Figure 1-7.

Figure 1-7:
This file management tool allows you to manipulate the files on your system.

In this particular case, all my Web files are in the www/aharrisbooks.net directory, so I click to see them. Figure 1-8 shows what you might see in an actual directory.

This page allows you to rename, upload, and edit existing files and change file permissions.

You can create or edit files with a simple integrated editor: build a new file with the Create File button. Type a filename into the text area and click the button. You can also click the edit button next to a file, and the file will open in the editor. In either case, the text editor shown in Figure 1-9 appears.

You can write an entire Web site using this type of editor, but the Web-based text editing isn't helpful, and it's kind of awkward. More often, you create your files on your own XAMPP system and upload them to the server when they're basically complete. Use server-side editing features for quick fixes only.

Figure 1-8:
Now, you
can see
some files
here.

Figure 1-9:
The hosting
service has
a limited
text editor.

What's with all the permissions?

Permissions are typically treated as binary numbers: 111 means "read, write, execute." This (111 value) is also a 7 permission because 111 binary translates to 7 in base ten (or base eight, but let's skip that detail for now).

A permission is read as three digits, each one a number indicating the permissions, so 644 permission means `rw- r-- r--`. This example can be translated as "The owner should be able to read and write this file. Everyone else can read it. Nobody can execute it."

If you don't understand this concept, don't worry about it. The guidelines are very simple: Make sure that each of your files has 644 permission and that each directory has 755 permission. That's all you really need to know.

Understanding file permissions

Most hosting services use Linux or Unix. These operating systems have a more sophisticated file permission mechanism than the Windows file system does. At some point, you may need to manipulate file permissions.

Essentially, the universe is divided into three populations: Yourself, your group, and everybody else. You can allow each group to have different kinds of permission for each file. Each of the permissions is a Boolean (true or false) value:

✦ **Read permission:** The file can be read. Typically, you want everybody to be able to read your files, or else you wouldn't put them on the Web server.

✦ **Write permission:** The file can be written, changed, and deleted. Obviously, only you should have the ability to write to your files.

✦ **Execute permission:** Indicates that the file is an executable program or a directory that can be passed through. Normally, none of your files is considered executable, although all your directories are.

Using FTP to manage your site

Most of the work is done on a local machine and then sent to the server in a big batch. (That's how I did everything in this book.) The standard Web-based file management tools are pretty frustrating when you want to efficiently upload a large number of files.

Fortunately, most hosts have the FTP (File Transfer Protocol) system available. *FTP* is a client/server mechanism for transferring files efficiently. To use it, you may have to configure some sort of FTP server on the host to find out which settings, username, and password you should use. Figure 1-10 shows the Freehostia Control Panel with this information displayed.

Figure 1-10: Configuring the FTP server.

You also need an FTP client. Fortunately, many free clients are available. I like FireFTP, for a number of reasons:

✦ **It's free and open source.** That's always a bonus.

✦ **It works as a Firefox plugin.** I always know where it is.

✦ **It's easy to use.** It feels just like a file manager.

Figure 1-11 shows FireFTP running in my browser.

Figure 1-11:
FireFTP is
a complete
FTP
program
that runs
inside
Firefox.

If you want to connect to your server with FTP, follow these steps:

1. **Look up the configuration settings.**

   You may have to dig around in the server documentation, but you should find the server name, username, and password to access your server. Sometimes, you have to configure these elements yourself.

2. **Create a profile for your server.**

   Use the Manage Accounts feature to create a profile using the FTP settings. Figure 1-12 shows a profile for my aharrisbooks account.

3. **Connect to the remote server.**

   FTP programs look a lot like the file explorer you might have on your machine, except that they usually have two file panels. The left panel represents the files on your local system, and the right panel shows files on the remote system.

4. **Navigate to the directories you're interested in.**

   If you want to move a file from the local system to the remote one, use the two file explorers to find the appropriate directory on each system.

Account Manager

Main | Connection | Advanced

Main Details

Account Name: aharrisbooks   Category: [▼]

Host: ftp.aharrisbooks.net

ID

Login: andhar50

Password: ●●●●●●

☐ Anonymous

Delete   OK   Cancel

Figure 1-12:
The profile
editor for
FireFTP.

5. **Drag the file to transfer it.**

   FireFTP automatically determines the type of transfer you need to make.

6. **Wait for the transfer to complete.**

   It usually takes some time to transfer a large number of files. Be sure the transfer is complete before you close the FTP window.

7. **Manipulate remote files.**

   You can right-click on the remote file system to display a context menu. This menu has commands for changing permissions, creating directories, and performing other handy tasks.

FTP is a completely unsecure protocol. Anything you transfer with FTP is completely visible to any bad guys sniffing the Internet. For this reason, some servers use a different protocol: Secure FTP (SFTP). FireFTP supports this and other protocols your server might use.

Naming Your Site

After you have a site up and running, you need to give it an address that people can remember. The Domain Name System (DNS) is sort of an address book of the entire Internet. DNS is the mechanism by which you assign a name to your site.

Understanding domain names

Before creating a domain name, you should understand the basics of how this system works:

✦ **Every computer on the Internet has an IP (Internet Protocol) address.** When you connect to the Internet, a special number is assigned to your computer. This *IP address* uniquely identifies your computer. Client machines don't need to keep the same address. For example, my notebook has one address at home and another at work. The addresses are dynamically allocated. A server needs a permanent address that doesn't change.

✦ **IP addresses are used to find computers.** Any time you request a Web page, you're looking for a computer with a particular IP address. For example, the Google IP address is `66.102.9.104`. Type it into your browser address bar, press Enter, and you see the Google main page.

✦ **DNS names simplify addressing.** IP numbers are too confusing for human users. The Domain Name System (DNS) is a series of databases connecting Web site names with their associated IP numbers. When you type `http://www.google.com`, for example, the DNS system looks up the text `www.google.com` and finds the computer with the associated IP.

✦ **You have to register a DNS name.** Of course, to ensure that a particular name is associated with a page, you need to register that relationship.

Registering a domain name

In this section, I show you how to register a domain using Freehostia.com. Check the documentation on your hosting service. Chances are that the main technique is similar, even if the details are different.

To add a domain name to your site, follow these steps:

1. **Log in to the service.**

Log in to your hosting service administration panel. You usually see a Control Panel something like the one shown in Figure 1-13.

2. **Find the domain manager.**

In Freehostia, the domain manager is part of the regular administration panel.

3. **Pick a subdomain.**

In a free hosting service, the main domain (`freehostia.com`, for example) is often chosen for you. Sometimes, you can set a subdomain (like `mystuff.freehostia.com`) for free. The page for managing this process might look like Figure 1-14.

Figure 1-13:
This Control Panel shows all the options, including domain and subdomain tools.

Figure 1-14:
Use this page to create a subdomain for your account.

**Book VIII
Chapter 1**

Managing Your
Servers

4. **Look for a domain search tool.**

   Often, you have a tool, like the one shown in Figure 1-15, that allows you to search for a domain.

5. **Search for the domain name you want.**

   You can type a domain name to see whether it's available.

Figure 1-15: I'm searching for aharris books.net — it seems like a good domain name!

6. **If the domain name is available to register and you want to own it, purchase it immediately.**

   If a domain is available to transfer, it means that somebody else probably owns it.

   Don't search for domains until you're ready to buy them. Unscrupulous people on the Web look for domains that have been searched and then buy them immediately, hoping to sell them back to you at a higher price. If you search for a domain name and then go back the next day to buy it, you often find that it's no longer available and must be transferred. I've also seen people offer to sell you a domain they do not own, buy it up, and sell it at a huge markup.

7. **Register the domain.**

   The domain-purchase process involves registering yourself as the domain owner. Figure 1-16 shows a typical form for this transaction. WHOIS information provides your information to people inquiring about the domain name.

Figure 1-16: Registering the domain name.

8. **Wait a day or two.**

   Your new domain name won't be available immediately. It takes a couple of days for the name to be registered everywhere.

9. **Remember to renew your domain registration.**

   Domain-name registration isn't expensive (typically about $10 per year), but you must renew it or risk losing it.

Managing Data Remotely

Web sites often work with databases. Your hosting service may have features for working with MySQL databases remotely. You should understand how this process works because it's often slightly different from working with the database on your local machine.

Creating your database

Often, a tool like the one shown in Figure 1-17 allows you to pick a defined database or create a new one.

Figure 1-17: You often have to create a database outside of phpMy Admin.

This database creation step happens because you don't have `root` access to MySQL. (If everybody had `root` access, chaos would ensue.) Instead, you usually have an assigned username and database name enforced by the server. On Freehostia, all database names begin with the username and an underscore. To create a new database, you need to provide a database name and a password. Usually, a MySQL user is created with the same name as the database name.

After you create the database, you can select it to work with the data in MySQL. Figure 1-18 shows the MySQL screen for my database on Freehostia.

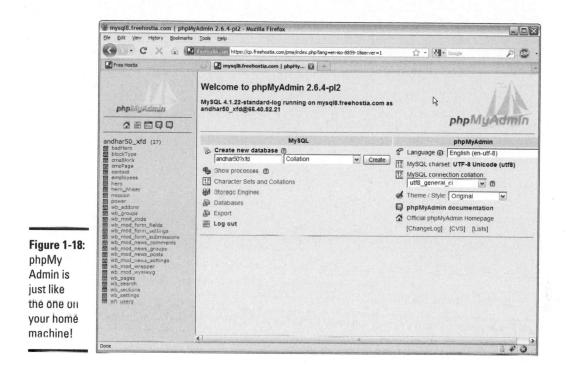

Figure 1-18: phpMy Admin is just like the one on your home machine!

If you look carefully, you see that Freehostia is still using MySQL 4. Therefore, not all SQL scripts in this book work correctly. The only significant problem is views because this feature wasn't included in MySQL 4. I include a version of the `buildHero4.sql` script on the CD-ROM that eliminates all references to views. Otherwise, the script is the same.

You can see from Figure 1-18 that phpMyAdmin is somewhat familiar if you read Book VI. Often, public servers remove the Privileges section because you aren't logged in as `root`. Everything else is basically the same. See Book VI for details on how to use phpMyAdmin to work with your databases.

Finding the MySQL server name

Throughout Book VI, I assume that the MySQL server is on the same physical machine as the Web server. This situation is common in XAMPP installations, but commercial servers often have separate servers for data. You may have to dig through the documentation or find a Server Statistics section to discover how your PHP programs should refer to your server.

Book VIII
Chapter 1

Managing Your Servers

By far the biggest problem when moving your programs to a remote server is figuring out the new connection. Make sure that you know the right combination of server name, username, and password. Test on a simple PHP application before working on a complex one.

Chapter 2: Planning Your Sites

A t some point, your Web efforts begin to grow. Rather than think about single Web documents, you begin to build more complex systems. Most real-life Web problems require a lot more than a single page to do the work. How do you make the transition to a site with many different but interconnected pages? How do you think through the process of creating a site that serves a specific purpose?

You might even be thinking about doing commercial Web development work. If so, it's definitely time to think about how to put together a plan for a customer.

Creating a Multipage Web Site

A complete Web site has these characteristics:

✦ **A consistent theme:** All the pages in a Web site should be about something — a product, a shop, a hobby. It doesn't matter much what the theme is, but the pages should be unified around it.

✦ **Consistent design:** The site should have a unified color scheme. All pages should have the same (or similar) layout, and the font choices and images should all use a similar style.

✦ **A navigation scheme:** Users must have a clear method to move around from page to page. The organization of the pages and their relationships should be clear.

✦ **A common address:** Normally, all pages in a site are on the same server and have a common DNS name so that they're easy to distinguish.

Obviously, the skills of Web design are critical to building a Web site, but a broader skill set is required when creating something larger than individual pages.

If you're starting to build a more complicated Web site, you need to have a plan, or else you won't succeed. This plan is even more important if you're building a site for somebody else.

Planning a Larger Site

Here are some questions you need to ask yourself when designing a larger Web site:

✦ **What's the point of the site?** The site doesn't have to be serious, but it does have to have a theme. If you don't know what your site is about, neither do your users (and they'll leave in a hurry).

✦ **Who am I talking to?** Web sites are a form of communication, and you can't communicate well if you don't understand your audience. Who is the primary target audience for this site?

✦ **Which resources do I have available?** Resources involve a lot more than money (but it helps). How much time do you have? Do you have access to a solid technical framework? Can you get help if you need it? Do you have all the copy and raw materials?

✦ **What am I trying to say?** Believe it or not, this question often poses a huge problem. Somebody says, "I need a Web site." When you ask what she wants on the site, she says, "Oh, lots of things." When you try to pin down the answers, though, people often don't know *what* they want their Web site to say.

✦ **What are the visual design constraints?** If you're building a page for a small business, it probably has some kind of visual identity (through brochures or signage, for example). The business owner often wants you to stick with the company's current branding, which may involve negotiating with graphic artists or advertisers the business has worked with.

✦ **Where will I put this thing?** Does the client already have a domain name? Will moving the domain name cause a problem? Does content that's already on the Web need to be moved? Do you already have hosting space and a DNS name in mind?

Understanding the Client

Often, a larger site is created at the behest of somebody else. Even if you're making a site for your own purposes, you should consider yourself a client. If the project is going to be successful, you need to know a few things about the client, as described in the following sections.

Ensuring that the client's expectations are clear

The short answer to the question of whether a client's expectations are clear is, "Not usually."

A client who truly understands the Internet and knows what it takes to realize her vision for the site probably doesn't need you. Most of the time, a client's own concepts of what should happen on the site are vague, at best. Here are some introductory questions you can ask to get a sense of your client's expectations:

✦ **What are you trying to say with this site?** If the Web site has a single message that can be boiled down to one phrase or sentence, find out what that message is.

✦ **Who are you trying to reach with this site?** Determine who the client expects to be the typical users of the site. Find out whether she expects others and whether the site has more than one potential type of user. (For example, customers and employees may need different things.)

✦ **What problem is this site trying to solve?** Sometimes, a Web site is envisioned as a solution to a particular problem (getting the schedule online or keeping an online newsletter updated, for example).

✦ **What kind of design framework is already in place?** Determine whether the organization already has some sort of branding and design strategy or whether you have freedom in this arena.

✦ **What is the time constraint?** Find out how quickly the client needs the site completed. Does the client want the entire project at one time, or can it be phased in?

✦ **Do you already have a technical framework in place?** Determine whether the project needs to work with an existing database, Web server, Web site, or domain name and whether you have complete access to those resources.

✦ **Are there security concerns?** First ask whether you will be asked to post data (personal information, credit card numbers, or Social Security numbers, for example) on the Internet that shouldn't be there. Run from any project that requires you to work with this potentially dangerous data, unless you're extremely comfortable with security measures.

✦ **How will you get the copy?** Any professional Web developer can tell you that the client usually promises to make the copy available immediately but rarely delivers it without a lot of pleading. If the content is available, it's often incomplete or incorrect. You need to have some plan for getting the material from the client, or else you cannot proceed past a certain point.

✦ **Does the client have a remuneration strategy?** If you will be paid for your work, find out how you will be paid and whether it's hourly or by the project. If you have a business arrangement, treat it as such and write out a contract. Even if the page is written for free for a friend, a written contract is a good idea because you don't want to ruin a friendship over something as silly as a Web site.

Delineating the tasks

Building a Web site can involve a lot of different tasks. Your contract should indicate which of these tasks is expected. This list describes the potential scope of the project:

✦ **Site layout:** Determine which pages the site has and how they're connected to each other.

✦ **XHTML coding:** Some projects simply require XHTML coding and CSS. Presumably, the copy has already been provided, and you simply need to convert it to XHTML format. This work isn't difficult, but it's tedious. Use a text editor with macro capability — after you create an XHTML template.

✦ **XHTML template design:** Devise an overall page design. The content isn't important here, but the general page design is the issue. This task requires sample data and an editor. It's normally done in conjunction with CSS templating.

✦ **CSS design:** After you have an XHTML template or two (so that you know the logical structure of the pages), you can work on the visual design. Start with sketches on paper and maybe images from a paint program. After you have a layout approved, write the CSS to implement it.

✦ **Data design:** If the project will have a database component, take some time to analyze (and, often, rebuild) the data structure to follow the normalization rules. Data work is difficult because it doesn't have a visual result, yet it's critical to the overall site. This step is usually put off until the end, and that decision often dooms Web projects. If you need data design, start it early.

✦ **Data implementation:** If the project has a data component, write and test the SQL code to build the database, including tables, views, and sample queries. You need time to write PHP code to connect the database to the XHTML front end.

✦ **Site integration and implementation:** It takes some effort to fit all the pieces back together and make them work. Usually, this process is ongoing. The site needs to be set up on a production server and then tested and launched.

✦ **Testing:** Testing your work with live users is critical. You can use formal usability studies, but failing that, you still learn a lot by asking people to use your system and watching them do it (with your mouth shut). This method is the best way to see whether your assumptions are correct and the site is doing what it needs to do.

For this discussion, I'm assuming you're building the entire site manually. In Chapter 3 of this minibook, I explain how to use content management systems to simplify the process of building large Web sites.

Understanding the Audience

Understanding your audience is one of the trickiest parts of Web planning. You need to anticipate the audience in a number of ways, as described in the following sections.

Determining whom you want to reach

Before you make a lot of design decisions, you need to think carefully about the type of person you're trying to reach in the Web site.

Try to anticipate the mindset that people have when they use a particular site. For example, one of my students simultaneously worked on two sites: one for a graduate program at a university and another for a spa and salon. She had to think quite differently about the users of the two sites, which had implications for how she approached each step of the process.

The graduate program page was part of a Web site for a university. The university already had its own style and branding guidelines, official colors, and a number of (evolving) standards. The potential users of this site were graduate students seeking online degrees. The focus of this site was all business. People were there to learn about the graduate program and set up their schedules. They wanted information about classes, instructors, and schedules, but they didn't want anything that interfered with the problem at hand. The writing was efficient and official, the color scheme was standard, and the layout was also official.

The spa and salon page had an entirely different feel. The owner loves design and spent long hours picking exactly the right paint color for the walls in the physical space. She's really happy with her brochure, and although she's not sure exactly what she wants, she knows when something isn't right. She wants to give her customers information about the salon, but more importantly, she wants them to get a sense of how invigorating, relaxing, and feminine the experience of visiting her salon can be.

These two sites, although they require the same general technical skills, demand vastly different visual and technical designs because the clients and their users are vastly different.

Ironically, someone could simultaneously be a graduate student and a patron of the salon, but the person would still have a different identity in these different sites. If you're going to a university site, in a student mindset, you want quick, reliable information. If, after you sign up for classes, you're looking for a salon, you likely want to be pampered.

Web sites are experiences. The design of the site should reflect the experience you're trying to give the user when he visits your site.

Finding out the user's technical expertise

Understanding the user isn't just an exercise in psychology. You also need to estimate the users' technical proficiency because it can have a major impact on your site. Consider these issues for the typical user:

+ **Whether the user has broadband access:** University students, hard-core gamers, and Web developers often have high-speed Internet access, so they don't mind a page with lots of video, multimedia assets, and large file sizes. (In fact, they may *expect* a page like this.) Lots of people still use dialup connections. If your audience has slower connections, every image creates a delay. Audio and video assets are completely unavailable to this group — and even make your site unattractive to them.

+ **Whether the user has a recent browser:** You have no way to predict which browser a user has, but think about whether your target audience has a reason to install any of the current browsers. By and large, grandmothers use whichever browsers were on their machines when they purchased them. (I do know some L337 H@XX0R grandmas, however.) If most people in your audience are still using the AOL browser — believe it or not, it's still used a lot — using advanced CSS and JavaScript tricks on your page may not be the best choice.

+ **Whether the user has a recent computer:** As technical people, we tend to assume that everyone else keeps up-to-date on technology. That's not necessarily an accurate assumption.

+ **Whether the user has certain proficiencies:** If you include a Flash animation, for example, the user might not have the right version of Flash installed. You have to decide whether it's reasonable to expect the user to install a plugin.

+ **Whether this will be a largely mobile application:** These days, every Web site should be considered a potential mobile site, but if a large percentage of your visitors will be using mobile devices to view your page, this will have implications on your design.

This process isn't about stereotyping, but you *must* consider the user while you're building a site. You want to match users' expectations and capabilities, if possible.

Of course, you're making assumptions here, and you may well be wrong. I once did some work for a club for retired faculty members, and I based my expectations on their being retired. I should have based my assumptions on their being professors. And they let me have it! Be willing to adjust your expectations after you meet real users. (For professional work, you *must* meet and watch real users use your site.)

Building a Site Plan

Often, the initial work on a major site involves creating a plan for the site design. I like to do this step early because it helps me see the true scope of the project. A *site plan* is an overview of a Web site. Normally, it's drawn as a hierarchy chart.

I was asked to help design a Web site for an academic department at a major university. The first question I asked was, "What do you want on the Web site?" I wrote down everything on a whiteboard, with no thought of organization. Figure 2-1 shows a (cleaned-up) version of that sketch.

Department Page Needs

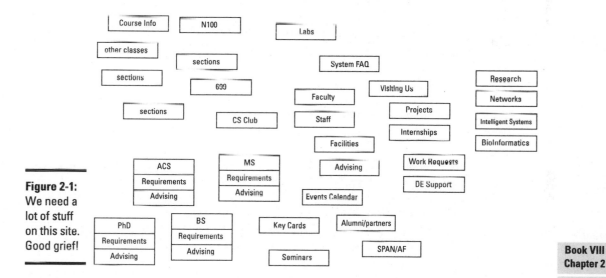

Figure 2-1: We need a lot of stuff on this site. Good grief!

For all the sketches in this chapter, I used Dia, the open-source drawing tool. An excellent tool for this kind of work, it's included on the CD-ROM so that you can play with it.

After all participants suggested everything they thought their site needed, I shooed them out of the room. Using only paper and pencil, I created a more organized sketch based on how *I* thought the information should be organized. My diagram looked like the one shown in Figure 2-2.

Book VIII
Chapter 2

Planning Your Sites

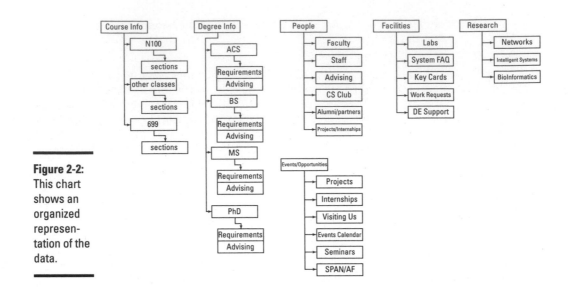

Figure 2-2:
This chart shows an organized representation of the data.

Creating a site overview

Keep these suggestions in mind while creating a site overview diagram:

✦ **Use the Law of Seven.** This law suggests that people generally can't handle more than seven choices at a time. Try not to have more than seven major segments of information at any level. Each of these can be separated into as many as seven chunks, and each of these can have seven chunks.

Note: Even this book uses the Law of Seven! (Well, sorta — this book has eight minibooks.) The monster you're holding is too intimidating to look at as just one book, but if you break it into smaller segments, it becomes easier to manage. Clever, huh?

✦ **Identify commonalities.** While you look over the data, general groupings emerge. In the university example, I could easily see that we had a lot of course data, degree information, information about faculty, and research. I wanted to consider a few other topics that didn't fit as well, until I realized that they could be grouped as events and opportunities.

✦ **Try to assign each topic to a group.** If you read Book VI, you probably recognize that I'm doing a form of *data normalization* here. This data structure isn't necessarily a formal one, but I'm using the same sort of thinking, so it could be. Clearly, I'm using the principle of functional dependency.

✦ **Arrange a hierarchy.** Group the topics from most general to most specific. For example, the term *course info* is very broad. N100 is a specific course, and it may have many sections (specific date, time, and instructor combinations). Thus, it makes sense to group sections under N100 and to group N100 under courses.

✦ **Provide representative data.** Not every single scrap of information is necessary here. The point is to have enough data so you can see the relationships among data.

✦ **Keep in mind that this diagram does *not* represent the site design.** When I showed this diagram to people, many assumed that I was setting up a menu structure, and they wanted a different kind of organization or menu. That's not the point yet. The purpose of this type of diagram is to see how the data itself fits together. Of course, this diagram tends to inform the page setup and the menu structure, but it doesn't have to.

✦ **Not each box is a page.** It might be, but it doesn't have to be. Later in the process, you can decide how to organize the parts of the site. For example, we decided to put all sections of N100 on one page with the N100 information using AJAX.

Building this sort of site diagram is absolutely critical for larger sites, or else you never really grasp the scope of the project. Have the major stakeholders look it over to see whether it accurately reflects the *information* you're trying to convey.

Building the site diagram

The site diagram is a more specific version of the site overview. At this point, you make a commitment about the particular pages you want in the system and their organizational relationship. Figure 2-3 shows a site diagram for the department site.

Figure 2-3: Now, you have a site diagram for the department site.

Semantic navigation

One idea that has been popular in Web design circles is the notion of *semantic navigation,* where you set up your menu structure so that it reflects the jobs people are trying to do, rather than reflect the hierarchy of your sites. For example, a university department site might have a menu for common student activities, alumni, and faculty.

This idea can be quite helpful if done properly, but don't try to set up your entire site this way because it involves too much duplication of data. (Students and faculty both need course information, but you don't want to post that in two different places.) Instead, set up your site in a normalized way, and then put another menu system on your site that allows users to choose the section of the site they want based on problems they're trying to solve. Then, you create the best of both worlds.

The site diagram is a bit different from the overview, for these reasons:

✦ **Each box represents a page.** Now, you have to make some decisions about how the pages are organized. Determine at which level of the overview you have separate pages. For example, are all the course sections on one page, or all the sections of N100? Does each section of each course have a different page? These decisions will help you determine which technologies to use in constructing the page.

✦ **The site diagram still doesn't need every page.** If you have 30 classes, you don't need to account for each one if you know where they go and they all have the same general purpose and design.

✦ **The navigation structure should be clear.** The hierarchy should give you a clear navigation structure. (Of course, you can, and often should, add a secondary navigation structure. See the sidebar "Semantic navigation.")

✦ **Name each box.** Each page should have a name. These box names translate to page titles and help you form a unified title system. This arrangement is useful for your navigation scheme.

✦ **Identify overall layout for each box.** Generally, a site uses only a few layouts. You have a standard layout for most pages. Often, the front page has a different layout (for news and navigation information). You may have specialty layouts, as well. For example, the faculty pages all have a specific layout with a prominent image. Don't plan the layout here — just identify it.

✦ **Sort out the order.** If the order of the pages matters, the site diagram is the place to work it out. For example, I organized the degrees from undergraduate to PhD programs.

The goal for this part of the site-planning process is to have a clear understanding of what each page requires. This information should make it easy for you to complete the data and visual design steps. The site diagram is an absolutely critical document. After you have it approved, print it and tape it to your monitor.

Creating Page Templates

If you've developed a site diagram, you should have a good feel for the overall requirements of the Web development project. You should know how many layouts you need and the general requirements for each one. Your next task is to think about the visual design. Here are some guidelines:

✦ **Get help if you need it.** Visual design is a skill that requires insight and experience. If you "design like a programmer" (I sure do!), don't be afraid to get help from a person who has design sensibility. You still need to translate the design into code, however.

✦ **Identify unifying design goals.** All pages on the site have certain characteristics in common. Find out the overall color scheme, whether you will have a logo, and whether all pages will have the same header and retain the same fonts throughout.

✦ **Identify a primary layout.** Generally, a Web site requires one major layout that's repeated throughout the site. Often, the main page does not use this primary layout, but most internal pages do. Determine, for example, which broad design elements can be shared by most of the pages, whether every page has a headline, whether you need columns, and how important images are.

✦ **Identify specialty designs.** The main page is often a bit different from the other pages because it serves as an overview to the site. Likewise, if you will be repeating certain kinds of pages (the course pages and faculty pages in my university example), you have to know how these designs differ from the primary layout. Keep design elements as consistent as you can because unity makes your job easier and ties the site pages together.

Sketching the page design

Do not write even a single line of code before sketching out some design ideas. Figure 2-4 shows a page sketch for my sample site.

Your page sketch gives you enough information to create XHTML and CSS code. It needs to start showing some detail, such as the following details:

✦ **Draw out each element on the page.** Any major page element (headlines, menus, columns) must be delineated.

✦ **Include the class or ID identifier for each element.** If you have a segment that will be used as a menu, name it "menu," for example. If you have a content area, identify that name now. Write all names directly on the diagram so that you're clear about what belongs where.

✦ **Include all relevant style information.** Describe every font, the width of every element (including measurement units), the foreground and background colors (with hex codes), the background images (including sizes), and anything else you might need in order to code CSS styles for the page.

✦ **Build a page sketch following these guidelines for each page template in your site.** If you have three page designs, for example, you need three separate diagrams.

Figure 2-4:
Here's a sample sketch for the standard template on this site.

These diagrams are finished only if they give you everything you need to build the XHTML and CSS templates. The idea is to do all your design work on paper and then implement and tweak your project with code. If you plan well, the coding is easy.

The design sketch isn't a page mock-up. It's not meant to look exactly like the page. Instead, it's a sketch that explains with text all the various details you need to code in XHTML and CSS. Often, designers produce beautiful mock-ups that aren't helpful in development because you need to know sizes and colors, for example. If you want to produce a mock-up, by all means do so, but also make a design sketch that includes things like actual font names and hex color codes so that you can re-create the mock-up with live code.

Building the XHTML template framework

With a page layout in place, you can finally start writing some code. Begin with your standard page layout diagram and create an XHTML template to implement the diagram in working code. The XML template is quite simple because most of the design should happen in the CSS. Keep these guidelines in mind:

✦ **Remember that the template is simply a framework.** The XHTML is mainly blank. It's meant to be duplicated and filled in with live data.

✦ **It has a reference to the style sheet.** External CSS is critical for large Web projects because many pages refer to the same style sheet. Make a reference to the style sheet, even though it may not actually exist yet.

✦ **Include all necessary elements.** The elements themselves can be blank, but if your page needs a list for a menu, add an empty list. If you need a content div, put it in place.

✦ **Create a prototype from the template.** You use the template quite a bit, but you need sample data in order to test the CSS. Build a prototype page that contains typical data. The amount of data should be typical of the actual site so that you can anticipate formatting problems.

It's very possible that you'll never manually put content in your template. There are several options for automating this process, which can be found in Chapter 4 of this minibook.

The XHTML template should be easy to construct because everything you need is in the page template diagram. Figure 2-5 shows an XHTML prototype.

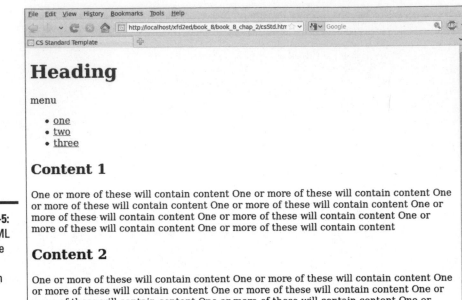

File Edit View History Bookmarks Tools Help

http://localhost/xfd2ed/book_8/book_8_chap_2/csStd.htm   Google

CS Standard Template

Heading

menu

- one
- two
- three

Content 1

One or more of these will contain content One or more of these will contain content One or more of these will contain content One or more of these will contain content One or more of these will contain content One or more of these will contain content One or more of these will contain content

Content 2

One or more of these will contain content One or more of these will contain content One or more of these will contain content One or more of these will contain content One or more of these will contain content One or more of these will contain content One or more of these will contain content
contact and footer info

Done   0 errors / 0 warnings

Figure 2-5: An XHTML prototype for my site (with no CSS attached yet).

Here's the XHTML code for my prototype:

```
<!DOCTYPE html PUBLIC "-//W3C//DTD XHTML 1.0 Strict//EN"
"http://www.w3.org/TR/xhtml1/DTD/xhtml1-strict.dtd">
<html lang="EN" dir="ltr" xmlns="http://www.w3.org/1999/xhtml">
  <head>
    <meta http-equiv="content-type" content="text/xml; charset=utf-8" />
    <title>CS Standard Template</title>
    <link rel = "stylesheet"
          type = "text/css"
          href = "csStd.css" />
  </head>

  <body>
    <div id = "all">
      <!-- This div centers a fixed-width layout -->
      <div id = "heading">
        <h1>Heading</h1>
      </div><!-- end heading div -->

      <div id = "menu">
        menu
        <ul>
          <li><a href = "">one</a></li>
          <li><a href = "">two</a></li>
          <li><a href = "">three</a></li>
        </ul>
      </div> <!-- end menu div -->
```

```
<div class = "content">
  <h2>Content 1</h2>
  One or more of these will contain content
  One or more of these will contain content
  One or more of these will contain content
  One or more of these will contain content
  One or more of these will contain content
  One or more of these will contain content
  One or more of these will contain content
  One or more of these will contain content
</div> <!-- end content div -->

<div class = "content">
  <h2>Content 2</h2>
  One or more of these will contain content
  One or more of these will contain content
  One or more of these will contain content
  One or more of these will contain content
  One or more of these will contain content
  One or more of these will contain content
  One or more of these will contain content
  One or more of these will contain content
</div> <!-- end content div -->

    <div id = "footer">
      contact and footer info
    </div> <!-- end footer div -->
  </div> <!-- end all div -->
  </body>
</html>
```

People commonly start writing pages at this point, but that's a dangerous idea. Don't use any real data until you're certain of the general XHTML structure. You can always change the style later, but if you create 100 pages and then decide that each of them needs another <div> tag, you have to go back and add 100 divs.

Creating page styles

With an XHTML framework in place, you can start working on the CSS. The best way to incorporate CSS is by following these steps:

1. **Begin with the page template diagram.**

It should have all the information you need.

2. **Load your XHTML prototype into Firefox.**

Nothing beats Firefox with the Web Developer CSS editor for CSS design because it lets you see your changes in real time. Honestly, you can use any browser you wish, but if you use another browser, you'll need to create the CSS file in a text editor and check it frequently in the browser. (Check Books II and III to see how Firefox and Web Developer simplify this task.)

3. **Implement the CSS from your diagram.**

   You should be *implementing* the design you already created, not *designing* the page. (That already happened in the diagramming process.)

4. **Save the design.**

   If you're using the Web Developer CSS editor, you can save your CSS directly into a file. If your XHTML template had an external style definition, this is the default save file. If you're editing CSS in a text editor, save it in the normal way so the browser will be able to read it. (See Book II for information on implementing external style sheets.)

5. **Test and tweak.**

   Things are never quite what they seem with CSS because browsers don't conform to standards equally. You need to test and tweak on other browsers, and you probably have to write a secondary style for IE exceptions.

6. **Repeat for other templates.**

   Repeat this process for each of the other templates you identified in your site diagram.

The result of this process should be a number of CSS files that you can readily reuse across your site.

Here's the CSS code for my primary page:

```
body {
  background-color: #000000;
}

#all {
  background-color: white;
  border: 1px solid black;
  width: 800px;
  margin-top:2em;
  margin-left: auto;
  margin-right: auto;
  min-height: 600px;
}

#heading {
  background-color: #A11204;
  color: #FFFFFF;
  height: 100px;
  font-size: 2em;
  padding-left: 1em;
  border-bottom: 3px solid black;
  margin-top: -1.5em;
}
```

```
#menu {
  background-color: #A11204;
  color: #FFFFFF;
  float: left;
  width: 100px;
  min-height: 500px;
}

#menu li {
  list-style-type: none;
  margin-left: -2em;
  margin-right: .5em;
  text-align: center;
}

#menu a {
  color: #FFFFFF;
  display: block;
  border: #A11204 3px outset;
  text-decoration: none;
}
#menu a:hover {
  border: #A11204 3px inset;
}

.content {
  border: 3px double #A11204;
  margin: 1em;
  margin-left: 110px;
  padding-left: 1em;
  padding-bottom: 1em;
  padding-right: 1em;
}

.content h2 {
  background-color: #A11204;
  color: #FFFFFF;
  text-align: right;
}

#footer {
  color: #FFFFFF;
  background-color: #000000;
  border: 1px solid #A11204;
  float: left;
  clear: both;
  width: 100%;
  text-align: center;
}
```

Figure 2-6 shows the standard template with the CSS attached.

Figure 2-6:
The XHTML template looks good with the CSS attached.

Building a data framework

The examples throughout this chapter assumed that a large Web project can be done in straight XHTML and CSS. That's always a good starting point, but if your program needs data or interactivity, you probably have a data back end.

Most data-enabled site plans fail.

The reason is almost always that the data normalization wasn't incorporated into the plan early enough, and the other parts of the project inevitably depend on a well-planned data back end.

If you suspect your project will involve a database, you should follow these steps early in the process (during the early site-planning phase):

1. **Identify the true data problem to be solved.**

Data gets complicated in a hurry. Determine why exactly you need the data on the site. Keep the data as simple as you can, or else you'll become overwhelmed.

2. **Identify data requirements in your site diagram.**

Find out where on the site diagram you're getting data. Determine which data you're retrieving and record this information on the site diagram.

3. **Create a third normal form ER diagram.**

   Don't bother building a database until you're sure that you can create an ER diagram in third normal form. Check Book VI, Chapter 3 for details on this process.

4. **Implement the data structure.**

   Create an SQL script that creates all the necessary data structures (including tables and views) and includes sample data.

5. **Create PHP middleware.**

   After the database is in place, you usually need PHP code to take requests, pass them to the database, and return the results. Most of the PHP code for the main site consists of simple queries from the database. If you can use AJAX or SSI, it simplifies the process because your PHP code doesn't have to create entire pages — it simply creates snippets of code.

   See Chapter 4 of this minibook for help on implementing these technologies.

6. **Consider update capabilities.**

   Usually, when you have a database, you need another part of the site to allow the client to update information. It's often an administrative site with password access. An administrative site is much more complex than the main site because it requires the ability to add, edit, and update records.

Fleshing Out the Project

If you completed all the steps in the preceding section, it becomes relatively easy to create the page: It's simply a matter of forming the copy into the templates you created, tying it all together, and launching on the site.

Making the site live

Typically, you do the primary development on a server that isn't in public view. Follow these steps to take the site to production:

1. **Test your design.**

   Do some usability testing with real users. Watch people solve typical problems on the site and see what problems they encounter.

2. **Proofread everything.**

   Almost nothing demolishes credibility as quickly as sloppy writing. Get a quality proofreader or copy editor to look over everything on the site to check for typos and spelling errors. If your page contains a specific type of content (technical information or company policy, for example), have an expert familiar with the subject check the site for factual or content errors.

3. **Prepare the online hosting environment.**

   Be sure that you have the server space to handle your requirements. Make a copy of your database and test it. Check the domain name to be sure that you have no legal encumbrances.

4. **Move your site online.**

   Move the files from your development server to the main server.

5. **Test everything again.**

   Try a *beta* test, where your page is available to only a few people. Get input and feedback from these testers and incorporate the best suggestions.

6. **Take a vacation. You earned it!**

Contemplating efficiency

When you start working with the site, you'll probably encounter repeated code. For example, each page may have exactly the same title bar. You obviously don't want to write exactly the same code for 100 different pages because it might change, and you don't want to make the change in 100 different places. You have three options in this case:

+ **Use AJAX to import the repeated code.** Follow the AJAX instructions in Chapter 4 of this minibook to import your header (or other repeated code).

+ **Use Server-Side Includes (SSI) to import code on the server.** If your server allows it, you can use the SSI technology to import pages on the server without using a language like PHP. SSI is explained in Chapter 4 of this minibook.

+ **Build the pages with PHP.** Put all segments in separate files and use a PHP script to tie them together. When you do this, you're creating a content management system, which is the topic of Chapters 3 and 4 of this minibook.

Chapter 3: Introducing Content Management Systems

In This Chapter

✔ Understanding the need for content management systems

✔ Previewing typical content management systems

✔ Installing a content management system

✔ Adding content to a content management system

✔ Setting up the navigation structure

✔ Adding new types of content

✔ Changing the appearance with themes

✔ Building a custom theme

*I*f you've ever built a large Web site, you'll probably agree that the process can be improved. Experienced Web developers have discovered the following maxims about larger projects:

✦ **Duplication should be eliminated whenever possible.** If you find yourself repeatedly copying the same XHTML code, you have a potential problem. When (not If) that code needs to be changed, you have a lot of copying and pasting to do.

✦ **Content should be separated from layout.** You've already heard this statement, but it's taken to a new level when you're building a large site. Separating *all* content from the layout would be helpful so that you could create the layout only one time and change it in one location.

✦ **Content is really data.** At some point, the content of the Web site is really just data. It's important data, to be sure, but the data can — and should — be separated from the layout code, and should be, if possible.

✦ **Content belongs to the user.** Developing a Web site for somebody can become a long-term commitment. If the client becomes dependent on the site, he frequently pesters you for changes. It would be helpful if the client could change his own content and ask you only for changes in structure or behavior.

✦ **A Web site isn't a collection of pages — it's a framework.** If you can help the client own the data, you're more concerned with the framework for manipulating and displaying that data. It's a good deal for you and the client.

A content management system (CMS) is designed to address exactly these issues, as this chapter will show you.

Overview of Content Management Systems

CMSs are used in many of the sites you use every day. As you examine these CMSs, you start to recognize them all over the Web. If you have your own server space, a little patience, and a little bit of knowledge, you can create your own professional-looking site using a CMS.

This list describes the general characteristics of a CMS:

- **It's written in a server-side language.** The language is usually PHP, but CMSs are sometimes written in other languages. Stick with PHP for now because it's described in this book, it's easy to use, and it's the most frequently used CMS language.

- **All content is treated as data.** Almost all the content of the CMS is stored in text files or (more commonly) a MySQL database. A CMS usually has few HTML files.

- **The layout consists of data, too.** The CSS and XHTML templates, and everything else the CMS needs, are also stored as data, in either text files or the database.

- **All pages are created dynamically.** When a user logs in to a CMS, she is normally talking to a PHP program. This program analyzes the current situation and generates an HTML document on the fly.

- **There are different levels of access.** Most CMSs allow anonymous access (like regular Web pages) but also allow users to log in for increased access.

- **The content can be modified from within the system.** Users with the appropriate access can modify the content of the CMS without knowing anything about PHP or databases. Often, you don't even need HTML or CSS.

- **The layout can be modified from within the system, too.** Most CMSs allow you to change the layout and design from within the system, although the process is usually more involved.

- **CMSs can be expanded.** Most CMSs are easily modified with hundreds of visual themes, add-in modules, and new capabilities available for free. In most cases, if you need something that isn't there, you can make it yourself.

- **Many of the best CMSs are open source.** CMSs are a shocking value. When you consider how much they can contribute to your online presence, it's amazing that most CMS programs are absolutely free.

Previewing Common CMSs

To get a true feel for the power of CMSs, you should test-drive a few. The wonderful resource www.opensourcecms.com allows you to log in to hundreds of different CMSs as a user and as an administrator to see how they work. I show you a few typical CMSs so that you can get a feel for how they work.

Moodle

Often, you have a special purpose in mind. For example, I wanted to teach an online course without purchasing an expensive and complicated course management system. I installed the special-purpose CMS Moodle. Figure 3-1 shows the Moodle screen for one of my courses.

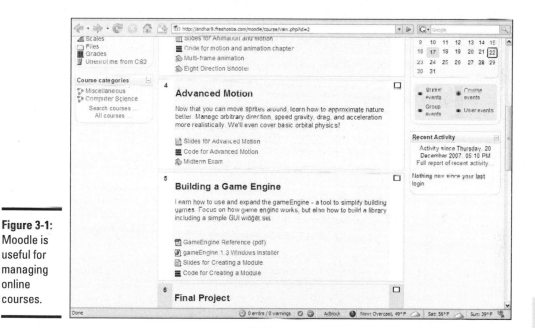

Figure 3-1: Moodle is useful for managing online courses.

Moodle has a lot of features that lends it to the educational setting:

✦ **Student and instructor management:** The system already understands the roles of student and instructor and makes appropriate parts of the system available.

✦ **Online assignment creation and submission:** One of the biggest problems with online courseware is getting assignments to and from students. Moodle has a complete system for handling this problem.

✦ **Online grade book:** When a teacher grades an assignment (online through Moodle), the student's grades are automatically updated.

+ **Online testing support:** Moodle has built-in modules for creating, managing, and scoring online quizzes and exams.

+ **Communication tools:** Moodle includes a *wiki* (a collaborative documentation tool), online chat, and forum tools you can set up for improved communication with your students.

+ **Specialized educational content:** Moodle was put together by hundreds of passionate (and geeky) teachers, so it has all kinds of support for various teaching methodologies.

Community-created software can be very good (as Moodle is) because it's built by people who know exactly what they want, and anybody with an idea (and the skills to carry them out) can add or modify the features. The result is an organic system that can often be better than the commercial offerings.

I find Moodle easier to use and more reliable than the commercial course management system that my university uses. I keep a Moodle backup for my classes because when the "official" system goes down, I can always make something available for my students.

WordPress

WordPress is another specialty CMS, meant primarily for blogging (short for *Web logging,* or keeping an online public diary). WordPress has become the dominant blogging tool on the Internet. Figure 3-2 shows a typical WordPress page.

Figure 3-2:
Woot! I'm
blogging!

WordPress takes one simple idea (blogging) and pushes it to the limit. Unregistered users see the blog output, but if you log in, you gain access to a complete set of tools for managing your online musings.

Figure 3-3 illustrates the administrator view of WordPress.

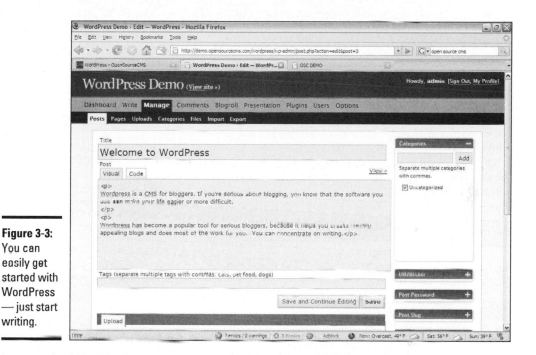

Figure 3-3: You can easily get started with WordPress — just start writing.

Additionally, you can change the layout and colors, add new templates, and do much more, as you can in a more traditional CMS.

Of course, hundreds of other specialized CMSs are out there. Before you try to build your own CMS from the ground up, take a look at the other available offerings and see whether you can start by using the work of somebody else.

Drupal

Drupal is one of the most popular multipurpose CMSs out there. Intended for larger sites, it's more involved than the specialty CMSs — although it can do almost anything.

Figure 3-4 shows a basic site running Drupal.

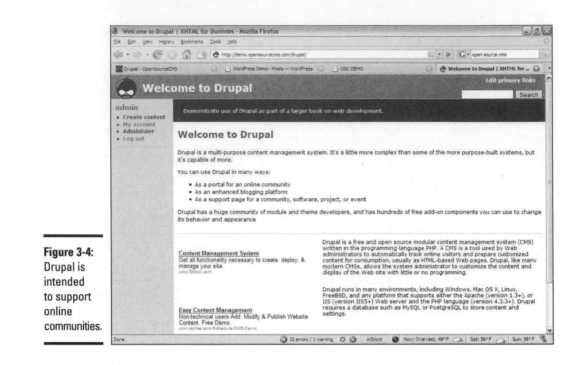

Figure 3-4:
Drupal is
intended
to support
online
communities.

Drupal was designed primarily for managing community Web sites. It is commonly used in the following types of sites:

✦ **Gaming sites:** Many game communities are based around a CMS like Drupal because it allows opportunities for users to share information, opinions, news, and files.

✦ **Software sites:** A CMS like Drupal is an ideal place to post information about your software, including downloads, documentation, and user support.

✦ **Forums:** Although you can find many dedicated forum packages, Drupal supports several good forum tools.

✦ **Blogging:** You can also use Drupal as a news site and a location to post your blog. You can add community features when you want or need them.

Drupal is powerful and extremely popular. However, this power has led to increased complexity. Learning everything you can do with Drupal will take some time and effort.

Building a CMS site with Website Baker

For the rest of this chapter, I take you through the installation and customization of a complete Web site using the Website Baker CMS. This is one of my favorite CMSs for a number of reasons:

✦ **It's easy to understand:** Systems like Drupal have gotten so complicated that you often require entire books on how to use them. Website Baker (as you'll see) is not complicated at all, even for somewhat advanced features.

✦ **It's easy to modify:** Website Baker uses a reasonably simple template system that's primarily XHTML and CSS (with a few PHP functions thrown in). This makes it very easy to adapt pages that were not designed in Website Baker to a CMS format.

✦ **It's easy to teach to clients:** When you're building a commercial site, it's critical that your customer learns how to manage the site. The easier you can make managing the site for the customer, the easier your job is down the road.

✦ **It's reasonably complete:** The basic install of Website Baker is not large, but you can customize your installation with hundreds of modules and templates to get exactly the look and behavior you want.

✦ **It's free and open source:** Like almost all the software I recommend, Website Baker is entirely free and open source, even for commercial use.

I focus on Website Baker in the upcoming section, but it's just an example CMS. Look over this section, but if you want to use a different CMS than Website Baker, by all means do so. You'll see the overall steps are pretty much the same regardless of the particular package you use.

Installing your CMS

A CMS package typically contains many different kinds of files. Most are primarily PHP programs with HTML/XHTML pages and CSS. Most CMSs also include databases written in MySQL. To install a CMS, you need to download these components and install them on your server.

1. **Download the latest version of Website Baker at `http://www.websitebaker2.org/en/home.php`.**

   Download the Zip file. (The CMS is all Web code, so it doesn't matter which operating system you use.)

2. **Create a subdirectory on your Web root.**

   If you use a local server, create a new subdirectory under `htdocs` (or wherever you save your Web files). If you're on a remote server, use FTP or the file management tool to create the subdirectory you want the files to go in.

3. **Copy all Website Baker files to the new directory.**

   The Zip file you download from Website Baker contains a `wb` directory. Copy all files and folders in this directory to your new directory.

4. Navigate to the new directory in your browser.

Be sure you have Apache and MySQL turned on. If you're on a local machine, be sure to use the `localhost` mechanism to find the directory.

If all is well, you see the Website Baker Installation Wizard, as shown in Figure 3-5.

Figure 3-5: The Website Baker Installation Wizard helps you get started.

Most CMSs work in a similar way: You install a set of base files to the server, and then the system helps you get the other systems configured. Here's how to install Website Baker:

1. Check system configuration.

The Step 1 section of the installation wizard ensures all the needed components are available on your server.

2. Ensure folders are writable.

The CMS will need to write files to the server. If you're in a Unix-based system, you may have to check the file permissions to ensure all files and folders specified in this section can be written to. Each specified file or folder can be set to 777 permission.

See Chapter 1 of this minibook for more on changing Unix permissions. (Even if you use a Windows or Mac at home, your Web server might use Linux or Unix.)

3. Set default settings.

Specify the path to the CMS, the default time zone, and the default language.

4. Specify your operating system.

Windows has its own way of doing things, so let Website Baker know whether you're using Windows or a Unix-based system. (Mac OSX and Linux are both Unix-based.)

5. Include database information.

Supply the information needed so Website Baker can get to your database. Supply a database name as well as the username and password you want to use to access the database. Check the Install Tables option to have Website Baker automatically build the database you need.

6. Enter the Web site name.

This name will appear on all the site's pages (but you can change it later).

7. Create an administrator account.

The admin account will have the ability to change the site. Create a user named admin with a password you can remember.

8. Install the CMS.

Press the Install Website Baker button to install the CMS. Figure 3-6 shows the installation wizard after I filled in the contents.

If all goes well, you're greeted by the administration page shown in Figure 3-7.

The final step of installing your CMS is to remove the install directory. This directory contains the scripts and tools you used to install the CMS. If you leave it in place, bad guys can reinstall your CMS from the Web and destroy your settings. Use your file management or FTP tool to delete the install directory from your Website Baker directory as soon as you're satisfied the installation went well. When you do this, the warning about the installation directory will disappear.

Instead of installing the CMS manually, many hosting services have automated installation scripts for popular CMSs that you can use. Freehostia has built-in support for Website Baker, but I find the automated systems tend to have older versions of the software. You should still know how to set up the CMS by hand.

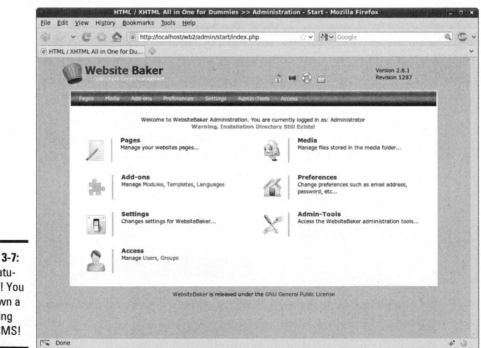

Figure 3-6:
The CMS
is ready to
install.

Figure 3-7:
Congratu-
lations! You
now own a
bouncing
baby CMS!

Getting an overview of Website Baker

The administration page (refer to Figure 3-7) is the control panel you and other administrators use to build the site. The administration page's tools are the foundation of the entire site:

✦ **Pages:** Where you add the primary content for the site. Each page is built here. Website Baker features a few standard page types, and you can install hundreds more through the module feature.

✦ **Add-ons:** The core installation of Website Baker is reasonably basic, but you can customize it in many ways. The most important techniques are to add new types of pages (modules) and new visual themes (templates). I describe both techniques later in this chapter.

✦ **Settings:** Allows you to change global settings for the site. You can modify the site name, description, theme, and other settings from this panel.

✦ **Access:** Allows you to add new users and groups and grant various users access to different parts of the system. For example, if you're setting up a site for a church, you might want the children's pastor to have access to only the site's children's ministry parts.

✦ **Media:** You can add images and video to your site. This section allows you to manage and upload the various media to your server.

✦ **Preferences:** Allows you to change a few more settings, including the e-mail address and password of the admin account.

✦ **Admin-Tools:** Contains advanced options for improving the administration experience.

Adding your content

The point of a content management system is to manage some content, so it's time to add pages to the system.

1. **From the administration page, choose Pages.**

A screen similar to Figure 3-8 appears.

2. **Type** main **as the first page name.**

Each page you create needs to have a name.

3. **Keep the page type WYSIWYG.**

You can make many different kinds of pages, but most of your pages will be the standard WYSIWYG format.

4. **Leave all other settings at their default.**

The other settings available here don't mean much until you have multiple pages.

Figure 3-8:
This page allows you to add, modify, and delete pages.

5. **Click the Add button to add the page.**

   A screen similar to Figure 3-9 appears.

Figure 3-9:
Now you're at a nice page editor.

Using the WYSIWYG editor

The purpose of the CMS is to make editing a Web site without any technical skills easy. You can give admin access to an HTML novice, and he can use the system to build Web pages with no knowledge of XHTML or CSS. The editor has a number of useful tools that make creating and editing much like working with a word processor.

✦ **Predefined fonts and styles:** The user can choose fonts and styles from drop-down menus, unaware that these options are taking advantage of predefined CSS styles.

✦ **The ability to add lists, links, and images:** The editor includes the ability to add lists, links, and images (and other types of content) without any knowledge of XHTML. If you add an image, the editor includes a wizard that helps you upload the image to the server. If you add a link, a wizard helps you specify the URL of the link.

✦ **Multiple paste options:** Many users create content in Microsoft Word. A Paste from Word button attempts to delete all the excess junk Word adds to a file and paste the content cleanly, which is a major lifesaver.

✦ **A plain source editor:** My favorite button on the WYSIWYG editor is the one that turns off the WYSIWYG features. The Source button displays the page as plain HTML/XHTML text. The automated features are nice, but I can usually build a page a lot faster and more accurately by hand. This feature is especially useful when the visual tools aren't doing what you want.

When you finish building your page, click the Save button to save the contents of the page.

Along the top of the editor is a series of icons: a house, a blue screen, a life ring, and a lock. Click the blue screen (which is the View icon) to open your new page and see it the way the user will see it. Figure 3-10 shows the results of my simple page.

The WYSIWYG page is the most commonly used page type (especially by nontechnical users) but it's not the only option. The standard edition of Website Baker also comes with a number of other default page types:

✦ **Code:** Interprets the page as PHP code. This is any easy way to enter any PHP code you wish, including database lookups. The code is interpreted as PHP, so if you want it to be HTML, you can just use a giant heredoc. Figure 3-11 shows a PHP snippet being written, and Figure 3-12 shows the results.

**Book VIII
Chapter 3**

Introducing Content
Management
Systems

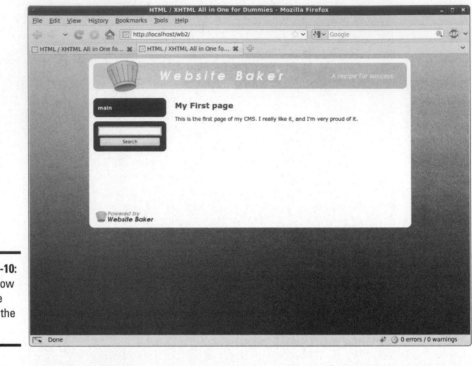

Figure 3-10:
This is how the page looks to the user.

Figure 3-11:
The code page allows you to write any PHP code you wish.

Figure 3-12:
How the
code page
looks to the
user.

✦ **Form:** Allows you to build a basic XHTML form without knowing any XHTML. The administrator can add all the normal form elements. Figure 3-13 shows the form editor in action. When the user enters form data, the content is automatically e-mailed to the administrator and stored in a database that can be retrieved via the CMS. This feature is one of the most important factors of a CMS because it's something that plain HTML Web sites simply can't do.

✦ **Menu Link:** This placeholder (it isn't really a page type) allows you to create a menu item that helps organize other pages. Use the parent attribute of a page to make it a child of a menu or an ordinary page. The menu structure adapts automatically.

✦ **News V3.5:** A blog feature that allows the user to write blog articles. I often use it for other things, such as sermon archives for church sites, specials of the week for commercial sites, and so on. A blog feature is good any time you're working with repetitive, dated material. You can add multiple blogs to the same site easily. Figure 3-14 shows the news page in action.

✦ **Wrapper:** This incredibly versatile page type allows you to do all kinds of interesting things. Essentially, it allows you to embed any page into the CMS. Figure 3-15 shows the wrapper used to embed a Google search into my site. The wrapper is handy when you want to access an external ordering or newsgroup system but keep within the visual structure of the CMS.

Book VIII
Chapter 3

Introducing Content
Management
Systems

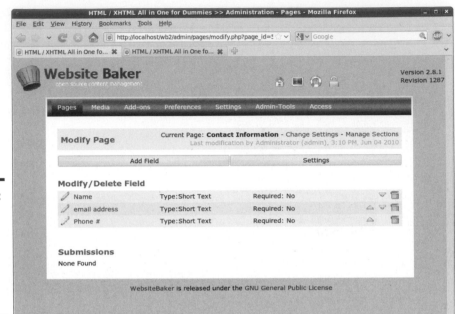

Figure 3-13:
The form editor simplifies creating forms and collecting form data.

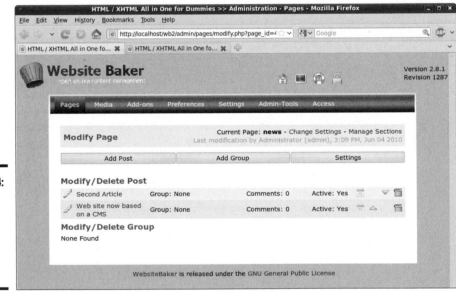

Figure 3-14:
The news page type allows you to build a blog-like document.

Figure 3-15:
Use the
wrapper
page type to
embed other
pages into
your system.

You are not limited to these page types. See the section "Adding new functionality" later in this chapter for information on how to add additional page types to your system.

Changing the template

One of the primary goals of a CMS is to separate the visual layout from the contents. So far, you've seen how to modify the contents, but you'll also want to change the appearance of the page. The visual settings of a site are all based on a *template* concept. You can easily overlay a new template onto the existing site without changing the contents at all.

1. **Log in as the administrator.**

Obviously, the administrator has the ability to change the template (although you can allow individual users to change their own templates).

2. **Go to the system menu.**

Templates are set in the system menu.

3. **Change template under Default Settings.**

Don't worry about the Backend Theme and Search Settings templates. It's best to leave these alone until you're a bit more experienced because they don't have a major impact on the user experience.

4. **Choose a template from the drop-down list.**

   All the templates installed in the system are available in a drop-down list. For this example, I chose the All CSS template (the default). See the section "Adding additional templates" for how to download and install templates that aren't already installed in the system.

5. **Preview the site with your new template in place.**

   Figure 3-16 shows the contents of the site with the All CSS template in place. The template essentially encapsulates core XHTML code and the CSS used to display each file.

Figure 3-16: The same site has a new look!

Adding additional templates

The standard installation of Website Baker includes only a few templates. Typically, you'll want to work with additional templates. Fortunately, there are hundreds of great templates available, and you can easily build your own. Here's how to add additional templates.

1. **Locate the template you want online.**

   A number of Web places offer great, free templates for Website Baker. My favorite is the Templates repository available at `http://www.web sitebaker2.org/template/pages/templates.php`. The templates in this archive are approved by the Website Baker community and meet minimum quality standards.

2. **Download a template or two that you like.**

   When browsing templates, remember that you will be able to modify them. If you don't like the particular colors or images, you can change them later. Save the downloaded Zip file somewhere on your local machine.

3. **Log in to Website Baker as admin.**

   Only the administrator can add new templates to the system.

4. **Navigate to the Templates page of the Add-ons section.**

   This is where you install and uninstall downloaded templates.

5. **Click the Browse button to locate the Zip file on your local system.**

   Load the entire Zip file containing the template onto the server.

6. **Click the Install button to begin the process.**

   You receive a notification when the installation is complete.

7. **Navigate to the Settings section.**

   Installing a template does not apply the template automatically.

8. **In Settings, apply the new template.**

   Specify the template to display from the drop-down list of templates.

9. **Preview your new look.**

   Use the Preview button (or reload the currently showing version of the CMS) to see the new look. Figure 3-17 shows my site with the Multiflex-3 template installed.

Figure 3-17: You can install any template onto your existing system.

The Multiflex-3 template is one of the most commonly used templates on the Internet. The original design (www.oswd.org/design/preview/id/3626) was built with plain XHTML/CSS implementation in mind but has been ported to nearly every CMS including Website Baker. The design is a solid and very flexible starting place. I've used it as the foundation of dozens of sites. Once you get to know it, you'll recognize it all over the place.

Adding new functionality

In addition to custom templates, you can add modules to your system. A module is a new page type that adds additional functionality. Dozens of add-ons are available at the Website Baker AMASP (All Modules and Snippets Project) at www.websitebakers.com.

The add-on modules include many new types of functionality, including online shopping modules, image galleries, event calendars, and many more. In addition to full-fledged modules, the AMASP also includes PHP snippets you can copy into your code for advanced functionality and *droplets,* which are small, self-contained PHP modules to add features to your site. It's probably best you start with full modules because they require the least effort to get working. As you become more proficient with Website Baker, you'll want to investigate how to add more features.

Many of my clients like to have image galleries. I use them for a number of things, including a simple form of an online catalog and for viewing sample work for craft or artist sites. Here's how to add a basic but full-featured image gallery:

1. **Find a module you wish to test.**

   Go to the AMASP site and browse the various modules until you find one you like; there's about a dozen. For this example, I'm looking at the (unimaginatively named) Image Gallery module. This one works very well, looks pretty good, and is very easy for my clients to use, so I almost always install it on commercial sites.

2. **Download the module.**

   Modules are installed much like templates. Download the module, which is usually PHP and HTML code in a Zip file, and then save the Zip file somewhere on your local file system.

3. **Log in as admin.**

   As usual, anything that involves changing the site requires administrator access.

4. **Navigate to the Add-ons section.**

   You add modules in the same section you add templates; that is, the Modules page of the Add-ons section.

5. Browse to find the Zip file you downloaded.

Click the Browse button to look on your local system for the Zip file containing the module. Click the Install button when you locate the file. Website Baker uploads the module to the server and places the files in the correct location.

6. A new page type will appear.

When you go to the Pages section, you see a new type of page. In this case, you can now add image galleries.

Building Custom Themes

Website Baker is an outstanding way to build a complex and fully featured Web site easily and quickly. With over a hundred templates, you're bound to find something you like. However, you almost never find something *exactly* the way you want it. This is especially important if you're developing for somebody else. Usually, you find a template that is close, but you still need to modify the colors and images. For that reason, it's important to understand the general structure of a Website Baker template and how to make your own.

Starting with a prebuilt template

Although it's possible to build a Website Baker template from scratch, it's generally not a good idea. It's much smarter to begin with a template that's close and add those features you need to make it your own. That way the general structure is already proven, and you only need to customize it to your specifications.

1. Find a starting template you like.

Often I have clients look over the Templates repository (`www.website baker2.org/template/pages/templates.php`) and tell me their favorite three templates. I also like to have them explain what they like or dislike about each template. I tell them we can change colors or banner graphics in a template, so to focus more on the general look and feel.

If you don't have another place to start, I like the templates built into the Website Baker core (especially All CSS and Round). Blank Template is especially designed for customizing. I often build commercial sites based on Multiflex-3 because it's well known throughout the Web community and has some great features.

2. Install the template on your local system.

It's much easier to work with a template on your local system than on a remote server.

3. Locate the local copy of the template.

Normally, templates are stored in the `wb/templates` directory of your server. Each template will have its own folder.

4. **Copy the folder of the template you want to modify.**

   It's generally smarter to work with a copy rather than the original. Paste the copied folder in the templates directory.

5. **Rename the new folder to reflect your new template name.**

   Your new template needs a different name than the original template.

At this point, you have a copy of the original template, but this copy will not be reflected in the CMS yet. You need to make a few changes before the new template is available. Before you do that, take a look at the file structure of a typical Website Baker template. Figure 3-18 shows my copy of the Multiflex-3 template.

Figure 3-18: Typical file structure for Website Baker templates.

One of the reasons I like Website Baker so much is how relatively simple the template structure is compared to other CMSs. The directory contains a relatively small number of files:

✦ `index.php`: This PHP file is the basic file that's used as the foundation of every page in the system. It's essentially an XHTML page with a few special PHP functions built in. You can edit any of the XHTML you wish, and the resulting changes will be reflected in every page of the site.

- ✦ **info.php:** This simple PHP file contains a number of variables used to control the overall behavior of the template. You'll make a few changes in this file to give your template an official name.

- ✦ **layout_setup.css:** This CSS file describes the CSS used for the overall page design. You can change the contents of this CSS file to change font colors or other big-picture CSS.

- ✦ **layout_text.css:** This CSS file is used to define the styles of the various text elements in the site. If you're looking for a class that isn't defined in layout_setup.css, you may find it here. *Note:* The names of the CSS files may change in other templates, but there will be at least one CSS file.

- ✦ **editor.css:** This file is used to modify the internal WYSIWYG editor. It describes how various elements are displayed in the editor.

- ✦ **images directory:** Often a template will include a number of images. These are stored in a subdirectory for convenience. You may need to change some of these images to create the look you're going for.

Some templates are more complex, some less so. Really, you can have as many or as few files as you want. You'll always need to have index.php and info.php. You'll almost always have at least one CSS page. You can have anything else you wish in the template, but nothing else is absolutely necessary.

Changing the info.php file

The info.php file contains a few PHP variables. You can modify these variables to identify this template as your own. You must change the template name to a unique value, and you can also change such variables as the developer name and version number. I typically claim any substantial changes I make to a template, but I always give credit to the original developer. It's great to stand on the shoulders of giants, and you should give them their due in the documentation. Here's the info.php file after I made a few changes:

```
<?php

/*

Website Baker Project <http://www.websitebaker.org/>
Copyright (C) 2004 2006, Ryan Djurovich

Website Baker is free software; you can redistribute it and/or modify
it under the terms of the GNU General Public License as published by
the Free Software Foundation; either version 2 of the License, or
(at your option) any later version.

Website Baker is distributed in the hope that it will be useful,
but WITHOUT ANY WARRANTY; without even the implied warranty of
```

```
MERCHANTABILITY or FITNESS FOR A PARTICULAR PURPOSE.  See the
GNU General Public License for more details.

You should have received a copy of the GNU General Public License
along with Website Baker; if not, write to the Free Software
Foundation, Inc., 59 Temple Place, Suite 330, Boston, MA  02111-1307   USA

*/


$template_directory = 'aio';
$template_name = 'aio';
$template_version = '1.1';
$template_platform = '2.x';
$template_author = 'Andy Harris, from Erik Coenjaerts (WB port)';
$template_license = '<a href="http://www.1234.info/webtemplates/">Open Source</
    a>';
$template_description = 'Original design from <a href="http://www.1234.info/
    webtemplates/">1234.info</a>. Ported to Website Baker by <a href="http://
    www.coenjaerts.com">Erik Coenjaerts</a>.';
$menu[1]='Main Menu';
$menu[2]='Top Menu';
$menu[3]='Extra Menu';
$block[2]='Sidebar';
$block[3]='News';

?>
```

Note that the template has the potential for three different types of menus and three blocks of information. ($block[1] is the main content block and is available by default.)

Modifying index.php

For the most part, you can leave index.php alone. However, there are a few modifications you might make. If you look over the file, it's basically plain HTML/XHTML with a few PHP functions thrown in. Generally, you can change the HTML code without any worries, but be more careful about the PHP code. The PHP code tends to call special functions defined in the Website Baker code base. Here are the functions and variables you're likely to run across:

✦ **TEMPLATE_DIR:** This constant contains the template directory. Use it to make links to the template directory.

✦ **WEBSITE_TITLE:** Use this constant to display the Web site name anywhere in your template.

✦ **PAGE_TITLE:** The title of the current page as defined in the menu.

✦ **WEBSITE_HEADER:** This constant displays the header defined in the admin panel.

✦ **show_menu(*menuID*):** This is a powerhouse of a function. It analyzes your site structure and uses it to build a navigation structure. It takes a parameter, which is the level of menu. (Typically the left menu is level 1 and the top menu is level 2, but this can be changed.) *Note:* Some templates use the more advanced show_menu_2() function, which has additional parameters, like the ability to define template code for how the menu displays.

✦ **page_content(*blockID*):** This function is used to display content for the current page. The parameter describes which block of content should display. Use 1 for the main page content, 2 for block 2, and so on.

✦ **page_footer():** Display the page footer identified in the admin panel.

Website Baker features many more constants and functions, but these are the basic ones used in nearly all templates. See the online documentation at www.websitebaker2.org for complete documentation. Other CMS systems use the same idea (XHTML templates with PHP functions embedded), but of course the function names are a bit different in a different CMS.

You may want to make other modifications of the default template. For example, the Multiflex-3 template includes multilanguage support and a large number of different "post it note" features. I generally remove the multilanguage content (because I only speak one language) and change all the "post it notes" to use the same CSS style (or remove them all).

Modifying the CSS files

Of course, the most powerful way to change the appearance of your pages is to modify the CSS files. Here's how:

1. **Identify the class you want to modify.**

   This can be surprisingly difficult in a system you didn't create. Use the Inspect feature of the Firebug extension to quickly identify which styles act on a particular element and what its class hierarchy is.

2. **Find the class definition in the CSS sheets.**

   Note that a system may have more than one CSS file, so find the one containing the class information you're interested in.

3. **Make incremental changes.**

   Make small changes and test frequently.

4. **Test on a local server.**

   You can make changes directly on the files in your local server. Just reload the page after every change to make sure the changes are being reflected. Of course, you need to have the template installed in your system.

Packaging your template

A template is nothing more than a set of PHP and CSS files (and perhaps some images and other files). It's pretty easy to port a template for installation. Just follow these steps:

1. **Create a stable version of the template.**

It doesn't have to be perfect before you package it, but at a minimum you need to change the `info.php` page to reflect the new template's name.

2. **Package the entire directory into a Zip file.**

Use a utility like IZArc for Windows or the Zip utility that comes installed with Linux or Mac. Save the Zip file with the same name as your template. *Note:* Don't include the template directory itself in the template; just include any contents of that directory (including subdirectories, if you have them).

3. **Install the template into your copy of Website Baker.**

Install your template the way you do any other template.

Chapter 4: Editing Graphics

In This Chapter

✔ **Introducing Gimp**

✔ **Managing the main tools**

✔ **Selecting image elements**

✔ **Working with layers**

✔ **Understanding filters**

✔ **Creating a tiling background**

✔ **Building banner images**

X HTML and CSS are powerful tools, but sometimes you still need to use a graphical editor to get the look you want. In this chapter you learn to use Gimp, a free and powerful graphic editor.

Using a Graphic Editor

You'll find using a graphical editor handy for a number of tasks:

✦ **Modifying an image:** The obvious use of a graphical tool is to modify or create an image that will be used on your Web page. This could involve changing the image size, correcting the color balance, or cropping the image.

✦ **Preparing a background image:** As I discuss in Book II, Chapter 4, background images can be distracting if you aren't careful. Making a lower contrast image (either lighter or darker than normal) might make sense so the text is easier to read. You might also want to prepare a tiled background.

✦ **Building banners:** Many Web sites include a special banner image that's prominent on every page. The banner image usually has a very specific size requirement.

✦ **Modifying existing graphics:** You might be modifying a template from the jQuery UI project (see Book VII, Chapter 4) or from a CMS (see Chapter 3 in this minibook). In both cases, you often have images that are close to, but not exactly, what you need.

✦ **Changing colors:** Frequently, you have the right pattern, but not the right colors. Modifying colors with a modern graphical tool is surprisingly easy.

Choosing an editor

Fortunately, great programs that make all these tasks quite easy to perform are available. Raster-based graphics editors are designed to solve exactly this type of problem and many more. A number of important graphics tools are used in Web development:

✦ **Adobe Photoshop:** The industry standard for Web graphics, and indeed for all digital imagery, Photoshop is powerful and capable but quite expensive. A slightly cheaper and less powerful version called Adobe Photoshop Elements is available.

✦ **Adobe Fireworks:** Designed specifically for Web developers, Fireworks features the ability to slice an image to make a graphical Web page from an image — and it's relatively inexpensive.

✦ **Windows Paint:** This simple image editor is available in all versions of Microsoft Windows. Although easy to use and already available to Windows users, Paint is relatively limited. It only supports a few image formats and doesn't have full support for transparent images or layers.

✦ **Paint.net:** A group of computer science students decided to create an improvement to Microsoft Paint that evolved into a very robust image-editing program. It is free (although, technically, not open source) and has all the features you might need for editing Web images. However, the primary version is available only for Windows.

✦ **Gimp:** A popular alternative to Photoshop, Gimp has all the features you might need for Web image editing. It is completely free, open source, and available for all major operating systems. For these reasons, I use Gimp throughout this chapter (and indeed throughout the book — nearly every graphic was created using Gimp).

People are passionate about their graphics programs. If you love Photoshop, you might find the Gimp interface strange and unfamiliar. I think learning how Gimp works is worth the time, but if you prefer, you can download GimpShop, a version of Gimp modified to use the same menus and keyboard shortcuts as Photoshop.

Note that in this list I'm only considering full-blown graphical editors. I describe image manipulation programs, such as IrfanView and XnView (which are simpler and have fewer features), in Book II, Chapter 4.

Introducing Gimp

If you haven't already installed Gimp, get a recent copy from this book's CD-ROM or www.gimp.org. Install the program and take a look at it. The Gimp interface's multiple windows are shown Figure 4-1.

Figure 4-1:
Gimp uses
a multiple
window
model.

 I have the Change Foreground Color dialog open in Figure 4-1, and I simply double-clicked on the foreground color in the main toolbox to open this dialog. Gimp tends to open a lot of dialogs, which might bother some people. Also, I want to illustrate how powerful the color chooser is. Like most features in Gimp, it has a lot of options.

The Toolbox is Gimp's main control panel. It manages all the tools you use to create images. Gimp also creates an image window, which contains the menu elements, but no image (by default). You can load an image into the Image window or create a new image.

Gimp sure seems cluttered . . .

Gimp doesn't reside in a single window like most programs. Instead, it uses a number of windows. Some find this jarring, but once you get used to it, this can be a useful feature. You can make any window as large or as small as you wish and combine windows to get less screen clutter. I configure Gimp in a way that combines the most common windows into the Toolbox, so I have one window showing the Toolbox and most of the dialogs and a separate window showing each picture I'm working on.

If you click the Configure Tab button (a small arrow at the top right of the tabs section), you can add new tabs to the main Toolbox window. I normally add my favorite tools (Navigation, Layers, Tool Options, and Brushes) to the Toolbox so the features are readily available and appear here instead of in separate windows.

**Book VIII
Chapter 4**

Editing Graphics

Creating an image

You choose the File⇨New menu command to create a new image. After you specify the size of your image, a new, blank image appears, as shown in Figure 4-2.

Figure 4-2: It's easy to create a new, blank image.

Working with existing images

It's very common in Web development to work with images that already exist. For example, I've built a couple of sites for office supply companies. It's nice to sprinkle the site with colorful images of staplers, Post-it notes, and the like. The question is, how do you get these graphics? If you're a skilled photographer or artist, you can create them yourself, but this takes more time and talent than I typically have. You could reuse images you find on the Web, but this is not respectful of these elements' owners.

The best solution is to use an image-supply site like www.freedigitalphotos. net or www.istockphoto.com. Be sure to search for royalty-free artwork, and check the license to ensure you can use and modify the work. I'm a big fan of stock art. Typically,

I can find a dozen images to spruce up a site for less than $20, and I have the satisfaction of knowing I'm completely legal. Often, stock art is designed for both print and digital use. Generally, you can purchase the smallest size for digital work, which is economical and perfectly fine for use on the Web. (**Note:** Monitors have much less resolution than printed paper, so you can get away with a smaller image.)

To reuse an image in a legitimate way, consider the following:

✔ **Acknowledge the source:** Generally, this acknowledgment isn't necessary for images you purchase, but it is polite if you receive an image free. You can place the acknowledgment in the source code.

✔ **Get permission if needed:** It's always best to get permission from the original developer. Sometimes this isn't possible or necessary, but you should always try.

✔ **Make the image your own:** Do something to modify the image. If it's a stock photo, this isn't necessary, but you might want to change the colors, move things around, and make the image fit the theme of your project a little better.

Of course, you can also load an existing image into Gimp. Gimp accepts all major image formats (and dozens more with optional plugins). Use the File➪Open menu command to open an image, or simply drag an image file onto the Gimp Toolbox.

Painting tools

Gimp includes a number of useful tools to create or modify an image. Figure 4-3 shows a few of these tools.

✦ **Pencil:** The Pencil tool is the standard drawing tool. It draws hard edges in the exact shape of the pen. You can choose from many pen shapes in the tool options panel (described in the next section).

✦ **Paintbrush:** The Paintbrush tool is similar to the Pencil tool, but it uses a technique called *anti-aliasing* to make smoother edges. Like the Pencil tool, the Brush tool can use many different pen shapes.

✦ **Eraser:** The Eraser tool is used to remove color from a drawing. If the current layer has transparency enabled, the eraser tool makes things transparent. If transparency is not turned on, the Eraser tool "draws" in the background color.

✦ **Airbrush:** The Airbrush tool allows you to paint with a virtual airbrush. You can modify the flow and size of the paint. This tool is especially effective with a pressure-sensitive drawing tablet.

✦ **Ink:** The Ink tool simulates a calligraphy brush. The speed of drawing indicates the width of the stroke. It seems quite realistic, because everything I draw with it looks just as bad as what I create when I try real calligraphy.

✦ **Clone:** The powerful Clone tool allows you to grab content from one part of an image and copy it to another part of the image. This tool is often used in photo retouching to remove scars and blemishes.

✦ **Fill:** The Fill tool is used to fill an area with a color or pattern. It has multiple options that allow you to pick the pattern, the color, and the method of filling. (You can fill the current selection or all areas with the same color, for example.)

✦ **Blend:** This Blend tool allows you to fill an area with color patterns, similar to the Fill tool. There are numerous options that allow you to determine what pattern is used and how it is distributed. (Many programs call this the Gradient tool.)

Figure 4-3: These tools are used to draw or modify an image.

A complex program like Gimp deserves (and has) entire books written about it. There's no way I can describe everything in this brief introductory chapter. Still, this should give you an indication of what you can do. Check the many excellent user tutorials at www.gimp.org/tutorials and the manual at www.gimp.org/docs.

Selection tools

Often, you'll be working on specific parts of an image. It's critical to have tools to help you grab a particular part of an image and work with it in isolation. Gimp (like any high-quality graphics tool) has a number of useful selection tools. Figure 4-4 shows where they are in the Toolbox.

✦ **Rectangle Select:** The Rectangle Select tool is used to (wait for it . . .) select rectangles. Rectangle selections are easy, and they're pretty common, so this is a good, basic selection tool.

✦ **Ellipse Select:** The Ellipse Select tool is like the Rectangle Select tool, but (you're catching on here) it selects ellipses. You can set the aspect ratio to 1:1 to select perfect circles.

✦ **Free Select:** Also called the Lasso tool, the Free Select tool allows you to draw a selection by hand. It takes an incredibly steady hand to use well, so it's usually only used for rough selections which are fine-tuned using other techniques.

✦ **Magic Select:** Also called the Fuzzy Select, the Magic Wand tool allows you to grab contiguous sections of similar colors. It's handy when you have a large section of a single color that you want to select. (You might want to select a white background and replace it with a pattern, for example.) Hold down the Shift key and make further selections if you want to select more than one color.

✦ **Select by Color:** Similar to the Fuzzy Select tool, the Select by Color tool grabs all the pixels of a chosen color, whether they're touching the selected pixel or not, and removes them. (It's ideal for use with a green screen, for example.)

✦ **Scissors Select:** The Scissors Select tool uses image-processing techniques to automatically select part of an image. Click along the edge of an element you want to select, and (if you're lucky) the selection will follow the edge. This works fine for high-contrast elements, but conditions have to be perfect.

✦ **Foreground Select:** The Foreground Select tool is a multipass tool that simplifies pulling part of an image from the rest. On the first pass, use the Lasso tool to choose the general part of the image you want to select. The image will show a selection mask with selected parts in white and nonselected parts blue. Click the colors you want to keep and then press Enter to commit the selection.

✦ **Bezier Select:** The Bezier Select tool is my favorite. Click an image to create a general outline of the selection. (You're actually making a *Bezier path,* which uses math formulas to draw a curved shape.) Modify the path until it's exactly how you want it and then you can convert it to a selection.

Magic Wand (Fuzzy)

Free (Lasso)   Select by color

Rectangle   Foreground

Bezier   Ellipse   Scissors

Figure 4-4:
These tools
are used for
selecting
parts of an
image.

Modification tools

A number of tools are used to modify parts of an image. Figure 4-5 illustrates the main modification tools:

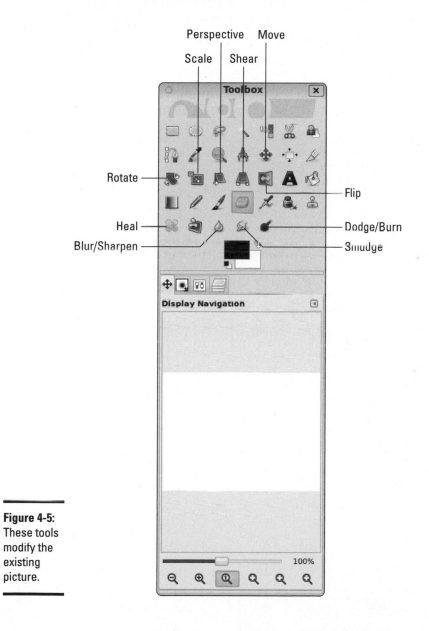

Figure 4-5:
These tools modify the existing picture.

✦ **Move:** This tool allows you to move a selection, a layer, or some other element.

✦ **Rotate, Scale, Shear, Perspective, and Flip:** These tools all apply trans-formations to a selection. Use them to rotate or resize a part of your image, or to change the perspective of a section so it appears to be on an angled surface, for example.

✦ **Heal:** This tool takes a sample area and applies it to other parts of an image (much like the Clone tool). It is often used in photo retouching to give skin a clean, unblemished look. It's great for fixing the rectangular artifacts that often appear in JPG images.

✦ **Blur/Sharpen:** This tool is used to blur (reduce contrast) or sharpen (increase contrast) a small part of the image selectively with the current pen. This tool is often used for quick touch-ups to remove scratches or other blemishes.

✦ **Smudge:** This allows you to push a color into adjacent pixels to clean up an image. I frequently use this tool when trying to build a tiled back-ground to help line pixels up in a seamless way.

✦ **Dodge/Burn:** This tool is named after a photography darkroom tool. It's used to darken or lighten parts of an image and to remove unwanted shadows.

Managing tool options

Most tools have options available. For example, when you choose the Pencil or Brush tool, you can select which brush tip to use. When you use the Fill tool, you can determine whether the tool fills with the current color or the current selection. You can also determine whether the tool fills with a color or a pattern.

You can see the Tool Options dialog for any tool by double-clicking the tool in the Toolbox. Generally, I dock the Tool Options dialog to the main Toolbox tabs because it's so frequently used.

Utilities

Gimp also comes with a number of handy utilities. The tools highlighted in Figure 4-6 have a variety of uses:

✦ **Color Selector:** The two overlapping rectangles show the current fore-ground and background color. Click one of the rectangles to pick a new color to work with. You can choose colors in a number of ways, using RGB and HSV schemes, as well as prefilled color palettes and a very cool watercolor tool.

✦ **Color Picker:** Allows you to determine the RGB value of any pixel on the image and pick that color as the current drawing color. It's very handy when you want to match colors precisely.

Perspective Clone   Color Selector

Color Picker   Measure   Align

Zoom   Move   Crop

Figure 4-6:
These tools
often come
in handy.

✦ **Zoom:** Allows you to quickly zoom in and out of your image. Drag around an area, and the selected area will fill the entire window. Hold down the Ctrl key while dragging to zoom out. Hold the center mouse button (often also the scroll wheel) to pan your zoomed-in view in any direction. It's very helpful to zoom in close when you're doing detail work.

✦ **Measure:** Drag the mouse on an image, and you can find the distance and angle between any two points. The Move tool is useful for precise placement.

✦ **Move:** Allows you to move a selection or layer.

✦ **Align:** The Align tool simplifies lining up various elements with each other.

✦ **Crop:** Used to crop unwanted border areas from an image.

✦ **Text:** Adds editable text to the image. The Text tool works with layers, so check the upcoming "Understanding Layers" section for more detail.

✦ **Perspective Clone:** This tool combines the Perspective tool and the Clone tool. Although it's cool, the applications are a bit rare, so I don't use it often in Web development.

Understanding Layers

Gimp has an astonishing variety of tools, but most of the interesting things you can do with a raster graphics tool involve a concept called *layers*. Layers are really pretty simple: Imagine the old animated movies (before digital animation was possible). Painters would create a large background, but the characters were drawn on transparent sheets (called *cels* in animation). A single frame of an animation might contain a single opaque background with a large number of mainly transparent layers on top. Each layer could be manipulated individually, providing a great deal of flexibility.

Any high-end graphics editor will support some form of layer mechanism. (In fact, support for layers is a primary differentiator between basic and advanced graphics tools.) Figure 4-7 shows the Layers panel in Gimp.

The primary area of the Layers panel is the window, showing a stack of layers. The background is on the bottom of the stack, and any other layers are on top. Anything on an upper layer obscures a lower layer. Imagine a camera at the top of the stack pointing down at the stack of layers. If a higher layer has transparency (as it usually does) the lower layer will show through any transparent pixels.

The Opacity slider in the Layers panel allows you to adjust the overall transparency of the layer. This can be useful for quickly lightening or darkening a layer, and for other effects, such as shadows.

Only one layer is active at a time. The current layer is highlighted in the window at the bottom of the Layers panel. Most operations will occur on the active layer only. Click a layer in the layers window to make that layer active.

Figure 4-7:
The Layers
panel allows
you to
manipulate
layers.

Be sure you know what layer is active. Many times I try to draw on a layer and nothing happens. I then typically scribble harder, thinking that will help. Almost always when this happens, I've selected the wrong layer and made a big mess somewhere. It's possible (and common) to have a layer active which is not visible. Fortunately, the Undo command (Ctrl+Z) is quite powerful. If in doubt, keep the Layers panel visible so you can tell what layer is active.

Each layer has two icons next to it that you can activate. The eye icon toggles the layer's visibility. The link icon allows you to link two or more layers together. Each layer also has a name. You can double-click the layer name to change it. This is especially useful when you have a complex image with many layers.

The bottom of the layers panel has the following buttons to help you manage various layers:

✦ **New Layer:** This button creates a new layer. The default type is transparent, but you can also choose to have the layer appear in the foreground or background color.

✦ **Up and down buttons:** Allow you to move a layer up or down in the stack. The position of a layer in the stack is important because higher layers have precedence.

✦ **Duplicate Layer:** Makes a copy of the currently active layer. If you're modifying a layer, working on a duplicate is a great idea because if you mess up, you still have a backup.

✦ **Anchor:** When you copy and paste a part of an image, the pasted segment is placed into a temporary layer. Use the anchor button to nail down the selection to the current layer.

✦ **Delete:** Allows you to delete the currently active layer. Be careful you delete the correct layer.

Introducing Filters

Digital editors include a number of other very useful tools. Generally, these tools apply mathematical filters to an image to change the image in some way. The standard installation of Gimp comes with dozens of filters, but here are a few most common to Web developers:

✦ **Blur filters:** Blur filters reduce the contrast between adjacent pixels to make the image less defined, and can often be used to hide imperfections or scratches. The most common blur is Gaussian blur, but there are many others, including Motion blur, which simulates the blur seen in a slow camera taking a picture of something moving quickly.

✦ **Unsharp mask:** A class of filters called *sharpen* filters are the opposite of blur filters. They increase contrast between adjacent pixels. I don't know why the sharpen filter is called the "Unsharp mask," but it is. *Note:* There is no "enhance" filter like the ones so common on crime dramas. Sadly, you can't just "zoom and enhance" endlessly to see the killer's eye color on the reflection of a spoon.

✦ **Colorize:** This marvelous tool allows you to keep the contrast of a layer and change the color, which can be perfect for changing the color of hair, eyes, or clothing.

✦ **Brightness/Contrast:** Lets you adjust the brightness (overall value) and contrast of a particular layer.

✦ **Color balance:** Allows you to adjust the relative amounts of red, green, and blue in a layer, which can be used to improve pictures with poor lighting.

Solving Common Web Graphics Problems

Gimp, and tools like it, can be used in many ways. The rest of this chapter is a cookbook of sorts, showing how to build a number of graphics commonly used in Web development.

Changing a color

Frequently, you'll have an image that's good, but not the right color. For example, you may want to change the color of a person's clothing, or make part of a logo fit the color scheme of the rest of your site. Gimp makes performing this effect quite easy:

1. **Load your starting image into Gimp and make any other adaptations you wish to the original image.**

2. **Use the Fuzzy Select tool to select the part you want to modify.**

   You might need to use the Shift key to add several variants of the color to the selection.

3. **Use the Copy command (Ctrl+C) to copy the section of the image you just selected.**

4. **Use the Paste command (Ctrl+V) to paste the selected area into a new layer.**

   The pasted area goes into a new "pseudo-layer" by default. In the Layers panel you'll see a layer called Floating Selection – Pasted Layer. Click the New Layer button and you'll create a new layer containing only the section you need.

5. **Colorize the new layer by applying the Colorize filter (Colors⇒Colorize).**

   Play with the color sliders until you get the color you want. Because you made the changes on a new layer, you can always remove or hide the layer to return to the original. (Or have several different color layers so you can play with various options.)

Figure 4-8 shows an example of this technique using an image of a glass of orange juice by Graur Razvan Ionut I found at FreeDigitalPhotos.net. The original image contained only the picture of orange juice, but I duplicated the juice glass and changed the color of the second glass to look like coffee. Of course you'll need to see this effect online or on the CD-ROM, because the color change will not be apparent in this black-and-white book.

Figure 4-8:
You can use the Colorize filter to change orange juice into coffee.

Building a banner graphic

Nearly every commercial Web site has a *banner graphic* — a special graphic, usually with a set size (900 x 100 is common), that appears on every page. Normally, if you're modifying a CSS template, you have a default banner graphic. You'll want to copy this graphic in order to start with the right size and shape.

You can build a banner many ways, but here's a simple technique you can modify (Figure 4-9 shows the banner's progression):

Figure 4-9: The steps for building a banner.

1. **Load or create the basic shape.**

   If you have a starting graphic to use, load it into Gimp. If not, create a new image of the size you need. Mine is 100 pixels tall by 900 pixels wide.

2. **Create a plasma background.**

   Use the Plasma filter (Filters⇨Render⇨Clouds⇨Plasma) to create a semi-random pattern. Use the New Seed and Turbulence buttons to change the overall feel. Don't worry about the colors; you remove them in the next step.

3. **After the plasma background is in place, use the Colorize filter to apply a color to the background.**

   Pick a color consistent with your theme. For this example, go for a lighter color because you're using shadows, which require a light background. Use the Lightness slider to make a relatively light color. (I'm going for a cloudy sky look, so I set Hue to 215, Saturation to 100, and Lightness to 75.)

4. Create a text layer using the Text tool.

Text in a graphic should be large and bold. The Text tool automatically creates a new layer. After you type your text, specify the font and size.

5. Duplicate the text layer.

In the Layers panel, make a copy of the text layer. Select the lower of the two text layers (which will become a shadow).

6. Blur the shadow.

With the shadow layer selected, apply the Gaussian blur (Filters⇨Blur⇨ Gaussian Blur).

7. Move the shadow.

Use the Move tool to move the relative positions of the text and the shadow. Typically, users expect a shadow to be slightly lower and right of the text (simulating light coming from the top left). The farther the shadow is from the text, the higher the text appears to be floating.

8. Make the shadow semitransparent.

With the shadow layer still selected, adjust the Opacity slider to about 50%. This will make the shadows less pronounced allow part of the background to appear through the shadow layer.

9. Season to taste; make additions based on your needs.

For example, one client wanted a picture of his sign to appear on the banner. I took a photo of the sign, brought it in as a layer, cleaned it up, and rotated and scaled the image until it fit in place.

10. Save in a reusable format.

The native format for images in Gimp is XCF. (I have no clue what XCF stands for, but every time I try to make up an acronym, it comes out dirty. There must be something wrong with me.) XCF stores everything — layers, settings, and all. If you need to modify the banner later (and you will), you'll have a good version to work from.

Choose File⇨Save As to save the file. If you specify the .xcf extension, Gimp automatically saves in the full format.

11. Export to a Web-friendly format.

Generally, I save banner graphics as PNG or GIF files. (Gimp supports both formats.) I prefer PNG unless the bottom layer has transparency (because some browsers still don't support the advanced transparency features of the PNG format). Do not save images containing text in JPG format. The JPG compression scheme is notorious for adding artifacts to text.

Normally, when you save to another format, a dialog box of options appears. If in doubt, go with the default values.

Figure 4-10 shows the final banner image. I included the XCF and PNG files on the CD-ROM and the Web site. Feel free to open my files in Gimp and experiment.

Figure 4-10:
This is a
simple but
reasonably
cool banner.

Building a tiled background

Often, you want a background image to cover the entire page. This can be harder than it seems because you don't know how large the page will be in the user's browser. Worse, large images can take a huge amount of space and slow down the user's experience. The common solution is to use a tiled image that's designed to repeat in the background. Gimp has some very useful tools for building tiled images.

Recall that the `background-repeat` CSS property allows you to specify how a background repeats. The default setting repeats the background infinitely in both the X and Y axes. You can also set the background to repeat horizontally (`repeat-x`), vertically (`repeat-y`), or not at all (`no-repeat`).

The goal of a tiled background is to make a relatively small graphic fill the entire page and look like a larger image. The secret is to create the image so it's difficult to see where the image repeats. Here's one way to make a tiled background in Gimp (Figure 4-11 shows the background's progression). Of course, you can adapt this technique for your own purposes.

Figure 4-11:
Building
a tiled
background
image.

1. **Create a new image.**

   The size of your image is important. Smaller images are much more efficient to download, but the pattern is much more obvious. Start with 256 by 256 pixels.

2. **Build a random pattern.**

   You can use the Plasma filter technique described in the previous section or try a similar technique by choosing Filters➪Render➪Clouds➪ Difference Clouds. The Difference Clouds filter creates a grayscale image but with a number of interesting options. The Tileable option creates a pattern that's ready to tile. Play with these options until you get something interesting.

3. **Adjust the contrast.**

   For the best effect, you want a relatively even distribution of values from light to dark. The easiest way to do this is through the automatic normalization tool (Colors➪Auto➪Normalize).

4. **Pick a gradient.**

   You'll add colors to your pattern using a technique called *gradient mapping*. Use the Gradient dialog (Windows➪Dockable Dialogs➪Gradients) to pick a gradient. Darker colors on your image map to colors on the left of the gradient, and lighter colors map to the left. You can adjust colors, so don't worry if the colors aren't exactly what you want. (If you want, you can make your own gradient with the gradient editor by clicking the Gradient dialog's New Gradient button.)

5. **Use the Gradient Map tool (Colors➪Map➪Gradient Map) to map the colors of the gradient to your cloud pattern.**

6. **Offset the image to check for tiling.**

   The easiest way to see whether the image tiles well is to offset the image. This puts the edges in the center so you can see how the image will look when multiple copies are next to each other. Open the Offset dialog by choosing Layer➪Transform➪Offset. The Offset dialog has a handy x/2, y/2 button. Click the button to see how your image looks.

7. **Clean the image if necessary.**

   If you chose the Tileable option when you built the cloud image, the new image will look fine. If not, you may have some visible seams. Use the Smudge and Clone tools to clean up these seams if necessary. Apply the Offset tool a second time to check whether your seams look good.

8. **Apply filters to get the effect you want.**

   You may want to colorize your image or blur it a bit to cover any artifacts of your cleanup. Remember that background images should be extremely dark or extremely light with very low contrast if you want readable text.

**Book VIII
Chapter 4**

Editing Graphics

9. **Test the image by saving the image in XCF format and a Web-friendly format (like PNG), build a simple page using the image as a background, and load the page into your browser to ensure it tiles the way you expect.**

Figure 4-12 shows a sample page containing my tiled image as the background.

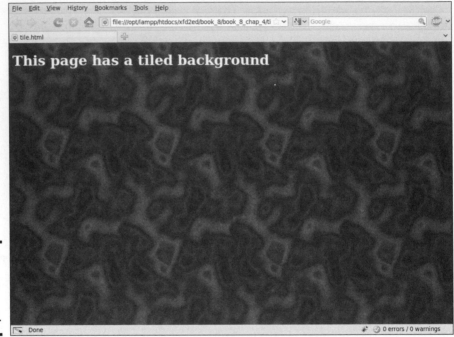

Figure 4-12:
This page features my new tiled background.

Chapter 5: Taking Control of Content

In This Chapter

✓ Approximating CMS with server-side includes (SSI)

✓ Reviewing client-side includes using AJAX

✓ Using PHP includes to build a basic CMS-style system

✓ Building a data-based CMS

✓ Creating a form for modifying content

Commercial sites today combine many skills and tools: XHTML, CSS, JavaScript, AJAX, databases, and PHP. This book covers many of these techniques. In this chapter you combine all these techniques to build your own content management systems. Some are very simple to build, and some are quite sophisticated.

Building a "Poor Man's CMS" with Your Own Code

The benefits of using a CMS are very real, but you may not want to make the commitment to a full-blown CMS. For one thing, you have to learn each CMS's particular way of doing things, and most CMSs force you into a particular mindset. For example, you think differently about pages in Drupal than you do in Website Baker (both described in Chapter 3 of this minibook). You can still get some of the benefits of a CMS with some simpler development tricks, as described in the following sections.

The examples in this chapter build on information from throughout the entire book. All of the CMSs (and pseudo-CMSs) built in this chapter use the design developed in Chapter 2 of this minibook.

Using Server-Side Includes (SSIs)

Web developers have long used the simple SSI (Server-Side Include) trick as a quick and easy way to manage content. It involves breaking the code into smaller code segments and a framework that can be copied. For example, Figure 5-1 shows a variation of the Web site developed in Chapter 2 of this minibook.

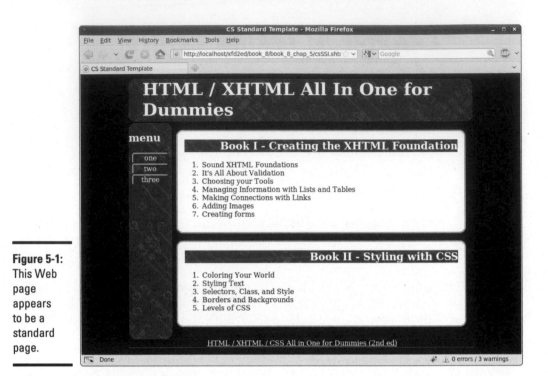

Figure 5-1:
This Web
page
appears
to be a
standard
page.

Even if you view the source code in the browser, you don't find anything
unusual about the page.

However, if you look at the code in a text editor, you find some interesting
discoveries:

```
<!DOCTYPE html PUBLIC "-//W3C//DTD XHTML 1.0 Strict//EN"
"http://www.w3.org/TR/xhtml1/DTD/xhtml1-strict.dtd">
<html lang="EN" dir="ltr" xmlns="http://www.w3.org/1999/xhtml">
  <head>
    <meta http-equiv="content-type" content="text/xml; charset=utf-8" />
    <title>CS Standard Template</title>
    <link rel = "stylesheet"
          type = "text/css"
          href = "csStd.css" />
  </head>

  <body>
    <div id = "all">
      <!-- This div centers a fixed-width layout -->
      <div id = "heading">
        <!--#include virtual = "head.html" -->
      </div><!-- end heading div -->

      <div id = "menu">
        <!--#include virtual = "menu.html" -->
      </div> <!-- end menu div -->

      <div class = "content">
```

```
      <!--#include virtual = "story1.html" -->
    </div> <!-- end content div -->

    <div class = "content">
      <!--#include virtual = "story2.html" -->
    </div> <!-- end content div -->

    <div id = "footer">
      <!--#include virtual = "footer.html" -->
    </div> <!-- end footer div -->
  </div> <!-- end all div -->
</body>
</html>
```

Some interesting things are happening in this code snippet:

+ **The page has no content!** All the actual content (the menus and the phony news stories) are gone. This page, which contains only structural information, is the heart of any kind of CSS — the structure is divorced from the content.

+ **A funky new tag is in place of the content.** In each place that you expect to see text, you see an `<!--#include -->` directive, instead. This special instruction tells the server to go find the specified file and put it here.

+ **The filename is unusual.** The server doesn't normally look for include tags (because most pages don't have them). Typically, you have to save the file with the special extension `.shtml` to request that the server look for include directives and perform them. (It's possible to use special server configurations to allow SSI with normal `.html` extensions.)

+ **Servers don't always allow SSI technologies.** Not every server is configured for Server-Side Includes. You may have to check with your server administrator to make this work.

The nice thing about Server-Side Includes is the way that it separates the content from the structure. For example, look at the code for the first content block:

```
<!--#include virtual = "story1.html" -->
```

This code notifies the server to look for the file story1.html in the current directory and place the contents of the file there. The file is a vastly simplified HTML fragment:

```
<h2>Book I - Creating the XHTML Foundation</h2>
<ol>
  <li>Sound XHTML Foundations</li>
  <li>It's All About Validation</li>
  <li>Choosing your Tools</li>
  <li>Managing Information with Lists and Tables</li>
  <li>Making Connections with Links</li>
  <li>Adding Images</li>
  <li>Creating Forms</li>
</ol>
```

Book VIII Chapter 5

Taking Control of Content

This approach makes it very easy to modify the page. If I want a new story, I simply make a new file, `story1.html`, and put it in the directory. Writing a program to do this automatically is easy.

Like PHP code, SSI code doesn't work if you simply open the file in the browser or drag the file to the window. SSI requires active participation from the server; to run an SSI page on your machine, therefore, you need to use localhost, as you do for PHP code.

Using AJAX and jQuery for client-side inclusion

If you don't have access to Server-Side Includes, you can use AJAX to get the same effect.

Figure 5-2 shows what appears to be the same page, but all is not what it appears to be.

Figure 5-2:
This time, I grabbed content from the client side using AJAX.

Figures 5-1 and 5-2 look identical, but they're not. I used totally different means to achieve exactly the same output, from the user's point of view.

The code reveals what's going on:

```
<!DOCTYPE html PUBLIC "-//W3C//DTD XHTML 1.0 Strict//EN"
"http://www.w3.org/TR/xhtml1/DTD/xhtml1-strict.dtd">
<html lang="EN" dir="ltr" xmlns="http://www.w3.org/1999/xhtml">
  <head>
    <meta http-equiv="content-type"  ="text/xml; charset=utf-8" />
    <title>CMS using AJAX</title>
    <link rel = "stylesheet"
          type = "text/css"
          href = "csStd.css" />
    <script type = "text/javascript"
            src = "jquery-1.4.2.js"></script>
    <script type = "text/javascript">
    //<![CDATA[
      $(document).ready(function() {
        $("#heading").load("head.html");
        $("#menu").load("menu.html");
        $("#content1").load("story1.html");
        $("#content2").load("story2.html");
        $("#footer").load("footer.html");
      });
    //]]>
    </script>
  </head>

  <body>
    <div id = "all">
      <!-- This div centers a fixed-width layout -->
      <div id = "heading">
      </div><!-- end heading div -->

      <div id = "menu">
      </div> <!-- end menu div -->

      <div class = "content"
           id = "content1">
      </div> <!-- end content div -->

      <div class = "content"
           id = "content2">
      </div> <!-- end content div -->

      <div id = "footer">
      </div> <!-- end footer div -->

    </div> <!-- end all div -->
  </body>
</html>
```

Once again, the page content is empty. All the contents are available in the same text files as they were for the Server-Side Includes example. This time, though, I used a jQuery AJAX call to load each text file into the appropriate element.

The same document structure can be used with very different content by changing the JavaScript. If you can't create a full-blown CMS (because the server doesn't allow SSI, for example) but you can do AJAX, this is an easy way to separate content from layout. See Book VII, Chapter 2 for more information on using jQuery and AJAX for page includes.

Building a page with PHP includes

Of course, if you have access to PHP, it's quite easy to build pages dynamically.

The `csInclude.php` program shows how this is done:

```
!DOCTYPE html PUBLIC "-//W3C//DTD XHTML 1.0 Strict//EN"
"http://www.w3.org/TR/xhtml1/DTD/xhtml1-strict.dtd">
<html lang="EN" dir="ltr" xmlns="http://www.w3.org/1999/xhtml">
  <head>
    <meta http-equiv="content-type" content="text/xml; charset=utf-8" />
    <title>CS PHP Includes</title>
    <link rel = "stylesheet"
          type = "text/css"
          href = "csStd.css" />
  </head>

  <body>
    <div id = "all">
      <!-- This div centers a fixed-width layout -->
      <div id = "heading">
        <?php include("head.html"); ?>
      </div><!-- end heading div -->

      <div id = "menu">
        <?php include("menu.html"); ?>
      </div> <!-- end menu div -->

      <div class = "content">
        <?php include("story1.html"); ?>
      </div> <!-- end content div -->

      <div class = "content">
        <?php include("story2.html"); ?>
      </div> <!-- end content div -->

      <div id = "footer">
        <?php include("footer.html"); ?>
      </div> <!-- end footer div -->
    </div> <!-- end all div -->
  </body>
</html>
```

As you can see, using PHP is almost the same as using the SSI and AJAX approaches from the last two sections of this chapter:

1. Start by building a template.

The general template for all three styles of page inclusion is the same. There's no need to change the general design or the CSS.

2. **Create a small PHP segment for each inclusion.**

    In this particular situation, it's easiest to write XHTML code for the main site and write a small PHP section for each segment that needs to be included.

3. **Include the HTML file.**

    Each PHP snippet does nothing more than include the appropriate HTML.

Creating Your Own Data-Based CMS

If you've come this far in the chapter, you ought to go all the way and see how a relational database can add flexibility to a page-serving system. If you really want to turn the corner and make a real CMS, you need a system that stores all the data in a data structure and compiles the pages from that structure dynamically. That sounds like a project. Actually, creating your own CMS neatly ties together most of the skills used throughout this book: XHTML, CSS, PHP, and SQL. It's not nearly as intimidating as it sounds, though.

Using a database to manage content

The first step is to move from storing data in files to storing in a relational database. Each page in a content management system is often the same structure, and only the data is different. What happens if you move away from text files altogether and store all the content in a database?

The data structure might be defined like this in SQL:

```sql
DROP TABLE IF EXISTS cmsPage;
CREATE TABLE cmsPage (
  cmsPageID INTEGER PRIMARY KEY AUTO_INCREMENT,
  title VARCHAR(30)
);

DROP TABLE IF EXISTS cmsBlock;
CREATE TABLE cmsBlock (
  cmsBlockID INTEGER PRIMARY KEY AUTO_INCREMENT,
  blockTypeID INTEGER,
  title VARCHAR(50),
  content TEXT,
  pageID INTEGER

);

DROP TABLE IF EXISTS blockType;
CREATE TABLE blockType (
  blockTypeID INTEGER PRIMARY KEY AUTO_INCREMENT,
  name VARCHAR(30)
);
```

```
DROP VIEW IF EXISTS pageView;
CREATE VIEW pageView AS
  SELECT
    blockType.name as 'block',
    cmsBlock.title as 'title',
    cmsBlock.content as 'content',
    cmsBlock.pageID as 'pageID',
    cmsPage.title as 'page'
  FROM
    cmsBlock, blockType, cmsPage
  WHERE
    cmsBlock.blockTypeID = blockType.blockTypeID;

INSERT INTO cmsPage VALUES (
  null,
  'main page'
);

INSERT into blockType VALUES (null, 'head');
INSERT into blockType VALUES (null, 'menu');
INSERT into blockType VALUES (null, 'content1');
INSERT into blockType VALUES (null, 'content2');
INSERT into blockType VALUES (null, 'footer');

INSERT INTO cmsBlock VALUES (
  null,
  1,
  'it\'s a binary thing',
  null,
  1
);

INSERT INTO cmsBlock VALUES (
  null,
  2,
  'menu',
  '
        <ul>
        <li><a href = "dbCMS.php?pageID=1">one</a></li>
        <li><a href = "dbCMS.php?pageID=2">two</a></li>
        <li><a href = "dbCMS.php?pageID=1">three</a></li>
      </ul>
  ',
  1
);

INSERT INTO cmsBlock VALUES (
  null,
  3,
  'Book I - Creating the XHTML Foundation',
  '
<ol>
  <li>Sound XHTML Foundations</li>
```

```
        <li>It\'s All About Validation</li>
        <li>Choosing your Tools</li>
        <li>Managing Information with Lists and Tables</li>
        <li>Making Connections with Links</li>
        <li>Adding Images</li>
        <li>Creating forms</li>
    </ol>
      ',
      1
);

INSERT INTO cmsBlock VALUES (
    null,
    4,
    'Book II - Styling with CSS',
    '
<ol>
    <li>Coloring Your World</li>
    <li>Styling Text</li>
    <li>Selectors, Class, and Style</li>
    <li>Borders and Backgrounds</li>
    <li>Levels of CSS</li>
</ol>
      ',
      1
);

INSERT INTO cmsBlock VALUES (
    null,
    5,
    null,
    'see <a href = "http://www.aharrisbooks.net">aharrisbooks.
      net</a> for more information',
      1
);
```

This structure has three tables and a view:

**Book VIII
Chapter 5**

**Taking Control
of Content**

- ✦ **The `cmsPage` table:** Represents the data about a page, which currently isn't much. A fuller version might put menu information in the page data so that the page would "know" where it lives in a menu structure.

- ✦ **The `cmsBlock` table:** Represents a block of information. Each block is the element that would be in a miniature HTML page in the other systems described in this chapter. This table is the key table in this structure because most of the content in the CMS is stored in this table.

- ✦ **The `blockType` table:** Lists the block types. This simple table describes the various block types.

- ✦ **The `pageView` view:** Ties together all the other information. After all the data is loaded, the `pageView` view ties it all together, as shown in Figure 5-3.

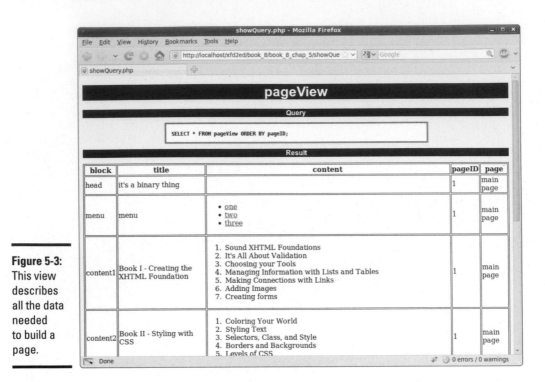

Figure 5-3:
This view describes all the data needed to build a page.

Most of the data is being read as HTML, but it's still text data. I included the entire SQL file, including the INSERT statements, on the CD-ROM as `buildCMS.sql`.

Writing a PHP page to read from the table

The advantage of using a data-based approach is scalability. In using all the other models in this chapter, I had to keep copying the template page. If you decide to make a change in the template, you have to change hundreds of pages. If you use data, you can write one PHP program that can produce any page in the system. All this page needs is a page-number parameter. Using that information, it can query the system, extract all the information needed for the current page, and then display the page. Here's the (simplified) PHP code for such a system:

```
<!DOCTYPE html PUBLIC "-//W3C//DTD XHTML 1.0 Strict//EN"
"http://www.w3.org/TR/xhtml1/DTD/xhtml1-strict.dtd">

<html lang="EN" dir="ltr" xmlns="http://www.w3.org/1999/xhtml">
  <head>
    <meta http-equiv="content-type" content="text/xml; charset=utf-8" />
    <title>dbCMS.php.</title>
    <link rel = "stylesheet"
          type = "text/css"
          href = "csStd.css" />
  </head>
```

```php
<?php

//get pageID from request if possible
$pageID = $_REQUEST["pageID"];
$pageID = mysql_real_escape_string($pageID, $conn);
if ($pageID == ""){
  $pageID = 1;
} // end if

//read current page information from the db
$conn = mysql_connect("localhost", "xfd", "xfdaio");
mysql_select_db("xfd");
$sql = "SELECT * FROM pageView WHERE pageID = 1";
$result = mysql_query($sql, $conn);

//populate local variables from db result
while ($row = mysql_fetch_assoc($result)){
  if ($row["block"] == "head"){
    $head = $row["title"];
  } else if ($row["block"] == "menu"){
    $menu = $row["content"];
  } else if ($row["block"] == "content1"){
    $c1Title = $row["title"];
    $c1Text = $row["content"];
  } else if ($row["block"] == "content2"){
    $c2Title = $row["title"];
    $c2Text = $row["content"];
  } else if ($row["block"] == "footer"){
    $footer = $row["content"];
  } // end if
} // end while

?>

  <body>
    <div id = "all">
      <!-- This div centers a fixed-width layout -->
      <div id = "heading">
        <h1>
          <?php print $head; ?>
        </h1>
      </div><!-- end heading div -->

      <div id = "menu">
        <?php print $menu; ?>
      </div> <!-- end menu div -->

      <div class = "content">
        <h2>
          <?php print $c1Title; ?>
        </h2>
        <p>
          <?php print $c1Text; ?>
        </p>
      </div> <!-- end content div -->

      <div class = "content">
        <h2>
          <?php print $c2Title; ?>
        </h2>
        <p>
          <?php print $c2Text; ?>
        </p>
      </div> <!-- end content div -->
```

```
        <div id = "footer">
          <?php print $footer; ?>
        </div> <!-- end footer div -->
      </div> <!-- end all div -->
    </body>
</html>
```

Here's the cool thing about dbCMS. This page is all you need! You won't have to copy it ever. The same PHP script is used to generate every page in the system. If you want to change the style or layout, you do it in this one script, and it works automatically in all the pages. This is exactly how CMS systems work their magic!

Looking at all the code at one time may seem intimidating, but it's quite easy when you break it down, as explained in these steps:

1. Pull the `pageID` number from the request.

If possible, extract the `pageID` number from the GET request. If the user has sent a particular page request, it has a value. If there's no value, get page number 1:

```
//get pageID from request if possible
$pageID = $_REQUEST["pageID"];
$pageID = mysql_real_escape_string($pageID, $conn);
if ($pageID == ""){
  $pageID = 1;
} // end if
```

Don't forget to escape the `pageID` data! Whenever you extract data from a page to use in a query, remember to escape the data to prevent injection attacks.

2. Query `pageView` to get all the data for this page.

The `pageView` view was designed to give you everything you need to build a page with one query.

If you're using MySQL 4 (without views), just copy the query from the view definition and insert it into your PHP code. The view is just a shortcut — it's never absolutely necessary.

3. Pull values from the query to populate the page.

Look at each response of the query. Then, look at the `block` value to see which type of query it is and populate local variables:

```
//read current page information from the db
$conn = mysql_connect("localhost", "xfd", "password");
mysql_select_db("xfd");
$sql = "SELECT * FROM pageView WHERE pageID = $pageID";
$result = mysql_query($sql, $conn);
```

4. Write out the page.

Go back to HTML and generate the page, skipping into PHP to print the necessary variables.

Allowing user-generated content

The hallmark of a CMS is the ability of users with limited technical knowledge to add content to the system. My very simple CMS illustrates a limited way to add data to the CMS. Figure 5-4 shows the `buildBlock.html` page. This page allows authorized users to add new blocks to the system and produces the output shown in Figure 5-5.

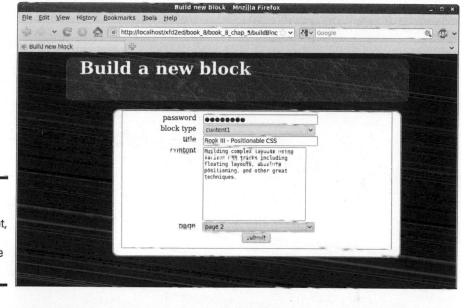

Figure 5-4: A user can add content, which updates the database.

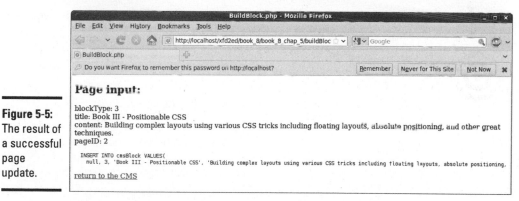

Figure 5-5: The result of a successful page update.

Book VIII Chapter 5

Taking Control of Content

After a few entries, a user can build a complete second page, which might look similar to Figure 5-6.

File   Edit   View   History   Bookmarks   Tools   Help

http://localhost/xfd2ed/book_B/book_8_chap_5/dbCMS.pl   Google

CS Basic CMS

page 2

one
two
three

Book III - Positionable CSS

Building complex layouts using various CSS tricks including floating layouts, absolute positioning, and other great techniques.

Book IV - JavaScript

introducing client-side code with JavaScript

see aharrisbooks.net for more information

Done   0 errors / 0 warnings

Figure 5-6:
This page is simply another set of page blocks added by the user.

The system is simple but effective. The user builds blocks, and these blocks are constructed into pages. First, look over the `buildBlock.html` page.

```
<!DOCTYPE html PUBLIC "-//W3C//DTD XHTML 1.0 Strict//EN" "http://www.w3.org/TR/
    xhtml1/DTD/xhtml1-strict.dtd">
<html xmlns="http://www.w3.org/1999/xhtml" xml:lang="en">
<head>
  <title>Build new block</title>
  <meta http-equiv="Content-Type" content="text/html;charset=UTF-8" />

  <link rel = "stylesheet"
        type = "text/css"
        href = "csStd.css" />

  <style type = "text/css">
  label {
    float: left;
    width: 10em;
    clear: left;
    text-align: right;
    padding-right: 1em;
  }

  input, select, textarea {
    float: left;
    width: 20em;
  }
```

```
      button {
        display: block;
        clear: both;
        margin: auto;
      }

    </style>
  </head>
  <body>
    <div id = "all">
      <div id = "heading">
        <h1>Build a new block</h1>
      </div>

      <div class = "content">
        <form action = "buildBlock.php"
              method = "post">
          <fieldset>

            <label>
              password
            </label>
            <input type = "password"
                   name = "password" />

            <label>block type</label>
            <select name = "blockType">
              <option value = "1">head</option>
              <option value = "2">menu</option>
              <option value = "3">content1</option>
              <option value = "4">content2</option>
              <option value = "5">footer</option>
            </select>

            <label>title</label>
            <input type = "text"
                   name = "title" />

            <label>content</label>
            <textarea name = "content"
                      rows = "10"
                      cols = "40"></textarea>

            <label>page</label>
            <select name = "pageID">
              <option value = "1">main page</option>
              <option value = "2">page 2</option>
            </select>

            <button type = "submit">
              submit
            </button>
          </fieldset>
        </form>
      </div>
    </div>
  </body>
</html>
```

This code is a reasonably standard HTML form. Here are the highlights:

✦ **Add CSS for consistency:** It's important that the user understands she is still in a part of the system, so I include the same CSS used to display the output. I also add local CSS to improve the form display.

✦ **Build a form that calls `buildBlock.php`:** The purpose of this form is to generate the information needed to build an SQL `INSERT` statement. The `buildBlock.php` program provides this vital service.

✦ **Ask for a password:** You don't want just anybody modifying your forms. Include a password to make sure only those who are authorized add data.

✦ **Get other data needed to build a block:** Think about the `INSERT` query you'll be building. You'll need to get all the data necessary to add a new record to the `cmsBlock` table.

Honestly, this page is a bit sloppy. I hard-coded the block types and page IDs. In a real system, this data would be pulled from the database (ideally through AJAX). However, I decided to go with this expedient to save space.

Adding a new block

When the page owner submits the `buildBlock.html` form, control is passed to `buildBlock.php`. This program reads the data from the form, checks the password, creates an `INSERT` statement, and passes the query to the database.

Here's the code and then the details:

```
<!DOCTYPE html PUBLIC "-//W3C//DTD XHTML 1.0 Strict//EN" "http://www.w3.org/TR/
    xhtml1/DTD/xhtml1-strict.dtd">
<html xmlns="http://www.w3.org/1999/xhtml" xml:lang="en">
<head>
  <title>BuildBlock.php</title>
  <meta http-equiv="Content-Type" content="text/html;charset=UTF-8" />
</head>
<body>
  <?php
//retrieve data from form
$password = filter_input(INPUT_POST, "password");
$blockType = filter_input(INPUT_POST, "blockType");
$title = filter_input(INPUT_POST, "title");
$content = filter_input(INPUT_POST, "content");
$pageID = filter_input(INPUT_POST, "pageID");

//clean input for sql use
$blockType = mysql_real_escape_string($blockType);
$title  = mysql_real_escape_string($title);
$content  = mysql_real_escape_string($content);
$pageID  = mysql_real_escape_string($pageID);

//check password
if ($password == "allInOne"){
  manageResults();
```

```
   } else {
     print "<h2>Unauthorized access...</h2>";
   } // end if

   function manageResults(){
     global $blockType, $title, $content, $pageID;

     //return output
     print <<<HERE
     <h2>Page input:</h2>
     <p>
       blockType: $blockType <br />
       title: $title <br />
       content: $content <br />
       pageID: $pageID
     </p>
HERE;

     //connect to db
     $con = mysql_connect("localhost", "xfd", "xfdaio");
     mysql_select_db("xfd");

     //build and submit query
     $query = <<<HERE
   INSERT INTO cmsBlock VALUES(
     null, $blockType, '$title', '$content', $pageID);
HERE;

     print "<pre>$query</pre>";

     $result = mysql_query($query);
     if ($result == -1){
       print mysql_error();
     } else {
       print "system updated";
     } // end if
   } // end function
   ?>
   <p>
   <a href = "dbCMS.php">return to the CMS</a>
   </p>
</body>
</html>
```

Here's how you use the PHP code with the HTML form to update the database:

1. **Retrieve data from the form.**

   Use the `filter_input` or `$_REQUEST` mechanism to extract all data from the previous form.

2. **Filter all input that's used in the query.**

   All form variables except the password are used in an SQL query, so pass each variable through the `mysql_filter_input()` function to prevent SQL injection attacks. (See Book V, Chapter 7 for information about SQL injection attacks and how to prevent them.)

3. **Check the password.**

   You obviously don't want just anybody to change your system. Check the password and continue only if the user is authorized.

4. **Print the form contents.**

   Ensure the form contents are what you expect before passing data to a database.

5. **Connect to the database.**

   Build a standard database connection so you can pass the query to the database.

6. **Build the query.**

   Send the query to the database. Check that the query contains the data you expect. (You might not print the actual query in a final pass, but it's great for debugging.) Also, send back the results of the `mysql_error()` function if something went wrong.

Improving the dbCMS design

Although the simple PHP/MySQL combination described in the last section is a suitable starting point, you probably want to do a bit more to make a complete CMS, because a better CMS might have the following features:

+ **Automatic menu generation:** The menu system in dbCMS is too static as it is. Your database should keep track of where each page is located in the system, and your menu code should be dynamically generated based on this information.

+ **Better flexibility:** To keep the code simple, I made only one page type, and the page always has exactly two content blocks. You'll want a much more flexible design.

+ **Error-checking:** This program isn't nearly robust enough for real use (yet). It crashes if the data isn't complete. Before you can use this system in a real application, you need a way to improve its "crash-worthiness."

+ **Improved data input:** The very basic input form described in this chapter is fine, but it could certainly be improved. Loading the block type and page data directly from the database would be better. It would also be nice if the user could create new block types. Still, this basic CMS shows how you can start building your own content systems.

Appendix A: What's on the CD

In This Appendix

- ✔ System requirements
- ✔ Using the CD
- ✔ What you'll find on the CD
- ✔ Troubleshooting

System Requirements

Make sure that your computer meets the minimum system requirements shown in the following list. If your computer doesn't match up to most of these requirements, you may have problems using the software and files on the CD. For the latest and greatest information, please refer to the ReadMe file located at the root of the CD-ROM.

- ✦ A PC running Microsoft Windows 98, Windows 2000, Windows NT4 (with SP4 or later), Windows Me, Windows XP, Windows Vista, or Windows 7.
- ✦ A Macintosh running Apple OS X or later.
- ✦ A PC running a version of Linux with kernel 2.4 or greater.
- ✦ An Internet connection
- ✦ A CD-ROM drive

If you need more information on the basics, check out these books published by Wiley Publishing, Inc.: *PCs For Dummies,* by Dan Gookin; *Macs For Dummies, 9th Edition,* by Edward C. Baig; *iMac For Dummies, 5th Edition,* by Mark Chambers; *Windows 95 For Dummies, Windows 98 For Dummies, Windows 2000 Professional For Dummies, Microsoft Windows ME Millennium Edition For Dummies, Windows Vista For Dummies, Windows 7 For Dummies,* all by Andy Rathbone.

Using the CD

To install the items from the CD to your hard drive, follow these steps.

1. **Insert the CD into your computer's CD-ROM drive. The license agreement appears.**

   Note to Windows users: The interface won't launch if you have autorun disabled. In that case, click Start⇨Run (For Windows Vista, Start⇨All Programs⇨Accessories⇨Run). In the dialog box that appears, type **D:\ Start.exe**. (Replace D with the proper letter if your CD drive uses a different letter. If you don't know the letter, see how your CD drive is listed under My Computer.) Click OK.

   Note for Mac Users: The CD icon will appear on your desktop, double-click the icon to open the CD and double-click the "Start" icon.

   Note for Linux Users: The specifics of mounting and using CDs vary greatly between different versions of Linux, and unfortunately we can't provide instructions for every version of Linux. Please see the manual or help information for your specific system if you experience trouble using this CD.

2. **Read through the license agreement and then click the Accept button if you want to use the CD.**

   The CD interface appears. The interface allows you to install the programs and run the demos with just a click of a button (or two).

What You'll Find on the CD

The following sections are arranged by category and provide a summary of the software and other goodies you'll find on the CD. If you need help with installing the items provided on the CD, refer back to the installation instructions in the preceding section.

Shareware programs are fully functional, free, trial versions of copyrighted programs. If you like particular programs, register with their authors for a nominal fee and receive licenses, enhanced versions, and technical support.

Freeware programs are free, copyrighted games, applications, and utilities. You can copy them to as many PCs as you like — for free — but they offer no technical support.

GNU software is governed by its own license, which is included inside the folder of the GNU software. There are no restrictions on distribution of GNU software. See the GNU license at the root of the CD for more details.

Trial, demo, or *evaluation* versions of software are usually limited either by time or functionality (such as not letting you save a project after you create it).

Most of the software mentioned in this book is available for all three operating systems. For space reasons, we have focused primarily on Windows and Mac versions. Please check the Web site (`www.aharrisbooks.net/xfd_2ed/resources.html`) for links to all software for other operating systems.

Author-created material

For Windows and Mac.

All the examples provided in this book are located in the Author directory on the CD and work with Macintosh, Linux, Unix and Windows 95/98/NT and later computers. These files contain much of the sample code from the book. The structure of the examples directory is

```
Author/Book 1/Chapter 01
```

Aptana Studio 2.0

Open source.

For Windows and Mac OS. A full-featured programmer's editor that greatly simplifies creating Web pages, CSS documents, and code in multiple languages.

Dia 0.97.1

Open source.

For Windows. A drawing tool suitable for site diagrams, flow diagrams, and other vector-drawing applications.

FileZilla 3.3.1

Open source.

For Windows and Mac OS. Having both client and server capabilities available, FileZilla is a free FTP alternative.

Firefox 3.6 and Extensions

Open source.

For Windows and Mac OS. I've included this powerful browser on the CD, but that's only part of the story. I recommend enhancing Firefox with numerous extensions. It's actually easier to install these extensions online than it is to include them on the CD. Once you've installed Firefox, please visit the resources Web page (`www.aharrisbooks.net/xfd_2ed/resources.html`) for links to the various extensions.

Web Developer Toolbar 1.1.8 adds all kinds of features for creating and testing pages; HTML Validator 0.7 checks your pages for standards-compliance; the FireBug 1.5 extension adds incredible features for JavaScript and AJAX debugging; and FireFTP is Mozilla's FTP client program.

GIMP 2.6
Open source.

For Windows. A professional-level graphics editor in a free package. It does everything the expensive graphics editors do.

HTML Tidy
Open source.

For Windows and Mac OS. HTML Tidy is an open source program and library for checking and generating clean XHTML/HTML. Binaries and source for a variety of platforms are available.

IrfanView 4.25
Freeware.

For Windows. A useful graphics viewer program.

IZArc 4.1
Freeware.

For Windows and Mac OS. A good freeware archive utility that supports a wide variety of archive formats.

jEdit
Open source.

For Windows and Mac OS. Written in Java, jEdit is a text editor built for programmers.

jQuery 1.4
Open source.

For Windows and Mac OS. A JavaScript Library that helps you transfer HTML documents, handle events, and includes AJAX features in your Web pages.

Komodo Edit

Open source.

For Windows and Mac OS. A handy text editor that supports PHP, Python, Ruby, Perl and Tcl, JavaScript, CSS, and HTML among other languages.

KompoZer 0.7.10

Open source.

For Windows and Mac OS. Useful for beginning and intermediate programmers, KompoZer is a Web authoring system that offers file management and WYSIWYG Web page editing.

Notepad++

Open source.

For Windows and Mac OS. The successor to Notepad, Notepad++ is a free source code editor that supports several languages.

SQLite 3.6.22

Open source.

For Windows and Mac OS. A powerful software library as well as SQL database engine.

WebsiteBaker 2.8.1

Open source.

For Windows and Mac OS. A free content management system for the beginning to intermediate programmer.

XAMPP 1.7.3

GNU version.

For Windows and Mac OS. XAMPP is a complete server package that's easy to install and incredibly powerful. This package includes the amazing Apache Web server, the PHP programming language, the MySQL database manager, and tons of useful utilities.

XnView 1.97

Open source.

For Windows and Mac OS. With XnView, you can view and convert a wide assortment of graphics and image files.

Troubleshooting

I tried my best to compile programs that work on most computers with the minimum system requirements. Alas, your computer may differ, and some programs may not work properly for some reason.

The two likeliest problems are that you don't have enough memory (RAM) for the programs you want to use, or you have other programs running that are affecting installation or running of a program. If you get an error message such as Not enough memory or Setup cannot continue, try one or more of the following suggestions and then try using the software again:

✦ **Turn off any antivirus software running on your computer.** Installation programs sometimes mimic virus activity and may make your computer incorrectly believe that it's being infected by a virus.

✦ **Close all running programs.** The more programs you have running, the less memory is available to other programs. Installation programs typically update files and programs; so if you keep other programs running, installation may not work properly.

✦ **Have your local computer store add more RAM to your computer.** This is, admittedly, a drastic and somewhat expensive step. However, adding more memory can really help the speed of your computer and allow more programs to run at the same time.

Customer Care

If you have trouble with the CD-ROM, please call the Wiley Product Technical Support phone number at (800) 762-2974. Outside the United States, call 1(317) 572-3994. You can also contact Wiley Product Technical Support at http://support.wiley.com. John Wiley & Sons will provide technical support only for installation and other general quality control items. For technical support on the applications themselves, consult the program's vendor or author.

To place additional orders or to request information about other Wiley products, please call (877) 762-2974.

Index

Special Characters and Numerics

A

F

O

Apple & Macs

iPad For Dummies
978-0-470-58027-1

iPhone For Dummies,
4th Edition
978-0-470-87870-5

MacBook For Dummies, 3rd
Edition
978-0-470-76918-8

Mac OS X Snow Leopard For
Dummies
978-0-470-43543-4

Business

Bookkeeping For Dummies
978-0-7645-9848-7

Job Interviews
For Dummies,
3rd Edition
978-0-470-17748-8

Resumes For Dummies,
5th Edition
978-0-470-08037-5

Starting an
Online Business
For Dummies,
6th Edition
978-0-470-60210-2

Stock Investing
For Dummies,
3rd Edition
978-0-470-40114-9

Successful
Time Management
For Dummies
978-0-470-29034-7

Computer Hardware

BlackBerry
For Dummies,
4th Edition
978-0-470-60700-8

Computers For Seniors
For Dummies,
2nd Edition
978-0-470-53483-0

PCs For Dummies,
Windows
7 Edition
978-0-470-46542-4

Laptops For Dummies,
4th Edition
978-0-470-57829-2

Cooking & Entertaining

Cooking Basics
For Dummies,
3rd Edition
978-0-7645-7206-7

Wine For Dummies,
4th Edition
978-0-470-04579-4

Diet & Nutrition

Dieting For Dummies,
2nd Edition
978-0-7645-4149-0

Nutrition For Dummies,
4th Edition
978-0-471-79868-2

Weight Training
For Dummies,
3rd Edition
978-0-471-76845-6

Digital Photography

Digital SLR Cameras &
Photography For Dummies,
3rd Edition
978-0-470-46606-3

Photoshop Elements 8
For Dummies
978-0-470-52967-6

Gardening

Gardening Basics
For Dummies
978-0-470-03749-2

Organic Gardening
For Dummies,
2nd Edition
978-0-470-43067-5

Green/Sustainable

Raising Chickens
For Dummies
978-0-470-46544-8

Green Cleaning
For Dummies
978-0-470-39106-8

Health

Diabetes For Dummies,
3rd Edition
978-0-470-27086-8

Food Allergies
For Dummies
978-0-470-09584-3

Living Gluten-Free
For Dummies,
2nd Edition
978-0-470-58589-4

Hobbies/General

Chess For Dummies,
2nd Edition
978-0-7645-8404-6

Drawing
Cartoons & Comics
For Dummies
978-0-470-42683-8

Knitting For Dummies,
2nd Edition
978-0-470-28747-7

Organizing
For Dummies
978-0-7645-5300-4

Su Doku For Dummies
978-0-470-01892-7

Home Improvement

Home Maintenance
For Dummies,
2nd Edition
978-0-470-43063-7

Home Theater
For Dummies,
3rd Edition
978-0-470-41189-6

Living the
Country Lifestyle
All-in-One
For Dummies
978-0-470-43061-3

Solar Power Your Home
For Dummies,
2nd Edition
978-0-470-59678-4

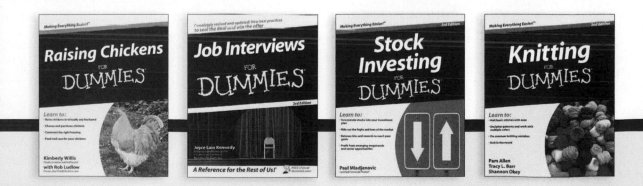

Internet

Blogging For Dummies,
3rd Edition
978-0-470-61996-4

eBay For Dummies,
6th Edition
978-0-470-49741-8

Facebook For Dummies,
3rd Edition
978-0-470-87804-0

Web Marketing
For Dummies,
2nd Edition
978-0-470-37181-7

WordPress
For Dummies,
3rd Edition
978-0-470-59274-8

Language & Foreign Language

French For Dummies
978-0-7645-5193-2

Italian Phrases
For Dummies
978-0-7645-7203-6

Spanish For Dummies,
2nd Edition
978-0-470-87855-2

Spanish
For Dummies,
Audio Set
978-0-470-09585-0

Math & Science

Algebra I
For Dummies,
2nd Edition
978-0-470-55964-2

Biology For Dummies,
2nd Edition
978-0-470-59875-7

Calculus For Dummies
978-0-7645-2498-1

Chemistry For Dummies
978-0-7645-5430-8

Microsoft Office

Excel 2010 For Dummies
978-0-470-48953-6

Office 2010 All-in-One
For Dummies
978-0-470-49748-7

Office 2010 For Dummies,
Book + DVD Bundle
978-0-470-62698-6

Word 2010 For Dummies
978-0-470-48772-3

Music

Guitar For Dummies,
2nd Edition
978-0-7645-9904-0

iPod & iTunes For
Dummies, 8th Edition
978-0-470-87871-2

Piano Exercises
For Dummies
978-0-470-38765-8

Parenting & Education

Parenting For Dummies,
2nd Edition
978-0-7645-5418-6

Type 1 Diabetes
For Dummies
978-0-470-17811-9

Pets

Cats For Dummies,
2nd Edition
978-0-7645-5275-5

Dog Training For Dummies,
3rd Edition
978-0-470-60029-0

Puppies For Dummies,
2nd Edition
978-0-470-03717-1

Religion & Inspiration

The Bible For Dummies
978-0-7645-5296-0

Catholicism For Dummies
978-0-7645-5391-2

Women in the Bible
For Dummies
978-0-7645-8475-6

Self-Help & Relationship

Anger Management
For Dummies
978-0-470-03715-7

Overcoming Anxiety
For Dummies,
2nd Edition
978-0-470-57441-6

Sports

Baseball
For Dummies,
3rd Edition
978-0-7645-7537-2

Basketball
For Dummies,
2nd Edition
978-0-7645-5248-9

Golf For Dummies,
3rd Edition
978-0-471-76871-5

Web Development

Web Design
All-in-One
For Dummies
978-0-470-41796-6

Web Sites
Do-It-Yourself
For Dummies,
2nd Edition
978-0-470-56520-9

Windows 7

Windows 7
For Dummies
978-0-470-49743-2

Windows 7
For Dummies,
Book + DVD Bundle
978-0-470-52398-8

Windows 7 All-in-One
For Dummies
978-0-470-48763-1

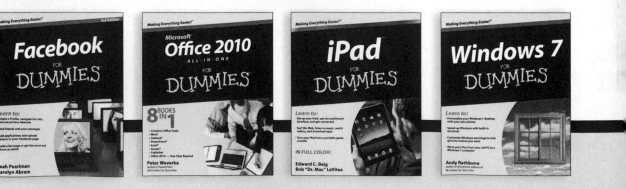

Available wherever books are sold. For more information or to order direct: U.S. customers visit www.dummies.com or call 1-877-762-2974.
U.K. customers visit www.wileyeurope.com or call (0) 1243 843291. Canadian customers visit www.wiley.ca or call 1-800-567-4797.

Notes

Notes